AFRICAN-AMERICAN
POLITICAL LEADERS

Revised Edition

Charles W. Carey, Jr.
Revised by Liz Sonneborn

Facts On File
An imprint of Infobase Publishing

Note on Photos

Many of the illustrations and photographs used in this book are old, historical images. The quality of the prints is not always up to current standards, as in some cases the originals are from old or poor quality negatives or are damaged. The content of the illustrations, however, made their inclusion important despite problems in reproduction.

African-American Political Leaders, Revised Edition

Facts On File, Inc.
An imprint of Infobase Publishing
132 West 31st Street
New York NY 10001

Library of Congress Cataloging-in-Publication Data

Carey, Charles W.
  African-American political leaders / Charles W, Carey, Jr.; revised by Liz Sonneborn—Rev. ed.
      p. cm. — (African Americans A to Z)
  Includes bibliographical references and index.
  ISBN 978-0-8160-8120-2 (acid-free paper) 1. African American politicians—Biography—Dictionaries. 2. African American political activists—Biography—Dictionaries. 3. African Americans—Biography—Dictionaries. 4. African American leadership—Dictionaries. I. Sonneborn, Liz. II. Title.
  E185.96.C18 2011
  973'.04960730922—dc22
  [B]   2010042294

Facts On File books are available at special discounts when purchased in bulk quantities for businesses, associations, institutions, or sales promotions. Please call our Special Sales Department in New York at (212) 967-8800 or (800) 322-8755.

You can find Facts On File on the World Wide Web at http://www.factsonfile.com

Text design by Joan M. Toro
Composition by Hermitage Publishing Services
Cover printed by Sheridan Books, Ann Arbor, Mich.
Book printed and bound by Sheridan Books, Ann Arbor, Mich.
Date printed: February 2011
Printed in the United States of America

10 9 8 7 6 5 4 3 2 1

This book is printed on acid-free paper.

CONTENTS

List of Entries   v

Introduction   vii

A to Z Entries   1

Bibliography and Recommended Sources   335

Entries by Office Held   338

Entries by Year of Birth   341

Index   345

LIST OF ENTRIES

Allen, Ethel
Anderson, Charles W.
Anderson, Charles W., Jr.
Archer, Dennis
Arnett, Benjamin
Arrington, Richard
Baker, Ella
Baker, Thurbert E.
Ballance, Frank
Barry, Marion
Belton, Sharon
Berry, Ted
Bishop, Sanford
Blackwell, Ken
Blackwell, Lucien
Blackwell, Unita
Bond, Julian
Booker, Cory
Bosley, Freeman
Bradley, Tom
Brooke, Edward
Brown, Corrine
Brown, Lee
Brown, Ron
Brown, Willie
Bruce, Blanche
Burke, Yvonne
Burris, Roland
Cain, Richard
Campbell, Bill
Cardozo, Francis

Carson, André
Carson, Julia
Cheatham, Henry
Chisholm, Shirley
Christian-Christensen, Donna
Church, Robert
Clarke, Yvette D.
Clay, William
Clay, William, Jr.
Clayton, Eva
Cleaver, Emanuel
Clyburn, James
Coleman, Michael
Collins, Barbara-Rose
Collins, Cardiss
Conyers, John
Crockett, George W.
Cummings, Elijah
Davis, Artur
Davis, Ben
Davis, Benjamin J.
Davis, Danny K.
Dawson, William
DeLarge, Robert
Dellums, Ron
DePriest, Oscar
Diggs, Charles
Dinkins, David
Dixon, Julian
Dixon, Sheila
Dymally, Mervyn

Elliott, Robert
Ellison, Keith
Espy, Mike
Evans, Melvin
Evers, Charles
Fattah, Chaka
Fauntroy, Walter
Fenty, Adrian M.
Fields, Cleo
Flake, Floyd
Ford, Harold
Ford, Harold, Jr.
Ford, James
Foster, Ezola
Franklin, Shirley
Franks, Gary
Fudge, Marcia L.
Fulani, Lenora
Gantt, Harvey
Gibson, Kenneth
Goode, W. W.
Gray, Bill
Gregory, Dick
Hall, Katie
Haralson, Jeremiah
Harmon, Clarence
Harris, Patricia Roberts
Hastie, William H.
Hastings, Alcee
Hatcher, Richard
Hawkins, Augustus

Hayes, Charles
Hayes, James
Henry, Aaron
Herenton, Willie
Herman, Alexis
Hilliard, Earl
Holder, Eric
Howard, Perry
Hyman, John
Jack, Hulan
Jackson, Alphonso
Jackson, Jesse
Jackson, Jesse, Jr.
Jackson, Lisa P.
Jackson, Maynard
Jackson Lee, Sheila
James, Sharpe
Jefferson, William
Johnson, Eddie Bernice
Johnson, Harvey
Jordan, Barbara
Kelly, Sharon Pratt Dixon
Keyes, Alan
Kilpatrick, Carolyn
Kilpatrick, Kwame
Kirk, Ron
Langston, John
Lee, Barbara
Leland, Mickey
Lewis, John
Long, Jefferson
Looby, Alexander
Lynch, John
Majette, Denise
Marsh, Henry
Martin, Louis
McCall, Carl
McKinney, Cynthia
Meek, Carrie
Meek, Kendrick

Meeks, Gregory
Metcalfe, Ralph
Mfume, Kweisi
Millender-McDonald, Juanita
Miller, Thomas
Mitchell, Arthur
Mitchell, Charles
Mitchell, Parren
Moore, Gwen
Morial, Dutch
Moseley Braun, Carol
Motley, Constance
Murray, George
Nagin, Ray
Napier, James
Nash, Charles
Nix, Robert
Norton, Eleanor Holmes
Nutter, Michael
Obama, Barack
O'Hara, James
O'Leary, Hazel
Owens, Major
Paige, Rod
Paterson, David
Patrick, Deval
Payne, Donald
Perry, Carrie
Pinchback, P. B. S.
Powell, Adam Clayton, Jr.
Powell, Colin
Powell, Debra
Rainey, Joseph
Rangel, Charles
Ransier, Alonzo
Rapier, James
Revels, Hiram
Rice, Condoleezza
Rice, Norm
Rice, Susan E.

Rogers, Joe
Ross, Don
Rush, Bobby
Savage, Gus
Schmoke, Kurt
Scott, Bobby
Sharpton, Al
Slater, Rodney
Smalls, Robert
Steele, Michael
Stokes, Carl
Stokes, Louis
Street, John
Sullivan, Louis
Thompson, Bennie
Towns, Edolphus
Tubbs Jones, Stephanie
Turner, Benjamin
Usry, James
Walls, Josiah
Washington, Harold
Washington, Walter
Waters, Maxine
Watson, Diane
Watt, Mel
Watts, J. C.
Weaver, Robert
Webb, Wellington
Wheat, Alan
White, George
White, Jesse
White, Michael
Wilder, Doug
Williams, Anthony
Williams, Avon
Williams, George
Williams, Hosea
Wynn, Albert
Young, Andy
Young, Coleman

INTRODUCTION

One of the most remarkable episodes in the history of U.S. politics is the rise to power of the African-American political leader. Although the first Africans to come to this country were treated as indentured servants, by the late 1600s they and their offspring had been relegated to a life of perpetual slavery. Released from bondage by the Civil War, African Americans continued to be despised by the vast majority of white northerners. Meanwhile, white southerners developed new, ingenious methods to deny blacks their rightful place in American society. Despite these obstacles, over the next 150 years African Americans carved out for themselves a significant role in the governance of their country, their states, and their localities.

1855–1877

The story of African-American political leaders begins in 1855, when John Langston was elected clerk of Brownhelm Township, a virtually all-white community in Ohio. Langston was later elected to several local offices in Oberlin, Ohio; the town was the home of Oberlin College, the first institution of higher education in the United States to accept black students and a hotbed of antislavery activity during the antebellum years. In 1866 Charles Mitchell and Edward G. Walker were elected to one-year terms in Massachusetts's lower house, thus becoming the first African Americans to serve as state legislators.

African-American political involvement began in earnest during Reconstruction (1867–77). States in the former Confederacy that wished to be readmitted as full equals into the Union were forced to abolish slavery and grant a measure of civil rights to ex-slaves, known collectively as freedmen. In 1867, 12 southern states (Tennessee, the exception, had been "reconstructed" during the Civil War) rewrote their constitutions so that African-American men could vote and hold political office.

For 11 years, African Americans in the South wielded a considerable amount of political power. In states with a black majority (South Carolina and Mississippi), freedmen took control of the state legislatures and began to make state government work for them. In both states, African Americans succeeded in getting important civil rights bills passed that guaranteed equal treatment before the law for all citizens, regardless of race. In some cases they were even able to legislate against racial discrimination in places that catered to the public. They also established public school systems that provided students of all races with the necessary literacy tools to make something of themselves.

Almost without exception, these black politicians belonged to the Republican Party. Formed in the 1850s to put an end to slavery, the Republican Party was the party of Abraham Lincoln, the Great Emancipator who had freed the slaves. Furthermore, it was the Republicans who recognized that the collective mind of the South needed to be reconstructed, at least in terms of race relations. To this end, the Radical Republicans who controlled Congress gained ratification of the Thirteenth, Fourteenth, and Fifteenth Amendments, all of which granted equal civil rights to freedmen. By contrast, the Democratic Party was considered, by blacks and whites alike, to be the party of secession, and southern Democrats seemed hell-bent on restoring white supremacy regardless of the price. Consequently, African Americans became Republicans because of what that party had done for them historically, and because they simply were neither recruited nor welcomed into the Democratic Party.

During Reconstruction, freedmen made the most radical gains in South Carolina. The black-controlled legislature implemented a program of land reform that redistributed thousands of acres of land from wealthy planters to more than 8,000 poor families, most of them headed by African Americans. Black politicians, most notably Francis Cardozo, served the state as lieutenant governor, secretary of state, treasurer, and attorney general. In addition, six African Americans— Joseph Rainey, Robert Elliott, Robert DeLarge, Richard Cain, Alonzo Ransier, and Robert Smalls—were elected to the U.S. House of Representatives.

Next to South Carolina, freedmen made the most conspicuous political gains in Mississippi. John R. Lynch served as speaker of the lower house of the state legislature and was later elected to the U.S. House. At a time when U.S. senators were chosen by the state legislators and not by the people at large, African-American state legislators successfully demanded that members of their race be elected to the U.S. Senate, and two, Hiram Revels and Blanche Bruce, served in this capacity.

Freedmen also made political gains in states where African Americans were a sizable minority. Although they never were able to control their state legislatures, a number of blacks were elected to the upper and lower houses of every state in the Lower South. In Louisiana, P. B. S. Pinchback was elected president pro tempore of the state senate and later served as the state's interim governor, while Charles Nash was elected to the U.S. House. In Alabama, Benjamin Turner, James Rapier, and Jeremiah Haralson were elected to the U.S. House, as were Georgia's Jefferson Long, Florida's Josiah Walls, and North Carolina's John Hyman.

During Reconstruction, state governments spent much more money than they ever had before. For the most part, this money went to create public school systems, which had not existed in the South before the Civil War, and in some cases to redistribute land to the poor of both races. Charges that increased funding, especially in states controlled by African-American politicians, was due to waste, mismanagement, fraud, and corruption are simply not true. Certainly, black politicians were as susceptible to temptation as their white brethren, but no more so. In fact, a dispassionate reading of the facts suggests that most African-American elected officials were too busy building a society in which blacks would be treated equitably to stuff their pockets with state dollars. And the charges that black politicians were, as a group, uncouth and uneducated is belied by the personal biographies of the leaders contained in this work. Although many black state and local politicians possessed only a rudimentary education, those African Americans who rose to positions of state and national leadership were just as well educated as the average white person, and a number of them possessed college degrees.

1877–1929

The end of Reconstruction in 1877 did not mark the end of African-American political involvement in the South. For 12 of the 18 years between 1883 and 1901, three black North Carolinians— James O'Hara, Henry Cheatham, and George White—represented the eastern part of their state in Congress, a black-majority district known generally as the "Black Second." Likewise, for several years between 1889 and 1897, African-American voters in eastern South Carolina's black-majority Seventh District were represented in Congress by Thomas Miller and George Murray. Langston served briefly in the 1890s as the congressional representative of a black-majority district centered around Petersburg, Virginia. James Napier served several terms as a city councilman in Nashville, Tennessee, while exercising considerable influence in that state's Republican Party. Benjamin Davis, Robert Church, and Perry Howard served for many years as leaders of the Republican Party in Georgia, Tennessee, and Mississippi, respectively. These three men exercised an iron grip on political patronage in their states whenever Republicans occupied the White House, which was usually the case during these years. And a number of competent blacks served in their state legislatures.

By 1901, however, most southern states had rewritten their constitutions so that, the Fourteenth Amendment notwithstanding, African Americans routinely were denied their constitutional rights to vote and hold office. Between 1901 and 1929, no African American served either in Congress or in the various state legislatures. Although blacks were permitted to vote in municipal elections, none held elective office in the localities, either.

The situation for northern blacks was not much better. Prior to the Great Migration that began just before World War I, few African Americans lived in the North, and so few opportunities existed for African Americans to get elected. The best opportunities existed in Ohio, where colleges like Oberlin and Wilberforce encouraged blacks to enroll and where a number of African Americans had settled after escaping slavery before the Civil War. As a result, racial prejudice, although it did exist, was not necessarily fatal to a black politician's chances. Although they only served one term apiece, Benjamin Arnett and George Williams attracted a number of white voters in

their campaigns for the Ohio state legislature. Charles Anderson never held an elected office, but he emerged as a political leader in New York because of his ability to turn out the African-American vote for Republican candidates.

1929–1967

In 1929 two major events changed the nature of African-American politics. First, Republican president Herbert Hoover began removing blacks from positions of influence in the state Republican committees in the South. He rooted out Benjamin Davis and Perry Howard and neutralized Robert Church so that the Republican Party would be more attractive to white voters in their states. While his actions failed to attract significant numbers of southern whites to the Republican Party, the racist attitude the actions demonstrated helped drive northern blacks into the Democratic Party. This shift of African-American political allegiance was accelerated in the 1930s by the Great Depression. While Republicans twiddled their thumbs and argued that relief efforts should be placed in the hands of state and local authorities, Democrats developed the New Deal, a series of federal spending programs designed to alleviate the misery of millions of Americans. During the New Deal, Hoover's successor, Democratic president Franklin D. Roosevelt, reached out to African Americans as no president had ever done before. One of Roosevelt's initiatives was the formation of the so-called black cabinet to advise him on minority affairs. Two of the cabinet's members were Robert Weaver, who later became secretary of housing and urban development, and William H. Hastie, who went on to become governor of the U.S. Virgin Islands.

Neither Roosevelt nor the New Deal did as much for African Americans as blacks had hoped, and so not all of them left the Republican Party because of the New Deal. Most southern blacks, for example, stayed in the party, mostly because their state Democratic organizations generally refused to nominate blacks for office. Two prominent southern black politicians who ran as Republicans during this period were Charles Anderson, Jr., a Kentucky state representative, and Alexander Looby, a city councilman in Nashville, Tennessee. A few, like James Ford and Ben Davis, joined the Communist Party and worked for an end to racial discrimination from within its ranks. Those who became Democrats were often disappointed with the results; in time, this disappointment led Ella Baker, Unita Blackwell, Aaron Henry, and others to found the Mississippi Freedom Democratic Party in 1964 as a vehicle for African-American political hopes. Nevertheless, the New Deal's promise was enough to induce the majority of northern blacks to leave the party of Lincoln and emancipation and become Democrats, and the New Deal's legacy generally was enough to keep them in.

The second major event of 1929 was the swearing-in of Oscar DePriest as the first black congressman elected from a northern state. His election was part of the wider exercise by blacks of their political muscle in the major cities of the North and West, where the Great Migration had led millions of African Americans to settle after 1910. Black-majority wards and congressional districts in cities like Chicago and New York gave black politicians increased opportunities to succeed in the electoral process. DePriest was succeeded in 1935 by Arthur Mitchell, the first black Democratic congressman, and in 1943 by William Dawson; all three were Chicagoans elected from Illinois' black-majority First District. In the 1940s three black New Yorkers—Ben Davis, Hulan Jack, and Adam Clayton Powell, Jr.—were elected to the New York city council, the state assembly, and Congress, respectively. In the 1950s Charles Diggs and Robert Nix were elected to Congress from Detroit and Philadelphia, respectively. In the early 1960s Augustus Hawkins and John Conyers were elected to Congress from Los Angeles and Detroit, respectively, while Constance Motley was elected to represent Harlem in the New York state senate. The rising importance of African-American vot-

ers in the 1960s induced President John F. Kennedy to appoint Louis Martin deputy chairman of the Democratic National Committee.

1967–1979

In 1967 four major events demonstrated that African Americans were on the verge of making important political gains. Edward Brooke took his seat in the U.S. Senate as the junior member from Massachusetts, thus becoming the first African American to serve in that body since 1881. Carl Stokes was elected mayor of Cleveland, Ohio, thus becoming the first elected African-American mayor of a major city. Richard Hatcher was elected mayor of Gary, Indiana, an industrial suburb of Chicago. Walter Washington was appointed president of the board of commissioners of Washington, D.C., thus becoming the de facto mayor of the nation's capital. Interestingly, of the four victories, only Hatcher's might be said to have resulted directly from the Civil Rights movement. Brooke, a Republican, got elected from a state whose population was overwhelmingly white and Democratic, and his voting record was indistinguishable from many of his white Democratic colleagues. Stokes got elected by an electorate that was almost two-thirds white. While Washington was appointed by President Lyndon B. Johnson over the objections of many white southern congressmen, he simply was the most qualified person for the job. Nevertheless, the victories indicated that African-American politicians could now gain major offices based on their accomplishments, not just their race.

Meanwhile, the election of African Americans to Congress from black-majority districts in northern and western cities accelerated. In this regard, black politicians benefited greatly from the Civil Rights movement. As a result of *Baker v. Carr* (1962) and *Reynolds v. Sims* (1964), two landmark decisions by the U.S. Supreme Court involving legislative apportionment, the states began reapportioning their congressional districts. As a result, a number of black-majority districts were created. In 1968 Shirley Chisholm, William Clay, and Louis Stokes were elected to the U.S. House of Representatives from Brooklyn, St. Louis, and Cleveland, respectively. In 1970 Ron Dellums, Ralph Metcalfe, Parren Mitchell, and Charles Rangel were elected to the House by the voters of Berkeley, California, Chicago, Baltimore, and New York City, respectively, while Walter Fauntroy was chosen by the District of Columbia's residents to serve as their nonvoting delegate in Congress. In 1971 these eight representatives joined Diggs, Nix, Hawkins, and Conyers to found the Congressional Black Caucus, a forum whereby African Americans in Congress could work together for their common goals. The following year, Yvonne Burke, Cardiss Collins, Barbara Jordan, and Andy Young were elected to Congress from Los Angeles, Chicago, Houston, and Atlanta, respectively. In 1974 Harold Ford was chosen to represent the voters of Memphis, Tennessee. In 1978 Julian Dixon, Bill Gray, and Mickey Leland won election to the House from Los Angeles, Philadelphia, and Houston, respectively.

African Americans also were being named in increasing numbers to important appointive positions. In 1977 Andy Young was named U.S. ambassador to the United Nations and Patricia Harris was appointed secretary of the U.S. Department of Housing and Urban Development. In 1979 Philadelphia city councilwoman Ethel Allen became Pennsylvania's secretary of state.

At the same time, black politicians were being elected to important positions in state and territorial governments. In the South, this development was also the direct result of the Civil Rights movement, which had worked tirelessly to register large numbers of African-American voters. By the mid-1970s this effort began to bear fruit, and black politicians were suddenly able to be elected to their state legislatures. Three who served in their state senates without going on to higher offices were Julian Bond, Avon Williams, and Hosea Williams. Melvin Evans became the first governor of the U.S. Virgin Islands to be elected by the resi-

dents of that territory. Roland Burris was elected state comptroller of Illinois; he would later be elected that state's attorney general.

While blacks were being elected to important national and state offices, voters were sending African Americans into the mayor's office as well, and not just in large cities with a black majority. In 1974, when Washington, D.C., gained home rule, Walter Washington was elected mayor. He was succeeded four years later by Marion Barry. The 1970s also saw the elections of Ted Berry in Cincinnati; Tom Bradley in Los Angeles; Maynard Jackson in Atlanta; Dutch Morial in New Orleans; Coleman Young in Detroit; Kenneth Gibson in Newark, New Jersey; Richard Arrington in Birmingham, Alabama; and Henry Marsh in Richmond, Virginia. Meanwhile, voters in smaller cities and towns were also electing black mayors, especially from southern communities where the Voting Rights Act of 1965 had a profound effect. In 1972, 13 black mayors met in Fayette, Mississippi, as the guests of Charles Evers to discuss their common problems. Two years later, at their annual meeting in Santee, South Carolina, the 20 mayors in attendance established the Southern Conference of Black Mayors. In 1976 "Southern" was changed to "National," and by 2000 membership had grown to 476, of whom 70 percent represented communities in the former Confederate states.

Last but not least, this period witnessed one of the most remarkable presidential campaigns in U.S. history—the election of 1968. Although Richard M. Nixon and Hubert H. Humphrey split all of the electoral votes between themselves, black comedian Dick Gregory polled 47,000 votes for president.

1980–1989
The political gains that African Americans made between 1967 and 1979 continued during the 1980s, but at an accelerated pace. Ironically, while blacks found it easier to get elected to political office during this decade, the whole concept of

affirmative action that had made their elections possible in many places now came under attack. The assault had begun rather obliquely during the Nixon administration (1969–77), but it escalated into an unapologetic full-blown siege during the Reagan administration (1981–89). Throughout the decade, African Americans in national, state, and local offices were forced to fight to retain the socio-economic gains they had been making steadily since the 1960s.

Meanwhile, the election of blacks to Congress continued unabated. In 1980 George W. Crockett and Mervyn Dymally were elected to represent Detroit and Los Angeles, respectively, while the voters in Chicago sent two new African-American representatives to Washington, Gus Savage and Harold Washington. In 1982 Major Owens and Edolphus Towns were elected from Brooklyn, New York, and Katie Hall and Alan Wheat were elected from Gary, Indiana, and Kansas City, Missouri, respectively. In 1983 Charles Hayes was chosen to take Harold Washington's seat. In 1986 Mississippi's Mike Espy and Georgia's John Lewis became the first African-American congressmen from their states since Reconstruction. That same year, Floyd Flake was sent to the House by the voters of Queens in New York City, while Kweisi Mfume was elected from Baltimore. In 1988 Donald Payne was sent to Congress by the voters of Newark, New Jersey.

At the same time, African Americans continued to perform credibly in state and local politics. The decade's first major victory in this regard came in 1980 when Willie Brown was elected speaker of the California state assembly. This period's last major victory came in 1989, when Doug Wilder was elected governor of Virginia. In between were the elections of Harold Washington, David Dinkins, W. W. Goode, Sharpe James, Carrie Perry, Kurt Schmoke, James Usry, Harvey Gantt, and Norm Rice as mayors of Chicago; New York City; Philadelphia; Newark, New Jersey; Hartford, Connecticut; Baltimore; Atlantic City, New Jersey; Charlotte, North Carolina; and Seat-

tle, respectively. In 1989 President George H. W. Bush acknowledged the growing importance of African-American voters in urban areas by appointing Louis Sullivan as secretary of the U.S. Department of Health and Human Services. Meanwhile, hundreds of African Americans were elected to positions in their state legislatures, including Don Ross of Oklahoma.

Ironically, the most impressive performance by an African-American political leader during this period was by one who never won an election. Jesse Jackson ran for the Democratic nomination for president in 1984 and 1988. He came close to winning the second time, when he finished second to Michael Dukakis. During the campaign he had won hundreds of delegates and several primaries. Perhaps most impressive—certainly most surprising—was his ability to attract white voters to his campaign. His success was yet another sign that African Americans were continuing to make slow but steady gains in the political arena based on their ability, not just their race.

1990 AND BEYOND

During the 1990s, African Americans began to rethink their unswerving allegiance to the Democratic Party. Many blacks perceived that Jesse Jackson had not been shown the proper respect at the 1988 Democratic National Convention, despite having come in second in the balloting for the presidential nomination. Others were upset that the Democratic Party had not done more for blacks over the years, especially in the face of the attack on civil rights that came about during the Reagan administration in the 1980s. And others had simply had enough of the Democratic Party's perceived tendency toward liberalism. By 1990 the black middle class had grown to unprecedented proportions, and as a group its members were just as attuned to class as they were to race. Many middle-class African Americans deplored the dependence of lower-class blacks on government assistance, and some even suggested that continued assistance was a clever ploy by whites to keep African Americans "in their place."

As African-American political leaders became more moderate in their views, many began to leave the Democratic Party. Gary Franks, J. C. Watts, Joe Rogers and Colin Powell joined the Republican Party, and Alan Keyes sought the Republican nomination for president in 1996. A few, such as Ezola Foster, joined the conservative Reform Party, while Lenora Fulani became a perennial candidate of the left-wing New Alliance Party. Many of those who remained Democrats began expressing a desire to move away from the party's traditional liberal agenda and toward the political center. A number of black Democrats in Congress joined the moderate Democratic Leadership Council and the fiscally conservative Blue Dog Coalition. While these groups continue to look to government to improve the lot of all Americans, they also seek an expanded role for private enterprise and local community groups in the quest for solutions to vexing socioeconomic problems.

One interesting feature of this period was the ability of African-American candidates to get elected by white-majority constituencies. This phenomenon can be attributed partly to the general public's increased acceptance of multicultural diversity, which itself was made possible in large part by the integration of the nation's public schools. However, another important factor is the rise of the black middle class. As African Americans began sharing more fully in the bounty of U.S. society, they began turning away from the radicalism of the 1960s and embracing the traditional political values of the white middle class. Thus, when black candidates spoke to the electorate about their hopes and dreams for the future, the message was increasingly one to which voters of both races could relate.

Meanwhile, African Americans continued to be elected to Congress in unprecedented numbers. In 1990 Barbara-Rose Collins, Eleanor Norton, William Jefferson, Maxine Waters, Lucien Blackwell, and Gary A. Franks were elected to Congress from Detroit, Washington, New Orleans, Los Angeles, Philadelphia, and Waterbury, Connecticut, respectively. In 1992 the South alone elected 13 new African-American congresspeople—Eva Clayton and Mel Watt (North Carolina), Sanford Bishop and Cynthia McKinney (Georgia), Corrine Brown, Alcee Hastings, and Carrie Meek (Florida), James Clyburn (South Carolina), Cleo Fields (Louisiana), Earl Hilliard (Alabama), Eddie Bernice Johnson (Texas), Bobby Scott (Virginia), and Bennie Thompson (Mississippi). Many of these southern representatives came from predominantly rural districts, thus adding a new dimension to the Congressional Black Caucus, which heretofore had focused mostly on urban affairs. Also elected to Congress that year were Bobby Rush from Chicago, Albert Wynn from the Maryland suburbs of Washington, and Carol Moseley Braun from Illinois, who became the first African American in 16 years to serve in the Senate. In 1994 four more African Americans were elected to Congress—Chaka Fattah from Philadelphia, Jesse Jackson, Jr., from Chicago, Sheila Jackson Lee from Houston, and J. C. Watts from rural Oklahoma. In 1996 Juanita Millender-McDonald, Elijah Cummings, Julia Carson, Donna Christian-Christensen, Danny K. Davis, Harold Ford, Jr., and Carolyn Kilpatrick were elected to Congress from Los Angeles, Baltimore, Indianapolis, the Virgin Islands, Chicago, Memphis, and Detroit, respectively. African Americans elected to Congress in 1998 included Gregory Meeks from New York City, Barbara Lee from Oakland, California, and Stephanie Tubbs Jones from Cleveland.

African Americans played a major role in getting Bill Clinton elected president in 1992. He acknowledged his debt to them the following year by appointing Mike Espy as secretary of agriculture, Ron Brown as secretary of commerce, and Hazel O'Leary as secretary of energy. After being reelected in 1996, in 1997 Clinton appointed Alexis Herman as secretary of labor and Rodney Slater as secretary of transportation.

As African Americans were getting elected to Congress and appointed to cabinet positions in unprecedented numbers, the same thing was happening at the state and local levels. In 1994 Carl McCall was elected state comptroller of New York. In 1998 Jesse White was elected Illinois secretary of state, Joe Rogers was elected lieutenant governor of Colorado, and Thurbert Baker was elected attorney general of Georgia. Meanwhile, the number of black mayors continued to grow with the elections of Sharon Pratt Dixon Kelly and Anthony Williams (Washington), Willie Herenton (Memphis), Michael White (Cleveland), Emanuel Cleaver (Kansas City, Missouri), Wellington Webb (Denver), James Hayes (Fairbanks, Alaska), Dennis Archer (Detroit), Freeman Bosley, and Clarence Harmon (St. Louis), Bill Campbell (Atlanta), Sharon Belton (Minneapolis), Willie Brown (San Francisco), Ron Kirk (Dallas), Lee Brown (Houston), Michael Coleman (Columbus, Ohio), Harvey Johnson, (Jackson, Mississippi), John Street (Philadelphia), and Debra Powell (East St. Louis, Illinois). Herenton, Cleaver, Webb, Hayes, Bosley, Belton, Willie Brown, Kirk, Lee Brown, and Coleman each were their city's first African-American mayor.

INTO THE TWENTY-FIRST CENTURY

The year 2001 saw the beginning of the administration of President George W. Bush. With the White House again under Republican control, the early years of the Bush administration could hardly be called auspicious for African-American politicians and voters, whom still overwhelmingly identified themselves as Democrats. President Bush, however, did make history by naming the first African-American secretary of state, the popular ex-general Colin Powell. Powell, as fourth in line to the presidency, became the highest-ranking black politician in U.S. history. When Powell stepped down at the start of Bush's second term, the president made another historic appointment. He replaced Powell with his National Security Advisor Condoleezza Rice, the first African-

American woman to serve in this post. Bush appointed two other black cabinet members—Secretary of Education Rod Paige and Secretary of Housing and Urban Development Alphonso Jackson.

In the early years of the 21st century, African Americans continued to increase their numbers in mayorships and in the U.S. House of Representatives, where black-majority cities and congressional districts largely supported African-American candidates. Successful mayoral candidates included Sheila Dixon (Baltimore), Shirley Franklin (Atlanta), Ray Nagin (New Orleans), and former Virginia governor Doug Wilder (Richmond). The House of Representatives saw the election of Yvette D. Clarke of New York, Marcia L. Fudge of Ohio, Kendrick Meek of Florida, and Gwen Moore of Wisconsin, among others. Especially notable were Keith Ellison of Minnesota and André Carson of Indiana, who were the first and second Muslims to serve in the U.S. Congress.

African Americans vying for statewide political office, however, initially struggled to get a foothold in the political climate of the new century. The election of 2002 could have been a historic one. Carl McCall of New York ran for governor of New York, and Ron Kirk ran for senator from Texas, but both were defeated. If McCall had won, he would have become the second elected African-American governor in U.S. history. If Kirk had won, he would have become the fifth African-American senator and the third elected by popular vote.

Despite these setbacks, a new breed of African-American politician was beginning to emerge. Prominent in this new generation of leaders was Artur Davis, who in 2002 successfully took on incumbent Earl Hilliard to win a seat in the U.S. House of Representatives. Others included three mayors—Cory Booker of Newark, New Jersey (elected in 2006), Adrian M. Fenty of Washington, D.C. (2006), and Michael Nutter of Philadelphia, Pennsylvania (2007). Perhaps the most impressive among this maverick group was Deval

Patrick. Without ever having held political office before, Patrick won the governorship of Massachusetts in 2006. What made this achievement all the more noteworthy was that Patrick achieved his electoral victory in a state in which African Americans made up only about 7 percent of the population. Patrick's win showed that the right kind of African-American politician now could expect support from both black and white voters.

This new breed of black officeholders possessed certain qualities that made them attractive to a broad swath of the electorate, while at the same time setting them apart from most African-American politicians of earlier eras. This younger group had attended top tier integrated colleges and universities, often studying political science or business management, instead of earning degrees from historically black colleges and seminaries. In their rhetoric, they concentrated on their hope for the future rather than on the injustices of the past. And they ran broad-based campaigns, hoping to attract a diverse group of supporters, rather than tailoring their messages to the specific needs of black voters.

Perhaps most important, this generation of leaders, born in the 1960s and 1970s, were too young to have strong memories of the Civil Rights era or personal experience with law-mandated segregation and harsh discrimination. Without these scars, they found it easier to fit into the political establishment. As products of Ivy League schools and other elite institutions, they were comfortable with white leaders, and white leaders were comfortable with them.

The success of these young politicians suggested that the electorate had fundamentally changed—that voters, especially young voters, were becoming more "color-blind" when they cast their ballots. However, there was also evidence that old prejudices, though dying, were not dead yet. This was most clear in the case of Harold Ford, Jr.'s run for the U.S. Senate in 2006. An attractive moderate Democrat from a political family, Ford seemed poised to become the next

senator from Tennessee, until the last weeks of the campaign, when the state Republican Party started running a television spot that tapped into old racial hatreds. In the ad, a young white woman in a cocktail dress asked the single Ford to call her. Conjuring up fears of miscegenation, the advertisement helped turn the course of the race. In the end, Ford lost his Senate run by a small margin to his white opponent.

Whereas Harold Ford, Jr.'s senatorial campaign was thwarted by last-minute concerns about race, Barack Obama's campaign for the presidency in 2008 was able to bypass those considerations and grab the greatest prize in American politics—the White House. Drawing lessons from Deval Patrick's successful gubernatorial run, Obama campaigned as an eternal optimist, as epitomized in his upbeat slogan, "Yes, We Can." Distressed by ongoing wars in Iraq and Afghanistan and frightened by a failing economy, voters were drawn to Obama's message of hope and promise of a better future. With his foreign-sounding name and his brown skin, he had at one time seemed an unlikely candidate. But by November 2008, these very things also suggested he was what many voters were looking for—an agent of change. On election day, the American people made history by choosing an African American as their new president.

The press was quick to announce that the United States had entered a new postracial era. Young African-American politicians, however, tended to bristle at the idea. They knew that, regardless of Obama's victory, it was still a struggle for black candidates to win over nonblack voters, and it would continue to be so for a long time to come. They also felt the term separated them from earlier generations of African-American politicians. The new breed of black leaders did not think they represented a dramatic break from the past, but instead the next stage in a slow but steady progression forward.

On his historic inauguration day, Obama made his own personal expression of thanks to the trail-

xvi   African-American Political Leaders

blazers who had come before him and made his own success possible. While a great crowd cheered for Obama as he prepared to give his inauguration speech on the Washington Mall, Obama turned to the man standing at his right—John Lewis, the great civil rights leader from Georgia who was then serving his 11th term in the U.S. House of Representatives. The two men briefly embraced as Lewis whispered his congratulations. Later, Lewis asked Obama to autograph a commemorative photograph as a keepsake of the event. The new president wrote, "Because of you, John. Barack Obama"—a simple note that yet said so very much.

A

Allen, Ethel
(Ethel D. Allen)
(1929–1981) *Pennsylvania secretary of state*

As a politician, Ethel Allen was unique. A practitioner of community medicine, she toted a gun while calling on patients in one of the nation's toughest neighborhoods. She was also a liberal, a feminist, and, as she described herself, a "BFR—a black female Republican, an entity as rare as a black elephant and just as smart."

Ethel Allen was born on May 8, 1929, in Philadelphia, Pennsylvania. Her father, Sidney, was a tailor, and her mother, Jean, was a homemaker. After graduating from a private girls' high school, Allen studied science and mathematics at West Virginia State College and received a B.A. in 1951. For the next seven years she worked as a chemist for the Atomic Energy Commission. During that same period she also did graduate work at Temple University and the University of Pennsylvania as part of her effort to get admitted to medical school. In 1958 she was accepted by the Philadelphia College of Osteopathic Medicine, and five years later she received the doctor of osteopathy (D.O.) degree. In 1964 she completed her internship at a hospital in Grand Rapids, Michigan, and returned to Philadelphia to open a medical practice. Calling herself a "ghetto practitioner," she worked with some of the city's poorest and most desperate people; on one occasion her waiting room furniture was stolen during office hours. Following passage of the Model Cities Act of 1966, she became medical director of the Spring Garden Community Center. This position required her to make house calls on indigent patients, and to protect herself from being assaulted by drug addicts she carried a pistol in her medical bag.

Allen's involvement in politics began at a young age. Her parents were members of the Democratic Party's 29th Ward Committee, and as a youngster she helped register voters and then get them to the polls. At age 19 she served as a page at the 1948 Democratic National Convention in Philadelphia. By 1952 she had come to identify herself as a Republican, and that same year she handled scheduling and appointments for Dwight D. Eisenhower's presidential campaign in Philadelphia. For a number of years thereafter she attended as many national conventions, Democratic and Republican, as she could.

By 1971, Allen had become quite concerned with Philadelphia's growing street crime problem. That same year, she ran for city council from the black-majority Fifth District against the Democratic incumbent. Promising to do everything he had not done and to do what he had done better, she easily won. As the council's only black female liberal Republican, she was usually outnumbered and outvoted. Nevertheless, she advocated equal

1

opportunity for women and disadvantaged minorities, and she pushed hard for programs that addressed the city's environmental, housing, and drug problems.

In 1975, Allen was reelected to the city council. The following year she gave a seconding speech to President Gerald Ford's nomination at the Republican National Convention. In 1978 she was urged to run for the U.S. House of Representatives, but she declined on the grounds that the position would force her to give up her medical practice, stop teaching community medicine at Hahnemann Medical College where she had taught for several years, and neglect the child for whom she was a legal guardian. Instead, she gave strong consideration to running for mayor of Philadelphia, but when the party's leaders demonstrated little enthusiasm for her candidacy, she chose not to run.

In February 1979, Allen accepted the position of secretary of state for Pennsylvania from newly elected Republican governor Richard Thornburgh. The position required her to supervise the regulation of charitable organizations, lobbyists, corporations, and 22 licensed professions and occupations. It also called for her to stand in for the governor as needed. During her nine-month term, she gave more than 100 speeches to enthusiastic gatherings around the state. In October, however, Thornburgh called on her to resign on the grounds that she had kept $1,000 in honoraria for two speeches written by a Department of State employee. She acknowledged the correctness of the charge but refused to step down, and in November she was fired.

In 1980, Allen went to work for the Philadelphia school system as a school clinician. She died on December 16, 1981, from complications related to open heart surgery, in Philadelphia. The Ethel D. Allen Elementary School in Philadelphia is named in her honor.

Further Reading

"Dr. Ethel Allen Dies; Held Pennsylvania Job." *New York Times*, December 18, 1981. Available online. URL: http://www.nytimes.com/1981/12/18/obituaries/dr-ethel-allen-dies-held-pennsylvania-job.html. Downloaded March 29, 2009.

Scott, Donald, Sr. "Allen, Ethel D." In *African American National Biography*, vol. 1, edited by Henry Louis Gates, Jr., and Evelyn Brooks Higginbotham. New York: Oxford University Press, 2008, pp. 87–88.

Anderson, Charles W.
(Charles William Anderson)
(1866–1938) *New York State Republican Party committeeman*

Although he never held elective office, in his day Charles Anderson was the most powerful African-American politician in New York. His ability to mobilize black voters for candidates of the Republican Party led in turn to his appointment to a number of highly visible and important government positions.

Charles William Anderson was born on April 28, 1866, in Oxford, Ohio, to Charles and Serena Anderson. He received a public school education in Oxford and Middletown, then attended the Spencerian Business College in Cleveland and the Berlitz School of Languages in Worcester, Massachusetts. At age 20 he moved to New York City to seek his fortune. At some point he married Emma Lee Bonaparte.

Shortly after his arrival in Manhattan, Anderson joined the Republican Party and became a "ward heeler," a dispenser of largesse from the local party machine to needy voters in return for their support at the polls. He was particularly effective among the city's African-American population, and in 1890 he was named president of the Young Men's Colored Republican Club of New York County. As a reward for his services, that same year the local Republican machine secured his appointment as a minor customs official with the Internal Revenue Service. He continued to prove his worth to the party, and to move up in the hierarchy of political patronage positions. In 1893 he became private secretary to the state treasurer, a position that allowed him to work behind the scenes to help secure passage of the New York Civil Rights Law of 1895. In 1895 he was appointed chief clerk of the state treasury and in 1898 supervisor of accounts for the state racing commission. In each of these positions he demonstrated considerable ability in getting the job done, and his work with the racing commission received special praise from Governor Theodore Roosevelt.

In 1904, Anderson founded the New York City Colored Republican Club for the purpose of returning Roosevelt to the White House. This move was a bit risky for Anderson to undertake, since it incurred the wrath of Thomas C. Platt, the Republican boss of New York City and an enemy of Roosevelt. On the other hand, it demonstrated Anderson's political acumen, because he understood that Platt's power was beginning to decline. The following year, Roosevelt demonstrated his gratitude by appointing Anderson collector of internal revenue for the Second District of New York. Because this district included Wall Street and Manhattan, it generated more revenue than any other district in the United States; consequently, Anderson's appointment to the post made him one of the most highly placed African Americans in the country. Over the next 10 years he oversaw its activities with great skill, earning high marks from the president as well as the New York business community. Not surprisingly, he appointed a number of African Americans to positions of responsibility and authority in the district. Meanwhile, he had been named to the state Republican committee, a post he held for 10 consecutive terms. During most of his tenure he was the only African American on the committee, but he made sure that blacks were given as many opportunities as possible to rise through the party's ranks.

In 1915, Anderson ran afoul of President Woodrow Wilson, a Democrat who also believed that federal jobs should be held by white men only.

Forced to resign as collector, he was appointed by the New York Agriculture Department to oversee its inspectors in New York City. In 1922, President Warren G. Harding, a Republican, made him collector of the newly created Third District in New York. He held this position until 1934, when poor health forced him to retire. He died on January 28, 1938, in New York City.

Further Reading

Meier, August. *Negro Thought in America, 1880–1915: Racial Ideologies in the Age of Booker T. Washington*. Ann Arbor: University of Michigan Press, 1963.

Osofsky, Gilbert. *Harlem: The Making of a Ghetto; Negro New York, 1890–1930*, 2nd ed. Chicago: Ivan R. Dee, 1996.

Williams, Patrick G. "Charles William Anderson." In *African American National Biography*, vol. 1, edited by Henry Louis Gates, Jr., and Evelyn Brooks Higginbotham. New York: Oxford University Press, 2008, pp. 121–123.

Anderson, Charles W., Jr.
(Charles William Anderson, Jr.)
(1907–1960) *state legislator from Kentucky*

Charles Anderson was Kentucky's first black legislator. At the time of his swearing-in in 1936, it had been 35 years since an African American had served in any southern state legislature. Before his tragic death, his many bills prompted the state legislature to ease racial discrimination in Kentucky.

Charles William Anderson, Jr., was born on May 26, 1907, in Louisville, Kentucky. His father, Charles W., Sr., was a physician, and his mother, Tabitha, was the state supervisor of black schools. As an infant, he moved with his family to Frankfort, the state capital, where he grew up. He received a B.A. from Kentucky State College (now University) in 1926, an A.B. from Wilberforce University in 1927, and an LL.B. (bachelor of laws degree) from Harvard University in 1931. Two years later he passed the Kentucky bar examination and joined a law partnership in Louisville. At some point he married Victoria McCall, with whom he had two children.

In the early 1930s, Anderson joined the Republican Party. By 1935 he had developed enough political acumen to get elected that same year to a seat in Kentucky's lower house. Reelected five times, he served a total of 11 years in the legislature.

As the state's only black legislator, Anderson served as a powerful force for the expansion of African-American civil rights. He was particularly effective in opening up the state's educational facilities to blacks. One of his first bills required each county to provide its black students with proper high school facilities; those that refused were required to pay the out-of-county tuition in a neighboring county's system. He sponsored bills that integrated state nursing schools and hospital internship and residency programs, and he led the drive to integrate Kentucky's institutions of higher learning. When the state continued to deny blacks admission to its law and medical schools, he cosponsored the Anderson-Mayer State Aid Act, which essentially paid the out-of-state tuition for black Kentuckians enrolled in professional schools. Other civil rights legislation sponsored by Anderson outlawed public lynchings and required state contractors to hire black employees.

Although Anderson was primarily interested in improving life for African Americans, he did not neglect other aspects of Kentucky life that he thought needed to be changed. He sponsored bills that allowed married women to work as teachers, provided that domestic workers be paid a minimum wage, and made electrocution, in place of hanging, the means of executing condemned criminals.

In 1946, Anderson resigned his seat to become assistant commonwealth attorney for Jefferson County, which includes Louisville. Although he never held elective office again, for the next 14 years he played an active part in the Civil Rights

movement in Kentucky. He served two terms as president of the Louisville chapter of the National Association for the Advancement of Colored People and worked with the Kentucky Commission on Human Rights to end the segregation of restaurants, theaters, and stores. In recognition of his achievements, he was commissioned a Kentucky Colonel, the first African American to receive this honor. In 1959 President Dwight D. Eisenhower appointed him an alternate delegate to the United Nations General Assembly. He died on June 14, 1960, in Shelbyville, Kentucky, when his car was struck by a train.

Further Reading

Booker, Teresa A. "Charles W. Anderson, Jr." In *African American National Biography*, vol. 1, edited by Henry Louis Gates, Jr., and Evelyn Brooks Higginbotham. New York: Oxford University Press, 2008, pp. 120–121.

Dunnigan, Alice A. *Fascinating Story of Black Kentuckians: Their Heritage and Tradition.* Washington, D. C.: Associated Publishers, 1982.

Horton, John B. *Not without a Struggle.* New York: Vantage Press, 1979.

Kentucky Commission on Human Rights. *Kentucky's Black Heritage.* Frankfort: The Commission, 1971.

Archer, Dennis
(Dennis Wayne Archer)
(1942–   ) *mayor of Detroit, Michigan*

Dennis Archer succeeded COLEMAN YOUNG as mayor of Detroit. During his eight-year tenure, he oversaw the city's economic upturn and a number of improvements in basic city services.

Archer was born on January 1, 1942, in Detroit. His father, Ernest, was a laborer, and his mother, Frances, was a homemaker. As an infant he moved with his family to Cassopolis, Michigan, where his parents took up farming. At age eight, he began working odd jobs after school to help support his family. He graduated from high school in 1959, and for the next six years he worked part-time while attending Wayne State University, the Detroit Institute of Technology, and Western Michigan University. In 1965, he received a B.S. in education from Western Michigan and accepted a position teaching emotionally disturbed children in the Detroit public school system. In 1967, he married Trudy DunCombe, with whom he has two children, and enrolled in the Detroit College of Law. He received a J.D. in 1970, and then practiced law for the next 16 years. In 1986, he was appointed a state supreme court judge, a position he held for four years.

Archer became involved in politics in the mid-1970s. By 1986, he had managed the campaigns of several local Democrats, including Coleman Young's successful reelection campaign for mayor in 1977 and GEORGE W. CROCKETT's successful reelection campaign for Congress in 1982. Archer retired from politics once he was appointed to the bench, but he returned to the political fray after only four years. As a justice, he had become increasingly concerned about the rising number of young African-American males living in Detroit who appeared in the state court system on charges related to drugs or violent crime. That same year, he resigned his judgeship, returned to the practice of law, and began making plans to run for mayor of Detroit so he could tackle the city's problems firsthand.

For two years, Archer sought the endorsement of Coleman Young, who seemed to be ready to retire from the mayor's office after five terms because of failing health. By 1992, Archer had grown tired of waiting for Young to step down, and he announced his plans to run against Young in 1993. Archer angered Young by criticizing his management style—Archer called it "cronyism"—and by promising to be more conciliatory in his dealings with Detroit's suburbs, which were predominantly white while the city itself was mostly black. Although Young eventually declined to run for reelection in 1993, he refused

to endorse Archer and instead gave his support to a rival candidate. Nevertheless, Archer was elected after a rather bitter campaign, during which it was suggested that Archer was not "black" enough to be Detroit's mayor. He took office in 1994.

As mayor, Archer focused on developing the city's economy. He established more cordial working relationships with the suburbs; one result was the merger of the area's bus systems, which gave inner-city residents better access to jobs in the suburbs where the demand for labor was high. He enticed the area's major employers to establish a job creation program for the city and succeeded in getting Chrysler to open a new automobile manufacturing plant within the city limits. He played a major role in removing the obstacles to the construction of several casinos on the city's riverfront. He convinced the federal government to designate Detroit an urban empowerment zone, thus qualifying the city for grants and tax incentives to attract new businesses. Partly as a result, General Motors and Compuware built their corporate headquarters in downtown Detroit while private investors built two new stadiums, one to keep the Detroit Tigers in town and the other to reclaim the Detroit Lions from the suburbs.

As Detroit's economic situation began to improve, Archer began working to improve municipal services. He helped lower the city's crime rate by hiring more police officers. However, he found it difficult to make city employees more responsive to the needs of the city's residents and the business community. In large part, this was because he refused to challenge the city's powerful employee unions by threatening to privatize some services, a strategy that has worked well in other major U.S. cities. Efforts to reform the city school system ran afoul of the state legislature, and he was unable to prevent a teacher walkout during the 1999–2000 school year. Efforts to improve garbage pickup and routine maintenance of streets and streetlamps worked well, but an initiative to increase the number of grocery and retail stores in the city's neighborhoods fell short of expectations.

Despite these setbacks, Archer's political star began to rise. At the Democratic National Convention in 1996, he cochaired the platform committee and seconded the nomination of President Bill Clinton. Archer was easily reelected in 1997 and seemed to have a brilliant political career ahead of him. However, the demands of running a major city kept him from spending enough time with his family, and in 2001 he declined to run for reelection. Shortly after leaving office in 2002, he assumed the presidency of the American Bar Association, the national organization of the legal profession. Two years later, Archer was appointed to an eight-year term on the board of trustees of Western Michigan University. He also served as the legal guardian of civil rights activist Rosa Parks for the year before her death in 2005.

Further Reading

Gurwitt, Rob. "Dennis Archer: A Softer Voice." *Governing* 7 (December 1993), p. 21.

Jones, Lisa C. "Dennis W. Archer: New Mayor in Motown." *Ebony* 50 (June 1995), p. 68.

Wilson, Sibyl Collins. "Archer, Dennis." In *African American National Biography*, vol. 1, edited by Henry Louis Gates, Jr., and Evelyn Brooks Higginbotham. New York: Oxford University Press, 2008, pp. 156–158.

Arnett, Benjamin

(Benjamin William Arnett)
(1838–1906) *Ohio state legislator*

Benjamin William Arnett was one of the first African Americans to serve in the Ohio state legislature, and the first to be elected from a white-majority district. He later became an important informal adviser to President William McKinley.

Arnett was born on March 6, 1838, in Brownsville, Pennsylvania. Little is known about his parents other than that his father, Benjamin, had African, Indian, and European ancestors. He received a rudimentary education in a one-room schoolhouse run by his uncle, Ephram Arnett, in Bridgeport. As a teenager, he worked as a freight handler and waiter and labored for awhile aboard steamboats on the Ohio and Mississippi Rivers. In 1858, he married Mary Louisa Gordon, with whom he had seven children; that same year he lost his left leg due to a cancerous tumor. He seems to have had no visible means of support for the next five years, when he became a schoolteacher. In 1865, he was licensed to preach in the African Methodist Episcopal (AME) Church, and in 1867 he was named pastor of a church in Walnut Hills, Ohio. Over the next 12 years, he held pastorates at increasingly larger churches in Toledo, Cincinnati, Urbana, and Columbus. In 1880, he was named general secretary of the AME General Conference, a position he held for eight years.

Arnett's political involvement began in 1864, when he joined the National Equal Rights League (NERL) and formed a chapter of the Faith and Hope League of Equal Rights in Brownsville. Two years later, he served as secretary of the NERL's national convention. Upon moving to Ohio, he joined the Republican Party and became actively involved in working to overturn that state's "Black Laws"; although not as restrictive as the racist Black Codes many southern states had passed following the abolition of slavery, these laws legalized segregation to the detriment of blacks. While his pastoral duties kept him from seeking elected office, his influence among Ohio Republicans gradually increased, and in 1880 he served as chaplain at the state convention.

In 1885, Arnett was narrowly elected to Ohio's lower house by the voters of Greene County, the vast majority of whom were not black. During his single term, he introduced a bill to abolish the Black Laws, and another to provide enough financial assistance to prevent Wilberforce University, one of the few colleges in the state that admitted African Americans, from declaring bankruptcy. He also became friends with U.S. congressman

William McKinley, the future president of the United States. Arnett served as chaplain at the Republican National Convention in 1896 that nominated McKinley, and he provided McKinley with the Bible upon which he took the oath of office in 1897. During McKinley's administration, the two consulted informally on several occasions concerning matters of race, and it was widely believed that Arnett exerted more influence on McKinley than any other African American.

Arnett retreated from partisan politics in 1888, when he was named bishop of the Seventh Episcopal District in South Carolina. Over the next 18 years, he served as bishop of districts in the Midwest and Northeast. However, he remained politically active by serving for a number of years as vice president of the Anti-Saloon League, a temperance organization. He played an important role in organizing chapters of black fraternal organizations, including the Sons of Hannibal and the Grand United Order of Odd Fellows, and was an active member of the National Negro Business League. He died on October 9, 1906, in Wilberforce, Ohio.

Further Reading

The African-American Experience in Ohio, 1850–1920. "Representative Benjamin W. Arnett (1836–1906)." Available online. URL: http://dbs.ohiohistory.org/africanam/page.cfm?ID=4446. Downloaded March 30, 2009.

Van Tine, Warren, and Michael Pierce. *Builders of Ohio: A Biographical History.* Columbus: Ohio State University Press, 2003.

Wright, Richard R., Jr. *The Bishops of the African Methodist Episcopal Church.* Nashville, Tenn.: A.M.E. Sunday School Union, 1963.

Arrington, Richard

(Richard Arrington, Jr.)
(1934–) *mayor of Birmingham, Alabama*

Richard Arrington was the first African-American mayor of Birmingham, Alabama. During his 20-year tenure, the city made much progress overcoming racial prejudice and diversifying its economy.

Arrington was born on October 19, 1934, in Livingston, Alabama. His parents, Richard and Ernestine, were sharecroppers. As a young boy, he moved with his family to Fairfield, on the outskirts of Birmingham, where his father had found a job as a steelworker. After finishing high school, he attended Miles College, a historically black institution in Birmingham, and he received an A.B. in science in 1955. Two years later, he received an M.S. in zoology from the University of Detroit and returned to Miles as an assistant professor in the science department. After teaching for six years, in 1963 he enrolled in the University of Oklahoma and received a Ph.D. in zoology four years later. In 1967, he returned to Miles, this time as an academic dean. Three years later, he became the executive director of the Alabama Center for Higher Education, a consortium of the state's historically black colleges, a position he held for nine years. In 1954, he married Barbara Jean Watts, with whom he had three children. They divorced in 1974, and the following year he married Rachel Reynolds, with whom he had two children.

Although Birmingham's population was divided almost evenly between blacks and whites, African Americans exercised very little political clout until the late 1960s. The Civil Rights movement changed all this, and in 1968 the city elected its first African-American city councilman. Arrington became involved in politics three years later, when he was also elected to city council. His primary focus while on council was to reduce the number of incidents involving police brutality against black citizens. Reelected in 1975, in 1979 he decided to run as a Democrat for mayor. He narrowly defeated his conservative Republican opponent in the general election, mostly because about 10 percent of the city's white voters cast their ballots for Arrington.

As mayor, Arrington focused on easing the racial tensions that had plagued Birmingham for decades and that had flared up in such an ugly manner during the mid-1960s. His first step toward doing this was to begin integrating the upper echelons of Birmingham's municipal government so that city hall reflected Birmingham's 50–50 racial makeup. By the time he left office in 1999, exactly half of the city's 24 department heads were African Americans, as were almost exactly half of the people in the police and fire departments and every other municipal agency. He also worked to overcome racial prejudice by assuaging the fears of the city's white business community. To this end, he lent the city's assistance to the Chamber of Commerce and various private investors seeking to diversify the local economy. For decades, Birmingham had been the steelmaking center of the South, but competition from overseas was beginning to eat into the market share of the city's mills. With Arrington's assistance, the city began to attract service industries such as banking and health care, and in time Birmingham joined Atlanta, Georgia, and Charlotte, North Carolina, as a regional center of such activity.

Arrington was reelected to five terms as mayor. Like other successful politicians, he was able to stay in power for so long by providing the voters with a consistently high quality of government services. Another factor in his success was the Jefferson County Citizens Coalition, in effect Arrington's political machine. Like many successful politicians, Arrington awarded his friends and punished his enemies via the dispensation of political patronage. Eventually, however, charges of cronyism and corruption began to surface. Arrington became known to many city residents

as "King Richard," and in 1992 an Atlanta contractor claimed that he had paid Arrington $5,000 in return for preference on a city bid. The result was a federal investigation, which Arrington charged was racially motivated. He stonewalled the investigation to the point that he was ordered to spend a night in jail for contempt. He dramatized his predicament by draping himself in chains and leading a protest march to the city jail from 16th Street Baptist Church, where four young black girls had been dynamited to death in 1963. Eventually all charges against him were dropped.

In 1999 Arrington decided not to seek reelection to a sixth term. He resigned a few months before his term ended so that his handpicked successor could run for election as the incumbent. After leaving office Arrington retired to private life. In 2008, he published his autobiography, *There's Hope for the World*.

Further Reading

Arrington, Richard. *There's Hope for the World: The Memoir of Birmingham, Alabama's First African-American Mayor.* Tuscaloosa: University of Alabama Press, 2008.

Fikes, Robert, Jr. "Arrington, Richard, Jr." In *African American National Biography,* vol. 1, edited by Henry Louis Gates, Jr., and Evelyn Brooks Higginbotham. New York: Oxford University Press, 2008, pp. 174–175.

Franklin, Jimmie L. *Back to Birmingham: Richard Arrington, Jr., and His Times.* Tuscaloosa: University of Alabama Press, 1989.

Manheim, James M. "Richard Arrington, 1934–   ." *Contemporary Black Biography* 24 (2000), pp. 7–9.

B

Baker, Ella
(1903–1986) *Mississippi Freedom Democratic Party cofounder*

Ella Baker never ran for political office. Nevertheless, she played a crucial role in Mississippi politics by serving as cofounder and chief adviser of the Mississippi Freedom Democratic Party, which enabled African Americans to challenge successfully for political office across that state.

Baker was born on December 13, 1903, in Norfolk, Virginia. Her father, Blake, was a waiter, and her mother, Georgianna, was a teacher. As a girl she moved with her family to a small, rural community in North Carolina where she grew up. She attended Shaw University in Raleigh with the intention of becoming a missionary, but when she graduated in 1927 she lacked the funds to travel overseas, so instead she moved to Harlem in New York City. She worked as a waitress and in a factory for two years before finding a job on the editorial staff of a black newspaper.

In 1932, Baker cofounded the Young Negroes' Cooperative League. This organization helped African-American consumers form cooperatives by which they could purchase better food for less money. For the next six years, she traveled the country as the League's national director and organized cooperatives in many cities. In 1938, she left the League to work for the National Association for the Advancement of Colored People (NAACP) as an assistant field secretary. Traveling throughout the South, she recruited new members for its local branches and raised money for its fight against racial segregation. Four years later, she took over as national field secretary and director of branches, but by 1946 she had become disillusioned with the organization. In part, she wanted the branches to exercise more control over their own affairs than the national leadership thought appropriate, but also she had become the primary caregiver for her eight-year-old niece and could no longer travel. Although she retained her membership in the NAACP, she resigned as national director and became a staff member with the American Cancer Society.

In 1954, Baker's niece turned 16, thus freeing Baker to resume her struggle to end segregation. Still disillusioned with the NAACP, however, the following year she cofounded In Friendship. This fund-raising group provided financial assistance to the Montgomery Improvement Association, which had organized an African-American boycott of city buses in Montgomery, Alabama. When the boycott succeeded in integrating Montgomery's places of public accommodations, she sought a way to transfer this success to other localities. Her efforts in this regard culminated in the founding of the Southern Christian Leadership Conference (SCLC) in 1957. Although Martin Luther

King, Jr., served as SCLC's head, it was Baker who organized the local chapters, coordinated their programs, and ran the central office in Atlanta, Georgia. Once again, she encountered philosophical differences with the organization's leadership, and for the same reason: SCLC's leaders wanted decisions to be made at the top by the charismatic King and his close circle of advisers, while she wanted the rank-and-file to enjoy greater autonomy.

Meanwhile, black students in the South were organizing sit-ins and boycotts of their own, and Baker concluded that they would be even more effective with some guidance and coordination. To this end, in 1960 she called for a conference of student leaders to be held at Shaw University; together they founded the Student Nonviolent Coordinating Committee (SNCC) with Baker as an adviser. Under her nominal direction, SNCC organized sit-ins and boycotts while also registering African Americans to vote.

By 1964, most blacks across the country had switched their political allegiance from the Republican Party to the Democrats. In black-majority Mississippi, however, the white-controlled state Democratic organization refused to abandon its segregationist policies. In order to provide a political home for the many new voters SNCC had registered, Baker suggested that SNCC form a new political party, the Mississippi Freedom Democratic Party (MFDP). That same year, she served as keynote speaker at the MFDP's inaugural convention in Jackson, then went to Washington, D.C., to organize its national office. From the nation's capital (and, after 1965, from Harlem), she raised funds and provided guidance to dozens of MFDP candidates who were elected to local offices across the state.

Baker continued to advise the MFDP until 1972, when it was able to normalize relations with the state's regular Democratic organization. For the remainder of her life, she served as adviser to a variety of liberation and human rights groups, especially the Mass Party Organizing Committee,

the African National Congress, and the Puerto Rican Solidarity Committee. She died on December 13, 1986, in New York City.

Further Reading

Crawford, Vicki L., et al., eds. *Women in the Civil Rights Movement: Trailblazers and Torchbearers, 1941–1965*. Brooklyn, N.Y.: Carlson Publishing, 1990.

Grant, Joanne. *Ella Baker: Freedom Bound*. New York: Wiley, 1998.

O'Malley, Susan Gushee. "Baker, Ella." In *African American National Biography*, vol. 1, edited by Henry Louis Gates, Jr., and Evelyn Brooks Higginbotham. New York: Oxford University Press, 2008, pp. 224–226.

Powledge, Fred. *Free at Last? The Civil Rights Movement and the People Who Made It*. Boston: Little, Brown, 1991.

Ransby, Barbara. *Ella Baker and the Black Freedom Movement: A Radical Democratic Vision*. Chapel Hill: University of North Carolina Press, 2003.

Baker, Thurbert E.

(1952–) *attorney general of Georgia*

In 1998, Thurbert Baker was elected attorney general of Georgia. It was the first time in the history of the state that an African American was elected to a statewide office.

Baker was born on December 16, 1952, in Rocky Mount, North Carolina. His mother, Mary, who was single, raised him on a farm; as a boy he helped support the family by picking cotton and tobacco on neighboring farms. He obtained enough financial aid to attend the University of North Carolina at Chapel Hill, receiving a B.A. in political science in 1975. Four years later he received a J.D. from Emory University in Atlanta, Georgia, and took up the private practice of law in Atlanta. He later became an attorney for the U.S. Environmental Protection Agency, and then he opened a law firm of his own. In 1988, he was elected as a Democrat to the first of five terms as one of DeKalb County's representatives in Georgia's lower house.

Baker's big political break came in 1990, as a result of his work for progressive Democrat Zell Miller's gubernatorial campaign. Miller took a liking to Baker, and following his election as governor, in 1991 he named Baker the assistant administration house floor leader. Two years later, he appointed Baker to the position of administration house leader. In these two roles, Baker introduced much of Miller's progressive legislation and then did the groundwork to get that legislation enacted into law. Among the many bills that Baker championed were ones toughening the penalties for drunk driving, speeding up the appeals process for condemned prisoners, reforming the welfare system so as to get recipients off the rolls and into jobs, creating a crime victims' bill of rights, and establishing the HOPE college tuition tax credit. Baker's toughest fight, which he won, involved the so-called two strikes bill, which mandated a sentence of life in prison without parole for anyone committing two unrelated violent felonies.

In 1997, Michael Bowers, the state attorney general, resigned from office to run for governor of Georgia. Miller appointed Baker to complete the remaining portion of Bowers's term, thus making Baker the favorite to win the general election the following year. Baker exhibited the same tough stance against crime he had as a legislator, and it propelled him to victory in the 1998 general election. By carrying 113 of the state's 159 counties, he became the first African American ever elected to a statewide office in Georgia.

As attorney general, Baker cracked down on consumer fraud, particularly that involving telemarketers operating from within the state. He had Georgia named as a plaintiff in the multistate suit against the tobacco industry for its role in damaging public health. He also convinced the legislature to pass tough laws against domestic violence, especially when it involved the elderly or was committed in view of a child. To demonstrate the seriousness of his crusade against domestic violence, he chaired the Violence Against Women Committee of the National Association of Attorneys General. Baker also created the Open Government Mediation Program, which has increased citizens' access to government meetings and records. In April 2009, Baker announced that he would be a candidate in Georgia's 2010 gubernatorial election.

Baker was reelected in 2002 and 2006. He and his wife, Catherine, have two children.

Further Reading

Manheim, James M. "Thurbert Baker, 1954– ." *Contemporary Black Biography* 22 (1999), pp. 26–28.
Office of the Attorney General of Georgia. "Thurbert E. Baker." Available online. URL: http://law.ga.gov/00/channel_title/0,2094,87670814_87670933,00.html. Downloaded April 15, 2009.

Ballance, Frank
(Frank Winston Ballance, Jr., Frank W. Ballance)
(1942–) *U.S. congressional representative from North Carolina*

Long one of the most influential African-American politicians in North Carolina, Frank Ballance served in the U.S. House of Representatives for only 18 months before a financial scandal ended his political career.

Ballance was born in tobacco-growing country in eastern North Carolina on February 15, 1942. The son of a sharecropper, he grew up in poverty in the segregated South. After enrolling at North Carolina Central University in Durham, Ballance became involved in the Civil Rights movement. During a protest march calling for school integration, he was assaulted with a club, leaving scars he would have for the rest of his life.

Graduating with a law degree in 1966, Ballance moved to the town of Warrenton to work at an African-American law firm with Theaoseus T.

Clayton. He became increasingly involved in local politics and helped organize voter registration drives. A Democrat, he briefly became a Republican, but returned to the Democratic Party before winning a seat in the North Carolina house of representatives. Serving in this body from 1983 to 1987, Ballance was the first African American from eastern North Carolina elected to the state legislature in almost 100 years. Beginning in 1989, Ballance went on to serve 14 years in the state senate.

In 1990, redistricting created a new African-American dominated legislative district along the eastern coast of North Carolina. Ballance considered running for the U.S. House of Representatives from this district, but instead deferred to EVA CLAYTON, the wife of his old law partner. Ballance not only supported Clayton's bid for office, but he also ran her successful campaign.

In 2002, after serving six terms, Clayton retired from Congress. At the age of 60, Ballance decided to run for her seat. He easily won both the Democratic primary and the general election. In Congress, Clayton worked to steer federal money for health care and education to his constituents. He also sought funds for portions of North Carolina that suffered damage from Hurricane Isabel in 2003.

Ballance declared his intention to run for reelection in 2004, but withdrew from the race only a few days later. Ballance then announced that he would retire on June 11, 2004, six months before the end of his term. He cited myasthenia gravis, a neural disorder, as the reason for early retirement from Congress.

At the time, however, the Federal Bureau of Investigation and state regulators were investigating possible misuse of taxpayer funds paid to the John A. Hyman Memorial Youth Foundation. This nonprofit drug treatment center—named after JOHN HYMAN, the first African American elected to Congress from North Carolina—had been cofounded in 1985 by Ballance, who also chaired its board of directors.

In September 2004, Ballance was indicted on federal corruption charges. He was accused of illegally funneling more than $100,000 from his charity to his law firm and to family members. Two months later, he pled guilty to one count of conspiracy to commit mail fraud and launder money. In October 2005, Ballance received a four-year prison sentence. He was released in June 2009 and allowed to serve the rest of his sentence at home.

Further Reading

Black Americans in Congress. "Frank W. Ballance, Jr." Available online. URL: http://baic.house.gov/member-profiles/profile.html?intID=130. Downloaded May 3, 2009.

Manheim, James M. "Frank W. Ballance, 1942– ." *Contemporary Black Biography* 41 (2004): pp. 20–22.

"National Briefing, South: North Carolina: First-Term Congressman Resigns." *New York Times*, June 9, 2004. Available online. URL: http://www.nytimes.com/2004/06/09/us/national-briefing-south-north-carolina-first-term-congressman-resigns.html?scp=1&sq=frank%20w.%20ballance&st=cse. Downloaded May 3, 2009.

Barry, Marion

(Marion Shepilov Barry, Jr.)
(1936–   ) *mayor of Washington, D.C.*

Marion Barry is one of the most controversial African-American politicians of all time. A leading civil rights activist turned politician, he is credited with helping to gain home rule for the District of Columbia, then fouling up the way its government works to the point that the federal government revoked home rule. His personal style, which included womanizing and drug use, continued to be controversial long after he left politics.

Barry was born on March 6, 1936, in Itta Bena, Mississippi. His parents, Marion and Mattie, were sharecroppers. Barry was four when his father died, and he moved with his mother to Memphis, Tennessee, where he grew up. He earned good enough grades to receive a scholarship to LeMoyne College, a black school in Memphis, where he received a B.S. in chemistry in 1958. Two years later, he received an M.S. in chemistry from Fisk University and then enrolled in the University of Tennessee. Over the next four years he pursued a doctorate in chemistry while teaching at various colleges.

While a student at Fisk, Barry helped organize the Nashville chapter of the National Association for the Advancement of Colored People (NAACP). In 1960, he helped organize Nashville's first lunch counter sit-in. That year he, ELLA BAKER, and others cofounded the Student Nonviolent Coordinating Committee (SNCC), with Barry as its first national chairman. In 1964, he dropped out of the University of Tennessee to work for civil rights full-time, and the following year he moved to Washington, D.C., to become director of the local SNCC chapter.

At the time, the District of Columbia was governed directly by Congress. The city's residents could not vote for their own mayor or city councilmen, so in 1966 Barry organized the "Free D.C." movement. Part of the movement included boycotting merchants who refused to put "Free D.C." posters in their store windows, a crude but effective way to gain some support from the business community while spreading the message. In 1967, he resigned from SNCC to found Youth Pride Inc., which found jobs for Washington's unemployed black youths. In 1972, he married Mary Treadwell; they divorced four years later. In 1978, he married Effie Slaughter. They divorced as well, and in 1992 he married Cora Masters.

Barry first ran for office in 1970 when he got elected to the citizen's board of the city's Pilot Police District Project, an effort to improve relations between Washington's black-majority population and its white-majority police force. The following year he was elected to the city board of education, and from 1972 to 1974 he served as its president. In 1974, the year after Washington gained limited home rule, he ran for a seat on the

city's first elected city council since the 1800s. For the next four years, he served as chairman of the council's committee on finance and revenue. In 1977, a group of radical Black Muslims attempted to take over the District Building, in essence Washington's city hall, and Barry was shot in the chest while trying to keep the terrorists from entering. He almost died, but by the time he recovered he had become a hero in the district, particularly to the poorer residents whom he had been trying to help for 10 years.

In 1978, Barry decided to run for mayor. The incumbent, WALTER WASHINGTON, was ready to retire from politics, but the city council president, Sterling Tucker, was considered the front-runner to take his place. Barry shocked the experts by polling more votes than Tucker in the Democratic primary, then sweeping his Republican opponent in the general election. He took office in early 1979.

Barry performed quite credibly during his first two terms as mayor. He balanced the city's budget, mollified the city's underprivileged residents by building new public housing and expanding existing job programs, and opened day care facilities for the children of government workers, many of whom lived in the city. To attract retailers who had abandoned downtown Washington after the riots of 1968, he implemented pro-business zoning and development practices. He also defused a teacher strike, got the city through a blizzard that threatened to cripple the entire district, and oversaw a sharp reduction in crime. He performed so admirably that in 1984 he was chosen to serve as president of the National Conference of Black Mayors, a position he held for four years.

Barry's reputation began to tarnish toward the end of his second term. A major riot at the city's prison in 1986 exposed serious problems of overcrowding in the prison and mismanagement in the mayor's office. Charges of corruption were made against his chief aide; a close female companion was arrested for selling cocaine; and questions were raised about the way Barry awarded city contracts. Despite these controversies, he was reelected to a third term in 1986. After his reelection, however, the controversies worsened. Two deputy mayors and 10 other city officials were charged with corruption. Treadwell, Barry's first wife, was convicted for misusing federal funds while working with Barry at Youth Pride. And in 1990, Barry was arrested for smoking cocaine on camera during a Drug Enforcement Agency sting operation. Later that year, he was convicted of cocaine possession and sentenced to six months in prison. His political career seemed over.

Just two years later, however, Barry made a miraculous comeback. His radical style, coupled with the real accomplishments he had made during his early days as mayor, endeared him to a majority of the district's residents, and in 1992 he was elected to the city council. Two years later, he defeated incumbent SHARON PRATT DIXON KELLY in the Democratic primary and his Republican opponent in the general election to win a fourth term as mayor.

Unfortunately for Barry, he had lost his magic touch as mayor. When he took office in 1995, the city was $1 billion in debt, thus forcing him to lay off city workers and reduce services drastically. The police had difficulty coping with rising crime, and in 1997 the school system opened three weeks late due to more than 11,000 fire code violations in 43 schools. Meanwhile, in 1995 Congress had established a financial control board with the authority to oversee the city's budget, thus forcing Barry to make regular visits to the House to ask, hat in hand, for more money. The situation continued to deteriorate amid allegations that Barry was misappropriating money, and in 1997 the federal government took over control of the district government. Barry was forced to relinquish most of his mayoral powers to the control board until such time as things improved.

In 1998, Barry declared that he would retire from politics when his term expired in 1999. He spent the next three years working as an investment banker. By 2002, however, Barry had decided to return to the political world, this time by running for city council. Only a month after announcing his candidacy, he pulled out of the race after it was reported that park police had discovered traces of crack cocaine in his car. Two years later, after the publicity had died down, Barry made another bid for city council. In the general election, he received 95 percent of the vote.

In 2006, Barry was sentenced to probation for failing to pay local and federal taxes. Nevertheless, he was easily reelected to his city council seat in 2008. Despite his popularity with the public, Barry has fallen out of favor with his fellow council members. On March 2, 2010, they voted unanimously to censure Barry and strip him of his chairmanship. The council's action resulted from an investigative report that found that Barry received $15,000 in exchange for awarding a city contract to his girlfriend. The city council has referred the allegation to the office of the U.S. attorney for further investigation.

Further Reading

Agronsky, Jonathan I. Z. *Marion Barry: The Politics of Race.* Latham, N.Y.: British American Publishing Company, 1991.

Barras, Jonetta R. *The Last of the Black Emperors: The Hollow Comeback of Marion Barry in the New Age of Black Leaders.* Baltimore: Bancroft Press, 1998.

Colburn, David R., and Jeffrey S. Adler. *African-American Mayors: Race, Politics, and the American City.* Urbana: University of Illinois Press, 2001.

Neumann, Caryn E. "Barry, Marion." In *African American National Biography*, vol. 1, edited by Henry Louis Gates, Jr., and Evelyn Brooks Higginbotham. New York: Oxford University Press, 2008, pp. 286–288.

Belton, Sharon
(Sharon Sayles Belton)
(1951–   ) *mayor of Minneapolis, Minnesota*

Sharon Belton was the first African American to serve as mayor of Minneapolis. Her two terms were devoted to economic development and crime prevention. After stepping down as mayor, she retired from politics.

Belton was born Sharon Sayles on May 13, 1951, in St. Paul, Minnesota. Her father was a car salesman, and her mother was an evangelist. In 1969, she graduated from high school and enrolled in Macalester College, receiving a B.A. four years later. In 1973, she went to work as a parole officer for the state department of corrections. That same year she had become the single mother of a child with brain damage, and for the next eight years she struggled to raise the child at home by herself. In 1981 she married Steve Belton, who adopted her child and with whom she had two children.

Belton's career in politics grew out of her efforts to combat violence against women. In 1978, she cofounded the first shelter for battered women in Minneapolis, and three years later she was elected president of the National Coalition Against Sexual Assault. When her two-year term expired in 1983, she was named associate director of the Minnesota Program for Victims of Sexual Assault. In this capacity, she helped open 26 centers for the victims of rape. Meanwhile, her advocacy of women's issues had brought her to the attention of a group of influential women in Minneapolis, who urged her to run for city council. Elected in 1984, she honed her political skills over the next five years, developing a reputation for conciliation and consensus-building. In 1989, she was elected council president, a position she held for four years.

As a former parole officer, Belton remained interested in the socioeconomic conditions that contribute to criminal behavior. A member of the Democrat-Farm-Labor Party (Minnesota's version of the Democratic Party), in 1993 she decided to become more involved in addressing these conditions by running for mayor of Minneapolis. Her campaign was aided immeasurably when she was endorsed by the outgoing mayor of 14 years, Don Fraser, who also helped her raise money. Despite her opponent's accusations that she was too passive a leader and too soft on crime, and the fact that

Minneapolis is almost 80 percent white, she won. Taking office in 1994, she hired more police and assigned them to high-crime areas. These areas tended to be poor neighborhoods with a high percentage of minority residents, but because of her race she was able to blunt charges of racial profiling. She also tried to deter crime in other ways. She worked to develop the city's economy by attracting new businesses to the central business district, and in the process she helped create more than 10,000 jobs. She implemented housing assistance and job training programs for poor families and established gun control and school truancy prevention programs. She also established a mayor's youth council to involve teenagers in crime prevention and community development. As a result of all these initiatives, the crime rate in Minneapolis dropped to its lowest in decades while property values rose and the local economy boomed.

Belton was reelected in 1997. Over the next four years her quiet leadership style was increasingly mistaken for passivity, and her critics began accusing her of ignoring the voters. She failed to counter these criticisms effectively in the media, and in 2001 she was defeated in her bid for a third term. Following the expiration of her term in 2002, she was named a senior fellow at the University of Minnesota's Hubert H. Humphrey Institute of Public Affairs. In 2010, Belton became the vice president of community relations and government affairs for Thomson Reuters, an information company based in New York City.

Further Reading
Luna, Christopher. "Sayles Belton, Sharon." *Current Biography* 62 (January 2001), pp. 73–76.

Berry, Ted
(Theodore Moody Berry)
(1905–2000) *mayor of Cincinnati, Ohio*

Ted Berry was the first African American to serve as Cincinnati's mayor. He was also a prominent civil rights lawyer and one of the generals of President Lyndon B. Johnson's "War on Poverty."

Berry was born on November 8, 1905, in Maysville, Kentucky. Nothing is known about his parents except that his mother, a deaf-mute housekeeper, was raped by his father, a white farmer. As a young boy he moved with his mother to Cincinnati where he grew up. To help support the family, he did a variety of odd jobs while attending school. After graduating as his high school's first black valedictorian, he went to work in a steel mill in Newport, just across the Ohio River in Kentucky. He also attended the University of Cincinnati, receiving an A.B. in 1928 and an LL.B. in 1931.

In 1932, Berry passed the bar examination, opened a law office in Cincinnati, and became legal counsel for the local chapter of the National Association for the Advancement of Colored People (NAACP). He argued many civil rights cases for the NAACP, and in 1937 he was admitted to the U.S. Supreme Court bar. In 1938 he married Johnnie Mae Newton, with whom he had three children. The following year he accepted the post of assistant prosecuting attorney for Hamilton County, which surrounds Cincinnati. In 1945 he gained a bit of national acclaim when he was asked to defend three black Army Air Corps pilots, part of a unit known today as the Tuskegee Airmen. These officers were being court-martialed for protesting their exclusion from the officers' club at Freeman Field in Seymour, Indiana. Although one of the three was convicted, Berry managed to get the other two acquitted.

By 1947, Berry had become one of Cincinnati's most distinguished African-American residents. He had gained a reputation as an astute lawyer and a brilliant public speaker, but also as a person who knew how to change things by working within the system. That same year he ran for city council as an independent; although he lost, the campaign set the stage for a second try two years later, which he won. His eight-year tenure on council was marked by controversy, only part of which was generated by his pro-civil rights activ-

ism. In 1953, as chairman of the finance committee, he led an attempt to impose a city income tax. Two years later he was elected vice-mayor as a result of the city's proportional representation voting system. According to this system, voters listed all the candidates in order of preference; the one with the most first-place votes was elected mayor; of those remaining, the one with the most first- and second-place votes was elected vice-mayor; and so on until all the council seats were filled. Because this system favored a minority candidate like Berry, the city's white voters became alarmed that he might be elected mayor in the next election. To prevent this, they forced a change to an at-large system, which worked against minority candidates. As a result, in 1957, instead of being elected mayor, Berry came in 14th out of 18 candidates and lost his seat on council.

Undaunted, Berry continued to work for change by founding the Community Action Commission, a local organization that sought to combat poverty by empowering the poor to help themselves. The program was so successful that in 1964 it came to the attention of R. Sargent Shriver, Jr., head of the Office of Economic Opportunity's "War on Poverty." The following year President Johnson appointed Berry director of the OEO's community action programs, which included Head Start and Job Corps and which operated on the same basic principles as those employed by the Community Action Commission. Although these projects failed to eliminate poverty as their proponents had hoped, they did much to alleviate the desperate condition of millions of disadvantaged Americans of all races.

Berry returned to Cincinnati after Johnson left office in 1969 and the "War on Poverty" ended. By now the racial climate in his hometown had changed significantly, and when a councilman died in 1970, Berry was appointed to fill his term. Meanwhile, Cincinnati had again changed the way it selected a mayor, and when he was elected to council in his own right in 1972, his fellow councilmen named him mayor. During his four-year tenure, he skillfully worked out compromises that benefited the interests of the poor, labor, and business.

In 1976, Berry retired from politics but remained active in the legal community. He joined the law firm of Tobias & Kraus, taught law at his alma mater, and served as the NAACP branch's general counsel. In the 1990s he cofounded the Center for Voting and Democracy in Cincinnati, and he led an unsuccessful movement to restore proportional representation. He spent his last few years in a nursing home in Loveland, Ohio, where he died on October 15, 2000.

Further Reading

Center for Voting and Democracy. "Death of Theodore Berry, Cincinnati's First Black Mayor and Champion of Proportional Representation, October 15, 2000." Available online. URL: http://www.fair-vote.org/pr/berry.htm. Downloaded April 12, 2009.

Cincinnati Enquirer. "Theodore M. Berry Showed Them the Way: Today's Leaders Remember Their Mentor." Available online. URL: http://enquirer. com/editions/2000/10/19/loc_berry_showed_them . html. Downloaded April 12, 2009.

Martin, Douglas. "Theodore Berry, 94, Civil Rights Pioneer, Dies." *New York Times,* October 17, 2000, p. B12.

Bishop, Sanford
(Sanford Dixon Bishop, Jr.)
(1947–) *U.S. congressional representative from Georgia*

Sanford Bishop is part of a growing breed of moderate black political leaders. Among other things, they are calling for fiscal conservatism in government and an expanded role for free-market forces in the solution of the nation's socioeconomic problems.

Sanford Dixon Bishop, Jr., was born on February 4, 1947, in Mobile, Alabama. His father, San-

ford, was a minister and college president, and his mother, Minnie, was a librarian. After finishing high school, he attended Morehouse College in Atlanta, Georgia, receiving a B.A. in 1968. He spent the next three years studying law at Emory University and received a J.D. in 1971. After a year in New York City, in 1972 he settled in Columbus, Georgia, where he opened a law firm that specialized in civil rights.

Bishop's involvement as a civil rights lawyer soon led him into politics. In 1976, he was elected to the first of seven terms in the state legislature, and in 1990 he was elected to the state senate. He served on the lower house's ways and means committee, and in this capacity he worked for measures that promoted jobs as well as a stronger, more diversified state economy. A moderate Democrat but a fiscal conservative, he introduced a bill in the senate to help people get off welfare by providing them with job training. He also introduced bills to raise the ethical standards of the state legislature.

Two things happened in 1992 to make Bishop the perfect candidate for the U.S. House of Representatives. First, Congress was rocked by a financial scandal. One of the benefits each senator and representative receives is a free checking account with overdraft protection. It was disclosed that hundreds of congresspeople had abused their privilege by being seriously overdrawn, in effect taking out unsecured, interest-free loans at taxpayer expense. The worst offenders faced the ire of their constituents at election time, and one of these offenders was Charles Hatcher, who represented Bishop's district. Because of ethics legislation Bishop had sponsored in the state senate, a number of people urged him to run for Hatcher's seat. Meanwhile, the census of 1990 had forced the Georgia legislature to redraw its congressional districts. In the process, it created a black-majority district centered around Columbus, where Bishop was the best-known African-American politician. He won the Democratic primary and the general

Sanford Bishop is one of a growing number of African-American congressmen who represent white-majority districts. *(Sanford D. Bishop, Jr.)*

money for projects that included flood relief and control, agriculture diversification, and new highways.

Meanwhile, the boundaries of Bishop's district had been challenged in court on the grounds that the district was gerrymandered in terms of race. In 1995 the U.S. Supreme Court ordered that the district be redrawn, and the result was a white-majority district. Many political pundits believed that Bishop had little chance of being reelected. Bishop, however, worked hard to demonstrate that his views differed little from those of his white constituents. He joined the National Rifle Association, which opposed gun control, emphasized his membership in the Blue Dog Coalition, a group of fiscally conservative House Democrats, and publicized his contributions to the district which had helped all of its residents. To the shock of many, he won reelection handily.

In 2010, Bishop was reelected to a 10th term. He remains one of the most conservative African Americans in the House of Representatives. Bishop is married to the former Vivian Creighton, with whom he has one child.

election with relative ease and took his seat in 1993. He was assigned to the committees on agriculture, intelligence, and veterans' affairs.

As a congressman, Bishop remained true to his moderate views. He supported measures to rid neighborhoods of crime and drugs, to clean up the environment, to improve the quality and accessibility of health care, and to maintain a strong military, but he insisted that these things be done within the constraints of a balanced budget. As a member of the agriculture committee, he oversaw the enactment of several important farm bills. Chief among them was the Farm Bill of 1996, which retained farm subsidies for peanut growers, many of whom live in Georgia, by employing market forces so that the net cost to the federal government was zero. He helped bring to his district more than $600 million in federal

Further Reading

Biographical Directory of the United States Congress. "Bishop, Sanford Dixon, Jr., 1947–   ." Available online. URL: http://bioguide.congress.gov/scripts/biodisplay.pl?index=B000490. Downloaded October 19, 2002.

Congressman Sanford D. Bishop, Jr., Official Web Site. Available online. URL: http://bishop.house.gov. Downloaded April 28, 2010.

Explorations in Black Leadership. "Sanford D. Bishop, Jr." Available online. URL: http://www.virginia.edu/publichistory/bl/index.php?uid=2. Downloaded April 19, 2009.

Grann, David. "Whose Bishop? A Race for the House: Georgia." *The New Republic* 215 (November 4, 1996): 18.

"Sanford Bishop." *Congressional Quarterly Weekly Report* 51 (January 16, 1993, supplement): 75.

Blackwell, Ken
(J. Kenneth Blackwell)
(1948–) *Ohio secretary of state*

Ken Blackwell has held a variety of offices in municipal, state, and national government. He made history in 2006 when he became the first African American to run for governor of Ohio on a major party ticket.

Blackwell was born on February 28, 1948. Raised in a Cincinnati public housing project, he won a football scholarship to the city's Xavier University. After graduating with a bachelor's degree in psychology and master's degree in education, Blackwell worked at Xavier, eventually becoming the university's vice president of community relations.

In 1977, Blackwell was elected to the Cincinnati city council, on which he remained for the next 10 years. Starting in 1979, he also served a two-year term as mayor. Aligning himself with the Republican Party, Blackwell was appointed undersecretary of the U.S. Department of Housing and Urban Development (HUD) from 1989 to 1990 by President George H. W. Bush. Blackwell then returned to Ohio to run for an open seat in the U.S. House of Representatives, but his campaign was unsuccessful. He rejoined the Bush administration in 1992 by accepting a post as the U.S. ambassador to the United Nations Human Rights Commission.

In 1994, Blackwell was appointed Ohio state treasurer to complete a vacated term and was elected to the position later that year. He thereby became the first African American in Ohio history to be elected to a statewide executive office. Four years later, Blackwell successfully ran for secretary of state of Ohio. While in the job, he acted as the national chairman for the 2000 presidential campaign of Steve Forbes. When Forbes dropped out, Blackwell publicly supported the Republican nominee George W. Bush.

In 2002, Blackwell was reelected to a second term as Ohio's secretary of state, a position whose responsibilities included overseeing state elections. In the 2004 election, he continued to serve as secretary of state while also acting as a chair of Bush's reelection campaign in Ohio. In the tight race, Bush won Ohio by a margin of only about 2 percent of the vote. Blackwell was subsequently named in a flood of lawsuits charging that minority voters in the state had been disenfranchised in an effort to manipulate the election's outcome.

Despite the criticism of his behavior during the 2004 election, Blackwell remained secretary of state even after he announced that he would run for governor in 2006, meaning that he would oversee an election in which he was a candidate. Running as a far right social and fiscal conservative, Blackwell courted religious and pro-gun groups. He won the Republican primary but lost the general election, receiving only 37 percent of the vote.

After his defeat, Blackwell remained a prominent Republican voice, both on the state and national level. He was frequently a guest on network and cable public affairs programs. He also coauthored with Ken Klukowski a book titled *The Blueprint: Obama's Plan to Subvert the Constitution and Build an Imperial Presidency* (2010). In 2009, Blackwell made a bid for the chairmanship of the Republican National Committee. He withdrew his name after the fourth ballot and endorsed MICHAEL STEELE, who eventually won the position.

Further Reading
Blackwell, J. Kenneth, and Ken Klukowski. *The Blueprint: Obama's Plan to Subvert the Constitution and Build an Imperial Presidency*. Guilford, Conn.: Lyons Press, 2010.

Dingle, Derek T. "Rise of the Black Republicans?" *Black Enterprise* 37 (November 2006): 100–109.

Nagourney, Adam. "At Key Moment, Diverse G.O.P. Leadership Choice." *New York Times,* January 10, 2009. Available online. URL: http://www.nytimes.com/2009/01/11/us/politics/11gop.html. Downloaded May 18, 2009.

Blackwell, Lucien
(Lucien Edward Blackwell)
(1931–2003) *U.S. congressional
representative from Pennsylvania*

Like CHARLES HAYES before him, Lucien Edward Blackwell came to politics by way of organized labor. A long-time president of his local union, Blackwell served for almost 20 years on the Philadelphia city council before moving on to a seat in the U.S. Congress.

Blackwell was born on August 1, 1931, in Whitsett, Pennsylvania. He finished high school in 1949, then briefly attended St. Josephs College in Philadelphia before going to work as a stevedore on the city's Delaware River waterfront. In 1953, he joined the U.S. Army and fought as an infantryman during the Korean War. Discharged the following year, he returned to the docks and was promoted to foreman. He got involved in Local 1332 of the International Longshoremen's Association, gradually working his way up through the union's ranks from trustee to vice president and business agent. In 1973, he was elected local president, a position he held for the next 18 years.

Blackwell's union activity led him into politics, and in 1973 he decided to run for office. He was elected as a Democrat to the state legislature, where he played a major role in establishing the Crisis Intervention Network as a means of dealing with gang-related crime. He left the legislature two years later after he was elected to the Philadelphia city council. He served on council for the next 17 years, during which time he worked to provide better jobs and housing for the city's minorities. He sponsored the city's Human Rights Bill as well as measures setting aside a certain percentage of city business for minority-owned enterprises. He also helped set up a public assistance program for homeless people. As a councilman, he is best remembered for his six-week fast in protest of insufficient maintenance and security in the city's public housing projects.

While on city council, he served a term as chairman of the council's finance committee, chairman of the Philadelphia Gas Commission, and commissioner of the Delaware River Port Authority. He ran for mayor in 1979 and 1991 but was defeated both times.

In 1991, BILL GRAY resigned from Congress to become executive director of the United Negro College Fund. Blackwell ran in the special election to fill the vacancy and was easily elected. He took his seat that same year and was assigned to a special task force investigating homelessness, which he called the "Shame of America." As a congressman, he focused on issues relating to labor. In 1993 he introduced a bill to establish a 30-hour workweek. At the time, many working people were being laid off because of a recession, and his bill was supported by organized labor because it promised to keep people on the job. He also sponsored a bill to protect the credit ratings of people who were laid off during a recession. On the local scene, he brought together state and local officials as well as religious and civic leaders to create a think tank to deal with Philadelphia's growing drug problem. Many of his constituents called him "Lucien with the Solution."

Blackwell was reelected to one term. In 1994 he was defeated in the Democratic primary by CHAKA FATTAH. After completing his term in 1995, Blackwell went to work for the city of Philadelphia as a lobbyist. He and his wife Jannie had four children. He died on January 24, 2003, in Philadelphia.

Further Reading
Biographical Directory of the United States Congress. "Blackwell, Lucien Edward, 1931–2003." Available online. URL: http://bioguide.congress.gov/scripts/ biodisplay.pl?index=B000517. Downloaded April 1, 2009.
Black Americans in Congress. "Lucien Edward Blackwell." Available online. URL: http://baic.house.gov/member-profiles/profile.html?intID=126. Downloaded April 3, 2009.

Clay, William L. *Just Permanent Interests: Black Americans in Congress, 1870–1992.* New York: Amistad Press, 1993.

"New Member Profile: Lucien E. Blackwell, D-Pa. (2)." *Congressional Quarterly Weekly Report* 49 (November 16, 1991): 3,406.

Blackwell, Unita

(1933–   ) *mayor of Mayersville, Mississippi*

Unita Blackwell was one of the first African-American mayors in the South. In addition to providing quality leadership to her own community, she contributed much to the development of mayors across the United States and around the world.

Blackwell was born on March 18, 1933, in Lula, Mississippi. Her parents were sharecroppers, and she spent most of her first 30 years chopping cotton on plantations in Mississippi, Arkansas, and Tennessee and peeling tomatoes in Florida. She managed to get an eighth-grade education by spending several months each year with relatives in West Helena, Arkansas, where black children were permitted to attend public school. She was married twice and had one child. In 1962, she took up residence in her first permanent home, a three-room shack in Mayersville, a town of about 500 people in Mississippi's Issaquena County.

Blackwell became involved in politics via the Civil Rights movement, which she joined shortly after settling in Mayersville. In 1963, she became one of the indigenous leaders of a voter registration drive organized by the Student Nonviolent Coordinating Committee (SNCC); in the process, she lost her job chopping cotton and was arrested more than 70 times. In 1964, she cofounded, along with ELLA BAKER, AARON HENRY, and others, the Mississippi Freedom Democratic Party (MFDP) to provide a political home for all the African American voters that SNCC had been registering since the previous year. That same year, she attended the Democratic National Convention as one of the MFDP delegates who attempted unsuccessfully to unseat Mississippi's regular Democratic delegation. In 1965, she filed suit against the Issaquena County Board of Education to force it to comply with the U.S. Supreme Court's 1954 ruling against segregated schools in *Brown v. Board of Education.* In 1967, she cofounded Mississippi Action Community Education as a means of helping small, black-majority towns incorporate so they could qualify for federal aid. During the 1970s, she worked for the National Council of Negro Women's low-income housing development program, recruiting people across the country to build their own homes under a special "sweat equity" program of the U.S. Department of Housing and Urban Development. In 1976, she was named to a four-year term as vice-chair of the state Democratic Party that she had challenged a decade earlier.

Blackwell first ran for political office in 1976, when she was elected mayor of Mayersville. Her first accomplishment as mayor was to have the town incorporated. She then obtained federal grant money to provide police and fire protection, build a public water system, pave the streets, install sidewalks and streetlamps, and construct decent housing for the elderly and disabled. Her success made her a role model for many other small-town African-American mayors, and in 1989 she was elected to a two-year term as president of the National Conference of Black Mayors. In 1991, she cofounded the Black Women Mayors' Conference as an offshoot of the NCBM and served as its first president. She served as Mayersville's mayor for more than 25 years.

In addition to her involvement in state and local politics, Blackwell played a role in international affairs as well. In 1973, she made a trip to the Republic of China with the actress Shirley MacLaine, whom she had met in the Civil Rights movement. Four years later she founded the U.S.-China People's Friendship Association and served as its president for six years. In 1984, she established an exchange program for mayors in the

United States and China. In 1979, she was appointed to the U.S. National Commission on the International Year of the Child.

In 1983, Blackwell achieved a personal goal when she received an M.A. in regional planning from the University of Massachusetts. Despite having never attended high school, she was admitted as part of the National Rural Fellows Program, which awarded her a scholarship and gave her credit based on her life experiences. In 1993, she ran for Congress but was defeated in the primary by BENNIE THOMPSON. Blackwell published her autobiography, *Barefootin': Life Lessons from the Road to Freedom*, in 2006.

In January 2008, Blackwell, suffering from the early stages of dementia, made national news when she disappeared from a hotel room in Atlanta while attending ceremonies to commemorate Martin Luther King Day. She was later found unharmed at the city's Hartsfield-Jackson International Airport.

Further Reading

Blackwell, Unita, with Joanne Prichard Morris. *Barefootin': Life Lessons from the Road to Freedom.* New York: Crown, 2004.

Civil Rights in Mississippi Digital Archive. "An Oral History with Unita Blackwell." Available online. URL: http://www.lib.usm.edu/~spcol/crda/oh/blackwell.htm. Downloaded April 1, 2009.

Hine, Darlene C., ed. *Facts On File Encyclopedia of Black Women in America.* New York: Facts On File, 1997.

Bond, Julian
(Horace Julian Bond)
(1940–   ) *Georgia state senator*

Julian Bond is perhaps the most perplexing African-American political leader of all time. Handsome, witty, and articulate, he is the first black to have his name placed in nomination for national office by a major political party. Less than a decade later, he had dropped from sight on the national political scene. Bond's interest in politics seems to have been motivated mostly by his larger interest in civil rights, while his personal ambitions tend more toward the "quiet arts" of poetry and scholarship.

Horace Julian Bond, popularly known by his middle name, was born on January 14, 1940, in Nashville, Tennessee. His father, Horace, was president of Fort Valley State College in Georgia and a scholar of national repute, and his mother, Julia, was a librarian. As an infant, he moved with his family from Fort Valley to Oxford, Pennsylvania, where his father served as president of Lincoln University and where he grew up. He finished high school in 1957 and enrolled in Morehouse College in Atlanta. He soon discovered that he had the ability to write poetry, and six of his poems were published while he was still in school.

Bond became involved in the Civil Rights movement in 1960, during his junior year at Morehouse. He and two fellow students founded the *Atlanta Inquirer*, a radical student newspaper, and the Atlanta Committee on Appeal for Human Rights. With Bond leading the way, the committee staged a sit-in at the cafeteria in Atlanta's city hall to protest the fact that it was segregated. Shortly thereafter, he was invited to attend the meeting at which the Student Nonviolent Coordinating Committee (SNCC) was founded. By 1961, he was devoting most of his time to directing the Civil Rights movement in Atlanta, and he dropped out of school to become SNCC's director of communications. That same year he married Alice Clopton, with whom he had five children. For the next three years, he edited SNCC's newspaper, *Student Voice*, and kept reporters across the Deep South well- provided with tapes and press releases.

The census of 1960 mandated that Georgia redraw the districts for its state legislature, and in the process several black-majority districts were created in Atlanta. In 1964, Bond ran for one of those seats and was elected easily. Shortly after the election, he made a statement critical of U.S.

involvement in Vietnam, and his fellow legislators voted almost unanimously to deny him his seat on the grounds of treason and disorderly conduct. After more than a year of legal battles, in 1966 the U.S. Supreme Court ordered that Bond be seated; the legislature relented but refused to let him speak from the floor.

The seating controversy made Bond a nationally known figure. His name recognition increased even more in 1968, when he led a black delegation to that year's Democratic National Convention. Following a bitter struggle with the Georgia Democratic Party's regular, mostly white delegation, Bond's group was awarded almost half the delegation's seats, a major victory for integration. Later at the convention, Bond was nominated for vice president, even though at age 28 he was too young by seven years to hold the office. Following the convention, he was mentioned prominently as being most likely to assume de facto control of the Civil Rights movement following the assassination of Martin Luther King, Jr. In a 1970 national poll of African Americans, Bond was their first choice for president.

Bond, however, had other plans. The national limelight seemed to hold little appeal for him, and although he was clearly interested in furthering civil rights, he had no intention of becoming the movement's leader. In 1971, he returned to Morehouse as a student and completed his B.A. He continued to serve in Georgia's lower house until 1975, when he won a seat in the state senate. That same year, he became president of the Atlanta chapter of the National Association for the Advancement of Colored People (NAACP). His disinterest in national affairs was clearly demonstrated in 1976, when he turned down a post in the administration of his fellow Georgian, President Jimmy Carter.

During his 22-year tenure in the state legislature, Bond focused on such mundane but important considerations as paving streets and improving garbage collection for his constituents. When he drew criticism for not getting involved in larger issues of interest to the African-American community, he replied that the protests of the Civil Rights movement had "moved indoors," and the goal now was to secure equal services as well as equal rights. In 1986, he stepped down from the state senate to campaign for the U.S. House of Representatives. When he lost the primary to JOHN LEWIS, he retired from politics. He taught for several years at Harvard, Drexel, and American Universities before becoming a full-time professor of history at the University of Virginia in 1989. He also divorced his wife that year, and in 1990 he married Pamela Horowitz. In 1998, he was elected chairman of the NAACP's national board of directors, on which he had served for a number of years. Stating that it was time "to let a new generation of leaders lead," Bond stepped down from the NAACP chairmanship in February 2009.

Further Reading

Bond, Julian. *A Time to Speak, a Time to Act: The Movement in Politics.* New York: Simon & Schuster, 1972.

Explorations in Black Leadership. "Julian Bond." Available online. URL: http://www.virginia.edu/publichistory/bl/index.php?uid=3. Downloaded April 9, 2009.

Neary, John. *Julian Bond: Black Rebel.* New York: Morrow, 1971.

Smith, Jessie C. *Black Heroes of the 20th Century.* Detroit: Visible Ink Press, 1998.

Sullivan, Patricia. "Bond, Julian." In *African American National Biography,* vol. 1, edited by Henry Louis Gates, Jr., and Evelyn Brooks Higginbotham. New York: Oxford University Press, 2008, pp. 473–474.

Booker, Cory
(Cory A. Booker)
(1969–   ) *mayor of Newark, New Jersey*

Years before Cory Booker was elected mayor of Newark, New Jersey, he was already considered a political star with the potential of making a name for himself on the national stage.

Booker was born in Washington, D.C., on April 27, 1969. He spent most of his youth in the affluent suburb of Harrington Park, New Jersey. Both his parents were executives at IBM.

Booker was an excellent student and was elected senior class president at his high school. He continued his education at Stanford University, in Palo Alto, California, where he was the student body president. After graduating in 1991, Booker was named a Rhodes Scholar. At Oxford University in England, he earned a second bachelor's degree in modern history.

After returning to the United States, Booker enrolled at Yale Law School in New Haven, Connecticut. During his last year at Yale, he moved to Newark, New Jersey, a city long plagued by widespread poverty and high crime rates. Booker moved into Brick Towers, a rundown housing project, where he lived for eight years. During that time, he joined with other activists to demand that the city government improve the living conditions in Newark's public housing. He also worked as a staff attorney for the Urban Justice Center.

Booker became convinced that Newark's poor would always be badly served until there was a drastic change in the city government. The idea inspired him to enter politics. Booker ran a successful campaign for the Newark Municipal Council in 1998. After the election, he immediately began challenging Mayor SHARPE JAMES and demanding improvements in Newark's police department and school system. After only four years on the council, Booker announced that he would try to unseat James in the 2002 mayoral election.

The campaign was the focus of the Academy Award–nominated documentary *Street Fight* (2005). The dramatic and fierce contest pitted Booker against important African-American leaders, such as JESSE JACKSON and AL SHARPTON, who viewed Booker as an upstart trying to usurp power from the old guard. James's supporters

fought hard against Booker, going so far as to initiate "whisper campaigns" suggesting that Booker was not who he said he was. At various times, voters were told that Booker was secretly white, gay, Jewish, and Republican. Booker lost the election, and James won a fifth term as mayor.

After his defeat, Booker became a partner in a law firm. He also worked for Newark Now, a nonprofit organization he founded to help Newark residents improve their neighborhoods. In 2006, Booker made his second bid for mayor. James declined to run but supported Booker's opponent, Ronald Rice. Since his previous campaign, Booker had drawn a great deal of attention from the media, which often touted him as the new face of African-American leadership. As a result, Booker's 2006 campaign attracted many contributors from outside Newark. Outspending his opponent by a ratio of 25 to 1, Booker won the election with a record-setting 72 percent of the vote.

At his inauguration, Booker promised to "lead our nation in an urban transformation." During his first year in office, he oversaw the opening of a new $375 million arena, part of Booker's greater plans for revitalizing Newark. But he also ran into unexpected problems. By the summer of 2007, because of a surprise budget deficit, Booker had to raise taxes and lay off hundreds of city workers, actions that infuriated many voters. He also had to deal with the aftermath of the brutal execution-style murders of three African-American college students in the usually quiet neighborhood of Ivy Hill. The slayings became national news and challenged Booker's optimistic views of Newark's future. As he admitted to the *New York Times*, "I still believe we're going to move the city forward but this is a powerful blow."

Although his first year as mayor deflated the high hopes of some supporters, Booker has since restored much of his sagging popularity. For instance, he was praised for pushing for new police procedures, which many Newark residents have credited with creating a 30 percent drop in the city's murder rate in 2008. This record helped

Booker easily win reelection in May 2010 with 59 percent of the vote. Booker's energy and charisma have also continued to attract positive media attention, suggesting that he will have a long career in the politics of New Jersey and perhaps beyond.

Further Reading

Boyer, Peter J. "The Color of Politics." *New Yorker,* February 4, 2008, pp. 38–47.

Ifill, Gwen. *The Breakthrough: Politics and Race in the Age of Obama.* New York: Doubleday, 2009.

Mayor Cory Booker, Official Web Site. Available online. URL: http://www.corybooker.com. Downloaded May 17, 2009.

Raab, Scott. "The Battle of Newark, Starring Cory Booker." *Esquire,* July 16, 2008. Available online. URL: http://www.esquire.com/features/cory-booker-0708. Downloaded May 17, 2009.

Bosley, Freeman
(Freeman Robertson Bosley, Jr.)
(1954–   ) *mayor of St. Louis, Missouri*

Freeman Bosley was the first African-American mayor of St. Louis, Missouri. Despite a relatively successful first term, he lost his bid for reelection to CLARENCE HARMON.

Freeman Robertson Bosley, Jr., was born on July 20, 1954, in St. Louis. His father, Freeman, owned a record company and managed a mattress factory, and his mother, Marjorie, was a teacher. After graduating from high school he enrolled in the University of St. Louis, receiving a B.A. in urban affairs and political science in 1976 and a J.D. from the university's law school in 1979. He worked for three years as an attorney for the Legal Services of Eastern Missouri, and in 1982 he became an associate in a local law firm.

Bosley became involved in politics through his father, who first ran for public office in 1973. Narrowly defeated for a seat on the city's board of aldermen, the elder Bosley ran again in 1977 and won. Both times, Bosley worked on his father's campaign. In 1982, he decided to run for office himself; that same year he was elected clerk of the city circuit court, a position he held for 10 years. In this position, he supervised 200 employees and managed an annual budget of $35 million.

In 1985, Bosley helped his father run for mayor of St. Louis. Both Bosleys were concerned about the future of St. Louis; like most cities in the 1980s, it was losing much of its population and jobs to the surrounding suburbs while its downtown and low-income neighborhoods were deteriorating. The incumbent mayor, Vincent Schoemehl, believed the damage could be fixed simply by revitalizing downtown to attract more tourists and businesses, but the Bosleys believed that much attention was owed the older neighborhoods as well. The elder Bosley had developed a reputation for being confrontational toward the city's white population, and he was easily defeated in the Democratic primary by Schoemehl. Shortly after the election, Bosley and his father began to lay the groundwork for another mayoral campaign, but this time with the younger Bosley as the candidate.

In 1992, Schoemehl decided to run for governor of Missouri instead of seeking reelection as mayor. Bosley was one of five Democrats to declare their candidacy for the mayoralty. Running on a platform that called for the continued renewal of downtown while also devoting major funding to residential redevelopment, Bosley won the Democratic primary and swept to victory in the general election. He took his seat in 1993.

Almost as soon as Bosley took office, the Mississippi and Missouri Rivers overflowed their banks in one of the worst floods in recorded history. Parts of St. Louis were underwater, and a significant portion of the city was without electricity or drinking water for days on end. Bosley spent most of his first year in office dealing with the problems caused by the flooding and trying to get the city back to normal. Not until 1994 was he able to begin implementing his own agenda for urban renewal.

Another major problem that Bosley was forced to deal with was the ongoing desegregation of the city's public schools. Since the 1960s St. Louis had bused, by court order, many of its black students to suburban schools while many city schools were left vacant. Bosley worked to put an end to this situation, calling it a waste of taxpayer money and an ineffective way to end segregation. In this effort he was aided greatly by WILLIAM CLAY, JR., who obtained the Missouri legislature's approval for a compromise solution to school segregation.

In terms of economic development, Bosley's most visible success was to lure a National Football League franchise back to St. Louis. Years earlier, the city had lost the St. Louis Cardinals to Phoenix, Arizona. With Bosley's help, a group of local investors was able to entice the Los Angeles Rams to move to St. Louis, where they became known as the St. Louis Rams. The coup was a major boost for the city's self-image as well as a major stimulus to tourism, but while the NFL was returning to St. Louis, several major corporations, among them Ralston-Purina, began making noises as if they were about to leave town, thus jeopardizing the success of his economic development efforts.

Bosley's political undoing came at the hands of his former chief of police, CLARENCE HARMON. Harmon, chief from 1991 to 1995, was generally believed to have done a good job of fighting crime in St. Louis. However, many blacks complained about the way the police force treated them, and the local chapter of the National Association for the Advancement of Colored People (NAACP) claimed that Harmon routinely treated white officers better than black officers. For two years Bosley and Harmon fought for control of the police department, until Harmon resigned from the department. Two years later, he ran against Bosley in the Democratic primary. It was an ugly contest; Harmon accused Bosley of misusing funds and patronizing his political cronies while Bosley accused Harmon of being "a traitor to his race." Harmon polled most of the white votes while Bos-

ley polled most of the black votes, with Harmon winning by a 56-43 margin.

After leaving office in 1998, Bosley returned to the private practice of law. In 2001, he ran in the Democratic primary for mayor; he outpolled Harmon but not Francis Slay, who went on to win the general election. Three years after his defeat, Bosley established his own law firm, Bosley & Associates. He and his wife, the former Darlynn Cunningham, have one child.

Further Reading
Kram, Mark. "Freeman Bosley, Jr." *Contemporary Black Biography* 7 (1994): 23–26.
St. Louis Mayors. "Freeman R. Bosley, Jr." Available online. URL: http://exhibits.slpl.lib.mo.us/mayors/data/dt44496704.asp. Downloaded April 10, 2009.
Weaver, Maurice. "Lawyer Wins in St. Louis." *Ebony* 48 (July 1993): 38.

Bradley, Tom
(Thomas Bradley)
(1917–1998) *mayor of Los Angeles, California*

Tom Bradley was the first African-American mayor of Los Angeles and the first black mayor of a white-majority city. Although his 20-year tenure was stormy at times, he is credited with overseeing the transformation of his city into an international trade center and the second-most important city in the country.

Bradley was born on December 29, 1917, in Calvert, Texas. His parents, Lee and Crenner, were sharecroppers. At age seven he moved with his family to Arizona, where they picked cotton, and then to Los Angeles where his father found work with the Santa Fe railroad. Several years later his father abandoned the family, and he and his siblings grew up in poverty. An excellent athlete in high school, in 1937 he won a track scholarship to the University of California at Los Angeles. After studying education for three years, in 1940 he dropped out to become a Los Angeles police officer. The following year he married Ethel Arnold, with whom he had three children.

Bradley served on the LAPD for 21 years. During his tenure he worked as a foot patrolman, a juvenile officer, and a vice-squad detective. He eventually was promoted to lieutenant, the first African American to attain that rank. Meanwhile, he had begun studying law at night, and in 1956 he received his LL.D. from Los Angeles's Southwestern University. After passing the bar examination in 1961, he retired from the LAPD and opened a law office.

As a policeman, Bradley had become aware of the city's many social and economic problems. Most of these problems stemmed from the fact that Los Angeles, like California, was growing tremendously as a result of immigration from the rest of the United States. In 1963 he decided to do what he could to solve these problems by running as a Democrat for city council. Although his district was two-thirds white, his experience on the LAPD and his stand on the issues impressed the voters, who elected him, thus proving that the city's biggest problems transcended race and ethnicity. As a councilman, he proved to be adept at building coalitions among a variety of groups, thus getting them to see past their differences and focus on their common problems. As the first black city councilman, however, he also worked to diminish racism in the LAPD; he was a vocal critic of the department's performance during the Watts riots in 1965, which saw the deaths of 34 people and the destruction of millions of dollars' worth of property.

By 1969, Bradley was politically strong enough to run for mayor. His opponent, Republican mayor Sam Yorty, was flamboyant, conservative, and popular, and he won by convincing voters that a Bradley victory would lead to a takeover by African-American militants like the Black Panthers. Four years later, however, when Bradley challenged Yorty again, such rhetoric fell on deaf ears, in large part because Mayor Yorty had failed to address the city's problems while Councilman

Bradley had pounded away at them. In 1973, Bradley won, polling nearly all of the black vote and nearly half of the nonblack vote, to become the city's first black mayor.

Bradley was reelected four times. In his own soft-spoken, low-keyed way, he got Los Angeles to change in dramatic and innumerable ways. He made Angelenos recognize the implications of the energy crisis of the early 1970s, implementing a number of energy-saving measures such as the expansion of public transportation. He facilitated the construction of Los Angeles International Airport and the city's downtown skyline. He opened the doors of city hall to minorities, hiring as city employees and appointing to city commissions a number of African Americans, Hispanics, and Asian Americans, both men and women. He addressed, with limited success, the racism that infected the LAPD, doing what he could to minimize its ill effects. He mobilized business and resident interests alike in order to reconstruct Watts and other areas of the city that had been destroyed during the Watts riots. And he overcame seemingly insurmountable odds to attract the 1984 Olympics to Los Angeles, which brought into the city more than $250 million after expenses.

Bradley's impressive achievements as mayor led him to run for governor of California twice, without success. In 1982 his opponent, state attorney general George Deukmejian, successfully portrayed him as a proponent of gun control, thus defeating him by a slim margin. Four years later he ran against Deukmejian again, but this time he lost so badly he vowed never to run for governor again.

Bradley's popularity began to fade in the late 1980s. Despite his many accomplishments, the city still suffered from overcrowding, air pollution, and crime. In 1989 he was fined $20,000 for accepting income as a director of two businesses that did business with the city, but his political undoing came about in 1992 as the result of the Rodney King incident. King was a black motorist who was beaten senseless by four white policemen during a traffic stop. By chance, the beating was videotaped, and the officers were put on trial for police brutality. Their acquittal led to five days of rioting in South Central L.A., part of the city's African-American community, that resulted in more deaths and greater damage than the Watts riots. Ironically, the investigation that followed placed much of the blame on Bradley, who was charged with doing too little to combat racism in the LAPD and for unwittingly inciting the riot by his intemperate remarks after the officers' acquittals.

In 1992, Bradley announced his retirement from politics effective the end of his term in 1993. For the remainder of his life he practiced law. He died on September 29, 1998, in Los Angeles.

Further Reading

Colburn, David R., and Jeffrey S. Adler. *African-American Mayors: Race, Politics, and the American City.* Urbana: University of Illinois Press, 2001.

Fritsch, Jane. "Tom Bradley, Mayor in Era of Los Angeles Growth, Dies." *New York Times*, September 30, 1998. Available online. URL: http://www.nytimes.com/1998/09/30/us/tom-bradley-mayor-in-era-of-los-angeles-growth-dies.html?scp=2&sq=tom%20%20bradley&st=cse. Downloaded March 29, 2009.

Nevin, Steven J. "Bradley, Tom." In *African American National Biography,* vol. 1, edited by Henry Louis Gates, Jr., and Evelyn Brooks Higginbotham. New York: Oxford University Press, 2008, pp. 528–530.

Payne, J. Gregory, and Scott C. Ratzan. *Tom Bradley, the Impossible Dream: A Biography.* Santa Monica, Calif.: Roundtable Publishing Company, 1986.

Brooke, Edward
(Edward William Brooke III)
(1919–) *U.S. senator from Massachusetts*

Edward Brooke was one of the most unusual politicians in U.S. history. A black Episcopalian Republican from the District of Columbia, he was elected attorney general and U.S. senator in Massachusetts, populated mostly with white Roman Catholic Democrats. As a senator, he was criticized for not taking a greater role in the Civil Rights movement and for not supporting his party at certain critical moments. He refused, however, to act "black" or "Republican" on the grounds that his duty called him to serve all his constituents, not just the ones who looked or thought like him.

Edward William Brooke III was born on October 26, 1919, in Washington, D.C. His father, Edward, Jr., was an attorney with the Veterans Administration, and his mother, Helen, was a homemaker. After graduating from high school, he studied sociology at Howard University and received a B.S. in 1941. Having served in the Reserve Officers Training Corps at Howard, upon graduation he was commissioned a second lieutenant in the U.S. Army and sent to Fort Devens, Massachusetts, to join the all-black 366th Combat Infantry Regiment. During World War II he saw action in North Africa and Italy; for bravery under fire he received the Bronze Star and the Distinguished Service Award and was promoted to captain. While in Italy he met Remigia Ferrari-Scacco; they were married in 1947 and had two children. After the war, he returned to Massachusetts and enrolled in Boston University Law School. In 1948, he received an LL.B., passed the bar examination, and opened a law office in Roxbury. The following year he received an LL.M. and moved his practice to Boston.

In 1950, Brooke was convinced by two army buddies to run for political office. He found it easier to pick the office—state representative—than the political party. The District of Columbia of his youth was administered entirely by the federal government, and the residents were not allowed to vote, even for local officials, until the early 1970s. Consequently, his parents had rarely discussed politics, so he had no idea what his political affiliations were. Since cross-filing was legal in Massachusetts, he decided to run in both party primaries. The Democratic primary had better-known candidates so he did poorly, but somehow he won the Republican primary. Although he lost the general election, he was encouraged enough to run again in 1952 as a Republican; once again he won the nomination but lost the election. A bit chastened by his failures, he decided to build up his law practice while also building up his name recognition. Over the next eight years he became heavily involved in a number of local civic and charitable organizations while holding national office in a veterans' group. By 1960, he was ready to run again, this time for secretary of state. Although he lost, he polled more than one million votes and was identified as a rising star in the state Republican Party.

In 1961, Brooke was appointed chairman of the Boston Finance Commission by newly elected Republican governor John A. Volpe. In theory, the commission was a watchdog agency over the city's government, but in practice it had become a source of political patronage. Under Brooke's leadership, however, it began investigating politicians and agencies and uncovered a considerable amount of graft and corruption in three major departments. The resultant publicity further increased his name recognition with the voters, and in 1962 he was elected attorney general. He continued to focus on exposing corrupt practices in government, and by the end of his second two-year term he had gained indictments against a former governor and a host of lesser officials. A liberal Republican (in the 1960s there were enough of these to constitute a sizable wing of the party), he also became a consumer advocate and an environmentalist, thus boosting his popularity even more.

During his early career, Brooke followed a course independent of his party and of his fellow African Americans. When the conservative wing seized control of the 1964 Republican National Convention and nominated Barry Goldwater for president, Brooke refused to support him. Follow-

ing Goldwater's disastrous defeat, in 1966 Brooke wrote *The Challenge of Change: Crisis in Our Two-Party System,* in which he called upon the Republicans to become more progressive and less conservative. Similarly, as attorney general he had ruled in 1963 that it was illegal for black students to protest segregated schools by boycotting school, and he threatened to prosecute them if they persisted.

In 1965, Brooke began campaigning for the U.S. Senate when Leverett Saltonstall announced he would not run for reelection in 1966. After gaining the support of his party's conservative wing, he handily defeated his Democratic opponent, a former governor who had been endorsed by Ted Kennedy, the state's other senator who was at the height of his popularity. It was the first time in history that an African American had been elected to the Senate by popular vote. He took his

Edward Brooke was the first of only two African Americans to be elected to the U.S. Senate in the 20th century. *(Library of Congress)*

seat in 1967 and was appointed to the banking and currency committee and the aeronautical and space sciences committee.

Brooke's maverick ways continued in the Senate. To the consternation of his fellow Republicans, he supported much of Democratic president Lyndon B. Johnson's Great Society legislation. Following the 1967 assassination of Martin Luther King, Jr., which incited rioting in more than 100 cities, he accepted Johnson's appointment to the Advisory Committee on Civil Disorders. He also pledged his basic support for Johnson's handling of the war in Vietnam but riled the president when he began calling for a halt to the bombing of the North. He became even more of a pariah to the Republicans after Richard M. Nixon, whom he had supported, assumed the presidency in 1969. One of the last liberal Republicans, Brooke continued to vote with the Democrats on most social issues while voting against three of Nixon's appointees to the Supreme Court. In 1973 he introduced a resolution calling for the appointment of a special prosecutor to investigate the Watergate affair, and he was the first senator to demand that Nixon resign once it became clear that the president had been a central player in that affair.

Brooke supported affirmative action, minority business development, and school integration, and he played a major role in outlawing housing discrimination via the Civil Rights Act of 1968. Nevertheless, his fellow African Americans in Congress perceived him as being "soft" on black issues. At best, he was a lukewarm member of the Congressional Black Caucus, which sought to unify its members in the struggle for expanded opportunities for African Americans. He was also slow to condemn white violence against blacks, particularly the 1970 police shooting of students at Jackson State College in Mississippi. He justified his position by reminding his black colleagues that, unlike theirs, his constituents were mostly white, and he had to serve their best interests, too.

Brooke was reelected in 1972. In 1978, the same year he divorced his first wife, he was defeated by his Democratic challenger, Paul Tsongas. In 1979 he retired from politics, married Anne Fleming (with whom he had one child), and returned to his law practice in Boston. Shortly thereafter he moved the practice to Washington, D.C.

In 2002, Brooke was diagnosed with breast cancer. Successfully treated, he has since worked to raise awareness of the rare occurrence of the disease in men. Brooke again made the national news in 2008, when journalist Barbara Walters revealed in her autobiography that she had had an affair with Brooke during the 1970s. He declined to comment on Walters's book.

In recognition of his service to the U.S. government, President George W. Bush awarded Brooke the Presidential Medal of Freedom in 2004. Five years later, Brooke received the Congressional Gold Medal from President Barack Obama. The Edward W. Brooke Courthouse in Boston, Massachusetts, is also named in his honor.

Further Reading

Biographical Directory of the United States Congress. "Brooke, Edward William, III, 1919– ." Available online. URL: http://bioguide.congress.gov/scripts/biodisplay.pl?index=B000871. Downloaded April 17, 2009.

Black Americans in Congress. "Edward William Brooke II." Available online. URL: http://baic.house.gov/member-profiles/profile.html?intID=125. Downloaded April 3, 2009.

Brooke, Edward W. Bridging the Divide: My Life. Piscataway, N.J.: Rutgers University Press, 2006.

Clay, William L. Just Permanent Interests: Black Americans in Congress, 1870–1992. New York: Amistad Press, 1993.

Cutler, John H. Ed Brooke: Biography of a Senator. Indianapolis, Ind.: Bobbs-Merrill, 1972.

Kinkead, Gwen. Edward W. Brooke, Republican Senator from Massachusetts. Washington, D.C.: Grossman Publishers, 1972.

Brown, Corrine

(1946–   ) *U.S. congressional representative from Florida*

In 1992 Corrine Brown, ALCEE HASTINGS, and CARRIE MEEK were elected to the U.S. House of Representatives from Florida. They were the first African Americans to represent the state in Congress since JOSIAH WALLS had left office 120 years earlier in 1873.

Corrine Brown was born on November 11, 1946, in Jacksonville, Florida. In 1965, she finished high school, gave birth to her only child, and enrolled in Florida A&M University. Four years later she received a B.S. in education and enrolled in the University of Florida, where she received an M.A. in 1971 and an Ed.S. in education in 1974. She taught briefly at the University of Florida before returning to Jacksonville to teach at Edward Waters College. In 1977 she joined the faculty at Florida Community College in Jacksonville and taught for five years. She then became a guidance counselor at FCC, a position she held until 1992.

Brown's concern for the poor, the underprivileged, and the elderly led her into politics. In 1982 she ran as a Democrat for a seat in the Florida legislature and won. She held this seat for the next 10 years, during which time she developed a reputation as an advocate for the needy. In 1992 she declared her candidacy for the U.S. House of Representatives. The state legislature had just redrawn the boundaries of its congressional districts, in the process creating a black-majority district in northeastern and central Florida that included that part of Jacksonville where Brown lived. She defeated several candidates in the Democratic primary and then easily won the general election. She took her seat in 1993 and was assigned to the committees on public works/transportation, veterans affairs, and government operations.

As a congresswoman, Brown sided with the moderate Democrats. She fought to preserve funding for educational programs such as Head Start and school lunches, supported the earned income tax credit for low-income families, and worked for passage of the Family and Medical Leave Act, which provides employees with unpaid leave to care for newborn children or sick relatives. At the same time, she supported measures that maintained a strong military and provided communities with more police officers while arguing in favor of a balanced budget. She used her influence on her assigned committees to obtain funding for a light-rail transportation project linking Jacksonville and Orlando and to expand Veterans Administration hospitals and cemeteries in Florida.

In 1998, Brown became involved in two minor scandals. Her daughter, Shantrel Brown, an attorney with the Environmental Protection Agency, had accepted an expensive automobile as a gift from Foutanga Sissoko, a Gambian millionaire. Sissoko had been jailed in Florida for bribing a U.S. customs official, and Brown had tried to get the Justice Department to release him to the authorities in his own country. That same year, it was disclosed that Brown had accepted a $10,000 contribution from Henry Lyons, a minister who had been indicted for theft, and then failed to properly document the contribution to election officials. In 1999, Brown's relationships with Sissoko and Lyons came under investigation by the House Ethics Committee.

Meanwhile, Brown had run into difficulty of another kind. The legality of her district had been challenged in court on the grounds that it had been gerrymandered in terms of race, and in 1995 the U.S. Supreme Court ordered that the district's boundaries be redrawn. The result was a district with a slight majority of whites. Nevertheless, in 1996 Brown was reelected with ease. Following the disputed presidential election in Florida in 2000, Brown became a vocal supporter of election reform. She was especially critical of the supposed miscounting of votes cast by African Americans and other minorities. In 2004, the House of Representatives voted to censure Brown and revoke her speaking privileges for a day after she referred to the 2000 election as a "coup d'état."

Brown became the first woman chosen to be vice-chair of the Congressional Black Congress in 2004. In 2010, she was reelected to a 10th term in Congress.

Further Reading

Biographical Directory of the United States Congress. "Brown, Corrine, 1946–   ." Available online. URL: http://bioguide.congress.gov/scripts/biodisplay. pl?index=B000911. Downloaded April 17, 2009.

Clay, William L. *Just Permanent Interests: Black Americans in Congress, 1870–1992.* New York: Amistad Press, 1993.

Congresswoman Corrine Brown, Official Web Site. Available online. URL: http://www.house.gov/corrinebrown. Downloaded April 17, 2009.

Foerstel, Karen. *Biographical Dictionary of Congressional Women.* New York: Greenwood Press, 1999.

Gill, LaVerne McCain. *African American Women in Congress: Forming and Transforming History.* New Brunswick, N.J.: Rutgers University Press, 1997.

Brown, Lee

(Lee Patrick Brown)
(1937–   ) *mayor of Houston, Texas*

Lee Brown followed a most unusual path to becoming an elected official. One of the nation's top law enforcement officials for more than 20 years, he worked for the mayors of Atlanta and New York City before eventually becoming the mayor of Houston.

Lee Patrick Brown was born on October 4, 1937, in Wewoka, Oklahoma, to Andrew and Zelma Brown. At age five he moved with his family to California's San Joaquin Valley where the family earned a living as migrant workers. A standout athlete in high school, he received a football scholarship to Fresno State University. In 1959, while still in school, he married Yvonne Streets, with whom he had four children (she died in 1992, and four years later he married Frances Young). In 1960, while still in school, he began working as a patrolman for the San Jose Police Department.

In 1961, Brown received a B.S. in criminology and went to work full-time as a San Jose police officer. By 1968 he had received master's degrees in sociology and criminology from San Jose State University, and he had worked on the police department's narcotics and vice squads. That same year, he obtained a one-year leave of absence from the department to establish a program in the administration of justice at Portland State University in Oregon. In 1970, he received a Ph.D. in criminology from the University of California at Berkeley, thus making him one of the best educated African-American law enforcement officials in the country.

In 1972, Brown left police work temporarily to teach criminal justice at Howard University in Washington, D.C. Three years later, he returned to the Portland, Oregon, area to be the sheriff of Multnomah County. In 1978, he was hired by Mayor MAYNARD JACKSON as public safety commissioner of Atlanta, Georgia. Four years later he was recruited to be the chief of police in Houston, Texas, and in 1990 Mayor DAVID DINKINS hired him to be the police commissioner for New York City. He left police work for good in 1992 when he returned to Houston to teach at Texas Southern University. In 1993, he was appointed by President Bill Clinton to serve as director of the White House Office of National Drug Control Policy. He left the post in 1996 to teach sociology at Rice University in Houston.

During his eight-year tenure as Houston's chief of police, Brown had worked to implement an innovative crime-prevention program which he called Neighborhood Oriented Policing (NOP). The program was designed to lower the city's high crime rate and reduce the incidences of police brutality by putting police officers into closer contact with the residents they were protecting. In effect, it was an attempt to return to the days of the "cop on the beat," who knew and was known by just about everyone in his assigned area. The program caught heavy flak from the city's police officers, who called NOP "Nobody on Patrol." However, minority residents took to NOP because it forced police officers to develop more cordial relationships with minorities. Although NOP never worked as well in Houston as Brown had hoped, it eventually became a model for law enforcement throughout the nation. It also gave him a reputation in Houston as a policeman who cared more about protecting people than about busting criminals.

Brown first tried to run for office in 1969, when he sought a seat on the San Jose city council. His application was denied, however, on the grounds that while in Oregon he had let his residency and voter registration lapse. In 1997, he ran for office for the second time, this time as a Democrat for mayor of Houston. He outdistanced his opponent, Republican Robert Mosbacher, Jr., by 16,000 votes and took office in early 1998.

As mayor, Brown focused on making city hall more knowledgeable about and responsive to the needs of citizens in all parts of Houston. To this end, he created 88 "super neighborhoods" with separate citizens councils and dedicated city staffers. He increased funding for after-school programs, oversaw the development of plans to renovate the city's three airports, and led the effort to secure a new stadium for the National League's Houston Astros. He also created much controversy by issuing an executive order banning discrimination based on sexual orientation for municipal workers. In 1998, the city council sued Brown to have his order overthrown, but the suit was dismissed by the state supreme court. Despite the controversy, the voters of Houston reelected Brown to two more two-year terms in 1999 and 2001. Because of term limits, Brown was compelled to leave office in 2004. He then founded the Brown Group International, which offers solutions to problems involving public safety, homeland security, and crisis management. In 2007, Brown was hired by New Orleans to conduct a study of its police department in an effort to bring down the city's high crime rate.

Further Reading

Brennan, Carol. "Lee Patrick Brown, 1937– ." *Contemporary Black Biography* 24 (2000), pp. 21–24.
Brown Group International. "Chairman & CEO Dr. Lee P. Brown." Available online. URL: http://www.bgi-intl.com/indexbrown.html#. Downloaded April 15, 2009.
Chappell, Kevin. "Houston's Lee P. Brown: A Can-Do Mayor for a Can-Do City." *Ebony* 54 (January 1999), pp. 96–98.
"Houston's First Black Mayor, Lee Brown, Wins a Third Term." *Jet* 101 (December 17, 2001): 4–5.

Brown, Ron
(Ronald Harmon Brown)
(1941–1996) *U.S. secretary of commerce*

Ron Brown was the first African American to lead a major political party. Under his direction, the Democrats were able to recapture the White House and retain their control of Congress. During his subsequent tenure as secretary of commerce, cut short by his untimely death, he did much to boost the export of U.S. goods and technologies around the world.

Ronald Harmon Brown was born on August 1, 1941, in Washington, D.C. His parents, William and Gloria, were college students. Shortly after his birth, the family moved to New York City where his father had gotten a job managing the Theresa Hotel in Harlem. Brown attended a series of private schools in which he was virtually the only black student, including Middlebury College in Vermont. At Middlebury he pledged a white fraternity and joined the ROTC. In 1962 he received a B.A. in political science and married Alma Arrington, with whom he had two children.

Following his discharge from the U.S. Army in 1967, Brown returned to New York City. He enrolled in St. John's University Law School and received a J.D. in 1970. Meanwhile, in 1968 he had gone to work for the National Urban League, a moderate civil rights organization, as a job training coordinator in New York City. He also served for two years as a district leader of the local Democratic Party in suburban Mount Vernon, New York. In 1973, the league sent him to Washington to lobby federal legislators on its behalf, which he did for the next six years. By 1979, Brown had developed a deep understanding of the white middle class, the Civil Rights movement, and the way things worked in Washington. This background would make him uniquely qualified to serve as a unifying and motivating force within the Democratic Party in years to come.

Brown began to play a larger role in the Democratic Party in 1979, when he was recruited to serve as deputy campaign manager for Senator Ted Kennedy's bid for the presidency. Although Kennedy lost, Brown made a name for himself as a savvy problem-solver. After a year as chief counsel of the Senate Judiciary Committee, in 1981 he was named chief counsel of the Democratic National Committee (DNC). The following year, he became its deputy chairman, a post he held for three years.

Brown left politics for three years beginning in 1985, during which he practiced law and lobbied on behalf of the clients of Patton, Boggs and Blow, a prestigious Washington law firm. He returned to politics with a vengeance in 1988, when he accepted an invitation from presidential candidate JESSE JACKSON to serve as his campaign manager. With Brown's help, Jackson came in a respectable second to Michael Dukakis. Because of Jackson's strong showing, he and his supporters hoped that Dukakis would select Jackson as his running mate. Instead, Dukakis chose Lloyd Bentsen, a U.S. senator and future secretary of the treasury, and he did so without even consulting the Jackson camp. At this point the party might have split into two hostile factions—many African Americans began speaking openly of leaving the Democratic Party—had not Brown engineered a meeting between Dukakis and Jackson. As a result of the meeting, the two sides were able to patch up their differences and unite for the upcoming campaign.

Brown's role at the 1988 national convention so impressed the party's leaders that in 1989 they elected him to chair the Democratic National Committee. This body has the primary responsibility of getting Democratic candidates elected to state and local offices around the country, and under Brown's capable leadership it worked wonders. Brown understood better than anyone else that everything the party did had to be geared to winning elections. Part of the party's problem, as he saw it, was that Democrats had been defined for decades by their opponents, the Republicans, as too liberal. Consequently, many Americans believed that the Democrats were the party of "tax and spend." Brown realized that, to be successful, the party needed a new image, and he worked very hard to cast it in a more moderate light. As a result of his influence, many state and local parties began moving away from liberal candidates and nominating moderate ones instead.

Under Brown's direction, the Democrats raised more money for federal, state, and local candidates than they had in recent years. As a result, he was able to oversee Democratic gains in Congress as well as in state and local offices around the country. During his tenure as DNC chair, DOUG WILDER of Virginia became the first black to be elected state governor by popular vote, and DAVID DINKINS became the first African-American mayor of New York City. Most impressively, Brown even managed to get the Democrats, a myriad and usually contentious bunch, to come together behind Bill Clinton, the model of a Brown moderate Democrat, at the 1992 national convention. As DNC chair, Brown played a key role in getting Clinton elected to the presidency that same year.

In large part, Clinton owed his election to African-American votes. To show his gratitude, he named three blacks to cabinet-level posts.

One of them was Brown, who took office in 1993 as secretary of commerce. The appointment drew heavy fire from the Republicans and the media, who charged that Brown was not qualified for the position and that his appointment was nothing more than a political kickback. Brown surprised most of his critics by charting a proactive course as secretary. Under his direction, Commerce Department officials signed favorable trade agreements worth billions of dollars with nations around the globe, including a $6 billion deal with the People's Republic of China. Brown himself led trade delegations, which normally included several chief executive officers of major U.S. corporations, to Africa, Asia, Europe, and the Middle East. Despite his successes, his opponents attempted to hound him from office by accusing him of influence peddling and shady business dealings before becoming secretary. In 1995, the Justice Department appointed an independent counsel to investigate these charges.

Unfortunately, the charges were dropped before they could be thoroughly investigated. In 1996, Brown led a trade delegation to the war-torn Balkans region in an effort to promote U.S. business interests that would also help to rebuild the local economies. On April 3, the delegation's airplane crashed near Dubrovnik, Croatia. Everyone on board, including Brown, was killed. The Department of Commerce, with the help of prominent business leaders, established the Ron Brown Award for Corporate Leadership in 1997.

Further Reading

Brown, Tracey L. *The Life and Times of Ron Brown: A Memoir.* New York: William Morrow, 1998.

Holmes, Steven A. *Ron Brown: An Uncommon Life.* New York: Wiley, 2000.

Walters, Ronald. "Brown, Ron." In *African American National Biography*, vol. 1, edited by Henry Louis Gates, Jr., and Evelyn Brooks Higginbotham. New York: Oxford University Press, 2008, pp. 638–639.

Brown, Willie
(Willie Lewis Brown, Jr.)
(1934–) *speaker of the California state assembly*

Willie Brown was speaker of the California state assembly longer than anyone else in the state's history. After stepping down as speaker, he became the first African-American mayor of San Francisco.

Willie Lewis Brown, Jr., was born on March 20, 1934, in Mineola, Texas. His father, Willie, Sr., was a laborer, and his mother, Minnie, was a domestic worker. By the time Willie was five both his parents had left town to find work, and he was raised by his maternal grandmother, Anna Lee Collins. He helped support himself by working in his grandmother's dance hall and saloon, helping his uncles make and sell moonshine, and picking beans on local farms. After finishing high school in 1951, he briefly attended Prairie View A&M College before moving to San Francisco, where another uncle lived, and transferring to San Francisco State University. He received a B.A. in 1955, then enrolled in Hastings College of Law to avoid being drafted. In 1958, he received a J.D. and married Blanche Vitero, with whom he has three children. He passed the bar examination the following year and opened a law office in a San Francisco storefront. For the next five years he specialized in defending pimps, prostitutes, and civil rights activists.

Brown became involved in politics in 1952, when he joined the Young Democrats at San Francisco State and worked as a volunteer for Adlai Stevenson, the Democratic candidate for president. He also became active in the National Association for the Advancement of Colored People, and in 1961 he helped lead a sit-in to protest segregated housing. The campaign brought him to the attention of the media, and the following year he decided to run for the state assembly. He campaigned for Haight-Asbury's seat, a neighborhood with a national reputation for its racial and ethnic

Willie Brown was the speaker of the California state assembly before becoming the first African-American mayor of San Francisco. *(Dennis De Silva)*

diversity. Undaunted by his loss, he worked hard to make himself known to the local voters, and when he ran for the same seat in 1964 he won.

As a state assemblyman, Brown worked hard to represent the peculiar interests of his constituents. Among his legislative successes were bills decriminalizing the possession of small amounts of marijuana and private sexual acts between consenting adults. He sponsored a bill requesting the U.S. Congress to grant American citizenship to Filipinos who had fought for the United States during World War II. He continued to work for civil rights, particularly promoting set-asides for minority-owned businesses in state contracts. In 1977, he successfully sponsored a bill requiring state-funded programs to provide benefits to qualified clients regardless of their race, ethnicity, gender, age, or disabilities. In 1993, he helped enact a bill

that prohibited insurance companies from discriminating against people with AIDS or other long-term health conditions.

In 1974, Brown mounted his first campaign for speaker of the assembly. Following his defeat, he began building a coalition of Democrats and Republicans that would eventually lead to victory. After two more failures, in 1980 he received the support of 28 Republicans and 23 Democrats, enough to win him the post. As the state's first black speaker, he opened doors for other African Americans in California's state government. He appointed black men as chief sergeant at arms, chaplain, and chief clerk, and black women as speaker's chief of staff and press secretary, all of which were firsts. He coauthored legislation requiring the state and its university system to divest themselves of investments in South Africa so long as apartheid existed in that nation.

Brown was speaker for 15 years, from 1980 to 1995. During that time, he successfully pushed bills to compensate crime victims, speed up the justice system, hold down medical costs for low-income families, make the wearing of seat belts compulsory, raise academic standards in public schools, and mandate stricter health testing of students. Despite his achievements, he was criticized repeatedly by non-allies, Republicans and Democrats alike, as being a flashy, flamboyant do-nothing who concentrated on defeating the bills of his enemies rather than on coming up with positive measures of his own. By state law, the speaker enjoys enormous powers over the day-to-day activities of the California assembly, and Brown used those powers to the fullest to reward his friends and punish his enemies.

In 1994, California voters approved term limits that forced Brown to step down from the state assembly the following year. He made plans to run for governor in 1996 but quickly discovered that the financial support for such a campaign would not be forthcoming. Instead, in 1995, he ran for mayor of San Francisco and won resoundingly. As mayor he continued to push for the same types of legislation that he worked for in the state assembly. He succeeded in requiring all city contractors to provide equal benefits to their employees' domestic partners, regardless of their sexual preference or marital status, and in making the municipal workforce more diverse. He also oversaw improvements to the municipal railway system and public housing and arranged for construction of a University of California campus in San Francisco.

After retiring from politics in 2004, Brown hosted a morning radio show on Air America and wrote a regular column for the *San Francisco Chronicle*. He also established the Willie L. Brown, Jr., Institute on Politics & Public Service at San Francisco State University. This nonprofit organization promotes discussion and debate on public policy issues.

Further Reading

Brown, Willie, and P. J. Corkery. *Basic Brown: My Life and Our Times*. New York: Simon and Schuster, 2008.

Holst, Arthur Matthew. "Brown, Willie." In *African American National Biography*, vol. 2, edited by Henry Louis Gates, Jr., and Evelyn Brooks Higginbotham. New York: Oxford University Press, 2008, pp. 12–13.

Richardson, James. *Willie Brown: A Biography*. Berkeley: University of California Press, 1996.

Bruce, Blanche
(Blanche Kelso Bruce)
(1841–1898) *U.S. senator from Mississippi*

Blanche Bruce was not the first African American to serve in the U.S. Senate, nor was he the first to be elected from Mississippi. He was, however, the first black to be elected to and serve a full term in the Senate. This achievement is all the more impressive when one considers that Bruce had once been a slave.

Blanche Kelso Bruce was born on March 1, 1841, in Farmville, Virginia. His mother, Polly, was a slave. His father's identity is unknown, but he was probably either Pettus Perkinson, Polly's master at the time of Bruce's birth, or a planter named Bruce, who had sold Polly to Perkinson before Bruce was born and whose surname Bruce took as his own upon attaining freedom. He grew up on small plantations in Virginia, Mississippi, and Missouri, each owned by Perkinson, and he was educated by the same tutor who taught Perkinson's son William. He worked as a hand in the tobacco fields and in a chewing tobacco factory, and he received some training as a printer.

Bruce gained his freedom during the Civil War by escaping from Missouri to Kansas, a free state. He took up residence in Lawrence, where he opened a school for blacks. He returned to Missouri in 1865, not long after that state abolished slavery, and set up a school for freedmen in Hannibal. For the next four years he worked in Hannibal as a printer's apprentice, studied briefly at Oberlin College in Ohio, and worked as a porter on a riverboat that plied the Mississippi River between St. Louis and Council Bluffs, Iowa.

In 1869, Bruce moved to Floreyville in Bolivar County, Mississippi, to take advantage of the economic and political opportunities being offered freedmen under Reconstruction. Almost immediately, he came to the attention of the district military commander, who appointed him a voter registrar for neighboring Tallahatchie County. He also joined the Republican Party and began recruiting large numbers of freedmen to the party's ranks. Bruce's physique was as impressive as his oratorical skills, and in 1870 he was made sergeant-at-arms of the Republican-controlled state senate. The following year he became the sheriff, tax collector, and county superintendent of education for Bolivar County, as well as a Floreyville alderman. In 1872, he was appointed to the board that oversaw construction and maintenance of levees in three Delta counties. He used

Blanche Bruce was a former slave who became the second African American to serve in the U.S. Senate. *(Library of Congress)*

the income from these positions to buy a 640-acre plantation near Floreyville, thus making himself one of Mississippi's most prominent black citizens. In 1874, he was elected to the state senate, and that same year he was chosen by the legislature to represent Mississippi in the U.S. Senate (prior to ratification of the Seventeenth Amendment in 1913, senators were elected by the state legislatures, not the voters at large).

Bruce was appointed to four congressional committees, including a select committee on Mississippi River improvements, and he chaired the select committee that investigated the failure of the Freedmen's Savings and Trust Company. Many African Americans had deposited money with this congressionally chartered bank, and when it failed in 1874 almost 70,000 black investors lost their savings. Under Bruce's leadership, the committee got the federal government to reimburse these investors for three-fifths of their losses.

Reconstruction came to an end during Bruce's term, and he spent much of his energy fighting to maintain the gains that freedmen had made. He introduced a bill to desegregate the U.S. Army, and he tried to secure federal funding for bounties for blacks who had served in the Union army and navy, industrial education for African-American students, and economic assistance for the Exodusters, black farmers who emigrated from the South to the Midwest during the late 1870s. He also called for a federal investigation into the brutal hazing of a black West Point cadet. In all of these endeavors, however, he was unsuccessful. In 1878, he married Josephine B. Wilson, with whom he had one child.

By 1881, when his term expired, the Democrats had gained control of the Mississippi state legislature, so Bruce did not attempt to gain reelection to the Senate. Instead, he remained in Washington and accepted an appointment as register of the U.S. Treasury, a position he held until Grover Cleveland, a Democrat, became president in 1885. He spent the next four years in Mississippi, building up his land holdings—at the time of his death he owned 3,000 acres—and overseeing the affairs of the state Republican Party. He also gave a number of speeches across the United States, in the process becoming one of the best-known African Americans in the country. In 1889, President Benjamin Harrison, a Republican, appointed him recorder of deeds for the District of Columbia, but he was forced to resign when Cleveland's second term began in 1893. For the next four years, he conducted business as an investment, insurance, and real estate agent in Washington. When William McKinley, a Republican, was elected president in 1896, it was rumored that Bruce would be appointed to his cabinet. Instead, Bruce was offered, and accepted, his old position at the treasury. He died on March 17, 1898, in Washington.

Further Reading

Biographical Directory of the United States Congress. "Bruce, Blanche Kelso, 1841–1898." Available online. URL: http://bioguide.congress.gov/scripts/biodisplay.pl?index=B000968. Downloaded April 14, 2009.

Black Americans in Congress. "Blanche Kelso Bruce." Available online. URL: http://baic.house.gov/member-profiles/profile.html?intID=127. Downloaded April 8, 2009.

Clay, William L. *Just Permanent Interests: Black Americans in Congress, 1870–1992.* New York: Amistad Press, 1993.

Dray, Philip. *Capitol Men: The Epic Story of Reconstruction Through the Lives of the First Black Congressmen.* Boston: Houghton Mifflin, 2008.

Graham, Lawrence Otis. *The Senator and the Socialite: The True Story of America's First Black Dynasty.* New York: HarperCollins, 2006.

Litwack, Leon F., and August Meier. *Black Leaders of the Nineteenth Century.* Urbana: University of Illinois Press, 1991.

Rabinowitz, Howard N., ed. *Southern Black Leaders of the Reconstruction Era.* Urbana: University of Illinois Press, 1982.

Burke, Yvonne

(Yvonne Braithwaite Burke)
(1932–   ) *U.S. congressional representative from California*

Yvonne Burke has set a number of milestones for African-American women in California. She was the first to serve in the state senate, the first to represent the state in Congress, and the first to chair the Los Angeles County Board of Supervisors.

Yvonne Braithwaite Burke was born Pearl Yvonne Watson on October 5, 1932, in Los Angeles, California. Her father, James, was a janitor, and her mother, Lola, was a realtor. She completed high school in 1949, then enrolled in the University of California at Berkeley. Two years later, she transferred to the University of California at Los Angeles and received a B.A. in political science in 1953. Three years later, she received a J.D. from the University of Southern California School of Law and opened a law office in Los Angeles. Over the next 10 years, she specialized in probate and real estate law while also working for the city of Los Angeles as deputy corporation commissioner, hearing officer for the police commission, and staff attorney for the commission that investigated the Watts riots of 1965. In 1957, she married Louis Braithwaite; they were divorced in 1964.

In 1966, Braithwaite ran as a Democrat for a seat in the California state assembly. When she won, she became the first African-American woman to serve in that body. Reelected twice, she

Yvonne Burke was one of many African Americans to represent California in the U.S. House of Representatives. *(Library of Congress)*

sponsored bills to end discrimination against women and minorities concerning job opportunities in the private sector and construction contracts in the public sector. She also worked to expand the rights of tenants, reform the state's prisons, and provide more funding for child health care and education.

The census of 1970 mandated that California redraw its congressional districts, and in the process a black-majority district was created in that part of Los Angeles where Burke lived. In 1972, the same year she married William Burke (with whom she has one child), she was elected to represent the district in Congress. Later that year, she gained national prominence as vice-chair of the Democratic National Convention.

Burke was assigned to the committees of interior and insular affairs and public works. While serving on the latter committee, she was responsible for amending the Alaska Pipeline Bill to include millions of dollars in minority set-asides. Reelected in 1974, she was assigned to the appropriations committee, where she continued to champion the cause of women and minorities. Her greatest victory in this regard was the Displaced Homemakers Act of 1977, which provided training for women entering the job market. In 1976, she was chosen to chair the Congressional Black Caucus, thus becoming the first woman to hold this position.

In 1978, Burke resigned from the House in order to campaign for attorney general of California. After losing the race, in 1979 she was appointed to a vacancy on the Los Angeles County Board of Supervisors. Her 1980 bid to win a full term of her own failed, so she returned to the private practice of law. In 1992, however, the voters returned her to the board, a position she held from 1992 to 2008. As a supervisor, she focused on the needs and education of children in the county's foster child programs.

The *Los Angeles Times* in 2007 reported that Burke did not live in the district she represented, a violation of laws governing city supervisors.

Burke denied the allegation but decided to retire from the board the following year. In 2009, a park in the beachfront community of Marina del Rey was named in her honor.

Further Reading

Abdullah, Melina. "Burke, Yvonne Brathwaite." In *African American National Biography*, vol. 2, edited by Henry Louis Gates, Jr., and Evelyn Brooks Higginbotham. New York: Oxford University Press, 2008, pp. 61–62.

Biographical Directory of the United States Congress. "Burke, Yvonne Braithwaite, 1932– ." Available online. URL: http://bioguide.congress.gov/ scripts/biodisplay.pl?index=B001102. Downloaded April 3, 2009.

Black Americans in Congress. "Yvonne Brathwaite Burke." Available online. URL: http://baic.house.gov/member-profiles/profile.html?intID=123. Downloaded April 9, 2009.

Clay, William L. *Just Permanent Interests: Black Americans in Congress, 1870–1992*. New York: Amistad Press, 1993.

Gill, LaVerne McCain. *African American Women in Congress: Forming and Transforming History*. New Brunswick, N.J.: Rutgers University Press, 1997.

Burris, Roland

(Roland W. Burris)
(1937–) *U.S. senator from Illinois*

Roland Burris was the first African American to be elected to a statewide position in Illinois. His victories and performance as state comptroller and attorney general helped pave the way for CAROL MOSELEY BRAUN's election to the U.S. Senate.

Burris was born on August 3, 1937, in Centralia, Illinois. His father, Earl, was a railroad worker, and his mother, Emma, was a homemaker. He finished high school in 1955, then enrolled in Southern Illinois University, earning a B.A. in political science four years later. In 1963, he received a law degree from Howard University and went to work for the U.S. Treasury Department as a federal bank examiner. A year later he moved to Chicago to work for Continental Illinois National Bank. Within a few years, he was named vice president in charge of minority loans.

Burris had decided to pursue a career in politics at age 16, as a result of his father's effort to desegregate the municipal swimming pool. As a politician, he seemed impervious to defeat. In 1968, he ran for a seat in the state legislature but finished dead last in a five-way contest. Vowing to build up a solid base of support for a future run, he became active in the National Association for the Advancement of Colored People, the Boy Scouts of America, the Chicago Urban League, and other civic groups. He also became an active member of the local Democratic Party organization, and in 1973 he played an important role in Dan Walker's election as governor. In return, Walker appointed him director of the department of general services. Three years later, Burris resigned to run for state comptroller but lost. He spent the next two years campaigning for the position while serving as national executive director of Operation PUSH, which had been founded by Chicago's JESSE JACKSON. In 1978, Burris was elected comptroller, the first statewide victory for an African American in Illinois. He was reelected to two terms.

In 1984, Burris made a bid for the U.S. Senate but finished a distant second in the Democratic primary. For the next six years, he worked for a Chicago law firm while preparing for his next campaign. By 1990, he was ready to run again, and this time he was elected state attorney general. He compiled an impressive record during his four-year term as the state's chief prosecutor by aggressively fighting corporate pollution, consumer fraud, elderly abuse, and illegal drugs.

Burris declined to stand for reelection in 1994, choosing instead to run for governor. After losing the Democratic primary in a hard-fought contest,

he returned to working as an attorney for a Chicago law firm. He ran for mayor of Chicago in 1995, but lost to the popular incumbent Richard M. Daley. In 1998, he ran for governor again; despite being unable to raise enough money to run even one television ad, he finished a respectable second in a six-way race. Undaunted by three straight losses, he ran for governor for the third time in 2002. As before, he was plagued by fund-raising problems and finished third in the primary.

Following the 2008 presidential election, Burris was suddenly thrust onto the national political stage. When BARACK OBAMA left his position as junior senator of Illinois to assume the presidency, the Illinois governor Rod Blagojevich was charged with appointing his successor. A corruption probe conducted by the Federal Bureau of Investigation (FBI) then taped conversations that suggested Blagojevich intended to sell the senate seat. Blagojevich was arrested on December 9, 2008, and impeached by the Illinois state senate on January 29, 2009. Before his removal from office, however, Blagojevich appointed Roland Burris to take over Obama's seat. Believing that Blagojevich's involvement tainted the appointment, the Democratic caucus in the Senate and President Obama urged Burris not to accept the post. Burris ignored their requests and took the oath of office on January 12, 2009.

Within weeks, news reports surfaced that, while Blagojevich was considering candidates for the vacant seat, his brother Rob asked Burris to help raise funds for the governor. The allegations brought a flood of demands for Burris's resignation, including ones from the editorial boards of the *Washington Post* and *Chicago Tribune*. Burris refused to resign from the Senate and denied any wrongdoing. In November 2009, the Senate Ethics Committee issued a letter that admonished Burris, but also stated that it would not level an ethics charge against him. Although Burris considered running for a full term in the Senate, he announced in July 2009 that he would retire when his current term was up in 2011.

Further Reading

Brennan, Carol. "Roland W. Burris." *Contemporary Black Biography* 25 (2000): 37–39.

Hulse, Carl, and David Stout. "Burris, Blocked from Taking Seat, Gains New Support." *New York Times,* January 6, 2009. Available online. URL: http://www.nytimes.com/2009/01/07/us/politics/07burris.html?hp. Downloaded April 19, 2009.

Kimmel, Leigh. "Burris, Roland." In *African American National Biography,* vol. 2, edited by Henry Louis Gates, Jr., and Evelyn Brooks Higginbotham. New York: Oxford University Press, 2008, pp. 75–77.

Toobin, Jeffrey. "The Replacement." *New Yorker,* March 23, 2009. Available online. URL: http://www.newyorker.com/reporting/2009/03/23/090323fa_fact_toobin. Downloaded April 15, 2009.

C

Cain, Richard
(Richard Harvey Cain)
(1825–1887) *U.S. congressional
representative from South Carolina*

Richard Cain was one of six African Americans
to represent South Carolina in Congress during
Reconstruction. An ordained minister, he was
mostly interested in land reform and in equal
rights for women as well as blacks.

Richard Harvey Cain was born on April 12,
1825, in Greenbriar County, Virginia (now West
Virginia). His father was African American and
his mother was Cherokee Indian; nothing is
known about them other than that they were free.
At age six, he moved with his family to Gallipolis,
Ohio, where he grew up. He received a basic education and went to work on an Ohio riverboat as
a teenager. At age 19, he was licensed to preach in
the Methodist Episcopal Church and moved to
Hannibal, Missouri, where he hoped to serve in a
ministerial capacity. The white congregation,
however, rejected his services, so he joined the
African Methodist Episcopal (AME) Church and
went to preach in Muscatine, Illinois, instead. In
1859, he was ordained a deacon, and he spent the
following year studying theology at Wilberforce
University in Ohio. In 1861, he was assigned to
Bridge Street Church in Brooklyn, New York, as
pastor, a position he held for four years. At some

point he married a woman named Laura, with
whom he had one child.

Cain became involved in politics in 1864 when
he attended a national convention of African
Americans in Syracuse, New York, which called
for the expansion of civil rights for blacks. After
the end of the Civil War, he was sent to Charleston, South Carolina, to reorganize the Emanuel
AME Church. While making Emanuel into the
largest AME church in the state, he became
involved in local politics. He attended the 1865
Colored People's Convention in Charleston,
which echoed the call of the Syracuse convention, and wrote one of its major documents,
"Address to the People of South Carolina," which
expressed the convention-goers' demand for equal
rights with whites. That same year, he joined the
Republican Party, the only major party that
accepted African Americans as members. From
1866 to 1868, he edited the party's newspaper,
the *South Carolina Leader;* for awhile he was
assisted by ROBERT ELLIOTT. His editorials argued
for a land reform program that would benefit the
landless poor of both races. When Reconstruction began in South Carolina in 1867, educated
blacks such as Cain were able to play important
roles in the governance of the state. In 1868, he
helped draw up the state's new constitution at a
convention held for that purpose and was elected
to the state senate. After losing his reelection bid

two years later, he was named chairman of Charleston's Republican Party.

Cain understood that, unless freedmen could somehow obtain property of their own, they would always remain second-class citizens. For this reason, he became a major supporter of land redistribution. While in the senate, he was instrumental in the establishment of a land commission for that purpose. When it failed to perform to his satisfaction, he decided to take matters into his own hands. In 1871, he financed the purchase of 2,000 acres near Charleston. Renaming the property Lincolnville, he subdivided it into 25-acre plots and resold them on credit. Unfortunately, Lincolnville was short-lived; the property was repossessed after Cain failed to make the first several payments. As a result of the fiasco, he was vilified by whites but lionized by blacks, whose support got him elected to the U.S. House of Representatives in 1872.

As a freshman congressman, Cain made little impact on the House's proceedings. He made several speeches in favor of expanded civil rights for blacks, to little effect. He did not stand for reelection in 1874, preferring to concentrate on church matters, but was returned to Congress for another term in 1877. During his second term, he outraged a number of congressmen of both parties by calling for a constitutional amendment to give women the vote. He introduced a bill that would set aside a portion of the proceeds from the sale of public land to fund public education, and to establish regular steamship service between the United States and Liberia, a West African country that had been colonized by freed American slaves. None of his bills, however, was passed.

Cain returned to Charleston in 1879 when his term expired. The following year he moved to Waco, Texas, to preside as bishop over the AME district comprising Texas and Louisiana. Shortly thereafter, he cofounded and served as president of Paul Quinn College in Waco. Several years later he was named bishop of New York, New Jersey, and Pennsylvania. In the mid-1880s, he retired to Washington, D.C., where he died on January 18, 1887.

Further Reading

Biographical Directory of the United States Congress. "Cain, Richard Harvey, 1825–1887." Available online. URL: http://bioguide.congress.gov/scripts/biodisplay.pl?index=C000022. Downloaded October 19, 2010.

Black Americans in Congress. "Richard Harvey Cain." Available online. URL: http://baic.house.gov/member-profiles/profile.html?intID=2. Downloaded April 4, 2009.

Clay, William L. *Just Permanent Interests: Black Americans in Congress, 1870–1992.* New York: Amistad Press, 1993.

Holt, Thomas C. *Black over White: Negro Political Leadership in South Carolina during Reconstruction.* Urbana: University of Illinois Press, 1977.

Lamson, Peggy. *The Glorious Failure: Black Congressman Robert Brown Elliott and the Reconstruction of South Carolina.* New York: W. W. Norton, 1973.

Campbell, Bill
(William C. Campbell)
(1953–   ) *mayor of Atlanta, Georgia*

Bill Campbell was the third African American to serve as mayor of Atlanta, Georgia. Although accounts vary as to whether he was the most (or least) capable, all observers seem to agree that he was the most controversial.

Campbell was born in 1953 in Raleigh, North Carolina. His father, Ralph, was a janitor, and his mother, June, was a secretary. After graduating from high school, he enrolled in Vanderbilt University, receiving a B.A. in history and political science in 1974. Three years later, he received a J.D. from Duke University Law School, and in 1978 he moved to Atlanta, Georgia, to practice law. In 1980, he went to work for the U.S. Department of Justice's Atlanta office as a prosecutor, but he returned to private practice a year later so that he could run for political office. While in law school, he married Sharon Tapscott, with whom he has two children.

In 1981, Campbell was elected as a Democrat to the Atlanta city council, where he served for the next 12 years. As a councilman, he introduced hundreds of measures, the most important of which was a tough ethics code for city employees, both elected and appointed. He also became a close ally of Mayor MAYNARD JACKSON, and he eventually served as Jackson's major spokesman on the council.

In 1993, the popular Jackson announced his intention to retire from politics after the expiration of his term the following year. Campbell was one of three candidates to declare for the office, and he quickly emerged as the front-runner. During the campaign, Campbell was accused of having accepted bribes in connection with the granting of a lucrative concessions contract at Atlanta's Hartsfield Airport, but he defused this issue by voluntarily taking a lie detector test, which he passed. He won the election easily and took office in 1994.

Campbell's first major challenge was to get Atlanta ready to host the 1996 Summer Olympic Games. When he took office, the city was $30 million in debt and preparations for the Games were far behind schedule. To make matters worse, the stadiums and arenas in which most events were to take place were surrounded by some of the worst slums in the nation. To combat these problems, Campbell convinced the voters to approve a $148 million bond issue for municipal repairs and urban renewal projects. Then he convinced the U.S. Department of Housing and Urban Development to designate Atlanta a federal empowerment zone, thus qualifying the city for $250 million in federal grants and millions more in tax incentives to private investors for various redevelopment projects. He helped make the inner-city neighborhoods more livable by channeling a major portion of the funds to low income housing and by implementing the Ticket-for-Kids program, which provided youth with free admission to a number of entertainment establishments and sporting events. He made the entire city safer by hiring retired police officers to

do paperwork on a part-time basis so the full-time officers could spend more time patrolling the streets, and by greatly increasing the number of police precincts, each with its own station. Meanwhile, Campbell had put his own people in charge of the Corporation for Olympic Development so that the needed improvements could be made on time. By the time the 1996 Summer Olympics were held, Atlanta had been rejuvenated, and the Games were a major success.

After the 1996 Olympics, Campbell turned his attention to economic development. He continued to pursue an initiative he had begun in 1995 of establishing stronger business ties between African-American entrepreneurs in Atlanta and the emerging nations of sub-Saharan Africa. Other initiatives to aid Atlanta's major businesses, most of which were white-owned, angered a number of his black constituents, who thought he should be spending more time furthering civil rights for black Atlantans. These critics were further angered when Campbell appointed a white chief of staff and cracked down on "Freaknik," a spring-break-type party for black college students that had disrupted downtown Atlanta annually for years. However, he also implemented an affirmative action program for the city of Atlanta that was so far-reaching that its opponents challenged it, unsuccessfully, in federal district court.

In an effort to cut the city's budget, Campbell explored the possibility of privatizing certain municipal services. In 1999, the operation of the city's water system was turned over to United Water. At the time, United Water's $420 million contract ($21 million annually for 20 years) was the largest privatization deal in U.S. history.

Campbell was reelected in 1997. Toward the end of his second term, he and his administration ran afoul of charges of corruption and fraud. In 2001, the city board of ethics found Campbell guilty of not disclosing $150,000 in speaking fees, but it chose not to punish him. Meanwhile, the state attorney general's office and the Federal Bureau of Investigation had begun investigating

Campbell and his associates on charges of corruption connected to the letting of city contracts under its minority contracts program. In 2002, after Campbell had left office, one of the contractors involved in the multimillion-dollar renovation of Atlanta's Hartsfield Airport confessed to having made $130,000 in illegal contributions to Campbell's reelection campaign. Campbell himself was never charged or indicted, and he labeled the investigations a racially motivated "inquisition."

Barred by law from seeking a third term, Campbell left office in early 2002. He went to work for an Atlanta radio station as an executive and as cohost of a morning news and public affairs talk show. He later moved to Palm Beach Gardens, Florida, where he briefly practiced law.

In 2004, Campbell was once again embroiled in legal troubles. Based on a five-year federal investigation into corruption during his tenure as mayor, he was indicted on charges of bribery and racketeering. Although Campbell was acquitted of these charges, in March 2006 he was convicted of tax evasion and subsequently sentenced to 30 months in a federal prison in Miami. Campbell was released in October 2008.

Further Reading

"Bill Campbell." *Current Biography* 57 (July 1996): 5–8.

Goodman, Brenda. "Split Verdict Ends Trial of Ex-Mayor of Atlanta." *New York Times,* March 11, 2006. Available online. URL: http://query.nytimes.com/gst/fullpage.html?res=9406E5D813 31F932A25750C0A9609C8B63. Downloaded April 23, 2009.

Cardozo, Francis
(Francis Louis Cardozo)
(1837–1903) *South Carolina state treasurer*

One of the most radical developments of Reconstruction was the redistribution of land from wealthy former Confederate officials in South Carolina to about 8,000 of the state's landless families. Of all the people who played a role in this redistribution, the one most instrumental in its success is Francis Cardozo, South Carolina's first African-American state official.

Francis Louis Cardozo was born on February 1, 1837, in Charleston, South Carolina. His mother, whose name and occupation are unknown, was a free black, and his father was probably either Jacob N. Cardozo, editor of a Charleston newspaper, or Jacob's brother Isaac, who worked in the city's customshouse. He received an elementary education in a Charleston school for free blacks. At age 12, he was apprenticed to a carpenter, and at age 17 he became a journeyman. By 1858, he had saved enough money to pay his tuition at the University of Glasgow, Scotland. He graduated in 1861, then spent the next three years studying at the London School of Theology and at a Presbyterian seminary in Edinburgh. He returned to the United States in 1864 to become the pastor of the Temple Street Congregational Church in New Haven, Connecticut. That same year he married Catherine Howell, with whom he had six children. In 1865, he returned to Charleston to be the director of the American Missionary Association's Saxton School and to cofound a year later the Avery Normal Institute, both of which catered to black students.

Cardozo's political career began in 1864 when he attended a national convention of African Americans in Syracuse, New York, that called for the expansion of civil rights for blacks. After moving to Charleston, he became involved in the affairs of South Carolina's Republican Party. In 1865, as a delegate to the Colored Peoples' Convention in Charleston, he drafted a petition to the state legislature demanding civil rights for freedmen via the repeal of the so-called Black Codes, legislation designed to keep African Americans in a state of quasi slavery.

In 1868, Cardozo was a delegate to the state constitutional convention. He chaired the education committee that drew up the plans for the state's first system of public education. He also argued successfully against the imposition of poll taxes, literacy tests, or any other kind of legal impediment that might keep freedmen from voting. Indeed, his main purpose at the convention was to write a constitution that could not possibly be interpreted in such a way as to deny African Americans their civil and political rights.

Cardozo emerged from the convention as one of the most prominent black politicians in the state. Later that same year, he was offered the Republican nomination for lieutenant governor. He declined, preferring instead to run for secretary of state; when he won, he became South Carolina's first black state official. His major accomplishment in this position, which he held for four years, was to reorganize the state land commission. Under the direction of ROBERT DELARGE from 1868 to 1871, the commission had acquired more than 10,000 acres of land, which it divided into small tracts and sold to approximately 3,000 landless poor families, who had eight years to repay their mortgages. By 1871, however, it became common knowledge that DeLarge has misused his powers as director to divert state funds into the pockets of himself and a group of friendly investors. Cardozo took over direct control of the commission that same year. Unable to find any records whatsoever of DeLarge's transactions, he nevertheless was able to sort out who owed what to whom. More important, by the end of 1872 he had placed another 5,000 families on redistributed land.

In 1872, Cardozo was elected state treasurer. Over the next four years, he set about imposing order on the state's chaotic financial affairs. In the process, he disbursed a considerable amount of money to fund the state's public education system, which had floundered because of his white predecessors' reluctance to part with the necessary funds. The state's finances were so confused, however, that in 1875 his white opponents accused him of fraud and corruption. Reelected to office in 1876, he resigned the following year to stand trial on charges that he had paid interest on state

bonds that had been issued fraudulently before he took office. Although it was never proved that he had benefited or participated in any way with the fraud, he was convicted and sentenced to two years in prison. He was pardoned by the governor before he could be jailed.

The year 1877 marked the end of Reconstruction, and with it came the departure of federal troops from South Carolina and other southern states. Once the troops were gone, nothing could stop whites from seizing control of the legislature and reversing the political and economic gains African Americans had made since 1865. In light of this development, Cardozo realized that his future was no longer in South Carolina. In 1878, he moved to Washington, D.C., where he went to work as a clerk in the Treasury Department. In 1884, he became principal of Washington's Colored Preparatory High School, and in 1891 he took over as principal of the M Street High School. He died in Washington on July 22, 1903. Cardozo Senior High School in northwest Washington, D.C., is named in his honor.

Further Reading

Holt, Thomas C. *Black over White: Negro Political Leadership in South Carolina during Reconstruction.* Urbana: University of Illinois Press, 1977.

Lamson, Peggy. *The Glorious Failure: Black Congressman Robert Brown Elliott and the Reconstruction of South Carolina.* New York: W. W. Norton, 1973.

McCarthy, Timothy P. "Cardozo, Francis Louis." In *African American National Biography,* vol. 2, edited by Henry Louis Gates, Jr., and Evelyn Brooks Higginbotham. New York: Oxford University Press, 2008, pp. 154–156.

Carson, André

(1974–) *U.S. congressional representative from Indiana*

In March 2008, four months after the death of his grandmother JULIA CARSON, André Carson won her seat in the House of Representatives in a special election. Born on October 16, 1974, Carson was raised by his grandmother in a rough area of Indianapolis. Seeing drug deals and gang members on the streets sparked in him an early interest in law and law enforcement. Carson earned his bachelor's degree in criminal justice management at Concordia University Wisconsin. He also holds a master's in business management from Indiana Wesleyan University.

Beginning in 1997, Carson worked for Indiana's Alcohol and Tobacco Commission for nearly 10 years. As an investigative officer, he helped prevent the sale of alcohol to minors. He also worked at his state's Department of Homeland Security in its antiterrorism unit.

Carson began his political career in August 2007. Patrice Abdullah, a member of the Indianapolis city council, lost his position because it was discovered he lived outside of the district. Carson was given the seat by district leaders, who held a special caucus to select Abdullah's replacement. A few months later, in November, he was elected to a full term on the council.

On December 15, 2007, Carson's grandmother Julia died. At the time of her death, she was serving her sixth term in Congress. Democratic leaders in Indianapolis suddenly had to choose a candidate for a special election for her congressional seat. André Carson was on their short list. His name recognition made him a good choice, even though his political experience included only a few months on the Indianapolis city council. Democratic leaders feared that left him vulnerable to the charge that, at only 34 years old, he was simply not ready for the job. Carson was also a convert to Islam, so some feared his religion would become an issue in the campaign. Despite these concerns, they chose Carson as the Democratic candidate. To the surprise of many, he won the special election handily, earning 52 percent of the vote. Sworn in using a bound copy of the U.S. Constitution, Carson was the second Muslim (after KEITH ELLISON) to serve in Congress.

Two months into filling out his grandmother's term, Carson won the Democratic primary, qualifying him for the 2008 general election. In that contest, Carson was again victorious. In January 2009, he began serving his first full term in Congress. He was reelected in 2010. Carson was named to the influential Financial Services Committee. He also worked toward achieving his two primary campaign promises—to improve the nation's health care system and to put an end to the war in Iraq. Carson is married to Mariama Carson, a schoolteacher, and they have one daughter.

Further Reading

Congressman André Carson, Official Web Site. Available online. URL: http://carson.house.gov. Downloaded May 9, 2009.
Kuglar, R. Anthony. "André Carson, 1974– ." *Contemporary Black Biography* 69 (2009): 21–23.

Carson, Julia
(Julia May Carson)
(1938–2007) *U.S. congressional representative from Indiana*

In 1997, Julia Carson became the second African American to represent Indiana in Congress. Like BARBARA LEE, her political career was furthered tremendously by many years of service as a congressional aide.

Carson was born Julia May Porter on July 8, 1938, in Louisville, Kentucky. Her mother was an unmarried teenager who supported Carson and herself by drawing welfare. As a girl, she moved with her mother to Indianapolis, Indiana, and contributed to their support by working a variety of odd jobs. She finished high school in 1955 and then worked a series of jobs before opening a clothing store in 1963. Two years later, the store went out of business, and she went to work as a staff assistant for Andy Jacobs, who represented Indianapolis in the U.S. Congress. She worked for

Jacobs for seven years, during which time she also attended Indiana University for two years. She was married briefly, but divorced after having two children.

Carson learned much about politics by serving as Jacobs's aide. Impressed with her ambition and organizational skills, he convinced her in 1972 to seek a political office of her own. That year she ran as a Democrat for the state legislature and won. Four years later, she was elected to the state senate, where she served for the next 14 years.

In 1990 Carson left the senate after she was elected trustee of Indianapolis's Center Township. This position put her in charge of distributing federal welfare payments in central Indianapolis. At the time she took over the program, her office was being held accountable for $17 million in improper payments. Over the next six years, she cleared up this financial mess and implemented sound management practices to ensure that it would not happen again. Meanwhile, she became a vocal supporter for changes in the welfare system. Having grown up on welfare, Carson was personally familiar with the way that clients abused the system as well as the way the system abused its clients. To solve both problems, she advocated making welfare recipients perform some sort of work in return for their money; not only would this requirement thin out the welfare rolls, but also it would help restore some sense of dignity and self-respect to those who were forced to live on welfare.

In 1996, Jacobs announced his retirement. Carson decided to run for his seat, despite the fact that only about 30 percent of the district's constituents were African American. With Jacobs's support, she won the Democratic primary and then eked out a narrow victory in the general election. She took her seat in 1997 and was assigned to the committees on financial services and veterans affairs.

Carson was reelected to Congress five times. As a congresswoman, Carson focused on legislation that protected children. She introduced the Responsible Fatherhood Act, which would fund federal and state programs that would provide opportunities for children to bond with their biological fathers. She introduced the National Defense Rail Act, which sought to preserve federal funding for Amtrak passenger rail service. And she reintroduced the Child Handgun Injury Prevention Act, which mandated that all handguns sold in the United States be equipped with trigger locks and load indicator devices. Carson was also a vehement opponent of the Iraq War.

In September 2007, in the middle of her sixth term in Congress, Carson was hospitalized with a leg infection. During her recovery, she was diagnosed with lung cancer. Carson died of the illness on December 15, 2007.

Further Reading
Biographical Directory of the United States Congress. "Carson, Julia May, 1938–2007." Available online. URL: http://bioguide.congress.gov/scripts/biodisplay.pl?index=C000191. Downloaded April 15, 2009.
Black Americans in Congress. "Julia May Carson." Available online. URL: http://baic.house.gov/member-profiles/profile.html?intID=43. Downloaded April 4, 2009.
Foerstel, Karen. *Biographical Dictionary of Congressional Women.* New York: Greenwood Press, 1999.
"Julia Carson, 69, U.S. Representative, Is Dead." *New York Times,* December 16, 2007. Available online. URL: http://www.nytimes.com/2007/12/16/us/16carson.html?_r=1&scp=1&sq=julia%20carson&st=cse. Downloaded April 3, 2009.

Cheatham, Henry
(Henry Plummer Cheatham)
(1857–1935) *U.S. congressional representative from North Carolina*

Henry Cheatham was the second African American to represent North Carolina's black-majority "Black Second" District. Like his predecessor,

JAMES O'HARA, as a congressman he did what he could to protect the civil rights of African Americans while advancing the economic interests of eastern North Carolina.

Cheatham was born on December 27, 1857, on a plantation near Henderson in Vance County, North Carolina. Little is known about his parents other than that his mother was a slave. He gained his freedom in 1865 when the Civil War ended, and for the next 10 years he worked as a farmhand and attended public school. At age 18, he moved to Raleigh to attend the teachers' college affiliated with Shaw University, and in 1882 he received a bachelor's degree from Shaw. For the next two years, he served as principal of a black school in Plymouth and helped found the North Carolina Orphanage for Negroes in Oxford. At some point during this period, he married Louise Cherry, with whom he had three children; he later married Laura Joyner, with whom he also had three children.

Cheatham's political career began in 1885, the same year he returned to Henderson. He immediately became involved with the Republican Party and was elected county registrar of deeds. He also took up the study of law, receiving an M.A. from Shaw in 1887, although he never practiced. In 1888 he ran for the U.S. House of Representatives from the so-called Black Second District, where a majority of voters were African American. A brilliant orator, he narrowly defeated his white Democrat opponent by convincing enough voters that the Democrats were planning to re-enslave the freedmen. He was reelected easily in 1890.

For most of his two terms, Cheatham was the only African American in Congress. Assigned to the committee on education, he introduced several bills to provide federal funding for public education. Most of his efforts, however, went into securing more federal money and jobs for his black constituents, at which he was quite successful. He also worked to improve conditions for farmers in his district by seeking federal agricultural aid and by voting for the McKinley Tariff of 1890, which protected tobacco, his state's main cash crop. Despite his oratorical skills, while in Congress he preferred to work behind the scenes, and in the process he became a well-known figure in the Republican Party. In 1892, he accepted an invitation to give a seconding speech to President Benjamin Harrison's renomination at that year's national convention.

During Cheatham's second term, the North Carolina legislature reapportioned its congressional districts, in the process eliminating the "Black Second." Having lost his black-majority constituency, he was not reelected in 1892, and his attempts to regain the seat in 1894 and 1896 failed. Following his return from Congress in 1893, he took up farming on some land he owned in Littleton. In 1897, he moved to Washington, D.C., and for the next four years he was registrar of deeds for the nation's capital. In 1901, he returned to his farm, then in 1907 he relocated to Oxford, North Carolina, to become superintendent of the orphanage he had cofounded 25 years earlier. He devoted the rest of his life to expanding and improving the institution's physical plant and instructional offerings. He died on November 29, 1935, in Oxford.

Further Reading

Anderson, Eric. *Race and Politics in North Carolina, 1872–1901: The Black Second.* Baton Rouge: Louisiana State University Press, 1981.

Biographical Directory of the United States Congress. "Cheatham, Henry Plummer, 1857–1935." Available online. URL: http://bioguide.congress. gov/scripts/biodisplay.pl?index=C000340. Downloaded March 28, 2009.

Black Americans in Congress. "Henry Plummer Cheatham." Available online. URL: http://baic.house.gov/member-profiles/profile.html?int ID=19. Downloaded April 11, 2009.

Clay, William L. *Just Permanent Interests: Black Americans in Congress, 1870–1992.* New York: Amistad Press, 1993.

Chisholm, Shirley
(Shirley Anita St. Hill Chisholm)
(1924–2005) *U.S. congressional
representative from New York, Presidential
candidate*

Shirley Chisholm was the first African-American
woman to serve in the U.S. House of Representatives. She was also the first African American and
the first woman to receive at least 10 percent of
the votes for president at a major political party's
national convention.

Chisholm was born Shirley Anita St. Hill on
November 30, 1924, in Brooklyn, New York. Her
father, Charles, worked in a bakery, and her
mother, Ruby, worked as a seamstress and housekeeper. From ages four to 10, she lived with her
maternal grandmother on the Caribbean island of
Barbados. After completing her secondary education in Brooklyn, she enrolled in Brooklyn College to study sociology and received a B.A. in
1946. In 1949, she married Conrad Chisholm;
they had no children. After graduating from
Brooklyn College, she continued her studies in
early childhood education at Columbia University, while teaching during the day in a nursery
school, and received an M.A. in 1953. Over the
next six years, she worked successively as a teacher's aide, teacher, and director for three different
child care facilities. In 1959, she became an educational consultant for the New York Department
of Social Services' day care division, a position she
held for five years.

While a student at Brooklyn College, Chisholm
had joined the 17th Assembly District Democratic
Club. During her senior year, she began working
politically with fellow club member Wesley M.
Holder. Holder was a Caribbean-born British subject who could not run for office himself, so he did
what he could to get other blacks elected to state
and local offices from New York City's blackmajority districts and wards. To this end, in 1953
Holder founded, with considerable help from
Chisholm, the Bedford-Stuyvesant Political

League. Unfortunately, Holder and Chisholm had
a falling-out shortly thereafter, and the league
folded within a few months.

Chisholm had little to do with politics for the
next seven years. By 1960, however, she had
become disgusted with the refusal of Democrats
in her assembly district to run African Americans
for office. That same year, she cofounded the
Unity Democratic Club, which sought to exercise
greater influence over the district's nomination
process. In 1962, the Unity Club got one member
elected to the state assembly and two more elected
to the party's district committee. Two years later,
when the assemblyman resigned to become a
municipal judge, the club got Chisholm nominated to take his place. In 1964, after a long, hard
campaign during which she received much support from women's social groups and civic clubs,
she took her seat in the state legislature. During
her four-year tenure as an assemblywoman, she
won two major legislative victories. One created
Search for Education, Elevation, and Knowledge
(SEEK), which provided financial and remedial
assistance for college-bound students of AfricanAmerican or Puerto Rican heritage, and the other
established an unemployment insurance program
for domestic workers.

Meanwhile, the New York legislature had reapportioned its congressional districts, thus creating
the black-majority 12th District around BedfordStuyvesant, Chisholm's neighborhood in Brooklyn. Although she was denied the support of her
party's leaders when she sought the nomination
for this seat in 1968, her performance in the state
assembly had gained her tremendous grassroots
support. She also reconciled with Holder, who
skillfully managed her low-budget, high-energy
campaign featuring the slogan "Fighting Shirley
Chisholm—Unbought and Unbossed." After edging out the leadership's anointed candidate in the
primary, in the general election she faced James
Farmer, the former national chairman of the Congress of Racial Equality. Farmer was well organized
and well funded, but he made the critical mistake

of making Chisholm's gender a campaign issue. Once again the women's social groups and civic clubs rallied to her support, and in 1969 she became the first African-American woman to take a seat in Congress. She wrote about her campaign experiences, as well as her first term in Congress, in *Unbought and Unbossed* (1970).

Chisholm was initially assigned to the committees on ways and means and on agriculture. She later served on the committees on veterans' affairs, education and labor, and rules. Most of her efforts, however, were focused on gaining federal funding for expanded social programs. Specifically, she sought to establish federal subsidies for day care centers, increase the minimum wage, refocus the War on Poverty to provide better job training, and implement a national version of SEEK. To pay for

Shirley Chisholm was the first African-American woman to serve in the U.S. House of Representatives. *(Library of Congress)*

these initiatives, she advocated a reduction in the military budget, and to this end she opposed the war in Vietnam. She also opposed most environmental bills on the grounds that they cost many low-income people their jobs. In 1971, she became a founding member of the Congressional Black Caucus.

In 1972, Chisholm ran for president of the United States. Although she professed to be a serious candidate for the post, in retrospect it seems more likely that her primary goal was to pave the way for another African American or woman to get elected to the White House later on. She campaigned heartily during the primary season, and even received 151 votes at the Democratic National Convention, but her fellow Democrats nominated peace candidate George McGovern instead. She wrote about her campaign experiences in *The Good Fight* (1973).

In 1978, Chisholm divorced her husband and married Arthur Hardwick. The following year he was involved in a near-fatal automobile accident, and several years after that he was diagnosed with cancer. Meanwhile, she found herself increasingly out of step with the new conservative mood in Congress resulting from the Reagan revolution. In 1982, after having been reelected six times, she announced her retirement from Congress, choosing instead to spend time with her ailing husband. After finishing her term in 1983, she taught political science and women's studies for four years at Mt. Holyoke College, then retired to her home in Williamsville, New York. She campaigned actively for JESSE JACKSON in his 1984 and 1988 runs for the presidency, and in 1984 she cofounded the National Political Congress of Black Women. In 1993, President Bill Clinton offered to nominate her as ambassador to Jamaica, but she declined on the grounds of poor health. Moving to Florida in 1991, Chisholm spent her retirement writing, lecturing, and reading political biographies. After suffering a series of strokes, she died at her home on January 1, 2005.

Further Reading

Barron, James. "Shirley Chisholm, 'Unbossed' Pioneer in Congress, Is Dead at 80." *New York Times*, January 3, 2005. Available online. URL: http://www. nytimes.com/2005/01/03/obituaries/03chisholm. html?pagewanted=1&sq=shirley%20chisholm &st=cse&scp=1. Downloaded April 3, 2009.

Biographical Directory of the United States Congress. "Chisholm, Shirley Anita, 1924." Available online. URL: http://bioguide.congress.gov/scripts/ biodisplay.pl?index=C000371. Downloaded April 3, 2009.

Black Americans in Congress. "Shirley A. Chisholm." Available online. URL: http://baic.house.gov/ member-profiles/profile.html?intID=24. Downloaded April 4, 2009.

Brownmiller, Susan. *Shirley Chisholm*. New York: Doubleday, 1970.

Canson, Patricia E. "Chisholm, Shirley." In *African American National Biography*, vol. 2, edited by Henry Louis Gates, Jr., and Evelyn Brooks Higginbotham. New York: Oxford University Press, 2008, pp. 279–281.

Clay, William L. *Just Permanent Interests: Black Americans in Congress, 1870–1992*. New York: Amistad Press, 1993.

Gill, LaVerne McCain. *African American Women in Congress: Forming and Transforming History*. New Brunswick, N.J.: Rutgers University Press, 1997.

Scheader, Catherine. *Shirley Chisholm: Teacher and Congresswoman*. Hillside, N.J.: Enslow Publishers, 1990.

Christian-Christensen, Donna

(Donna Marie Christian-Green, Donna Marie Christian, Donna Marie Christian-Christensen) (1945–   ) *delegate to U.S. House from Virgin Islands*

Like her predecessor, MELVIN EVANS, Donna Christian-Christensen became the Virgin Islands' nonvoting delegate in the U.S. House of Representatives after a long career as a physician.

While in Congress, she has worked to improve the economy and the health care in her island constituency.

Christian-Christensen was born Donna Marie Christian on September 19, 1945, in Teaneck, New Jersey. Her father, Almeric, was a district court judge for the Virgin Islands, and her mother, Virginia, was a homemaker. In 1962, she finished high school and enrolled in St. Mary's College in Indiana. After receiving a B.S. four years later, she enrolled in George Washington University School of Medicine and received an M.D. in 1970. After four years as an intern and resident at the Pacific Medical Center in San Francisco, California, and Howard University Medical Center in Washington, D.C., she returned to the island of St. Croix, where she had grown up, to open a medical practice. From 1975 to 1980, she served in various capacities with the U.S. Virgin Islands Department of Health. In 1980, she took over as director of the Nesbitt Clinic in Frederiksted, and in 1987 she became the medical director of St. Croix Hospital. In 1988, she was named territorial assistant to the Virgin Islands' commissioner of health, and in 1994 she was appointed acting commissioner. In 1974, she married Carl Green, with whom she had two children; they divorced six years later. In 1998, she married Chris Christensen.

Christian-Christensen became involved in politics in 1980, when she got involved with the Democratic Party as vice-chair of its Virgin Islands territorial committee. In 1984, she was elected to a two-year term on the islands' board of education and was chosen to serve on the Democratic National Committee. In 1988, she was named to the U.S. Virgin Islands Status Commission. This body was charged with investigating whether the Virgin Islands should gain statehood, remain a territory, or be granted independence.

Christian-Christensen first ran for the Virgin Islands' nonvoting seat in Congress in 1994, but she was defeated by Victor O. Frazer. Two years later, she ran against Frazer again and won. She took her seat in 1997 and was assigned to the committees on resources and small business. She has been reelected to three terms.

As a delegate, Christian-Christensen focused on raising the consciousness of her colleagues as to the effect of federal legislation on her constituents. For example, a tariff treaty between the United States and the European Union proposed to eliminate tariffs on rum. While this was a small feature of the overall treaty, it threatened to destroy the Virgin Islands' rum industry, the most important part of the islands' economy after tourism. She also worked to secure more federal funding for the islands, especially in the form of Medicaid and child-care benefits; she claimed that Virgin Islanders received only one-tenth what they would have received in such payments had they lived in one of the 50 states. In addition, her committee assignments have involved her in affairs related to public health and telecommunications. She is the former chair of the natural resources subcommittee on insular affairs, which oversees issues involving the U.S. Virgin Islands, Puerto Rico, and other offshore territories.

Further Reading

Biographical Directory of the United States Congress. "Christensen, Donna Marie Christian, 1945– ." Available online. URL: http://bioguide.congress. gov/scripts/biodisplay.pl?index=C000380. Downloaded April 8, 2009.

Congresswoman Donna M. Christensen, Official Web Site. Available online. URL: http://www.donna christensen.house.gov. Downloaded April 3, 2009.

Foerstel, Karen. *Biographical Dictionary of Congressional Women.* New York: Greenwood Press, 1999.

Church, Robert

(Robert Reed Church, Jr.)
(1885–1952) *Tennessee Republican Party committeeman*

Unlike many southern Republicans of his day, Robert Church was not primarily interested in claiming more than his share of federal patronage jobs. Instead, he used his influence within the party to improve the lives of his fellow African Americans. In the process, he spent a considerable portion of his own personal fortune and eventually lost it all.

Church was born on October 26, 1885, in Memphis, Tennessee. His father, Robert, Sr., was a banker and businessman, and his mother, Anna Sue, was a school principal. He attended private schools in Memphis, Ohio, and Illinois, then graduated from the Packard School of Business in New York City in 1904. After working for three years as a banker's apprentice on Wall Street, in 1907 he returned to Memphis to become a manager in the family businesses, which included the Solvent Savings Bank and Trust Company and more than 300 parcels of real estate. In 1911, he married Sara Johnson, with whom he had one child.

In 1911, Church became involved in politics by backing the mayoral candidacy of Democrat Edward H. Crump, a reform candidate and a moderate on matters of race. Although Tennessee's constitution virtually barred African Americans from voting in state and national elections via literacy tests and poll taxes, blacks could still vote in municipal elections. In return for Crump's promise to build parks and pave streets in black neighborhoods, Church promised to give Crump the support of the Colored Citizens Association of Memphis. Crump won the election, and Church got hooked on politics. Despite his connection with Crump, he joined the Republican Party, and the following year he was named a delegate to its national convention.

In 1912, Robert Church, Sr., died and left Church and his sister in charge of the family estate, which was valued at more than $1 million. Church was elected president of the bank, but his desire to effect political change led him to resign the next year. Instead, he concentrated on turning the black citizens of Memphis into full-fledged voters. By 1916, he had organized the Lincoln

League and turned it into a black Republican machine. With his leadership and financial backing, the league helped black citizens register to vote by teaching them enough to pass the literacy tests and by paying their poll taxes. That same year, the league ran a black candidate for Congress; although he lost, his respectable showing encouraged Church and the league to try harder. It also secured for Church a seat on the state Republican executive committee. In 1920, the league was able to turn out enough black voters to carry the city and the state for the Republican national ticket, the first time this had happened since the end of Reconstruction in 1877. As a result of this showing, Church became a party hero and was granted considerable influence over the distribution of political patronage jobs in Tennessee.

Church never sought political office for himself; indeed, he turned down at least two appointments to cushy federal commissions. Instead, he seemed entirely motivated by his desire to involve his fellow African Americans more fully in political affairs, spending much of his personal fortune in the process. Since it was politically impossible to appoint blacks to patronage positions in the South, he recommended only those whites he believed were not racially prejudiced. Likewise, he continued to support Crump as long as the mayor's administration treated African Americans evenhandedly. As a result, the Memphis city government under Crump spent millions of dollars on public improvements and services for its black residents, while the federal government contributed funding for two black housing projects.

Church's influence began to wane in 1929 as the result of Herbert Hoover's election to the presidency. Hoover wanted to attract more white voters to the Republican Party in the South, but he knew this would never happen as long as blacks held influential positions in the party apparatus. Although Hoover was able to remove BENJAMIN DAVIS and PERRY HOWARD, black Republican leaders in Georgia and Mississippi, respectively,

from their positions for alleged corrupt practices, he never was able to remove Church. Nevertheless, Hoover's unwillingness to work with Church diminished his political influence. He lost virtually all of his influence following the election of Franklin D. Roosevelt to the presidency in 1932. At the strong urging of his wife Eleanor, Roosevelt made greater concessions to African Americans than any president ever had before. As a result, more and more black voters across the country, including Memphis, became Democrats.

The Great Depression hit Church particularly hard. He had come to rely on the income from his rental property for his financial support, but the inability of his tenants to pay rent, coupled with higher municipal tax assessments, resulted in his tax bill's being higher than his rental income. In 1938, he moved to Philadelphia, Pennsylvania, and two years later to Chicago, Illinois; by 1941 the city of Memphis had seized all of his property for nonpayment of back taxes. He supported himself for awhile by working for various Republican candidates and organizations in Philadelphia and Chicago. In 1944, he accepted a paid position as organizer of the Republican American Committee, whose intent was to get Republicans in Congress to support the permanent creation of the Fair Employment Practices Committee and other civil rights legislation sponsored by Democrats. In 1952, he returned to Memphis to reclaim his position in the state Republican Party, but before he could achieve this he died of a heart attack on April 17, 1952, in Memphis.

Further Reading
Boschert, Thomas A. "Church, Robert Reed, Jr." In *African American National Biography,* vol. 2, edited by Henry Louis Gates, Jr., and Evelyn Brooks Higginbotham. New York: Oxford University Press, 2008, pp. 286–287.

Church, Annette E., and Roberta Church. *The Robert R. Churches of Memphis: A Father and Son Who Achieved in Spite of Race.* Memphis: A. E. Church, 1979.

Lamon, Lester C. *Blacks in Tennessee, 1791–1970.* Knoxville: University of Tennessee Press, 1981.

Scott, Mingo, Jr. *The Negro in Tennessee Politics and Governmental Affairs: 1865–1965, The Hundred Years Story.* Nashville, Tenn.: Rich Printing Co., 1965.

Clarke, Yvette D.
(Yvette Diane Clarke)
(1964–   ) *U.S. congressional representative from New York*

In 2006, Democrat Yvette D. Clarke became the U.S. House representative for District 11 in Brooklyn, New York, a position once held by legendary congresswoman SHIRLEY CHISHOLM.

Yvette Diane Clarke was born in Brooklyn on November 21, 1964. Her father was an engineer and architect with the Port Authority of New York and New Jersey. Her mother, Una, had an early career as a day care administrator. Una S. T. Clarke eventually entered New York City politics. Representing the heavily Caribbean neighborhoods of Flatbush and East Flatbush, she became the first Jamaican-born member of the city council.

Yvette D. Clarke attended Edmund R. Murrow High School, where she was voted vice president of her senior class. Her excellent grades earned her a scholarship to Oberlin College in Ohio. While at Oberlin, she served as an intern in Washington, D.C., for Representative MAJOR OWENS, who took over Chisholm's congressional seat in 1983. Clarke spent her last semester at Brooklyn's Medgar Evers College.

In 1987, Clarke was hired by the Erasmus Neighborhood Federation as a child-care specialist. She later worked as an aide for two state legislators and as the director of a youth program for a health service workers' union. In 1995, Clarke became the director of business development for the Bronx Empowerment Zone. Charged with working to economically revitalize the South Bronx, she oversaw a budget of $51 million.

Forced to leave the city council because of term limits, Una Clarke in 2000 staged an unsuccessful bid for Owens's seat in the House of Representatives. The same year, Yvette Clarke entered city politics by running for the council seat vacated by her mother. Clarke beat out five challengers in the primary and easily won the general election in her heavily Democratic district. She became the first woman in New York history to take over her mother's seat in the city council.

After less than three years in this post, Clarke announced that she would run against Owens in the 2004 primary. Clarke failed to beat the incumbent, but her second place showing convinced her to run again in 2006, after Owens decided to retire from Congress. The hotly contested primary race pitted her against Owens's son Chris, state senator Carl Andrews, and councilman David Yassky. During the campaign, Clarke was criticized for falsely claiming that she graduated from Oberlin, when in fact she left the college six credits shy of earning a degree. Nevertheless, she won the support of the majority of the district's Caribbean voters and important endorsements from several unions. After winning the primary, Clarke sailed through the November election, capturing 89 percent of the vote.

In the House of Representatives, Clarke has served on the Education and Labor Committee, the Homeland Security Committee, and the Small Business Committee. Her voting record supported increasing children's access to health care, revitalizing public housing, and allowing rehabilitated drug convicts to apply for student loans. In 2010, she was reelected to a third term.

Further Reading
Congresswoman Yvette D. Clarke, Official Web Site. Available online. URL: http://clarke.house.gov. Downloaded April 28, 2009.

Hicks, Jonathan P. "In Her Mother's Footsteps, and Now in Shirley Chisholm's, Too." *New York Times,* September 14, 2006. Available online. URL: http://www.nytimes.com/2006/09/14/nyregion/14yvette.html. Downloaded April 28, 2009.

Clay, William

(William Lacy Clay)

(1931–) *U.S. congressional representative from Missouri*

William Clay was the first African-American congressman from Missouri. Throughout his political career he focused on winning and guaranteeing equal opportunity for blacks.

Clay was born on April 30, 1931, in St. Louis, Missouri. His father, Irving, was a welder, and his mother, Luella, was a homemaker. At age 13, he took a job as a janitor to help support his family; later, while still in school, he worked as a tailor and salesman in a clothing store. After graduating from high school, he enrolled in St. Louis University; he majored in history and political science and received his B.S. in 1953. That same year, he married Carol Johnson, with whom he has three children, and joined the U.S. Army. He spent most of his two-year enlistment fighting segregation on southern army bases. One of his protests came to the attention of CHARLES DIGGS, who launched a congressional investigation that ended the worst abuses. In 1955, he returned to St. Louis. Over the next four years, he sold insurance, but his real work was to struggle for equal rights for African Americans.

In 1959, Clay joined the Democratic Party and ran for city alderman from the black-majority 26th Ward, handily defeating the white incumbent. That same year, he was named business representative of St. Louis's chapter of the State, Local and Municipal Workers' Union. As alderman, he worked to gain equal employment opportunities for blacks. After opening the doors of city hall's personnel office to more blacks in search of city jobs, he tackled the discriminatory hiring practices of private employers. In 1963, he was jailed for several months for picketing a local bank that refused to hire blacks. Shortly after his release, he introduced and won passage for the city's first fair employment act. In 1964, he resigned as alderman, although he remained active in politics as his ward's Democratic committeeman. He maintained his union connections by serving as education coordinator of the local pipe-fitters' union. Meanwhile, he supported his family by selling real estate.

In 1968, the Missouri legislature redistricted the state so that most of St. Louis's African-American population ended up in the black-majority First Congressional District. Running on his record as a civil rights activist and union supporter, Clay easily won the primary and the general election. He took his seat in Congress in 1969 and was assigned to the committee on education and labor.

As a congressman, Clay continued to work for equal opportunity for blacks. He saw himself as the representative of all African Americans between the Mississippi River and the Rocky Mountains, since he was the only black congressman from that part of the country. He protested police brutality against blacks in Chicago, Illinois, and Jackson, Mississippi, and he investigated the Federal Communications Commission on the grounds that it tolerated discrimination against black newspeople. When Vice President Spiro T. Agnew criticized black leaders for criticizing the Nixon administration's attempts to nullify the gains made by African Americans during the Kennedy and Johnson administrations, Clay accused Agnew of being "seriously ill" and an "intellectual misfit." He was a vocal opponent of the war in Vietnam on the grounds that black troops were fighting to preserve rights for Asians that they themselves did not possess at home. In 1971, he became a founding member of the Congressional Black Caucus.

In the 1970s, Clay was assigned to the committee on the post office and civil service, and in 1993 he became its chairman. He made postal reform one of his pet projects, attacking the U.S. Postal Service for unsafe working conditions, consistently exceeding its budget, and trying to blame postal rate increases on Congress rather than on its own inability to hold down costs.

Clay demonstrated an interest in issues other than civil rights and postal reform. He sponsored the act that made it easier to become vested in company pension plans as well as guaranteeing one's rights to a deceased spouse's pension. He tried to amend the Hatch Act of 1939, which prohibited federal employees from participating in partisan politics, to allow such employees to politick on their own time. He was a major mover behind getting the Parental and Medical Leave Act of 1993 enacted; this act granted several weeks of unpaid leave for purposes of caring for newborns or seriously ill family members. In keeping with his pro-labor stance, he sponsored legislation requiring factories to give their employees advance notice of any plant closings and to protect the jobs of striking workers. In 1993, he published *Just Permanent Interests: Black Americans in Congress, 1870–1992.*

Clay was reelected to Congress 15 times. In 2000 he declined to run for reelection and was succeeded by his son, WILLIAM CLAY, JR. He resides in St. Louis. His autobiography, *Bill Clay: A Political Voice at the Grass Roots,* was published in 2004.

Further Reading

Biographical Directory of the United States Congress. "Clay, William Lacy, Sr., 1931– ." Available online. URL: http://bioguide.congress.gov/scripts/biodisplay.pl?index=C000488. Downloaded April 3, 2009.

Black Americans in Congress. "William Lacy (Bill) Clay, Sr." Available online. URL: http://baic.house.gov/member-profiles/profile.html?intID=25. Downloaded April 8, 2009.

Clay, William L. *Bill Clay: A Political Voice at the Grass Roots.* St. Louis: Missouri Historical Society Press, 2004.

———. *Just Permanent Interests: Black Americans in Congress, 1870–1992.* New York: Amistad Press, 1993.

Clay, William, Jr.

(William Lacy Clay, Jr.)
(1956–) *U.S. congressional representative from Missouri*

In 2001, William L. Clay, Jr., joined HAROLD FORD, JR., as the U.S. House of Representatives' second African American son to hold a seat that his father had held. As in Ford's case, he did so by taking the seat of his retired father.

Clay was born on July 27, 1956, in St. Louis, Missouri. His father was WILLIAM CLAY, and his mother, Carol, was a homemaker. At age 13, he moved to Washington, D.C., following the election of his father to the U.S. House of Representatives. He graduated from high school in 1974, and for the next nine years he worked a variety of jobs during the day while attending night school at the University of Maryland. In 1983, he received a B.S. in government and politics and returned to St. Louis. In 1993, he married Ivie Lewellen, with whom he has two children.

In essence, Clay's involvement in politics began when his father was first elected to office in 1959. He learned much about governing simply by observing his father in action, and he learned about campaigning for office by assisting in his father' reelection efforts every two years. At some point, he decided to pursue a political career of his own, and in 1983 he made his first bid for public office. Having just resettled in St. Louis that same year, he was elected as a Democrat to the state house of representatives. He served in the lower house for eight years, during which he served a term as chair of the labor committee. In 1991, he was elected to the state senate, where he chaired the financial committee during the latter part of his nine-year tenure.

During his 17 years in the Missouri state legislature, Clay authored several important acts. One ended the 30-year battle over desegregating the St. Louis public school system. Another provided thousands of teenagers with jobs and job training

He took his seat in 2001 and was assigned to the committees on financial services and government reform.

As a congressman, Clay focused on many of the issues that had concerned him as a state legislator. He pushed for passage of a federal hate crimes bill, and he sought passage of legislation that would extend health care benefits to workers who had been laid off from their jobs. He also worked to increase federal expenditures on environmental cleanup projects, and obtain prescription drug benefits for senior citizens, and he helped secure preliminary approval for the National Housing Trust Fund. Other issues of concern to Clay included expanding voter registration, cracking down on predatory lending, and introducing financial literacy programs into public schools. He was also a vocal critic of the Iraq War.

In 2010, Clay was reelected to a sixth term. He is married to Ivie Lewellen Clay, with whom he has two children.

Further Reading

Biographical Directory of the United States Congress. "Clay, William Lacy, Jr., 1956– ." Available online. URL: http://bioguide.congress.gov/scripts/biodisplay.pl?index=C001049. Downloaded April 16, 2009.

Congressman William Lacy Clay, Official Web Site. Available online. URL: http://lacyclay.house.gov. Downloaded April 24, 2009.

"William Lacy Clay Jr., D-Missouri (1). New Member Profile." CQ Weekly 58 (November 11, 2000): 2,686.

William Clay, Jr., was elected to a seat in the U.S. House of Representatives that had been held for years by his father, William L. Clay. *(William Clay, Jr.)*

as part of a violence prevention program. Yet another established Family Development Accounts; this program allowed low- income families to deposit tax-exempt money into tax-free accounts as a means of saving for such investments as a college education, buying a home, or starting a small business. He also wrote Missouri's first hate crime act, as well as the revisions that included sexual orientation, gender, and disability under its provisions.

In 2000, Clay's father announced his retirement from Congress after more than 30 years in office. That same year Clay declared his candidacy for the seat. Needless to say, he received his father's enthusiastic endorsement. This, coupled with his own impressive career in the state legislature, enabled him to succeed his father with ease.

Clayton, Eva

(Eva McPherson Clayton)
(1934–) *U.S. congressional representative from North Carolina*

In 1993, Eva Clayton and MEL WATT became the first African Americans to represent North Carolina in the U.S. House of Representatives since

1901, when GEORGE WHITE left office. Unlike Watt and many of her black colleagues in Congress, Clayton came from a rural district, and she championed the interests of small farmers.

Clayton was born Eva McPherson on September 16, 1934, in Savannah, Georgia. Her father was an insurance salesman, and her mother was a homemaker. As a young girl, she moved with her family to Augusta where her father had been transferred. After finishing high school, she enrolled in Johnson C. Smith University, where she received a B.S. in biology in 1956. That same year she married Theaoseus Clayton, with whom she has four children, and settled in Warren County, North Carolina. In 1962, she received an M.S. in biology and general science from North Carolina Central University. She then enrolled in the University of North Carolina Law School but dropped out after the birth of her fourth child. She stayed in Chapel Hill to serve as director of the University of North Carolina's Health Manpower Development Program.

In 1974, Clayton became the executive director of the Soul City Foundation. The foundation was the creation of civil rights activist Floyd McKissick, and its purpose was to build an all-black community, known as Soul City, in Warren County. It was funded primarily by a $14 million bond issue backed by the U.S. Department of Housing and Urban Development under its New Towns program. During Clayton's tenure, Soul City ran into serious financial difficulty, and in 1977 she left the foundation to accept the position of assistant secretary for community development for the North Carolina Department of Natural Resources and Community Development. Four years later, she founded Technical Resources International, a management and consulting firm specializing in economic development.

Clayton made her first bid for political office while still in law school. In 1968, she ran unsuccessfully in the Democratic primary for a seat in the U.S. Congress. She remained active in local party affairs, and in 1976 she played a major role in Jim Hunt's successful campaign for governor. In 1982, she made her second run for public office, and this time she won a seat on the Warren County Board of Commissioners. Almost immediately she was named to chair the commission, a position she held for eight years. During this period, she helped recruit new businesses that brought 900 new jobs and more than $500 million in investments to the county. In 1990, she was declared the state's outstanding county commissioner.

In 1992, Walter B. Jones, who represented Clayton's district in the U.S. House of Representatives, died in office. Clayton ran against Jones's son in the primary, winning a narrow victory. She had an easier time in the general election, and took her seat in Congress that same year. She was assigned to the committees on agriculture and small business.

As a congresswoman, Clayton's major focus has been the welfare of her constituents, many of whom are small tobacco or peanut growers and small family farmers. She opposed the North American Free Trade Agreement because she feared that competition from farmers in Mexico would mean the loss of farming jobs in her district. She played a major role in securing passage of the Agriculture Research Act, which provided funds for research and crop insurance. She got the Department of Agriculture to make money available to poor farmers who were unable to get the credit they needed to keep farming. She opposed the Republican Party's "Freedom to Farm" initiative in 1996, which sought to phase out farm subsidies, and she repeatedly worked to thwart measures to cut back, directly or indirectly, on the production of tobacco.

In other areas, Clayton has fought to preserve federal funding for affordable housing, another major need of her rural constituents. She also worked to fend off cutbacks in social services such as food stamps, job training, and health care. In 1998, she became actively involved in the National Campaign to Prevent Teenage Pregnancy. In 2000, she was reelected to Congress for the fourth time. She declined to run for reelection in 2002. Following the completion of her term in 2003, she joined the United Nations Food Agriculture Organization as a special adviser to the director-general. She left this position after three years and has since reestablished her consulting firm, Eva Clayton Associates International, Inc., in Raleigh, North Carolina. In 2007, Clayton organized the first North Carolina Hunger Forum, which set the goal of cutting the rate of hunger in the state by 50 percent by 2015.

Further Reading

Biographical Directory of the United States Congress. "Clayton, Eva M., 1934–   ." Available online. URL: http://bioguide.congress.gov/scripts/biodisplay. pl?index=C000494. Downloaded April 3, 2009.

Black Americans in Congress. "Eva M. Clayton." Available online. URL: http://baic.house.gov/member-profiles/profile.html?intID=42. Downloaded April 10, 2009.

Clay, William L. *Just Permanent Interests: Black Americans in Congress, 1870–1992.* New York: Amistad Press, 1993.

Gill, LaVerne McCain. *African American Women in Congress: Forming and Transforming History.* New Brunswick, N.J.: Rutgers University Press, 1997.

Neuman, Nancy M. *True to Ourselves: A Celebration of Women Making a Difference.* San Francisco: Jossey-Bass Publishers, 1998.

Cleaver, Emanuel
(Emanuel Cleaver II)
(1944–   ) *U.S. congressional representative from Missouri*

Emanuel Cleaver was the first African-American mayor of Kansas City, Missouri. Like many black political leaders, he came to politics by way of the pulpit and the Civil Rights movement.

Cleaver was born on October 26, 1944, in Waxahachie, Texas. As a boy, he moved with his family to Wichita Falls where he grew up. After finishing high school, he attended Murray State College on a football scholarship but transferred to Prairie View A&M College after injuring his knee. In 1968, he received a B.S. in sociology and enrolled in St. Paul School of Theology in Kansas City, receiving an M. Div. in 1974. As a seminarian he was assigned to St. James United Methodist Church, a congregation of 47 parishioners that met in a soon-to-be-condemned building. Under his energetic leadership, St. James became one of the largest congregations in Kansas City, with more than 2,000 parishioners meeting in an $8-million sanctuary.

In 1968, while still a theology student, Cleaver founded the Kansas City chapter of the Southern Christian Leadership Conference, the civil rights group headed by Dr. Martin Luther King, Jr. As its head, Cleaver led the chapter in its efforts to combat racism in Kansas City. At first he was something of a firebrand; he once organized a sleep-in on the lawn of an upscale department store to protest homelessness, and in 1972 he resigned in disgust from the board of directors of the local YMCA because of what he called its "institutionalized racism." In 1973, he filed the first desegregation lawsuit against the city school district, but over the years, he developed the ability to build bridges rather than burn them, thus making his efforts even more productive. By the late 1970s, Cleaver had emerged as one of the black community's leading voices of moderation without surrendering anything in terms of effectiveness.

As with many African-American pastors, Cleaver's involvement in civil rights led him into politics. In 1979, he was elected to a seat on the Kansas City city council. Over the next 12 years, he served terms as chairman of the plans and zoning committee and of the policy and rules committee. In 1987, he was appointed mayor pro tem, in essence making him the council's vice chair.

In 1991, Cleaver ran as a Democrat for mayor of Kansas City. By then he had become truly adept at crossing racial lines to achieve consensus and progress on perplexing problems. Although Kansas City's population was about 25 percent black, race was not an issue during the mayoral campaign, and Cleaver was able to win by a 57-43 margin. He took office that same year.

As mayor, Cleaver focused on building up the local economy. He played a major role in attracting new industry to Kansas City, and during his tenure Transamerica, Gateway, Citicorp, and Harley-Davidson opened manufacturing, distribution, or regional headquarters operations in the city. He helped win federal designation of Kansas City as an enhanced enterprise zone, which led to a $25 million construction grant for an industrial park near a Hispanic neighborhood plagued by high unemployment. To make the city more attractive to companies looking for a "big city" atmosphere, he oversaw plans to upgrade the public school system, improve Kansas City International Airport, and expand cultural offerings such as the Jazz Hall of Fame, the convention center, and the city zoo.

In terms of social issues, Cleaver sponsored the inclusion of more women and minorities in the workings of the municipal government. He appointed the city's first female mayor pro tem, he appointed a number of African Americans and Hispanics to city boards and commissions, and he got the city council to toughen the municipal code on sexual harassment. He also oversaw the establishment of more recreational opportunities in all parts of the city, but especially in minority neighborhoods.

Cleaver played a part in national politics as well. A longtime member of the Democratic National Committee, in 1992 he served on President-elect Bill Clinton's transition team. In 1996, Cleaver was elected to a two-year term as president of the National Conference of Black Mayors.

Cleaver was reelected mayor in 1995. He declined to run for reelection in 1999 and left office that same year. After a brief stint as a special urban adviser to the U.S. Department of Housing and Urban Development, he devoted himself to his duties as senior pastor of St. James UMC.

Cleaver returned to politics by successfully running for the House of Representatives in 2004. He was reelected to a fourth term in 2010. As a congressman, Cleaver has served on the Financial Services Committee and the Speaker's Select Committee on Energy Independence and Global Warming. He and his wife, Dianne, have four children.

Further Reading

Congressman Emanuel Cleaver II, Official Web Site. Available online. URL: http://www.house.gov/cleaver. Downloaded April 12, 2009.

Nichols, Jomel. "Emanuel Cleaver, 1944– ." *Contemporary Black Biography* 4 (1993), pp. 42–44.

Poinsett, Alex. "Minister Wins in Kansas City." *Ebony* 46 (September 1991): 68.

St. James United Methodist Church. "Emanuel Cleaver, II." Available online. URL: http://www.stjamesumc.com/pastorsecleaver.html. Downloaded April 3, 2009.

Clyburn, James
(James Enos Clyburn)
(1940–) *U.S. congressional representative from South Carolina*

In 1993, James Clyburn became the first African American to represent South Carolina in Congress in more than 90 years. Coincidentally, that last black congressman, GEORGE MURRAY, was Clyburn's great-uncle.

Clyburn was born on July 21, 1940, in Sumter, South Carolina. His father, E. L., was a minister, and his mother, Almeta, was a homemaker. In 1957 he finished high school and enrolled in South Carolina State University, receiving a B.S. in education in 1962. That same year, he married Emily England, with whom he has three children. For the next three years, he taught history in a Charleston public high school, then in 1965 he went to work as an employment counselor for the state employment security commission. A year later, he became director of Charleston's neighborhood youth corps and new career projects. In 1968, he was named executive director of the state commission for farm workers, a position he held for three years.

In 1971, Clyburn joined Governor John West's staff as the special assistant for human resources development. Three years later, West appointed him head of the state commission of human affairs, a position he held for 18 years. As commissioner, he focused on ending all types of discrimination. He played a major role in the enactment of the state's bill of rights for handicapped citizens in 1983 and a fair housing law in 1989. He also developed a string of political contacts and allies across the state. He attempted to use these contacts to his advantage by twice running for state secretary of state in the 1980s, but both times he was defeated by slim margins.

In 1992, the South Carolina state legislature redrew its congressional districts, in the process creating a black-majority district in the eastern part of the state. Robin Tallon, the incumbent of the old district that had included much of the black-majority district, declined to run for reelection because he believed it was time once again for an African American to represent South Carolina in Congress. Clyburn defeated four other challengers to win the Democratic nomination, then easily defeated his Republican opponent in the general election. He took his seat in 1993 and was assigned to the transportation and infrastructure committee.

As a congressman, Clyburn worked hard to alleviate the poverty and economic depression that pervaded much of his district. When the military closed several bases in his district, he worked to have the areas in which they were located designated enterprise communities, thus providing tax breaks and incentives for businesses that would open or relocate in them. He fought against raising excise taxes on cigarettes, since

many farmers in his district depended on tobacco for their livelihood. He won millions of dollars in federal money for infrastructure improvement projects in his district such as new highways, airport repair, harbor dredging, and watershed protection.

Like President Bill Clinton and other moderate Democrats, Clyburn supported efforts to rethink such classic liberal programs as affirmative action and welfare. He was not interested in ending these programs, but rather he wanted to fine-tune them so that they better served the interests of all Americans, especially the ones the programs were intended to help. To this end, he supported efforts to raise the minimum wage and to enact the Livable Wage Act of 1995. Unlike many Democrats, he also supported a balanced federal budget and term limits for congressmen.

In 1998, Clyburn was elected to a two-year term as chair of the Congressional Black Caucus. The following year he was appointed to the prestigious House Appropriations Committee.

Following the 2006 election, when Democrats took control of the House of Representatives for the first time in 12 years, the House Democratic Caucus unanimously voted Clyburn the majority whip. Clyburn was the second African American (after BILL GRAY) to hold this position, the third most powerful in the House. In 2010, he was reelected to a 10th term in Congress.

Further Reading

Biographical Directory of the United States Congress. "Clyburn, James Enos, 1940– ." Available online. URL: http://bioguide.congress.gov/scripts/biodisplay.pl?index=C000537. Downloaded April 22, 2009.

Congressman James E. Clyburn, Official Web Site. Available online. URL: http://clyburn.house.gov. Downloaded April 24, 2009.

Cooney, Jessica Benton. "CQ and A: An Interview with House Majority Whip James E. Clyburn." CQ Politics, April 3, 2007. Available online. http://www.cqpolitics.com/wmspage.cfm?doc

ID=news-000002484252. Downloaded April 24, 2009.

Explorations in Black Leadership. "James Clyburn." Available online. URL: http://www.virginia.edu/publichistory/bl/index.php?uid=7. Downloaded April 22, 2009.

"James E. Clyburn." *Congressional Quarterly Weekly Report* 51 (January 16, 1993 supplement): 135.

Coleman, Michael
(Michael Bennett Coleman)
(1955–   ) *mayor of Columbus, Ohio*

Michael Coleman was the first African-American mayor of Columbus, Ohio. A longtime member of the Columbus city council, he showed a particular interest in renovating the city's inner neighborhoods.

Coleman was born in 1955 in Indianapolis, Indiana. His father, John, was a physician, and his mother, Joan, was a homemaker. At age three, he moved with his family to Toledo, Ohio, where he grew up. After graduating from high school in 1973, he enrolled in the University of Cincinnati, receiving a B.A. in political science four years later. In 1980, he received a J.D. from the University of Dayton Law School and moved to Columbus to work as an attorney in the Ohio attorney general's office. Two years later, he became a legislative aide to Ben Espy, a Columbus city councilman. Coleman eventually joined a local law firm and involved himself in a leadership role with a number of community organizations such as the Downtown Development Corporation, the Community Housing Network, and the Columbus Youth Corps.

In 1992, Espy was appointed to fill a vacancy in the Ohio state senate, and Coleman was chosen to take Espy's place on the city council. A year later, he was elected to a full term of his own. As a councilman, he developed a reputation as a consensus-builder and as someone who knew the workings of the municipal government inside and out. He worked to revitalize Columbus's inner-city neighborhoods by establishing vehicles such as the Urban Infrastructure Recovery Fund, the Neighborhood Partnership Program, and the Urban Growth Corporation. He also worked to provide additional funding for a mentoring program to assist minority youth and to establish a system of bicycle paths across the city. Reelected in 1997, that same year he was chosen by his fellow councilmen to be council president.

In 1998, Coleman ran as a Democrat for lieutenant governor of Ohio. His loss did not dampen his desire to seek higher political office, and in 1999 he announced his candidacy for mayor of Columbus. He defeated Espy in the Democratic primary, and then beat his Republican rival in the general election by a 60-40 margin. Late that year, he began his four-year term as the city's first African-American mayor and its first Democratic mayor in 28 years.

Michael Coleman was the first black mayor of Columbus, Ohio. *(Michael R. Coleman)*

As mayor, Coleman inherited a federal lawsuit against the city police department for systematic police brutality. He addressed the problem by working quietly with the embattled chief of police to overhaul the department. He also provided each squad car with a video camera to record each traffic stop in an effort to get officers to reform their ways. He then focused on continuing his main work as a councilman, revitalizing the central city neighborhoods. His major effort in this area was Neighborhood Pride, a program whereby code enforcement officers, police, and street sweepers take one neighborhood at a time and work to clean it up thoroughly. Part of the program included low- interest, city-backed loans to low-income homeowners who needed to make basic repairs to their property. In terms of economic development, he devoted much energy to getting Columbus into the movies by appealing to a number of Hollywood film moguls to shoot all or part of their productions in central Ohio.

In 2003, Coleman ran unopposed for a second term as Columbus's mayor. Two years later, he announced that he would seek the Democratic nomination in the 2006 gubernatorial race. Within months, he dropped out due to family obligations. He won his third term as mayor in 2007. Coleman and his ex-wife, Frankie, have three children.

Further Reading

Brennan, Carol. "Michael B. Coleman, 1955(?)– ." *Contemporary Black Biography* 28 (2001): 53–54.

Mayor Michael B. Coleman, Official Web Site. Available online. URL: http://mayor.columbus.gov. Downloaded April 18, 2009.

Collins, Barbara-Rose

(1939–) *U.S. congressional representative from Michigan*

Barbara-Rose Collins once described herself as a "little person," and in many respects this was true.

She got involved in politics because, as a mother, she was concerned about her children's futures. During the course of her political career, however, she demonstrated that even a "little person" can make the system work if that person gets involved and strives to make things better.

Collins was born Barbara-Rose Richardson on April 13, 1939, in Detroit, Michigan, to Lamar and Versa Richardson. After graduating from high school in 1957, she studied for several semesters at Wayne State University, after which she worked at Wayne State as a purchasing agent for the physics department. In 1958 she married Gary Collins, with whom she had two children; he died in 1972.

Collins got involved in politics in 1970 when she became concerned about the poor quality of both the schools her children attended and the education they were receiving. She ran for a seat on the Detroit school board and won. For the next three years she worked to get the city to commit more resources to public education. In 1974, she stepped down from the school board to take a position on Detroit's human rights commission.

Meanwhile, Detroit was experiencing the same thing as most U.S. cities; "white flight" to the suburbs and the closing of plants all over the city were resulting in a shrinking tax base and increased urban decay. In 1975, Collins decided to do what she could about these problems by running as a Democrat for the state legislature. She won, and for the next seven years she held a seat in the lower house. During that time, she chaired the standing committee on urban affairs, and she used this position to call attention to the plight of America's cities. She also cofounded and chaired the Michigan Legislative Black Caucus.

In 1982, Collins won election to the Detroit city council. Over the next eight years, she worked hard to improve conditions in her hometown. She chaired a task force on litter and cleanup, and authored ordinances regulating the cleanup of toxic waste sites. She also chaired a task force on teenage violence and juvenile crime.

In 1988, Collins challenged incumbent George W. Crockett for his seat in Congress. She lost, but after he announced his resignation effective the end of his term in 1990, she ran again and won. She took her seat the following year and was assigned to the committees on the post office/civil service and public works/transportation.

As a congresswoman, Collins continued to push for federal aid for cities. She spoke out forcefully against foreign aid for the former communist nations of Eastern Europe while U.S. cities continued to be plagued by crime, drugs, joblessness, homelessness, and violence. She focused attention on the contributions of homemakers and other unpaid workers; her Unremunerated Work Act called on the Bureau of Labor Statistics to develop a way to measure the value of such work so that it can be more fully appreciated. She also sponsored legislation requiring food-processing plants to put expiration dates on their products, providing more funding for sex education in the public schools, and providing funding for insurance for pregnant women.

Collins was reelected to Congress twice. During her third term, she came under the scrutiny of the Justice Department for firing a staff member. The staffer alleged that he had been fired because he was a homosexual, and the investigators found in his favor. Meanwhile, the House Ethics Committee was investigating the financial reports for her campaigns and office expenses for alleged irregularities. Partly as a result of these controversies, she was defeated in the 1996 primary by Carolyn Kilpatrick. Collins returned to Detroit after her term expired in 1997, taking up residence in the house she had lived in as a little girl. She was later reelected to the Detroit city council in 2001 and 2005. Plagued by various health problems, Collins retired from the city council in 2009.

Further Reading

Biographical Directory of the United States Congress. "Collins, Barbara-Rose, 1939– ." Available online. URL: http://bioguide.congress.gov/scripts/ biodisplay.pl?index=C000633. Downloaded April 3, 2009.

Black Americans in Congress. "Barbara-Rose Collins." Available online. URL: http://baic.house.gov/ member-profiles/profile.html?intID=41. Downloaded April 10, 2009.

Brown, Roxanne. "Barbara-Rose Collins Wins in Motown." *Ebony* 46 (January 1991): 104.

Foerstel, Karen. *Biographical Dictionary of Congressional Women.* New York: Greenwood Press, 1999.

Gill, LaVerne McCain. *African American Women in Congress: Forming and Transforming History.* New Brunswick, N.J.: Rutgers University Press, 1997.

Collins, Cardiss

(Cardiss Robertson Collins)
(1931–) *U.S. congressional representative from Illinois*

Cardiss Collins served in the U.S. Congress for 24 years, longer than any other African-American woman. In addition to equal opportunity, she fought to protect the rights of women and children and to make air travel safer.

Collins was born Cardiss Robertson on September 24, 1931, in St. Louis, Missouri. Her father, Finley, was a laborer, and her mother, Rosia Mae, was a nurse. At age 10, she moved with her family to Detroit, Michigan, where she grew up. In 1949, she graduated from high school and moved to Chicago. After working for several years in low-paying, dead-end jobs, she enrolled in Northwestern University and studied business and accounting at night. Although she never graduated, her coursework made it possible for her to obtain a position as a secretary with the Illinois Department of Labor. She eventually transferred to the state department of revenue and worked her way up to revenue auditor. In 1958, she married George W. Collins, with whom she had one child.

In 1964, George Collins was elected to the Chicago board of aldermen, and in 1970 he won election to the U.S. House of Representatives. Cardiss Collins, his biggest supporter, was actively involved in his political career and served on the Democratic committee for the 24th Ward. In 1972, George Collins was killed in a plane crash, and Collins was urged by her fellow Democrats to run in the special election to choose his successor. She won handily and took her deceased husband's seat in 1973. She was assigned to the committees on government operations and energy and commerce.

As a congresswoman, Collins championed the rights of women and children. During her first term, she introduced legislation outlawing gender discrimination by lenders. Later, she conducted an investigation into collegiate compliance with Title IX of the Education Amendments of 1972, which mandated gender equity in college sports. The investigation prompted her to introduce the Equity in Athletics Disclosure Act of 1993, which forced colleges and universities to provide greater athletic opportunities for women students. In 1990, she authored the legislation that authorized Medicare to pay for mammograms and Pap smears, and the following year she succeeded in getting Congress to declare October National Breast Cancer Awareness Month. She cosponsored the Family and Medical Leave Act of 1991, which permitted mothers who had just given birth to take six weeks of unpaid leave. She wrote the Child Safety Protection Act of 1993, which mandated warning labels for toys and established safety standards for bicycle helmets. In 1994, she became the unofficial leader of the pro-abortion rights forces in their struggle to defeat the so-called Hyde Amendment, which prohibited the use of federal funds for abortion. She also played a major role in the expansion of child care facilities for federal workers.

Collins was active in other areas as well. Not surprisingly, given the circumstances of her husband's death, she focused on airline safety. She cosponsored the Airport and Airway Safety, Capacity and Expansion Act of 1987; at her insis-

tence, the act provided for set-asides for businesses owned by minorities and women, thus guaranteeing that such businesses would receive a certain minimum percentage of work contracted under the act. In the 1980s, she called attention to the discriminatory hiring practices of the Justice Department, the Federal Trade Commission, the National Endowment for the Humanities, and the airline industry, thus forcing them to do a better job of complying with federal equal employment opportunity regulations. In a similar vein, she prompted a 1990 Government Accounting Office investigation into the advertising practices of the Department of Defense (DoD). The investigation showed that the DoD placed very few recruitment ads with minority-owned television and radio stations even as it was targeting minorities, and this prompted a reversal of the policy.

Collins was reelected to 11 full terms of her own. At various times, she chaired subcommittees on government activities and transportation, manpower and housing, telecommunications and finance, and commerce, consumer protection and competitiveness, as well as the Congressional Black Caucus. She declined to run for reelection in 1996. In 2004, Cardiss was named chairperson of the Task Force on Television Measurement, established by Nielsen Media Research to improve representation by people of color in its television rating system.

Further Reading

Biographical Directory of the United States Congress. "Collins, Cardiss, 1931– ." Available online. URL: http://bioguide.congress.gov/scripts/biodisplay. pl?index=C000634. Downloaded on October 18, 2010.

Black Americans in Congress. "Cardiss Collins." Available online. URL: http://baic.house.gov/member-profiles/profile.html?intID=40. Downloaded April 12, 2009.

Clay, William L. *Just Permanent Interests: Black Americans in Congress, 1870–1992.* New York: Amistad Press, 1993.

Kaptur, Marcy. *Women of Congress: A Twentieth- Century Odyssey.* Washington: Congressional Quarterly, 1996.

Smith, Jessie C. *Epic Lives: One Hundred Black Women Who Made a Difference.* Detroit: Visible Ink Press, 1993.

Conyers, John

(John Conyers, Jr.)

(1929–　) *U.S. congressional representative from Michigan*

When John Conyers was elected to Congress in 1965, he was the youngest member in that body. Thirty-seven years later, he had become one of its deans. Along the way he became known as a champion of civil rights, a proponent of peace, and a watchdog over government spending.

Conyers was born on May 16, 1929, in Detroit, Michigan. His father, John Sr., was an automobile assembly line worker and a union organizer, and his mother, Lucille, was a homemaker. After graduating from high school in 1947, he joined his father on the Lincoln- Mercury assembly line as a spot welder. The following year, he joined the U.S. Army National Guard and began taking night courses at Wayne State University. In 1950, his unit was called to active duty; over the next four years he graduated from officers' candidate school, served as a second lieutenant in the Corps of Engineers, and fought in Korea during the Korean War. He returned to Wayne State in 1954, receiving his B.A. in 1957 and his LL.B. in 1958. After passing the bar examination the following year, he and two partners opened a law firm in Detroit. While the firm specialized in criminal matters and landlord-tenant disputes, he also served as general counsel for the Detroit Trade Union Leadership Council.

Conyers's political career began in college when he joined the Young Democratic Club and got elected precinct delegate to the state organizing committee. In 1959, he became a legislative assistant to John Dingell, Jr., at the time a state representative. Two years later, he left his practice and Dingell's office to become a referee for the state workmen's compensation department.

In 1963, Conyers decided to make his first run for office. Rather than enter a state or local race, he chose to compete for Michigan's newly established First Congressional District, a combination of two former districts in Detroit that was largely composed of middle-class African Americans and black auto workers. The party leadership, however, refused to support his candidacy on the grounds that he was too young (he was 34) and too inexperienced politically. Undaunted, he quit his state position and began campaigning full-time. By making maximum use of his union contacts, he defeated the leadership's candidate by a few dozen votes in the primary, then swept to victory in the general election. When he took office in 1965, he was the youngest member of Congress.

Assigned to the judiciary committee, Conyers quickly became a champion of civil rights. He played an important role in bringing the Voting Rights Act of 1965 to the House floor, and he supported the efforts of the Mississippi Freedom Democratic Party to secure those rights for its African-American residents. In 1969, he sponsored a bill to make Martin Luther King, Jr.'s birthday a federal holiday; reintroduced several times, the bill was finally enacted 14 years later. In the 1970s, he conducted several fact-finding missions to Alabama and Mississippi to determine how the Voting Rights Act was being implemented and sponsored several bills to make the act tougher. In 1971, he cofounded the Congressional Black Caucus, which was formed in large part to unite black opposition to President Richard M. Nixon's efforts to roll back the gains African Americans had made under Presidents John F. Kennedy and Lyndon B. Johnson. He also initiated the Department of Justice's national study of police brutality against blacks and was the original sponsor of the Hate Crimes

Statistics Act, by which data related to crimes involving racial, religious, and sexual prejudice were tabulated. Among his most recent civil rights initiatives were the Civil Rights Act of 1991, the National Voter Registration Act of 1993, and the Traffic Stops Statistics Study Act of 1999; this last act is an attempt to end racial profiling in routine traffic stops by police officers. He has also introduced bills to examine the effects of slavery on modern African Americans and to determine the feasibility of paying reparations to the descendants of slaves.

Although Conyers was a loyal supporter of Johnson's Great Society agenda, he was a staunch opponent of American military involvement in Vietnam. He was one of a few congressmen who repeatedly voted against appropriations bills for the war effort, maintaining that the war was unconstitutional because it had never been declared by Congress. He contributed to three books attacking the war: *American Militarism* (1970), *War Crimes and the American Conscience* (1970), and *Anatomy of an Undeclared War* (1972). His opposition to war in general surfaced again in the 1980s when, as chairman of the committee on government operations, he opposed President Ronald Reagan's efforts to fund the multibillion-dollar Strategic Defense Initiative on the grounds that it would not work and that the money was more urgently needed for social programs.

Once the struggles to gain civil rights and to end the war in Vietnam were largely won, his interests turned to other matters. He has written bills on a wide range of issues. Some of them include giving the Environmental Protection Agency cabinet status, placing warning labels on alcoholic beverages, doubling death benefits to police officers and firefighters killed in the line of duty, creating chief financial officers for each federal agency so that the mismanagement of funds might be better avoided, making violent criminals pay reparations to their victims, outlawing violence against women, and preserving jazz.

In 1989, Conyers ran a losing campaign against COLEMAN YOUNG for mayor of Detroit. The following year he married Monica Esters, with whom he has two children. As the judiciary committee's senior member, in 1994 he took over as chairman. More recently, Conyers has been a leading advocate for health care reform, particularly for the implementation of a universal health care system. Since the presidential election of 2000, he has also fought for election reform and the protection of voting rights. Conyers presided over the House Judiciary Committee's investigation into voting irregularities in Ohio during the 2004 election. Its findings were published in *What Went Wrong in Ohio* (2005).

An outspoken critic of the Iraq War, Conyers repeatedly challenged the foreign and domestic policies of the administration of George W. Bush. He and his staff compiled *The Constitution in Crisis* (2007), a lengthy report that criticized the administration's handling of the war and detailed the erosion of civil liberties during Bush's tenure in office. In early 2009, Conyers introduced legislation calling for a "truth commission" to investigate abuses of power during the Bush era.

Conyers supported BARACK OBAMA during the 2008 presidential campaign. In 2010, he was reelected to his 23rd congressional term.

Conyers became indirectly involved in a political scandal when his wife, the former president of the city council of Detroit, pled guilty to conspiring to commit bribery in June 2009. Monica Conyers was sentenced to 37 months in prison in March 2010.

Further Reading

Biographical Directory of the United States Congress. "Conyers, John, Jr., 1929– ." Available online. URL: http://bioguide.congress.gov/scripts/bio display.pl?index=C000714. Downloaded October 19, 2010.

Conyers, John C., Jr., and Staff. *The Constitution in Crisis: The High Crimes of the Bush Administration and a Blueprint for Impeachment.* New York: Skyhorse Publishing, 2007.

Explorations in Black Leadership. "John Conyers, Jr." Available online. URL: http://www.virginia.edu/publichistory/bl/index.php?uid=9. Downloaded April 20, 2009.

Lindsey, Fred. "Conyers, John, Jr." In *African American National Biography*, vol. 2, edited by Henry Louis Gates, Jr., and Evelyn Brooks Higginbotham. New York: Oxford University Press, 2008, pp. 393–395.

Miller, Anita, ed. *What Went Wrong in Ohio: The Conyers Report on the 2004 Presidential Election*. Chicago: Academy Chicago Publishers, 2005.

Crockett, George W.
(George William Crockett, Jr.)
(1909–1997) *U.S. congressional representative from Michigan*

Elected to the U.S. House of Representatives at the age of 71, George Crockett was the oldest freshman congressman in U.S. history. As a congressman, he gained a reputation as a vocal critic of the foreign policy of President Ronald Reagan and George H. W. Bush.

Crockett was born on August 10, 1909, in Jacksonville, Florida. His father, George, was a carpenter, and his mother, Minnie, was a homemaker. He finished high school in 1927 and enrolled in Morehouse College, receiving an A.B. four years later. For the next three years he studied at the University of Michigan Law School. In 1934, he received a J.D., opened a law office in Jacksonville, married Ethelene Jones, with whom he had three children, and moved his practice to Fairmont, West Virginia.

Crockett devoted most of his legal career to working for civil rights and equal opportunity. In West Virginia he met and became good friends with U.S. senator Matthew M. Neely, who in 1939 arranged for Crockett to go to Washington to work as an attorney for the Justice Department. Almost immediately he was reassigned to the Labor Department, and in 1943 he was named a hearing examiner of the Fair Employment Practices Committee. In this capacity, he worked to ensure that the hiring practices of government contractors did not discriminate against African Americans. In 1944, he moved to Detroit to establish an equal opportunity division for the International United Auto Workers. Two years later he cofounded a law firm that became famous for defending communists and other leftists whom the federal government had accused of subversion. On one occasion he defended COLEMAN YOUNG; on another he defended his client with such vigor that Crockett was sentenced to four months in federal prison for contempt of court. He also served as vice president of the National Lawyers Guild and chaired its Mississippi Project, which provided free legal services to civil rights workers who had been jailed in that state.

Crockett became involved in politics in 1966, when he was elected as a Democrat to a Detroit judgeship. He continued to work for equal rights from the bench by refusing to jail civil rights workers who had run afoul of the law, instead releasing them on their own recognizance. In 1978, he retired from the Detroit court, and for the next two years he served as a visiting judge on the Michigan court of appeals and as corporation counsel for the city of Detroit. In 1980, following CHARLES DIGGS's resignation from Congress, Crockett ran in the special election to fill the unexpired portion of Diggs's term as well as a full two-year term. His performance as a judge had earned him the respect of Detroit's African-American community, and he was elected easily. He took his seat that same year and was assigned to the committees on the judiciary and foreign affairs.

Despite his advanced years, Crockett quickly earned a reputation as one of Congress's most liberal members. He was the first congressman to publicly advocate the legalization of drugs such as marijuana and heroin. He was arrested for demonstrating against apartheid in front of the South African embassy in Washington, and he authored the Mandela Freedom Resolution, which called on South Africa to release Nelson Mandela from prison. He argued for U.S. recognition of the Palestine Liberation Organization as the legitimate representative of the Palestinians while most government officials considered it to be nothing more than a band of terrorists. He sued the Reagan administration to keep it from sending troops into El Salvador, and he opposed the U.S. invasions of Grenada and Panama.

Crockett was reelected to four terms. In 1990, he announced his intention to retire from Congress. Following the completion of his term in 1991, he remained in Washington, where he died on September 7, 1997.

Further Reading

Biographical Directory of the United States Congress. "Crockett, George William, Jr., 1909–1997." Available online. URL: http://bioguide.congress. gov/scripts/biodisplay.pl?index=C000919. Downloaded March 28, 2009.

Black Americans in Congress. "George William Crockett." Available online. URL: http://baic.house. gov/member-profiles/profile.html?intID=39. Downloaded March 30, 2009.

Clay, William L. *Just Permanent Interests: Black Americans in Congress, 1870–1992.* New York: Amistad Press, 1993.

Cummings, Elijah
(Elijah Eugene Cummings)
(1951–   ) *U.S. congressional representative from Maryland*

In 1996, Elijah Cummings was elected to represent Baltimore, Maryland, in Congress. He held the same seat that had been occupied previously by PARREN MITCHELL and KWEISI MFUME.

Cummings was born on January 18, 1951, in Baltimore, Maryland. His father, Robert, worked in a chemical plant, and his mother, Ruth, was a homemaker. He graduated from high school in 1969 and enrolled in Howard University, where he received a B.A. in political science four years later. He then attended the University of Maryland Law School and received a J.D. in 1976. That same year he opened a law practice in Baltimore. He was later married and divorced and has two children.

In a sense, Cummings's political career began in college, where he served as sophomore class president, student government treasurer, and student government president. As an attorney, he became involved in the local affairs of the Democratic Party, and in 1983 he was ready to run for office. That same year, he was elected to the Maryland House of Delegates, where he served for the next 13 years. In 1984, he was named to chair the Maryland Legislative Black Caucus, and in 1995 he was named speaker pro tempore, the second-highest position in Maryland's lower

Elijah Cummings represents Baltimore, Maryland, in the U.S. House of Representatives. *(Elijah E. Cummings)*

house. As a state legislator, he served on the committees on constitutional/administrative law and economic matters. He is particularly remembered for helping to establish a "boot camp" for juvenile offenders, and for pushing through a bill banning liquor advertisements on inner-city billboards. Outside of his committee interests, he worked to improve health care availability and employment opportunities for poor urban residents.

In 1995, Kweisi Mfume announced his intention to resign from Congress in order to become head of the National Association for the Advancement of Colored People. A special election was held in early 1996 to replace him, and Cummings was one of 32 candidates from both parties. Superior name recognition, several key endorsements, and a well-funded campaign chest won him the primary and the special election. He took Mfume's seat in early 1996, and then won the general election later that year for a full term of his own. Cummings has since been reelected six times.

As a congressman, Cummings focused on issues related to education, crime prevention, and health. After visiting many of the public schools in his district, he began working to bring increased access to the Internet and other technological upgrades to the public schools. He opposed school vouchers, which would provide public funding for private schools. He opposed the death penalty as a means of deterring crime, preferring instead to ameliorate the socioeconomic conditions that often serve as a breeding ground for crime. He cosponsored the Violence Against Women Act of 1999 as a means of preventing spousal abuse. As cochair of the House AIDS Working Group, he authored the HIV Prevention Outreach Act of 1997; this act legalized federal funding for needle-exchange programs as a means of slowing down the spread of AIDS, especially in the nation's African-American communities. He cosponsored the Traffic Stops Statistics Study Act of 1999; many young African-American male motorists were complaining about being stopped, searched, and arrested arbitrarily, and this act was intended to prevent law enforcement officials from harassing blacks on racial grounds. Cummings has represented Maryland's Seventh District for eight terms.

Further Reading

Biographical Directory of the United States Congress. "Cummings, Elijah Eugene, 1951." Available online. URL: http://bioguide.congress.gov/scripts/biodisplay.pl?index=C000984. Downloaded April 3, 2009.

Congressman Elijah E. Cummings, Official Web Site. Available online. URL: http://cummings house/gov. Downloaded April 29, 2010.

Kalb, Deborah. "Cummings Wins Mfume Seat. New Member Profile." *Congressional Quarterly Weekly Report* 54 (April 20, 1996): 1,070.

D

Davis, Artur

(1967–   ) *U.S. congressional representative from Alabama*

Hailed for his youth and energy, Artur Davis took on Alabama's Democratic establishment to win a seat in the U.S. House of Representatives from the state's seventh congressional district. Born on October 9, 1967, Davis grew up in a poor area on the west side of Montgomery, Alabama. (He once quipped to *Time* magazine, "I was born where both sides of the track were wrong.") His father abandoned the family when he was two, leaving his mother, a schoolteacher, and his grandmother to raise him. Davis credited his mother with igniting his interest in politics by taking to see the state capitol building when he was 10 years old.

After graduating from Jefferson Davis High School, Davis received a scholarship to Harvard University, in Cambridge, Massachusetts, from which he graduated with honors in 1990. He then attended Harvard Law School. While a student, he worked for the Southern Poverty Law Center and served as an intern for U.S. senator Howell Heflin. Also while in law school, he became acquainted with fellow student BARACK OBAMA, who would later play a role in Davis's political career.

Beginning in 1994, Davis worked as an assistant U.S. prosecutor in Montgomery for four years. He then joined the private law firm of Johnston Barton Proctor & Powell, based in Birmingham, Alabama. After careful deliberation, Davis in 1999 decided to run for the U.S. House of Representatives by challenging the Democratic incumbent EARL HILLIARD for his seat. Davis was dismissed as brash and inexperienced by longtime Hilliard supporters. Raising less than $100,000 for his campaign, Davis lost to Hilliard in the primary.

Despite the defeat, Davis still sensed that Hilliard was vulnerable. Some poorer constituents were growing disillusioned with Hilliard, but more important, the district had been redrawn to eliminate some areas where he had enjoyed his greatest support. Announcing his candidacy in the 2002 race, Davis raised about $1 million, much of it from Jewish voters who objected to some statements Hilliard had made about U.S. policy toward Israel. Hilliard, however, maintained the support of the state's Democratic leadership and of national African-American leaders such as AL SHARPTON and Martin Luther King III. After a brutal and sometimes vicious campaign, Davis won the Democratic primary with 56 percent of the vote. With no Republican candidate in the race, he overwhelmingly won the general election. In 2008, he was reelected to his fourth term.

In Congress, Davis served on the influential House Ways and Means Committee. He worked to improve public housing and to expand access to health care and education. Davis also coauthored a bill calling for the construction of an interstate through the so-called Black Belt region of central Alabama.

In 2007, Davis was an early supporter of the presidential campaign of Barack Obama. His decision to endorse Obama went against his state's party leadership, which overwhelmingly threw its support to Democratic candidate Hillary Clinton. When Obama won the 2008 Democratic primary in Alabama, Davis was vindicated in his belief that both black and white Alabamans could embrace an African-American candidate.

Davis announced on February 9, 2009, that he would run for governor of Alabama in the 2010 election. Despite his political success, detractors doubted a black candidate would be able to win the office once held by segregationist George Wallace. But Davis was confident that the electorate in Alabama had fundamentally changed since Wallace's day—a notion supported by Wallace's daughter, Peggy Wallace Kennedy, who endorsed Davis's candidacy. In an interview with *Time* in 2008, Davis cited Obama's ascent as evidence that it was time for young African-American politicians in the South to become more ambitious: "But just as COLIN POWELL and CONDOLEEZZA RICE helped pave the way for Barack Obama, Barack Obama's candidacy is paving the way for other black candidates to run in their states."

Davis optimism about this gubernatorial bid proved unfounded. On June 1, 2010, he lost the democratic primary to Ron Sparks, Alabama's agricultural commissioner. Davis received only 38 percent of the vote. His decisive defeat was largely blamed on his inability to win over the state's black political establishment. The day after the primary Davis announced that he would not run for political office again.

Further Reading
Congressman Artur Davis, Official Web Site. Available online. URL: http://arturdavis.house.gov. Downloaded May 22, 2009.
Gray, Steven. "Can Alabama Spark a Democratic Revival in the South?" *Time*, April 28, 2009. Available online. URL: http://www.time.com/time/nation/article/0,8599,1893149,00.html. Downloaded May 22, 2009.
Ifill, Gwen. *The Breakthrough: Politics and Race in the Age of Obama.* New York: Doubleday, 2009.

Davis, Ben
(Benjamin Jefferson Davis, Jr.)
(1903–1964) *city councilman in New York City*

Ben Davis is the only African American to be elected as a Communist. Although his party affiliation actually helped him get elected at first, in the end it was responsible for driving him out of office and into a federal prison.

Davis was born on September 8, 1903, in Dawson, Georgia. His father, BENJAMIN J. DAVIS, was a newspaper publisher, and his mother, Jimmie (also known as Willa), was a homemaker. At age six he moved with his family to Atlanta, where he grew up. He was educated at Morehouse College's secondary school, Amherst College (B.A., 1925), and Harvard Law School (LL.B., 1928). He emerged from college a proud young black man who bristled at the way southern blacks were treated by southern whites. While home from college one year, he had been arrested for refusing to move out of the white section of a trolley; he would have been jailed had not his father, an important figure in the state Republican Party, intervened on his behalf. Rather than return immediately to the Jim Crow South, he spent the first three years out of college working with black newspapers in Baltimore, Maryland, and Chicago, Illinois. In 1932, he returned to Atlanta, passed the state bar examination, and opened a law office.

One of Davis's first clients was Angelo Herndon, a black Communist who had been arrested for inciting an "insurrection." In fact, all he had done was distribute Communist literature while leading a protest in support of expanded poor relief, but

Ben Davis was the only African American ever elected to public office as a Communist. *(Library of Congress)*

under Georgia law Herndon's crime was punishable by death. Davis lost the case in a trial that was remarkable for the total lack of respect shown for him and his client because of their race. Although he got Herndon a sentence of "only" 20 years (and then got him freed after five years of appeals), he was outraged by the entire proceeding, which illustrated all too graphically the situation in general for African Americans in the South. By 1933 Herndon had convinced him that the best way to strike at racial discrimination was to become a Communist, since the Communist Party was the only one that espoused racial equality.

In 1935, Davis closed his law office and went to work in the Communist Party's headquarters in New York City. For the next seven years, he edited

several party newspapers, including the *Harlem Liberator,* the *Negro Liberator,* and the *Daily Worker.* He also cofounded the National Negro Congress (NNC), a Communist-backed organization that, for awhile, counted among its members several leaders of the National Association for the Advancement of Colored People. Another NNC cofounder was ADAM CLAYTON POWELL, JR., at the time a city councilman, with whom he developed a close relationship.

As a result of the census of 1940, the New York legislature created a black-majority congressional district centered around Harlem. In 1943, when Powell began to campaign for this seat in the election of 1944, he persuaded Davis to run for his city council seat. With the support of Powell and a host of other prominent African Americans, in 1943 he ran for city council as a Communist. Emphasizing the antidiscriminatory policies of the Communist Party, and by contrast the support given racial discrimination by both major parties, he easily won. In 1945 he was reelected to a four-year term.

As a city councilman, Davis picked up where Powell had left off as a champion of the city's African-American residents. He worked for rent control, lower bus fares, and higher pay for black teachers. He called for investigations of segregated housing, the substandard condition of hospitals and fire protection in Harlem, and the brutal treatment of black suspects by white policemen. He also called for an end to segregation in major league baseball and supported the creation of the state of Israel; this last position gained him favor with Manhattan's Jewish population.

During World War II, when the United States was allied with the Soviet Union, Davis's being a Communist had not been an issue, but during the early years of the cold war, when the Soviet Union went from being an ally to the enemy, his party allegiance cost him dearly. In 1948, he was indicted by a federal grand jury for violating the Smith Act, which made it illegal to belong to any group that espoused the violent overthrow of the United States government. In 1949, two months before the city council elections, he was found guilty and sentenced to five years in prison. He ran for reelection anyway but was soundly defeated by a black candidate who had been endorsed by both the Democrats and the Republicans. Shortly after the election but before his term had expired, he was expelled from the council by unanimous vote.

Davis was released from the federal penitentiary in Terre Haute, Indiana, in 1954. That same year, he married Nina Stamler, with whom he had one child. He continued to be active in the Communist Party, serving as national secretary, national committeeman, and chairman of the New York state party, the largest in the nation. In 1962, he was indicted by another federal grand

jury, this time for not registering the party as an agent of the Soviet Union as required by the McCarran Internal Security Act. He died on August 22, 1964, in New York City.

Further Reading

Biondi, Martha. *To Stand and Fight: The Struggle for Civil Rights in Postwar New York City.* Cambridge, Mass.: Harvard University Press, 2003.
———. "Davis, Benjamin Jefferson." In *African American National Biography,* vol. 2, edited by Henry Louis Gates, Jr., and Evelyn Brooks Higginbotham. New York: Oxford University Press, 2008, pp. 564–565.
Davis, Benjamin J. *Communist Councilman from Harlem: Autobiographical Notes Written in a Federal Penitentiary.* New York: International Publishers, 1990.
Foster, William Z. *History of the Communist Party of the United States.* New York: Greenwood Press, 1968.
Horne, Gerald. *Black Liberation/Red Scare: Ben Davis and the Communist Party.* Newark: University of Delaware Press, 1994.

Davis, Benjamin J.
(Benjamin Jefferson Davis)
(1870–1945) *Georgia Republican Party chairman*

Benjamin Davis never held a government position of any kind. Nevertheless, as a national committeeman during the 1920s, he was one of the most powerful politicians in the South because he controlled the dispensation of political patronage in Georgia.

Davis was born on May 27, 1870, in Dawson, Georgia. His parents, Mike and Katherine, were farmers and ex-slaves. He received a sixth-grade education, then worked for a time as a bricklayer and teacher. At some point he went to work for Tom Loyless, a white printer in Dawson who taught him the trade, after which he opened his own printing shop. In 1898 he married a woman named Jimmie Porter, with whom he had two children.

In 1903, Davis began publishing a weekly newspaper called the *Independent*. The paper catered to Georgia's African-American population by running stories about black church, club, and social doings, features and advertisements touting black-owned businesses, and editorials condemning such racially discriminatory evils as convict labor, disfranchisement, and lynchings. The paper's militant stance made it very popular with blacks—within a year it had attracted almost 100,000 readers—and very unpopular with whites, who banned it from a number of small Georgia towns. One such town sent back a bundle of papers with a death threat for Davis; undaunted, he immediately jumped in his car, drove to the town, and personally distributed in its main street the very papers that had been returned. By 1909, his operation had grown to the point that he felt it necessary to relocate to Atlanta. Three years later, he was instrumental in the development in downtown Atlanta of Odd Fellows Block, a collection of office buildings that became the center for the city's black professionals. Thanks to his growing wealth and prestige, he became one of Atlanta's leading African-American citizens.

Davis joined the Republican Party while still living in Dawson, and in 1908 he attended the Republican national convention as a delegate. He was appointed secretary of the state party's executive committee shortly after moving to Atlanta, mostly because of his ability to mobilize black voters for Republican candidates in that city, where African Americans could still vote in municipal elections. In 1916, he argued at the Republican national convention that the platform must include a plank calling for decreased congressional representation for those states that disfranchised African Americans. In 1925, he was named state chairman and national committeeman; the chairmanship gave him control over the distribution in his state of political patronage jobs, such as postmasterships and positions with the Internal Revenue Service, whenever the Republicans controlled the White House. By 1928, despite having never run for office, he was one of the most powerful political leaders in the South.

Davis's position of power, however, did not go unchallenged. White applicants for federal positions complained to the Ku Klux Klan that they had been forced to grovel before this fearless, imperious black man. In response, the Klan burned crosses in front of his mansion, threw rocks through his windows, and slashed his tires. More seriously, he was challenged by President Herbert Hoover, who desired to increase the Republican Party's appeal to white southerners by ridding its leadership of blacks. In 1929, Hoover arranged for Davis to appear before a U.S. Senate special committee investigating campaign expenditures. For a week, he was interrogated by hostile senators, in particular Walter George, a Georgia Democrat who wanted to know what had happened to $2,000 that Hoover had given Davis for campaign expenses. When Davis could not produce receipts nor offer a reasonable explanation for why he had no receipts, Hoover forced him to resign from his party posts.

Davis continued to play an important, if diminished, role in the Georgia Republican Party. He remained a force in Atlanta municipal elections until 1932, when he stopped publishing the *Independent* because of declining circulation, and he served as a delegate to the national convention through 1944. In 1943, at age 73, he was named president of the Young Men's Republican Club of Georgia. For the most part, however, after his embarrassment in 1929 he devoted his time and energy to charitable work, serving as a leader of the Grand United Order of Odd Fellows, the Knights of Pythias, and the Baptist Layman's League of Georgia. He died on October 28, 1945, in New York City while visiting his son, BEN DAVIS. The minister who officiated at his funeral in Atlanta was the father of MAYNARD JACKSON.

Further Reading

Carey, Charles W., Jr. "Davis, Benjamin J." In *African American National Biography,* vol. 2, edited by Henry Louis Gates, Jr., and Evelyn Brooks Higginbotham. New York: Oxford University Press, 2008, pp. 563–564.

Horne, Gerald. *Black Liberation/Red Scare: Ben Davis [Jr.] and the Communist Party.* Newark: University of Delaware Press, 1994.

Walton, Hanes. *Black Republicans: The Politics of the Black and Tans.* Metuchen, N.J.: Scarecrow Press, 1975.

Davis, Danny K.

(1941–   ) *U.S. congressional representative from Illinois*

During the 1990s, many African-American political leaders began turning away from the Democratic Party's liberal policies and moving toward more moderate positions. One black politician who resisted this move was Danny K. Davis, who gained a reputation as one of the more liberal members of Congress.

Davis was born on September 6, 1941, in Parkdale, Arkansas. His parents, H. D. and Mazzie, were cotton farmers. After finishing high school, he attended Arkansas AM&N College (now the University of Arkansas at Pine Bluff) and received a B.A. in 1961. That same year, he moved to Chicago, Illinois, and found a job as a postal clerk. A year later, he obtained a position as a teacher and guidance counselor in the Chicago public school system. In 1968, he received an M.S. from Chicago State University, and the following year he was named director of training at the Martin Luther King Neighborhood Health Center on Chicago's West Side. In 1971, he joined the West Side Health Planning Organization as a manpower consultant, and he was named its executive director the following year. In 1976, he became a special assistant to the president of the Miles Square Community Health Center, a position he

held for three years. During this period, he also served a term as president of the National Association of Community Health Centers.

Davis became involved in politics in the mid-1970s when he cofounded and served as the first president of the Westside Association for Community Action. The purpose of the organization was to gain a greater voice for African-American residents in Chicago local government, which at the time was controlled by white politicians in both the Democratic and Republican parties. In 1979, he was elected as a Democrat to the city board of aldermen, a position he held for 11 years. During this period he was a main participant in the so-called council wars that pitted the board of aldermen's black members against its white members in the never-ending struggle over the allocation of city services and patronage positions. Within this context, he was a strong supporter of HAROLD WASHINGTON, who became Chicago's first black mayor in 1983. In 1990, he was elected to the Cook County board of commissioners, where he served for six years.

Early on, Davis set his sights on higher elective offices than alderman or commissioner. In 1984, he ran for Congress against the popular incumbent, CARDISS COLLINS, but was defeated. A second run against Collins two years later also ended in defeat, as did a campaign for mayor against the popular incumbent Richard Daley, Jr., in 1991. His political ambitions received a boost in 1993; having cochaired Democratic President Bill Clinton's 1992 campaign in Illinois, Davis was rewarded by being named to the board of directors of the National Housing Partnership. The partnership exercised considerable influence over public housing in Chicago, thus enhancing Davis's political clout in his hometown.

In 1996, Collins announced her decision to retire from Congress, and Davis once again declared his candidacy. He easily defeated the other seven challengers in the Democratic primary and coasted to victory in the general election. He took his seat in 1997 and was assigned to the committees on government reform and small business.

As a congressman, Davis sided with the liberal wing of the Democratic Party. He introduced legislation to increase federal funding for community health care centers and public housing. He supported a decrease in military spending and an increase in the minimum wage. He also worked to protect social programs such as welfare and affirmative action from being dismantled by the Republicans, who had gained control of the House in 1994. One of his legislative successes established transportation services between the inner cities and the suburbs. The program made it possible for urbanites who owned no cars to commute to work in the suburbs, where blue-collar workers were in great demand. Other successes included obtaining more federal money for youth summer employment and more jobs and investments for low-income communities.

In 2010, Davis was reelected to a 10th term. He is married to the former Vera Garner, with whom he has two children. Following the 2008 election, Illinois junior senator and president-elect BARACK OBAMA vacated his U.S. Senate seat. In late December 2008, Illinois governor Rod Blagojevich contacted Davis and asked if he would be willing to take over Obama's position. Davis later admitted that he was interested in serving in the Senate, but he refused because Blagojevich had been accused of previously trying to sell the seat. As Davis told the *New York Times*, "I felt that if I was to take the appointment I would spend so much of my time deflecting and defending the position that it would take away from my real reason for being involved in politics and political life: to try and find solutions to problems."

Further Reading

Biographical Directory of the United States Congress. "Davis, Danny K., 1941– ." Available online. URL: http://bioguide.congress.gov/scripts/bio display. pl?index=D000096. Downloaded April 15, 2009.

Congressman Danny K. Davis, Official Web Site. Available online. URL: http://www.davis.house. gov. Downloaded April 15, 2009.

"Danny K. Davis, D-Ill. (7). New Member Profile." *Congressional Quarterly Weekly Report* 55 (January 4, 1997): 57.

Davey, Monica, and Rachel I. Swarns. "Tough Calculus for Blagojevich on Senate Seat." *New York Times,* December 31, 2008. Available online. URL: http:// www.nytimes.com/2009/01/01/us/01illinois.html?_ r=1&hp. Downloaded April 23, 2009.

Dawson, William

(William Levi Dawson)
(1886–1970) *U.S. congressional representative from Illinois*

William Dawson served in the U.S. House of Representatives for 27 years. During his tenure, he became the first African American to chair a permanent congressional committee. Had he so desired, he could also have been the first black to serve in the cabinet.

Dawson was born on April 26, 1886, in Albany, Georgia. His father, Levi, was a barber, and his mother, Rebecca, was a homemaker. He completed his secondary education at a Methodist missionary school in Albany, then enrolled in Fisk University where he received his B.A. in 1909. Finding little opportunity for an educated black man in the segregated South, in 1912 he boarded the train for Chicago, Illinois. He enrolled in the Kent School of Law and supported himself by doing various jobs for Crip Woods, a black politician in the 14th Ward. In 1917, he joined the U.S. Army and saw action in France during World War I as a first lieutenant. He returned to Chicago after the war to study law at Northwestern University, and in 1920 he passed the Illinois bar examination and opened a law office in the city's black-majority Second Ward. In 1922, he married Nellie Brown, with whom he had two children.

Dawson became an active member of the Republican Party in the early 1920s. By 1928, he figured he had made enough reputation for himself to run for Congress from Illinois's black-majority First District. The party's nomination, however, went to Martin B. Madden, the white incumbent. When Madden died during the campaign, Dawson was passed over again, this time in favor of OSCAR DEPRIEST, who won the election. Somewhat chastened by the whole experience, Dawson became a loyal follower of DePriest. He was rewarded two years later by being named to the party's state central committee. In 1933, he was elected to represent the Second Ward on the city board of aldermen, a post he held for six years.

In 1938, Dawson lost his second bid for Congress, this time to DePriest's successor, the Democrat ARTHUR MITCHELL. By now, Chicago's African-American population was gradually changing its party allegiance from Republican to Democrat, mostly because of the latter party's support for the New Deal. In 1939, when Dawson lost his alderman's seat to a Democrat, he decided to make the switch also, especially after Mayor Edward J. Kelly offered to make him the party's Second Ward committeeman. Over the next four years, Dawson built a strong Democratic organization in his own and neighboring wards in Chicago's South Side. When Mitchell declined to run for reelection in 1942, Dawson's organization carried him to victory.

Dawson was reelected to the House 13 times. During his entire tenure, he was the senior black member of that body, and until EDWARD BROOKE took his seat in the U.S. Senate in 1967, he was the highest elected black official in the nation. In 1949, he became, by virtue of seniority, the chairman of the committee on government operations, thus making him the first black chairman of a permanent congressional committee. Despite these high-level positions, he was not a flamboyant leader, preferring instead to work behind the scenes for small victories that eventually added up to something large. As committee chairman, he worked to end racial discrimination among defense contractors. He also opposed regressive income taxes, which hurt poor African Americans, and the poll tax, which kept African Americans from voting.

Dawson believed that the Democratic Party offered blacks their best chance of upward political mobility, and so he supported the party without question. This support generated flak among some African Americans, particularly those who saw the Democrats as the mainstay of segregation in the South and those who opposed the Johnson administration's policy in Vietnam because a disproportionate number of blacks were dying there. As a conciliator and compromiser, he was a bit out of step with the Civil Rights movement; in 1966 he called Dr. Martin

William Dawson represented Chicago, Illinois, in the U.S. House of Representatives. *(Library of Congress)*

Luther King, Jr., an "outside agent" for leading a protest march in Chicago. And he was a lukewarm participant in the Democratic Select Committee, an early incarnation of the Congressional Black Caucus, because he considered it to be too militant.

Meanwhile, Dawson continued to exert tremendous influence in Chicago politics and within the Democratic Party. As the leading African-American member of the city's Democratic machine, he exercised considerable control over the distribution of political patronage jobs. His organization continued to control the black voters of the South Side, who often delivered the deciding votes in important elections. The South Side is credited with getting Richard J. Daley elected mayor in 1955, as well as putting Illinois in President Harry S. Truman's column in 1948 and in President John F. Kennedy's column in 1960. In recognition of his importance to the party, he was named to a series of increasingly influential party positions: assistant chairman of the national committee in 1944, chairman of the national convention's Negro Division in 1948, and vice-chair of the national committee in 1950. In 1961, Kennedy offered to make him postmaster general; had he accepted, he would have been the first African-American cabinet official.

In 1962, at age 76, Dawson fell ill while campaigning and never fully recovered. He declined to run for reelection in 1970, instead giving his support to RALPH METCALFE. He died on November 9, 1970, in Chicago.

Further Reading

Biographical Directory of the United States Congress. "Dawson, William Levi, 1886–1970." Available online. URL: http://bioguide.congress.gov/scripts/biodisplay.pl?index=D000158. Downloaded March 28, 2009.

Black Americans in Congress. "William Levi Dawson." Available online. URL: http://baic.house.gov/member-profiles/profile.html?intID=27. Downloaded April 1, 2009.

Clay, William L. *Just Permanent Interests: Black Americans in Congress, 1870–1992.* New York: Amistad Press, 1993.

Clayton, Edward T. *The Negro Politician.* Chicago: Johnson Publishing, 1964.

Granger, Bill, and Lori Granger. *Lords of the Last Machine.* New York: Random House, 1987.

DeLarge, Robert

(Robert Carlos DeLarge)
(1842–1874) *U.S. congressional representative from South Carolina*

During Reconstruction, white southerners complained bitterly about black politicians who made big promises while leading their states to financial ruin because of dishonesty and/or incompetence. Although the vast majority of African-American politicians in the 1870s did not fit this stereotype, Robert DeLarge was one who came close.

DeLarge was born on March 15, 1842, in Aiken, South Carolina. His father, a tailor, and his mother, a cloak maker, were free blacks; their names are unknown. He attended a primary school in North Carolina and graduated from Wood High School, a school for free blacks in Charleston. By the time he was 18 he had worked as a tailor, farmer, and barber. During the Civil War he was employed as a clerk by the Confederate navy, but later he found it politically expedient to donate most of the salary he had earned in this position to the state Republican Party. At some point he married—the date of the marriage and the name of his wife are unknown—and had one child. By the end of the war, he was a prominent member of Charleston's black elite.

In 1865, DeLarge became an agent for the Freedmen's Bureau. He also got involved in politics, serving as chairman of the credentials committee of that year's Colored Peoples' Convention in Charleston. This meeting endorsed legal rights for African Americans and political rights for black men and condemned the so-called Black

Codes, legislation that tried to keep freedmen in a state of quasi slavery. A flamboyant orator, DeLarge made several speeches in favor of universal public education and universal manhood suffrage that excited the convention-goers and made him an important figure among black politicians.

The establishment of Reconstruction in South Carolina in 1867 gave African Americans such as DeLarge the opportunity to play more active roles in state politics. In 1867, he chaired the platform committee of the state Republican Party, of which African Americans constituted a majority, and the following year he served as a member of three standing committees of the state constitutional convention. He impressed black voters by insisting on measures to implement integrated public education and redistribute land to the state's poor of both races. Meanwhile, he impressed white voters by opposing the further confiscation of land owned by former Confederates and opposing the granting of voting rights to blacks and whites who could not pass a literacy test.

In 1868, DeLarge was elected to the state legislature, which named him chairman of the ways and means committee. In 1870, he was appointed head of the state's land commission, thus gaining the opportunity to implement his own radical proposals for redistributing land to impoverished farmers. Within a year, he announced that nearly 2,000 small tracts carrying eight-year mortgages had been made available to "the impoverished people of the state." Shortly after his announcement, however, it became evident that DeLarge had misused his powers as commissioner by engaging in a number of land transactions that enriched himself and his cronies while bilking the state. Charges of gross mismanagement led to his forced resignation in 1871. He was never brought to trial, however, because his successor, FRANCIS CARDOZO, could find no records of DeLarge's transactions as commissioner, fraudulent or otherwise.

Despite the controversy over his land dealings, in 1871 DeLarge was elected to the U.S. House of Representatives, defeating his white opponent,

Robert DeLarge was a Reconstruction-era congressman from South Carolina. *(Library of Congress)*

Christopher C. Bowen, by a slender margin. He added to his reputation as a political moderate by insisting on federal enforcement of the Fourteenth Amendment, which guaranteed equal rights to African Americans, while supporting the removal of voting restrictions on former Confederates. While in Congress, he began to flirt with the notion of black nationalism, stating on several occasions that African Americans were Republicans only because no other party was open to them. He demurred, however, when asked if he supported the creation of a "black man's party." The result was to demean his stature among white Republicans and assimilationist blacks while confusing militant blacks as to where he stood on the issue.

Meanwhile, Bowen had challenged DeLarge's election. After an investigation that lasted 17 months, the House Committee on Elections ruled that the contest between DeLarge and Bowen was so rife with fraud and corruption that neither man deserved the contested seat. DeLarge was forced to resign on January 24, 1873, less than six weeks before the expiration of his term.

Shortly after his return to South Carolina, DeLarge was appointed a magistrate in Charleston. He declined to run for the House again, and his seat was won by ALONZO RANSIER. He died from consumption (tuberculosis) on February 14, 1874, in Charleston.

Further Reading

Biographical Directory of the United States Congress. "DeLarge, Robert Carlos, 1842–1874." Available online. URL: http://bioguide.congress.gov/scripts/biodisplay.pl?index=D000208. Downloaded March 28, 2009.

Black Americans in Congress. "Robert Carlos De Large." Available online. URL: http://baic.house.gov/member-profiles/profile.html?intID=3. Downloaded April 10, 2009.

Clay, William L. *Just Permanent Interests: Black Americans in Congress, 1870–1992.* New York: Amistad Press, 1993.

Dray, Philip. *Capitol Men: The Epic Story of Reconstruction Through the Lives of the First Black Congressmen.* Boston: Houghton Mifflin, 2008.

Holt, Thomas C. *Black over White: Negro Political Leadership in South Carolina during Reconstruction.* Urbana: University of Illinois Press, 1977.

Lamson, Peggy. *The Glorious Failure: Black Congressman Robert Brown Elliott and the Reconstruction of South Carolina.* New York: W. W. Norton, 1973.

Dellums, Ron
(Ronald Vernie Dellums)
(1935–   ) *U.S. congressional representative from California, mayor of Oakland*

During his 27 years in Congress, Ron Dellums was one of that body's most outspoken opponents of U.S. military policy. His efforts helped reduce the threat of nuclear holocaust while imposing a certain measure of sanity on the military budgeting process.

Dellums was born on November 24, 1935, in Oakland, California. His father, Vernie, was a longshoreman, and his mother, Willa, was a clerical worker. After graduating from high school in 1954, he spent two years in the U.S. Marines, then returned home to attend college. He studied social work while receiving an A.A. from Oakland City College in 1958, a B.A. from San Francisco State College in 1960, and an M.S.W. from the University of California at Berkeley's Graduate School of Social Welfare in 1962. That same year, he married Leola Higgs, with whom he has three children. Over the next six years, he worked as a psychiatric social worker for the California Department of Mental Hygiene, program director for the Bayview Community Center in San Francisco, assistant director and director of San Francisco's Hunters Point Youth Opportunity Council, planning consultant for the Bay Area Social Planning Council, and director of the San Francisco Economic Opportunity Council's Concentrated Employment Program. In 1968, he became a senior consultant for manpower specialization programs with Social Dynamics, a Bay Area firm.

During his early career as a social worker, Dellums impressed the people around him as someone who truly cared for the underprivileged and who was willing and able to change the system on their behalf. Having received the endorsements of everyone from the local Democratic Party to the Community for New Politics, in 1967 he ran for and won a seat on the Berkeley city council. At the time, Berkeley was perhaps the most radical community in America, serving as home to "flower power" hippies as well as "black power" Black Panthers, and Dellums's agenda of "poor power," coming as it did toward the end of President Lyndon B. Johnson's War on Poverty, found a number of ready allies.

The political climate favoring "poor power" changed in 1969, however, with the swearing-in of

President Richard M. Nixon. The following year, Dellums decided to pursue his agenda at the national level by running for the U.S. House of Representatives. By now, he had become an outspoken opponent to the war in Vietnam on the grounds that it diverted much-needed funds from programs like the War on Poverty; he had even gone so far as to address an international conference at which the representatives of Southeast Asian communist liberation fronts were in attendance. His victory was virtually assured when Vice President Spiro T. Agnew assailed him for being an unreconstructed radical, which Berkeley residents interpreted as high praise. He took his seat in 1971 and was assigned to the committee on the District of Columbia.

Ron Dellums, longtime congressman from California's Bay Area and one-term mayor of Oakland, is an outspoken opponent of excessive military spending. *(Library of Congress)*

As a freshman congressman, Dellums attacked the military-industrial complex with all his might. Having campaigned on an anti–Vietnam War platform, he began holding his own hearings on U.S. policy in Vietnam as well as on racism in the military. In 1973, the powers-that-be in the House appointed him to the committee on the armed services in the hope that this would mollify his opposition to military spending. It did not; instead, it gave him access to the information he needed to attack what he saw as unnecessary defense programs. In 1979, he began arguing against the use of tactical nuclear weapons; his opposition helped initiate the round of negotiations with the Soviet Union that culminated in the 1987 Intermediate Nuclear Forces Treaty, which called for the destruction of both countries' short-range nuclear missiles. In 1981, he created a major stir when he introduced an alternative military budget that eliminated funding for several long-range missile programs as well as for the development of the B-1 bomber. His ability to oppose military spending increased in 1983 when he became the chairman of the subcommittee on military installations and facilities, in 1991 when he was appointed to the committee on intelligence, and in 1993 when he became chairman of the armed services committee. In 1983, he published *Defense Sense: The Search for a Rational Military Policy,* which outlined his views on the dangers to American society of diverting funding from social programs to military spending. Although he was not always able to derail projects that he thought were misguided, he did succeed in forcing Pentagon officials to present reasoned arguments for their pet projects in order to get them funded.

Although Dellums's primary focus was on defense spending, he did not neglect other matters. In 1971, he introduced a resolution banning U.S. investment in South Africa; a similar resolution was eventually passed in 1986 and helped bring about an end to apartheid. He also worked to defend the gains made in civil rights during the

1960s from conservative attacks during the Nixon and Reagan administrations. From 1979 to 1993, he chaired the committee on the District of Columbia, and from 1988 to 1991 he chaired the Congressional Black Caucus.

Dellums was reelected to Congress 13 times, in most instances by a landslide. In 1998 he resigned his seat. Dellums established a lobbying firm in Washington, D.C., but returned to politics in 2005 when he announced that he would run for mayor of Oakland, California. Dellums was elected with just over 50 percent of the vote.

As mayor, Dellums has worked to lower the city's crime rate by hiring more police officers and reorganizing the police department. Nevertheless, Dellums's administration drew harsh criticism from the public and the press, especially after the shooting deaths of four officers by a parolee in March 2009. Faced with widespread criticism of his job performance, Dellums decided not to run for reelection in 2010.

Further Reading

Biographical Directory of the United States Congress. "Dellums, Ronald Vernie, 1935–   ." Available online. URL: http://bioguide.congress.gov/scripts/biodisplay.pl?index=D000222. Downloaded April 8, 2009.

Black Americans in Congress. "Ronald V. Dellums." Available online. URL: http://baic.house.gov/member-profiles/profile.html?intID=38. Downloaded April 12, 2009.

Clay, William L. *Just Permanent Interests: Black Americans in Congress, 1870–1992.* New York: Amistad Press, 1993.

Dellums, Ronald V., and H. Lee Halterman. *Lying Down with the Lions: A Public Life from the Streets of Oakland to the Halls of Power.* Boston: Beacon Books, 2000.

Levy, Sholomo B. "Dellums, Ron." In *African American National Biography,* vol. 2, edited by Henry Louis Gates, Jr., and Evelyn Brooks Higginbotham. New York: Oxford University Press, 2008, pp. 644–646.

Swain, Carol M. *Black Faces, Black Interests: The Representation of African Americans in Congress,* enlarged ed. Cambridge Mass.: Harvard University Press, 1995.

DePriest, Oscar
(Oscar Stanton DePriest)
(1871–1951) *U.S. congressional representative from Illinois*

The political career of Oscar DePriest served to open and close epochs in the history of black political leaders. On the one hand, he was the first African-American congressman to be elected from a northern state and the first of a rising tide of black congressmen to hold office after 1929. On the other hand, he was one of the last black Republicans to serve in Congress; none were elected to Congress for 32 years after he left office in 1935, and of 75 black elected congressmen between then and 2008, only three were Republican.

DePriest was born on March 9, 1871, in Florence, Alabama. His father, Neander, was a farmer and teamster, and his mother, Martha, was a laundress. In 1878 his family joined the Great Exodus, the migration of African Americans from the South to the Midwest, and settled in Salina, Kansas. At age 17, having completed a two-year business course at Salina Normal School, he moved to Chicago, Illinois. After a series of odd jobs, he found work as a house painter. By 1898, the year he married Jessie Williams, with whom he had one child, he was operating his own home repair and renovation business.

In the late 1890s, DePriest became actively involved in the Republican Party. As a reward for his success in recruiting Chicago's growing African-American community to the party's ranks, in 1904 he was elected to the Cook County Commission. Reelected in 1906, he became embroiled in a factional dispute with Martin B. Madden, the Republican congressman from Illinois's black-majority First District; thus, he was defeated in

Oscar DePriest represented Illinois in the U.S. Congress. He was the first African-American congressman elected from a northern state. *(Library of Congress)*

1908 and prevented from running for the state legislature. Undaunted by this temporary setback, he remained active in the party. Meanwhile, he expanded his business activities to include the buying and selling of real estate, and as property values in the city rose, so did his bank account. Once he reconciled with Madden in 1912, he was poised, politically and financially, to become a major political player in Chicago.

In 1915, DePriest returned to the campaign trail as a candidate for city alderman from the black-majority Second Ward. He campaigned for months, lining up support among the party faithful and community leaders. He campaigned especially hard among women, who in 1913 had received the right to vote in municipal elections. He easily defeated two white candidates to become the city's first African-American alderman. In this position, he worked to gain more political patronage jobs for blacks and introduced a civil rights ordinance. In 1917, his enemies had him arraigned on charges of bribery; he had accepted a campaign contribution from a gambling joint in return, it was claimed, for protection against police raids. Although he was found

not guilty, the incident set back his career for several years. He was kept from running for reelection and was defeated in his next two tries to reclaim his seat.

DePriest continued to be active in party activities in the hope that one day he could return to office. He served as a delegate to the 1920 Republican National Convention, actively supported the reelection campaigns of Madden and Chicago mayor William "Big Bill" Thompson, and served as committeeman for the black-majority Third Ward. In 1928, his patience was rewarded. Madden died while seeking reelection, and DePriest was chosen in mid-race to take his place. The party closed ranks behind him, and the following year he took his seat as the first black congressman since 1901.

DePriest served on the committees on enrolled bills, Indian affairs, and invalid pensions. His most successful legislative initiative prohibited racial discrimination in the Civilian Conservation Corps, an important source of jobs during the Great Depression. He also secured more money for improving Howard University's physical plant. His other race-related bills, however, failed to be enacted. An antilynching bill that made a lynching the legal responsibility of the county in which it occurred died in committee, although it received the support of at least one southern governor. A bill providing for a change of venue for defendants who were unlikely to receive a fair trial because of their race or religion also died in committee, as did one awarding a $75 monthly pension to ex-slaves.

As the only African American in Congress, DePriest was the center of several racial controversies. His wife's attendance at a White House tea for congressional wives caused an uproar, but he used the publicity to raise money for the National Association for the Advancement of Colored People. As a congressman, he was entitled to eat in the House dining room, but when Senator James Heflin from Alabama attempted to bar him from the Senate's facility, he declared that Heflin was not man enough to keep him from eating wherever he pleased. He was unable, however, to gain congressional dining privileges for his black staff members, although such privileges were routinely granted to white staffers. And on several occasions he toured the South, speaking out against racial discrimination despite more than one threat against his life.

DePriest was reelected in 1930 and 1932. Being a Republican, he opposed most New Deal federal relief programs, preferring instead to give such responsibility to the states and localities. About one-third of his black constituents were of the opposite opinion, however, and in 1934 they and the district's white voters rejected him in favor of his Democratic challenger, ARTHUR MITCHELL. He remained active in local Republican affairs, serving as a delegate to the 1936 national convention and as Third Ward alderman from 1943 to 1947. Meanwhile, he continued to operate his real estate business until his death on May 12, 1951, in Chicago.

Further Reading

Biographical Directory of the United States Congress. "DePriest, Oscar Stanton, 1871–1951." Available online. URL: http://bioguide.congress.gov/ scripts/ biodisplay.pl?index=D000263. Downloaded March 28, 2009.

Black Americans in Congress. "Oscar DePriest." Available online. URL: http://baic.house.gov/member-profiles/profile.html?intID=28. Downloaded March 28, 2009.

Clay, William L. *Just Permanent Interests: Black Americans in Congress, 1870–1992.* New York: Amistad Press, 1993.

Gosnell, Harold F. *Negro Politicians: The Rise of Negro Politics in Chicago.* Chicago: University of Chicago Press, 1967.

Mann, Kenneth E. "Oscar Stanton DePriest: Persuasive Agent for the Black Masses." *Negro History Bulletin* 35 (October 1972): 134–137.

Diggs, Charles
(Charles Coles Diggs, Jr.)
(1922–1998) *U.S. congressional representative from Michigan*

Charles Diggs was the first African American to represent Michigan in the U.S. Congress and the first chairman of the Congressional Black Caucus. He devoted his political career to gaining civil rights for blacks both at home and abroad. Unfortunately, his career was cut short when, like his father, he was convicted and jailed for fraud.

Diggs was born on December 2, 1922, in Detroit, Michigan. His father, Charles Sr., owned a funeral home, and his mother, Mamie (also spelled Mayme), was a homemaker. After studying at the University of Michigan for two years, in 1942 he transferred to Fisk University. The following year he was drafted into the U.S. Army and was assigned to the Air Corps; by the end of World War II he had risen to the rank of second lieutenant. After the war, he returned to Detroit and enrolled in the Wayne College of Mortuary Science. When he graduated in 1946, he went to work with his father and enrolled in the University of Detroit School of Law.

Diggs's first foray into politics stemmed from a perceived insult to his father. In addition to being a successful businessman, Diggs Sr. was also a popular state senator. In 1948, he was convicted on two counts of bribery and imprisoned, leaving his son to run the family business. When Diggs Sr. was released after serving 15 months, he ran for reelection and won; the senate, however, refused to seat him because he was a felon. The entire episode outraged Diggs, who vowed to avenge his father's reputation by getting elected to his former seat. Although still a law student, he campaigned vigorously; this effort, coupled with his father's record of service to his constituents, propelled him to victory in the Democratic primary and the general election. In 1951, just

Charles Diggs was the first African American to represent Michigan in Congress. *(Library of Congress)*

months after graduating from law school, he took his father's seat in the state senate.

As a senator, Diggs earned a reputation as a pro-labor legislator, which stood him in good stead in working-class Detroit. In 1954, he decided to run for the 13th District's seat in the U.S. House of Representatives. At first, this decision seemed to be utter foolishness: He was politically inexperienced, he was running in a white-majority district, the Democratic incumbent had given his constituents many years of faithful service, the most likely Republican challenger was the son of the owner of the city's most prestigious newspaper, and in the last 50 years only four blacks from the entire country had been elected to Congress. Undaunted, Diggs ran hard while his opponents took him lightly; to their astonishment, it was he and not they who was sworn in in 1955. He was reelected 11 times.

Diggs was first appointed to the committees on interior and insular affairs and veterans affairs. He showed more interest, however, in the workings of the committee on foreign relations. Specifically, he spoke out forcefully for improved U.S. relations with the black nations of Africa, which were just throwing off centuries of colonial rule. In 1957, he accompanied Vice President Richard M. Nixon on a tour of Africa, and two years later he was appointed to the foreign relations committee. He used his new assignment to oppose U.S. military aid to Portugal and South Africa, which he contended would be used primarily to thwart black nationalism in Angola, Mozambique, and South Africa, as well as the purchase of chrome from Rhodesia (modern Zimbabwe), which at the time was being governed under apartheid-like conditions. In 1973, he organized a $30 million relief effort for the Sahel, the impoverished region south of the Sahara Desert that was in the throes of a famine. These efforts and others earned him the sobriquet "father of African-American foreign relations."

Diggs also devoted himself to improving civil rights for blacks in the United States. In the 1950s, he traveled repeatedly to Mississippi to investigate firsthand the ongoing struggle for civil rights; he was staying at the home of AARON HENRY when it was bombed by segregationists. After *Brown v. Board of Education* overturned the legal underpinnings for segregated schools in 1955, he called for extending the decision to cases involving transportation. In 1963, he was appointed to the committee on the District of Columbia, which oversaw the local government of Washington, D.C., whose population was overwhelmingly black. As committee chairman, he played a crucial role in passing the 1973 home rule bill that granted the city's residents the right to elect their own mayor and city council. In 1971, having become the most senior African American in the House, he cofounded and served as first chairman of the Congressional Black Caucus. This body strove to enhance the impact of black representatives on the workings of the House by providing a forum within which they could work as a group.

Diggs also experienced his share of personal troubles. In 1960, he divorced his first wife, Juanita Rosario, with whom he had three children, and married Anna Johnston. In 1971, he divorced her and married Janet Hall. In 1978, he was convicted on 29 counts of income tax evasion, mail fraud, and payroll kickbacks involving his congressional staff; he was censured by the full House and jailed in 1980 when the Supreme Court refused to hear his appeal. Upon his release from prison after serving seven months, he opened a funeral home in Hillcrest Heights, Maryland, a suburb of Washington. He died on August 24, 1998, in Hillcrest Heights.

Further Reading

Biographical Directory of the United States Congress. "Diggs, Charles Coles, Jr., 1922–1998." Available online. URL: http://bioguide.congress.gov/scripts/biodisplay.pl?index=D000344. Downloaded March 28, 2009.

Black Americans in Congress. "Charles Coles Diggs, Jr." Available online. URL: http://baic.house.gov/member-profiles/profile.html?intID=29. Downloaded March 28, 2009.

Clay, William L. *Just Permanent Interests: Black Americans in Congress, 1870–1992.* New York: Amistad Press, 1993.

Dubose, Carolyn P. *The Untold Story of Charles Diggs: The Public Figure, the Private Man.* Arlington, Va.: Barton Publishing, 1999.

Parker, Pearl T. *A Political Activist: Charles Coles Diggs Jr., Michigan's First Black Congressman.* Nashville: Tennessee State University Press, 1984.

Dinkins, David
(David Norman Dinkins)
(1927–) *mayor of New York City*

David Dinkins was the first African-American mayor of New York City. A calm, dignified man, he did much to ease the tensions caused by the city's own brand of confrontational politics. Despite his best efforts to manage the city's problems, he was one of the first African-American mayors of a major city to be denied reelection.

Dinkins was born on July 10, 1927, in Trenton, New Jersey. His father, William, was a barber, and his mother, Sally, was a domestic worker. When he was six years old, his parents divorced and he moved with his mother to Harlem in New York City. Shortly thereafter, however, he returned to his father's home in Trenton, where he grew up. After graduating from high school in 1945, he was drafted into the U.S. Army but transferred to the Marine Corps. Discharged in 1946, he took advantage of the G.I. Bill and enrolled in Howard University. In 1950 he received a B.S. in mathematics and went to Rutgers University to pursue graduate work, but after a semester he dropped out and became an insurance salesman. In 1953, he married Joyce Burrows, with whom he has two children, and enrolled in Brooklyn Law School. After receiving an LL.B. in 1956, he passed the bar examination and joined a law firm in Harlem.

Dinkins became involved in politics at the urging of his father-in-law, Daniel Burrows, who had once represented Harlem in the state assembly. Burrows was impressed by Dinkins's intelligence, self-assurance, and easygoing manner, so he introduced him to his friends in the Carver Democratic Club. The Carver Club was a major vehicle for getting black politicians from Harlem elected to state and local offices, and Dinkins soon became the protégé of its leader, J. Raymond Jones. After years of giving his untiring efforts and loyal support to the club's candidates, in 1965 Dinkins received the club's backing to run for state assemblyman. He declined to run for reelection after completing his two-year term, choosing instead to serve as the club's president, a position he held for the next 30 years. In 1972, he was appointed president of the city's board of elections; during his two-year term he effected several procedural changes that made it easier for people to register to vote.

In 1975, Dinkins was offered the post of deputy mayor of New York City, an appointive position. He was forced to turn down the offer when it was disclosed that he had paid no income taxes from 1969 to 1972. Calling the nonpayment an oversight, he quickly paid up in full with interest, then accepted the post of city clerk, a largely ceremonial position that he held for the next 10 years. In 1977 and 1981, he ran for borough president of Manhattan and lost both times in a landslide. Undaunted by these embarrassing defeats, in 1985 he ran again and won. As borough president, he proceeded with great deliberation on issues such as pedestrian safety and school decentralization, and on several occasions he was accused of studying a problem to death. His moderation in office, however, endeared him to the voters, who found him a refreshing change from the "ready, fire, aim" style of a number of the city's politicians.

In 1989, Dinkins decided to run for mayor of New York City. The incumbent, Edward I. Koch, was running for an unprecedented fourth term and was considered to be unbeatable by many observers. However, Dinkins knew that Koch had lost much support in the African-American community because of budget cuts that adversely affected their neighborhoods. After narrowly defeating Koch in the Democratic primary, he bested Rudolph Giuliani, at the time a federal district attorney, in the general election.

When Dinkins took over as mayor in 1990, New York City was facing difficult times. Expenditures far exceeded revenues, which made it difficult to introduce programs to deal with the city's high unemployment and crime rates. Nevertheless, he tackled these problems at his usual deliberate pace, drawing representatives from all factions of the city into the decision-making process. In this manner, he was able to cut services and reduce the city's payroll in such a way that minimized the damage done to any one constituency. So well did this program work that in 1992 the city was able to pay its bills and provide essential services while holding a small amount of money in reserve.

Dinkins also did much to defuse racial tensions in the city. He established an all-civilian police complaint review board that helped improve police-community relations. In 1991, a vehicle driven by a leader of the Jewish community in Brooklyn struck and killed a young black pedestrian in Queens. Before the situation could escalate into a full-blown race riot, Dinkins arrived on the scene and appealed to the angry crowd to go home and let justice run its course. He remained on the scene for several days until the protests subsided, then did what he could to reconcile the black and Jewish communities with one another. In 1992, he kept African-American rage over the Rodney King affair (see TOM BRADLEY) from exploding into widespread rioting, as it did in some cities. Throughout his four-year term, he acted as a peacemaker, using his charm and dignified approach to politics to bring differing factions to the table and help them work out their differences.

By 1993, New York City was experiencing financial difficulties once again. Despite Dinkins's best efforts, the city was operating at a deficit of more than $2 billion. He was attacked on the one hand for cutting too many jobs and services, and on the other hand for increasing taxes by $800 million to pay for the jobs and services he had not cut. His deliberate pace was now seen as procrastination, and his appointment of several incompetent people to important city positions was seen as cronyism. Although he easily won the Democratic primary, he narrowly lost his bid for reelection to Giuliani.

After leaving office in 1994, Dinkins was named a visiting professor at Yale University. Later that year he accepted teaching positions at Columbia University's School of International and Public Affairs and the Barnard-Columbia Center for Urban Research and Policy. Since his retirement from politics, Dinkins has endorsed two candidates in New York City mayoral races—Mark

Green in 2001 and Fernando Ferrer in 2005. In 2008, he supported Hillary Clinton during the Democratic presidential primary.

Further Reading

Colburn, David R., and Jeffrey S. Adler, eds. *African-American Mayors: Race, Politics, and the American City*. Urbana: University of Illinois Press, 2001.

NYC 100. "Elected Mayors of New York City, 1898–1998." Available online. URL: http://www. ci.nyc. ny.us/html/nyc100/html/classroom/hist_info/mayors.html#dinkins. Downloaded April 8, 2009.

Perry, Huey. *Race, Politics, and Governance in the United States*. Gainesville: University of Florida Press, 1996.

Rich, Wilbur C. *David Dinkins and New York City Politics: Race, Images, and the Media*. Albany: State University of New York Press, 2006.

Smith, Jessie Carney, ed. *Black Heroes of the 20th Century*. Detroit: Visible Ink, 1998.

Dixon, Julian
(Julian Carey Dixon)
(1934–2000) *U.S. congressional representative from California*

At the time of his death, Julian Dixon was one of the most powerful African Americans in government. Nevertheless, he was virtually unknown outside his congressional district and the halls of Congress, largely because of his quiet approach to politics.

Dixon was born on August 8, 1934, in Washington, D.C. As a young boy he moved with his parents to Los Angeles, California, where he grew up. After graduating from high school in 1953, he worked at various jobs for four years before joining the U.S. Army in 1957. In 1960, he was discharged at the rank of sergeant and returned to Los Angeles. He enrolled in Los Angeles State College (now California State University at Los Angeles) and received a B.S. in 1962. Over the next five years

he worked various day jobs while studying law at night at Southwestern University. In 1967, he received an LL.B. and opened a law office in Los Angeles.

Dixon became involved in politics in the early 1970s when he became a legislative aide to MERVYN DYMALLY, at the time a California state senator. In 1972, when YVONNE BURKE decided to run for Congress, Dixon ran for her former seat in the state assembly. Over the next six years he gained a reputation as a hardworking legislator who got things done by working behind the scenes rather than by drawing attention to himself. He authored or sponsored a number of bills to reform education and criminal justice while championing equal opportunity for minorities. In 1978, when Burke retired from Congress to run for state attorney general, Dixon again ran for her former seat. Although he faced seven other hopefuls, he managed to win largely because the state's Democratic leadership supported his candidacy and saw to it that his campaign was amply funded. He took office in 1979 and was assigned to the committees on ethics and appropriations.

Dixon's legislative interests as a congressman were wide-ranging. In addition to writing the first bill to impose economic sanctions against South Africa, he authored bills to provide humanitarian aid and development capital to southern Africa and to fund scholarships in the United States for disadvantaged South African youths. During the 1990s, he gained federal support for a mass-transit project in Los Angeles and aid for California communities hurt by cuts in defense spending following the end of the cold war. He also continued to push for legislation that advanced equal opportunity in the areas of education, employment, housing, and health care. He chaired the Congressional Black Caucus from 1983 to 1985.

Dixon possessed a low-key demeanor and the consummate ability to defuse a tense situation. As a result, the Democratic leadership called upon him repeatedly to handle tough situations. In 1984, he was named chairman of the rules committee of the Democratic National Convention in anticipation of a series of challenges to the seating of delegates by JESSE JACKSON, who was running for president. Dixon handled the challenges in a way that maintained both fairness and decorum. In 1985, he was chosen to chair the ethics committee just prior to the House's investigation of Speaker Jim Wright, who eventually resigned over almost 70 charges of ethics violations. Once again, Dixon kept the proceedings from turning into a media circus, instead steering them toward an equitable outcome. In 1995, he was named chairman of the committee on the District of Columbia, which oversees the local government of the nation's capital. At the time, Washington's deficit was about $1 billion, and the city's residents had just reelected MARION BARRY mayor despite his having served a prison term on charges related to drug abuse. That same year, Dixon led the move to place the city's budget in the hands of a federally appointed control board until such time as the city's financial affairs could be straightened out.

Dixon was reelected to 10 terms in Congress without once facing a serious challenger. His power in Washington and his popularity at home were such that he was requested several times to run for mayor of Los Angeles. He was married to the former Bettye Lee, with whom he had one child. He died of a heart attack on December 8, 2000, in Los Angeles.

Further Reading

Biographical Directory of the United States Congress. "Dixon, Julian Carey, 1934–2000." Available online. URL: http://bioguide.congress.gov/scripts/biodisplay.pl?index=D000373. Downloaded March 28,2009.

Black Americans in Congress. "Julian Carey Dixon." Available online. URL: http://baic.house.gov/member-profiles/profile.html?intID=37. Downloaded April 1, 2009.

Clay, William L. *Just Permanent Interests: Black Americans in Congress, 1870–1992.* New York: Amistad Press, 1993.

Dixon, Sheila
(1953–) *mayor of Baltimore, Maryland*

In 2007, Sheila Dixon became the first woman ever to serve as the mayor of Baltimore, Maryland. She also made history eight years earlier, when became the first African-American woman named president of Baltimore's city council.

Born on December 27, 1953, Dixon was raised in Baltimore and educated at city public schools. Her father was a car dealer, and her mother was local political activist. One of Dixon's first experiences in politics was working with her mother on KWEISI MFUME's 1978 campaign for a seat on the city council.

After graduating from Towson State University, Dixon began a career in education. She worked as a kindergarten teacher and as an educator in a program to help dropouts obtain a GED. In the 1980s, Dixon began a business venture involving importing and selling purses from Kenya. This enterprise led to a job with the Maryland Department of Business and Economic Development as an international trade specialist.

Dixon earned a master's degree in education management from Johns Hopkins University in 1985. But increasingly she was drawn toward a new career path in city politics. In 1987, she ran for the city council, winning the seat vacated by Mfume after he was elected to the U.S. House of Representatives. Dixon became known in the council for her outspokenness. In one notorious meeting in 1991, she took off her shoe, waved it at her mostly white and male colleagues, and shouted, "You've been running things for the last 20 years—now the shoe is on the other foot. See how you like it."

Dixon was elected president of the city council in 1999 and held this position for seven years. In 2006, when her mentor, Mayor Martin O'Malley, became Maryland's governor, Dixon automatically succeeded him according to the rules of the city charter. In November 2007, she was elected to a full term as mayor, earning an impressive 87 percent of the vote in the general election.

As mayor, Dixon addressed Baltimore's high violent crime rate by forming a task force to focus on getting illegal guns off the street. She also worked to reduce homelessness, increase treatment options for substance abusers, improve run-down neighborhoods, and beautify the city through street cleaning programs and community murals. Dixon paid particular attention to public health issues by implementing a citywide smoking ban and promoting fitness and nutritional education, especially among children.

Early in her tenure as mayor, Dixon was dogged by allegations of nepotism. She was also accused of giving city jobs and contracts to relatives. In early 2009, Dixon's reputation was further tainted when she was indicted on 12 counts of perjury, fraud, theft, and misconduct. Prosecutors accused her of not reporting gifts she received from developers involved in city projects, including thousands of dollars spent on trips and other expensive items by Dixon's one-time boyfriend Ronald Lipscomb. Dixon was also charged with asking developers for gift cards for needy families, but which she instead used herself. On December 1, 2009, a jury found her guilty of fraudulent misappropriation. She was sentenced to four years probation. As part of her plea agreement, Dixon resigned effective February 4, 2010.

Further Reading

Brennan, Carol. "Sheila Dixon, 1953– ." *Contemporary Black Biography* 68 (2009): 59–61.

Linskey, Annie. "Dixon Attorneys Argue Case for Dismissal of Charges." *Baltimore Sun*, April 24, 2009. Available online. URL: http://www.baltimoresun.com/news/local/baltimore_city/bal-dixon0423,0,3605941.story. Downloaded May 6, 2009.

Dymally, Mervyn
(Mervyn Malcolm Dymally)
(1926–) *U.S. congressional representative from California*

Mervyn Dymally was the first African American elected to the California state assembly. Over the years he also served as state senator, lieutenant governor, and congressman.

Dymally was born on May 12, 1926, in Cedros, Trinidad, British West Indies. His father, Hamid, ran an insurance agency, and his mother, Andreid, was a homemaker. He completed his secondary education in San Fernando in 1944, then went to work for *The Vanguard*, the newspaper of Trinidad's oil workers' union. In 1946, he enrolled in Lincoln University in Jefferson City, Missouri, to study journalism, but he transferred a year later to Chapman College in California and then to California State University at Los Angeles. Over the next seven years he worked part-time while majoring in special education. In 1954, he received a B.A., became a U.S. citizen, settled in Compton, California, and took a position with the Los Angeles public school system teaching children who were educationally handicapped. In 1968, he married Alice Gueno, with whom he had two children.

Dymally become active in politics in 1960, when he worked as a field coordinator for John F. Kennedy's presidential campaign. In 1962, he ran as a Democrat for the California state assembly. When he won, he became the first African American ever elected to that body. In addition to performing his duties as an assemblyman, he went on a State Department–sponsored tour of Africa to speak about U.S. democracy. He was reelected two years later, and in 1966 he was elected to the state senate. Throughout his 12 years in the state legislature, he championed equal opportunity for minorities and improved education for all Californians. During his tenure in the senate, he chaired the senate's committee on social welfare and attended California State University at Sacramento, receiving an M.A. in government in 1969.

In 1974, Dymally was elected lieutenant governor of California. In this position, he chaired the state commission for economic development and worked to bring new industries to the Golden State. Meanwhile, he continued his education by receiving a Ph.D. in human behavior from U.S. International University in San Diego in 1978.

In 1979, Dymally stepped down as lieutenant governor to run in the following year's election for South Los Angeles County's seat in the U.S. Congress. After defeating the incumbent and three other challengers in the Democratic primary, he easily won the general election. He was assigned to the committees on foreign affairs, post office and civil service, and the District of Columbia.

As a congressman, Dymally took a particular interest in U.S. relations with African and Caribbean nations. He worked closely with CHARLES DIGGS and other African-American congresspersons to increase U.S. aid to African nations and to foster better trade relations between the United States and Africa. As a congressman, he traveled extensively in Africa, visiting more than 40 nations, several of them repeatedly. As for his work in the Caribbean, he is best remembered for trying to normalize relations between the United States and Cuba by meeting with Fidel Castro, the communist leader of Cuba. He also worked to expand opportunities for minorities, and pushed for government set-asides, guaranteed percentages of government contract work, for minority-owned companies in energy-related industries. From 1987 to 1989, he chaired the Congressional Black Caucus.

Dymally was reelected five times. He declined to run for reelection in 1992, and after his term expired the following year he returned to his home in Compton. Over the next decade, he served as president of Dymally International Group, a consulting and financial advisory firm, acted as the Republic of Benin's honorary consul in California, lobbied for several African nations, and taught at Central State University in Ohio. In 2002, at age 76, Dymally resumed his political career as a California state assemblyman. After serving in the assembly for six years, he ran for the California State Senate in 2008 but was defeated in the Democratic primary.

Further Reading

Biographical Directory of the United States Congress. "Dymally, Mervyn Malcolm, 1926– ." Available online. URL: http://bioguide.congress.gov/scripts/biodisplay.pl?index=D000592. Downloaded April 8, 2009.

Black Americans in Congress. "Mervyn Malcolm Dymally." Available online. URL: http://baic.house.gov/member-profiles/profile.html?intID=36. Downloaded April 8, 2009.

Clay, William L. *Just Permanent Interests: Black Americans in Congress, 1870–1992.* New York: Amistad Press, 1993.

Dymally, Mervyn M., ed. *The Black Politician: His Struggle for Power.* Belmont, Calif.: Duxbury Press, 1971.

Musgrove, George Derek. "Dymally, Mervyn." In *African American National Biography,* vol. 3, edited by Henry Louis Gates, Jr., and Evelyn Brooks Higginbotham. New York: Oxford University Press, 2008, pp. 126–128.

E

Elliott, Robert
(Robert Brown Elliott)
(1842–1884) *U.S. congressional representative from South Carolina*

Robert Elliott led the Republican Party in South Carolina during the 1870s. During this period, he also served as a U.S. congressman and as speaker of the state legislature. His accomplishment is all the more remarkable when one considers that, for his entire life, Elliott was a subject of the British Crown.

The facts about Elliott's first 25 years remain unclear, but the following account seems most likely. He was born on August 11, 1842, in Liverpool, England. The names and occupations of his parents, who were West Indian, are unknown. After finishing his education in the English public school system, he worked for awhile as a printer's apprentice before joining the Royal Navy. In 1866, he deserted his ship in Boston, Massachusetts, and went to work as a typesetter. In 1867, he relocated to Charleston, South Carolina. That same year, he became associate editor of RICHARD CAIN's newspaper, the *South Carolina Leader,* and married Grace Lee Rollin. They had no children.

Despite his lack of American citizenship (his claim that he had been born in Boston was not scrutinized until the late 20th century), Elliott immediately became involved in politics. In 1867,

Reconstruction was just beginning, and he was chosen to serve as a delegate to the convention that would rewrite the state constitution. At the convention, he emerged as a champion of freedmen's rights by demanding equality for African Americans in the most forceful of terms. He led the fights for state-funded compulsory education and against measures that would require voters to pay a poll tax and pass a literacy test, both of which he knew would keep poor freedmen from voting. He also refused to countenance a measure requiring that debts incurred for the purchase of slaves be repaid. His resultant popularity among black voters, who constituted a majority of the state Republican Party, led to several impressive accomplishments. That same year, he came in third in the first round of balloting for lieutenant governor at the state Republican convention, he was named to the Barnwell County Board of Commissioners, and he was elected to South Carolina's lower house. After finishing second in the balloting for Speaker of the House, he was appointed to the committee on privileges and elections and made chairman of the committee on railroads. Also in 1868, he was admitted to the South Carolina bar and opened a law office in Columbia. In 1869, he was named assistant adjutant general and was put in charge of recruiting a state-funded black militia to combat the terrorist activities of the Ku Klux Klan. In

1870, he became chairman of the Republican nominating convention, a post he held throughout the decade. As chairman, he made sure that African Americans got their share of the nominations. At his insistence, in 1870 the party nominated three blacks—JOSEPH RAINEY, ROBERT DELARGE, and Elliott—for the U.S. House of Representatives and another black for lieutenant governor.

In 1870, Elliott was elected to the first of two consecutive terms in Congress. He served on the Education and Labor Committee and the Committee on the Militia. Because of his strong belief in equal rights for African Americans, he aligned himself with the Radical Republicans, whom he saw as the best friends the freedmen had. A powerful orator, he was an outspoken opponent of relaxing the political restrictions against former Confederates and a strong supporter of the Enforcement Act of 1872, which protected black southerners from being intimidated at the polls by the Ku Klux Klan and related groups. In 1874, he held his own in a debate on the House floor with Alexander Stephens, the former vice president of the Confederate States of America, concerning what became the Civil Rights Act of 1875, which made it a federal offense for places of public accommodation to discriminate against African Americans.

By 1874, black Republicans were losing control of South Carolina to white Democrats, who were making gains at their opponents' expense by accusing them of political chicanery and incompetence. As chairman of the state's Republican executive committee, he felt it necessary to resign from Congress and return to South Carolina in order to help stem the rising tide of white rule and the threat of black disfranchisement. In 1874, he was elected to the state house and served as its speaker until 1876, when he was elected attorney general.

Although Elliott was hugely popular with South Carolina's black voters, he was despised by white South Carolinians because of his militant insistence on civil rights for African Americans. In 1877, when the federal government withdrew its troops from South Carolina and Reconstruction came to an end, white supremacists, via the Ku Klux Klan and the Democratic Party, gained control of the state legislature. One of the new legislature's first acts was to force Elliott to give up the attorney generalship.

Although he never held elective office again, Elliott continued to work on behalf of the Republican Party in South Carolina, serving as leader of its delegation to the national convention in 1880. Meanwhile, in 1879 he had closed his law office for lack of business and accepted a position as a special inspector of customs in Charleston for the U.S. Treasury Department. In 1881, he moved to New Orleans, Louisiana, where he opened another law office and worked briefly as a federal treasury agent. He died from malaria on August 9, 1884, in New Orleans.

Further Reading

Biographical Directory of the United States Congress. "Elliott, Robert Brown, 1842–1884." Available online. URL: http://bioguide.congress.gov/scripts/biodisplay.pl?index=E000128. Downloaded March 28, 2009.

Black Americans in Congress. "Robert Brown Elliott." Available online. URL: http://baic.house.gov/member-profiles/profile.html?intID=4. Downloaded March 28, 2009.

Clay, William L. *Just Permanent Interests: Black Americans in Congress, 1870–1992.* New York: Amistad Press, 1993.

Dray, Philip. *Capitol Men: The Epic Story of Reconstruction Through the Lives of the First Black Congressmen.* Boston: Houghton Mifflin, 2008.

Holt, Thomas C. *Black over White: Negro Political Leadership in South Carolina during Reconstruction.* Urbana: University of Illinois Press, 1977.

Lamson, Peggy. *The Glorious Failure: Black Congressman Robert Brown Elliott and the Reconstruction of South Carolina.* New York: W. W. Norton, 1973.

Ellison, Keith

(1963–   ) *U.S. congressional representative
from Minnesota*

On January 4, 2007, Keith Ellison became the first
Muslim member of the U.S. Congress. He was
born in Detroit, Michigan, on August 4, 1963. His
father was a psychiatrist and his mother was a
social worker. Both were heavily involved in community activism, which inspired Ellison to pursue
a career in law.

After graduating from Jesuit High School, Ellison attended Wayne State University in Detroit.
While there, he read *The Autobiography of Malcolm X*. Moved by Malcolm X's story, Ellison
decided to convert from Catholicism to Islam at
the age of 19. Ellison graduated from Wayne State
with a bachelor's degree in economics in 1986. He
married his high school girlfriend, Kim, with
whom he eventually had four children.

The Ellisons moved to Minneapolis so he could
enroll in law school at the University of Minnesota. After graduating, he joined the Minneapolis
law firm of Lindquist and Vennum, before becoming the executive director of the Legal Rights
Center, a nonprofit firm for low-income clients. In
1998, he started his own practice within the firm
of Hassan and Reed. While practicing law, Ellison
was the host of a public affairs radio program in
Minneapolis.

In 2002, Ellison was elected to the Minnesota
state legislature. He proposed numerous bills,
some inspired by suggestions from his constituents. Ellison helped repeal a law that criminalized
homelessness, opposed legislation against same-
sex marriage, and worked to increase funding to
public schools. Ellison was elected to a second
term in 2004.

In 2006, Ellison decided to run for the seat in
the U.S. House of Representatives vacated by the
retiring Martin Sabo. During the campaign, Ellison's candidacy became a national issue because
of his religion. Right-wing pundits and legislators
rushed to attack Ellison for being a Muslim. When

he was interviewed by Glenn Beck on the cable
news network CNN, Beck asked Ellison to "prove
to me that you are not working with our enemies."
Ellison responded, "There's no one who's more
patriotic than I am, and so you know, I don't need
to prove my patriotic stripes." Throughout the
campaign, Ellison emphasized that, although he
was proud of being a Muslim, he was running
above all as a candidate with a track record of
getting things done. Ellison won the election with
56 percent of the vote.

As Ellison was about to take office, another
media frenzy broke out. New members of Congress are officially sworn in en masse, but each has
an individual ceremony for publicity purposes. At
these ceremonies, Congress members often place
a hand on the Bible or on another book, such as a
legal text or a Jewish prayer book. Ellison opted to
use a copy of the Qur'an, the holy book of Islam,
that was once owned by President Thomas Jefferson. His decision prompted another round of outrage from Republican lawmakers and conservative
commentators. For instance, Dennis Prager in a
column on the Web Site Townhall.com declared
that "the act undermines American culture."

Ellison weathered the media storm and settled
into his role as a freshman congressman. In the
House of Representatives, he pushed for a national
health care system, opposed predatory lending
practices, and demanded an immediate with-
drawal of U.S. military troops from Iraq. In March
2007, he met with Secretary of State CONDO-
LEEZZA RICE to discuss how he could help improve
the United States' image to Muslims worldwide.

In November 2008, Ellison was reelected. The
same month, ANDRÉ CARSON of Indiana became
the second Muslim elected to Congress. In an
interview with *The Progressive*, Ellison acknowledged that "we've broken a threshold." But he
added that, "in another sense," his and Carson's
faith was simply "not that important because at
the end of the day we all have to serve the public.
We all have to deliver." In 2010, Ellison was
reelected to a third term.

Further Reading

Congressman Keith Ellison, Official Web Site. Available online. URL: http://ellison.house.gov. Downloaded May 19, 2009.

Pal, Amitabh. "Keith Ellison: The Progressive Interview." *The Progressive* 72 (October 2008): 33–38.

Espy, Mike
(Alphonso Michael Espy)
(1953–   ) *U.S. secretary of agriculture*

Mike Espy was the first African American to represent Mississippi in Congress in the 20th century. He was also the first black from the Deep South to serve in a cabinet-level position.

Espy was born on November 30, 1953, in Yazoo City, Mississippi. His parents, Henry and Willie Jean, owned a chain of funeral homes. He graduated from high school in 1971 and enrolled in Howard University, receiving a B.A. four years later. In 1978, he received a J.D. from the University of Santa Clara School of Law. That same year he accepted a position in Yazoo City as managing attorney for Central Mississippi Legal Services. In 1980, he became the assistant secretary of state for the state's Public Lands Division, and four years later he was appointed assistant state attorney general for the Consumer Protection Division. In 1978, he married Sheila Bell, with whom he had two children; they were divorced in 1988. In 1999, he married Portia Ballard, with whom he had one child.

In a sense, Espy's political career began in high school when he was elected senior class president of a mostly white class. As prominent black businessmen, his father and grandfather were well-connected politically in the African-American community; their connections thought highly of Espy as a political candidate. Espy himself used the many contacts he made while working for the state government to prepare a run for public office. He paid some dues in 1983 by serving as district coordinator for the Democratic candidate for attorney general. It was rumored that Espy would run for governor in 1985, but instead he decided to stand for election to Congress.

In 1985, Espy resigned from the state and began to campaign in the black-majority Second Congressional District. He defeated two white candidates in the 1986 Democratic primary, then squeezed out a narrow victory over the Republican incumbent. In 1987 he took his seat as the first black congressman from Mississippi in more than 100 years. He was assigned to the committees on agriculture and the budget.

As a congressman, Espy championed the residents of the Mississippi Delta. During his first term in Congress, he got the federal government to establish the Lower Mississippi Delta Commission. The purpose of the commission was to study poverty in the Delta and to stimulate its economy. The commission immediately proposed an ambitious economic development plan that Espy got enacted as the Lower Mississippi River Valley Delta Development Act of 1988. This act provided economic development for river communities between the Gulf of Mexico and the Ohio River. Part of its plan was to increase the production of pond-raised catfish, which Espy began promoting to the government with a vengeance. He convinced the U.S. Army to serve catfish once a week at all its bases, and he got June 25 declared National Catfish Day. He later established the Lower Mississippi Delta Congressional Caucus as a means for the region's congressmen to speak with one voice, and he served as its first chairman. The caucus's most important accomplishment was to amend the Housing and Community Development Act of 1990 to include special provisions for fighting poverty in the Delta.

Espy was reelected three times. He managed to do this by appealing to both his black and white constituents. Economic development was a key accomplishment; however, Espy also espoused certain conservative measures that rural Mississippians applauded. He supported school prayer, the death penalty, and a balanced budget amendment. He showed his opposition to gun control by appearing in a pro-gun advertisement for the National Rifle Association, of which he was a member. At the same time, he opposed increases in military spending and supported abortion rights.

Following the election of Bill Clinton, a Democrat, to the presidency in 1992, Espy began lobbying for a cabinet-level position. He was unable to convince Clinton to appoint him secretary of housing and urban development; that post went to a Hispanic, Henry G. Cisneros. However, Espy's background in agriculture and his success in working with congressmen made him the logical candidate for secretary of agriculture. In 1993, he resigned his seat in the House to accept the secretaryship.

Espy's first move as secretary was to downsize the U.S. Department of Agriculture. He believed it was too big, and therefore unable to respond in a timely fashion to the needs and wants of either farmers or consumers. Next, he modernized the USDA's methods for inspecting meat by hiring more meat inspectors and mandating safer methods for handling raw meat and poultry products. He played a key role in negotiating agricultural trade agreements with other countries, and even met with leaders of the People's Republic of China in an effort to sell them more American wheat.

Despite his accomplishments, Espy's term as secretary came to a short end. In 1994, it was rumored that he had accepted inappropriate gifts from Tyson Foods, a major poultry processor, and Sun-Diamond Growers, a major fruit and vegetable grower, in exchange for postponing stricter poultry handling procedures and a ban on a particular pesticide. An independent counsel was established to investigate the charges. Despite his denials of any wrongdoing, the evidence uncovered by the counsel compelled Clinton to ask Espy to resign. In 1997, Espy was indicted on 39 counts of accepting gifts, although three of the most serious charges were dropped later that year. In 1998, Espy was cleared of all wrongdoing following a

seven-week trial. For their roles in the scandal, Tyson and Sun-Diamond were fined for dispensing illegal gratuities.

Following his resignation in 1994, Espy moved to Jackson, Mississippi, to work as an attorney for Crosthwait Terney, a law firm. Later he became associated with Butler Snow, the state's largest law firm, and the Farm Foundation, a think tank on matters related to agriculture, the food system, and rural communities. More recently, Espy has established his own law and agricultural consulting firms. He continues to be mentioned as a future candidate for governor or attorney general of Mississippi.

Further Reading

Biographical Directory of the United States Congress. "Espy, Albert [sic] Michael, 1953–   ." Available online. URL: http://bioguide.congress.gov/scripts/biodisplay.pl?index=E000218. Downloaded April 12, 2009.

Black Americans in Congress. "Alphonso Michael (Mike) Espy." Available online. URL: http://baic.house.gov/member-profiles/profile.html?intID=35. Downloaded April 9, 2009.

Clay, William L. *Just Permanent Interests: Black Americans in Congress, 1870–1992.* New York: Amistad Press, 1993.

Espy, Mike. *Promise Made, Promises Kept.* Manhattan: Kansas State University Press, 1993.

Whitaker, Charles. "Mike Espy: Bruised but Unbowed." *Ebony* 54, no. 6 (April 1999): 98–100.

Evans, Melvin
(Melvin Herbert Evans)
(1917–1984) *governor of the U.S. Virgin Islands*

Melvin Evans was the first elected governor of the territory of the U.S. Virgin Islands. He also served as a delegate to Congress and as a foreign ambassador.

Evans was born to Charles and Maude Evans on August 7, 1917, in Christiansted, St. Croix,

U.S. Virgin Islands. He attended high school in Charlotte Amalie on St. Thomas, then enrolled in Howard University, receiving a B.S. in 1940 and an M.D. in 1944. After completing his internship in New York City, he returned to the Virgin Islands to become physician in charge of the municipal hospital in Frederiksted on St. Croix. In 1945, he married Mary Phyllis Anderson, with whom he had four children. In 1948, he moved to Washington, D.C., to serve as senior assistant surgeon for the U.S. Public Health Service. Two years later, he returned to the hospital in Frederiksted, and in 1951 he was named assistant commissioner of health for the Virgin Islands and chief municipal physician for the island of St. Croix. In 1958, he was promoted to commissioner of health, and the following year he was named chairman of the Virgin Islands Board of Medical Examiners. In 1966, he took a leave of absence from both positions to study public health at the University of California at Berkeley. Upon receiving an M.P.H. the following year, he opened a private medical practice on St. Croix.

Evans became involved in government in 1962, when he was appointed chairman of the Governor of the Virgin Islands' Commission of Human Resources. At the time, the residents of the Virgin Islands, a U.S. territory, could elect their own legislators, but the territorial governor was appointed by the president of the United States. In 1969, President Richard M. Nixon named Evans to the governorship. The following year, he ran successfully for governor as a Republican under the provisions of the Virgin Islands Elective Governor Act of 1968, which gave Virgin Islanders the right to elect their own governor. In 1973, he was elected to a one-year term as chairman of the Southern Governors' Association.

As governor, Evans concentrated on gaining federal grants to improve roads, housing, and education. Unfortunately, his administration was marred by a crime wave that nearly crippled the islands' economy. In 1972, black militants murdered eight white tourists on a St. Croix golf course, and over the next two years other black supremacists assaulted white tourists on the three major islands of the U.S. Virgin Islands. Tourism, the Virgin Islands' major industry, plummeted precipitously, and thousands of hospitality workers became unemployed. Evans tried to play down the situation by blaming the media for making it appear worse than it was. Otherwise, he was perceived by the voters as doing little to address the situation. As a result, his 1974 bid for reelection as territorial governor failed, and he stepped down following the expiration of his term the following year.

In 1978, Evans was elected to the House of Representatives as the Virgin Islands' nonvoting delegate. He served on the committees on the armed services, interior and insular affairs, and merchant marine and fisheries. He successfully lobbied his fellow congressmen for more money for public education and health care for the Virgin Islands. He also managed to get the islands defined as a state for law enforcement purposes, so that additional federal funding could be made available to the islands' police departments.

Evans was defeated in his bid for reelection in 1980, and he resigned his office immediately following the election. In 1981, President Ronald Reagan appointed him ambassador to Trinidad and Tobago. He held this position until his death from a heart attack on November 27, 1984, in Christiansted.

Further Reading

Biographical Directory of the United States Congress. "Evans, Melvin Herbert, 1917–1984." Available online. URL: http://bioguide.congress.gov/scripts/biodisplay.pl?index=E000254. Downloaded March 28, 2009.

Black Americans in Congress. "Melvin Herbert Evans." Available online. URL: http://baic.house.gov/member-profiles/profile.html?intID=79. Downloaded March 28, 2009.

Hill, Roger. *Melvin H. Evans*. St. Croix, V.I.: CRIC Productions, 1987.

Moolenaar, Ruth. *Profiles of Outstanding Virgin Island-ers,* 3rd ed. St. Thomas, V.I.: Virgin Islands Department of Education, 1992.

University of the Virgin Islands Libraries. "Evans, Melvin Herbert." Available online. URL: http://webpac. uvi.edu/imls/pi_uvi/profiles1972/Governors/Evans_ MH/shtml. Downloaded March 29, 2009.

Evers, Charles

(James Charles Evers)
(1922–) *mayor of Fayette, Mississippi*

Charles Evers is not as well known as his younger brother, Medgar Evers, the civil rights activist who was assassinated in 1963. However, Charles picked up where his brother had left off, and by 1989 he had become one of the most successful African-American political leaders in Mississippi.

Evers was born on September 4, 1922, in Decatur, Mississippi. His father, Jim, was a laborer, and his mother, Jessie, was a domestic worker. In 1941, he dropped out of high school to join the U.S. Army, and he served during World War II in the Philippines. Discharged in 1945, he returned to Decatur and finished high school, and the following year he enrolled in Alcorn A&M College (now Alcorn State University).

In 1950, he married Manie Magee, with whom he had four children, and received a B.A. in social sciences. In 1951, after a year in Korea with his Army Reserve unit, he moved to Philadelphia, Mississippi, where he made ends meet by teaching school, working in his great-uncle's funeral home, and selling bootleg liquor. Over the next five years, he gave up teaching to become a full-time businessman, and by 1956 he had bought the funeral home, opened a hotel and gas station, started a taxi company, and gone to work as a disc jockey.

When Evers, while on the air, began urging blacks to register to vote, he was fired and then tried on a number of trumped-up charges. After selling his businesses and home to pay his legal fees, in 1957 he moved to Chicago, Illinois. Before

long, he had opened a liquor store and tavern and was part-owner of an apartment house. He returned to Mississippi in 1963 after the assassination of Medgar Evers. Outraged by his brother's death, he took over Medgar's position as field director of the state chapter of the National Association for the Advancement of Colored People, a position he held for six years. That same year, he organized an economic boycott in the Mississippi Delta that resulted in the desegregation of a hospital and the hiring of a number of blacks to various law enforcement and business positions.

In 1964, Evers, ELLA BAKER, UNITA BLACKWELL, AARON HENRY, and others founded the Mississippi Freedom Democratic Party (MFDP) to provide African-American voters with an alternative to the regular Democratic Party, which was antagonistic toward black participation in the electoral process. In 1965, following passage of the Voting Rights Act, he moved to Fayette in Jefferson County, a black-majority county in the Delta that had virtually no black voters. By the end of the year, he had enticed almost 2,700 African Americans to register. For the next three years, he worked hard to duplicate this success in other black-majority counties in southwest Mississippi, and to campaign for black candidates when they could get on the ballot. In 1966, he managed the campaign of Robert L. Williams; by winning a seat on the Jefferson County School Board, Williams became the state's first African American to be elected to political office since Reconstruction ended in 1877.

By 1968, Evers was probably the best-known African-American politician in the Mississippi Delta. That same year he decided to run for Congress from the state's Third District, which encompassed the southwest corner of the state. As the only black among seven candidates, he polled the most votes; however, he failed to win a majority, and he lost in the runoff to the runner-up. Buoyed by the high turnout of black voters, the following year he ran for mayor of Fayette, narrowly winning against his white opponent.

Evers's biggest challenge as mayor was to get the town's residents, black and white, to work together for the common good. Although blacks outnumbered whites, whites dominated the business community, and any perceived shift by Evers toward "black power" would have sent them packing, leaving the community an economic shambles. To his credit, he managed to incorporate blacks into city government without alienating whites. He also managed to attract new businesses, clean up a number of eyesores, and put the city budget in the black. In 1971, he ran for governor as a Loyalist Democrat, a black moderate who rejected both the radicalism of the MFDP and the conservatism of the regular Democratic apparatus. After losing, he returned to running Fayette and did such a good job that he was reelected repeatedly, serving as mayor for 20 years.

In 1972, Evers hosted a conference of 13 African-American mayors from communities across the South. The meeting proved to be so fruitful a means for finding solutions to common problems that the mayors in attendance decided to meet yearly. At their 1976 conference, they incorporated as the National Conference of Black Mayors; by 2000 membership had grown to more than 450.

Although the Loyalist Democrats reached a rapprochement with the state's regular Democratic organization in 1976, Evers never felt entirely comfortable as a member of the party's fold. In 1989, he left the party and became a Republican, a shocking move given that party's efforts to roll back civil rights during the Nixon and Reagan administrations. The shift amounted to political suicide; the Republicans gave him lukewarm support, and his former Democratic allies abandoned him. He lost his bid for reelection that same year and retired from politics. He remains in Fayette, supporting himself by the income from the Medgar Evers Shopping Center, which he owns.

Further Reading

Evers, Charles. *Evers.* New York: World Publishers, 1971.

Evers, Charles, and Andrew Szanton. *Have No Fear: The Charles Evers Story.* New York: John Wiley & Sons, 1997.

Haskins, James. *A Piece of the Power: Four Black Mayors.* New York: Dial Press, 1972.

Michel, David. "Evers, Charles." In *African American National Biography,* vol. 2, edited by Henry Louis Gates, Jr., and Evelyn Brooks Higginbotham. New York: Oxford University Press, 2008, pp. 612–613.

F

Fattah, Chaka

(1956–) *U.S. congressional representative from Pennsylvania*

Chaka Fattah got involved in electoral politics when he was a schoolboy. Since then, he has held positions in local, state, and federal government. His primary concern has been to improve educational opportunities for low-income minority students.

Fattah was born Arthur Davenport on November 21, 1956, in Philadelphia, Pennsylvania. His father, Russell, was a U.S. Army sergeant, and his mother, Frances, was a journalist. His parents divorced when he was young, and he was raised by his mother. When he was 12, his mother remarried, and she and her new husband changed the family's last name to Fattah. They also renamed the children, with Fattah being named after the legendary African warrior Chaka Zulu. The Fattahs settled in West Philadelphia and turned their residence into the House of Umoja, a home for gang members whom the Fattahs hoped to save from the street. The House of Umoja soon proved to be too small to house everyone who wanted to live in it, so Fattah took action himself. The house was surrounded by dozens of rundown, vacant row houses that were owned by a local bank. Although only 14 years old, Fattah convinced the bank's president to donate several of the houses to the

House of Umoja. Shortly thereafter, Congressman BILL GRAY helped his mother get a federal grant to fix up the homes.

Fattah became involved in politics while in junior high school. He first campaigned for mayoral candidate Hardy Williams, in the process learning the basics of getting out the vote. He also worked on Gray's reelection campaigns. As a high school student, he cofounded the Youth Movement to Clean Up Politics, a junior version of the Black Power movement in Philadelphia. The organization worked to register African-American voters and get them to the polls on election day. After high school, he attended the Community College of Philadelphia and the University of Pennsylvania's Wharton Community Education Program. In 1978, he made his first bid for public office by running for the board of city commissioners. Although only 22 years old, and therefore three years too young to hold the position legally, he ran an energetic campaign and came in fourth out of 24 candidates.

After serving for several years as the assistant director of the House of Umoja, in 1980 Fattah went to work for the city's office of housing and community development as special assistant to the director. Two years later he made his second bid for public office by challenging Nicholas Pucciarelli for his seat in the state assembly. Pucciarelli was a prominent politician with a strong base and the support of the Democratic Party. Undaunted, Fattah drew on his experience as a grassroots politician and put together a grassroots campaign that resulted in victory. Although one of the youngest members of the assembly, he sponsored seven bills that were enacted into law. Among them were measures to implement job training and to protect the rights of people without credit. He served in the state assembly for six years; during this time he received an M.A. in government administration from the University of Pennsylvania's Fels School for State and Local Government.

In 1988, Fattah won a seat in the Pennsylvania senate. He used his influence to get a number of corporations and institutions to make advance payments on their wage taxes so that the city of Philadelphia could meet its payroll during a funding crunch. He also worked to get low-income families transferred out of the slums and into single-family homes in decent neighborhoods. He then developed a program whereby the federal government would rebuild the nation's 100 largest cities over the next 10 years. As chairman of the senate education committee, he spearheaded efforts to get more students into college. He also designed and implemented Read to Lead, a state-funded summer reading program for elementary students.

In 1991, Gray retired from Congress in midterm, and Fattah declared his candidacy for the seat. He lost the special election to LUCIEN BLACKWELL but retained his seat in the state senate. In 1994, Fattah ran against Blackwell again, and this time he won. He was assigned to the committees on appropriations and House administration.

As a congressman, Fattah focused on obtaining more federal aid for higher education. In 1998 he successfully sponsored GEAR UP, a partnering program between colleges and universities and low-income high school students. Other education-related successes were the William H. Gray College Completion Grant, which offers financial assistance to low-income minority students who might otherwise have to drop out of college, and the reauthorization of the Higher Education Act, which increased student aid and lowered interest rates on student loans. He also played a key role in the enactment of bills to assist economic growth in Africa and the Caribbean, help local communities fight against drug abuse, and help the District of Columbia regain its financial stability. Fattah opposed the Iraq War during the administration of President George W. Bush. In the 2008 presidential election, he endorsed BARACK OBAMA.

While still serving in Congress, Fattah announced in 2006 that he would run for mayor of Philadelphia. His candidacy was cut short when he came in fourth in the Democratic primary. In

Chaka Fattah has long represented Philadelphia in Congress. *(Chaka Fattah)*

2008, however, Fattah was triumphant in his bid for reelection. He was reelected in 2010 to his ninth term in the House of Representatives.

Twice divorced, he is married to the former Renee Chenault and has three children.

Further Reading

Biographical Directory of the United States Congress. "Fattah, Chaka, 1956– ." Available online. URL: http://bioguide.congress.gov/scripts/biodisplay. pl?index=F000043. Downloaded April 8, 2009.

Fenno, Richard F. *Going Home: Black Representatives and Their Constituencies.* 2nd ed. Chicago: University of Chicago Press, 2003.

Zook, Nathan. "Fattah, Chaka." In *African American National Biography,* vol. 3, edited by Henry Louis Gates, Jr., and Evelyn Brooks Higginbotham. New York: Oxford University Press, 2008, pp. 233–234.

Fauntroy, Walter
(Walter Edward Fauntroy)
(1933–) *delegate to U.S. House from the District of Columbia*

Walter Fauntroy was the first African American to represent Washington, D.C., in Congress. Despite being a nonvoting delegate, he used his position to lobby successfully for increased political rights for the city's residents. He also played a prominent role in JESSE JACKSON's first campaign for the presidency.

Fauntroy was born on February 6, 1933, in Washington, D.C. His father, William, was a government clerk, and his mother, Ethel, was a homemaker. After finishing high school in 1950, he enrolled in Virginia Union University and received a B.A. in 1955. Having discerned a calling to the ministry as a youth, he enrolled in Yale University School of Divinity and received a B.D. in 1958. Two weeks after he graduated from Yale, the pastor at his church in Washington, New Bethel Baptist, died. He was chosen to take over as the new pastor, and he served in this capacity for more

than 43 years. In 1958, he married Dorothy Sims, with whom he has two children.

As pastor, Fauntroy became a leader in the Civil Rights movement in Washington. During the first two years of his ministry, he organized picket lines in front of stores that refused black patronage and led the city's Interdenominational Ministers Alliance in protest of the eviction of African-American tenants from a prime piece of downtown real estate that was scheduled to be redeveloped. His successes came to the attention of Martin Luther King, Jr., whom he had met in college, and in 1960 King asked him to become director of the Southern Christian Leadership Conference's Washington branch. In this capacity Fauntroy organized the SCLC's lobbying efforts in Congress and with the various segments of the executive branch. He also helped organize the famous 1963 March on Washington. In 1966, he founded the Model Inner City Community Organization as a means of cleaning up Washington's slums and addressing other questions of social justice in the nation's capital.

Fauntroy's involvement in Washington affairs and his lobbying efforts on behalf of the SCLC won the approval of President Lyndon B. Johnson. At the time, residents of the District of Columbia, about 85 percent of whom were African American, could vote for president and vice president but could not participate in any other elections. Governed directly by the federal government, their city council was Congress and their mayor was the president. In 1967, Johnson got Fauntroy started in politics by appointing him vice chairman of Washington's city council, essentially a presidential advisory group. In 1970, Congress passed the District of Columbia Delegate Act, thus giving Washington residents a nonvoting delegate in the U.S. House of Representatives. That same year, Fauntroy won the Democratic primary and the general election for this office. In 1971, he took his seat and was assigned to the committee on the District of Columbia.

Walter Fauntroy served in the U.S. House of Representatives as a nonvoting delegate from the District of Columbia. *(Library of Congress)*

Fauntroy used his position in Congress to gain greater political rights for district residents. He and U.S. senator EDWARD BROOKE formed a national coalition to get black voters to write their congressmen and request them to support home rule for Washington, specifically the establishment of an elected mayor and city council. As a result, the House District Committee drafted legislation establishing home rule; however, John L. McMillan, the committee's chairman, refused to send the legislation to the House for a vote. So, in the congressional election of 1972, Fauntroy campaigned among McMillan's black constituents and got enough of them to vote against McMillan, who then lost. He then persuaded the other members of the committee to release the legislation, and in 1974 his efforts finally came to fruition. That same year, WALTER WASHINGTON was

elected mayor of Washington, along with a complete slate of city councilmen, albeit with limited authority to run the city in accordance with the wishes of its residents.

Fauntroy next turned his attention to getting voting representation in Congress for the district. His biggest obstacle was that such representation was unconstitutional and could only be achieved by amending the Constitution. Undaunted, Fauntroy began lobbying his fellow congresspersons, and in 1978 he succeeded in getting them to approve an amendment proposal to give the district two seats in the Senate and proportional representation in the House. The proposal was then sent to the states for ratification but failed to gain enough support. The measure was defeated, not because of racism (as some charged) but because of partisan politics, pure and simple. Washington was a Democratic stronghold during presidential elections, and Republicans across the country feared that ratifying the amendment would give the Democrats two more votes in the Senate. In 1987, he attempted to revive the proposal, but the Republican- controlled Congress showed little interest in it.

In 1981, Fauntroy was named chairman of the Congressional Black Caucus, which he had cofounded 10 years earlier. For two years, he led the caucus's opposition to the policies of President Ronald Reagan, who sought to undo many of the gains made by African Americans over the previous 15 years. Although the caucus succeeded in making Martin Luther King's birthday a national holiday, most of the rest of its agenda under Fauntroy's chairmanship failed to be enacted. By the end of his chairmanship in 1983, he had become convinced that the time was right for an African American to mount a serious run for the presidency, if for no other reason than to establish a national forum on the African-American condition. Not wishing the position for himself, he convinced Jesse Jackson, his former SCLC comrade, to run and then signed on as a campaign strategist. Although Jackson performed well in the 1984 Democratic primaries, he fell short of gaining the party's nomination. Meanwhile, the national forum Jackson's candidacy was supposed to engender failed to materialize to Fauntroy's satisfaction.

After 1984, Fauntroy focused his attention on foreign affairs. As a member of the House Banking Committee, he initiated a congressional examination of the Third World's mounting debt problem. He also played an important role in attacking apartheid in South Africa and human rights violations in Haiti and Zaire.

In 1990, after almost 20 years in Congress, Fauntroy resigned his seat to run for mayor of Washington. His campaign failed to excite much interest, and he was defeated in the Democratic primary by SHARON PRATT DIXON KELLY. Since his defeat he has opened a lobbyist consulting firm whose clients have included South Africa's African National Congress. Fauntroy continues to serve as pastor of the New Bethel Baptist Church in Washington, D.C.

Further Reading

Biographical Directory of the United States Congress. "Fauntroy, Walter Edward, 1933–   ." Available online. URL: http://bioguide.congress.gov/scripts/biodisplay.pl?index=F000046. Downloaded April 9, 2009.

Black Americans in Congress. "Walter Edward Fauntroy." Available online. URL: http://baic.house.gov/member-profiles/profile.html?intID=78. Downloaded April 8, 2009.

Clay, William L. *Just Permanent Interests: Black Americans in Congress, 1870–1992.* New York: Amistad Press, 1993.

Spelman, Duncan. *Walter E. Fauntroy, Democratic Representative from District of Columbia.* Washington: Grossman, 1972.

Fenty, Adrian M.

(1970–   ) *mayor of Washington, D.C.*

In 2007, 36-year-old Adrian M. Fenty was inaugurated as the youngest mayor in the history of Washington, D.C. Born on December 6, 1970, Fenty grew up in the nation's capital in a family of three boys. For much of his youth, his father Phil stayed home with the children, while his mother Jan supported the family by working as a special education teacher. When Fenty was a teenager, his parents opened Fleet Feet, an athletic shoe store where he and his brothers worked nights and weekends. Also during his teens, Fenty was introduced to marathon running by his father. Fenty has since become an avid runner, frequently entering marathons and triathlons.

After graduating from high school, Fenty attended Oberlin College in Ohio, where he majored in English and economics. He then returned to Washington, D.C., to study law at Howard University. There, he met his wife Michelle. The Fentys have three children.

In 1996, Fenty began working as a probate lawyer. At the same time, he became increasingly interested in civic affairs. After moving to the Crestwood area, he joined the 16th Street Neighborhood Association and became a member of the city's Advisory Neighborhood Commission.

In 2000, Fenty made his first bid for elective office. He ran for the city council from Ward 4, a position that had been held by Charlene Drew Jarvis for more than 20 years. Fenty took to the pavement, going door to door to persuade voters to support his candidacy. The personal touch paid off. In the Democratic primary, he was elected by a 57-43 percent margin. Fenty then easily won the general election in his heavily Democratic ward. He was reelected in 2004.

While a city councilman, Fenty got a reputation for quickly responding to his constituents' needs and complaints. When he failed to get a speedy reaction from city agencies, he was known for trying to solve problems himself, going so far as filling in potholes and fixing broken street lamps. Fenty also became known for his strained relationship with his fellow council members. At council meetings, he spoke little and often sent e-mails to his office, completely ignoring the discussion at hand.

In 2006, after only six years on the council, Fenty announced his decision to run for mayor. In the Democratic primary, his challenger was Linda Cropp, the city council chair. Fenty returned to his old campaign strategy of making personal appeals to voters. During the campaign, he estimated that he had knocked on the doors of half the homes in the D.C. area. Once again, the approach led to victory, first in the primary, and then in the general election.

Soon after being sworn in, Fenty set out to tackle one of Washington, D.C.'s most vexing problems—its failing school system. With the support of the council, he took over the city schools and reassigned many of the school board's responsibilities to a new school chancellor. Fenty also pursued an aggressive plan to increase development deals citywide.

Over all, Fenty's first term drew mixed reviews. He was credited with improving local schools and decreasing the city's homicide rate. But Fenty was also widely criticized for his unwillingness to deal with Washington's budget troubles and his handling of city services during a series of heavy snowstorms in early 2010. Despite a dramatic drop in approval ratings, Fenty decided to run for reelection to second term. Early in the Democratic primary, it became clear that Fenty no longer appealed to middle-class black voters. They largely threw their support to City Council Chairman Vincent C. Gray, leading to Fenty's surprise defeat. In his first public remarks after the primary election, Fenty stated that he did not expect to run for elected office again.

Further Reading

Jaffe, Harry. "Adrian Fenty: Born to Run." *Washingtonian* magazine, November 2008. Available online. URL: http://www.washingtonian.com/print/articles/6/173/9958.html. Downloaded May 9, 2009.

Manheim, James M. "Adrian M. Fenty, 1970– ." *Contemporary Black Biography* 60 (2007): 60–62.

Williams, Vanessa. "See How He Runs." *Washington Post,* August 31, 2006. Available online. URL: http://www.washingtonpost.com/wp-dyn/content/article/2006/08/30/AR2006083003248.html. Downloaded May 9, 2009.

Fields, Cleo
(1962–) *U.S. congressional representative from Louisiana*

By age 34, Cleo Fields had served six years in the Louisiana state senate and four years in the U.S. House of Representatives. Then he retired from public life after losing his bid for governor of Louisiana, but less than a year after leaving politics, he was elected to the state senate.

Fields was born on November 22, 1962, in Port Arthur, Louisiana. His father, Isidore, was a dock worker, and his mother, Alice, was a homemaker. His father died when he was four, after which the family moved to Baton Rouge. Fields worked several jobs while in high school, and a position with the Mayor's Office of Youth Opportunity helped him pay his way through college. He received a B.A. in mass communications from Southern University in 1984, then enrolled in Southern's law school and received a J.D. three years later.

Fields's political career began while he was still in law school. In 1986, he began campaigning for a seat in the Louisiana senate. His opponent, Republican Richard Turnley, had served in the senate for years, and he seemed to be well-liked by his constituents. Many political observers considered Turnley to be unbeatable, and no Democrat other than Fields would challenge him. Fields countered Turnley's advantages by running a high-energy campaign that mobilized scores of college students, and he barely beat Turnley in the general election. In 1987, the same year he completed his education, he took a seat in the senate. At age 24, he was its youngest member, and he was occasionally mistaken for a page.

As a state senator, Fields sponsored several bills to toughen the state's laws against the use and distribution of illegal drugs in the vicinity of schools. He worked to protect the environment from the petrochemical companies that line the Mississippi River between Baton Rouge and New Orleans. He played an important role in getting African Americans hired into a number of state jobs. He gained passage of an inner-city economic development program to benefit Baton Rouge, among other cities, and he chaired the committee that redrew the state's congressional districts following the census of 1990. As chairman, he oversaw the successful effort to create a black-majority district centered around Baton Rouge, his hometown.

Fields first ran for Congress in 1990. Undaunted by his defeat, he ran again in 1992 and won. He left the senate to take his seat the following year and was assigned to the committees on small business and banking, finance, and urban affairs. He quickly emerged as one of the most liberal congressman in the House. He supported abortion rights, increased funding for public health, and reductions in the military budget following the end of the cold war. He introduced bills to increase funding for education and to protect consumers from the fraudulent practices of financial institutions. Back home, he established the Congressional Classroom, a program that taught elementary students about government while also developing leadership skills and self-esteem.

During his four years in Congress, Fields was involved in three controversies. The first concerned his district, which he had played a major role in shaping. On a map it looked like a "Z," and its legality was challenged in federal court on the grounds that it had been gerrymandered on the basis of race. It was redrawn in time for the election of 1992, which Fields won. The second concerned the alleged abuse of power. Several critics charged him with using his positions on the small business and finance committees to entice businesses to relocate to his district. The most damaging controversy concerned a newsletter he sent to

his constituents. In 1995, he declared his candidacy for governor of Louisiana, and the newsletter was attacked as a thinly veiled piece of campaign literature.

Fields's candidacy for governor generated controversy in other ways as well. P. B. S. PINCHBACK had served as governor during Reconstruction, but many critics, Democrats as well as Republicans, stated openly that Louisianans were not ready to elect a black governor. They were surprised when Fields won the Democratic primary in a crowded race. His Republican opponent, Mike Foster, refused to take Fields's candidacy lightly. Foster appealed vigorously to the conservative portion of the electorate without raising the question of race. He also attacked the newsletter as just another example of government waste, a charge that the Fields campaign could never counter. Foster's smart campaign, coupled with the lukewarm support given Fields by state Democrats, led to Fields's defeat in the general election.

Fields chose not to run for reelection to Congress in 1996. Upon leaving office the following year, he returned to Baton Rouge. He founded a general consulting firm, Cleo Fields and Associates, with himself as president and CEO. In 1997, he returned to politics, winning election to his old seat in the state senate. Fields remained in office until 2007, when the Louisiana State Supreme Court ruled that he could not run for reelection because of term limits. He is married to the former Debra Horton, with whom he has two children.

Further Reading

Biographical Directory of the United States Congress. "Fields, Cleo, 1962– ." Available online. URL: http://bioguide.congress.gov/scripts/biodisplay. pl?index=F000110. Downloaded April 8, 2009.

Black Americans in Congress. "Cleo Fields." Available online. URL: http://baic.house.gov/member-profiles/profile.html?intID=77. Downloaded April 8, 2009.

Clay, William L. *Just Permanent Interests: Black Americans in Congress, 1870–1992.* New York: Amistad Press, 1993.

"Introducing Cleo Fields." *Ebony* 44 (November 1988): 180–181.

Flake, Floyd
(Floyd Harold Flake)
(1945–   ) *U.S. congressional representative from New York*

Reverend Floyd Flake was an anomaly among his black colleagues in Congress. He placed greater faith than they did in the free enterprise system as a vehicle for improving the lot of African Americans. Instead of federal entitlement programs, he preferred that the government assist private self-help programs, like the ones that had been so successful at his church.

Flake was born on January 30, 1945, in Los Angeles, California. His father, Robert, was a janitor, and his mother, Rosie, was a homemaker. As a young boy, he moved with his family to Houston, Texas, where he grew up. In 1963, he graduated from high school and enrolled in Wilberforce University, receiving a B.A. in 1967. For the next three years, he did social work and sold tobacco products and copiers while preparing for the ministry at Payne Theological Seminary in Dayton, Ohio. In 1970, he was named associate dean of students and director of student activities at Lincoln University in Pennsylvania. Three years later, he became dean of students and university chaplain at Boston University.

In 1976, Flake moved to New York City to become pastor of Allen African Methodist Episcopal (AME) Church in Queens. Under his leadership, the church developed a number of important community outreach programs including a senior citizen complex, a health clinic, a home care agency, a housing construction corporation, a bus company, a school, and two Head Start programs. His vision for the church was that it could provide the sort of financial and social underpinning its members needed to change their neighborhoods for the better without having to rely on government.

In early 1986, the U.S. representative for Flake's district, Joseph Addabbo, died while in office. Flake was urged by a number of his fellow Queens clergymen to run in the special election to fill the remainder of Addabbo's term. Undaunted by his loss, to Alton R. Waldon, Flake ran even harder for the regular election in 1986. This time he received the support of Mayor Ed Koch, whom Flake had campaigned for on several occasions. Koch's endorsement gained Flake a number of key votes among his Italian and Jewish constituents, which led to his victory. He took his seat in 1987 and was assigned to the committees on small business and banking/finance/urban affairs.

As a congressman, Flake focused on issues related to housing. In 1990 he introduced the Peace Dividend Housing Act; this act diverted funds from the military budget, which could be reduced because the cold war had ended, to public housing projects. He wrote several of the provisions in the Housing Programs Reauthorization Act, which focused on improving public housing, and the Home Ownership Plan Encouragement Act, which focused on improving private housing. He is best remembered for writing the Bank Enterprise Act of 1994. This act provided incentives for financial institutions to invest in destabilized urban and rural economies, and it increased significantly the flow of capital for commercial and residential lending into struggling communities.

Despite being a Democrat, Flake often found himself allied with conservative Republicans. He was one of a very few Democrats who supported the Republicans' Contract with America, a package of conservative reform legislation. In so doing, however, he won the inclusion of important pledges to improve the lot of urban Americans, pledges not included in the contract's original version. He supported the Republican-backed Community Renewal Act, which used free-market principles such as tax breaks to improve conditions in urban neighborhoods. He bucked the Congressional Black Caucus and New York City's public school teachers and administrators by supporting school vouchers. Most opponents viewed vouchers as a way for conservative whites to avoid sending their children to integrated schools, but Flake saw them as providing a powerful incentive to public schools to improve the effectiveness of their classrooms and to instill their students with values and discipline.

Unlike most African Americans, Flake rejected reliance on the government as the primary strategy by which blacks could achieve success. He pointed to the success of his church at helping African Americans get ahead and offered it as a model in place of government entitlement programs. Conservative Republicans embraced his ideas while liberal Democrats were less sure what to make of them.

Flake was reelected five times. While in Congress, he continued to fulfill his duties as a full-time minister. In 1994, he earned a doctorate in ministry from the United Theological Seminary. In 1997, he resigned in midterm in order to devote himself more completely to Allen AME. He later became a senior fellow at the Manhattan Institute for Policy Research, a think tank for developing and promoting ideas about greater economic choice and individual responsibility. In 2002, he was appointed president of Wilberforce University in Ohio. He is married to the former Elaine McCollins, with whom he has four children.

Further Reading

Baker, Russ. "The Ecumenist," *The American Prospect* 11, no. 5 (January 17, 2000): 26–32.

Biographical Directory of the United States Congress. "Flake, Floyd Harold." Available online. URL: http://bioguide.congress.gov/scripts/biodisplay.pl?index=F000184. Downloaded April 9, 2009.

Black Americans in Congress. "Floyd Harold Flake." Available online. URL: http://baic.house.gov/ member-profiles/profile.html?intID=76. Downloaded April 10, 2009.

Explorations in Black Leadership. "Floyd Flake." Available online. URL: http://www.virginia.edu/ publichistory/bl/index.php?uid=10. Downloaded April 9, 2009.

Flake, Floyd, and Donna M. Williams. *The Way of the Bootstrapper: Nine Action Steps for Achieving Your Dreams.* San Francisco: HarperSanFrancisco, 1999.

Ford, Harold
(Harold Eugene Ford, Sr.)
(1945–   ) *U.S. congressional representative from Tennessee*

Harold Ford was the first African American to represent Tennessee in the U.S. Congress. At the time of his election, he was the youngest person ever elected to Congress. He also serves as head of the Ford family, one of the state's leading political dynasties.

Ford was born on May 20, 1945, in Memphis, Tennessee. His father, Newton, owned a funeral home, and his mother, Vera, was a homemaker. After finishing high school in 1963, he enrolled in Tennessee State University, receiving a B.S. four years later. In 1969, he received an A.A. in mortuary science from John Gupton College and went to work for his father. That same year he married Dorothy Bowles, with whom he has three children. In 1982 he received an M.B.A. from Howard University.

Ford became involved in politics in 1964, when he worked on his father's unsuccessful campaign for the Tennessee state legislature. In 1970, he was elected as a Democrat to the first of two terms in the general assembly. He distinguished himself during his second term by chairing a select committee that investigated local utility companies that refused to provide service to minorities and the poor.

In 1974, Ford ran for Memphis's seat in the U.S. House of Representatives. His opponent was

Daniel Kuykendall, the Republican incumbent who staunchly supported President Richard M. Nixon throughout the Watergate hearings. Ford's campaign linked Kuykendall to Nixon, whose popularity by then was abysmal, and lambasted the incumbent for neglecting the needs of his Memphis constituents. Following a hard-fought campaign, Ford was elected by fewer than 800 votes, thus becoming the state's first black congressman. He took his seat in 1975 and was assigned to the committees on banking, currency and housing, and veterans' affairs.

During his second term, Ford was appointed to the prestigious committee on ways and means. As chairman of the subcommittee on health, he worked to increase federal funding for health care for the poor and elderly. After 1981, he chaired the subcommittee on public assistance and unemployment compensation. He is best remembered for chairing the subcommittee on welfare reform during the Clinton administration, when the entire welfare system underwent a major overhaul.

As Tennessee's only African-American congressman, Ford was also the unofficial head of the Ford family. The family has controlled politics in Memphis since 1974; on the same day Ford was elected to Congress, his brother John was elected to the state senate and his brother Emmitt was elected to the state assembly. His brothers Michael and James were later elected to the Memphis city council. The family has maintained its hold on the loyalty of Memphis's black voters, who constitute a slight majority, by rewarding supporters with political appointments, paying close attention to the needs of constituents, and turning out the vote on election days for themselves and the local candidates of their choice.

Ford's political reputation was tarnished somewhat in 1990, when he was charged with 18 counts of bank and mail fraud. The charges involved more than $1.2 million in alleged political payoffs disguised as bank loans. His first trial, in 1990, ended in a hung jury, while his second trial, in 1993, ended in his acquittal. Despite his innocence, he was pressured to step down as chairman of the House subcommittees.

Ford was reelected 10 times. In 1996, he announced that he would retire upon the completion of his current term. He was succeeded by his son, HAROLD FORD, JR. Upon returning to Memphis, he opened a consulting firm that specializes in lobbying Congress and federal agencies on behalf of the health, transportation, and telecommunications industries. He continues to be an important figure in Memphis politics.

Further Reading

Biographical Directory of the United States Congress. "Ford, Harold Eugene, 1945– ." Available online. URL: http://bioguide.congress.gov/scripts/biodisplay.pl?index=F000261. Downloaded April 9, 2002.

Black Americans in Congress. "Harold Eugene Ford, Sr." Available online. URL: http://baic.house.gov/member-profiles/profile.html?intID=74. Downloaded April 8, 2009.

Clay, William L. *Just Permanent Interests: Black Americans in Congress, 1870–1992.* New York: Amistad Press, 1993.

Ford, Harold, Jr.
(Harold Eugene Ford, Jr.)
(1970–   ) *U.S. congressional representative from Tennessee*

Harold Ford, Jr., was a second-generation congressman. Like his father, HAROLD FORD, Ford was elected to Congress at a relatively young age. Unlike his father (but like many African Americans of his own generation), Ford has emerged as more of a political centrist than a traditional liberal.

Ford was born on May 11, 1970, in Memphis, Tennessee. His mother, Dorothy, worked for the U.S. Department of Agriculture. Between 1975 and 1997, the senior Ford represented Memphis in the U.S. House of Representatives, so Ford grew up in both Memphis and Washington, D.C. After finishing high school in 1988, he enrolled in the University of Pennsylvania, receiving a B.A. in American history four years later. He then went to the University of Michigan Law School and received a J.D. in 1996.

Ford comes from a thoroughly political family. Harold Ford, Sr., and his four brothers were lifelong politicians: John served in the Tennessee senate, Emmitt served in the state legislature, and Michael and James served on the Memphis city council. Together they constituted the Ford family, and they maintained a tight grip on the loyalty of Memphis's black voters. The Ford Family's winning ways were predicated upon its philosophy of delivering the goods. The family made sure to reward supporters with political appointments, pay close attention to the needs of constituents, and turn out the vote on election days for themselves and the local candidates of their choice. The younger Ford learned these lessons by watching his father and uncles in operation.

Not surprisingly, Ford became interested in politics at a young age. When he was five, he remarked to his mother during his father's swearing-in ceremony that he wanted to grow up to be a congressman, too. The senior Ford took him to meetings of the Congressional Black Caucus, and he became personally acquainted with such important African-American congressmen as CHARLES RANGEL. In 1992, just graduated from college, he coordinated his father's reelection campaign. Following the election, he joined president-elect Bill Clinton's transition team as a special assistant for justice and civil rights. In 1993, he served as a special assistant in the U.S. Department of Commerce's Economic Development Administration. In 1994, he served once again as his father's campaign manager.

In 1996, Ford made his own run for political office. His father had announced his retirement, and Ford declared his candidacy to succeed him. Although he was far younger than the other can-

didates, his name recognition took him a lot further; he had buttons and T-shirts printed up that simply said, "Jr." Not surprisingly, he won an easy victory. He took his father's seat in 1997 and was assigned to the committees on education/workforce and government reform/oversight.

As a congressman, Ford focused on improving education. He supported wholeheartedly the underlying assumptions of the No Child Left Behind Act of 2001, which calls for increased funding for public schools as well as greater accountability from them regarding the achievements of K–12 students. He wrote a bill to make college affordable by making such college- related expenses as tuition, fees, and room and board tax deductible. These ideas were eventually passed into law via their inclusion in the Economic Growth and Tax Relief Reconciliation Act of 2001. Other Ford initiatives include bills to help consumers better understand and be protected by the credit reporting system, to cover the cost of prescription drugs under Medicare, and to expand the opportunity to perform national and community service by increasing funding for the AmeriCorps national service program. In 2000 Ford delivered the keynote address at the Democratic National Convention, and in 2004 he was reelected to his fifth term in the House of Representatives.

Ford is one of a growing breed of young African-American Democrats looking for ways to transcend the political status quo. Many black voters and politicians have become disappointed with the lack of progress on issues of special interest to them during the 1980s, when the Republicans under presidents Ronald Reagan and George Bush rolled back many of the gains made during the Civil Rights movement. To a degree, they blame the Democrats for this situation. They perceive that the Democratic Party has taken the black vote for granted and therefore has not taken a stronger pro-African-American position. At the same time, they perceive that the major problems facing the nation are more related to economic class than to race. To this end, Ford and other representatives of his generation are working to achieve progress through moderate organizations such as the New Democrat Coalition as well as the Blue Dog Coalition, a group of fiscally conservative House Democrats. Less liberal than their leaders, they have broken with House Democratic leadership on a number of issues such as a balanced budget and school prayer.

In early 2006, Ford formally announced his candidacy for the U.S. Senate. He easily won the Democratic primary, but faced formidable opposition from Republican candidate Bob Corker in the general election. Ford enjoyed a slight lead before, late in the campaign, the Republican Party ran an advertisement that implied Ford was a womanizer who sought out the company of white women. The ad was widely denounced as racist, but soon after it started airing, Corker pulled ahead in the polls. Corker subsequently won the election by less than 3 percentage points.

After his defeat, Ford was hired as a news analyst by the Fox News Channel and by MSNBC. In 2007, he became a vice chairman of the brokerage firm Merrill Lynch and was appointed to a visiting professorship at the University of Texas at Austin named in honor of Texas congresswoman BARBARA JORDAN. The same year, Ford became the chairman of the Democratic Leadership Council, a nonprofit organization representing centrist Democratic politicians. In early 2010, it was widely rumored that Ford would run for the Senate in New York State, but in an op-ed article featured in the *New York Times* on March 1, he announced that he had decided not to enter the campaign.

Further Reading

Biographical Directory of the United States Congress. "Ford, Harold, Jr., 1970– ." Available online. URL: http://bioguide.congress.gov/scripts/biodisplay. pl?index=F000262. Downloaded October 19, 2002.

Black Americans in Congress. "Harold Ford, Jr.." Available online. URL: http://baic.house.gov/member-profiles/profile.html?intID=75. Downloaded April 12, 2009.

Clemetson, Lynette. "Losing the Old Labels." *Newsweek* 139, no. 4 (January 28, 2002): 50–51.

Idani, Michaeljulius. "Ford, Harold, Jr." In *African American National Biography*, vol. 3, edited by Henry Louis Gates, Jr., and Evelyn Brooks Higginbotham. New York: Oxford University Press, 2008, pp. 313–314.

Kolbert, Elizabeth. "Next Generation: Harold E. Ford, Jr." *New Yorker* 75, no. 31 (October 18–25, 1999): 135.

Ford, James
(James William Ford)
(1893–1957) *candidate for U.S. vice president*

By the 1920s, many African Americans had become dissatisfied with the Republican Party. Despite being the party of Lincoln, the Great Emancipator, the party was perceived as having turned its back on black people. Most African Americans sought a new home in the Democratic Party, but a few became communists instead. The most prominent African-American Communist was James Ford, three-time party candidate for vice president.

Ford was born James William Foursche on December 22, 1893, in Pratt City, Alabama. His father, Lyman, was a steelworker, and his mother, Nancy, was a domestic worker. When Ford was a boy, the family name was changed by a white policeman who was unable to spell "Foursche." At age 13, Ford went to work as a water boy for the company that employed his father. In 1914, he graduated from high school and enrolled in Fisk University, but he dropped out three years later to enlist in the U.S. Army. He served in France during World War I as a noncommissioned officer and radio engineer in the Signal Corps. Discharged in 1919, he returned to Fisk and received a B.A. the following year. In 1920 he moved to Chicago, Illinois, in search of a job in the radio industry. Denied a skilled position because of his race, he eventually landed a job as a parcel dispatcher with the U.S. Post Office, which he held for the next seven years. At some point he married (his wife's name is not known) and fathered three sons; he and his wife later separated under circumstances unknown. He later married a woman whose name is given alternately as Mary and Reva.

The radicalization of Ford began in the 1920s. Previously, he had subscribed to the self-help creed of Booker T. Washington, who had argued fervently that the best way for African Americans to overcome racism was to get an education, work hard, and get ahead economically. In Chicago, Ford began to suspect that it was more complicated than that. As a means of combating racial prejudice within the post office, he joined the postal workers' union and began rising through its ranks. He also joined the Trade Union Educational League, an arm of the American Communist Party. In 1925, he helped organize the left-wing American Negro Labor Congress, and the following year he became a full-fledged party member.

Like BEN DAVIS, Ford found a home in the Communist Party. Marxist doctrine emphasized class struggle and fostered solidarity among all oppressed people regardless of race. Communist leaders believed that African Americans were particularly amenable to being radicalized, and they worked assiduously to recruit black workers into communist organizations. Ford's militant stance won him many followers, but it also got him into trouble with postal and union leaders alike. In 1927, he lost his job, allegedly as a result of being framed by a supervisor and a union leader whose bigotry he had criticized.

After being fired, Ford moved to Harlem in New York City, headquarters of the Communist Party USA. That same year he traveled to Moscow as a delegate to the International Labor Union (ILU) convention and was elected to its executive committee. He returned to Moscow the following year and was appointed to the Commu-

nist International's Negro Commission. Upon returning to New York City, he helped organize the Trade Union Unity League, the U.S. branch of the ILU, and served as leader of its Negro Department. Meanwhile, he was arrested in 1929 for protesting the U.S. incursion into Haiti and in 1932 for participating in the Bonus March whereby World War I veterans marched on Washington, D.C., to demand payment of the bonus they had been voted by Congress in 1924.

In 1932, Ford was nominated by the Communist Party to run for vice president of the United States and he toured the nation with William Z. Foster, the party's presidential nominee. During this and later campaigns, Ford called on white Americans to recognize that African Americans had a right to a decent and secure livelihood and to full equality in all aspects of society. He and Foster received more than 100,000 votes in the election of 1932, but they were defeated by millions of votes to the Democratic candidate, Franklin Delano Roosevelt. He returned to New York City after the election to assume control of the party's Harlem section. In 1936, he was nominated for vice president again, running this time with Earl Browder, and again received more than 100,000 votes. In 1938, he ran for the U.S. Senate, and in 1940 he ran a third time for vice president. This time he and Browder received fewer than 50,000 votes.

Although Ford never ran for election after 1940, he remained active in the affairs of the Communist Party and its related organizations. He died on June 21, 1957, in New York City.

Further Reading

Ford, James W., and James S. Allen. *The Negroes in a Soviet America*. New York: Workers Library Publishers, 1935.

Foster, William Z. *History of the Communist Party of the United States*. New York: Greenwood Press, 1968.

Logan, Rayford W., and Michael R. Winston, eds. *Dictionary of American Negro Biography*. New York: W. W. Norton, 1982.

Opdycke, Sandra. "Ford, James William." In *African American National Biography,* vol. 3, edited by Henry Louis Gates, Jr., and Evelyn Brooks Higginbotham. New York: Oxford University Press, 2008, pp. 316–317.

Record, Wilson. *The Negro and the Communist Party.* Chapel Hill: University of North Carolina Press, 1951.

Foster, Ezola

(1938–   ) *candidate for U.S. vice president*

During the 1980s, a number of African Americans began turning to the political right in an effort to overcome what they deemed to be the failure of affirmative action. These black conservatives espoused a return to traditional American values, emphasizing personal responsibility and initiative in place of overly relying on federal assistance. In 2000, Ezola Foster became the most visible of these conservative blacks when she was chosen to run as vice president on the Reform Party ticket.

Foster was born on August 9, 1938, in Maurice, Louisiana. Her father was in the military, and her mother was a homemaker. At age two, she moved with her family to Houston, Texas. When she was five, her parents divorced, and for the next 13 years she divided her time between her mother's home in Houston and the home of her maternal grandparents, Doris and Anastasia Catalon, in Maurice. In 1956, she graduated from high school in Houston and enrolled in Texas Southern University, receiving a B.S. in business education in 1960. That same year, she moved to Los Angeles, California. In 1963, after working for three years as a legal secretary, she became a teacher in the Los Angeles Unified School District. For the next 33 years, she taught high school English, business, and typing. In 1973, she earned an M.S. in school management and administration from Pepperdine University, and thereafter she also worked as a school administrator. In 1977, she married Chuck Foster, with whom she has three children; an earlier marriage was annulled.

Foster became active in politics while in college. She joined the Democratic Party in 1959 and for 17 years worked for party candidates in Houston and Los Angeles. In 1976, she realized that, while her own political views were becoming increasingly conservative, the Democratic Party in general was becoming increasingly liberal. That same year, she left the party and joined the Republicans. For the next 17 years, she worked as hard for Republican candidates as she once had for Democrats. In 1984 and 1986, she ran for a seat in the California state assembly, losing both times to MAXINE WATERS.

Meanwhile, Foster continued to drift toward the right. In 1987, she founded and became president of Black Americans for Family Values, a conservative group that opposed the erosion of morals in American life, particularly the deemphasis on religious training in the public schools (the group later dropped "Black" from its name). In 1994, she spoke out in favor of Proposition 187, the controversial California initiative to deny education and other government benefits to illegal aliens. She also defended the Los Angeles Police Department after four white officers were accused of violating the civil rights of Rodney King, the black motorist whom they had beaten when he refused to cooperate during a routine traffic stop. When she left teaching in 1996, she accepted a position as traveling speaker for the John Birch Society, an anticommunist organization that also promotes various ultraconservative causes.

At some point, Foster met Pat Buchanan, who had assumed the leadership of the Republican far right at the party's national convention in 1992. Despite differences of race and gender, the two found themselves to be ideological soul mates. When Buchanan sought the Republican nomination for president in 1996, Foster cochaired his campaign. She left the Republican Party in 1996, then joined Buchanan three years later in the Reform Party. This party had been founded by H. Ross Perot in 1992 as a vehicle to promote his own presidential ambitions, but it had survived two unsuccessful Perot candidacies to emerge as the voice of staunch conservatives. In 2000, Buchanan named her national cochair of Independents for Buchanan, his effort to capture the Reform Party's nomination for president. Upon winning the nomination, he named Foster his running mate.

As a candidate for vice president, Foster pledged to reform public education. In particular, she espoused reducing the influence of the federal government, which she claimed had ruined public education. She decried school lunches and the banning of school prayer as just two examples of government efforts to convert schools into "socialist training camps." She also spoke out against immigration, condemned homosexuality, demanded that English be made the nation's official language, and called for the implementation of the Jeffersonian idea that "that government is best which governs least." The Buchanan-Foster ticket polled almost 450,000 popular votes nationwide but failed to win any electoral votes.

In 2001, Foster ran for the congressional seat left vacant by the death of JULIAN DIXON. Her bid to become the first Reform Party candidate elected to Congress was not realized. In 2002, Foster joined the conservative Constitution Party, which, according to its Web site, seeks to "restore [the U.S.] government to its Constitutional limits and [its] law to its Biblical foundations."

Further Reading

Faryna, Stan, et al. *Black and Right: The Bold New Voice of Black Conservatives in America.* Westport, Conn.: Praeger, 1997.
Foster, Ezola, with Sarah Coleman. *What's Right for All Americans.* Waco, Tex.: WRS Publishing, 1995.
The Washington Post. "Ezola Foster: Pat Buchanan's Far Right Hand." Available online. URL: http://fluoridationcenter.org/papers/2000/washingtonpost091300.htm. Downloaded April 8, 2009.

Franklin, Shirley
(Shirley Clarke Franklin, Shirley Clarke)
(1945–   ) *mayor of Atlanta, Georgia*

On January 7, 2002, Shirley Franklin was sworn in as Atlanta's first female mayor. She also became the first African-American woman to lead a major Southern city.

Born Shirley Clarke on May 10, 1945, she was raised in Philadelphia, Pennsylvania. As a girl, she had little interest in becoming a politician, but instead hoped to become a professional dancer. After graduating from the Philadelphia High School for Girls, Franklin attended Howard University in Washington, D.C. While in college, she volunteered to work in the office of Congresswoman SHIRLEY CHISHOLM. In 1968, Franklin received a bachelor's degree in sociology from Howard. The following year, she earned a master's at the University of Pennsylvania.

In 1972, she married David McCoy Franklin. The couple settled in Atlanta, Georgia. They had three children before divorcing in 1986.

Franklin was introduced to Atlanta politics when her husband worked on the campaign of MAYNARD JACKSON, who became the city's first black mayor in 1974. Franklin joined the city government as the commissioner of cultural affairs in 1978. From 1982 to 1990, she served as the city manager under Mayor ANDREW YOUNG. Responsible for the daily operations of Atlanta's government, she was the first female manager of such a large city in the United States. Her visibility in this post earned her the nickname "Mayor Shirley."

Beginning a third term as mayor, Maynard Jackson appointed Franklin the executive officer of operations in 1990. She left this job the following year to become a member of the Atlanta Committee for the Olympic Games. For five years, she helped prepare the city to host the Olympic Summer Games in 1996.

After the Olympics, she founded Shirley Clarke Franklin & Associates, a consulting firm. Franklin also joined the Georgia Regional Transportation Authority as vice chairman. She resigned from this position in 2000 when she announced her intention to run for mayor.

Later, Franklin told *Newsweek* that she made the decision "very reluctantly." Although others in city government had pushed her to run, she worried about living in the limelight. To gain confidence and to introduce herself to voters, Franklin campaigned for two years. She proved especially adept at fund-raising. She received twice as many campaign contributions as her main rival, Atlanta city council president Rob Pitts. Even so, the race remained close. In the end, however, Franklin won enough votes to become mayor without having to face a runoff.

From the start, Mayor Shirley Franklin had to work hard to restore the voters' confidence in the city government. Her predecessor, BILL CAMPBELL, had been under investigation for corruption. Franklin signaled that her administration would be different by establishing a new ethics code for municipal employees. She also demonstrated that she wanted to be responsive to citizens' needs by establishing the popular "pothole posse." This team of workers repaired Atlanta's long neglected city streets. Franklin's greatest challenge, however, was to reduce Atlanta's growing budget deficit. She conducted a massive audit, funded through contributions from the private sector, to determine how the budget could be cut.

Franklin won reelection in 2005 by a landslide. The management skills she displayed in her first term also earned her national media attention. *Time* magazine named her one of the five best big-city mayors, and *U.S. News & World Report* featured her in an issue focusing on the best leaders of 2005. The same year, she received the Profiles in Courage Award from the John F. Kennedy Library Foundation.

Budget troubles continued to plague Franklin during her second term. As a general economic downturn cut into tax revenues, she pushed through unpopular measures such as laying off city employees and raising property taxes. Prevented from running for a third consecutive term by law, she stated that she was "determined to leave this city on firm financial footing." After leaving officer, Franklin accepted a professorship at Spelman College. Many in Atlanta political circles believe that Franklin will one day run for governor.

Further Reading

LaBalle, Candace. "Shirley Clarke Franklin, 1945– ." *Contemporary Black Biography*, 34 (2002): 53–56.
"Meet the Mayor: Atlanta Mayor Shirley Franklin." City of Atlanta Online. Available online. URL: http://www.atlantaga.gov/Mayor/Meet.aspx. Downloaded May 21, 2009.

Franks, Gary
(Gary Alvin Franks)
(1953–) *U.S. congressional representative from Connecticut*

At the time of his election to Congress, Gary Franks was the highest-ranking elected African-American Republican in the United States. As a black conservative Republican, he represented the growing mistrust among African-American political leaders with the Democratic Party's ability and willingness to help black Americans.

Franks was born on February 9, 1953, in Waterbury, Connecticut. His father, Richard, was a factory worker and his mother, Jenary, was a homemaker. He finished high school in 1971 and then enrolled in Yale University, where he received a B.A. four years later. From 1975 to 1986, he worked as a manager in the industrial and labor relations departments of three major corporations headquartered near New York City. In 1986, he formed GAF Realty in Waterbury to take advantage of the local real estate boom. In 1990, he married Donna Williams, with whom he has two children.

Franks got involved in politics in 1985 when he was elected as a Republican to the Waterbury board of aldermen. The following year he ran for state comptroller but lost. His defeat did not cost him his seat on the board, however, and he held this position until 1990. During this period, he served as president pro tempore of the board and as vice chair of the zoning board, and he was a member of the environmental control and civil rights commissions. In 1987, he challenged unsuccessfully for the chairmanship of the state Republican Party.

In 1989, Franks announced his candidacy for western Connecticut's seat in the U.S. House of Representatives. The following year, when he went into the Republican caucus to determine the nominee, he was last of the five candidates in terms of delegates. After nine ballots, however, the other four had eliminated each other, and Franks emerged victorious. The general election campaign also generated much heat. His Democratic opponent was Toby Moffett, a former four-term congressman who had resigned to run for the U.S. Senate. Moffett, a white liberal, lambasted Franks, a black conservative, for his weak support for the Civil Rights Act of 1990. Meanwhile, Franks blasted Moffett for his spendthrift Democratic ways and called for fiscal conservatism in government. As Booker T. Washington, the famous black leader, had done earlier in the century, Franks called for increased self-sufficiency from all Americans and asked that the government provide help, not handouts, to minorities. Although Franks's district was 96 percent white, his emphasis on conservative values resonated more loudly with his white, upper-class constituents, and he won. He took his seat in 1991 and was assigned to the committee on policy.

As a conservative Republican, Franks encountered much hostility from African Americans in general and from the Congressional Black Caucus in particular, but he held true to his conservative values and worked diligently for welfare reform. He introduced a bill requiring single mothers on welfare to identify the fathers of their children or risk losing benefits. He also worked to rebuild the nation's deteriorating urban centers by introducing a bill offering incentives to private companies investing in downtown businesses.

Franks was reelected to Congress twice. He was voted out of office in 1996, seemingly because he did not campaign very hard for reelection. He returned to Waterbury after his term expired in 1997. The following year he ran against Christopher Dodd, Connecticut's long-time U.S. senator, but lost. After his defeat, Franks returned to his real estate business.

Further Reading

Biographical Directory of the United States Congress. "Franks, Gary A., 1953–   ." Available online. URL: http://bioguide.congress.gov/scripts/biodisplay. pl?index=F000348. Downloaded April 8, 2009.

Black Americans in Congress. "Gary A. Franks." Available online. URL: http://baic.house.gov/ member-profiles/profile.html?intID=73. Downloaded April 9, 2009.

Clay, William L. *Just Permanent Interests: Black Americans in Congress, 1870–1992.* New York: Amistad Press, 1993.

"Connecticut Elects First Black Republican Congressman in 56 Years." *Ebony* 46 (January 1991): 110.

Franks, Gary. *Searching for the Promised Land: An African American's Optimistic Odyssey.* New York: ReganBooks, 1996.

Fudge, Marcia L.
(1952–   ) *U.S. congressional representative from Ohio*

After the sudden death of Representative STEPHANIE TUBBS JONES, the elite of Cleveland's Democratic Party drafted attorney Marcia L. Fudge to take her place in Congress. Fudge was born in Cleveland, Ohio, on October 29, 1952. Excelling as a student and an athlete, Fudge graduated from Shaker Heights High School in 1971. She continued her education at Ohio State University, where she earned a bachelor of science in business administration in 1975. Fudge later studied law at Cleveland State University.

In addition to working in a private legal practice, Fudge made use of her legal and business education in several posts in city and state government. She served as the director of the Cuyahoga County budget commission and as the budget and finance director for the country prosecutor, who at the time was Tubbs Jones. She and Fudge became close friends as well as colleagues. In 1998, Tubbs Jones was elected to the U.S. House of Representatives, winning the 11th congressional district seat that had been long held by LOUIS STOKES. She asked Fudge to join her in Washington, D.C., and work as her chief of staff.

After a year, Fudge returned to the Cleveland area with the intention of running for municipal judge. Instead, she was recruited to campaign for mayor of Warrensville Heights, a modest city east of Cleveland with a largely African-American population. Winning the election, Fudge became the first black woman to serve as the city's mayor. During her nine-year tenure in office, some 200 new houses were constructed in Warrensville Heights and its retail sector grew and prospered.

On August 19, 2008, Representative Tubbs Jones suffered a brain aneurysm. She died the following day. Fudge had never expressed an interest in national politics, yet many of Tubbs Jones's supporters pushed for Fudge to take over her friend's congressional seat. Fudge was hesitant. Although they shared views about how government could improve people's everyday lives, the two women had very different temperaments. Like many politicians, Tubbs Jones was outgoing and magnetic. Fudge was much more reflective and reserved. She, however, had earned a reputation as a diligent public servant. As Fudge told the *Cleveland Plain Dealer*, "I work. That is what I do. I don't go to work to do anything other than the best job that I can do."

Nearly 300 Democratic Party leaders in the Cleveland area met to choose a nominee for the 11th district race. They considered five candidates, but Fudge had received the endorsement of many local mayors and of former congressman Louis Stokes. With their support, Fudge emerged as the consensus choice after only one round of voting. On November 4, 2008, Fudge won the election against the Republican challenger, Thomas Pekarek, by taking 85 percent of the vote.

Two weeks later, Fudge won a second electoral contest. By Ohio law, a special election had to be held to select a replacement for Tubbs Jones during the final weeks of her term. Fudge's name was only one on the ballot, so she won 100 percent of the 9,000 votes cast. Because of the special election, Fudge was sworn into office six weeks before any of the other members of her freshmen congressional class. Fudge promised her constituents to work toward creating jobs, building small businesses, and improving health care and education. During her first full term, she was appointed to the Education and Labor and Science and Technology committees. She was reelected in 2010.

Further Reading

Congresswoman Marcia L. Fudge, Official Web Site. Available online. URL: http://fudge.house.gov. Downloaded May 7, 2009.

Perkins, Olivera. "Marcia Fudge, with Style of Her Own, Takes Congressional Seat." *Cleveland Plain Dealer*, November 19, 2008. Available online. URL: http://blog.cleveland.com/metro/2008/11/marcia_fudge_with_style_of_her.html. Downloaded May 7, 2009.

Fulani, Lenora
(Lenora Branch Fulani)
(1950–) *presidential candidate*

Lenora Fulani was a perennial independent candidate for statewide office in New York. In 1988, she made history by becoming the first African-

American candidate for president to appear on the ballot in all 50 states and the District of Columbia.

Fulani was born Lenora Branch on April 25, 1950, in Chester, Pennsylvania. Her father, Charles, was a railroad baggage handler, and her mother, Pearl, was a nurse. After graduating from high school in 1968, she moved to Long Island, New York, to attend Hofstra University, receiving a B.A. in psychology in 1971. That same year she got married, and she and her husband both changed their last name to Fulani, the name of a West African tribe; they had two children before divorcing in 1979. In 1972, she received an M.A. from Columbia University's Teachers College and went to work as a guest researcher at Rockefeller University. She also began working on her doctorate in developmental psychology at the City University of New York, which she received in 1984.

In the late 1970s, Fulani met psychologist Fred Newman. Newman practiced what he called Social Therapy, which uses a performatory clinical approach to eradicate mental illness by ridding patients of prejudices such as racism, sexism, and homophobia. As a means to applying his work to society as a whole, Newman had founded the New Alliance Party (NAP), which Fulani joined in 1980. Shortly thereafter she became the director of community clinics for Newman's Institute for Social Therapy and Research.

In 1982, the NAP began running candidates for political offices, and Fulani was chosen to run for lieutenant governor of New York. Three years later, she ran for mayor of New York City, and in 1986 she was a candidate for governor of New York. In the gubernatorial race, she polled 25,000 votes, which was almost as many as the party's presidential candidate had polled nationwide two years earlier. In 1988, Fulani ran for president; NAP activists got enough voters to sign her petitions that her name appeared on the ballot in all 50 states and the District of Columbia. Her platform billed her as a staunch supporter of gay rights and socialism, and it included pledges to cut the

military budget in half, raise corporate taxes, and provide free health care to all American citizens. She received 240,000 votes and qualified for more than $900,000 in federal matching funds. In 1990 she ran again for governor of New York but lost.

As a candidate, Fulani had an ambivalent relationship with the Democratic Party. Throughout her career she criticized the party for paying lip service only to the needs and wants of African Americans, and she castigated the party elite when it refused to make JESSE JACKSON its vice-presidential candidate in 1988. Nevertheless, in 1992 she ran as a Democrat in the New Hampshire presidential primary. Following her defeat (she received 402 votes), she campaigned for the presidency on the NAP ticket. This time her name was on the ballot in 45 states, and she received 217,000 votes. In 1994, she entered the New York Democratic primary for governor and received 142,000 votes (21 percent).

Following her primary defeat, Fulani attended a meeting of the Federation of Independent Voters in Arlington, Virginia. Most of the federation's members were former supporters of H. Ross Perot, the independent candidate for president in 1992. Their purpose was to found a third party that could win elections by consolidating the efforts of independents from around the country. The meeting gave birth to the Patriot Party, which later became known as the Reform Party. Fulani helped fold the NAP into the Patriot Party and ran as its candidate in the 1994 general election for New York's lieutenant governor. The following year, she helped get Perot's name on the ballot in all 50 states as the Reform Party's candidate for president, then campaigned for him up until the election of 1996. In 1998, she ran a third time for lieutenant governor of New York, this time on the Reform Party ticket.

In 1999, Fulani shocked the political pundits when she endorsed the candidacy of Pat Buchanan, the archconservative who gained the Reform Party's nomination for president in 2000. Buchanan responded by naming her cochair of his national campaign. Fulani defended her action by explaining that, while she did not see eye to eye with Buchanan on many issues, she agreed with him on the necessity of forging an anti–big government, anti–big business alliance among working-class Americans of all colors. In her opinion, breaking the "collar barrier" would lead inevitably to breaking the "color barrier." The differences between the right-wing Buchanan and the left-wing Fulani, however, were too great to overcome, and they broke shortly after declaring their mutual support. The break came after Buchanan refused to support Fulani in her bid to become the party's national chair. She resigned from his campaign and threw her support to his chief rival for the Reform Party's presidential nomination, John Hagelin, the candidate of the former Natural Law Party.

Following Hagelin's defeat, Fulani also continued to work for a multiracial, pro-reform, national political party as chair of the Committee for a Unified Independent Party, which she had cofounded in 1994. In 2001, Fulani endorsed Republican Michael Bloomberg for mayor of New York and encouraged the city's Independence Party members to lend him their support. Fulani, however, became embroiled in a power struggle within the Independence Party, when in 2005 opponents criticized her for making what they called an anti-Semitic remark. Remaining a controversial yet influential figure in New York City politics, Fulani has frequently written columns for daily newspapers and appeared on radio and television shows.

Further Reading

"Dr. Lenora Fulani Enters Race for President but Will Quit if Dems Pick Jackson." *Jet* 73 (February 1, 1988): 28.

Fulani, Lenora B. *The Making of a Fringe Candidate.* New York: Castillo International, 1993.

"Fulani, Lenora." *Current Biography* 61 (March 2000): 53–59.

McIntire, Mike. "Fulani Loses Independence Party Role over Comments on Jews." *New York Times,* September 19, 2005. Available online. URL: http://www.nytimes.com/2005/09/19/nyregion/metrocampaigns/19fulani.html?scp=4&sq=fulani&st=cse. Downloaded April 23, 2009.

Robbins, Tom. "Mike's Awkward Ally." *Village Voice,* September 6, 2005. Available online. URL: http://www.villagevoice.com/2005-09-06/news/mike-s-awkward-ally. Downloaded April 23, 2009.

G

Gantt, Harvey
(Harvey Bernard Gantt)
(1943–   ) *mayor of Charlotte, North Carolina*

Harvey Gantt was the first African-American mayor of Charlotte, North Carolina. In 1990, he came very close to becoming the first African-American senator from the South since Reconstruction.

Gantt was born on January 14, 1943, in Charleston, South Carolina. His father, Christopher, was a shipyard worker, and his mother, Wilhelmenia, was a homemaker. After finishing high school in 1961, he enrolled in Iowa State University. He left after a year because of the harsh winters, but in order to attend a public university in his home state he had to battle the forces of segregation. In 1963, he obtained a court order permitting him to become the first black student at Clemson University, and two years later he received a bachelor's degree in architecture. He spent the next five years at the Massachusetts Institute of Technology, receiving an M.A. in urban planning in 1970. After graduation he went to work as a planner for the Soul City Foundation. The foundation was the creation of civil rights activist Floyd McKissick, and its purpose was to build an all-black community, known as Soul City, in Warren County, North Carolina. A year later,

Gantt relocated to Charlotte where he and a partner formed an architectural firm.

In 1974, Gantt was appointed to the Charlotte city council to complete the term of Fred Alexander, the council's only black member, who had just been elected to the state senate. Almost immediately, Gantt began working to get the council to change the way its members were elected. Instead of having all members elected to at-large seats, he succeeded in having some members elected from districts, thus giving minority voters more representation on the council. He was elected to a full term of his own in 1975 and reelected in 1977. He declined to run in 1979, choosing instead to run for mayor of Charlotte. At the time, Charlotte was one of the fastest growing cities in the Sun Belt, but the growth threatened to outstrip the city's ability to plan for it. Gantt ran on a platform of managed growth, but his message held little appeal for city residents who saw only the potential of a business boom. Following his defeat, he remained out of office until 1981, when he was reelected to city council.

In 1983, Gantt made a second run for mayor. This time the problems of unmanaged growth were more visible, and his platform of managed growth held more appeal for the voters. The result was a surprising win for Gantt, who polled 52 percent of the total vote and about one-third of the white vote. The campaign was significant in that neither Gantt nor his Republican opponent raised the issue of race. Gantt refused help from national black leaders, preferring instead to campaign on his own merits as a local politician. He credited his victory to the citizens of Charlotte, which he categorized as a "New South" city where race was finally ceasing to be the overarching issue.

As mayor, Gantt worked to improve municipal services while holding the line on tax increases. As part of his economic development program, he helped win the city a franchise in the National Basketball Association, the Charlotte Hornets. He also worked to renovate the city's decaying central business district and its minority neighborhoods. Despite his efforts to manage the city's growth, he never managed to successfully address the problem of traffic congestion, which seemed only to get worse. Reelected in 1985, he was defeated two years later, mostly because of citizen discontent over the traffic problem.

In 1990, Gantt declared his candidacy for the Democratic nomination for one of North Carolina's seats in the U.S. Senate. The challenge drew the attention of the national media because the seat was held by Republican Jesse Helms, arguably the most conservative member of the Senate. To the surprise of most observers, Gantt outpolled two other challengers in the Democratic primary, and then he defeated his other challenger in the runoff, thus winning the right to face Helms. Throughout the campaign, Gantt characterized himself as the candidate of the enlightened New South and Helms as the candidate of the benighted Old South. At first, Helms simply ignored Gantt, but as election day drew nearer and the polls suggested that Gantt might actually win, Helms went on the offensive. The Helms campaign accused Gantt of several financial improprieties, while the Gantt campaign accused the Republicans of using scare tactics to keep black voters from the polls. Much to Gantt's disgust, Helms and his supporters managed to make race the central issue of the campaign. By

the time the votes were counted, Gantt had lost by the narrow margin of 53-47.

After the election, Gantt retired to private life, devoting himself to his architectural practice, his wife Cindy, and their four children. He remained active in state politics, serving on the executive council of the state Democratic Party as a Democratic national committeeman.

Further Reading

Brabham, Robin. "Gantt, Harvey." In *African American National Biography*, vol. 3, edited by Henry Louis Gates, Jr., and Evelyn Brooks Higginbotham. New York: Oxford University Press, 2008, pp. 434–435.

Elliot, Jeffrey M. *Black Voices in American Politics*. New York: Harcourt Brace Jovanovich, 1986.

Magnuson, Ed. "Carolina's Great Black Hope." *Time* 135 (June 18, 1990): 18.

Ryan, Bryan. "Harvey Gantt, 1943– ." *Contemporary Black Biography* 1 (1992): 72–74.

Whitaker, Charles. "Harvey Gantt." *Ebony* 41 (April 1986): 82.

Gibson, Kenneth
(Kenneth Allen Gibson)
(1932–) *mayor of Newark, New Jersey*

Kenneth Gibson was the first African American to be elected mayor of a major northeastern city, and the first black to be elected president of the U.S. Conference of Mayors. During his 16 years as mayor of Newark, New Jersey, he greatly reduced crime and infant mortality. He failed, however, to solve the problem of how to maintain services in the face of falling revenues, a common problem for big-city mayors in the late 20th century.

Gibson was born on May 15, 1932, in Enterprise, Alabama. His father, Willie, was a butcher, and his mother, Daisy, was a seamstress. At age eight he moved with his family to Newark. In 1951, he graduated from high school, got married, and enrolled in the Newark College of Engineering (NCE). For the next five years, he attended classes at night while working in a factory during the day and playing the saxophone on weekends. In 1956, he was drafted into the U.S. Army and spent most of the next two years in Hawaii with an engineering battalion. While in Hawaii, he got divorced and was awarded custody of his two children. Returning to Newark in 1958, he married Muriel Cooke, worked for the state highway department, and reenrolled in NCE. He received a B.S. in structural engineering in 1962, then took a position as an engineer and administrator for the Newark Housing Authority. Over the next four years he worked his way up to chief structural engineer. Meanwhile, he became heavily involved in the community, serving as head of the Business and Industry Coordinating Council, which helped employers find prospective employees and vice versa, and vice president of the United Community Corporation, which oversaw the implementation of programs for the city's underprivileged.

In 1966, Gibson got involved in politics by running as a Democrat for mayor of Newark. At the time, the city ranked among the nation's worst in terms of crime, substandard housing, and infant mortality, problems which particularly beset its African-American residents. Newark's mayor, Hugh Addonizio, seemed to be doing little to solve these and other problems. Gibson made his decision to run just six weeks before the election, but his last-minute, low-budget campaign—which he characterized as "a civil rights demonstration"— still managed to appeal to about 20 percent of the voters. He spent the next four years lining up supporters and campaign funds for a second run. His chances were strengthened immeasurably when, in his position as an administrator for the housing authority, he uncovered widespread corruption in city hall. A state prosecutor whom Gibson had informed conducted an investigation that led to indictments of Addonizio and nine other city officials on 66 counts of extortion and income tax evasion. When the election was held in 1970, Gibson won handily.

As mayor, Gibson focused on improving the city's public health services. To this end, he opened seven community health centers that, among other things, offered comprehensive testing for infants. The centers played a crucial role in reducing the incidence of tuberculosis and venereal disease while dramatically cutting the infant mortality rate. He also allocated more money for such services as garbage collection and street sweeping. Reelected in 1974, he focused his second term on making the city a safer place to live. Three years later, Newark's serious crime rate ranking had fallen from first to 23rd among cities with populations greater than 300,000. He also instituted an affirmative action program that gave promotions to a number of the city's black employees. These successes led to his reelection in 1978 and 1982, as well as to his election in 1976 as president of the U.S. Conference of Mayors. They also induced him to run for governor of New Jersey in 1981 and 1985, but he showed poorly in both contests.

Despite his successes, Gibson had his failures as well. The problems of the 1960s—including serious riots in 1968—had started an exodus of the city's middle-class residents to the suburbs. As the city's tax base shrunk, he was forced to lay off city workers and raise property taxes. Although these measures eliminated budget deficits, they also mandated cuts for the city's public school system, which was already underfunded. As a result, the exodus to the suburbs continued unabated, and along with it went most of the small businesses that catered to the city's middle and working classes. During Gibson's tenure, the population fell by almost 70,000, and by 1986 the city had only one supermarket and no movie theaters. And while the economy improved for the city's financial district, it worsened for the city's blue-collar workers.

By 1986, Newark residents were ready for a new mayor. Despite Gibson's impressive list of achievements, he lost his bid for a fifth term to SHARPE JAMES. After completing his term, he founded Gibson Associates, a Newark-based construction management consulting firm. In 1998, he ran unsuccessfully for county executive of Essex County (Newark is the county seat of Essex). Two years later, he and two associates were indicted by a federal grand jury on 18 counts of conspiracy, bribery, fraud, and income tax evasion involving a $50 million project his company had undertaken for Essex County's Irvington Township school district. In 2002, he pleaded guilty to one count of tax evasion and was sentenced to three years' probation.

Further Reading

Fried, Joseph P. "Four-Term Newark Leader Won't Second-Guess Mayor." *New York Times*, January 20, 2005. Available online. URL: http://www.nytimes.com/2005/01/30/nyregion/30folo.html. Downloaded April 15, 2009.

Haskins, James. *A Piece of the Power: Four Black Mayors*. New York: Dial, 1972.

Joint Center for Political Studies. *Profiles of Black Mayors in America*. Chicago: Johnson Publishing, 1977.

Goode, W. W.

(Woodrow Wilson Goode)
(1938–   ) *mayor of Philadelphia, Pennsylvania*

W. W. Goode was the first African American to be elected mayor of Philadelphia, Pennsylvania. At first, he was lauded by virtually all of the city's residents for his strong leadership and innovative programs. Unfortunately, a bungled eviction crippled his effectiveness and brought his political career to an early end.

Goode was born on August 19, 1938, in Seaboard, North Carolina. His parents, Albert and Rozella, were sharecroppers. By age 12, he had moved with his parents to Philadelphia. After graduating from high school, he enrolled in Morgan State University and received a B.A. in 1961. He then joined the U.S. Army and was discharged in 1963 with the rank of captain. Over the next five years, he worked a variety of jobs while studying public administration at the University of Pennsylvania's Wharton School of Business, receiving an M.P.A. in 1968. For the next 10 years, he served as executive director of the Philadelphia Council for Community Advancement, a nonprofit organization that sought to improve housing conditions for the city's disadvantaged.

Goode became actively involved in government in 1978 when he was appointed chairman of the state public utility commission. Within a year of his appointment, a potentially disastrous accident occurred at Pennsylvania's Three Mile Island nuclear power plant. It was his responsibility as chairman to investigate the accident while also convincing the public that its safety was not and had not been compromised. He handled an extremely sensitive situation with considerable aplomb, and in 1980 he was offered the position as Philadelphia's managing director. In this position, he directed the day-to-day operation of the city's departments.

Unlike his predecessors, Goode met frequently with community leaders across Philadelphia in an effort to make sure that the service needs of all of the city's residents were met. Over the next three years, he did much to improve basic services like sanitation while eliminating some of the worst examples of urban blight. He also made a number of important political contacts, who were impressed with his dedication and his ability to get things done. By 1983, he had developed enough of a following that he decided to run for mayor of Philadelphia. Running as a Democrat, he captured virtually all the black vote and a sizable percentage of the white vote to win easily.

During the first year of his tenure, Goode could do no wrong. He developed a highly successful program, called "Seizing Control of Our Destiny," to attract new industry to the city. He eased racial tensions considerably by appointing a cabinet to study and make recommendations about problems such as crime, housing, and unemployment. He got the city council to repeal an unpopular mercantile tax, pushed through the completion of the city's rapid transit system, and even convinced the owner of the Philadelphia Eagles to keep the team in town.

In 1985, however, Goode lost his golden touch. The beginning of the end started when a group of black radicals called MOVE took up residence in a West Philadelphia row house. After numerous complaints from the neighbors concerning MOVE's back-to-nature lifestyle, the police attempted to evict MOVE. When the members of MOVE refused to leave peacefully, Goode authorized the dropping of a bomb on the roof of their house. The resulting explosion demolished the house and killed seven adults and four children. It also started a fire that destroyed an additional 60 homes and caused millions of dollars in property damage. At first, Goode denied any responsibility for the fiasco, but when his own handpicked investigating commission cited him for negligence and poor leadership for authorizing the bomb, his credibility was severely damaged and his effectiveness as mayor was crippled.

Nonetheless, Goode managed to win reelection in 1987. His second term was marred throughout by a city council that refused to take his lead. Time and again, the council voted down his proposals to increase revenue or to implement new programs, thus bringing the city's government to a standstill. Meanwhile, the economic downturn of the late 1980s had a disastrous effect on Philadelphia, as it did on most large cities. Revenues dwindled while expenses increased, resulting in a major budget deficit by 1990. Goode managed to float a $150 million loan from several banks and pension funds, but the loan was perceived by Philadelphians as making the situation worse instead of better. By 1991, he was being vilified in the media and elsewhere for being a weak, ineffectual leader. Prohibited by law from seeking reelection a second time, he left office quietly when his term expired in early 1992.

In 1992, Goode went to work for the U.S. Department of Education's Office of Intergovernment and Interagency Affairs as a deputy assistant regional secretary. In this capacity, he oversaw the agency's community service activities in New York, New Jersey, Puerto Rico, and the Virgin Islands. Five years later he was named to a similar position in the agency's Region Three, which includes Pennsylvania, Maryland, Delaware, Virginia, West Virginia, and the District of Columbia. He also began teaching political science and urban policy at Eastern College in St. Davids, Pennsylvania. By 2002, he had become an ordained Baptist minister and was employed as senior adviser on faith-based initiatives for Public/Private Ventures, for whom he directed Amachi, a program that provides mentors for the children of prisoners. In 2006, Goode won the Purpose Prize, which recognizes Americans over the age of 60 who find innovative solutions to long-standing social problems.

Further Reading

Bowser, Charles W. *Let the Bunker Burn: The Final Battle with MOVE.* Philadelphia: Camino Books, 1989.

Goode, W. Wilson, and Joann Stevens. *In Goode Faith.* Valley Forge, Pa.: Judson Press, 1992.

Matthew, Arthur. "Goode, W. Wilson." In *African American National Biography,* vol. 3, edited by Henry Louis Gates, Jr., and Evelyn Brooks Higginbotham. New York: Oxford University Press, 2008, pp. 542–543.

Gray, Bill
(William Herbert Gray III)
(1941–) *U.S. congressional representative from Pennsylvania*

Despite his relatively short career in elective politics, Bill Gray established himself as one of the most powerful African-American political leaders of the 1980s. His name was mentioned prominently in Democratic circles as being a potential candidate for U.S. vice president, but he gave up politics to concentrate on his pastoral duties and to improve educational opportunities for blacks.

Gray was born on August 20, 1941, in Baton Rouge, Louisiana. His father, William, Jr., was a doctor, and his mother, Hazel, was a high school teacher. As a child he moved with his family to St. Augustine and Tallahassee, Florida, where his father served as president of two black colleges, then in 1949 to Philadelphia, Pennsylvania, where he grew up. After graduating from high school in 1959, he attended Franklin and Marshall College, receiving a B.A. in history four years later. In 1964, he became a pastor at Union Baptist Church in Montclair, New Jersey. Meanwhile, he continued to study, receiving an M.Div. from Drew Theological Seminary in 1966 and an M.A. in theology from Princeton University in 1970. From 1966 to 1972, he served as Union's senior pastor and taught religion at several New Jersey colleges. In 1972, the year after he married Andrea Dash (with whom he had three children), he assumed the pastorate of Bright Hope Baptist Church in Philadelphia. He took over the church from his father, who in turn had taken it over from his father, William Gray, Sr., the church's founding pastor.

Gray became involved in politics in 1976 when he ran against ROBERT NIX, Philadelphia's first African-American congressman. Nix had served in Congress for 18 years, and Gray had worked as a Nix intern while at Franklin and Marshall. Undaunted by his defeat in the Democratic primary, two years later he ran against Nix again, and this time he won. He took his seat in 1979 and was appointed to the committees on foreign affairs, the budget, and the District of Columbia.

As a congressman, Gray worked with his black colleagues to protect the gains made by African Americans over the previous two decades. This task was made much harder after 1981, when Republican president Ronald Reagan sought to build up the U.S. military at the expense of social programs. Gray's major success in this area was to secure $300 million in set-asides, guaranteed percentage of government contract work, for minority- and female-owned businesses on contracts put out by the Agency for International Development. He also demonstrated an interest in African affairs, authoring legislation that provided U.S. aid to impoverished villages via the African Development Foundation. He also wrote the House versions of the Anti-Apartheid Acts of 1985 and 1986; these acts greatly restricted U.S. investments in South Africa as long as apartheid remained in effect.

Gray's ability to get what he wanted via compromise propelled him up the ranks of House Democrats. In 1985, in only his fourth term, he was named chairman of the budget committee. He obtained consensus on needed budgetary reforms by cutting programs he personally supported, thus prompting other congressmen to follow suit. In 1989, he was elected House Majority Whip, thus becoming the third-highest-ranking Democrat in the House. In this capacity, he was responsible for creating unity among his fellow Democrats and making sure they voted in important roll calls.

Gray was reelected to six terms. In 1991 he declined to run for reelection, choosing instead to become president and chief executive officer of the United Negro College Fund, now known as College Fund/UNCF. Over the next six years he raised more than $300 million for fund- sponsored scholarships and established the Frederick D. Patterson Research Institute to collect and analyze data concerning the performance of African-American students. In 1994, President Bill Clinton appointed him special adviser to the president and secretary of state on Haiti. In this capacity he helped establish the democratic regime of Haitian president Jean-Bertrand Aristide, for which the nation of Haiti awarded him a Medal of Honor. More recently, Gray has been on the board of directors of several companies including Dell, Pfizer, and J. P. Morgan Chase. He continues to serve as pastor of Bright Hope.

Further Reading

Biographical Directory of the United States Congress.
"Gray, William Herbert, III, 1941–   ." Available
online. URL: http://bioguide.congress.gov/scripts/
biodisplay.pl?index=G000402. Downloaded April
8, 2009.

Black Americans in Congress. "William Herbert Gray
III." Available online. URL: http://baic.house.
gov/member-profiles/profile.html?intID=71.
Downloaded April 7, 2009.

Clay, William L. *Just Permanent Interests: Black Americans in Congress, 1870–1992.* New York: Amistad
Press, 1993.

Explorations in Black Leadership. "Bill Gray." Available online. URL: http://www.virginia.edu/public
history/bl/index.php?uid=15. Downloaded April
8, 2009.

Smith, Jessie Carney. *Black Heroes of the 20th Century.*
Detroit: Visible Ink Press, 1998.

Gregory, Dick
(Richard Claxton Gregory)
(1932–   ) *presidential candidate*

In 1968, two African Americans ran for president
of the United States. One was Eldridge Cleaver,
the well-known leader of the Black Panthers, a
militant black group centered in Northern California's Bay Area. The other was Dick Gregory, a
nationally acclaimed comedian.

Gregory was born on October 12, 1932, in St.
Louis, Missouri. His father, Presley, was a cook,
and his mother, Lucille, was a domestic worker.
After finishing high school in 1951, he attended
Southern Illinois University for three years on a
track scholarship. In 1954, he was drafted into the
U.S. Army; following his discharge two years later,
he returned briefly to Southern Illinois before
moving to Chicago. For 18 months, he worked a
series of jobs before landing a gig in 1958 as a
stand-up comedian at a black nightclub. Three
years later, he had became one of the nation's
most popular comedians, appearing regularly at

nightclubs across the country and on the most
popular television talk shows. Part of his popularity stemmed from his unique routine, which poked
fun at black and white racial stereotypes and at
segregation in general. In 1959, he married Lillian
Smith, with whom he had 10 children.

In 1962, Gregory took an active role in the
Civil Rights movement by going to Mississippi to
take part in a voter registration drive. Over the
next five years, he balanced his career as a top-
flight comedian with his growing involvement
with the movement, lending his name and presence to several marches in the South. In 1965, he
was shot accidentally by blacks while trying to
defuse the Watts riots in Los Angeles, California.
During this period, he also began calling attention to the plight of reservation American Indians
and protesting U.S. military involvement in
Vietnam.

Gregory became involved with politics in 1967,
when he decided to run as a write-in candidate for

Comedian Dick Gregory made an unsuccessful bid for
the White House. *(Library of Congress)*

mayor of Chicago. His unsuccessful campaign promised to end the racism that permeated the city, particularly the police department, under Mayor Richard Daley's administration. The following year, he declared his candidacy as a write-in candidate for president of the United States; Mark Lane, an attorney, freelance writer, and documentary filmmaker, was his running mate. His party affiliation, the Freedom and Peace Party, was a takeoff on the Peace and Freedom Party, the political arm of the Black Panthers. After he declared his candidacy, one faction of the Peace and Freedom Party nominated Gregory for president and Dr. Benjamin Spock, the noted pediatrician and peace activist, for vice president, and got the pair on the ballot in several states (the other faction nominated Eldridge Cleaver).

Not surprisingly, Gregory's campaign was laced with humor. He declared that his first executive order would be to paint the White House black, and that his foreign policy would focus on sending "money and food to needy people in foreign lands—like Mississippi and Alabama." He used a facsimile of a one-dollar bill as campaign literature, with Gregory's face replacing George Washington's. The Treasury Department seized piles of the "bills" on the grounds that they were counterfeit, but Gregory argued that, until the Treasury Department actually put a black person's face on a U.S. note, nothing that had his smiling visage on it could possibly qualify as counterfeit money. Although he came nowhere close to winning, he managed to poll more than 45,000 votes, mostly in California. Following his defeat, he declared himself "president-in-exile" and hosted several "inaugural" events.

Gregory never ran for political office again. He continued to work for equal rights for African Americans and American Indians, and to protest the Vietnam War. He also devoted himself to issues such as world hunger, capital punishment, drug abuse, and poor health care in the African-American community. In 1973, he gave up performing as a comedian and moved with his family to a 400-acre farm in Plymouth, Massachusetts. In the 1980s, he developed the Slim-Safe Bahamian Diet, a weight-loss program that eventually netted him millions of dollars. He donated most of this money to civil rights groups and other causes that he supported. Gregory continues to be a popular speaker at colleges and universities.

Further Reading

Dick Gregory Global Watch. "Biography: Dick Gregory for the People... ." Available online. URL: http://www.dickgregory.com/about_dick_gregory.html. Downloaded April 9, 2009.

Explorations in Black Leadership. "Dick Gregory." Available online. URL: http://www.virginia.edu/publichistory/bl/index.php?uid=16. Downloaded April 26, 2009.

Gregory, Dick, with Robert Lipsyte. *Nigger: An Autobiography.* New York: Washington Square Press, 1964.

———, with Shelia P. Moses. *Callus on My Soul: A Memoir.* Atlanta: Longstreet Press, 2000.

Moses, Shelia Patrice. "Gregory, Dick." In *African American National Biography,* vol. 3, edited by Henry Louis Gates, Jr., and Evelyn Brooks Higginbotham. New York: Oxford University Press, 2008, pp. 631–633.

H

Hall, Katie
(Katie Beatrice Green)
(1938–) *U.S. congressional representative from Indiana*

Katie Hall was the first African American to represent Indiana in the U.S. Congress. She is best remembered for introducing the bill that made the birthday of Martin Luther King, Jr., a national holiday.

Hall was born Katie Beatrice Green on April 3, 1938, in Mound Bayou, Mississippi, to Jeff and Bessie Green. She finished high school in 1956 and enrolled in Mississippi Valley State University, receiving a B.S. in 1960. The following year, she moved to Gary, Indiana, where she taught social studies in the public schools until 1975. In 1968, she received an M.S. from Indiana University. In 1957, she married John Hall, with whom she had two children.

Hall became involved in politics in 1966 when she worked for RICHARD HATCHER's first mayoral campaign. After his victory, she became increasingly involved in the affairs of the local Democratic Party and helped Hatcher get reelected four years later in 1970. In 1974, she decided to run for office herself and was elected that same year to the Indiana state legislature. In 1976, she was elected to the state senate, where she served for six years. Because of her background in education,

she was chosen to chair the senate committee on education.

In 1982, Adam Benjamin, Jr., U.S. congressman from Indiana's First District, died in office. Hall was nominated to run in a special election to fill his seat for the remainder of his term as well as the next two-year term. She defeated her Republican opponent handily, thus becoming the first African American to represent Indiana in the U.S. Congress. She took her seat in 1982 and was assigned to the committees on the post office/civil service and public works/transportation.

In 1983, Hall introduced a bill to make the birthday of Martin Luther King, Jr., a national holiday. Similar bills had been introduced in the past, but nothing had ever become of them. Hall succeeded where the others had failed for several reasons. Unlike the 1960s and 1970s, when previous bills had been introduced, in 1983 there was a sizable contingent of African Americans in Congress, and the Congressional Black Caucus threw its weight behind the bill. Second, by 1983 enough African Americans had registered to vote that they constituted a significant proportion of the voting population, and the leaders of both major parties perceived that the bill's defeat would have negative repercussions at the polls in upcoming elections. Third, Hall devoted herself to getting the bill passed, and she worked tirelessly to convince her fellow legislators to vote for it. Introduced in July, the bill passed the House in August and the Senate in October. It was signed into law that November by President Ronald Reagan.

Hall served only one term in Congress. She lost her bid for renomination in 1984 and returned to Gary the following year. In 1986 and 1990, she tried to regain her seat in Congress, but both attempts failed. In 1985, Hall was named vice chair of the Gary Housing Board of Commissioners and elected city clerk. While serving in this position, Hall pled guilty to mail fraud in 2002 and was sentenced to house arrest and probation.

Further Reading

Biographical Directory of the United States Congress. "Hall, Katie Beatrice, 1938–   ." Available online. URL: http://bioguide.congress.gov/scripts/bio display.pl?index=H000058. Downloaded April 10, 2009.

Black Americans in Congress. "Katie Beatrice Hall." Available online. URL: http://baic.house.gov/member-profiles/profile.html?intID=70. Downloaded April 12, 2009.

Catlin, Robert A. "Organizational Effectiveness and Black Political Participation: The Case of Katie Hall." *Phylon* 46 (September 1985): 179–192.

Gill, LaVerne McCain. *African American Women in Congress: Forming and Transforming History.* New Brunswick, N.J.: Rutgers University Press, 1997.

Haralson, Jeremiah

(1846–1916) *U.S. congressional representative from Alabama*

In his heyday, Jeremiah Haralson was considered to be one of the most powerful African-American politicians in the South. This estimation, however, was based upon his powerful oratory, not his accomplishments as a legislator.

Haralson was born on April 1, 1846, on a plantation near Columbus, Georgia. Nothing is known about his parents except that they were slaves. By age 13, he had been bought and sold three times,

his third master being John Haralson of Selma, Alabama. He taught himself how to read and write, and after the Civil War he took up farming in Dallas County, the county surrounding Selma.

Haralson got involved in politics in 1867, the year Reconstruction began. From the very start, he proved to be a political maverick. Unlike most African Americans, who joined the Republican Party because it had brought them freedom, he became a Democrat. He used his considerable abilities as a public speaker to recruit freedmen to the party, but when his efforts failed he joined the ranks of the Republicans in 1869. He immediately devoted himself to the task of getting a black man elected to public office. In 1870, he married Ellen Norwood, with whom he had one child, and chaired the district convention that nominated BENJAMIN TURNER for the U.S. House of Representatives. When the same convention denied him the nomination for state representative, he decided to run as an independent. Thus, the election of 1870 saw Haralson campaigning arduously for a Republican for Congress while also running as an independent for the state lower house; it is a testament to his political and oratorical skills that both he and Turner won. Two years later, he returned to the Republican Party, and this time he gained its nomination for state senator.

Haralson proved to be as fearless a legislator as he was an orator. In 1872, while speaking at a convention in New Orleans, he declared to a black audience that the Democrats would put all the freedmen to death if that party won that year's presidential election. In 1873, he sponsored a bill in the state senate that would have outlawed discrimination in any school or place of public accommodation in Alabama on the grounds of race. In essence, the same bill was passed by the Congress in the form of the Civil Rights Act of 1875. Haralson's version, however, was not enacted, and it, along with his intemperate oratory, earned him the enmity of white Republicans. Meanwhile, his party-jumping raised issues of party loyalty in the minds of many black Republi-

Jeremiah Haralson was elected to the U.S. House of Representatives from Alabama. *(Library of Congress)*

can leaders, and he eventually became involved in a factional dispute with JAMES RAPIER, Alabama's second black congressman, over the dispensation of political patronage in the state. However, he remained a favorite of black voters because of fiery oratory and his racial pride. He frequently derided his African-American opponents for being only half-black, since many of them had a white father, and he once remarked that he could never be interested sexually in a white woman unless she was wealthy.

In 1874, Haralson became the third African American to be elected to the U.S. House of Representatives from Alabama. As a congressman, he proved to be a disappointment. Appointed to the committee on public expenditures, he introduced a number of bills and resolutions, none of which passed. Oddly, given his powers as an orator, he never made a speech before the assembled House.

Although he supported what became known as the Civil Rights Act of 1875, he distressed many of his constituents by voting to restore the political rights of former Confederates and by developing a friendship with Jefferson Davis, former president of the Confederacy.

In 1876, Haralson was forced to run for reelection against Rapier, who had just moved into Haralson's district. Much to his chagrin, the Republicans gave the nomination to Rapier. As before, he ran anyway as an independent, but this time the effect was to split the black vote between Rapier and himself, thus allowing their white Democratic opponent to win. He campaigned for a return to the House in 1878 but was defeated when voter fraud denied him the votes of two heavily black wards in his hometown.

In 1879, Haralson accepted a position with the U.S. Treasury Department as collector of customs in Baltimore, Maryland. When his term expired a year later, he became a clerk in the Interior Department in Washington, D.C. In 1882, he transferred to the Pension Bureau but resigned in 1884 to make one last run for Congress. Following his defeat, he moved to Louisiana where he took up farming once again. In 1904, he moved to Arkansas to become a federal pension agent. He returned to Selma in 1912, then spent the next four years in Texas, Oklahoma, and Colorado, where he was engaged in a coal mining enterprise. In 1916, he went on a hunting trip and never returned; it is presumed that he died in the wilderness near Denver and that his body was devoured by wild beasts.

Further Reading

Bailey, Richard. *Neither Carpetbaggers nor Scalawags: Black Officeholders during the Reconstruction of Alabama, 1867–1878.* 5th ed. Montgomery, Ala.: New South, 2007.

Biographical Directory of the United States Congress. "Haralson, Jeremiah, 1846–1916." Available online. URL: http://bioguide.congress.gov/scripts/biodisplay.pl?index=H000179. Downloaded March 28, 2009.

Black Americans in Congress. "Jeremiah Haralson." Available online. URL: http://baic.house.gov/member-profiles/profile.html?intID=5. Downloaded March 30, 2009.

Clay, William L. *Just Permanent Interests: Black Americans in Congress, 1870–1992.* New York: Amistad Press, 1993.

Harmon, Clarence
(1940–   ) *mayor of St. Louis, Missouri*

Clarence Harmon succeeded FREEMAN BOSLEY as mayor of St. Louis, Missouri. Despite a number of significant accomplishments, he was not reelected to a second term.

Harmon was born in 1940 in St. Louis. After finishing high school, he enlisted in the U.S. Army, serving as a paratrooper in the 101st Airborne Division. He returned to St. Louis after being honorably discharged and in 1969 he became a city police officer. He also enrolled part-time in St. Louis Community College, and over the next 19 years he received a B.S. from Northeast Missouri State University and an M.A. in criminal justice administration and a master's degree in public administration from Webster University.

In 1988, having previously served as head of the department's special operations, Harmon was promoted to area commander. In this capacity he helped to implement a community-oriented policing program similar to the one developed in Houston, Texas, by LEE BROWN. In 1991, Harmon was named secretary of the city board of police commissioners, and a few months later he was promoted to chief of police. As chief, he fought against the prevailing promotion system, which emphasized an officer's political connections rather than ability, education, or on-the-job achievement. His efforts to involve the community in crime prevention and detection, begun while he was an area commander, resulted in a gradual but steady reduction in the crime rate.

Despite his accomplishments, Harmon ran afoul of Freeman Bosley, who was elected mayor in 1993. Part of the problem resulted from the way Harmon allegedly treated his African-American police officers. Some of them had complained to the local chapter of the National Association for the Advancement of Colored People that Harmon gave preference to white officers over black officers. Bosley, the city's first African-American mayor, had been elected because of his strong support in the black community. He pressured Harmon to end this practice, while Harmon resisted Bosley's efforts to exert control over the department. After two years of bickering between the two, in 1995 Harmon resigned from the force. For the next two years, he worked as director of business development and market research for United Van Lines. Meanwhile, despite his lack of political experience, he began to formulate plans to challenge Bosley for mayor. In 1996, Harmon announced his intention to run in the Democratic primary the following year.

In the months leading up to the primary, members of Bosley's staff were accused of mishandling funds related to a midnight basketball program run by the city's parks and recreation department. The program itself did not set well with white voters to begin with. To many of them, the program symbolized Bosley's excessive advocacy of black interests in the city, and charges of corruption related to the program did nothing to improve its or Bosley's popularity with white voters. As white support for Harmon mounted, Bosley began to attack him for cozying up to whites and even went so far as to call him "a traitor to his race." In the primary, Harmon received most of the white votes while Bosley received most of the black votes, with Harmon winning by a 56-43 margin. He then swept to victory in the general election and took office in 1997.

As mayor, Harmon worked hard to promote economic development. His office played a major role in getting several large corporations, such as Ralston-Purina, to stay in St. Louis, and it helped several others with their plans to expand. Downtown Now!, a Harmon initiative, helped revitalize the central business district. He oversaw the development of a plan encouraging the private renovation of abandoned buildings into loft condominiums and rental units. In the transportation area, he helped secure construction of a new runway for Lambert–St. Louis International Airport and a new multimodal transportation hub.

Despite these accomplishments, Harmon remained an unpopular mayor. His lack of political skills served him poorly when it came time to smooth ruffled feathers or to arrive at consensus on a given question. By the end of his four-year term, he had alienated most of the white voters without being able to attract very many black voters. In the 2001 Democratic primary, he polled a mere 5 percent of the vote, being outdistanced by Bosley and by Francis Slay, who went on to win the general election.

After leaving office in 2001, Harmon taught American policy and municipal government at Southern Illinois University at Carbondale. The following year he began teaching criminal justice at St. Louis University. He is married to the former Janet Kelley and has four children.

Further Reading

Golus, Carrie. "Clarence Harmon, 1940(?)–   ." *Contemporary Black Biography* 26 (2001): 71–73.
Mahtesian, Charles. "Race Reversal." *Governing* 11 (November 1997): 72.

Harris, Patricia Roberts
(1924–1985) *U.S. secretary of housing and urban development*

Patricia Harris was the first African-American woman to serve as an ambassador to a foreign country. She was also the first black woman to hold a cabinet-level position.

Harris was born Patricia Roberts on May 31, 1924, in Mattoon, Illinois. Her father, Bert, was a railroad dining car waiter, and her mother, Hildren (also known as Chiquita), was a homemaker. During the Great Depression her father left the family, and around the time she finished elementary school she moved to Chicago with her mother and brother. In 1941, she graduated from high school and enrolled in Howard University, where she received an A.B. in political science and economics. In 1945, she returned to Chicago to work as a program director for the local Young Women's Christian Association while studying industrial relations at the University of Chicago. Four years later she returned to Washington, D.C., to become assistant director of the American Council for Human Rights. In 1953, she took over as executive director of Delta Sigma Theta national sorority. Two years later, she married William B. Harris; they had no children.

By all accounts, Harris had a brilliant mind as well as the self-discipline and self-assurance to get things done. Nevertheless, by age 33 she remained unsure as to which direction her career should take. Her husband, an attorney, convinced her to become a lawyer, and in 1957 she enrolled in George Washington University Law School. She received a LL.B. in 1960 and then went to work for the U.S. Department of Justice's criminal division. In 1961, she returned to Howard University as associate dean of students, and in 1963 she began teaching full-time in Howard's law school.

Throughout the various twists and turns of her professional career, Harris remained a staunchly loyal member of the Democratic Party. Having experienced plenty of racial discrimination as a child, she had come to believe that black people had a patriotic duty to fight against racial injustice via the democratic system. Meanwhile, her positions with the American Council for Human Rights and Delta Sigma Theta had made her an opinion leader for African-American women across the country. Although her status as a resident of the District of Columbia prevented her from voting in national, state, or local elections until the 1970s, she campaigned whenever and wherever she could for Democratic candidates. By 1959, when she resigned as director of Delta Sigma Theta, she had become one of the most influential African-American women in the party.

President John F. Kennedy recognized Harris's ability, loyalty, and leadership by naming her to chair the National Women's Committee for Civil Rights. In this position, she helped gain grassroots support for the legislation that became known as the Civil Rights Act of 1965. Her efforts toward securing its passage were recognized in 1964, when she was chosen to second President Lyndon B. Johnson's nomination at the Democratic National Convention. That same year she was named by Johnson to the Commission on the Status of Puerto Rico, which sought to determine whether that island should be granted statehood, independence, or continued commonwealth status. She demonstrated sufficient diplomatic skill on this ticklish assignment to be appointed by Johnson in 1965 as ambassador to Luxembourg. This two-year assignment was followed by appointments as a delegate to the 1967 and 1969 sessions of the United Nations General Assembly. Meanwhile, she had returned to Howard Law School in 1967 as a professor and served briefly as its dean. In 1970, she left the school and joined a D.C. law firm.

In 1977, President Jimmy Carter named Harris as secretary of the U.S. Department of Housing and Urban Development. For the next three years, she worked hard to transform the department's focus. Previously, it had renewed urban areas by bulldozing slums and then constructing immense public housing projects in their place. This strategy had the unfortunate side effect of displacing and dispersing an area's residents, which made it difficult to create a sense of community in the new project. Although Harris continued to oversee new construction in places where more housing was needed, she insisted on renovating rundown neighborhoods whenever possible because this option did not turn the neighborhood's residents into refugees. She also expanded the Urban Homesteading Plan, which encouraged middle-class suburbanites to relocate to the cities,

and secured funding for Urban Development Action Grants, which made it easier for retail merchants to do business in the inner cities.

In 1979, Harris was asked by Carter to replace Joseph A. Califano as secretary of the Department of Health, Education, and Welfare. When Congress created a separate Department of Education the following year, she stayed on as head of the renamed Department of Health and Human Services. In 1981, she resigned following the election of President Ronald Reagan and returned to George Washington Law School as a professor. In 1982 she ran for mayor of Washington against incumbent MARION BARRY but lost. She died from cancer on March 23, 1985, in Washington.

Further Reading

Johnson, Judith R. "Harris, Patricia Roberts." In *African American National Biography*, vol. 4, edited by Henry Louis Gates, Jr., and Evelyn Brooks Higginbotham. New York: Oxford University Press, 2008, pp. 90–91.

Lynn, Laurence E., and David deF. Whitman. *The President as Policymaker: Jimmy Carter and Welfare Reform.* Philadelphia: Temple University Press, 1981.

Murray, Pauli. *Song in a Weary Throat.* New York: Harper, 1987.

Smith, Jessie Carney, ed. *Black Heroes of the 20th Century.* Detroit: Visible Ink, 1998.

Hastie, William H.
(William Henry Hastie, Jr.)
(1904–1976) *governor of the U.S. Virgin Islands*

William H. Hastie is best remembered as an effective advocate for civil rights and as the first African American to become a federal judge. In addition, however, he was only the second black, and only one of five African Americans to date, to serve as a governor.

Hastie was born on November 17, 1904, in Knoxville, Tennessee. His father, William, Sr., was a clerk in the U.S. Pension Office (today the Department of Veterans Affairs), and his mother, Roberta, was a teacher. In 1916, he moved with his family to Washington, D.C., where his father had been transferred. After graduating from Amherst College in 1925, he taught for two years in Bordentown, New Jersey, then enrolled in Harvard University Law School. In 1930, he received his LL.B., returned to Washington, passed the bar examination, joined the law firm of William L. and Charles H. Houston, and began teaching at Howard University Law School. Two years later, he reenrolled at Harvard, rooming with ROBERT WEAVER while earning his doctorate in judicial sciences. In 1933, he returned to Washington to teach at Howard Law School and to become an assistant solicitor for the U.S. Department of the Interior. Two years later, he married Alma Syphax; they had no children. They were later divorced, and in 1945 he married Beryl Lockhart, with whom he had two children.

As assistant solicitor, Hastie was primarily concerned with insular affairs, particularly those of the U.S. Virgin Islands. These Caribbean islands had been purchased from Denmark in 1917 to protect the Panama Canal from German aggression during World War I. They were administered by the U.S. Navy until 1931, when they were transferred to the jurisdiction of the Interior Department. Hastie and others were given the assignment of drawing up a scheme of civilian government for the islands; their efforts were passed into law as the Virgin Islands Organic Act of 1936. The following year, he was appointed federal district judge for the Virgin Islands, thus becoming the first African-American federal judge. He served in this capacity until 1939, when he resigned to become dean of the Howard Law School.

During the 1930s, in addition to his duties as solicitor and law professor, Hastie had argued many civil rights cases in the federal courts. This experience made him an expert on race relations in the United States, and in 1940 Secretary of War Henry L. Stimson appointed him a civilian aide and assigned him to conduct a survey of race relations

William H. Hastie *(left)* was the first African American to serve as governor of a U.S. territory. He is shown here in a 1942 meeting with Undersecretary of War Robert Patterson. *(Library of Congress)*

in the armed forces. Hastie's report revealed that the Army Air Corps (today the U.S. Air Force) was the most segregated branch of the service. His recommendations for change, however, were mostly ignored, and in 1943 he resigned in protest.

Meanwhile, Hastie had become involved once again with the Virgin Islands. In 1942, President Franklin D. Roosevelt had appointed him to the Caribbean Advisory Committee, which coordinated the social and economic activities of the Virgin Islands and Puerto Rico with the activities of Great Britain's Caribbean colonies. Four years later, President Harry S. Truman nominated him for governor of the Virgin Islands. When the U.S. Senate gave its consent, he became the second African American to serve as a governor (P. B. S. PINCHBACK was the first). His background as a federal judge and college dean, coupled with his total lack of political experience, made his tenure as governor a rough one, as he was not used to dealing with constituents who by right could disagree with him. He did, however, win two important victories. Many of the islands' prominent residents were white, but he convinced the legislature to pass a civil rights bill that outlawed discrimination on the basis of race or color. Before his tenure as governor, the legislature had approved acts appointing its own members to administrative boards and tribunals in violation of the principle of separation of powers. Unlike his predecessors, who merely complained about the practice, he sued successfully in federal district court to have the practice stopped.

In 1949, Hastie resigned as governor to accept an appointment to the Third Circuit Court of Appeals, which included the Virgin Islands in its jurisdiction. In 1968, he became the court's chief judge and served in this capacity until he resigned three years later. He devoted his remaining years to lecturing and raising money on behalf of law firms that fought for the rights of consumers and minorities and to protect the environment. He died on April 14, 1976, in Norristown, Pennsylvania.

Further Reading

Marvis, B. *William H. Hastie: Educator and Politician.* New York: Chelsea House Publishers, 2002.

McGuire, Phillip. *He, Too, Spoke for Democracy: Judge Hastie, World War II, and the Black Soldier.* New York: Greenwood Press, 1988.

Truman Presidential Museum & Library. "Oral History Interview with Judge William H. Hastie." Available online. URL: http://www.trumanlibrary.org/oralhist/hastie.htm. Downloaded March 28, 2009.

Ware, Gilbert. *William Hastie: Grace under Pressure.* New York: Oxford University Press, 1984.

Hastings, Alcee

(Alcee Lamar Hastings)

(1936–   ) *U.S. congressional representative from Florida*

Alcee Hastings made one of the more remarkable comebacks of any public official in U.S. history. Impeached and removed from office as a federal judge, he was elected to the U.S. House of Representatives, where he has served several terms.

Hastings was born on September 5, 1936, in Altamonte Springs, Florida, to Julius and Mildred Hastings. He finished high school in 1954 and enrolled in Fisk University, where he received a B.A. four years later. He attended Howard University School of Law for the next two years before transferring to Florida A&M University, where he received his J.D. in 1963. For the next 13 years, he practiced law in Fort Lauderdale, gaining a reputation as a first-class civil rights attorney. In 1977, he was appointed to a judgeship on the Broward County Circuit Court. Two years later, President Jimmy Carter tapped him to serve as a federal judge for Florida's Southern District.

Hastings's career as a tenured federal judge ran into trouble after only two years. In 1981, he was indicted by a grand jury on charges that he had accepted a $150,000 bribe in return for reducing the sentences of two convicted mobsters. He was acquitted of the charges in 1983. Then a special investigating committee for the circuit court of appeals that oversaw Hastings's court charged Hastings with perjuring himself and fabricating the evidence that led to his acquittal. The committee recommended that the case be handed over to the U.S. Congress for impeachment hearings. In 1988, the House voted 413-3 to impeach Hastings, and the following year the Senate voted 69-26 to remove him from the bench. Hastings appealed the Senate's decision in federal district court. In 1992, that court ruled that the Senate had handled the trial improperly and ordered that Hastings be reinstated. In 1993, the U.S. Supreme Court overturned the lower court's decision and upheld the Senate's conviction.

Having left the bench in 1989, Hastings decided to seek another public office. In 1990, he ran for Florida secretary of state but lost. Undaunted by his defeat, two years later he ran for Congress. He barely won a bitterly contested Democratic primary, and then won a convincing victory over his Republican opponent in the gen-

Alcee Hastings represented southern Florida in Congress. *(Alcee L. Hastings)*

eral election. He took his seat in the House of Representatives just days after the Supreme Court upheld his conviction by the Senate. His colleagues in the House contemplated banning him from Congress because of his conviction. They were dissuaded from acting when a federal judge ruled that the conviction did not preclude Hastings from holding another federal position. He was assigned to the committees on foreign affairs and merchant marine/fisheries.

As a congressman, Hastings focused on eliminating job discrimination. He authored a bill that allows employees to use circumstantial evidence to support claims of discriminatory employment practices. He worked for passage of the so-called Cesar Chavez Workplace Fairness Act, which prohibited companies from firing striking workers. He pushed for the hiring of more black narcotics agents on the grounds that they are better able to penetrate those black neighborhoods where drug abuse is prevalent.

Somewhat surprisingly, given the large number of Hispanics in his district, Hastings emerged as a foe of immigration. He supported efforts to bolster the Immigration and Naturalization Service and the Coast Guard so that these agencies could do a better job of preventing illegal aliens from entering the country. He also worked to deny social benefits to undocumented aliens.

Hastings received high marks from his constituents for his services to the district. Among other things, he was instrumental in getting more federal funding for new roads in rapidly growing South Florida and in getting legislation passed that would protect the Everglades from developers. In 2010, Hastings, the divorced father of three children, was reelected to a 10th term.

Further Reading

Biographical Directory of the United States Congress. "Hastings, Alcee Lamar, 1936– ." Available online. URL:http://bioguide.congress.gov/scripts/biodisplay.pl?index=H000324. Downloaded April 15, 2009.

Clay, William L. *Just Permanent Interests: Black Americans in Congress, 1870–1992.* New York: Amistad Press, 1993.

Congressman Alcee L. Hastings, Official Web Site. Available online. URL: http://www.alceehastings.house.gov. Downloaded April 8, 2009.

Volcansek, Mary L. *Judicial Impeachment: None Called for Justice.* Urbana: University of Illinois Press, 1993.

Hatcher, Richard
(Richard Gordon Hatcher)
(1933–   ) *mayor of Gary, Indiana*

Richard Hatcher was one of the nation's first African-American big-city mayors. For 20 years, he governed Gary, Indiana, by getting blacks and whites to cooperate with one another instead of working at cross-purposes. In the process, he helped Gary get rid of its reputation as "Sin City" and recast itself in a new image.

Hatcher was born on July 10, 1933, in Michigan City, Indiana. His father, Carlton, worked in a railcar foundry, and his mother, Catherine, was a homemaker. After graduating from high school in 1951, he worked in his father's foundry for a year, then enrolled in Indiana University on a track scholarship. In 1956, he received a B.S., then enrolled in Valparaiso University Law School. After receiving an LL.B. in 1959, he settled in Gary while working as a clerk in an East Chicago law firm. In 1961, he opened a law office in Gary. That same year, he took a part-time position as deputy prosecutor in the Lake County, Indiana, criminal court. He struggled to find enough clients to make his law practice a success, however, and in 1962 he relocated it to Gary.

Hatcher became involved in politics in 1958, while still a law student. He ran as a Democrat for justice of the peace of the local township and came in fourth out of 10 candidates. His next campaign came in 1963, when he decided to run for an at-large seat on Gary's city council. At the time, the city's population was 55 percent African American, yet the city council was predominantly white. As a member of a civil rights group called Muigwithania (the name means "we are together" in Swahili, and was the name of an East African newspaper that espoused black liberation in the 1920s), Hatcher was committed to reforming his adopted city. The previous year, the mayor had been arrested for accepting kickbacks on city contracts, and the city in general had a reputation for being a hotbed of gambling and prostitution. Hatcher particularly wanted to commit Gary's government to improving life for black residents, most of whom lived in a huge midtown slum. Undaunted by the local Democratic committee's refusal to back his candidacy (not because he was black but because he promised to eliminate graft and corruption), he ran as an independent. Hatcher and Muigwithania mobilized a number of first-time black voters, who supported him at the polls in record numbers, thus ensuring his election. He proved to be

an energetic go-getter, as evidenced by his election as city council president after only one year on council.

In 1966, Hatcher began his campaign for mayor. His bid received a strong boost in the black community when he was invited to meet with Vice President Hubert H. Humphrey to talk about the concerns of African Americans. Nevertheless, local Democrats remained unimpressed, in large part because the incumbent mayor, Martin Katz, was also a Democrat and was seeking reelection. Once again, Hatcher and Muigwithania campaigned hard in the black community, winning the Democratic primary when Katz and another white candidate split the white vote. Despite this victory, the Democratic committee still refused to support Hatcher in the general election, choosing instead to back his Republican challenger. Disappointed but not surprised, Hatcher used his connections with Humphrey to gain support from the National Democratic Club and various national Democratic officeholders, many of whom campaigned on Hatcher's behalf. An attempt by local election officials to alter the voter rolls illegally was thwarted by the FBI and the Justice Department, and in the general election Hatcher won by fewer than 2,000 votes to become Gary's first black mayor.

As mayor, Hatcher worked ceaselessly to improve Gary. He hired professional city administrators to run the various departments, and he introduced competitive bidding for city contracts. He reorganized the police force by hiring more black officers, and he greatly reduced prostitution and gambling in the downtown area by implementing crime prevention units. He also obtained grants from the federal government and the Ford Foundation to renovate and build almost 6,000 new public housing units, pave almost 1,000 blocks of city streets, improve garbage collection services, build three new parks, and provide vocational training and jobs for thousands of inner-city youths. He also worked to reduce smokestack emissions from the mills of

U.S. Steel, Gary's largest employer. As downtown Gary became safer and cleaner, new businesses located to the city, and several that had left in the early 1960s returned. The centerpiece of Hatcher's efforts to revitalize the city's economy was the Genesis Convention Center, which was built in the heart of downtown in 1982. Perhaps most important, he fostered a new attitude of cooperation between blacks and whites that permitted the city to move ahead instead of continuing to stagnate. The voters rewarded Hatcher for his accomplishments by reelecting him to four consecutive terms. On the national level, he served as head of the National Conference of Black Mayors from 1978 to 1982.

By 1987, however, Hatcher's magic touch had worn off. He had been Gary's mayor for 20 years, and many residents perceived that his efforts to revitalize their city were no longer paying off. When he lost his bid for renomination in that year's Democratic primary, he declined to run in the general election. He finished out his term, then in 1988 he opened a consulting firm. A year later, he became a professor of law at his alma mater, Valparaiso. In 1991, he ran again for mayor of Gary but was defeated in the primary. Hatcher has since become the board director and president of the National Civil Rights Hall of Fame.

Further Reading

Colburn, David R., and Jeffrey S. Adler. *African-American Mayors: Race, Politics, and the American City.* Urbana: University of Illinois Press, 2001.

Drotning, Phillip T., and Wesley W. South. *Up from the Ghetto.* New York: Cowles, 1970.

Haskins, James. *A Piece of the Power: Four Black Mayors.* New York: Dial Press, 1972.

Poinsett, Alex. *Black Power, Gary Style: The Making of Mayor Richard Gordon Hatcher.* Chicago: Johnson Publishing, 1970.

Simmonds, Yussuf. "Richard G. Hatcher." *Los Angeles Sentinel,* July 10, 2008. Available online. URL: http://www.lasentinel.net/Richard-G.-Hatcher.html. Downloaded April 25, 2008.

Hawkins, Augustus

(Augustus Freeman Hawkins)
(1907–2007) *U.S. congressional representative from California*

Augustus Hawkins was the first African-American congressman from California. During his 56 years of public service in the California senate and the U.S. Congress, he authored a number of important pieces of social legislation, thus making him one of the most effective black political leaders of all time. He remains, however, one of the least known of those leaders, largely because of his preference to work behind the scenes rather than call attention to himself.

Hawkins was born on August 31, 1907, in Shreveport, Louisiana. His father, Nyanza, was a pharmacist, and his mother, Hattie, was a homemaker. At age 10, he moved with his family to Colorado and then to Los Angeles, California, where his father reopened his pharmacy. After graduating from high school, he studied economics at the University of California at Los Angeles and received a B.A. in 1931. He then enrolled in the University of Southern California's Institute of Government and went to work with his brother as a real estate agent. In 1941, he married Pegga Smith; they had no children.

Hawkins's involvement in real estate gave him a keen awareness of the economic difficulties facing Los Angeles's black, Asian, and Hispanic minorities, especially in the early days of the Great Depression. This awareness led him into politics, and in 1932 he became a Democrat and campaigned for Franklin D. Roosevelt for president and for Upton Sinclair for governor. By 1934, he had become sufficiently well-known in his community and the party to run for the state senate. His Republican opponent had held his seat for 16 years and was considered unbeatable, so Hawkins promised to lower the streetcar fares if elected. The ploy worked; however, both he and the voters quickly found out that a freshman state senator pulled very little weight with the city transit company. Fortunately, this incident led him to be very careful about making campaign promises in the future.

Hawkins served in the senate for 28 years. During his tenure, he authored more than 100 bills; most of them concerned "minority" issues such as constructing more public housing, eliminating urban blight, establishing day-care centers, and providing domestics and other low-wage workers with a minimum wage, worker's compensation, disability insurance, and old age pensions. Most of his bills passed, in large part because he chaired, at various times, the important committees on public utilities, labor and capital, and rules. His greatest success involved passage of a fair employment practices act.

By 1962, Hawkins had enough seniority to be a serious contender for speaker of the senate. However, he had come to the realization that many of the problems facing minorities in California were faced by minorities all over the country. Desiring to do something about them on a national scale, he decided instead to run for the U.S. House of Representatives. He took his seat in Congress in 1963 and was assigned to the committees on House administration and on education and labor. Reelected 13 times, he chaired House administration from 1981 to 1985 and education and labor from 1983 to 1990.

As in the California senate, Hawkins authored a number of important pieces of social legislation. He wrote that part of the Civil Rights Act of 1964 that outlawed discriminatory hiring practices and established the Equal Employment Opportunity Commission. He sponsored the Elementary and Secondary Education Act of 1970, which provided $1.3 billion in federal aid to schools with a high percentage of low-income students. He cosponsored the Humphrey-Hawkins Full-Employment and Balanced Growth Act of 1978, which set national goals of 3 percent inflation and 4 percent unemployment and required the president, Congress, and Federal Reserve Board to cooperate in developing policies to achieve these goals. He wrote the Fair Housing Amendments Act of 1988,

which prohibited discrimination against the disabled and, in most cases, families with children. He cosponsored the Elementary and Secondary School Improvement Amendments of 1988, which provide for bilingual education as well as improved education for children with social disabilities and for Indians living on reservations. He also played a prominent role in passing legislation to reform the juvenile justice system and to provide needy public school students with subsidized meals. In 1971, he became a cofounder of the Congressional Black Caucus.

A loyal Democrat, Hawkins was a vocal opponent of the Nixon administration's war effort in Vietnam. While on a fact-finding mission there in 1970, he and another congressman discovered that Viet Cong captives were being brutalized in Con Son prison. Their disclosure of the prison's activities led to it being closed shortly thereafter. He was also vociferous in his opposition to the "Reagan Revolution" in the 1980s, which sought to eliminate funding for the very types of social programs he had battled for during his entire political career.

In 1990, at age 83, Hawkins retired from politics. He returned to Los Angeles where he serves as a director of the Hawkins Family Memorial Foundation for Educational Research and Development, which he established in 1969. Three months after turning 100, Augustus Hawkins died on November 10, 2007.

Further Reading

Biographical Directory of the United States Congress. "Hawkins, Augustus Freeman, 1907– ." Available online. URL: http://bioguide.congress.gov/scripts/biodisplay.pl?index=H000367. Downloaded April 9, 2009.

Black Americans in Congress. "Augustus Freeman (Gus) Hawkins." Available online. URL: http://baic.house.gov/member-profiles/profile.html?intID=30. Downloaded April 8, 2009.

Clay, William L. *Just Permanent Interests: Black Americans in Congress, 1870–1992*. New York: Amistad Press, 1993.

Hoel, Janet E. *Augustus F. Hawkins, Democratic Representative from California.* Washington: Grossman Publishers, 1972.

Luther, Claudia, and Valerie J. Nelson. "Augustus F. Hawkins: 1907–2007—A Pioneer for Black Lawmakers in L.A." *Los Angeles Times,* November 13, 2007. Available online. URL: http://articles.latimes.com/2007/nov/13/local/me-hawkins13. Downloaded April 9, 2009.

Hayes, Charles
(Charles Arthur Hayes)
(1918–1997) *U.S. congressional representative from Illinois*

Most political leaders arrive at a career in politics after studying and practicing law. Charles Hayes was an exception to his rule, having entered politics after a long career as a blue-collar worker and labor organizer.

Hayes was born on February 17, 1918, in Cairo, Illinois. In 1935, he graduated from high school and went to work as a machine operator. Shortly thereafter, he became a charter member of Local 1424 of the United Brotherhood of Carpenters and Joiners of America. He enjoyed union work more than operating a machine, and he soon gained a reputation as a good organizer. In 1940 he was elected to a two-year term as local president.

By 1943, Hayes had left the machine shop and taken a job in a meatpacking plant. That same year he was offered a position on the grievance committee of the local of the United Packinghouse Workers of America. For the next 36 years, he was active in the affairs of the UPWA. He became a field representative in 1949 and director of its District One in 1954. In 1968, the UPWA merged with several meat cutters' unions to form the United Food and Commercial Workers Union. Hayes retained his position as district director, and in 1979 he took on the additional duties of international vice president. He held both positions until 1983, when he retired from union work in order to run for political office.

Like most union leaders, Hayes worked hard to obtain better wages and working conditions for working people. As an African-American union leader, he used his positions in the unions to obtain more and better jobs and promotions for blacks in the workplace. He made it a point to seek out black union members who, like him, had a flair for union work, and then worked to get them promoted into leadership positions in the unions. In 1972, he cofounded the Coalition of Black Trade Unionists to give African-American union members an independent voice within the ranks of labor and to force organized labor to give more attention to minority interests. He served as the CBTU's executive vice president from its founding until 1986.

In 1983, HAROLD WASHINGTON was elected mayor of Chicago. Hayes played a key role in Washington's election by mobilizing the labor vote. He was particularly effective at raising money from black union members and getting them to work for Washington's campaign. At the time, Washington represented Chicago's Southside in Congress, home to a large percentage of the city's African-American working class, and he resigned from the House following his election. Fourteen challengers, including Hayes, announced their candidacy for the remainder of Washington's term. Hayes, however, was personally selected by Washington to be his successor, and he became the front-runner when Washington endorsed him. After winning the Democratic primary with 45 percent of the vote, he swept to victory in the special election and he took his seat in Congress in late 1983. He was assigned to the committees on education/labor and small business.

As a congressman, Hayes continued to champion the cause of the working class. His most ambitious endeavor in this regard was to introduce a bill ratifying an Economic Bill of Rights. The need for such a measure had been suggested by President Franklin D. Roosevelt but was never seriously addressed. Had it passed, Hayes's program would have given all Americans the rights to a job at a living wage, equal pay for equal work, collective bargaining, and a good education, among others.

Other Hayes initiatives included legislation to encourage students to stay in school, and to provide increased federal funding for vocational training and job placement. He was particularly interested in improving working conditions for workers in the postal system. He is best remembered for writing and shepherding through Congress the School Improvement Act of 1987. This act provided millions of federal dollars to public schools across the country for computers, textbooks, and supplies.

Hayes was reelected to Congress four times. In 1992, it was disclosed that he was involved in the House banking scandal. Hundreds of congressmen had written thousands of bad checks, creating numerous overdrafts in their congressional bank accounts. These overdrafts amounted to interest-free loans, and the American public was outraged by what it perceived to be a gross abuse of congressional privilege at taxpayer expense. As a result, he failed to get renominated in 1992, losing in the Democratic primary to BOBBY RUSH. He returned to Chicago when his term expired the following year.

Hayes was married three times and had two children. Two marriages ended with the death of his spouse, and one ended in divorce. Hayes remained active in labor affairs until his death on April 8, 1997, in Hazel Crest, Illinois.

Further Reading

Biographical Directory of the United States Congress. "Hayes, Charles Arthur, 1918–1997." Available online. URL: http://bioguide.congress.gov/scripts/biodisplay.pl?index=H000388. Downloaded March 28, 2009.

Black Americans in Congress. "Charles Arthur Hayes." Available online. URL: http://baic.house.gov/member-profiles/profile.html?intID=69. Downloaded April 1, 2009.

Clay, William L. *Just Permanent Interests: Black Americans in Congress, 1870–1992.* New York: Amistad Press, 1993.

Isaacs, McAllister, 3rd. "TW's 1998 Leader of the Year: Charles A. Hayes." *Textile World* 148, no. 10 (October 1998), pp. 34–36.

Hayes, James
(James C. Hayes)
(1946–   ) *mayor of Fairbanks, Alaska*

In 1992, James Hayes ran virtually unopposed for the office of mayor of Fairbanks, Alaska. After winning, he became the first African American to serve as mayor of an Alaskan community.

Hayes was born on May 25, 1946, in Sacramento, California. At age nine, his parents divorced, and he moved with his mother, Juanita, to Fairbanks. As a boy, he helped support the family by shining shoes and delivering newspapers. After finishing high school in 1965, he enrolled in the University of Alaska in nearby College and received a B.A. in education in 1970. He taught fifth grade in Fairbanks for two years, then worked briefly as the Alaska bureau director of the President's Council on Youth and Job Opportunity and as deputy director of the governor of Alaska's manpower planning division. In late 1972, he returned to Fairbanks as an associate attorney-investigator for the attorney's general's office of consumer protection, a position he held for 20 years. In the meantime, he became more involved in his church, Lily of the Valley Church of God in Christ. In 1974 he married Chris Parham, daughter of the church's pastor, with whom he has two children. He was ordained a minister in the Church of God in Christ in 1982, and he went on to serve as Lily of the Valley's assistant pastor and, when his father-in-law died in 1997, pastor.

Hayes became involved in politics in 1973, when he was elected to a term on the Fairbanks North Star Borough board of education. He declined to run for reelection in order to concentrate on his other duties but returned to the political fray in 1987. That same year, he won a seat on the Fairbanks city council. Over the next five years, he earned a reputation for being a fiscal and social conservative. He advocated an increase in city taxes to offset the results of years of deficit spending by previous administrations, and he helped to renegotiate several union contracts with municipal employees so that the proposed tax increase would be minimal. He also called for the statewide repeal of the law legalizing the recreational use of marijuana.

In 1992, Wayne Nelson, mayor of Fairbanks, announced that he would not seek reelection that year. Hayes, a Democrat, was the only candidate of either party to file before the deadline, and he easily won in the general election against a last-minute write-in candidate. As mayor, Hayes's biggest problem was finding enough money in the city budget to pay for snow removal. He also worked hard to promote Fairbanks as a tourist destination, endlessly touting its beautiful scenery and balmy summers, when the temperature can climb into the upper 80s. He frequently traveled to the state capital in Juneau to lobby for the needs of the state's northern residents, with generally positive results.

Hayes was reelected in 1995 but also the voters voted to give him more power than any other Alaska mayor. While transferring some of the city manager's powers to the mayor's office, in 1995 the voters approved of giving the mayor the power to break ties on city council decisions. Reelected in 1998, he declined to run again in 2001, citing the demands of the job and of his pastorate.

Several years after leaving office, Hayes was investigated for misusing federal grants he received for the LOVE Social Services tutoring and mentoring center, which he operated. He was ultimately found guilty of diverting approximately $450,000 for personal use and for the construction of a new building for his church. In May 2008, he was sentenced to five and a half years in federal prison. His wife, Murilda "Chris" Hayes,

was given a sentence of three years for her role in the scandal.

Further Reading
Johnson, Anne J. "James C. Hayes, 1946– ." *Contemporary Black Biography* 10 (1996): 94–97.
Eshleman, Christopher, "Former Mayor, First Lady, Sentenced to Federal Prison," *Fairbanks Daily News-Miner,* May 2, 2008. Available online. URL: http://www.newsminer.com/news/2008/may/02/hayeses-sentenced-jim-5-12-chris-3-years. Downloaded April 9, 2009.

Henry, Aaron
(Aaron Edd Henry)
(1922–1997) *Mississippi state representative*

Aaron Henry is best known as a leading figure of the Civil Rights movement in Mississippi. Equally important, however, is the role he played in state politics by cofounding two political parties and serving seven terms in the state legislature.

Henry was born on July 2, 1922, in Dublin, Mississippi. His parents, Edd and Mattie, were sharecroppers. He spent his youth helping his parents in the cotton fields and attending schools for blacks in nearby Clarksdale. After graduating from high school, he joined the U.S. Army and served during World War II in Hawaii. Discharged after the war, he used the G.I. Bill to pay his way through Xavier University in New Orleans, Louisiana, receiving a B.A. in pharmacology in 1950. That same year, he became a partner in a Clarksdale drugstore and married Noelle Michael, with whom he had one child. Within a few years he had become one of the most prominent African Americans in Clarksdale.

Mississippi in the 1950s was a hotbed of white racism, and Henry resolved to do what he could to combat it. In 1954, he joined the state chapter of the National Association for the Advancement of Colored People (NAACP). The following year, he cofounded and became chairman of the

Aaron Henry spoke before the credentials committee at the Democratic National Convention. A leader in the struggle for civil rights in Mississippi, he served seven terms in the state legislature. *(Library of Congress)*

Council of Federated Organizations (COFO), an umbrella organization that sought to coordinate the in-state activities of the major civil rights groups, these being the NAACP, the Student Nonviolent Coordinating Committee, the Southern Christian Leadership Conference, and the Congress of Racial Equality.

In 1960, Henry was named president of the state NAACP chapter, a position he held for the next 33 years. The following year, he helped guide the first of several statewide campaigns to register African-American voters and provide them with a rudimentary political education. In 1961, when the Freedom Riders attempted to desegregate white-only facilities at the bus station in Jackson, the state capital, he was arrested with them and then helped plan their legal defense. Later that year, he organized a black boycott of Clarksdale stores that refused to hire or serve African Americans.

Henry's efforts to end segregation made him a marked man. During his career he was arrested more than three dozen times, more often than not on trumped-up charges. On one occasion, he was convicted of sexually harassing a white hitchhiker, but the conviction was overturned on appeal. In addition, his drugstore was firebombed and his wife was fired from her job as a teacher. According to legend, before civil rights activist Medgar Evers was murdered in 1963, his assailants flipped a coin to determine whether Evers or Henry would be assassinated.

Undaunted, Henry continued to press for political equality for Mississippi's African-American population. In late 1963, COFO sponsored "Freedom Vote," a mock election that provided Mississippi's black voters with some practical experience at the polls. Approximately 80,000 voters, or more than three times the number of registered black voters, "elected" Henry governor by a landslide. The turnout was so encouraging that COFO decided to expand its registration efforts during the "Freedom Summer" of 1964. To provide a congenial home for new black voters, that same year Henry, ELLA BAKER, UNITA BLACKWELL, CHARLES EVERS, and others founded the biracial Mississippi Freedom Democratic Party, with Henry as chairman. The MFDP created a stir at the 1964 Democratic National Convention when it unsuccessfully tried to unseat the state's regular party delegation. Later that year, Henry tried to run for the U.S. House of Representatives as an independent, but election officials refused to put his name on the ballot. In 1965, he won another mock election, this time to the U.S. Senate.

In 1965, Henry left the MFDP on the grounds that it was becoming too radical to achieve any good. That same year he cofounded the Loyalist Democrats, a group of black moderates who sought to achieve some accommodation with the regular Democratic state apparatus. As leader of the Loyalists, Henry led their delegation to the national conventions of 1968 and 1972. By 1976, he had co-engineered a merger between the Loyalists and the regulars, thus making it possible for African Americans to run for public office in Mississippi with the full support of the state Democratic Party.

In 1980, Henry succeeded in getting the courts to force the state to reapportion the state legislature, thus creating a number of black-majority districts. In 1982, he was elected from one of the districts. For the next 14 years, he served in the state legislature as a champion for programs to improve housing, health care, employment, and child care.

In 1996, Henry retired from politics. He accepted a position as chairman of the board of MINACT, Inc., which operates eight Job Corps centers in seven states. He died on May 19, 1997, in Jackson.

Further Reading

Hamlin, Françoise N. "Henry, Aaron E." In *African American National Biography*, vol. 4, edited by Henry Louis Gates, Jr., and Evelyn Brooks Higginbotham. New York: Oxford University Press, 2008, pp. 192–193.
Henry, Aaron, with Constance Curry. *Aaron Henry: The Fire Ever Burning.* Jackson: University Press of Mississippi, 2000.

Herenton, Willie
(Willie Wilbur Herenton)
(1940–   ) *mayor of Memphis, Tennessee*

In 1991, Willie Herenton became the first African-American mayor of Memphis, Tennessee. Herenton was born on April 23, 1940, in Memphis. His parents separated when he was young, and he was raised in the country outside Memphis by his mother and grandmother. As a boy, he helped support the family by picking cotton. After finishing high school, he enrolled in LeMoyne-Owen College in Memphis on a work-study program and received a B.S. in education in 1963. For the next four years, he taught elementary school in the Memphis public school system. In 1967, the year after he received an M.A. from Memphis State University, he was promoted to principal. In 1971, he received a Ph.D. from Southern Illinois University. Three years later, he was named deputy superintendent of schools, and in 1979 he became superintendent, a position he held for 12 years. As superintendent, he implemented an innovative program that greatly reduced teacher turnover in inner-city schools.

In 1990, the population of Memphis was almost 60 percent African American. The city's black voters had managed to elect African Americans to represent them in the U.S. Congress in the person of HAROLD FORD, who served from 1975 to 1997, and his son HAROLD FORD, JR., who took his father's place in the House of Representatives in 1997. However, they had not yet been able to elect a black mayor. In 1991, a number of Memphis's black voters held the African American People's Convention for purposes of nominating one of their own to run for mayor. Herenton emerged from the convention as their overwhelming preference, and with their support he ran as a Democrat against Richard Hackett, the Republican incumbent. Herenton won the hard-fought contest by less than 150 votes, and he took office in mid-1991.

As mayor, Herenton worked to improve the delivery of municipal services to all city residents. He worked to lower the crime rate by hiring hundreds of additional police officers and establishing more than a dozen mini-precincts in high-crime areas. He allocated enough money to the school board to build and repair a number of schools, and most important, to air-condition every classroom. His economic development program brought in thousands of new jobs and attracted more than $1 billion in downtown

Willie Herenton was the mayor of Memphis, Tennessee. *(G. Hings/Skipworth)*

redevelopment projects. Part of his program encouraged the establishment of minority-owned businesses via set-asides and other incentives. He oversaw the development of the city's first master plan for its park system, which included significant upgrades and repairs.

Herenton was easily reelected in 1995. During his second term, he came into conflict with the powerful Ford family; led by Congressman Harold Ford, the Ford family had established a formidable political organization in Memphis. The conflict arose mainly over who would control the city's African-American voters. It manifested itself in such matters as a pay raise for city employees belonging to the Memphis local of the American Federation of State, County, and Municipal Employees. When Herenton ran for reelection in 1999, one of his 14 opponents was Joe Ford, the family's candidate. To the surprise of many, Herenton won the election by receiving almost half of the total vote. He continued to press forward with the initiatives of his first term, and in 2003 *American City & County* magazine named him its 2002 Municipal Leader of the Year. In 2007, Herenton became the first mayor of Memphis to be elected to five consecutive terms. He resigned from office on July 30, 2009, in order to run for the House of Representatives from Tennessee's Ninth Congressional District. After a highly combative campaign, Herenton was soundly defeated by the incumbent candidate, Steve Cohen, in the Democratic primary.

Herenton is married to the former Ida Jones, with whom he has three children.

Further Reading

Charlier, Tom. "Herenton Wins Unprecedented 5th Term as Memphis Leader." *Memphis Commercial Appeal*, October 5, 2007. Available online. URL: http://www.commercialappeal.com/news/2007/oct/05/still-the-one-mayorherenton-wins-unprecedented-8. Downloaded April 23, 2009.
Golus, Carrie. "Willie W. Herenton, 1940–   ." *Contemporary Black Biography* 24 (2000), pp. 76–78.

Pohlmann, Marcus D., and Michael P. Kirby. *Racial Politics at the Crossroads: Memphis Elects Dr. W. W. Herenton.* Knoxville: University of Tennessee Press, 1996.

Herman, Alexis
(Alexis Margaret Herman)
(1947–) *U.S. secretary of labor*

Alexis Herman was one of four African Americans appointed by President Bill Clinton to his cabinet. Both before and after her appointment as secretary of labor, she worked actively to improve job opportunities for women and minorities.

Herman was born on July 16, 1947, in Mobile, Alabama. Her father, Alex, was a businessman, and her mother, Gloria, was a teacher. After graduating from high school in 1965, she enrolled in Edgewood College in Madison, Wisconsin. Two years later, she transferred to Spring Hill College in Mobile, and a year after that to Xavier University in New Orleans, where she received a B.A. in 1969. She spent two years as a social worker for two different faith-based community outreach organizations in Mobile, and in 1971 she went to work for a job training program based in Pascagoula, Mississippi. In all these positions, she worked to desegregate schools and workplaces.

In 1972, Herman was hired by the Southern Regional Council to become director of its Atlanta-based Minority Women Employment Program; in this position, she worked to place qualified black women in management positions, mostly in the private sector. Under her direction, the program was so successful that in 1974 the Department of Labor decided to increase its funding to make it nationwide, with her as the national director. Her accomplishments in this position brought her to the attention of Democratic president Jimmy Carter, who in 1977 appointed her director of the Department of Labor's Women's Bureau. She resigned as the bureau's director in 1981, following the inauguration of Republican president Ronald Reagan. She remained in Washington as head of her own marketing and management consulting firm.

Herman became interested in politics while in school; her father had sued the Alabama Democratic Party to gain access for African Americans to its state primary, and he later became the state party's first black ward committeeman. She herself became an active member of the party, one reason she was selected for the Labor Department post. She remained active in the party's affairs after leaving government service in 1981, and in 1989 she was recruited by RON BROWN to work for the Democratic National Committee. She served for two years as the DNC's chief of staff, and in 1991 she was named deputy chair. The following year, she served as chief executive officer of the Democratic National Convention Committee, which was charged with making all the arrangements for the party's 1992 national convention at New York City's Madison Square Garden.

Following his election in 1992, President Bill Clinton named Herman as deputy director of his transition team. Shortly after taking office in early 1993, he appointed her director of the Office of Public Liaison. In this capacity, she served as Clinton's public relations manager. She played a key role in getting the controversial Dr. Jocelyn Elders confirmed as Surgeon General and in drumming up support within the law enforcement community for Clinton's 1994 crime bill. She also arranged informal weekly meetings, called "confabs," with Democratic leaders who at first were hostile to the Clinton administration, and she served as Clinton's unofficial ambassador to African Americans in general and the Congressional Black Caucus in particular. In 1996, Clinton described her as "my eyes and ears, working to connect the American people [to the president]."

Following his reelection in 1996, Clinton nominated Herman as secretary of labor. Like all Clinton nominees, she was scrutinized heavily by congressional Republicans. A central issue in her confirmation hearing was her role in scheduling the confabs, which critics condemned as illegal fund-raisers. She survived this and other charges (one news service erroneously identified her as being a lesbian) to take office in mid-1997.

As secretary, Herman focused on making the American workforce as competitive in the international labor market as it could be. To this end, she helped secure a tax credit for senior citizens who got job education and training. She also worked for increased funding for high-tech training, workplace safety, a higher minimum wage, affirmative action, employment programs for at-risk youth, and programs to help welfare recipients become employed. The highlight of her career in these areas was the enactment of the Workplace Investment Act of 1998. She also handled a number of labor disputes, the most significant being the United Parcel Service (UPS) strike of 1997. The strike had threatened to cripple the nation's economy, as virtually every business in the United States shipped and received packages via UPS. Herman averted this situation by taking an active part in the strike negotiations, thus helping to end the strike after only 10 days.

In 2001, Herman stepped down as secretary of labor following the election of Republican president George W. Bush. Since that time she has chaired the Coca-Cola Company's diversity task force, served as a senior adviser to Toyota Motor Sales, written an Internet advice column for job seekers, and served as CEO of New Ventures, Inc., a not-for-profit organization that works with the employment challenged. She is married to Charles Franklin.

Further Reading

Langston, Donna. *A to Z of American Women Leaders and Activists.* New York: Facts On File, 2002.

Simmonds, Yussuf. "Alexis M. Herman." *Los Angeles Sentinel,* May 29, 2008. Available online. URL: http://www.lasentinel.net/Alexis-M.-Herman.html. Downloaded April 20, 2008.

United States Department of Labor. "Alexis M. Herman." Available online. URL: http://www.dol.gov/ oasam/programs/history/herman.htm. Downloaded April 20, 2009.

Whigham-Desir, Marjorie. "The Magnolia Mediator." *Black Enterprise* 30 (May 2000): 143–148.

Hilliard, Earl
(Earl Frederick Hilliard)
(1942–   ) *U.S. congressional representative from Alabama*

In 1992, Earl Hilliard became the first African American to represent Alabama in Congress since JEREMIAH HARALSON left office in 1877. He served in Congress for five terms.

Hilliard was born on April 9, 1942, in Birmingham, Alabama, to William and Iola Hilliard. After finishing high school in Birmingham, he entered Morehouse College and received a B.A. in 1964. In 1967, he received a J.D. from Howard University Law School and returned to Birmingham. He taught for a year at Miles College and then spent two years as an assistant to the president of Alabama State University. Meanwhile, he was completing course work for an M.B.A., which he received from the Atlanta University School of Business in 1970. That same year, he became a partner in a Birmingham law firm. In 1966 he married Mary Franklin, with whom he has two children.

As an attorney, Hilliard worked for equal opportunity for minorities, which led him into local politics. By 1974, the Civil Rights movement had registered enough African-American voters in Birmingham to make possible the election of blacks to the state legislature. That same year, Hilliard, running as a Democrat, won a seat in the lower house. The following year, he cofounded and served as the first chair of the Alabama Black Legislative Caucus. In 1980, he was elected to the state senate. He remained in that body for 12 years, during which time he chaired the committees on judiciary and commerce/transportation/ utilities. He successfully pushed bills that provided more state funds for Alabama's historically black colleges and universities and that made available more scholarship money for minority students.

The census of 1990 mandated that Alabama redraw its congressional districts. In the process of doing so, the state legislature created a black-majority district centered around the Birmingham neighborhood where Hilliard lived. In 1992, he declared his candidacy for the seat and narrowly won the Democratic primary. After an easy win in the general election, he took his seat in 1993 and was assigned to the committees on small business and agriculture.

As a congressman, Hilliard sided with the liberal Democrats. He supported socialized medicine as a means of providing national health care and chaired several committees related to rural health care. He pushed for increased federal funding for black colleges and college students, and he has gone on record as supporting reparations payments to the descendants of slaves. At home, he was able to get the federal government to designate three impoverished areas as "enterprise zones," thus qualifying businesses that relocated to them for special tax breaks and other incentives. He also played an instrumental role in restoring ferry service to Gees Bend, Alabama, a small black community on the Alabama River downstream from Selma. In 1962, many of the town's residents had participated in the civil rights march in Selma that turned into the bloody riot that made Selma infamous. Selma's white residents retaliated by cutting off ferry service to Gees Bend, and for 30 years the residents of the black community had to drive 40 miles to reach the nearest shopping of any consequence.

Hilliard was reelected to five terms in Congress. During his tenure, he became embroiled in several minor scandals. In 1995, the *New York Times* labeled him Congress's "most frequent flyer" because of the number of overseas trips he has made at taxpayer expense. In 1999, the House Ethics Committee opened an investigation into the financial affairs of his congressional office

after it was disclosed that his staff included the relatives of several prominent Birmingham politicians. Meanwhile, his liberal views seemed to turn off a number of his constituents. His 2002 bid for reelection was denied when he lost the Democratic primary to ARTUR DAVIS, a moderate African-American candidate. Hilliard returned to Birmingham and resumed his law practice.

Further Reading

Biographical Directory of the United States Congress. "Hilliard, Earl Frederick, 1942– ." Available online. URL: http://bioguide.congress.gov/scripts/biodisplay.pl?index=H000621. Downloaded April 9, 2009.

Black Americans in Congress. "Earl Frederick Hilliard." Available online. URL: http://baic.house.gov/member-profiles/profile.html?intID=68. Downloaded April 7, 2009.

Clay, William L. *Just Permanent Interests: Black Americans in Congress, 1870–1992.* New York: Amistad Press, 1993.

"Earl F. Hilliard." *Congressional Quarterly Weekly Report* 51 (January 16, 1993 supplement): 37.

Holder, Eric
(Eric H. Holder, Jr.)
(1951–) *U.S. attorney general*

In 2009, Eric Holder became the first African American to serve as attorney general of the United States. Born on January 21, 1951, he grew up in the middle-class neighborhood of East Elmhurst in Queens, New York. His parents, both immigrants from Barbados, instilled him in a strict work ethic and respect for education. After attending an elementary school for gifted children, he was accepted into Stuyvesant, one of the most prestigious public high schools in the United States.

Holder continued his education at Columbia University, where he studied American history. On weekends, he volunteered for a Harlem youth program and took underprivileged teenagers on trips to New York's cultural institutions. After receiving his bachelor's degree in 1973, Holder attended Columbia Law School. As he explained to the *New York Times,* "The law inevitably is wound up with some great political movements, social movements. I wanted to be a part of that."

Following graduation, Holder joined the staff of the U.S. Department of Justice. For 12 years, he served in its Public Integrity Section, which was charged with prosecuting high-level corruption cases. In 1988, President Ronald Reagan appointed him to the superior court of the District of Columbia. After five years on the bench, he was tapped by President Bill Clinton to serve as the U.S. attorney for Washington, D.C. In this position, he oversaw the fraud investigation of Illinois congressman Dan Rostenkowski.

In 1997, Holder was promoted to deputy attorney general, working under Attorney General Janet Reno. Acting on his advice, Reno permitted special prosecutor Kenneth Starr to investigate the relationship between White House intern Monica Lewinsky and President Clinton—a decision that ultimately led to Clinton's impeachment. Holder was also at the center of the controversy involving Clinton's presidential pardon of financier Marc Rich, who had fled the United States after being charged with tax evasion. The pardon drew criticism from the press and from Republican leaders, especially when it was reported that Rich's ex-wife had made large donations to Clinton's presidential library. Holder was forced to appear before the House Committee on Oversight and Government Reform. Holder's legal advice on the question of whether to grant the Rich pardon was a tepid "neutral leaning towards favorable," but the outgoing administration suggested he was responsible for the decision. Disturbed by questions regarding his integrity, Holder told the committee, "I have been angry, hurt, and even somewhat disillusioned by what has transpired over the past two weeks with regard to this pardon."

Holder left public service for the private sector. In 2001, he became a partner at the Washington law firm of Covington & Burling. While there, his clients included Chiquita, Merck, and the National Football League.

In 2004, Holder attended a dinner party at which he met BARACK OBAMA, then the junior senator from Illinois. According to Holder, the two men immediately "clicked." Holder and Obama became friends, and when Obama declared his candidacy in the 2008 presidential election, he asked Holder to become a cochairman of his campaign. Well known in Washington political circles, Holder was instrumental in Obama's fund-raising efforts there. Holder also served on the advisory team that helped select Senator Joe Biden as Obama's running mate.

Following his electoral victory, Obama asked Holder to become attorney general. Holder was sworn into office on February 3, 2009. One of his first acts as attorney general was the dismissal of the indictment against Senator Ted Stevens on charges of corruption. Although the Justice Department prosecutors had secured a conviction, they were accused of prosecutorial misconduct during the trial.

Holder has drawn fire from some conservative critics for his positions on the treatment of terrorism suspects. One of his more controversial actions was to announce that Khalid Sheikh Mohammed and other conspirators involved in the September 11, 2001, attacks would be tried in federal court in New York City. During Obama's first term, Holder also worked to build a criminal case against BP (British Petroleum) for its role in the 2010 Gulf of Mexico oil spill and to challenge an Arizona law intended to curb illegal immigration.

Holder is married to Sharon Malone, an obstetrician. They have three children.

Further Reading

Hernandez, Javier C. "Holder, High Achiever Poised to Scale New Heights." *New York Times,* November 30, 2008. Available online. URL: http://www.nytimes.com/2008/12/01/nyregion/01holder.html. Downloaded May 20, 2009.

Johnston, David. "Eric H. Holder, Jr." *New York Times,* November 11, 2008. Available online. URL: http://www.nytimes.com/2008/11/12/us/politics/11web-holder.html?scp=3&sq=eric%20holder&st=cse. Downloaded May 20, 2009.

Longstreth, Andrew. "Making History." *The American Lawyer,* June 1, 2008. Available online. URL: http://www.law.com/jsp/tal/PubArticleTAL.jsp?id=1202421743636. Downloaded May 20, 2009.

Howard, Perry
(Perry Wilson Howard)
(1877–1961) *Mississippi Republican Party chairman*

For eight years, Perry Howard was chairman of the Mississippi Republican Party even though he did not live in Mississippi. This strange situation was made possible by the disfranchisement of African Americans throughout the South and the ability of Republican presidential candidates to win consistently.

Howard was born on June 14, 1877, in Ebenezer, Mississippi. His father, Perry, was a businessman and local politician who had cofounded Ebenezer, and his mother, Sallie, was a homemaker. After receiving his A.B. from Rust College in 1898, he briefly studied law at Fisk University, then began teaching mathematics at Alcorn A&M College. From 1901 to 1905, he also studied law at the University of Chicago and received his LL.B in 1905. After graduation, he gave up teaching and opened a law office in Mississippi. In 1907, he married Wilhelmina Lucas with whom he had three children.

In 1905, Howard followed in his father's footsteps by joining the Republican Party. He worked his way up the ranks of the state organization, and in 1912 he was named a delegate to the party's national convention. As a reward for his loyalty, in 1921 President Warren G. Harding, a Republican, appointed him special assistant to the U.S. attorney general. That same year, he moved to Washington, D.C., where he resided for the rest of his life.

At the time, disfranchisement kept most African Americans from voting, so the Republican Party in Mississippi, indeed in every southern state other than Tennessee, had virtually no chance of winning an election. However, it served as the vehicle by which federal patronage jobs, like postmasterships and positions with the Internal Revenue Service, were distributed whenever the Republicans controlled the White House, which they did for all but 16 years between 1860 and 1932. Thus, it makes a bit of sense that in 1924 Howard was named chairman of the Mississippi state executive committee, even though he no longer resided there, as well as national committeeman. For the next eight years, he reigned supreme over the Mississippi Republican Party, controlling the dispensation of patronage jobs in his home state from his office in the nation's capital.

In 1929, Howard came under fire when Herbert Hoover was elected president. Hoover wanted to build up the Republican Party in the South, but he knew that as long as African Americans, particularly absentee ones like Howard, controlled the state mechanisms, whites would never join the party. Under Hoover's direction, Howard was indicted in federal court for selling federal jobs to the highest bidder. The indictment forced him to relinquish his position in the attorney general's office. He was finally acquitted in 1932, but by then his position as state chairman had been sufficiently undermined and he was forced to resign. He remained a national committeeman, however, until 1960; for a number of years he was the senior delegate to the national convention, and in that capacity he served as chairman of committees.

Howard remained in Washington after resigning as state chairman. He and two partners opened the law firm of Cobb, Howard, and Hayes, and he maintained his practice until his death on February 2, 1961, in Washington.

Further Reading

Jackson, David H., Jr. "Howard, Perry Wilson." In *African American National Biography,* vol. 4, edited by Henry Louis Gates, Jr., and Evelyn Brooks Higginbotham. New York: Oxford University Press, 2008, pp. 341–343.

Walton, Hanes. *Black Republicans: The Politics of the Black and Tans.* Metuchen, N.J.: Scarecrow Press, 1975.

Hyman, John

(John Adams Hyman)
(1840–1891) *U.S. congressional representative from North Carolina*

John Hyman was the first African American elected to the U.S. Congress from North Carolina. He devoted his entire political career to advancing the cause of freedmen. Unfortunately, his career and his personal life were plagued by recurring charges of corruption.

Hyman was born on July 23, 1840, near Warrenton in Warren County, North Carolina. Nothing is known about his parents except that they were slaves. During the first 25 years of his life, he was bought and sold eight times. He was taught to read and write by a Warrenton jeweler and his wife who had purchased him in 1861 to work as a janitor. When their illegal tutoring of Hyman was discovered later that year, they were run out of town and Hyman was forcibly sold to a planter in Alabama. When the Civil War ended in 1865, he returned to Warren County and took up farming; within two years he was also operating a small country store. At some point, he married an unknown woman, with whom he had four children.

Hyman's political career began in 1866 when he served as a delegate to the Freedmen's Convention of North Carolina, which sought equal rights for the state's ex-slaves. He also joined the Republican Party, and the following year he was a delegate to the party's state convention, at which he was named to the executive committee. He was also appointed registrar for Warren County, and in this capacity he went about registering African Americans to vote as well as to join the Republicans. In 1868, he attended the state constitutional convention where he worked to ensure the civil, political, and economic rights of freedmen.

In 1868, Hyman was one of the five blacks elected to the North Carolina state senate. During his six-year tenure in that body, he gained a reputation as an unequivocal supporter of black civil rights. Unlike many other black politicians in the South, he adamantly opposed restoring ex-Confederates to their full political rights. He also opposed the removal from office of Governor William H. Holden, who was impeached in 1872 by the senate's white majority for prosecuting Ku Klux Klan members who had harassed black voters. He also worked hard for the residents of his district, using his influence to have a state prison built in Warrenton. This victory was tainted by charges made by his white Democratic opponents that he had used bribery and corruption to clinch the deal. He was later implicated, but never brought to trial, in a scandal involving the misappropriation of funds raised via the sale of railroad stock.

Hyman first tried to run for the U.S. House of Representatives in 1872, but he was denied his party's nomination. In 1874, he gained the party's nod and defeated his white Democratic opponent in the election. He served on the committee on manufactures and introduced a total of 14 bills, resolutions, and petitions. Most of them involved protecting or expanding the civil rights of African Americans; however, several called for federal relief for Cherokee Indians still living in North Carolina. Surprisingly, he rarely spoke before the House on behalf of his measures, and none of them were enacted.

In 1876, Hyman was again denied his party's nomination for Congress, so he did not run for reelection. Instead, he accepted an appointment with the U.S. Treasury Department as a collector of internal revenue in his congressional district. He also returned to farming, but he was forced to sell his land to make good the debts he had incurred while living in the nation's capital. When his term expired in 1878, he opened a liquor store in Warrenton. In 1879, he was removed from his post as superintendent of the Warrenton Negro Methodist Church's Sunday school when it was discovered he had mismanaged the school's funds. A year later, he returned to Washington where he worked as an assistant mail clerk for 10 years. In 1889, he went to work as a clerk in the Agriculture Department's seed dispensary. He died from a stroke on September 14, 1891, in Washington.

Further Reading

Biographical Directory of the United States Congress. "Hyman, John Adams, 1840–1891." Available online. URL: http://bioguide.congress.gov/scripts/biodisplay.pl?index=H001025. Downloaded March 28, 2009.

Black Americans in Congress. "John Adams Hyman." Available online. URL: http://baic.house.gov/member-profiles/profile.html?intID=6. Downloaded April 7, 2009.

Christopher, Maurine. *Black Americans in Congress*, rev. and expanded ed. New York: T. Y. Crowell, 1976.

Clay, William L. *Just Permanent Interests: Black Americans in Congress, 1870–1992.* New York: Amistad Press, 1993.

Reid, George T. "Four in Black: North Carolina's Black Congressmen, 1874–1901." *Journal of Negro History* 64 (summer 1979): 229–243.

J

Jack, Hulan
(Hulan Edwin Jack)
(1906–1986) *president of Manhattan borough, New York City*

For seven years, Hulan Jack was the highest elected official in Manhattan, the center of the world's financial markets and the most expensive piece of real estate in the world. The first African American to hold this office, he worked hard to improve life for the borough's residents. Unfortunately, his career was cut short when he became embroiled in two political scandals that may have been designed to remove him from office because of his race.

Jack was born on December 23, 1906, on the Caribbean island of St. Lucia, at the time a British possession. His father, Ratford, was a minister, and his mother, Emily, was a homemaker. As a boy, he moved with his family to his father's successive pastorates in St. Vincent, British Guiana, Cuba, and Barbados. His father was a member of the Universal Negro Improvement Association (UNIA), founded in 1914 by the black nationalist Marcus Garvey. The association's headquarters was in Harlem, and in 1923 Jack accompanied his father to a UNIA meeting in New York City. Awed by life in the United States, he remained in Harlem after his father returned home. He supported himself via a succession of odd jobs while attending high school at night. After receiving his diploma in 1929, he studied business administration for three years at the City College of New York. He then went to work in a paperboard box factory as a box cutter, eventually working his way up to vice president of sales. In 1934, he married Gertrude Hewitt, with whom he had one child. She died in 1937, and four years later he married Almira Wilkinson, with whom he also had one child.

Jack became a naturalized American citizen in 1931 and immediately got involved in local politics. He joined the Democratic Party and became one of its best organizers in the black precincts. By 1940, New York Democrats had realized that Harlem was becoming increasingly black, and they decided to run a black candidate to represent Harlem in the state assembly. Jack got the party's nod, defeated his Republican opponent, and took his seat in 1941. Reelected five times, his tenure in the state assembly was relatively colorless.

In 1953, Jack decided he could play a greater role within the political system by holding elective office closer to home. That same year, he campaigned for the presidency of the borough of Manhattan; when he won, he became the first African American to hold the office and the highest elected black local official in the nation. He immediately set about implementing an ambitious plan to renovate the borough's aging transportation systems, sewers, and other public services and to construct more public housing. Not surprisingly, several of these projects generated much public controversy. His plan to construct a sunken four-lane highway through the middle of Washington Square Park met with a frenzy of protest from the neighborhood's residents. When Horace Stoneham, owner of the New York Giants, decided to move the team to San Francisco, California, Jack tried to keep them in town by planning a 110,000-seat stadium over a six-block section of the New York Central's railroad tracks. Unfortunately, the project's exorbitantly high price tag doomed it to failure and the Giants moved anyway.

A consummate politician, Jack sailed through such controversies and was reelected in 1957. Shortly thereafter, he ran into a political problem he could not surmount; a contractor had performed $4,500 of renovations to Jack's apartment and then refused to accept payment. This matter eventually came to the attention of the press, and in 1960 Jack was convicted of accepting an illegal gift and forced to resign as borough president.

Despite his disgrace, Jack remained active in the Democratic Party. He also worked to have his name cleared, but although he got his sentence suspended, his conviction was never overturned. He did manage, however, to convince his constituents that he had been framed because of his race, and in 1968 they reelected him to the state assembly. Unfortunately, two years later he became involved in another scandal, this one concerning conflict of interest charges related to a community service firm in which he was a partner. He was convicted and sentenced to three months in jail. Although he later got the conviction overturned, this sorry episode ended his public career. In 1980, he involved himself in one last controversy by endorsing the candidacy of Lyndon H. LaRouche, Jr., for the Democratic Party's presidential nomination. LaRouche was a nationally known economist who argued for a fundamental restructuring of the world's economic, monetary, and fiscal systems so that emerging nations would have a better

chance to thrive; he was eventually jailed for conspiring against the U.S. government.

Jack died on December 19, 1986, in New York City.

Further Reading

Clayton, Edward T. *The Negro Politician—His Success and Failure.* Chicago: Johnson Publishing Co., 1964.
Jack, Hulan. *Fifty Years a Democrat: The Autobiography of Hulan E. Jack.* New York: New Benjamin Franklin House, 1982.
Smith, Jessie Carney. *Black Firsts.* Detroit: Gale Research, 1994.

Jackson, Alphonso
(Alphonso R. Jackson)
(1945–) *U.S. secretary of housing and urban development*

As the head of the Department of Housing and Urban Development (HUD) from 2004 to 2008, Alphonso Jackson was one of the few African Americans to serve in the cabinet of President George W. Bush.

Jackson was born on September 9, 1945, in Marshall, Texas. The youngest of 12 children, he grew up in poverty but managed to get a good education. He received a bachelor's degree in political science and a master's degree in educational administration from Northeast Missouri State University. Jackson also earned a law degree from Washington University in St. Louis.

In the early 1980s, Jackson served as the executive director of the St. Louis Housing Authority. Known in Republican political circles in Missouri, he was tapped to oversee the U.S. Department of Public and Assisted Housing for Washington, D.C. in 1987. Two years later, he became the first African American to head the housing authority of Dallas, Texas. During his seven-year tenure, Jackson worked to repair dilapidated public housing and battled homeowners and city council members to construct new housing projects for low-income families in predominantly white neighborhoods. Although Jackson was widely credited with substantially improving Dallas's public housing, he was criticized for his aggressive style. Jackson courted controversy by accusing various city officials of racism and, in one instance, assaulting a political opponent.

From 1996 to 2000, Jackson worked in the private sector as the president of American Election Power-TEXAS. In early 2001, however, he was called to Washington, D.C., by his friend and onetime neighbor, President George W. Bush. Jackson was named the deputy secretary of HUD, working under Secretary Mel Martinez. After Martinez left HUD to run for the U.S. Senate, Bush nominated Jackson to become the new head of the department.

In his second year on the job, Jackson made a stunning statement during an address to a group of business leaders in Dallas. He said that he had denied a government contract to a company because its head was not a Bush supporter. "Why should I reward someone who doesn't like the president, so they can use funds to try to campaign against the president?" Jackson asked. Because awarding contracts based on party affiliation is a violation of federal law, Jackson's comments stirred an uproar in Washington. Jackson tried to quell the situation by claiming he made the story up, but he continued to be dogged by allegations that he was misusing his position by handing out lucrative contracts to reward political allies. By early 2008, the FBI was investigating charges that he had directed federal funds for the rebuilding of public housing in post-Katrina New Orleans to personal friends.

On March 31, 2008, Jackson announced that he was leaving his post at HUD. He cited family concerns as his reason for stepping down, but press accounts assumed he was motivated more by a call for his resignation by two members of Congress. Jackson was not formally charged with any crime, although his name emerged in another

later scandal dating from his tenure at HUD. In March 2009, a congressional report fingered Jackson as one of several politically powerful people given extremely favorable home loans from mortgage lender Countrywide Financial allegedly to curry their influence in debates over lending practices. The Justice Department, however, closed its investigation into the matter in May 2010 without filing any charges against Jackson.

Further Reading

Brennan, Carol. "Alphonso R. Jackson, 1946– ." *Contemporary Black Biography* 48 (2005): 96–98.
Swarns, Rachel L. "As HUD Chief Quits, a Look at Close Ties." *New York Times,* April 18, 2008. Available online. URL: http://www.nytimes.com/2008/04/18/washington/18jackson.html. Downloaded May 1, 2009.

Jackson, Jesse
(Jesse Louis Jackson)
(1941–) *presidential candidate*

Before the election of President BARACK OBAMA in 2008, Jesse Jackson was the most successful African-American presidential candidate. Jackson won several Democratic primaries and came in second at the 1988 Democratic National Convention. His success has made him a respected voice of African Americans ever since.

Jackson was born Jesse Louis Burns on October 8, 1941, in Greenville, South Carolina. His mother, Helen Burns, was a teenager, and his father, Noah Robinson, was her married next-door neighbor. When Jesse was two, his mother married Charles Jackson, who adopted Jackson and gave him his last name. After graduating from high school in 1959, he turned down an offer to play professional football; instead, he accepted a football scholarship at the University of Illinois in Chicago. A year later he transferred to North Carolina A&T College (now University) in Greensboro. Shortly thereafter, he joined the

Congress of Racial Equality (CORE), and by his senior year he had become a leader of the local student Civil Rights movement. That same year, he became a field representative for CORE and was elected president of the North Carolina Intercollegiate Council on Human Rights. While in college, he married Jacqueline Davis, with whom he has five children. In 2001, it was revealed that he had also fathered a child out of wedlock.

Jackson received a B.A. in sociology in 1964 and then spent the next two years at the Chicago Theological Seminary. During this period, he joined the Southern Christian Leadership Conference (SCLC) and became a loyal follower of Dr. Martin Luther King, Jr. Jackson helped organize the 1965 protest march from Selma to Montgomery, Alabama, and in 1966 he played a major role in organizing an SCLC protest in Chicago. That same year, he left the seminary to serve as the Chicago coordinator of the SCLC's Operation Breadbasket, a program designed to win economic and political power for poor people. As director, Jackson proved adept at getting stores and businesses located in black neighborhoods to hire more blacks and to carry more goods manufactured by minority companies. The following year, he took over as the program's national director, a position he held for four years. In 1968, the same year he was ordained a Baptist minister, he helped organize the Poor People's Campaign, which included a march on the nation's capital. The protesters erected Resurrection City, a tent city on the Mall near the Lincoln Memorial, and chose Jackson to serve as their city manager.

Jackson was with King when the latter was assassinated in Memphis, Tennessee, in 1968. Exactly what Jackson did after the shooting has been hotly debated; some claim he cradled the dying King in his arms and heard his last words, while others claim he was nowhere near King when he was shot. Whatever happened, the general public believed that Jackson was now leading the Civil Rights movement, much to the dismay of the SCLC leadership. For the next three years,

many civil rights leaders fumed that Jackson was using the movement to advance his own personal agenda, and in 1971 he was suspended from the SCLC. The suspension arose over charges that Jackson had misappropriated the proceeds from a Black Expo he had run in Chicago to benefit minority business owners. The charges were unfounded, but they caused him to break with the SCLC for good.

In 1971, Jackson formed Operation PUSH (People United to Save Humanity). In essence, PUSH was Operation Breadbasket without the SCLC. PUSH put together what later became known as the Rainbow Coalition, a group of blacks, whites, Hispanics, and Native Americans working together to rid the nation of poverty, racism, militarism, and class divisions. In 1976, he formed PUSH-Excel, a program aimed at getting teenagers to avoid drugs and premarital sex. He traveled the country giving motivational speeches to young people, and he became famous for the slogan he got his audiences to shout repeatedly, "I Am … Somebody!"

Jackson became involved in electoral politics in 1971, when he ran for mayor of Chicago against the incumbent, Richard Daley. Unable to gain support from either major party, he formed the Bread 'n' Butter Party to serve as his campaign vehicle. Jackson's campaign also failed to gain the support of the city's African-American political leaders, mostly because he never bothered to consult with them before announcing his candidacy. As a result, he lost badly. Twelve years later, he got involved in the mayoral race again, but this time on behalf of HAROLD WASHINGTON. Jackson is credited with helping Washington win by registering more than 100,000 black first-time voters, then convincing them to vote for Washington.

In 1984, Jackson announced his candidacy for president. Operating on the theory that "the old minorities constitute a new majority," he christened his campaign organization the Rainbow Coalition. Jackson's candidacy was not taken seriously until he pulled a major diplomatic coup. In the late 1970s, he had traveled extensively throughout the Middle East while working for peace in that region, and had met with Yasser Arafat, the Palestinian leader. During the 1984 presidential campaign, a U.S. military pilot was shot down over Lebanon and was being held hostage in Syria. Jackson used his influence with Arafat and other Arab leaders to get the pilot released. By the time of the Democratic National Convention, Jackson had captured several hundred delegates in the primaries, a respectable total but nowhere close to achieving victory.

Jackson spent the next four years preparing for a second run at the presidency. He moved to Washington, D.C., where he continued to develop the Rainbow Coalition into a national organization for raising money and getting out the vote. By 1988, he was ready to take on the other six contenders for the Democratic nomination. Jackson ran extremely well in the primaries, winning several and pulling off a major upset in the Michigan primary. Despite his achievement, he still did not win the nomination, coming in second to Michael Dukakis.

Jackson and his followers hoped that his second-place showing at the convention would earn him a spot as the Democratic Party's vice-presidential candidate. Instead, Dukakis chose Lloyd Bentsen, one of the party's longtime leaders. The announcement that Bentsen had been chosen greatly disappointed the Jackson forces, who were not even consulted as to the choice. For many African Americans, it was a bitter disappointment. Black voters had been expressing some discontent with the party's failure to do more for African Americans. Jackson's rejection led many of them to consider forming a third party, one that would be more directly attuned to the needs and wants of the nation's black residents. This did not happen, however; shortly after the announcement, Dukakis and Jackson met and patched up their differences. Jackson was invited to address the convention, and when it came his turn to speak he gave a rousing speech in support of the Dukakis-Bentsen ticket. He also dropped several hints that the Democrats needed to stop taking the African-American vote for granted.

Jackson never ran for president again, but he did remain a highly visible spokesman for African-American inclusion in the political process. In 1990 he was named to serve as a "shadow senator" for the District of Columbia as part of its effort to win statehood. In 1992, he enthusiastically backed President Bill Clinton's candidacy for the White House and played a major role in getting Clinton elected. In 1998, Clinton made Jackson a special envoy and sent him to Africa to promote democracy. Two years later Clinton awarded Jackson the Presidential Medal of Freedom. He also returned to Chicago Theological Seminary to complete the few courses he needed for his M.A. in theology, which he received in 2000.

Jackson's influence in American politics began to wane, especially after 2001, when it was revealed that he had fathered a child out of wedlock with a member of his staff. Nevertheless, he continued to maintain a high profile, appearing regularly on radio and television to discuss human rights issues in the United States and abroad. By the beginning of the 21st century, Jackson's distinguished career in politics and public service had long since secured his legacy as one of the most significant African-American leaders of the post–civil rights era.

Further Reading

Colton, Elizabeth O. *The Jackson Phenomenon: The Man, the Power, the Message.* New York: Doubleday, 1989.

Frady, Marshall. *Jesse: The Life and Pilgrimage of Jesse Jackson.* New York: Simon and Schuster, 2006.

Jackson, Jesse, with Roger D. Hatch and Frank E. Watkins. *Straight from the Heart.* Philadelphia: Fortress Press, 1987.

Stanford, Karin L. *Beyond the Boundaries: Reverend Jesse Jackson in International Affairs.* Albany: State University of New York Press, 1997.

Jackson, Jesse, Jr.

(Jesse Louis Jackson, Jr.)
(1965–) *U.S. congressional representative from Illinois*

Jesse Jackson, Jr., has taken up where his father left off. Despite being one of the most influential African-American political leaders ever, JESSE JACKSON never held a political office. Jesse Jr., on the other hand, was elected to Congress at the age of 30 and promises to enjoy a long and successful public career.

Jackson was born on March 11, 1965, in Greenville, South Carolina. His mother, Jacqueline, is a homemaker. After graduating from high school, he turned down football scholarships to several big-name colleges to attend his father's alma mater, North Carolina A&T University. He received a B.S. in business management in 1987, then, like his father, enrolled in the Chicago Theological Seminary. Unlike his father, he received an M.A. in theology from the school after only three years. He next enrolled in the University of Illinois College of Law and received a J.D. in 1993. He then went to work as field director for the Rainbow Coalition and Operation PUSH, both of which had been founded by his father. Over the next two years, he modernized and computerized the operations, created a voter education program, and established many new local chapters of Operation PUSH. In 1991, he married Sandra Jackson, with whom he has one child.

As a boy, Jackson accompanied his father on many political and diplomatic missions. He spoke on his father's behalf before the 1988 Democratic National Convention and campaigned for a number of his father's political allies, most notably JOHN CONYERS and MAXINE WATERS. He also made several tours of the national lecture circuit on his own. In 1994, he relocated to Chicago and began planning a run for a seat in Congress. His plans were greatly simplified when Mel Reynolds, the incumbent he

Jesse Jackson, Jr., represents Chicago in the U.S. House of Representatives. *(Jesse L. Jackson, Jr.)*

had planned to challenge, was convicted of having sexual relations with an underage campaign worker and resigned from office. Jackson won a hard-fought Democratic primary against three other contenders, largely because of his success at appealing to younger voters. During the special general election, he shrugged off charges of having accepted money from an alleged gang member as well as from a union that was being investigated by the federal government for its alleged ties to organized crime. He took his seat in 1995 and was assigned to the committee on banking and financial services.

As a congressman, Jackson worked to end the death penalty, partly because minorities are much more likely to be put to death for their crimes than nonminorities. He helped establish a center at the National Institutes of Health for researching problems peculiar to the health of minorities. He sponsored the HOPE for Africa Act of 1999, which offers federal aid to African nations both to combat the AIDS epidemic and to improve trade relations with the United States. He has proposed that the Bill of Rights be amended to include the rights to quality public education and quality health care. His arguments in this regard are spelled out in his book, *A More Perfect Union: Advancing New American Rights*. A loyal Democrat, he worked hard to remove Republican Newt Gingrich, who had become speaker of the House in 1996, from office; he was later rewarded by being reassigned to the prestigious appropriations committee. As a means of providing jobs for his constituents, many of whom were laid off by corporations relocating out of Chicago, he has supported the construction of a new airport on the south side of Chicago. Jackson was a vocal opponent of the 2002 U.S. invasion of Iraq. With five other representatives, he launched a lawsuit, alleging that the war was unconstitutional. The suit was rejected by a district court judge in Boston, Massachusetts.

A critic of longtime Chicago mayor Richard M. Daley, Jackson considered running against him in 2007 but chose instead to remain in Congress. He was reelected to his ninth term in 2010.

After Illinois senator Barack Obama was elected president in 2008, Jackson was considered to be a strong candidate to serve the remainder of Obama's term. Rod Blagojevich, the governor of Illinois, instead appointed ROLAND BURRIS to the post. Blagojevich, however, was accused of attempting to sell the position, and the House Ethics Committee launched an investigation into whether Jackson had agreed to help raise funds for Blagojevich in exchange for the senate seat. In May 2010, Jackson was subpoenaed by Blagojevich lawyers to testify in the former governor's criminal trial for bribery.

Further Reading

Biographical Directory of the United States Congress. "Jackson, Jesse. L., Jr., 1965–   ." Available online. URL: http://bioguide.congress.gov/scripts/bio display.pl?index=J000283. Downloaded April 20, 2009.

Congressman Jesse L. Jackson, Jr., Official Web Site. Available online. URL: http://www.house.gov/ jackson. Accessed April 20, 2009.

Draper, Robert. "The Son." *Gentlemen's Quarterly* 71, no. 7 (July 2001): 146–153.

Jackson, Jesse, Jr., and Frank E. Watkins. *A More Perfect Union: Advancing New American Rights*. New York: Welcome Rain Publishers, 2001.

Jackson, Lisa P.
(1962–   ) *U.S. administrator of the Environmental Protection Agency*

In January 2009, Lisa P. Jackson became the first African American to head the Environmental Protection Agency (EPA)—a federal agency employing 18,000 people charged with protecting the environment and public health.

Born in Philadelphia, Pennsylvania, on February 8, 1962, Jackson was adopted as a baby and raised in New Orleans, Louisiana. A self-described geek, she graduated first in her class from St. Mary's Dominican High School. She continued her education at Tulane University and Princeton University, where she earned a bachelor's and master's degree in chemical engineering.

After graduating, Jackson began her career with the EPA. For 16 years, she worked first at the agency's headquarters in Washington, D.C., and later at its regional office in New York City. Jackson's duties included overseeing the cleanup of hazardous waste sites under the Superfund program and directing efforts to enforce EPA regulations.

In 2002, Jackson was named an assistant commissioner for compliance and enforcement with the New Jersey Department of Environmental

Protection (DEP). She also held the post of assistant commissioner for land use management before New Jersey governor Jon Corzine tapped her to head the entire department. Overseeing the DEP was a challenging position. During her tenure as its commissioner, Jackson had to cope with budget cuts and staff reductions while setting and enforcing needed environmental regulations. The position also required battling with powerful state legislators and influential builders and developers. Jackson gained a reputation for negotiating her way through potential political minefields and working out compromises that placated business interests without diluting the department's regulatory responsibilities. Jackson, however, drew some fire from environmental groups for pushing to farm out the cleanup of some hazardous waste sites to private contractors.

While in the New Jersey state government, Jackson was a vocal critic of the EPA under the Republican administration of President George W. Bush. She joined with officials in other states to sue the administration for preventing states from enacting tough fuel efficiency standards. Jackson once declared, "When it comes to the auto industry, the EPA apparently is the Emissions Permissions Agency."

In part because of her demonstrated political savvy, Governor Corzine asked Jackson in late October 2008 to become his chief of staff. She was both the first woman and first African American to hold that position. Jackson began the job on December 1, a few weeks after she had been tapped by President-elect BARACK OBAMA to serve on his transition team as an expert on energy and the environment. On December 15, Obama formally nominated Jackson as the administrator of the EPA.

During her confirmation hearing, Jackson implicitly criticized the Bush administration for its politicization of the EPA. "If I am confirmed, political appointees will not compromise the integrity of EPA's technical experts to advance particular regulatory outcomes," she stated. Jackson also voiced her commitment to the five primary environmental goals of the Obama administration: to reduce greenhouse gas emissions, to reduce other air pollutants, to deal with the problems posed by toxic chemicals, to clean up waste sites, and to protect water quality.

Jackson was officially confirmed on January 23, 2009. She thereby became the first African American, the second New Jerseyan, and the fourth woman entrusted with command of the EPA. Within weeks, Jackson signaled that she would work to aggressively address the problem of global warming, an initiative that a *New York Times* editorial dubbed "an astonishing turnaround" from the previous administration's environmental policies. The many challenges Jackson has since faced included organizing the EPA's response to the environmental disaster caused by the 2010 Gulf of Mexico oil spill.

Further Reading

Kocieniewski, David. "The New Team: Lisa P. Jackson." *New York Times*, December 11, 2008. Available online. URL: http://www.nytimes.com/2008/12/11/us/politics/11web-jackson.html. Downloaded May 1, 2009.

U.S. Environmental Protection Agency. "Administrator Lisa Jackson." Available online. URL: http://www.epa.gov/administrator/biography.htm. Downloaded May 1, 2009.

Jackson, Maynard
(Maynard Holbrook Jackson, Jr.)
(1938–2003) *mayor of Atlanta, Georgia*

Maynard Jackson was the first African-American mayor of Atlanta, and the first black to be elected mayor of a major southern city. During his three terms, Atlanta made major strides toward becoming the city that was "too busy to hate."

Jackson was born on March 23, 1938, in Dallas, Texas. His father, Maynard Sr., was a Baptist minister, and his mother, Irene, was a teacher. At age seven he moved with his family to Atlanta, where his father had been appointed pastor of Friendship Baptist Church. After finishing his sophomore year in high school, he was accepted into an early admissions scholar program at Morehouse College, and at age 18 he received a B.A. He worked for a year as a claims examiner for the Ohio State Bureau of Unemployment Compensation in Cleveland, then spent four years selling encyclopedias in Ohio, Massachusetts, and New York. In 1961, he decided to study law at North Carolina Central University, where his mother taught French. While in law school, he married Burnella Burke, with whom he has two children. After receiving an LL.B in 1964, he returned to Atlanta to work as a general attorney for the National Labor Relations Board. In 1968, he became managing attorney and director of community relations for the Emory Community Legal Services Center, which provided pro bono legal services to local residents.

Jackson became interested in politics following the assassination of Martin Luther King, Jr., in 1968. Just two months later, he began his political career by entering, at the last minute, the Democratic primary as a candidate for the U.S. Senate. Not surprisingly, the political neophyte was beaten badly by the longtime incumbent, Herman Talmadge. However, Jackson shocked everyone by carrying the city of Atlanta. He also attracted the votes of a number of poor white farmers and received some support from labor unions. Buoyed by his strong showing among these groups, the following year he ran for vice-mayor of Atlanta. He won by capturing most of the black vote and about one-third of the white vote, and took office in early 1970.

In 1973, Jackson entered the race for mayor of Atlanta against Sam Masell, the white incumbent, and nine other candidates. Although Jackson gained the most votes in the election, he failed to gain a majority, thus setting the stage for a runoff against Masell. The runoff degenerated into a race-baiting campaign where both candidates appealed openly to their own racial constituencies. In the end, Jackson won by sweeping the black vote and garnering about one-fourth of the white vote.

Shortly after taking office in early 1974, Jackson oversaw sweeping changes in the way Atlanta was governed and managed. After the mostly white board of aldermen was replaced with a biracial city council, he was able to hire a professional city administrator and reorganize the city into 24 planning districts that sought out citizen input via neighborhood meetings. He demoted the city's police chief for being racially insensitive, then replaced him with a black activist who hired more black police officers; by the end of Jackson's first term, the crime rate in Atlanta had declined significantly. He also implemented affirmative action programs in other city departments and oversaw a number of public works projects, each of which featured set-asides for minority-owned businesses.

Reelected in 1977, Jackson was barred by the city charter from seeking a third consecutive term. After leaving office in 1982, he returned to the practice of law. His firm specialized in legal issues related to the sale of state and municipal bonds, and he benefited greatly from his connections with other African-American mayors. During the 1980s, he also served as the founding chairman of the Atlanta Economic Development Corporation and as chairman of the Atlanta Urban Residential Finance Authority.

In 1989, Jackson ran for a third term, easily defeating two other black candidates to succeed ANDY YOUNG. Jackson's focus during his first two terms had been to make the system work more fairly for all of Atlanta's citizens. But the gains made by African Americans during his and Young's tenure allowed him to focus his third term on such issues as building more public housing, attracting new businesses and industries, and addressing the growing problems of drug abuse and AIDS.

Despite a generally successful third term, Jackson declined to run for reelection in 1993, citing health problems related to his heart. After leaving office in 1994, he founded Jackson Securities, an investment firm specializing in public bonds. In 2001, Jackson tried for the chairmanship of the Democratic National Committee (DNC); he withdrew and instead was named chairman of the DNC's Voting Rights Institute. In September 2002, Jackson set up an organization to increase voter turnout. He died June 23, 2003.

Further Reading

Braukman, Stacy. "Jackson, Maynard." In *African American National Biography*, vol. 4, edited by Henry Louis Gates, Jr., and Evelyn Brooks Higginbotham. New York: Oxford University Press, 2008, pp. 457–458.

Colburn, David R., and Jeffrey S. Adler. *African-American Mayors: Race, Politics, and the American City*. Urbana: University of Illinois Press, 2001.

Joint Center for Political Studies. *Profiles of Black Mayors in America*. Chicago: Johnson Publishing, 1977.

Rice, Bradley R. "Maynard Jackson (1938–2003)." New Georgia Encyclopedia. Available online. URL: http://www.georgiaencyclopedia.org/nge/Article.jsp?id=h-1385. Downloaded March 28, 2009.

Stone, Clarence N. *Regime Politics: Governing Atlanta, 1946–1988*. Lawrence: University Press of Kansas, 1989.

Jackson Lee, Sheila

(1950–) *U.S. congressional representative from Texas*

Sheila Jackson Lee is the latest in the long line of distinguished African Americans to represent Houston in the U.S. Congress. In this regard, she follows BARBARA JORDAN and MICKEY LELAND, both of whom had previously held her seat in the House.

She was born Sheila Jackson on January 12, 1950, in New York City. After graduating from high school in 1968, she entered Yale University and received a B.A. in political science four years later. She then enrolled in the University of Virginia School of Law and received a J.D. in 1975. That same year, she married Elwyn Lee, with whom she has two children, and opened a law office in Houston, Texas. After two years of private practice, she accepted a position as staff attorney with the U.S. House Select Committee on Assassinations. In 1980, she went to work as an attorney for Houston's United Energy Resources, a position she held for seven years. In 1987 she was named an associate municipal court judge for the city of Houston.

Jackson Lee's career as a legislator began in 1990, when she was elected to a seat on the Houston city council. As a councilwoman, she chaired the city's human relations committee. Reelected

Sheila Jackson Lee represented Houston, Texas, in Congress. *(Sheila Jackson Lee)*

two years later, she was forced out of office in 1994 by a term limits law. That same year she declared her candidacy for the U.S. House. She easily defeated incumbent Craig Washington in the Democratic primary and her Republican opponent in the general election. She took her seat in 1995 and was assigned to the committees on science and the judiciary.

As a congresswoman, Jackson Lee demonstrated an interest in a number of areas. She passed legislation instructing the National Science Foundation to donate surplus computers and scientific equipment to public schools. She sponsored legislation to increase funding for the African Development Foundation and to address human rights violations in Ethiopia. She worked to establish a senior enlisted woman in the U.S. Army to investigate charges of sexual harassment by male officers against female soldiers. She spearheaded the passage of the Date Rape Prevention Drug Act, which outlaws the use of gamma hydroxybutyrate, a drug sometimes used to render young women unconscious. She successfully worked to establish the Office of Special Populations within the Agency for Health Research and Quality to gather statistical information related to the health of minorities, women, children, and the elderly. She pushed for legislation making it a federal offense to switch babies at birth, a practice that was becoming increasingly prevalent during the 1990s. She founded the bipartisan Congressional Children's Caucus, which pushes for legislation related to a wide range of issues from adoption to the payment of child support and alimony. Jackson Lee also launched the Dr. Mae C. Jemison Grant Program, which aids institutions in encouraging women of color to pursue careers in aeronautics. As for local matters, she gained millions of dollars in federal money for a flood control project for the Houston suburbs.

As a member of the House Judiciary Committee, Jackson Lee has devoted much energy to revising the nation's immigration laws. As a member of the committee, she came to the nation's attention in 1998 during President Bill Clinton's impeachment hearings. She was one of the president's most vocal supporters, and she clashed openly on several occasions with Republican members of the committee. More recently, Jackson Lee has been an outspoken advocate for bringing an end to genocide in the Darfur region of Sudan. On April 28, 2006, she was arrested during a protest outside of Sudan's embassy in Washington, D.C.

In 2010, Jackson Lee was reelected to a ninth term in the House of Representatives. She is married to Dr. Elwyn C. Lee, and they have two children.

Further Reading

Biographical Directory of the United States Congress. "Jackson-Lee, Sheila, 1950–   ." Available online. URL: http://bioguide.congress.gov/scripts/bio display.pl?index=J000032. Downloaded April 13, 2009.

Congresswoman Sheila Jackson Lee, Official Web Site. Available online. URL: http://jacksonlee.house. gov. Downloaded April 13, 2009.

Gill, LaVerne McCain. *African American Women in Congress: Forming and Transforming History.* New Brunswick, N.J.: Rutgers University Press, 1997.

"U.S. Representative: Sheila Jackson Lee." *Ebony* 54 (March 1999): 100.

James, Sharpe

(1936–   ) *mayor of Newark, New Jersey*

Sharpe James was mayor of Newark, New Jersey, from 1986 to 2008. During his time in office, he oversaw the transformation of Newark from, in his words, "a city you couldn't give away to a city that everybody wants."

James was born on February 20, 1936, in Jacksonville, Florida. His father died when he was an infant; shortly thereafter, his mother, Beulah, moved the family to Newark, where she opened a restaurant. After finishing high school in 1954, he enrolled in Montclair State College and received a B.S. in education in 1958. He spent the next two years in Germany with the U.S. Army, then enrolled in Springfield College in Massachusetts, receiving an M.S. in education in 1961. He then returned to Newark to teach in the public school system, where he met and married Mary Mattison. They have three children. In 1968, he joined the faculty of Newark's Essex County College, and for the next 18 years he taught education while serving as athletic director.

James became involved in politics in 1970, when he was elected as a Democrat to represent Newark's South Ward on city council. For the next 16 years, he served as the council's conscience, voting against such excesses as municipal automobiles and exorbitant pay increases for councilmen. His tenure on city council coincided with KENNETH GIBSON's tenure as mayor of Newark, whose efforts to revive Newark James supported. By 1986, however, it had become clear to James that Gibson's earlier successes had faded and that new leadership was needed to move the city forward. That same year, James ran for mayor against Gibson, who many political pundits thought was a shoo-in for a fifth term. They were surprised when James prevailed at the polls and took office later that year.

As mayor, James developed several new schemes for revitalizing Newark. The one that seemed most ridiculous to many New Jerseyans was his plan to build a performing arts complex in downtown Newark, which heretofore had been a "Sahara of the beaux arts." Undaunted by the laughter, he pursued his vision doggedly for 10 years, and in 1997 the Jersey Performing Arts Center opened as one of the largest arts centers in the United States. The center spurred further development along the city's Passaic River waterfront. Other James-inspired projects included a rapid-transit line connecting downtown to Newark International Airport, a research/laboratory complex similar to North Carolina's Research Triangle Park, and several revitalized residential

neighborhoods in close proximity to the city's colleges. During his tenure as mayor, Newark's crime fell precipitously, more than 25,000 new jobs were attracted, more than 3,000 public housing units were either built or rehabilitated, and a comprehensive citywide recycling program was initiated. The city was named a Most Livable City and an All-America City and won the Environmental Protection Administrator's Award. In 2002, James was reelected to a fifth consecutive term.

James also held various state and national offices, including vice president of the New Jersey Conference of Mayors and president of the National League of Cities. In 1995, he was named commissioner of the state redevelopment authority. In 1999, he was elected state senator; his refusal to step down as mayor, insisting instead on holding both offices simultaneously, drew howls of protest from his political opponents, which he ignored. In March 2006, James announced that he would not run for a sixth term as mayor. The following spring, he declined to seek reelection as state senator. Between these two announcements, reports surfaced that James was under federal investigation for fraud. In April 2008, he was convicted of helping his mistress purchase city property at a fraction of its worth. Three months later, James was sentenced to 27 months in prison. He was released in April 2010 after serving 18 months.

Further Reading

Feuer, Alan, and Nate Schweber. "Former Newark Mayor Is Sentenced to 27 Months." *New York Times,* July 20, 2008. Available online. URL: http://www.nytimes.com/2008/07/30/nyregion/30james.html?pagewanted=1&sq&st=cse%22sharpe%20james%22&scp=3. Downloaded April 9, 2009.

James, Sharpe. *Mayor Sharpe James, Leading Newark into the 21st Century.* Newark, N.J.: Keim Printing, 1987.

New Jersey Performing Arts Center Women's Board. *Bricks, Mortar, and Spirit: The Endurance of Newark: Remembering the Past, Heralding the Future: A Four Part Seminar.* Newark, N.J.: The Board, 1998.

Jefferson, William
(William Jennings Jefferson)
(1947–   ) *U.S. congressional representative from Louisiana*

In 1991, William Jefferson became the first African American to represent Louisiana in Congress in more than 100 years. Jefferson was born on March 14, 1947, in Lake Providence, Louisiana. His father, Mose, was a handyman, and his mother, Angeline, was a homemaker who also served as president of the local PTA. As a young boy, Jefferson helped his family make ends meet by picking cotton for neighboring farmers. After finishing high school in 1965, he enrolled in Southern University A&M College and received a B.A. in English and political science four years later. In 1969, he was accepted into Harvard University Law School, receiving a J.D. in 1972. Over

William Jefferson was the first black Louisianan to serve in Congress since Reconstruction. *(William J. Jefferson)*

the next three years, he clerked for a federal district judge in New Orleans and served as a legislative assistant to J. Bennett Johnson, a U.S. senator from Louisiana. In 1976, he cofounded Jefferson, Bryan and Gray, a law partnership in New Orleans. This practice eventually became the largest minority law partnership in the South.

In 1979, Jefferson ran successfully for the Louisiana senate. Over the next 12 years, he served on the state bond commission and the finance committee, and he was eventually named to chair the governmental affairs committee. As a senator, he established a solid reputation as an able legislator. Meanwhile, his political ambitions had outgrown the state senate. In 1982 and 1986, he ran for mayor of New Orleans but was defeated both times.

In 1990, Lindy Boggs, who represented New Orleans in the U.S. Congress, announced that she would not stand for reelection. Jefferson was one of 12 candidates who ran for the Democratic nomination to replace her. His toughest challenger was Marc Morial, son of former New Orleans mayor DUTCH MORIAL. After a hard-fought contest in which he and Morial faced each other in a runoff election, Jefferson emerged victorious. He held on to win in the general election and took his seat in 1991. He was assigned to the committees on the merchant marine/fisheries, public works, and education/labor.

Jefferson was a strong and early supporter of Bill Clinton's presidential candidacy. Like Clinton, Jefferson was a moderate Democrat, and he sometimes angered his African-American colleagues for looking to the private sector to help solve some of the nation's social ills. When Clinton was elected in 1992, Jefferson's position in Congress was enhanced tremendously. In only his second term, he was named to the prestigious Ways and Means Committee, which exerts a great deal of control over the government's ability to tax and spend.

Jefferson used his position on Ways and Means to provide government assistance to minority-owned small businesses. He called attention to the so-called digital divide, the growing gap between middle- and upper-class families that own computers and lower-class families that do not, and he authored legislation that provided tax breaks to lower-income families in order to help them afford computers and related equipment. He fought against so-called environmental racism, whereby such undesirable but necessary facilities like toxic waste dumps are located near lower-income neighborhoods. He played a prominent role in the enactment of the Africa Growth and Opportunity Act and the New Markets Initiative. The former stimulated bilateral investments and trade between the United States and the developing nations of sub-Saharan Africa. The latter made available more than $20 billion in home equity loans and other tax incentives to promote home buying and business investment in lower-income communities.

Meanwhile, Jefferson continued to set his sights on higher elective office. He considered running for governor of Louisiana in 1991 and 1995, only to back away at the last moment. In 1999, he threw his hat in the ring, but he was defeated soundly by incumbent Republican governor Mike Foster. Because of the timing of the election, he was able to keep his seat in Congress.

In 2002, Jefferson returned to Congress and was reelected two years later. During his eighth term, he became the subject of a federal investigation into bribery and corruption. On August 3, 2005, investigators raided his home and found $90,000 hidden in his freezer. Within weeks, the scandal was soon overshadowed by the flooding of much of New Orleans in the aftermath of Hurricane Katrina. The following year, however, several associates of Jefferson pled guilty to aiding and abetting bribery.

Despite the growing scandal, Jefferson was reelected in November 2006. Eight months later, he was indicted on 16 charges of bribery, racketeering, and money laundering. Jefferson vigorously denied his guilt, and his legal team managed to delay the trial until after the 2008 election. Nevertheless, Jefferson lost his bid for reelection to the Republican candidate, Anh Cao, despite the fact that his district was overwhelmingly Democratic.

On August 5, 2009, Jefferson was found guilty of 11 counts of bribery and related crimes. He was subsequently sentenced to 13 years in prison. Jefferson vowed to appeal his conviction.

Further Reading
Biographical Directory of the United States Congress. "Jefferson, William Jennings, 1947– ." Available online. URL: http://bioguide.congress.gov/ scripts/ biodisplay.pl?index=J000070. Downloaded April 15, 2009.

Black Americans in Congress. "William J. Jefferson." Available online. URL: http://baic.house.gov/ member-profiles/profile.html?intID=98. Downloaded April 23, 2009.

"Louisiana Elects First Black Congressman since Reconstruction Era." *Ebony* 46 (January 1991), p. 108.

Nossiter, Adam. "Voters Oust Indicted Congressman in Louisiana." *New York Times*, December 7, 2008. URL: http://www.nytimes.com/2008/12/07/us/07 louisiana.html?scp=1&sq=nossiter%20%22voters%20oust%22&st=cse. Downloaded April 23, 2009.

Patterson, Donna A. "Jefferson, William Jennings." In *African American National Biography*, vol. 4, edited by Henry Louis Gates, Jr., and Evelyn Brooks Higginbotham. New York: Oxford University Press, 2008, pp. 518–519.

Johnson, Eddie Bernice
(1935–) *U.S. congressional representative from Texas*

In 1993, Eddie Bernice Johnson became the fourth African American to represent Texas in Congress. She later became the second woman to chair the Congressional Black Caucus.

Johnson was born on December 3, 1935, in Waco, Texas, to Lee and Lillie Mae Johnson. In 1952, she finished high school and went off to St. Mary's College at the University of Notre Dame. After receiving a nursing diploma three years later, she returned to Texas to work in the psychiatric ward of the Veterans Administration Hospital in Dallas. In 1967, she received a B.S. in nursing from Texas Christian University, and shortly thereafter she was promoted to chief psychiatric nurse. In 1956, she married Dawrence Kirk, with whom she had one child; they were divorced in 1970.

By 1972, Johnson had grown weary of what she perceived to be the state's lack of interest in public health care as well as the slow rate of progress toward integration. She decided to address these issues as a politician, and that same year she ran for the state legislature as a Democrat. Since she was a black woman, her candidacy was discounted by the political pundits. They were amazed, therefore, when she won by a wide margin. Elected to a second term in 1974, she was chosen to chair the labor committee. Despite holding this important post, she found it quite difficult to make headway against the white male power structure that controlled the Texas house. While a representative, she returned to school and received a master's degree in public administration from Southern Methodist University in 1976.

In 1977, Johnson resigned in the middle of her third term to accept an invitation from Democratic president Jimmy Carter to serve as a regional director of the Department of Health, Education, and Welfare. She held this position until the inauguration of Republican president Ronald Reagan four years later. In 1981, she founded Eddie Bernice Johnson and Associates, a real estate firm specializing in business relocation and expansion.

The rise of the AIDS epidemic in the United States, coupled with the Reagan administration's lack of interest in combating it, induced Johnson to return to politics. In 1986, she won a seat in the Texas senate. Over the next six years, she pushed bills providing AIDS patients with legal access to

Eddie Bernice Johnson represented Dallas, Texas, in Congress and chaired the Congressional Black Caucus. *(Eddie Bernice Johnson)*

health care. She also authored bills to regulate diagnostic radiology centers, require drug testing in hospitals, and prohibit hospital kickbacks to referring doctors. She also worked to improve the housing situation for low-income families. She sponsored a bill to permit local governments to make renovations to substandard rental units and charge the cost of repairs to the landlords, and another to create a commission to hear complaints about discriminatory housing practices.

Johnson played a prominent role on the committee that realigned the state's congressional districts following the census of 1990. In the process, a black-majority district centered on Dallas County, where she lived, was crafted out of portions of several other districts. The new district was unpopular enough with the incumbents of the affected districts and their supporters, but then Johnson made matters worse by declaring her candidacy for the district's seat in Congress. Her opponents complained loudly and bitterly that she had gerrymandered the district to ensure her own election, but she generally ignored them as she swept to victory in 1992. She took her seat in 1992 and was assigned to the committees on public works/transportation and science/space/technology.

As a congresswoman, Johnson continued to focus on health care. In particular, she sponsored bills to double the National Science Foundation's budget and to increase funding for HIV/AIDS research. In other areas, she worked to make the tax code fairer to the average taxpayer/employee without investment income, and to make the Small Business Administration more effective at promoting the interests of small businesses.

Johnson has also worked to promote human rights around the world. She has authored or coauthored more than 120 bills that have been signed into law. In 2000, she was elected to a two-year term as chair of the Congressional Black Caucus. In 2010, she was reelected to a 10th term in Congress.

Further Reading

Biographical Directory of the United States Congress. "Johnson, Eddie Bernice, 1935– ." Available online. URL: http://bioguide.congress.gov/scripts/biodisplay.pl?index=J000126. Downloaded April 9, 2009.

Clay, William L. *Just Permanent Interests: Black Americans in Congress, 1870–1992.* New York: Amistad Press, 1993.

Congresswoman Eddie Bernice Johnson, Official Web Site. Available online. URL: http://ebjohnson.house.gov. Downloaded April 9, 2009.

Foerstel, Karen. *Biographical Dictionary of Congressional Women.* New York: Greenwood Press, 1999.

Gill, LaVerne McCain. *African American Women in Congress: Forming and Transforming History.* New Brunswick, N.J.: Rutgers University Press, 1997.

Johnson, Harvey
(Harvey Johnson, Jr.)
(1947–   ) *mayor of Jackson, Mississippi*

Harvey Johnson was the first African-American mayor of Jackson, Mississippi. His election generated much controversy, but it also held out hope for the future of race relations in the Magnolia State.

Johnson was born in 1947 in Vicksburg, Mississippi. His father was a garbage collector and his mother was a domestic worker. After graduating from high school, he attended Tennessee State University and received a B.A. in political science in 1969. He then attended the University of Cincinnati and received a master's degree in political science in 1972. After graduation, he returned to Mississippi and settled in Jackson, where he went to work as the executive director of the Mississippi Institute for Small Towns. In this position, he oversaw the development and implementation of water, sewer, and housing projects for communities across the state. Over the next 20 years, he taught political science at Jackson State University, worked as a state tax commissioner, and served as a commissioner on the state gaming board.

Johnson made his first bid for political office in 1993 when he ran for mayor. He was defeated in the Democratic primary by Kane Ditto, a moderate who did much to soothe racial tensions in Jackson. Four years later, Johnson tried again, and this time he won the primary and the general election.

After taking office in 1997, Johnson vowed to make Jackson the "Best of the New South." He worked to improve the day-to-day delivery of services by the municipal government by focusing on collecting garbage, repairing streets, making city clerks more customer oriented, and improving the city's financial standing. In terms of economic development, he worked to bolster the city's African-American business community and to renovate downtown Jackson. Plans included a $70 million convention center, completed in 2009, and a telecommunications conference and training center. This controversial project required the approval of the state legislature and had been long debated. Johnson's pro-business attitude stimulated the creation of the Downtown Jackson Partners, a group of private investors that planned to build apartments, a hotel, and some stores and renovate a number of residential buildings in a 60-block area. His most innovative measure was to develop a Civil Rights Driving Tour to emphasize the city's important role in the Civil Rights movement. The tour includes 55 sites and spans four decades of civil rights history; among the stops is the home where Medgar Evers, the brother of CHARLES EVERS, was assassinated. Another Johnson innovation was a "partnership in support of diversity" with Butler Snow, the state's largest law firm. The partnership provided information to city contractors and other businesses about how to diversify their staffs, broaden their recruitment and selection practices, and expand their lists of vendors and subcontractors.

Not surprisingly in a city where the Civil Rights movement was fought as bitterly as anywhere, Johnson's election created a great deal of controversy. At least one member of the white community called on his fellow whites to abandon Jackson, and by 2001 it was estimated that "white flight" was costing the city almost 1,000 white residents each year. In 2001, one of Jackson's white representatives to the state legislature introduced a bill allowing citizens of cities with populations of more than 100,000 to dissolve their city government and merge with a surrounding county. Although the representative denied that his bill targeted Jackson, it was the only city large enough to be affected. For his part, Johnson helped outrage white residents by approving of a city council resolution condemning the state flag, which features the Confederate flag in one corner.

Despite all the controversy, Johnson was reelected in 2001. Facing mounting criticism over Jackson's high crime rate, Johnson, however, ran into trouble in his next reelection bid in 2005. In the primary, he was soundly defeated by rival Frank Melton, who went on to win the general election.

In January 2009, Jackson announced his intention to run for a third term as mayor. The crowded Democratic field already had eight candidates, including Melton. As a candidate, Jackson promised to place a priority on economic development and to increase staff in the police and fire departments. After winning the Democratic primary in a runoff, he easily defeated his opponents in the general election.

Further Reading

Chappell, Kevin. "Harvey Johnson: First Black Mayor of Jackson, Mississippi." Ebony 52 (August 1997): 76.

Golus, Carrie. "Harvey Johnson, Jr., 1947(?)–   ." Contemporary Black Biography 24 (2000): 98–99.

Lynch, Adam. "The 2009 JFP Interview with Harvey Johnson." Jackson Free Press, March 11, 2009. Available online. URL: http://www.jacksonfree press.com/index.php/site/comments/the_2009 _jfp_interview_with_harvey_johnson_jr. Downloaded April 24, 2009.

Jordan, Barbara
(Barbara Charline Jordan)
(1936–1996) *U.S. congressional representative from Texas*

Barbara Jordan was the first African American from Texas to serve in the U.S. Congress. A powerful orator who exuded charisma, she was thought by many to have a good chance of becoming the first African-American president. Unfortunately, in her late 30s she was stricken with leukemia, and shortly thereafter she withdrew from politics.

Jordan was born on February 21, 1936, in Houston, Texas. Her father, Benjamin, was a Baptist minister, and her mother, Arlyne, was a homemaker. After finishing high school in 1952, she enrolled in Texas Southern University, a black college, where she studied political science and starred on the debate team. Jordan and TSU shocked the collegiate debate world when they battled the Harvard University debaters to a tie. After receiving a B.A. in 1956, she was admitted to Boston University Law School, receiving an LL.B. three years later. She then returned to Houston to open a law office.

Jordan became involved in politics in 1960 when she campaigned for John F. Kennedy, the Democratic candidate for president. She remained active in the affairs of the Democratic Party after his election and eventually became speaker of the Harris County Democratic organization. By 1962, she was ready to run for office, mostly because she had decided that the best way to put an end to racial discrimination was to attack it in the halls of power. Her campaign for the state house of representatives that year ended in failure, as did a similar attempt two years later. By 1966, however, Houston's voting districts had been redrawn, and most of the voters who had supported her in her first two campaigns ended up in the same senatorial district. When she ran for the state senate in 1966, she was elected by a two-to-one margin, thus becoming the first African American to sit in that body since Reconstruction.

During her six-year tenure in the Texas senate, Jordan sponsored a number of bills related to equal opportunity. She also worked to protect the environment and to improve the lot of the working class. In 1972, she was elected president pro tempore of the senate, and was made honorary Governor for a Day. As "governor," she proclaimed September Sickle Cell Disease Control Month.

The census of 1970 mandated the redrawing of Texas's congressional districts, and in the process a black-majority district was created in Houston. Jordan ran for this seat in 1972 and won easily, thus becoming the first African American from Texas to sit in the U.S. Congress. She was assigned to the committees on the judiciary, government operations, and steering and policy.

Almost immediately, Jordan became a nationally known figure because of her partici-

In 1976, congresswoman Barbara Jordan delivered the keynote address at the Democratic National Convention. *(Library of Congress)*

pation in the hearings related to Nixon administration scandals. Following the 1973 resignation of Vice President Spiro T. Agnew on charges related to corruption, President Richard M. Nixon chose Gerald R. Ford to take his place. As a member of the House Judiciary Committee, Jordan questioned Ford rather sharply about his civil rights record, and in the end voted against his approval. In 1974, she sat on the House judiciary panel that investigated Watergate, and her penetrating questioning of witnesses was televised across the nation, elevating her to celebrity status.

Jordan was easily reelected in 1974. During her second term, she sponsored an extension of the Voting Rights Act of 1965 that gave Hispanics and other minorities the same protections afforded to African Americans under the original act. She also sponsored two acts that eliminated certain exceptions to the antitrust laws, thus lowering the prices of consumer goods. In 1976, she delivered the keynote address at the Democratic National Convention, thus becoming the first African American to do so.

Despite her incredible popularity, Jordan declined to run for reelection in 1976, largely because she was suffering from the early stages of leukemia and multiple sclerosis but partly because she was ready to move on to other endeavors. In 1979, she was appointed professor of ethics at the Lyndon Baines Johnson School of Public Affairs at the University of Texas at Austin, a position she held until 1995. In 1991, she was appointed special counsel for ethics to the governor of Texas, and in 1994 she was named to chair the U.S. Commission on Immigration Reform.

Although her health was not good during the last 20 years of her life, Jordan remained a powerful public speaker until her death. In 1985, she was named the Best Living Orator, and in 1992 she again delivered the keynote speech at the Democratic National Convention. She died on January 17, 1996, in Austin.

Further Reading

Black Americans in Congress. "Barbara Jordan." Available online. URL: http://baic.house.gov/member-profiles/profile.html?intID=67.   Downloaded March 28, 2009.

Clay, William L. *Just Permanent Interests: Black Americans in Congress, 1870–1992.* New York: Amistad Press, 1993.

Fenno, Richard F. *Going Home: Black Representatives and Their Constituents.* 2nd ed. Chicago: University of Chicago Press, 2003.

Gill, LaVerne McCain. *African American Women in Congress: Forming and Transforming History.* New Brunswick, N.J.: Rutgers University Press, 1997.

Holmes, Barbara A. *A Private Woman in Public Spaces: Barbara Jordan's Speeches on Ethics, Public Religion, and Law.* Harrisburg, Pa.: Trinity Press International, 2000.

Jordan, Barbara, and Shelby Hearon. *Barbara Jordan, a Self-Portrait.* Garden City, N.Y.: Doubleday, 1979.

Rogers, Mary B. *Barbara Jordan: American Hero.* New York: Bantam Books, 1998.

Sherman, Max, ed. *Barbara Jordan: Speaking the Truth with Eloquent Thunder.* Austin: University of Texas Press, 2007.

K

Kelly, Sharon Pratt Dixon
(Sharon Pratt Dixon, Sharon Pratt)
(1944–) *mayor of Washington, D.C.*

In 1991, Kelly, known as Sharon Pratt Dixon at the time, took office as mayor of Washington, D.C. Her single term was sandwiched between terms of MARION BARRY.

Kelly was born Sharon Pratt on January 30, 1944, in Washington, D.C. Her father, Carlisle, was an attorney, and her mother, Mildred, was a homemaker. When she was four years old her mother died, and she went to live with her grandmother and aunt, Hazel and Aimee Pratt, who also resided in Washington. She graduated from high school in 1961 and enrolled in Howard University. Four years later, she received a B.A. in political science, and in 1968 she received a J.D. from Howard University Law School. While at Howard she became acquainted with PATRICIA ROBERTS HARRIS, who taught law at Howard and served briefly as dean of the law school. After a brief stint as house counsel for the Joint Center for Political Studies, in 1971 she joined her father's law firm. In 1976, she went to work for the Potomac Electric Power Company as an associate general counsel. Three years later, she became the director of consumer affairs, and in 1983 she was named a vice president, a position she held for seven years. In 1967, she married Arrington

Dixon, with whom she had two children; they divorced in 1982. In 1991, she married James Kelly III. This marriage also ended in divorce in 1999.

Kelly became involved in politics in 1968, when she helped with her husband's campaign for D.C. school board. Although he lost, they remained involved in the affairs of the local Democratic Party. In 1974, she helped him run for office again, and this time he was elected to the D.C. city council. Three years later, when Patricia Harris was named secretary of housing and urban development, Kelly was chosen to succeed her as one of D.C.'s representatives on the Democratic National Committee (DNC). In 1982, she managed Harris's unsuccessful campaign for mayor. Reelected to three additional terms on the DNC, in 1985 Kelly was named its treasurer, a post she held for four years.

Kelly began to think about running for elective office in the late 1980s as a result of what she perceived to be happening with the District of Columbia's local government. Long a ward of the federal government, in 1973 D.C. had been granted the right to elect its own mayor and city council and to run its own local affairs. In 1979, Marion Barry had been elected mayor, and for several years he had performed well. By 1990, however, Barry was in serious trouble. Charges of gross mismanagement and corruption in his administration, coupled with his own arrest on drug charges, forced him from office. In 1990, Kelly and a host of others declared their candidacies for Barry's job. Of the group, she had the least amount of experience, having never served in a public capacity. She turned this liability into an asset, however, by running as an outsider, claiming legitimately to have had nothing to do with the mess that Barry and his associates had created. She promised to "clean house with a shovel, not a broom." The voters responded to her message, and she took office in 1991.

As mayor, Kelly succeeded in obtaining $100 million in additional funds from the federal government, by far the city's major landlord, with which to operate the D.C. government. She used the money to upgrade office equipment and communications systems, much of which did not work or did not exist when she took office. Other achievements, however, were hard to come by. She had promised to streamline government by laying off unnecessary upper-level managers, but she failed to perceive the political clout that these managers possessed. Programs to reduce the murder rate, drug abuse, and homelessness failed to achieve the expected results. To make matters worse, Congress cut D.C.'s budget by $42 million, citing its displeasure with what it perceived to be continuing mismanagement. In fact, much of what Congress perceived as mismanagement was actually inexperience. Most of the employees she inherited from Barry remained staunchly loyal to their former boss, and Kelly had great difficulty attracting and retaining a team of able advisers who were loyal to her. By 1994, the voters were expressing their displeasure quite vocally, and some of them mounted a campaign to have her recalled before her term expired. Meanwhile, Barry's political star was beginning to rise again. He had been elected to city council in 1992, and he used this position as a platform to run for mayor again. In 1994, he easily defeated Kelly in her bid for reelection.

After leaving office in 1995, Kelly taught for a year at Harvard University's Institute of Politics.

In 2002, she established Pratt Consulting, a management consulting firm that specializes in assisting companies and governments in projects dealing with homeland security. She remained involved in D.C. politics but only as a private citizen.

Further Reading

Atwater, Deborah F. "Kelly, Sharon Pratt." In *African American National Biography*, vol. 5, edited by Henry Louis Gates, Jr., and Evelyn Brooks Higginbotham. New York: Oxford University Press, 2008, pp. 57–58.
Smith, Jessie Carney, ed. *Epic Lives: One Hundred Black Women Who Made a Difference.* Detroit: Visible Ink Press, 1993.

Keyes, Alan
(Alan Lee Keyes)
(1950–) *presidential candidate*

Alan Keyes was the first African American to run for president of the United States as a Republican. He has since become one of the leading conservative voices in American society.

Keyes was born on August 7, 1950, in New York City. His father was in the military, and he moved with his family to wherever his father was stationed. He graduated from high school in San Antonio, Texas, in 1969, and enrolled in Cornell University. He left after his freshman year to spend a year in Paris, France, and then enrolled in Harvard University, receiving a B.A. in political science in 1972 and a Ph.D. in political science in 1979. In 1978, he had accepted a position as a foreign service officer with the U.S. State Department. In 1981, he married Jocelyn Marcel, with whom he has three children, and settled in the Maryland suburbs of Washington, D.C.

Over the next nine years, Keyes rose through the ranks of the State Department, serving as a desk officer for southern African affairs, a member of the department's policy planning council, ambassador to the United Nations Educational, Scientific, and Cultural Organization (UNESCO), and assistant secretary of state for international organizational affairs. In this latter position, he was the highest ranking African American in the State Department. He resigned from government service in 1987 following a dispute with a superior over the allocation of U.S. funds to various UN organizations; during the dispute, Keyes claimed that he was insulted racially.

In a sense, Keyes's political career began when he was in high school. He was elected president of the student council as well as president of the American Legion Boys Nation. By this time, he had developed strongly conservative views to go along with his remarkable oratorical and writing skills. As the Boys Nation's president, he delivered a number of resounding speeches in support of U.S. involvement in Vietnam. He also won a national essay contest by writing on the same subject. He left Cornell partly because he had spoken against black militants who had taken over the student center and who retaliated by threatening him with bodily harm. As a State Department employee, he defended President Ronald Reagan's decision not to impose economic sanctions against South Africa because of apartheid. Keyes's support for Reagan in this regard earned him the denunciations of a great many African-American political leaders.

Keyes first ran for office in 1988, when he declared his candidacy for one of Maryland's seats in the U.S. Senate. He won the Republican nomination but lost the general election to a popular liberal Democrat, Paul Sarbanes; still, Keyes polled about 38 percent of the vote, an impressive showing for a political neophyte's first statewide campaign. After the election he became president of Citizens Against Government Waste, a conservative Washington-based group. He also mounted a nationwide speaking tour, during which he claimed to be a "moral populist." As a speaker, Keyes earned high praise for his style, if not his message, which was that Americans must return to old-fashioned family values in order to preserve their position in the world and at home.

Keyes ran again for the Senate in 1992. Once again, he secured the Republican nomination, and once again he lost to a popular liberal Democrat, this time Barbara Mikulski. After the election, he became a talk show host for WCBM Radio in the D.C. suburb of Owings Mills. Broadcasting for three hours each weekday, he espoused his conservative views with mesmerizing oratory, and before long his show, called "America's Wake-Up Call" and "The Alan Keyes Show," became nationally syndicated. As a result, Keyes became a hero to the so-called Christian right, which thoroughly endorsed his attacks on abortion and his calls for a return to old-fashioned family values.

Buoyed by the support he received from his millions of listeners, in 1995 Keyes declared his candidacy for the Republican nomination for president of the United States. His campaign speeches focused almost entirely on moral issues, especially abortion, which he condemned unequivocally. He campaigned tirelessly in the various state primaries, and argued vociferously that he should be included in debates among the party's major candidates. Despite his energetic style, he was a distant also-ran by the time of the Republican National Convention. In 2000, he sought the nomination a second time, but with the same result.

After the election, he continued to espouse conservative family values in his talk show and on national speaking tours. In 2002, he briefly hosted a television show, *Alan Keyes Is Making Sense,* on MSNBC.

Keyes returned to politics in August 2004, when he became the Republic nominee for the junior U.S. senator from Illinois. He was a last-minute replacement for the previous Republic candidate, Jack Ryan, who had become embroiled in a sex scandal. Losing to Democratic nominee BARACK OBAMA, Keyes received only about 27 percent of the vote.

In 2008, Keyes made a third quixotic bid for the presidency. After Arizona senator John McCain secured the Republican nomination, Keyes switched his affiliation to the Constitution Party, which selected Chuck Baldwin as its candidate. Keyes then formed America's Independent Party (AIP). He appeared as the AIP's presidential nominee on the ballot in three states and received a total of approximately 48,000 votes.

Further Reading

Idani, Michaeljulius. "Keyes, Alan." In *African American National Biography*, vol. 5, edited by Henry Louis Gates, Jr., and Evelyn Brooks Higginbotham. New York: Oxford University Press, 2008, pp. 71–73.

Keyes, Alan. *Masters of the Dream: The Strength and Betrayal of Black America.* New York: William Morrow, 1995.

Stengel, Richard. "Moralist on the March." *Time* 146 (September 4, 1995): 33.

Kilpatrick, Carolyn

(Carolyn Cheeks Kilpatrick)
(1945–   ) *U.S. congressional representative from Michigan*

In 1997, Carolyn Kilpatrick succeeded Barbara-Rose Collins in the U.S. House of Representatives. While Collins focused on the plight of America's cities, Kilpatrick involved herself in everything from banking and transportation to foreign affairs.

Kilpatrick was born Carolyn Jean Cheeks on June 25, 1945, in Detroit, Michigan, to Marvell and Willa Mae Cheeks. After graduating from high school, she worked as a secretary while studying at Ferris State College. In 1965, she earned an A.A. and enrolled in Western Michigan University. Two years before receiving a B.S. in 1972, she accepted a position teaching business education in the Detroit public school system. She continued her education while teaching, receiving a M.S. in

education administration from the University of Michigan in 1977. In 1968, she married Bernard Kilpatrick, with whom she had two children; they later divorced.

Kilpatrick became involved in politics in 1973, when she served as a community organizer for Coleman Young's first campaign for mayor of Detroit. She later served as the coordinator of political action for the Shrine of the Black Madonna Pan-African Orthodox Christian Church and was elected to the Detroit school board. In 1978, she was elected to a seat in the Michigan state legislature. Over the next 18 years, she championed increased funding for public education and transportation projects.

In 1991, Collins resigned from the Detroit city council after being elected to Congress. That same year, Kilpatrick ran for her vacant seat on council. A loyal ally of Mayor Young, she was expected to win easily. However, a last-minute scandal involving the nonpayment of employee taxes by a printing company she owned tipped the scales in her opponent's favor. Three years later, her bid for a seat in the state senate was thwarted unintentionally by the incumbent, David Holmes. Kilpatrick filed to run thinking that Holmes intended to retire, but he filed at the last minute so she withdrew. Eight days later, Holmes died, and she was unable to refile. In 1996, she again ran for Collins's seat, this time before it was vacated. Collins had become embroiled in scandals involving the House Ethics Committee and the U.S. Justice Department, and Kilpatrick defeated her easily in the Democratic primary. Kilpatrick won the general election, took her seat in 1997, and was assigned to the committees on banking/financial services and oversight.

As a congresswoman, Kilpatrick has focused on legislation related to her committee duties. During her first term, she was mostly involved with reforming the banking system, revitalizing the U.S. Department of Housing and Urban Development, and overseeing federal participation in urban development. Later, she was assigned to the House

Security Office in honor of civil rights activist Rosa Parks.

Kilpatrick was elected to serve a two-year term as chairwoman of the Congressional Black Congress in 2006. Two years later, she narrowly won a sixth term in the House of Representatives. She was not so lucky in her next campaign. Running for reelection in 2010, Kilpatrick lost the Democratic primary to state senator Hansen Clarke. Her defeat was largely attributed to the tarnishing of her reputation by the legal troubles and imprisonment of her son KWAME KILPATRICK, the former mayor of Detroit.

Further Reading

Biographical Directory of the United States Congress. "Kilpatrick, Carolyn Cheeks, 1945– ." Available online. URL: http://bioguide.congress.gov/ scripts/ biodisplay.pl?index=K000180. Downloaded April 15, 2009.

Congresswoman Carolyn Cheeks Kilpatrick, Official Web Site. Available online. URL: http://www. house.gov/kilpatrick. Downloaded April 20, 2009.

Foerstel, Karen. *Biographical Dictionary of Congressional Women.* New York: Greenwood Press, 1999.

Taylor, Deborah Lois. "Kilpatrick, Carolyn Cheeks." In *African American National Biography,* vol. 5, edited by Henry Louis Gates, Jr., and Evelyn Brooks Higginbotham. New York: Oxford University Press, 2008, pp. 79–80.

Kilpatrick, Kwame
(1970–) *mayor of Detroit, Michigan*

In 2002, Kwame Kilpatrick, at 31, became the youngest person ever to be elected mayor of Detroit, Michigan. In 2008, his last year in office, he became the only sitting mayor in the city's history to be charged with a felony.

Kilpatrick was born in Detroit on June 8, 1970. Both his parents were involved in politics. His father, Bernard Kilpatrick, held several local positions, including Wayne County commissioner.

Carolyn Kilpatrick represented Detroit, Michigan, in Congress. *(Carolyn Cheeks Kilpatrick)*

Appropriations Committee, which oversees federal spending for such diverse agencies as the National Transportation Safety Board and the Peace Corps. Outside of committee work, she had worked for greater involvement for minority-owned media outlets and advertising firms in the telecommunications industry. Kilpatrick has also sought to force the Department of Defense to allocate a portion of its advertising budget to minority businesses.

To aid her constituents, Kilpatrick has helped direct federal funds to local programs to improve transportation, health care, and housing options. Through her efforts, the National Aeronautics and Space Administration (NASA) established a science and engineering program for public school students at Detroit's Wayne State University. In 2005, she introduced a bill that, when passed, named her district's Federal Homeland

His mother, CAROLYN KILPATRICK, served in Michigan's state legislature and later became a member of the U.S. House of Representatives.

After attending public school in his hometown, Kilpatrick enrolled at Florida A&M in Tallahassee. With a bachelor's degree in political science, Kilpatrick returned to Detroit with his wife Carlita. The couple would eventually have three children.

While studying at the Detroit School of Law, Kilpatrick was elected to Michigan's house of representatives. He took the seat his mother vacated in order to campaign for the U.S. Congress. When Mayor DENNIS ARCHER announced he would not seek a third term, Kilpatrick declared that he would run for the city's highest office. With the support of unions and business leaders, Kilpatrick came from behind to win both the Democratic primary and the general election.

Young and energetic, Kilpatrick promised to take Detroit in a new direction by resolving its budget crisis and lowering its high crime rate. But almost from the start, his administration was preoccupied by scandal. During his first term, reporters discovered that Kilpatrick had leased a SUV for his family with $25,000 of taxpayer money at a time when Detroit's government was slashing thousands of jobs. He also ran up $200,000 of spa, hotel, and restaurant bills on a city credit card. In 2002, rumors spread about a wild party he hosted at the governor's mansion. The later murder of an exotic dancer who was said to have attended the party added further grist for the rumor mill.

Despite growing doubts about Kilpatrick's ability to lead, he was reelected in 2006. Throughout his second term, he was dogged by a civil lawsuit brought by two former police officers. They claimed Kilpatrick improperly fired them for investigating the conduct of several of his bodyguards. At the trial, Kilpatrick appeared on the stand and, under oath, lied about a sexual affair he had had with his chief of staff, Christine Beatty. The jury found for the plaintiffs and awarded the policemen $6.5 million. Kilpatrick

said he would appeal the verdict but instead made a secret agreement with the officers, offering them $8.4 million in taxpayers' money in exchange for keeping quiet about his affair. In January 2008, the press obtained access to 14,000 text messages between Kilpatrick and Beatty issued on city-owned pagers. The often-graphic messages made it clear that Kilpatrick had committed perjury.

In September 2008, Kilpatrick made a deal with prosecutors. He agreed to plead guilty to two counts of obstruction of justice. As punishment, he would serve four months in jail and be on probation for five years. Kilpatrick resigned his position, and Kenneth Cockrel, Jr., president of the city council, became the interim mayor. On October 28, 2008, the day he began serving his sentence, Kilpatrick announced to the press, "I want to tell you, Detroit, that you done set me up for a comeback."

After 99 days in jail, Kilpatrick was released on February 3, 2009. However he was back in court the following year. Kilpatrick had hidden assets to avoid paying the $1 million in restitution he had been ordered to give the city of Detroit, thereby violating his probation. On March 25, 2010, Kilpatrick was sentenced to 18 months to five years in prison. The former mayor's legal troubles grew even worse when, on June 23, 2010, a federal grand jury indicted him on 19 counts of fraud and tax evasion. Kilpatrick was accused of using money from his nonprofit organization, Kilpatrick Civic Fund, illegally to pay for campaign and personal expenses. If found guilty, Kilpatrick could spend decades in prison.

Further Reading

Hakim, Danny. "In Troubled Detroit, Mayor's Race Is a Referendum on Style. *New York Times,* July 10, 2005. Available online. URL: http://www.nytimes.com/2005/07/10/national/10detroit.html. Downloaded May 8, 2009.

Marks, Alexandra. "'Hip Hop Mayor' Aims to Rev Motor City Engine." *Christian Science Monitor,* August 7, 2002. Available online. URL: http://

www.csmonitor.com/2002/0807/p01s03-uspo.
htm. Downloaded May 10, 2009.

Stephey, M. J. "Kwame Kilpatrick." *New York Times,*
October 28, 2008. Available online. URL: http://
www.time.com/time/politics/article/0,8599,
1854335,00.html. Downloaded May 10, 2009.

Kirk, Ron
(Ronald Kirk)
(1954–   ) *mayor of Dallas, Texas; U.S. trade
representative*

Ron Kirk was the first African-American mayor of
Dallas, Texas. In 2002, he came very close to
becoming the first African-American senator
from the South since Reconstruction.

Kirk was born on June 27, 1954, in Austin,
Texas. His father was a postal worker and his
mother was a teacher. After graduating from high
school, he enrolled in Austin College. He became
fascinated with the political process in 1974,
when he served an internship as a legislative aide
to the speaker of the house at the Texas Constitutional Convention. He received a B.A. in political science and sociology in 1976 and then
enrolled in the University of Texas School of
Law; while in law school he served another political internship, this time with the Texas legislature. In 1979, he received a J.D. and went to work
as an attorney for a Dallas law firm. After a two-
year stint in Washington, D.C., as a legislative
aide to U.S. senator Lloyd Bentsen, Kirk returned
to Dallas in 1981 to be assistant city's attorney.
Because of his legislative experience, he soon
became the city's chief lobbyist as well, working
to gain the approval of state legislators for measures of particular interest to Dallas. In 1988, he
married Matrice Ellis, with whom he has two
children. The following year, he returned to the
private practice of law.

Over the next several years, Kirk remained in
the public sphere by chairing the state's general
services commission, which oversees all state pur-
chases. He also served as executive committee
member of the Dallas Regional Mobility Commission and as a director of the Texas State Fair.
In 1994, the Texas secretary of state resigned to
accept a federal judgeship, and Kirk was named
to serve out the remainder of his term. Although
he did a creditable job in the position, he declined
to run for a term of his own in 1995 because he
had decided to run that same year for mayor of
Dallas.

Kirk's political experience to date had taught
him that substantive sociopolitical change was
most easily achieved at the local level, and to this
end he campaigned as a force for positive change.
Kirk attracted the support of the white business
community by promising to make Dallas an international city so that it could take maximum
advantage of the North American Free Trade
Agreement, which removed many of the trade
barriers between the United States and Mexico.
At the same time, he won the support of African
Americans and Hispanics by arguing that Dallas
must learn to appreciate diversity in order to
become an international city. He polled more
votes that the other five challengers combined
and took his office in 1995.

As mayor, Kirk focused on improving the city's
business climate. He targeted 400 businesses for
growth, reduced government regulations for small
businesses, and established a response team to
help businesses deal with the remaining regulations. He oversaw economic development efforts
that attracted $3.5 billion in new investments to
Dallas, which in turn helped create 45,000 new
jobs, about a quarter of which were created in the
city's minority neighborhoods. His most visible
achievement in this regard was the construction
of a downtown arena that allowed the city to keep
the NBA Dallas Mavericks and attract the NHL
Minnesota North Stars. The result was a business
boom that boosted the city's tax revenue without
having to raise taxes. Much of this new revenue
went to fight crime, which fell to its lowest level in
20 years, improve streets and bridges, and establish

new parks. Other Kirk-led initiatives include a first-time buyer program whereby the city assisted 3,200 low-income families to buy their own homes. As a result of these accomplishments, Kirk was overwhelmingly reelected in 1999.

Although Kirk had previously said that the only elected office he ever wanted was the mayoralty of Dallas, in 2002 he set his sights higher. That same year, Phil Gramm, the state's longtime Republican U.S. senator, announced that he would not run for reelection in 2002. Shortly thereafter, Kirk resigned as mayor and declared his candidacy for Gramm's seat. He won the Democratic nomination after Tony Sanchez, the Democratic nominee for governor, endorsed Kirk over his Hispanic challenger, Victor Morales. The endorsement won Kirk the support of many Hispanic voters, which propelled him to a 60-40 victory over Morales. Buoyed by the victory, Kirk then took on his Republican challenger, Texas attorney general John Cornyn.

After a tough race, Kirk was defeated by a margin of 57-43.

Returning to private life, Kirk worked as a lawyer and lobbyist until January 2009, when President-elect BARACK OBAMA nominated him for U.S. Trade Representative. Sworn in on March 20, 2009, Kirk became the first African American ever to hold this position.

Further Reading
"Ex-Dallas Mayor Ron Kirk Wins U.S. Senate Nomination." *Jet* 101 (April 29, 2002): 20–21.

Gillman, Todd J. "Biggest Challenge for Ron Kirk May Come from U.S." *Dallas Morning News*, April 9, 2009. Available online. URL: http://www.dallasnews.com/sharedcontent/dws/news/politics/national/stories/040909dnmetkirk.3f9555d.html. Downloaded April 23, 2009.

Massaquoi, Hans J. "Introducing: Ron Kirk: First Black Mayor of Dallas." *Ebony* 50 (September 1995): 32.

L

Langston, John
(John Mercer Langston)
(1829–1897) *U.S. congressional representative from Virginia*

John Langston was the first African American elected to public office and the first black congressman from Virginia. Throughout his career he strove mightily to secure equal rights and educational opportunities for African Americans.

Langston was born on December 14, 1829, near Louisa Court House in Louisa County, Virginia. His father, Ralph Quarles, was a wealthy white planter, and his mother, Lucy Jane Langston, was a former slave who had been freed by Quarles. In 1834, both his parents died, but not before Quarles had made arrangements for him and his siblings to go live with longtime family friend William D. Gooch in Chillicothe, Ohio, thus evading their possible enslavement under the provisions of Virginia law. However, when Gooch moved to Missouri, a slave state, in 1839, Langston was forced to remain in Ohio and fend for himself. Over the next five years, he boarded with various families in Chillicothe and Cincinnati, supporting himself as a farmhand and bootblack and attending private schools for blacks when he could. In 1844, at age 14, he enrolled in the college preparatory program at Oberlin College, the only college in the United States that admitted African Americans.

He studied theology and received his B.A. in 1849 and his M.A. in 1852. He then took up the study of law and passed the Ohio bar examination in 1854. That same year, he married Caroline Wall, with whom he had five children, bought a farm in Brownhelm Township near Oberlin College, and opened a law office in Oberlin.

Langston became interested in politics in 1848 when he joined the antislavery movement and began attending black civil rights conventions. In 1852, he began campaigning for local candidates in Ohio, although he was not affiliated with any political party. A charismatic orator, he soon learned how to appeal to a mostly white audience. In 1855, he joined the Free-Soil Party and was elected Brownhelm's clerk, thus becoming the first African American to hold an elective office. The following year, he moved to Oberlin, and over the next 14 years he served that township in various elected positions, including town councilman and secretary of the board of education.

Meanwhile, Langston had become increasingly involved in the antislavery movement and in obtaining equal rights for free blacks. In 1858, he organized and led the Ohio State Anti-Slavery Society and voiced his support for John Brown's efforts to provoke a slave insurrection by raiding Harper's Ferry in 1859. During the Civil War, he recruited hundreds of blacks to serve in African-American regiments in the Union army and then worked to secure their impartial treatment while in uniform. In 1864, he was elected president of the National Equal Rights League, a forerunner of the National Association for the Advancement of Colored People (NAACP). In 1867, he presided over a national black convention in Washington, D.C., that demanded full citizenship for African Americans. That same year, he became the Freedmen's Bureau educational inspector-general; in this capacity he spent the next two years checking on the bureau's schools throughout the South while also registering freedmen to vote and getting them involved in the Republican Party on the state and local levels. In addition, he helped Senator Charles Sumner draft certain provisions of what became known as the Civil Rights Act of 1875, which outlawed racial discrimination by establishments that catered to the general public.

In 1869, Langston moved to Washington to become the first dean of Howard University's law school. Over the next six years, he established it as a quality program while also serving for two years as the school's vice president and acting president. As a reward for his loyal support of the Republican Party, in 1871 he was appointed to the District of Columbia's board of health, serving for six years as its legal adviser. In 1877, he was appointed U.S. minister and consul general to Haiti, and he spent the next six years working to improve relations between the United States and the world's first black republic. In 1885, he returned to the United States to serve as president of the Virginia Normal and Collegiate Institute in Petersburg, the state's teachers' college for African Americans. He was forced to resign by his white Democrat opponents in the state legislature after only two years.

In 1888, Langston decided to run for Congress from Virginia's Fourth District, a black-majority district centered around Petersburg. Although he "lost" to his Democrat opponent, he challenged the results and was eventually seated by the House in late 1890, just in time to serve the last three months of his term. He devoted his efforts to fighting the disfranchisement of black voters in the South, introducing a bill that would reduce the congres-

sional delegations of states that denied voting rights to African Americans for whatever reasons, including failure to pass literacy requirements.

Langston was denied reelection in 1890, and when his term expired the following year he remained in Washington. He practiced law in the nation's capital until his death there on November 15, 1897.

Further Reading

Biographical Directory of the United States Congress. "Langston, John Mercer, 1829–1897." Available online. URL: http://bioguide.congress.gov/scripts/biodisplay.pl?index=L000074. Downloaded March 28, 2009.

Black Americans in Congress. "John Mercer Langston." Available online. URL: http://baic.house.gov/member-profiles/profile.html?intID=18. Downloaded March 28, 2009.

Cheek, William, and Aimee Lee Cheek. *John Mercer Langston and the Fight for Black Freedom, 1829–65.* Champaign: University of Illinois Press, 1996.

Clay, William L. *Just Permanent Interests: Black Americans in Congress, 1870–1992.* New York: Amistad Press, 1993.

Langston, John Mercer. *From the Virginia Plantation to the National Capitol.* New York: Arno Press, 1969, reprint.

Litwack, Leon, and August Meier, eds. *Black Leaders of the Nineteenth Century* Urbana: University of Illinois Press, 1988.

Merida, Kevin. "The 'Obama Before Obama.'" *Washington Post,* June 7, 2008. Available online. URL: http://www.washingtonpost.com/wp-dyn/content/article/2008/06/06/AR2008060604509.html?nav=rss_email/components. Downloaded March 28, 2009.

Lee, Barbara

(1946–) *U.S. congressional representative from California*

In 1998, Barbara Lee was elected to take the place of RON DELLUMS as Oakland's representative in the U.S. Congress. She had previously worked as Dellums's chief aide, and she promised "to continue fighting the good fight" in the Dellums tradition.

Lee was born on July 16, 1946, in El Paso, Texas. At age 14, she moved with her family to San Fernando, California, on the outskirts of Los Angeles. After finishing high school, she worked at various jobs until 1967, when she moved to Oakland. She eventually returned to school, receiving a B.A. from Oakland's Mills College in 1973 and an M.S.W. in social welfare from the University of California at Berkeley in 1975. While in graduate school she cofounded a community health center in Berkeley.

Lee became involved in politics in 1973 when she spent a year as an intern on Dellums's staff. After graduating from the University of California at Berkeley, she joined the staff on a full-time basis. Over the next 15 years, she worked in Dellums's offices in Oakland and Washington, D.C., and in 1979 she was appointed his chief of staff. In 1990, with Dellums's encouragement, she ran as a Democrat for the California state assembly and won. Six years later, she won a seat in the state senate. During her eight years as a state legislator, she sponsored 67 bills that were enacted into law. These bills covered a wide range of issues involving education, public safety, environmental protection, health, labor, and women's rights. Perhaps the most noteworthy was a bill establishing a nonviolent conflict-resolution program in the state's public schools. She also cofounded and served as president of the California Commission on the Status of African American Males, the California Legislative Black Caucus, and the National Conference on State Legislatures Women's Network.

In 1998, Dellums, who had served in Congress for 27 years, decided in midterm to retire. A special election was held to replace him, and Lee declared her candidacy. She was quickly endorsed by Dellums, who had been grooming Lee to replace him; one of the reasons he encouraged her to run for office in 1990 was so that she could gain the necessary legislative experience to take his place in

A former congressional aide to Ron Dellums, Barbara Lee took Dellums's place when he retired from Congress. *(Barbara Lee)*

Congress. Dellums and Lee had much in common philosophically and politically; both had master's degrees in social welfare from the same university, both had come of age in the unique sociopolitical climate of the Oakland-Berkeley area, and both were committed to working for peace and social justice throughout the world. She easily won the special election and the general election later that same year. She took her seat in 1998 and was assigned to the committees on banking/financial services and international relations.

As a congresswoman, Lee seemed to pick up where Dellums left off. She was one of a few congresspeople who voted against renewing U.S. bombing raids against Iraq, and the only one to vote against involving the United States in bombing raids against Serbia. She made highly publicized trips to Cuba, which the United States had placed under a trade embargo as a means of toppling Fidel Castro's communist regime, and to Grenada, which U.S. troops had invaded in the 1980s to expel a pro-Marxist regime. She worked to redirect the nation's priorities, and its budgetary allocations, away from global military involvement and toward the creation of "livable communities in a peaceful world." She sponsored legislation to address the global AIDS/HIV crisis, to provide all Americans with universal health care, to make home ownership more accessible to low-income buyers, to construct affordable housing for those who cannot otherwise buy homes, and to provide public schools with more mental health and social work counselors, among other things.

Following the terrorist attacks of September 11, 2001, Barbara Lee was the only member of Congress to vote against U.S. House Resolution 64, which authorized President George W. Bush to use military force in response. Lee explained her dissenting vote by stating, "We must not rush to judgment. Far too many innocent people have already died." Lee's stance led to death threats and harsh criticism from conservative media figures. But her vote and her opposition to the war in Iraq only seemed to increase her popularity among her constituents. In 2010, Lee was reelected to a seventh full term and chosen to chair the Congressional Black Caucus.

Further Reading

Abdullah, Melina. "Lee, Barbara." In *African American National Biography*, vol. 5, edited by Henry Louis Gates, Jr., and Evelyn Brooks Higginbotham. New York: Oxford University Press, 2008, pp. 187–188.

Biographical Directory of the United States Congress. "Lee, Barbara, 1946– ." Available online. URL: http://bioguide.congress.gov/scripts/biodisplay.pl?index=L000551. Downloaded October 19, 2010.

Congresswoman Barbara Lee, Official Web Site. Available online. URL: http://lee.house.gov. Downloaded April 20, 2009.

Explorations in Black Leadership. "Barbara Lee." Available online. URL: http://www.virginia.edu/publichistory/bl/index.php?uid=31. Downloaded April 20, 2009.

Whitting, Sam. "Facetime: Giving Peace a Chance, Local Rep. Barbara Lee on Her National Following." *San Francisco Chronicle*, March 23, 2003. Available online. URL: http://www.sfgate.com/cgi-bin/article.cgi?file=/chronicle/archive/2003/03/23/CM260023.DTL. Downloaded April 21, 2009.

Leland, Mickey

(George Thomas Leland, Jr.)
(1944–1989) *U.S. congressional representative from Texas*

"Mickey" Leland is better known as a humanitarian than as a politician. During his 10 years in the U.S. Congress, he did much to focus the attention of the nation and the world on the plight of starving refugees in East Africa.

Leland was born on November 27, 1944, in Lubbock, Texas. His father, George, was a laborer, and his mother, Alice, was a teacher. His father abandoned the family shortly after his birth, after which he moved with his mother to Houston where he grew up. After finishing high school in 1963, he worked part-time while attending Texas Southern University, receiving a B.S. in pharmacy in 1970. For the next two years he taught clinical pharmacy at Texas Southern.

While in college, Leland had developed a strong desire to contribute to the Civil Rights movement. In 1973, he decided that the best way to change the system was to become a part of it, so that same year he ran for the Texas state legislature and won. For the next five years, he worked diligently to expand opportunities for minorities. In 1978, when BARBARA JORDAN announced her intention to retire from the U.S. House of Representatives, Leland ran for her seat and won. He took office in 1979 and was assigned to the interstate and foreign commerce committee and the post office and civil service committee.

As a congressman, Leland continued to work for equal opportunity. His greatest success in this area was to open up the nation's telecommunications industry to minority entrepreneurs, and to get more black actors and actresses into television. He also sought to do something for the nation's dispossessed. When conservatives opened fire on the printing of government forms in English and Spanish, he fought to preserve them, offering his remarks on the House floor in Spanish. Another Leland measure sought to provide assistance to homeless people; although it failed to pass, several of its provisions were enacted as part of the Stewart B. McKinney Homeless Assistance Act. Yet another bill provided tax incentives to companies that contributed to food banks. He also made a number of trips to Appalachia and Indian reservations to call attention to living conditions there. He chaired the Congressional Black Caucus from 1985 to 1986.

By 1983, the same year he married Alison Walton, with whom he had three children, Leland's primary focus had shifted to Africa, which was being ravaged by racism, warfare, and famine. He worked to strengthen sanctions against South Africa as long as apartheid held sway in that nation. He authored legislation that provided $800 million in nonmilitary aid to the nations of sub-Saharan Africa. As chairman of the Select Committee on Hunger from 1984 to 1989, he made several fact-finding trips to East Africa to determine where U.S. humanitarian aid was most needed.

Leland considered himself to be a citizen of the world, not just of the United States. To this end, he ignored the global politics that motivated many U.S. policy makers during the cold war. He established cordial relations with Marxist leaders in East Africa and Latin America in the hope of normalizing relations between their countries and the United States so that starving refugees could be better helped. As a result of his relationship with Cuba's Fidel Castro, he was able to secure the release of nine Americans who had been imprisoned in Cuba for various offenses.

Leland was reelected five times. He died on August 7, 1989, when his airplane crashed near Gambela, Ethiopia, during a tour of relief operations in East Africa.

Further Reading

Biographical Directory of the United States Congress. "Leland, George Thomas (Mickey), 1944–1989." Available online. URL: http://bioguide.congress. gov/scripts/biodisplay.pl?index=L000237. Downloaded March 28, 2009.

Black Americans in Congress. "George Thomas (Mickey) Leland." Available online. URL: http:// baic.house.gov/member-profiles/profile.html? intID=66. Downloaded April 4, 2009.

Clay, William L. *Just Permanent Interests: Black Americans in Congress, 1870–1992.* New York: Amistad Press, 1993.

Lewis, John
(John Robert Lewis)
(1940–) *U.S. congressional representative from Georgia*

During the 1960s, John Lewis was one of the most fearless leaders of the Civil Rights movement. In 1986, he became the first African-American congressman from Georgia since the end of Reconstruction.

Lewis was born on February 21, 1940, in Troy, Alabama. His parents, Eddie and Willie Mae, were farmers. After graduating from high school, he enrolled in the American Baptist Theological Seminary in Nashville, Tennessee. He became involved in the Civil Rights movement in Nashville, and in 1960 he attended the organizational meeting that founded the Student Nonviolent Coordinating Committee (SNCC). In 1961, he graduated from the seminary and became one of the first Freedom Riders, a group of blacks and

John Lewis *(front row, far right)* was the first African American to represent Georgia in Congress since Reconstruction. Second from left is Andrew Young. *(Library of Congress)*

sympathetic whites who attempted to desegregate bus facilities in the South. In 1965, he took part in the Selma to Montgomery march, during which he received a fractured skull. He also helped plan the famous 1963 March on Washington and was elected to succeed MARION BARRY as SNCC's chairman. During the course of his civil rights career, he was jailed 40 times.

Lewis left SNCC three years later to work for the Field Foundation, and from 1970 to 1977 he directed its voter education project for the Southern Regional Council. Under his leadership, the project recruited huge numbers of new African-American voters. Meanwhile, in 1967 he had earned a B.A. in religion and philosophy from Fisk University in Nashville. The following year, he married Lillian Miles, with whom he has one child.

In 1976, ANDY YOUNG resigned from Congress to accept President Jimmy Carter's appointment as U.S. ambassador to the United Nations. Lewis decided to run for Young's seat, but his low-key campaign failed to rouse enough voters for him to defeat Wyche Fowler, a white liberal Democrat. The following year, Carter named Lewis the director of operations for ACTION, a federal agency that coordinated the activities of almost 250,000 volunteers. In 1980, he became the community affairs director of the National Consumer Co-op Bank of Atlanta, Georgia. Two years later, he was elected to a seat on the Atlanta city council. During his two terms, he worked to improve municipal services in the city's minority neighborhoods.

In 1986, Fowler retired from Congress, and Lewis decided once again to run for the seat. This time he mounted a more aggressive campaign, and he narrowly defeated the odds-on favorite JULIAN BOND in the Democratic primary. He easily won the general election and took his seat in 1987. He was assigned to the committees on public works and interior/insular affairs.

As a freshman congressman, Lewis managed to obtain a $300 million federal office building for downtown Atlanta. He worked to improve life for inner-city residents and eventually served as cochair of the Congressional Urban Caucus. Meanwhile, he built a strong "rainbow" coalition within his district between working-class blacks and conservative whites that permitted him to get reelected. He eventually was assigned to the Ways and Means Committee and named one of the Democratic Party's House leaders.

The rollback of affirmative action programs under the Nixon and Reagan administrations, coupled with the Republican Party's Contract with America in the 1990s, disillusioned a number of African-American leaders about the possibility of creating a truly integrated society. Many of them have called for what amounts to a separate sphere for blacks in American society in the form of minority set-asides, black-majority districts, and the like. Not Lewis. He never opposed affirmative action programs and indeed supported them vigorously, but at the same time he remained committed to the goal of creating a "beloved society," where a person's race means nothing. In the late 1990s, he began calling for affirmative action programs that targeted class instead of race. As for black-minority districts, he called for the creation of districts that gave black candidates a good chance of winning, but only if they could appeal to their white constituents as well. By the same token, he urged that white-majority districts include a healthy number of minority voters whenever possible, so that white candidates would have to reach out to blacks in order to win.

Lewis has been criticized for being too trusting of the good intentions of white liberals, and for supporting the Democratic Party too closely even while it fails to do more for African Americans. Indeed, he has authored a relatively small number of bills, preferring instead to work for passage of bills that the Democratic Party leadership supports. Ironically, his role as a floor leader has given

him a great deal of influence over the types of bills he is asked to support, and he is routinely consulted by the party leadership as to what shape important legislation should take.

During the 2008 presidential election, Lewis initially supported Hillary Clinton. But by February 2008, when it was clear BARACK OBAMA was running more than a symbolic campaign, he switched his endorsement to Obama. On the day Obama was elected president, Lewis won his 12th term in the House of Representatives. He was reelected in 2010.

Further Reading

Biographical Directory of the United States Congress. "Lewis, John R., 1940–   ." Available online. URL: http://bioguide.congress.gov/scripts/biodisplay.pl?index=L000287. Downloaded April 18, 2009.

Congressman John Lewis, Official Web Site. Available online. URL: http://johnlewis.house.gov. Downloaded April 20, 2009.

Lewis, John R. *Walking with the Wind: A Memoir of the Movement.* New York: Simon & Schuster, 1998.

Remnick, David. "The President's Hero." *New Yorker,* February 2, 2009. Available online. URL: http://www.newyorker.com/talk/comment/2009/02/02/090202taco_talk_remnick. Accessed April 20, 2009.

Smith, Robert C. "Lewis, John." In *African American National Biography,* vol. 5, edited by Henry Louis Gates, Jr., and Evelyn Brooks Higginbotham. New York: Oxford University Press, 2008, pp. 224–225.

Wilentz, Sean. "The Last Integrationist." *The New Republic* (July 1, 1996), pp. 19–26.

Long, Jefferson
(Jefferson Franklin Long)
(1836–1901) *U.S. congressional representative from Georgia*

Jefferson Long was the first African American to represent Georgia in the U.S. Congress. He was also the first black congressman to make a speech before the House. Despite these accomplishments, his congressional career lasted less than seven weeks.

Long was born on March 3, 1836, in Knoxville, Crawford County, part of Georgia's "black belt" region. The names of his mother, a slave, and father, a white man, are unknown, as are most details about his early life. He taught himself how to read and write, and by 1860 he had married Lucinda Carhart, with whom he had seven children. He also had moved to Macon where he earned a living as a merchant and tailor.

After the Civil War, Long became a champion of freedmen's rights. By 1867, he was making speeches for the Georgia Equal Rights and Educational Association urging blacks to register to vote in the upcoming election of 1868. He campaigned

strenuously for the Republican ticket in that election, and shortly thereafter he was named to the Republican state central committee. In 1869, he cochaired a convention of 200 African-American delegates that called for integrated public education, higher wages for farm laborers, and better contractual terms for tenant farmers and sharecroppers.

In late 1870, Samuel F. Gove, the congressman from Long's district, was declared unfit to serve by the House of Representatives. The Republican Party nominated Long to fill the remainder of Gove's term, which expired in early 1871. The campaign was marred by violence perpetrated against blacks by the Ku Klux Klan and related groups, but Long fearlessly spoke out during the campaign against the shotgun-and-rope tactics of

Jefferson Long *(standing, right)* was the first African American to represent Georgia in Congress. He is shown here with the other African-American senators and representatives of the 41st and 42nd Congress. *(Library of Congress)*

the opposition. His courage inspired freedmen to go to the polls on December 22 in numbers sufficient to elect him.

Long was sworn in on January 16, 1871, making him the second African American to serve in the House. On February 1, he made his only speech before that body, a ringing condemnation of a bill to remove some of the political restrictions against former Confederates. Long had just fought a bloody campaign against such people, and in no uncertain terms he acquainted his fellow congressmen with the folly of the action they were about to take.

When his term expired on March 3, 1871, Long returned to Macon. Although he never ran for public office again, he played an active role in the state Republican Party and was a delegate to the national conventions from 1872 to 1880. But by 1880, he had become disgusted with the party's efforts to recruit white voters by giving nominations and positions of leadership to whites, a minority among Republicans, rather than blacks. That same year, he supported the gubernatorial candidacy of Alfred H. Colquitt, the Democratic incumbent, because Colquitt had worked harder to stop antiblack violence in Georgia than had the state's white Republicans. Long fought against white control of the party, and the resultant loss of African-American influence within it, until 1884, when he resigned. His subsequent efforts to organize black voters independent of either party failed.

Long helped found the Union Brotherhood Lodge, a black self-help fraternity headquartered in Macon with branches across Georgia. With the help of a son, he continued to run his tailor shop until he died in Macon on February 4, 1901.

Further Reading

Biographical Directory of the United States Congress. "Long, Jefferson Franklin, 1836–1901." Available online. URL: http://bioguide.congress.gov/scripts/biodisplay.pl?index=L000419. Downloaded March 28, 2009.

Black Americans in Congress. "Jefferson Franklin Long." Available online. URL: http://baic.house.gov/member-profiles/profile.html?intID=7. Downloaded March 27, 2009.

Clay, William L. *Just Permanent Interests: Black Americans in Congress, 1870–1992*. New York: Amistad Press, 1993.

Drago, Edmund L. *Black Politicians and Reconstruction in Georgia: A Splendid Failure.* Athens: University of Georgia Press, 1992.

Dray, Philip. *Capitol Men: The Epic Story of Reconstruction through the Lives of the First Black Congressmen.* Boston: Houghton Mifflin, 2008.

Mathews, John M. "Jefferson Franklin Long: The Public Career of Georgia's First Black Congressman." *Phylon* 42 (June 1981): 145–156.

Looby, Alexander
(Zephaniah Alexander Looby)
(1899–1972) *city councilman in Nashville, Tennessee*

Like JAMES NAPIER, Alexander Looby was an important figure in Nashville's local government. Both served on its city council for a number of years and were active in the expansion of civil rights for its African-American citizens. In recognition of their contributions to the city's black community, in 1978 the city's African-American legal fraternity renamed itself the Napier-Looby Bar Association.

Looby was born on April 8, 1899, in Antigua, British West Indies. The occupations of his parents, John and Grace, are unknown. Orphaned at age 15, he worked his way to the United States as a ship's cabin boy, settling in Bedford, Massachusetts, in 1914. After working his way through Howard University (B.A., 1922), Columbia University (bachelor of law, 1925), and New York University (J.D., 1926), in 1926 he moved to Nashville, Tennessee, to teach economics at Fisk University. Three years later, he passed the state bar examination and opened a law office in Memphis. In

1932, he moved his practice to Nashville and founded Kent College of Law for black students. In 1934, he became a naturalized citizen and married Grafta Mosby.

As an attorney, Looby was a leader of the Civil Rights movement in Tennessee. In the 1930s, he struggled unsuccessfully to integrate the University of Tennessee's graduate schools of law and pharmacy. In the 1940s, he successfully defended 23 African Americans accused of attempting to murder four police officers during a race riot. In the 1950s, he and AVON WILLIAMS, among others, successfully argued *McSwain v. Board of Anderson County, Tennessee* before the U.S. Supreme Court, thus forcing the county to integrate its public schools. In the 1960s, he successfully defended the African-American "sit-in" demonstrators who integrated the lunch counters of downtown Nashville. And in the 1970s, he and Williams convinced a federal district court judge to integrate Nashville's public schools via a massive busing plan.

Although better known for his work as a civil rights activist, Looby was also one of the few successful black politicians in Tennessee before the 1970s. A Republican, he first ran for office in 1943; although he polled the most votes in a multicandidate election for Nashville city council's Fifth Ward seat, he failed to gain a majority and lost the runoff election to a white opponent by a hefty margin. Eight years later, he ran again, but this time he won. Reelected in 1955 and 1959, he worked from the inside to desegregate the city's courts, schools, and places of public accommodation, and to win equal pay for African-American teachers. In 1962, he campaigned for a seat on the Tennessee Supreme Court but lost in the primary. Later that year, however, when Nashville and Davidson County voted to consolidate their governments, he was the only black elected to the metropolitan council. He was reelected to several terms.

Looby retired from politics in 1971, having served in Nashville's local government for 21 consecutive years. Although his health had become poor—he had to use a wheelchair for the last several years of his life—he continued to practice law until his death on October 8, 1972, in Nashville.

Further Reading

Doyle, Don H. *Nashville since the 1920s.* Knoxville: University of Tennessee Press, 1985.

Lovett, Bobby L., and Linda T. Wynn, eds. *Profiles of African Americans in Tennessee.* Nashville: Local Conference on Afro-American Culture and History, 1996.

Sarvis, Will. "Leaders in the Court and the Community: Z. Alexander Looby, Avon N. Williams, Jr., and the Legal Fight for Civil Rights in Tennessee, 1940–1970." *Journal of African American History* 88 (Winter 2003), pp. 42–58.

Scott, Mingo. *The Negro in Tennessee Politics and Governmental Affairs, 1865–1965: The Hundred Years Story.* Nashville: Rich Printing Co., 1965.

Tennessee State University Digital Library. "Z. Alexander Looby (1899–1972)." Available online. URL: http://www.tnstate.edu/library/digital/ looby.htm. Downloaded March 23, 2009.

Lynch, John
(John Roy Lynch)
(1847–1939) *U.S. congressional representative from Mississippi*

John Lynch was the first African American to represent Mississippi in the U.S. House of Representatives. In addition to being a successful politician, he enjoyed successful careers as a real estate investor, lawyer, and military officer.

Lynch was born on September 10, 1847, on a plantation near Vidalia, Louisiana, just across the Mississippi River from Natchez, Mississippi. His father, Patrick Lynch, was the white overseer of the plantation, and his mother, Catherine White, was a slave. At some point, Patrick Lynch purchased White and her children by him and they lived together as a family, although state law required that White and the children remain enslaved. Then Patrick Lynch became deathly ill, so he transferred title to John, his mother, and siblings to a friend, William Deal, who promised to treat them as free people. Instead, Deal sold the family to Alfred W. Davis, a planter in Natchez. Lynch served as Davis's valet until he incurred the displeasure of Mrs. Davis, after which he was sent to work in the fields. He was freed from slavery in 1863 when Union troops captured Natchez.

For the next three years, Lynch worked at a variety of odd jobs, most of which had something to do with serving the Union army of occupation. In 1866, he became a photographer's messenger, learned how to develop photographs, and then was hired to manage a rival photography shop. Over the next two years, he acquired a grammar school education and developed an intense interest in studying law.

Lynch became involved in politics shortly after Reconstruction began in 1867. Within a year, since the Democrats refused to admit freedmen, he had joined the local Republican Party, and was speaking in favor of the new state constitution, which greatly broadened the civil rights of African Americans. His eloquent speeches came to the attention of Adelbert Ames, the Republican governor, and in 1869 he made Lynch a justice of the peace in Natchez. That same year, Lynch was elected to Mississippi's lower house, where he served on the judiciary committee and the committee on elections and education. Reelected to a second term in 1871, he was named speaker of the house. As speaker, he earned a reputation as a fair-minded presider who kept things moving without injuring anyone's dignity. He also used his position to exercise enormous influence over the redistricting process and was able to ensure the Republicans five safe congressional districts to the Democrats' one. In 1872, at the age of 26, he was elected to the first of three terms in the U.S. House of Representatives.

In Congress, Lynch served on the committees overseeing mines and mining as well as expenditures in the Interior Department. He introduced a number of bills intended to provide federal aid for various projects back home, most of which did not pass. However, he impressed his colleagues with his knowledge of parliamentary procedure, something few black congressmen possessed. A dynamic orator, he argued forcefully on several occasions for passage of the Civil Rights Act of 1875, which outlawed discrimination against African Americans on juries and in places of public accommodation.

Lynch was reelected in 1874, but his strong support for the civil rights bill outraged many white Republicans who denied him reelection in 1876. He spent the next four years tending to his real estate investments, which he had begun acquiring in 1869. He ran for Congress again in 1880 but "lost" to his white Democrat opponent. Lynch successfully challenged the outcome on grounds of fraud, and he was seated in 1882 in time for the second session of his term. He lost his bid for reelection in 1882 and returned to Natchez when his term expired the following year.

Although Lynch never held elected office again, he remained active in the affairs of the state Republican Party. He served as chairman of its executive committee from 1881 to 1889 and attended every national convention between 1884 and 1900 as a state delegate. He was elected temporary chairman of the 1884 national convention and became the first African American to deliver the keynote address before the convention of a major party.

Lynch remained active in other areas as well. In 1884, he married Ella W. Somerville, with whom he had one child. He continued to build up his land holdings, and by 1905, when he disposed of his properties, he owned more than a dozen lots in Natchez and four plantations in adjacent Adams County. In 1889, he was appointed auditor of the treasury for the Navy Department, a post he held for four years. He then took up the study of law, and in 1896 he was admitted to the Mississippi bar. He practiced law in Natchez and in

Washington, D.C., for the next two years. In 1898, he served as a paymaster of volunteers during the Spanish-American War. He continued to work as a paymaster for the army after the war; he was commissioned a captain in 1901 and promoted to major in 1906. By 1911, he had served as paymaster at posts in Nebraska, California, and the Philippines. He retired from the army in 1911 and moved to Chicago, Illinois. The following year, his first wife having died, he married Cora Williamson. In 1915, he was admitted to the Illinois bar, and he practiced law in Chicago until shortly before his death. He also wrote two books about Reconstruction as well as his memoirs. He died in Chicago on November 2, 1939.

Further Reading

Biographical Directory of the United States Congress. "Lynch, John Roy, 1847–1939." Available online. URL: http://bioguide.congress.gov/scripts/bio display.pl?index=L000533. Downloaded March 28, 2009.

Black Americans in Congress. "John Roy Lynch." Available online. URL: http://baic.house.gov/member-profiles/profile.html?intID=8. Downloaded March 27, 2009.

Clay, William L. *Just Permanent Interests: Black Americans in Congress, 1870–1992.* New York: Amistad Press, 1993.

Franklin, John Hope, ed. *Reminiscences of an Active Life: The Autobiography of John Roy Lynch.* Chicago: University of Chicago Press, 1970.

Rabinowitz, Howard N., ed. *Southern Black Leaders of the Reconstruction Era.* Urbana: University of Illinois Press, 1982.

M

Majette, Denise
(Denise L. Majette)
(1955–) *U.S. congressional representative from Georgia*

In 2004, one-term congresswoman Denise Majette made history by becoming the first African American nominated to run for the U.S. Senate in Georgia.

A native of Brooklyn, New York, Majette was born on May 18, 1955. Her mother was a teacher, and her father was a real estate agent, although he dreamed of becoming a lawyer. His ambition fueled Majette's own childhood fascination with the law. She was also inspired by the Civil Rights movement, which convinced her that knowledge of the law could help her effect real social change.

Majette attended Yale University in New Haven, Connecticut, and graduated in 1976 with a bachelor's degree in history. She continued her education at Duke University School of Law, in Durham, North Carolina. Majette worked for the Legal Aid Society in Winston-Salem, before moving to Stone Mountain, Georgia, to take a job as a law clerk in the superior court of DeKalb County. She also clerked for Robert Benham, who later became the first African-American chief justice of the Georgia Supreme Court. After three years as a partner in the law firm of Jenkins, Nelson & Welch, Majette was appointed state court judge. During her 10 years on the bench, she became well known in Atlanta's legal community.

In 2002, Majette announced that she would challenge Congresswoman CYNTHIA MCKINNEY in the Democratic primary for the House seat representing Georgia's 4th district. Majette sensed that McKinney's sometimes extreme rhetoric, especially concerning U.S. foreign policy, had made her vulnerable. Although inexperienced in politics, Majette learned on the campaign trail how to go head-to-head with the combative McKinney. But Majette was helped far more by McKinney's missteps. McKinney courted the ire of conservative pundits by implying that President George W. Bush had known in advance about the terrorist attacks of September 11, 2001. McKinney's widely publicized comments helped Majette win the primary by a healthy margin of 16 points. She easily won the general election in November.

As a congresswoman, Majette served on the Budget, Small Business, and Education and Workforce committees. She worked to increase funding for Head Start and for programs to protect women from domestic violence. She also sponsored a bill to designate Arabia Mountain in DeKalb County as a national heritage site. Majette claimed that she helped direct approximately $250 million of federal money to her district.

In early 2004, Majette decided to run for the U.S. Senate seat being vacated by Zell Miller. Although Majette was largely unknown outside of the Atlanta area, she managed to win the Democratic primary. In the general election, however, she was soundly defeated by her Republican rival, three-term congressional representative Johnny Isakson.

Majette returned to Georgia in 2005, once again working as a judge in DeKalb County. The following year, she ran an unsuccessful race for Georgia's superintendent of schools. She has since joined the real estate firm of Chapman Realty in Brunswick, Georgia. Majette is married to Rogers J. Mitchell, Jr., and they have two sons.

Further Reading

Black Americans in Congress. "Denise L. Majette." Available online. URL: http://baic.house.gov/member-profiles/profile.html?intID=165. Downloaded May 3, 2009.

Manheim, James M. "Denise Majette, 1955–   ." *Contemporary Black Biography* 41 (2004): 129–131.

Marsh, Henry

(Henry L. Marsh III)
(1933–   ) *mayor of Richmond, Virginia*

Henry Marsh was the first African-American mayor of Richmond, Virginia. At the height of his power, he was mentioned as a possible candidate for vice president. Instead, he served out his political career on the Richmond city council and in the Virginia state senate.

Marsh was born on December 10, 1933, in Richmond, Virginia. His mother died when he was five, and he spent the next several years living with relatives in Isle of Wight County. He returned to Richmond to live with his father while attending high school; one of his classmates was DOUG WILDER. He completed high school in 1952, then spent the next four years at Virginia Union University, receiving a B.A. in

sociology in 1956. In 1961, he received a law degree from Howard University. That same year, he joined the law firm of Oliver W. Hill and Samuel Tucker, the two most prominent civil rights lawyers in Virginia. For the next 20 years, he played a key role in many of the state's school desegregation cases as well as other litigation involving civil rights.

As in many U.S. cities, during the 1960s Richmond's white population decreased when many whites relocated to the suburbs. As whites moved out, the percentage of the population that was African American increased. The result was more political power in city government for blacks. Marsh took advantage of this demographic shift in 1966, when he ran successfully as a Democrat for a seat on Richmond's city council from a black-majority district. Four years later, the heightened importance of the African-American electorate was acknowledged when Marsh was chosen by his fellow councilmen to serve as vice-mayor.

Meanwhile, the city tried to increase its dwindling tax base by annexing a mostly white part of Chesterfield County. In 1970, black activists led by Curtis Holt challenged the move in federal court on the grounds that it was intended primarily to dilute black voting power in the city. For seven years, the court battle dragged on. Finally, in 1977, an agreement was reached. The court allowed the annexation, but it ordered the city to redraw its electoral districts so that blacks were more fairly represented on city council. The city was then divided into nine single-member districts, five of which had a black majority. When the newly elected council convened in 1977, the five black councilmen chose Marsh to be the new mayor.

At the time, the mayor of Richmond was a part-time, ceremonial position. The mayor was chosen by the councilmen from among the councilmen and had little to do with the operation of city government other than to preside over council meetings. All that changed under Marsh. He led the effort to oust the longtime city manager, who seemed disinclined to take orders from a black mayor. He then won the appointment of a city manager who welcomed Marsh's input regarding the city's day-to-day operations.

Marsh also began lobbying for federal assistance for Richmond. He had been one of President Jimmy Carter's first supporters in Virginia, and when Carter took office in 1977 he looked favorably on Richmond's applications for aid. Marsh cofounded Richmond Renaissance and the Metropolitan Economic Development Council, both of which oversaw multimillion-dollar downtown renewal projects that relied largely on federal aid. He also secured enough federal money to open a number of recreation centers, day care facilities, and senior citizens centers.

The flow of federal money was cut off in 1981, following the election of Republican president Ronald Reagan. A number of city programs had to be cut, which caused Marsh to come under attack from all sides. In 1982, he lost the mayor's office to Roy A. West, a black councilman who had the support of the four white councilmen. For the next nine years, Marsh and West squabbled with each other over who best represented Richmond's African Americans. Nevertheless, most of the innovations and initiatives Marsh had introduced during his tenure remained in place.

In 1991, after 25 years on city council, Marsh decided to run instead for the state senate. He won with ease and was reelected four times. As a state senator, he served on the committees on transportation, rehabilitation and social services, courts of justice, and local government. He is married to the former Diane Harris, with whom he has three children.

Further Reading

Brennan, Carol. "Henry L. Marsh III." *Contemporary Black Biography* 32 (2002): 111–113.
Explorations in Black Leadership. "Henry Marsh Interview." Available online. URL: http://www.virginia.edu/publichistory/bl/index.php?uid=22. Downloaded April 9, 2009.

Martin, Louis
(Louis Emanuel Martin)
(1912–1997) *Democratic National Committee deputy chairman*

As a political adviser to three presidents, Louis Martin was one of the most powerful and least known African-American politicians of all time. Keeping himself out of the limelight, the "godfather of black politics," as the *Washington Post* dubbed him, did much to advance the political agenda of black Americans in general while promoting the political careers of a number of black Americans in particular.

Martin was born on November 18, 1912, in Shelbyville, Tennessee. His father was a Cuban-born doctor, and his mother was a homemaker. As was the practice among African-American women at the time, his mother went back to her hometown to give birth and then returned to her home in Savannah, Georgia, where Martin grew up. After graduating from high school, he enrolled in Fisk University; he later transferred to the University of Michigan to study journalism and received a B.A. in 1934. He spent the next two years as a freelance writer based in Havana, Cuba, then went to work for the *Chicago Defender,* one of the nation's foremost African-American newspapers. In 1937, the same year he married Gertrude Scott, (with whom he had five children), the *Defender's* owners sent him to Detroit to cofound, edit, and publish the *Michigan Chronicle.* While with the *Chronicle,* he cofounded the National Newspaper Publishers Association, a group of black publishers, and served as its first president. In 1947, he returned to the *Defender* to become editor-in-chief, a position he held for 12 years. In 1959, he went to Lagos, Nigeria, to spend a year as editorial adviser to Amalgamated Press (today Fleetway Press), a British periodical publishing company.

Martin became a vocal proponent of the Democratic Party because of the New Deal, which promised a better life for all Americans, including blacks. He editorialized in favor of its policies and candidates in the *Chronicle* and, later, the *Defender*. Because of his strong support for the party and his influence in the African-American community, in 1960 he was recruited to work for John F. Kennedy's presidential campaign. At his urging, Kennedy placed a sympathy call to Coretta Scott King when her husband, Martin Luther King, Jr., was jailed in Atlanta, Georgia, for a minor traffic violation. Martin also made sure word of the call was publicized in black churches the weekend before the election, thus generating a tremendous amount of goodwill for Kennedy among African Americans. So impressed was Kennedy by this stratagem that, following his narrow victory in 1960, he appointed Martin deputy chairman of the Democratic National Committee. For the duration of the Kennedy administration, Martin advised Kennedy on political matters related to race; he was the first African American to enjoy direct daily access to the president of the United States.

Unlike Kennedy's other aides, Martin retained his influential position after Lyndon B. Johnson took over the presidency in 1963 following Kennedy's assassination. He worked just as diligently for Johnson as he had for Kennedy. He convinced a number of Democratic senators that the continued goodwill of African Americans toward party candidates hinged upon passage of a comprehensive civil rights package. When the Civil Rights Act of 1964 was enacted (followed by the Voting Rights Act of 1965), a good deal of the credit belonged to Martin. Johnson reaped the benefit of the Civil Rights Act in the election of 1964; he won in a landslide, partly because he captured 96 percent of the African-American vote. In turn, Martin used his heightened influence with Johnson to lobby successfully for the appointment of a number of blacks to prominent positions, including Thurgood Marshall, the first African-American Supreme Court justice, and ROBERT WEAVER, the first African-American cabinet member.

Martin resigned from the Democratic National Committee after the election of 1968 put the Republican candidate, Richard M. Nixon, in the White House. Although he returned once again to the *Defender* to serve as editor, he also remained involved in politics. In 1970, he cofounded the Washington-based Joint Center for Political and Economic Studies to provide training and technical assistance to black elected officials, and he served as its chairman for eight years. In 1978, he left the *Defender* and the Joint Center to become a special assistant to President Jimmy Carter. In this position, he advised Carter about potential black appointees to federal judgeships and played a major role in 37 such appointments.

When the Carter administration ended in 1981, Martin became assistant vice president for communications for Howard University. In 1987, he returned to Chicago to work for his wife's public relations company, Calmar Communications. In 1990, he retired to Diamond Bar, California; he died on January 27, 1997, in nearby Orange.

Further Reading

"In Memoriam, Louis Martin, 1912–1997." *Focus* 25, no. 1 (January 1997): 2–9.

Niven, Steven J. "Martin, Louis." In *African American National Biography*, vol. 5, edited by Henry Louis Gates, Jr., and Evelyn Brooks Higginbotham. New York: Oxford University Press, 2008, pp. 414–416.

Poinsett, Alex. *Walking with Presidents: Louis Martin and the Rise of Black Political Power*. Lanham, Md.: Madison Books, 1997.

McCall, Carl
(H. Carl McCall)
(1935–   ) *New York state comptroller*

Carl McCall was the first African American elected to state office in New York. In 2002, he made a bid to become only the second African American to be elected popularly as governor of a state.

McCall was born in 1935 in Boston, Massachusetts. At some point his father abandoned the family, and his mother supported McCall and his five siblings on welfare. After finishing high school, he attended Dartmouth College on a scholarship. He received a B.A. and then studied theology at Andover Newton Theological Seminary and the University of Edinburgh in Scotland. He was ordained a minister by the United Church of Christ and became the pastor of Metropolitan United Methodist Church in New York City's Harlem. Like many Harlem pastors before him, McCall quickly became a social and political activist. He founded and served as president of the Inner City Broadcasting Corporation, which sought to find more jobs for blacks in the media. He also worked to improve the standard of living of Harlem's residents, and in 1966 he was named commissioner of New York City's Council Against Poverty, a position he held for three years.

McCall got involved in politics in 1974 when he ran successfully for the New York state senate. Reelected twice, he declined to run for a fourth term; instead, in 1979 he accepted an appointment as deputy ambassador to the United Nations in charge of special political affairs. Two years later, he ran for lieutenant governor in the Democratic primary but was defeated. He then went to work as a senior vice president for WNET-TV, a public television station, but left in 1982 when he was appointed head of the state's human rights division and named to the board of commissioners of the Port Authority of New York and New Jersey. In 1985, he returned to the private sector as a vice president of Citicorp/Citibank, a position he held for eight years. From 1991 to 1993, he served as president of the New York City Board of Education.

In 1993, Edward Regan retired during midterm as state comptroller, and the state legislature appointed McCall to complete the term. The appointment gave him control over the administration of the state's finances and oversight over the financial affairs of the state's localities. Since the comptroller is independent of the governor, the appointment made McCall the second most powerful state

official in New York. Among his many duties was the administration of the New York State Common Retirement Fund. To this end, he combined a strong sense of fiduciary responsibility with an equally strong sense of community responsibility. Under his aegis, the retirement fund doubled in size to more than $100 billion. In the process, he invested a significant portion of the fund's monies in businesses that were either minority- or female-owned or located in economically depressed areas of the state.

As comptroller, McCall appointed 87 women and minorities to positions of responsibility in the comptroller's office. He used the fund's position as a major stockholder in Texaco Inc. to force that corporation to apologize for and reverse the discriminatory hiring practices that had become public knowledge in 1996. He played a major role in preserving state funding for the state's university system, and he oversaw a number of studies on such diverse topics as school finance and welfare reform, truancy in the public schools, and the economic implications of such events as the East Asian economic crisis and the attacks on the World Trade Center.

As comptroller, McCall was no stranger to controversy. Twice he sued the governor to prevent him from drawing monies out of the retirement fund to use to supplement the state budget. He also sued New York City's mayor Rudolph Giuliani when the mayor barred McCall's auditors from inspecting the accounts of several city agencies. Giuliani, a Republican, maintained that the audits were politically motivated; nevertheless, McCall prevailed and the audits went ahead.

McCall was elected to a term as comptroller in his own right in 1994 and reelected in 1998. In 2000, he declared his candidacy for governor, a race that would not be contested until 2002. He spent the intervening two years raising money and courting support, especially in the African-American community. Despite high hopes, he polled only 33 percent of the vote, thus losing the election to his Republican opponent.

McCall returned to private life after the election, although he remained an influential figure in New York City politics. McCall has also served on the board of directors of the New York Stock Exchange, Tyco International, and TAG Entertainment. He is married to Joyce Brown and has one child.

Further Reading

Idani, Michaeljulius. "McCall, H. Carl." In *African American National Biography*, vol. 5, edited by Henry Louis Gates, Jr., and Evelyn Brooks Higginbotham. New York: Oxford University Press, 2008, pp. 466–468.

Sanchez, Brenna. "H. Carl McCall." *Contemporary Black Biography* 27 (2001), pp. 132–134.

McKinney, Cynthia

(Cynthia Ann McKinney)
(1955–) *U.S. congressional representative from Georgia, presidential candidate*

In 1996, Cynthia McKinney became the first African American to be elected to Congress from a white-majority district in the Deep South. She is also one of a few daughters who have followed their fathers into a political career.

McKinney was born on March 17, 1955, in Atlanta, Georgia. Her father, Billy, is a longtime state legislator, and her mother, Leola, was a nurse. After finishing high school, she enrolled in the University of Southern California and received a B.A. in international relations in 1978. She spent the next six years doing graduate work at Georgia State University and the University of Wisconsin. From 1985 to 1988, she taught political science at Clark Atlanta University and Agnes Scott College. In 1980, she married Coy Grandison, with whom she had one child; they separated in 1986 and were later divorced.

Because her father was a politician, McKinney was exposed to the ins and outs of political life as a child. She studied and taught politics for a num-

ber of years, and then in 1986 she decided to run for the Georgia legislature, in large part because her father encouraged her to do so. She lost, but in 1988 she ran again and was elected. During the four years that she served alongside her father in the state assembly, she focused on achieving equal opportunity for minorities and women. In this regard, she is best remembered for her efforts to get the legislature to redraw its state and federal voting districts, following the census of 1990, in a way that empowered a greater number of black voters. She also pushed for increased awareness and funding for HIV/AIDS research, and for the construction of a high-speed rail system linking the state's cities.

In 1992, McKinney was elected to Congress from a black-majority district that included a portion of Atlanta. She took her seat the following year and was assigned to the committees on international relations and banking/financial services. As a congresswoman, she focused on human rights, both inside and outside the United States. She sponsored the Arms Transfers Code of Conduct of 1997, which prohibits the sales of military weapons to dictators, many of whom had come to power in postcolonial Africa. She was a strong proponent of strengthening economic ties between the United States and sub-Saharan Africa, especially Liberia, which had been settled largely by freed slaves from the United States. She also served as head of the Women's Caucus Task Force on Children, Youth and Families.

McKinney found herself at the center of several controversies while in Congress. On two occasions, in 1996 and 1998, she created a media stir by complaining publicly about her treatment at the hands of White House security personnel. Both times the Secret Service failed to accord her the privileges and respect due a congressperson; she claimed that the incidents were racially motivated, and she demanded (and received) apologies from the White House. In 2002, she was one of a few congresspeople who spoke out against the Bush Administration's handling of the war against

Cynthia McKinney represented a white-majority congressional district in the U.S. House of Representatives. *(Cynthia A. McKinney)*

terrorism that arose in the wake of the attacks of September 11, 2001. Her particular concern was that U.S. military intelligence and surveillance were being used inappropriately against U.S citizens, and in the process the federal government threatened to turn the United States into a police state. She insisted on an investigation into what the federal government had known about the probability of such attacks before they occurred; her call suggested that the Bush Administration should have known that the attacks were about to take place and yet did nothing to prevent them. She condemned Israel's treatment of the Palestinians, and indirectly the Bush Administration's support for Israel, insisting that the Palestinians were not terrorists but a legitimate national group that should be granted a homeland.

McKinney's district had been created under the provisions of the Voting Rights Act. In 1994, it was redrawn when that act was challenged successfully in the U.S. Supreme Court. That same year she was forced to run for reelection from a white-majority district that encompassed much of rural north-central Georgia as well as several suburbs of Atlanta. To just about everyone's surprise, she won. In 2000, she was reelected to a fifth term. Her bid for reelection in 2002 was denied when she lost the Democratic primary to DENISE MAJETTE. When Majette ran for the U.S. Senate in 2004, McKinney was elected to replace her in the House. During her sixth term, she continued to criticize the Bush administration, especially for its conduct in the Iraq War and its response to Hurricane Katrina.

In March 2006, McKinney was involved in an altercation with a security officer in the Capitol Building. The incident was widely reported in the mainstream media, with conservatives taking the opportunity to paint McKinney as unpredictable and unstable. Even with this negative publicity, in June 2006 McKinney managed to win the Democratic primary in her district, although not by a large enough margin to avoid a runoff. In the runoff election, she was defeated by Hank Johnson, who won her old seat in November.

Disillusioned with the Democratic Party, McKinney announced in December 2007 that she would run for president in the 2008 election on the Green Party ticket. She received approximately 160,000 votes in the general election.

Further Reading

Biographical Directory of the United States Congress. "McKinney, Cynthia Ann, 1955– ." Available online. URL: http://bioguide.congress.gov/scripts/ biodisplay.pl?index=M000523. Downloaded April 13, 2009.

Black Americans in Congress. "Cynthia Ann McKinney." Available online. URL: http://baic.house. gov/member-profiles/profile.html?intID=64. Downloaded April 13, 2009.

Clay, William L. *Just Permanent Interests: Black Americans in Congress, 1870–1992.* New York: Amistad Press, 1993.

Foerstel, Karen. *Biographical Dictionary of Congressional Women.* New York: Greenwood Press, 1999.

Gill, LaVerne McCain. *African American Women in Congress: Forming and Transforming History.* New Brunswick, N.J.: Rutgers University Press, 1997.

Meek, Carrie

(Carrie Pittman Meek)
(1926–   ) *U.S. congressional representative from Florida*

In 1992, Carrie Meek, CORRINE BROWN, and ALCEE HASTINGS were elected to the U.S. House of Representatives from Florida. It marked the first time since Reconstruction that an African American had represented the state in Congress.

Meek was born Carrie Pittman on April 29, 1926, in Tallahassee, Florida. Her father, William, was a sharecropper, and her mother, Carrie, was a domestic worker. After graduating from high school, she attended Florida A&M University where she starred in track and field and received a B.S. in biology and physical education in 1946. Two years later, she received an M.S. in physical education and public health from the University of Michigan. She then returned to Florida to teach biology and coach women's basketball at Bethune-Cookman College in Daytona Beach. In 1958, she went back to Tallahassee to teach at her alma mater, Florida A&M, but left three years later to become a biology professor and the director of women's athletics at Miami-Dade Community College in Miami. In 1968, she was named associate dean for community service and assistant to the president for literacy and public affairs programs. She was married and divorced twice and has three children.

Meek began thinking about a career in politics in the mid-1960s, when she became involved in the federal government's Model Cities program.

This program offered federal subsidies for urban redevelopment pilot programs in several dozen U.S. cities. The basic idea was to rebuild the most blighted areas while also addressing their social and economic problems via job training, school improvement, and a combination of experimental self-help and professional assistance programs. Meek was impressed by the Miami project's scope, but she also was depressed by the lack of focus that resulted in a general lack of progress. Her involvement in the program taught her that local people had to gain greater access to the decision-making process at all levels of government, but as yet she was not ready to run for office.

In 1979, Dade County's representative in the state legislature died in office, and Meek was persuaded to run in the special election to fill the remainder of the term. Despite her total lack of experience in politics, she beat out 11 other contenders to win the seat. Once elected, she realized that she had no idea what a state legislator was supposed to do, so she simply did her best to serve as a spokesperson for her constituents, many of whom lived at or below the poverty level. She did a good enough job at this that she was reelected to a full term the following year, and to the state senate in 1982, where she served for 11 years. As a state senator, she worked to increase state funding for public education, to establish set-asides in government contracts for businesses owned by minorities or women, and to make it easier for the working poor to own their own homes. Toward the end of her tenure in the senate, she chaired the educational subcommittee, which oversaw the state's $10 billion public school budget.

In 1992, Meek was elected to the U.S. House of Representatives. She was assigned to the prestigious appropriations committee, which funds all executive branch programs and independent agencies. She used her position on the committee to speak up for the poor. Specifically, she fought for job training and economic opportunity programs while the committee was looking to cut back on social spending, and she secured $195 million for housing assistance for the elderly. She helped enact legislation making domestic workers eligible for Social Security while requiring the employers of domestic workers to pay Social Security taxes on their earnings. She also worked to have the Census Bureau use scientific sampling methods as a way to establish more accurately the number of poor and homeless people, believing that proper counts are a necessity, since many federal programs base their apportionments to the various localities on the number of such people. She worked to ease immigration restrictions on Haitian refugees and to provide supplemental security income to aged, blind, or handicapped legal aliens. In 1993, she secured more than $100 million in federal aid for families displaced by Hurricane Andrew, which had devastated much of her district in the days before the election of 1992. In 2002, she was reelected to a sixth term. She retired from Congress the following year because of her health. She was succeeded in her district by her son, KENDRICK MEEK.

After retiring from politics, Meek established the Carrie Meek Foundation. This nonprofit organization sponsors programs to improve education, housing, and health care and to promote economic development and community empowerment. Beginning in 2008, the foundation has awarded Carrie Meek Education Scholarships to hundreds of low-income students in Miami.

Further Reading

Biographical Directory of the United States Congress. "Meek, Carrie Pittman, 1926– ." Available online. URL:http://bioguide.congress.gov/scripts/biodisplay.pl?index=X000000. Downloaded April 9, 2009.

Black Americans in Congress. "Carrie P. Meek." Available online. URL: http://baic.house.gov/member-profiles/profile.html?intID=63. Downloaded April 9, 2009.

Carrie Meek Foundation. Available online. URL: http://www.carriemeekfoundation.org. Downloaded April 9, 2009.

Foerstel, Karen. *Biographical Dictionary of Congressional Women.* New York: Greenwood Press, 1999.

Gill, LaVerne McCain. *African American Women in Congress: Forming and Transforming History.* New Brunswick, N.J.: Rutgers University Press, 1997.

Meek, Kendrick
(Kendrick B. Meek)
(1966–) *U.S. congressional representative from Florida*

The son of U.S. representative CARRIE MEEK, Kendrick Meek carved out his own political career by taking over his mother's Florida congressional seat. Born on September 6, 1966, Meek grew up in Miami. As a teenager, he served as a page in Florida's statehouse. Meek attended Florida A&M University in Tallahassee on a football scholarship and graduated in 1989 with a bachelor's degree in criminal justice. He joined the highway patrol, eventually rising to the rank of captain.

Long interested in a political career, Meek made a successful bid for a seat in the Florida house of representatives in 1994. Four years later, he was elected to the state senate. Although his famous mother initially helped Meek win over voters, he soon drew support for his willingness to take on the Florida political establishment, especially Florida governor Jeb Bush. Meek strongly opposed Bush's "One Florida" program, which would effectively end affirmative action policies at state colleges and universities. With another state legislator, Tony Hill, he went to Bush's office and asked to meet with the governor. According to Meek, Bush "barked at us as though we were children" and told the lawmakers they better get some blankets because they were in for a long wait. Meek and Hill did just that. They staged a sit-in for the next 25 hours—a gambit that was widely reported in the press and proved extremely embarrassing to the governor.

In 2002, Meek scored another political victory with his campaign to add an amendment to the state constitution that would limit class size in public schools. He drew support for the idea by circulating a petition, which was signed by 500,000 Floridians. Voters eventually approved Meek's amendment at the ballot box.

On July 7, 2002, Meek's mother announced that she was retiring from the U.S. Congress. He decided to run for her seat, aided by Carrie Meek's political friends and allies. Her late announcement left little time for anyone else to launch a campaign. Running unopposed, Kendrick Meek won the election. He was reelected three times.

As a congressman, Meek served on the influential House Ways and Means Committee. He has advocated increasing federal aid to Haiti, improving emergency response systems, and creating more affordable housing. In January 2009, he announced his intention to run for the U.S. Senate, seeking the seat vacated by the retiring Mel Martinez. Meek explained that the election of. President BARACK OBAMA had helped inspire his senate run: "I learned from President Obama that you can win against impossible odds if you put together the right team, have the right strategy and be straight with people." Despite Meek's confidence, he was defeated, winning only 20 percent of the vote.

Meek is married to Leslie Dixon. The couple has two children.

Further Reading

Congressman Kendrick B. Meek, Official Web Site. Available online. URL: http://kendrickmeek.house. gov/index.shtml. Downloaded May 20, 2009.

Manheim, James M. "Kendrick Meek, 1966– ." *Contemporary Black Biography* 41 (2004): 152–154.

Meeks, Gregory
(Gregory Weldon Meeks)
(1953–) *U.S. congressional representative from New York*

In 1998, Gregory Meeks was elected to represent Queens in the U.S. Congress. He was one of a growing number of moderate black political leaders who espoused bettering life for African Americans via free market mechanisms rather than by government assistance only.

Meeks was born on September 25, 1953, in Harlem in New York City. His father, James, was a cabdriver and handyman, and his mother, Mary, was a homemaker. In 1971, he graduated from high school and enrolled in Adelphi University, receiving a B.A. four years later. He spent the next three years at Howard University Law School and received a J.D. in 1978. He then returned to New York City, settling in the middle-class neighborhood in Queens where his parents had recently moved. His first job out of law school was as an assistant district attorney for Queens County. In 1980, he was named a special narcotics prosecutor for New York City, and in 1984 he became a staff

Congressman Gregory Meeks represents the borough of Queens in New York City. (*Gregory W. Meeks*)

attorney for the state investigations commission. The following year, he was appointed judge of the state workers' compensation board, a position he held for seven years.

Meeks became involved in politics shortly after moving to Queens, when he and his mother established a neighborhood association in order to obtain better city services. He then cofounded a political club that eventually became known as the Thurgood Marshall Regular Democratic Club. He supported the club's candidates for elective office for several years, and in 1991 he won its support for a bid for city council. He lost the election, but the following year he ran for the state assembly and won. He served three terms in the assembly, during which he focused on issues related to labor and transportation. In 1997, he married Simone-Marie Lipscomb with whom he has three children.

In 1997, FLOYD FLAKE, who represented much of Queens in the U.S. Congress, resigned his position in order to devote more time to his duties as pastor of the largest church in Queens. A number of hopefuls stepped forward to take his place, but Flake gave his support to Meeks, who eventually won the special election held in 1998. He took his seat that same year and was assigned to Flake's position on the House Banking Committee. After being elected to a full term of his own later in that year's general election, he was assigned to the committee on international relations as well. In 2010, he was elected to a seventh full term.

As a congressman, Meeks sided mostly with the moderate wing of the Democratic Party. As a representative of a middle-class, black-majority district, he worked for improvements in the lot of African Americans. However, like Flake, he believed this could best be done via economic development rather than government handouts. Consequently, Meeks supported efforts to stimulate business in black communities, so that in time these communities would become self-sufficient and no longer need government assistance. To this end, he worked to create an economic development zone in his district and to revitalize the central business district of Jamaica in Queens.

Further Reading
Biographical Directory of the United States Congress. "Meeks, Gregory W., 1953– ." Available online. URL: http://bioguide.congress.gov/scripts/bio display.pl?index=M001137. Downloaded April 9, 2009.
Congressman Gregory W. Meeks, Official Web Site. Available online. URL: http://www.house.gov/meeks. Downloaded April 15, 2009.
"Gregory W. Meeks D-N.Y. (6). New Member Profile." *Congressional Quarterly Weekly Report* 56 (February 7, 1998): 332.

Metcalfe, Ralph
(Ralph Harold Metcalfe)
(1910–1978) *U.S. congressional representative from Illinois*

Like OSCAR DePRIEST, ARTHUR MITCHELL, and WILLIAM DAWSON before him, Ralph Metcalfe represented the black-majority Illinois First District in the U.S. House of Representatives. Because of the times during which they served, his predecessors believed they had to practice big-city machine politics in order to gain small advantages for their African-American constituents. Metcalfe, however, served during a different time, and he was able to repudiate the Chicago Democratic machine and develop into an outspoken, unapologetic champion for equal rights.

Metcalfe was born on May 29, 1910, in Atlanta, Georgia. His father, Clarence, was a laborer, and his mother, Mamie, was a dressmaker. As a young boy he moved with his family to Chicago, Illinois, where he grew up. A national high school sprint champion at age 19, he received a track scholarship to attend Marquette University. In addition to being the national collegiate champion for three straight years (1932–34), he was a two-time Olympian. He won a silver and a bronze medal at

Former Olympic gold medalist Ralph Metcalfe represented Chicago in Congress. *(Library of Congress)*

the 1932 Los Angeles Games, and a gold and a silver medal at the 1936 Berlin Games. After receiving a B.A. in 1936, he enrolled in the University of Southern California and received an M.A. in physical education in 1939. For the next four years, he taught political science and coached the track team at Xavier University, an all-black institution in New Orleans, Louisiana. In 1943, he joined the U.S. Army and served during World War II as a first lieutenant in the Army Transportation Corps. He returned to Chicago after the war to work for the Chicago Commission on Human Relations as the director of its civil rights department. In 1947, he married Madalynne Young, with whom he had one child. In 1949, he was appointed commissioner of the state athletic commission, a position he held for four years.

Metcalfe joined the Democratic Party in 1949, and for the next four years he served as an assistant precinct captain. His loyalty and hard work

in getting out the vote was rewarded in 1953 when he was named a Third Ward committeeman. This position made him an important cog in the city's Democratic machine and gave him a small role in the dispensation of municipal jobs. Two years later, he was elected to the board of aldermen, and for the next 15 years he served as a loyal ally to Richard J. Daley, the city's powerful Democratic mayor. During his tenure, he served as president pro tempore of the board of aldermen, as chairman of the board's building and zoning committee, and as chairman of the city's planning commission.

In 1970, Dawson decided not to run for reelection. Instead, he urged the party to nominate Metcalfe; it did, and he won handily. He took his seat in 1971 and was assigned to the committee on the merchant marine and fisheries and the committee on interstate and foreign commerce. During his four terms, however, he focused his attention on federal housing. Most important, he worked to outlaw the practice known as "redlining," whereby private companies refused to issue loans or homeowners insurance to residents in black-majority neighborhoods, and to ensure the safety of residents in federal housing projects. He also sponsored bills to help minority-owned businesses and to make health care more accessible for the poor. In addition, he played an important role in drafting and enacting the legislation that gave ownership of the Panama Canal to Panama.

As an alderman, Metcalfe had been accused by many of Chicago's African Americans of being Daley's stooge, who they perceived had done little for them. Once he became a congressman, however, Metcalfe declared his independence from the Chicago Democratic machine and began confronting Daley head-to-head over a host of race-related issues. At least part of the confidence to do this came in 1971, when Metcalfe and 12 other African-American congresspeople founded the Congressional Black Caucus as a means of supporting one another in the struggle for equal rights. The following year, in response to repeated charges of police brutality against Chicago's blacks, he conducted a highly publicized investigation and offered the protection of his office to those who would testify to their own victimization. In 1975, he refused to support Edward Hanrahan, Daley's handpicked candidate for Cook County state attorney, because six years earlier Hanrahan had led a raid on the Chicago branch of the Black Panther Party that left one Black Panther dead. Enraged, Daley backed Metcalfe's opponent in the 1976 primary, but by then Metcalfe had become a hero in the African-American community and he was easily renominated and reelected.

In 1978, Metcalfe ran unopposed for the Democratic nomination for his seat in Congress. He died of a heart attack before the election, on October 10, 1978, in Chicago.

Further Reading

Biographical Directory of the United States Congress. "Metcalfe, Ralph Harold, 1910–1978." Available online. URL: http://bioguide.congress.gov/scripts/biodisplay.pl?index=M000675. Downloaded April 15, 2009.

Black Americans in Congress. "Ralph Harold Metcalfe." Available online. URL: http://baic.house.gov/member-profiles/profile.html?intID=63. Downloaded April 13, 2009.

Clay, William L. *Just Permanent Interests: Black Americans in Congress, 1870–1992.* New York: Amistad Press, 1993.

Cornfield, Michael, and Susan Baker. *Ralph H. Metcalfe, Democratic Representative from Illinois.* Washington, D.C.: Grossman, 1972.

Mfume, Kweisi

(1948–) *U.S. congressional representative from Maryland*

Kweisi Mfume is one of a few people in American history who have made the metamorphosis from street thug to national association president. In the process he passed up a promising political career.

Mfume was born Frizzell Gray on October 24, 1948, in Baltimore, Maryland. His father was Rufus Tate, but he lived with his mother and stepfather, Mary Elizabeth and Clifton Gray, in nearby Turners Station. In 1960, his stepfather left the family, and Gray moved with his mother and sisters to Baltimore. When he was 16, his mother died and he took on three jobs to help support himself and his sisters. He eventually dropped out of school, became a numbers runner, and joined a street gang. By age 20, he had fathered five children by three different women.

One day, Gray was hanging out on a Baltimore street corner when Congressman PARREN MITCHELL happened to meet him. The two conversed for awhile, and then Mitchell told Gray to stop being part of the problem and start being part of the solution. Gray was so impressed with Mitchell that he vowed to do exactly that. After earning a high school equivalency diploma, he enrolled in the Community College of Baltimore, earning an associate's degree in 1974. That same year, he went to work as a radio personality, enrolled in Morgan State University, and changed his name to Kweisi Mfume, which is Ibo for "conquering son of kings." Two years later, he received a B.A. in political science from Morgan State. In 1984, he earned an M.A. in liberal arts from Johns Hopkins University.

As a radio talk show host, Mfume repeatedly criticized the Baltimore city council for pushing downtown redevelopment while ignoring the pressing problems of black neighborhoods. One caller suggested to him, half in jest, that Mfume run for city council himself. Mfume took up the caller's dare, and in 1978 he ran a no-frills campaign. He made up for his lack of money by campaigning door-to-door, and he so impressed the voters in his district that he won a narrow victory in the election. During his four terms as councilman, he locked horns on many occasions with Mayor Donald Schaefer, the future governor of

Maryland, but to no avail. Eventually he learned the art of compromise, and as he did he was able to win more concessions from Schaefer and the council for programs for the city's black residents. He also got the city to divest itself of its investments in South Africa until after apartheid was abolished, and he won significant set-asides for minority businesses in city contracts.

In 1986, Mitchell announced his retirement from Congress, and Mfume decided to run for the seat. Despite attempts to smear him because of his unsavory past, he won resounding victories in both the Democratic primary and the general election. In 1987, he was sworn in and assigned to the committee on banking, finance, and urban affairs.

As a congressman, Mfume focused on addressing the problems of the nation's inner cities. During his term (1993–94) as chairman of the Congressional Black Caucus, he presented President Bill Clinton with a list of the caucus's nonnegotiable demands; most of them had something to do with federal aid for inner cities or the poor. He wrote, in part or in whole, several acts to benefit minority businesses, including the Financial Institutions Reform and Recovery Act and the Minority Business Development Act. He also worked to expand the rights of minorities in general by playing major roles in securing the passage of the Americans with Disabilities Act and the Civil Rights Act of 1991.

Mfume was reelected to Congress four times. He seemed to be headed toward a prominent role in the House and was rumored to be a candidate for Speaker. Instead, he resigned from Congress in 1995 to become the president and chief executive officer of the National Association for the Advancement of Colored People. The NAACP had fallen on hard times, and Mfume felt he could do more to promote equal opportunity by reviving it than by remaining in Congress. He took charge of the organization in 1996, and within a year he had raised enough money to pay off its debt of $4.5 million. He then initiated a major member-

ship drive that brought in thousands of new members. Lastly, he implemented a six-point action agenda that focused on civil rights, political empowerment, educational excellence, economic development, health, and youth outreach.

Mfume left the NAACP in 2004. The following year, he attempted a political comeback by running for U.S. senator. Mfume, however, lost the Democratic primary, thus ending his hope of returning to Congress. In 2010, Mfume was named executive leader of the National Medical Association, which represents the interests of more than 30,000 African-American doctors.

Further Reading

Biographical Directory of the United States Congress. "Mfume, Kweisi, 1948– ." Available online. URL: http://bioguide.congress.gov/scripts/biodisplay.pl?index=M000687. Downloaded April 9, 2009.

Black Americans in Congress. "Kweisi Mfume." Available online. URL: http://baic.house.gov/member-profiles/profile.html?intID=61. Downloaded April 9, 2009.

Clay, William L. *Just Permanent Interests: Black Americans in Congress, 1870–1992.* New York: Amistad Press, 1993.

Haywood, Richette L. "Can Kweisi Mfume Turn the NAACP Around?" *Ebony* 52 (January 1997): 94–96.

Mfume, Kweisi, and Ron Stodghill. *No Free Ride: From the Mean Streets to the Mainstream.* New York: One World, 1996.

Millender-McDonald, Juanita
(1938–2007) *U.S. congressional representative from California*

Like several other African-American political leaders, Juanita Millender-McDonald was elected to Congress after a successful career as a public school teacher. Throughout her political career, she focused on improving transportation for southern California.

Millender-McDonald was born Juanita Millender on September 7, 1938, in Birmingham, Alabama. Her mother died when she was three, and she moved with her father and siblings to Los Angeles, California, where she grew up. After finishing high school, she worked a variety of jobs in the Los Angeles area, and in the 1970s she settled in the nearby community of Carson. In 1981 she received a B.S. in business administration from the University of Redlands, and for the next seven years she taught high school business in the Los Angeles Unified School District. After receiving an M.A. in educational administration from California State University in 1988, she became one of the school district's textbook writers. She was later named director of the district's gender equity programs.

Millender-McDonald became involved in the affairs of the local Democratic Party after settling in Carson. She campaigned loyally for the party's candidates in the Los Angeles area, and in 1984 she was named a delegate to the Democratic National Convention. In 1990, she decided to run for office herself and was elected to a seat on the Carson city council. She was named mayor pro tempore by her council colleagues the following year; one of her first acts was to make the post of mayor an elected rather than an appointed post. Her second act was to try to do something about the scheduling of the Southern Pacific Railroad's trains, which caused interminable rush-hour delays in Carson and nearby Alameda.

In 1992, Millender-McDonald was elected to the California state assembly's lower house. She devoted most of her four-year tenure to battling the Southern Pacific, which had refused her requests to reschedule its trains during rush hour. She eventually won support for a $1.8 billion transportation project known as the Alameda Corridor. This project eased congestion by rerouting the Southern Pacific's tracks, but getting it approved required much hard struggle with the railroad and its allies in the state assembly. The key to victory was a bill she pushed through the assembly authorizing the use of eminent domain

to acquire the rights to Southern Pacific property. She also played a major role in getting the Alameda Corridor designated a national transportation artery, thus making available federal funding for the project. She also chaired the committees on insurance and revenue/taxation and worked to reform urban education.

In early 1996, Walter Tucker, who represented Millender-McDonald's district in the U.S. House, resigned from office after being convicted of extortion and income tax fraud. A special election was held to replace him, and Millender-McDonald was one of eight Democrats who declared their candidacies. She won the special election and took her seat in Congress that same year. In late 1996 she was elected to a full term of her own and assigned to the committees on transportation/infrastructure and small business.

As a congresswoman, Millender-McDonald focused on protecting the Alameda Corridor's status and funding until it could be completed. In other areas, she called on the Federal Aviation Administration to end discrimination against women in airport control towers, and she worked to get more government set-asides for female-owned businesses. In 1997, she called for a complete investigation into allegations that the Central Intelligence Agency was involved in the crack cocaine trade in southern California as a means of financing its covert operations. Millender-McDonald was reelected to a sixth term in 2006. On April 22, 2007, she succumbed to colon cancer, leaving behind her husband, James McDonald, and five adult children. Millender-McDonald was 68.

Further Reading

Biographical Directory of the United States Congress. "Millender-McDonald, Juanita, 1938– ." Available online. URL: http://bioguide.congress.gov/scripts/biodisplay.pl?index=M000714. Downloaded April 9, 2009.

Black Americans in Congress. "Juanita Millender-McDonald." Available online. URL: http://baic.

house.gov/member-profiles/profile.html?
intID=47. Downloaded April 9, 2009.

Foerstel, Karen. *Biographical Dictionary of Congressional Women.* New York: Greenwood Press, 1999.

"Juanita M. McDonald, D-Calif. (37). New Member Profile." *Congressional Quarterly Weekly Report* 54 (March 30, 1996): 904.

Miller, Thomas
(Thomas Ezekial Miller)
(1849–1938) *U.S. congressional representative from South Carolina*

Thomas Miller was one of the last African-American congressmen from South Carolina during the 19th century. Like most black politicians laboring in that century's post-Reconstruction period, he spent most of his career fighting against disfranchisement and working to enhance educational opportunities for black students.

Miller was born on June 17, 1849, in Ferrebeeville, South Carolina. His parents, Richard and Mary, were free blacks; their occupations are unknown. He was so light-skinned, especially compared to his parents, that it was rumored throughout his life that he was the illegitimate son of a white couple who had given him to the Millers to raise as their own. Shortly after his birth, his parents moved to Charleston, where he grew up. He contributed to the family's upkeep by selling newspapers while attending a succession of schools for free blacks. During the Civil War, he was impressed into the Confederate army as a servant and military laborer. Freed by Union troops in 1865, he accompanied them to New York City after the war. He completed his secondary education at the Hudson School in New York and graduated from Pennsylvania's Lincoln University in 1872. That same year, he returned to South Carolina and settled in Beaufort; however, he spent much of the next three years in Columbia, the state capital, where he studied law and briefly attended the University of South

Carolina. In 1874, he married Anna Hume, with whom he had nine children. After passing the bar examination the following year, he opened a law office in Beaufort.

In 1872, Miller joined the Republican Party and became active in its affairs in Beaufort County, where African-American voters constituted a sizable majority. That same year, he was elected to the county school commission, then in 1874 he won a seat in the state legislature's lower house. One of the state's few black politicians to survive the end of Reconstruction in 1877, he held this seat for six years, serving with distinction throughout. In 1880, he was elected to the state senate, and later that year he received the Republican nomination for lieutenant governor. He did not run, however, because widespread white violence against black voters convinced the party's leaders not to contest statewide offices. He resigned from the senate in 1882 to concentrate on his law practice, but he remained active in party politics. In 1884, he accepted the post of state chairman of the Republican Party, and in 1886 he won his old seat in the lower house.

In 1888, Miller ran for the state's Seventh District seat in the U.S. House of Representatives. After "losing" to his white Democrat opponent, he appealed the election to the Republican-controlled House. Although the House found in his favor, it did not do so until 1890, and he was not seated until just before the expiration of his term. He served long enough to give an impassioned speech on the House floor defending the accomplishments of freedmen and opposing the restriction of the voting rights of African Americans, as was then being countenanced throughout the South. Reelected in 1890, he was denied his seat by the state supreme court on a technicality. In those days, the parties and not the states printed ballots and operated the polling places, and the court ruled that Miller's ballots were the wrong shade of white. His appeal to the House, now dominated by Democrats, was rejected. He ran again in 1892 but lost the nomination to GEORGE MURRAY.

Despite these setbacks, Miller remained active in politics. In 1894 he was elected to one last term in the lower house. In 1895, he was one of only five African Americans to serve as delegates to the state constitutional convention. Joined by ROBERT SMALLS, he argued long and loud against whites who wanted to disfranchise blacks, but his pleas were ignored and the constitution was rewritten in such a way that it effectively prevented most blacks from voting.

Miller did succeed in getting South Carolina to found a new black college and to place its operation entirely in the hands of African Americans. Known then as the Colored Normal, Industrial, Agricultural and Mechanical College of South Carolina, but today as South Carolina State University, it opened in Orangeburg in 1896 with Miller as its first president. Over the next 15 years, he developed the school into a first-rate teacher's college and training institute. He was forced to resign in 1911 when the Democratic candidate for governor, whom he had opposed, was elected.

Miller retired to Charleston where he lived until 1923. He spent the next 11 years in Philadelphia, Pennsylvania, then returned to Charleston where he died on April 8, 1938.

Further Reading

Biographical Directory of the United States Congress. "Miller, Thomas Ezekial, 1849–1938." Available online. URL: http://bioguide.congress.gov/scripts/biodisplay.pl?index=M000757. Downloaded March 23, 2009.

Black Americans in Congress. "Thomas Ezekial Miller." Available online. URL: http://baic.house.gov/member-profiles/profile.html?intID=47. Downloaded March 25, 2009.

Clay, William L. *Just Permanent Interests: Black Americans in Congress, 1870–1992.* New York: Amistad Press, 1993.

Holt, Thomas C. *Black over White: Negro Political Leadership in South Carolina during Reconstruction.* Urbana: University of Illinois Press, 1977.

Tindall, George Brown. *South Carolina Negroes, 1877–1900.* Reprint. Columbia: University of South Carolina Press, 2003.

Mitchell, Arthur
(Arthur Wergs Mitchell)
(1883–1968) *U.S. congressional representative from Illinois*

Arthur Mitchell was the first African American elected to the U.S. Congress as a Democrat. Prior to Mitchell, virtually all black politicians had belonged to the party of Lincoln, the Republican Party. After Mitchell's election in 1934, however, only three out of 75 black elected congressmen were Republicans.

Mitchell was born on December 22, 1883, near Lafayette in Chambers County, Alabama. His parents, Taylor and Alma, were farmers and ex-slaves. As a boy, he came to hate farming, so at age 14 he ran away to Tuskegee Institute. He paid his tuition by working as a farmhand and as an office boy for Booker T. Washington, the institute's president. Washington taught that African Americans could best achieve equality via economic, not political, activity, and he served as Mitchell's role model throughout his political career.

After graduating from Tuskegee, Mitchell received a teacher's certificate from Snow Hill Normal and Industrial Institute and began teaching in the state's rural schools for blacks. In 1908, he founded Armstrong Agricultural College in West Butler; as its first president, he modeled it after Tuskegee. Meanwhile, in 1904 he had married Eula King, with whom he had one child. She died in 1909, and two years later he married Annie Harris, with whom he had no children. In 1917, he left Armstrong to serve in the U.S. Army during World War I. After being discharged, he studied law at Columbia and Harvard universities. Although he did not graduate from either school, in 1927 he passed the bar examination in Washington, D.C, and opened a law office there.

In 1927, Mitchell joined the Republican Party, the party of choice for African Americans. The following year he went to Chicago, Illinois, to campaign for Herbert Hoover, the party's presidential nominee, and OSCAR DEPRIEST, who was running for Congress from Illinois's black-majority First District. He liked Chicago so much that he moved his law practice there shortly after the election. At first, he hoped to get elected to public office as a Republican, but factional disputes with DePriest squashed all his attempts. In 1932, he joined the Democratic Party, partly because it offered him greater opportunities for political advancement but also because he despaired of Republican efforts to end the Great Depression, which was having a particularly deleterious effect on African Americans. In 1934, he lost the party's nomination to Harry Baker, a white Democrat who had been active in the party for years. When Baker died during the campaign, the party was forced to advance Mitchell as its candidate. Meanwhile, DePriest had alienated many black voters by not supporting the Democrats' New Deal programs; they and the district's white voters supported Mitchell, who narrowly won.

Despite his support for the New Deal, Mitchell was a conservative at heart. His tutelage at the feet of Booker T. Washington made him seek redress for racism in the New Deal's economic programs that promised to improve the lots of all Americans, regardless of color. He did, however, introduce several race-related bills, including a relatively weak antilynching bill that died in committee. He also called for an end to racial discrimination in the U.S. Civil Service and appointed blacks to the two military academies. As long as he showed strong support for the New Deal, he continued to do well with his constitu-

ents, who reelected him three times. In 1936, he became the first African American to speak from the floor of a Democratic convention when he seconded the renomination of President Franklin D. Roosevelt, the New Deal's chief architect.

Ironically, Mitchell's greatest claim to fame had little to do with politics. In 1937, while riding through Arkansas on a first-class railroad ticket, he was ordered into the second-class coach for black passengers in accordance with Arkansas law. He took his case all the way to the U.S. Supreme Court, which decided in *Mitchell v. United States et al.* (1941) that the "separate but equal" railcar accommodations endorsed by *Plessy v. Ferguson* (1896) were no longer constitutional. It was a small but important victory in the campaign against racial discrimination, and Mitchell became a hero in the national African-American community as a result.

Unfortunately, the case alienated Chicago's conservative white Democrats, who denied Mitchell the party's endorsement for reelection in 1942. Faced with the prospect of a tough primary campaign, the 59-year-old Mitchell decided to retire from politics. Shortly thereafter, he moved to a farm near Petersburg, Virginia. His wife died in 1947, and the following year he married Clara Smith. When not farming, he toured the South speaking on behalf of the Southern Regional Council, a moderate group that promoted racial harmony. He died on May 9, 1968, in Petersburg.

Further Reading

Biographical Directory of the United States Congress. "Mitchell, Arthur Wergs, 1883–1968." Available online. URL: http://bioguide.congress.gov/scripts/biodisplay.pl?index=M000805. Downloaded April 24, 2009.

Black Americans in Congress. "Arthur Wergs Mitchell." Available online. URL: http://baic.house.gov/member-profiles/profile.html?intID=31. Downloaded March 27, 2009.

Clay, William L. *Just Permanent Interests: Black Americans in Congress, 1870–1992.* New York: Amistad Press, 1993.

Nordin, Dennis S. *The New Deal's Black Congressman: A Life of Arthur Wergs Mitchell.* Columbia: University of Missouri Press, 1997.

Mitchell, Charles
(Charles Lewis Mitchell)
(1829–1912) *Massachusetts state legislator*

In 1866, Charles Lewis Mitchell and Edward Garrison Walker were elected to the Massachusetts state legislature. They were the first African Americans to serve in a state legislature, having been elected a full two years before blacks were elected to the southern legislatures during Reconstruction.

Mitchell was born on November 10, 1829, in Hartford, Connecticut. His parents, whose names are not known, were free blacks of some standing in local African-American society. Although he had no formal education, he did learn how to read and write at a time when such skills were by no means universal. He also learned how to set print on a printing press, and as a young man he worked as a typesetter with a Hartford printer. In 1853, he moved to Boston, Massachusetts, partly in search of a better job and partly because Boston was home to a much larger and more vibrant African-American community. He quickly found a position at *The Liberator*, the famous abolitionist newspaper published by William Lloyd Garrison, where he worked as a typesetter for the next 10 years.

In 1863, Mitchell enlisted as a private in the 55th Massachusetts Infantry, a black regiment in the Union army. Almost immediately, he was promoted to sergeant and assigned to the headquarters company of the First Brigade, where he was put in charge of the regiment's printing. In 1864, he was transferred to a combat company and lost his right foot during the fighting at Honey Hill, South Carolina. After spending some time in a New York City hospital, he was sent to recuperate in a hospital in Worcester, Massachusetts, where he finished out the Civil War. In 1865, he was discharged and awarded a disability pension for life.

In 1866, Mitchell ran as a Republican for a seat in the Massachusetts General Court, the lower house of the state legislature. A gifted speaker and war hero, he faced little opposition and was elected to a one-year term. During his tenure in the general court, he spoke eloquently on several occasions concerning the right of black citizens to enjoy legal and social equality with whites.

After completing his term of office in 1867, Mitchell returned to the printing trade. Meanwhile, he remained active in the local affairs of the Republican Party. Two years later, he received a political appointment to serve as an inspector at the Treasury Department customhouse in Boston. He was later promoted to clerk, a position he held until he retired in 1899.

Throughout his life, Mitchell was active in the affairs of the Grand Army of the Republic, the national group of Union veterans of the Civil War. He was also active in various groups that sought to improve relations between blacks and whites. In 1877, he married Nellis Brown. They had no children. In 1879, he served as a pallbearer at William Lloyd Garrison's funeral. In 1898, he helped raise an African-American company for service in the Spanish-American War. He died at his home in Roxbury, Massachusetts, on April 13, 1912.

Further Reading
Johnson, Robert, Jr. "Mitchell, Charles." In *African American National Biography*, vol. 5, edited by Henry Louis Gates, Jr., and Evelyn Brooks Higginbotham. New York: Oxford University Press, 2008, pp. 627–628.

Logan, Rayford W., and Michael R. Winston, eds. *Dictionary of American Negro Biography.* New York: W. W. Norton, 1982.

Ploski, Harry A., and James Williams, eds. *The Negro Almanac: A Reference Work on the African American.* Detroit: Gale Research, 1989.

Mitchell, Parren

(Parren James Mitchell)
(1922–2007) *U.S. congressional representative from Maryland*

Parren Mitchell was the first African American to represent Maryland in Congress. His major contribution was the establishment of the 10 percent set-aside for minority-owned businesses in several major federal public works projects.

Mitchell was born on April 29, 1922, in Baltimore, Maryland. His father, Clarence, was a hotel waiter, and his mother, Elsie, was a homemaker. After graduating from high school in 1940, he joined the U.S. Army, rose to the rank of captain, and served in Europe during World War II. Discharged in 1946, he returned to Baltimore and attended Morgan State College on the G.I. Bill. After receiving a B.A. in 1950, he enrolled in the University of Maryland at Baltimore County and received an M.A. in sociology in 1952. He then taught sociology at Morgan State until 1954, when he became the supervisor of probation for the Baltimore city courts. In 1963, he was named executive secretary of the Maryland Commission on Interracial Problems and Relations; in this position he ensured compliance with state law forbidding racial discrimination in places of public accommodation. In 1965, he was appointed director of Baltimore's Community Action Agency (CAA), and for the next three years he oversaw the city's antipoverty programs. In 1968, he returned to Morgan State as assistant director of the Urban Affairs Institute.

For most of his professional career, Mitchell had worked with people who had been marginalized economically. The programs of President Lyndon B. Johnson's Great Society, which Mitchell had become acquainted with as the CAA's director, had done much to alleviate the worst conditions they encountered. By 1968, however, those programs were in danger of coming to an end, especially in the wake of Johnson's decision not to seek reelection in 1968. Inspired to do something to ensure the continuity of the Great Society, Mitchell decided to run for public office despite his lack of political involvement.

In 1968, Mitchell ran for the U.S. House of Representatives from Maryland's Seventh District, which at the time had a white majority. Not surprisingly, he failed to win the Democratic Party's nomination against the incumbent, Samuel N. Friedel. Undaunted by his poor showing, he became more involved in community affairs, thus becoming better known, and in 1970 he made a second run for Congress. This time, Friedel was faced with a white challenger, Carl Friedler, as well. While Friedel and Friedler battled it out for the white vote, Mitchell garnered virtually all of the African-American vote, which gave him a narrow plurality in the primary. He then went on to defeat his Republican challenger in the general election and took his seat in Congress in 1971. By the time he came up for reelection, his district had

Parren Mitchell was the first African American to represent Maryland in Congress. *(Library of Congress)*

been redrawn so that it had a black majority. He was reelected to seven terms without once facing a serious challenger.

Mitchell served on the committees on small business, the budget, and banking, finance and urban affairs. He was particularly active on the small business committee, and became its chairman in 1981. He used his position on this committee to improve dramatically opportunities for minority businesspeople. In 1976, he wrote legislation that required state and local governments seeking federal money for public utilities projects to set aside 10 percent of each project for minority-owned contractors. In 1980, he succeeded in appending a similar rider to the Surface Transportation Assistance Act, thus making it possible for minorities to participate in a significant way in the construction of billions of dollars worth of highways. For thus championing the interests of African-American businesspeople, he became known as "Mr. Minority Enterprise."

Mitchell also was active in other areas of interest to African Americans. He succeeded in getting the United States to contribute $25 million to the African Development Bank, which loaned money to various community improvement projects in Africa. He was able to get the budget for the Elementary and Secondary Education Act increased by $150 million; much of the increase went to improve education in school districts where minorities were in the majority. In 1978, he got the Small Business Administration's budget increased by $271 million; most of the increase was used to assist minority-owned small businesses. He also helped to create more than 100,000 summer jobs for minority youth and helped defeat a proposal that would have established a sub-minimum wage for people under the age of 18. In 1971, he cofounded the Congressional Black Caucus.

Mitchell declined to run for reelection in 1986. When his term expired the following year, he became the chairman of the Minority Business Enterprise Legal Defense and Education Fund,

which he cofounded in 1980. On May 28, 2007, Mitchell died of complications from pneumonia.

Further Reading
Biographical Directory of the United States Congress. "Mitchell, Parren James, 1922." Available online. URL: http://bioguide.congress.gov/scripts/biodisplay. pl?index=M000826. Downloaded April 11, 2009.

Black Americans in Congress. "Parren James Mitchell." Available online. URL: http://baic.house.gov/member-profiles/profile.html?intID=60. Downloaded April 11, 2009.

Clay, William L. *Just Permanent Interests: Black Americans in Congress, 1870–1992.* New York: Amistad Press, 1993.

Kupferstein, Linda M. *Parren J. Mitchell, Democratic Representative from Maryland.* Washington, D.C.: Grossman, 1972.

Moore, Gwen
(Gwendolynne S. Moore)
(1951–) *U.S. congressional representative from Wisconsin*

Gwen Moore was the first African American and second woman elected to the U.S. Congress from Wisconsin. In April 18, 1951, she was born into a large family living in a poor neighborhood of Racine, Wisconsin. Her mother, a schoolteacher, emphasized the importance of education and dreamed that her daughter would one day take a seat in the state legislature. Although shy as a young woman, Moore showed an early interest in politics while serving as the student council president of her high school.

During her first year at Marquette University in Milwaukee, Moore became pregnant. She struggled to support her daughter on welfare and food stamps while pursuing her studies. In 1978, after eight years in college, she graduated with a bachelor's degree in political science. Moore joined the Volunteers in Service to America

(VISTA) program and helped establish a community credit union. Her efforts earned her the VISTA Volunteer of the Decade award for 1976 to 1986.

In the 1980s, Moore worked for the city of Milwaukee and for several Wisconsin state agencies. She soon parlayed her interest in community affairs into a career in politics. In 1988, she won a seat in the state assembly. After two terms, in 1992, she became the first African-American woman elected to the state senate. While in the state legislature, Moore spoke out against the police's handling of the case of mass murderer Jeffrey Dahmer. Moore, who had lived two blocks away from Dahmer, said that the police had refused to investigate her neighbors' complaints about him. She also stirred up controversy in late 2001 when she became angry at being asked to show identification when entering the state capitol building. She complained to the governor that the new security measure "disenfranchises people who come to their Capitol."

Known for her advocacy for poor and minority citizens, Moore ran as a Democratic candidate for the U.S. House of Representatives in 2004. She defeated her Republican challenger, Gerald Boyle, by winning approximately 70 percent of the vote. As a congresswoman, Moore served on the Budget, Small Business, and Financial Services committees. She largely focused her energies on trying to improve the economic and employment opportunities for low-income workers. Remembering the needs of the poor in the inner-city neighborhood in which she grew up, she worked to support small businesses, create new jobs, expand educational opportunities, and increase access to affordable health care and housing. Moore also fought for protections from predatory lending practices and for the rights of victims of domestic abuse.

In 2008, Moore was reelected to her third term. She has three children and three grandchildren, all of whom live in her district in Wisconsin.

Further Reading

Clarke, Robyn D. "Striving For More: Gwen Moore Worked Her Way from Welfare to Washington." *Black Enterprise* (June 2005): 290.

Congresswoman Gwen Moore, Official Web Site. Available online. URL: http://www.house.gov/gwenmoore. Downloaded May 1, 2009.

Explorations in Black Leadership. "Gwen Moore." Available online. URL: http://www.virginia.edu/publichistory/bl/index.php?uid=38. Downloaded May 1, 2009.

Morial, Dutch

(Ernest Nathan Morial)
(1929–1989) *mayor of New Orleans, Louisiana*

"Dutch" Morial was the first African-American mayor of New Orleans. Five years after his death, his son Marc Morial was elected mayor of New Orleans.

Morial was born on October 9, 1929, in New Orleans, Louisiana. His father, Walter, was a cigar maker, and his mother, Leonie, was a tailor. The descendant of light-skinned Creoles, he got the nickname "Dutch" because his father thought he looked like the little boy on the label of Dutch Boy house paint. He graduated from high school in 1948, having spent the year between his freshman and sophomore years at sea. Upon receiving a B.A. from Xavier University in New Orleans in 1951, he enrolled in Louisiana State University Law School and became its first African-American graduate three years later. He served two years in the U.S. Army as an intelligence officer, then in 1957 he became a partner in a New Orleans law firm. In 1955, he married Sybil Haydel, with whom he had five children.

As an attorney, Morial worked hard to end racial segregation in New Orleans via the courts. By 1965, he had won court orders to integrate the city's public schools, taxicabs, and recreational facilities. That same year, he was appointed assistant district attorney for New Orleans, and in this capacity he continued to pursue a judicial cure for racial injustice.

Meanwhile, Morial had gotten involved in the affairs of the state Democratic Party. In 1959, he ran unsuccessfully for a seat on the party's state central committee. Undaunted, he redoubled his involvement in party affairs, thus building up his political reputation and skills. In 1967, he ran again, this time for state representative, and won, thus becoming the first African American to serve in the Louisiana legislature in almost 100 years. As the lower chamber's only black member, he kept a low profile; however, he worked assiduously behind the scenes and as a member of the legislative committee for changes beneficial to blacks. He also worked to abolish the death penalty and to give the vote to 18-year-olds. He declined to run for reelection in 1969, choosing instead to campaign for a seat on the New Orleans city council. He lost, but the following year he was named a judge on the city's juvenile court. In 1974, he was elected to the state's Fourth Circuit Court of Appeals but resigned three years later to run for mayor.

Although New Orleans has a large African-American population, Morial knew he could not rely on its votes alone to gain victory. Consequently, he campaigned on a platform of rejuvenating New Orleans's economy, thus gaining substantial support in the white community. He took office in 1978 and immediately set about keeping his campaign promises. During his two terms as mayor, he created an office of economic development to attract new industries while retaining old ones. One of its accomplishments was to secure enough federal funding to complete a 7,500-acre industrial district, which led to an increase of thousands of jobs and a building boom in downtown New Orleans. He also established an office of minority business development that awarded a greater share of city contracts to small and minority-owned businesses. Perhaps the most visible accomplishment of his tenure was the renovation of the city's waterfront, a project that

included the construction of much retail space. He also balanced the budget, in the process wiping out a $40 million deficit.

By law, New Orleans's mayors could serve only two consecutive terms. In 1985, Morial attempted to have this law overturned by referendum, but the measure was rejected. When his second term expired in 1986, he returned to the private practice of law. He remained active in the Democratic Party by serving as a national committeeman and, in 1988, as an adviser to Michael Dukakis, the party's candidate for president. He died of a heart attack on Christmas Eve, 1989, in New Orleans.

Further Reading

Colburn, David R., and Jeffrey S. Adler. *African-American Mayors: Race, Politics, and the American City.* Urbana: University of Illinois Press, 2001.

Hirsch, Arnold R. *Dutch Morial: Old Creole in the New South.* New Orleans: College of Urban & Public Affairs, University of New Orleans, 1990.

Weber, Bret A. "Morial, Ernest Nathan 'Dutch.'" In *African American National Biography,* vol. 6, edited by Henry Louis Gates, Jr., and Evelyn Brooks Higginbotham. New York: Oxford University Press, 2008, pp. 25–26.

Moseley Braun, Carol
(Carol Moseley, Carol Moseley-Braun)
(1947–   ) *U.S. senator from Illinois, presidential candidate*

In 1993, Carol Moseley Braun became the first African American elected to the U.S. Senate as a Democrat. During her six years in office, she was the highest-ranking elected black political leader in the United States.

Moseley Braun was born Carol Moseley on August 16, 1947, in Chicago, Illinois. Her father, Joseph, was a policeman, and her mother, Edna, was a medical technician. Her parents divorced when she was 16, and she and her mother moved in with her grandmother, who lived in Oakwood, one of the worst neighborhoods in Chicago. She moved out two years later to attend the University of Illinois, receiving a B.A. in political science in 1967. Five years later, she received a J.D. from the University of Chicago Law School and went into private practice. In 1974, she was named an assistant U.S. attorney for the northern district of Illinois, a position she held for four years. In 1973, she married Michael Braun, with whom she had one child; they divorced in 1987.

In 1978, Moseley Braun was elected to the first of five terms in the Illinois state legislature. As a legislator, she worked to improve public education and to outlaw racial discrimination in housing and private clubs. She introduced the bills that forced the state of Illinois to divest itself of its investments in South Africa and to redraw its voting districts so that representation in the legislature was apportioned fairly. After 1983, she became a close ally of Chicago mayor HAROLD WASHINGTON, and she served as his official liaison with the state legislature. She held several leadership positions in the lower house and twice won the Independent Voters of Illinois's Best Legislator Award. When she left the house, she had developed a reputation for leadership and bipartisan consensus-building.

In 1986, Moseley Braun tried to run for lieutenant governor, but she failed to obtain the necessary support from the Democratic Party. The following year, she joined Washington on the "Dream Ticket," a slate of Democratic candidates for various municipal posts in Chicago and Cook County that was balanced by race and gender. She was elected recorder of deeds for the county, a post she held for four years.

In 1991, Moseley Braun decided to run for the U.S. Senate. She was motivated to do so by the Senate confirmation hearings concerning Supreme Court nominee Clarence Thomas. During the hearings, Thomas was accused of sexual harassment by Anita Hill, a law professor and former aide to Thomas. By voting to confirm Thomas, the Senate outraged millions of women

because it demonstrated what was perceived as the male-dominated Senate's callous disregard for the veracity as well as the feelings of women. Illinois senator Alan J. Dixon, who was up for reelection, had voted to confirm, and Moseley Braun determined to do her best to unseat him.

The political pundits gave Moseley Braun little chance to win the 1992 Democratic primary. In addition to Dixon, she was running against millionaire Al Hofeld. Both men had much more money than she did, and Dixon, a longtime incumbent, had the support of the party. Fortunately for Moseley Braun, her male opponents ignored her and instead attacked one another. This left her free to concentrate on the issues, which she did with knowledge and confidence. To the surprise of many, she received more votes than either Dixon or Hofeld, thus securing the nomination. She easily defeated her Republican opponent in the general election and took her seat in the Senate in 1993. She was assigned to the judiciary, small business/banking, and housing/urban affairs committees.

Moseley Braun generated much controversy during her first years in the Senate. She came under attack for mishandling campaign donations and was investigated as a result. While on a trip to Africa, she paid a personal call on Nigeria's dictator, General Sani Abacha. Abacha had been accused of human rights violations, and her visit was roundly condemned by members of both parties. She is best remembered for opposing the copyright renewal of the insignia of the United Daughters of the Confederacy (UDC). The insignia featured the Confederate flag, and the renewal was sponsored by powerful conservative Republican senator Jesse Helms. Moseley Braun singlehandedly took on Helms and the UDC, and in a moving speech before the Senate outlined the deep-seated opposition that African Americans had to the Confederate flag. As a result of her speech, the renewal was denied.

Toward the end of her term, Moseley Braun had put most of the controversy behind her and had developed a good working relation with her fellow senators. In 1995, she was appointed to the finance committee.

Moseley Braun ran for reelection in 1998 but lost to her Republican opponent. After stepping down the following year, she served briefly as an adviser to the U.S. Department of Education. In late 1999, she was appointed and confirmed as U.S. ambassador to New Zealand. Following the inauguration of Republican president George W. Bush in 2001, she resigned her ambassadorship and returned to Chicago.

In 2000, Moseley Braun returned to politics by running for the Democratic presidential nomination. Although her bid was unsuccessful, she became the second African-American woman in history to seek the nomination (SHIRLEY CHISHOM, in 1972, was the first). The following year, Moseley Braun began teaching political science at Morris Brown College in Georgia and at DePaul University in Illinois. She also established a business consulting firm in Chicago and founded Good Food Organics, a company that produces and markets organic coffees, teas, and spices.

Moseley Braun announced that she was making a second bid for the presidency in 2003. She withdrew from the race in January 2004 after losing the Iowa caucus. In September 2010, Moseley Braun once again threw her hat into the ring by announcing that she would run for mayor of Chicago in 2011.

Further Reading

Biographical Directory of the United States Congress. "Moseley-Braun, Carol, 1947– ." Available online. URL: http://bioguide.congress.gov/scripts/biodisplay.pl?index=M001025. Downloaded April 1, 2009.

Black Americans in Congress. "Carol Moseley-Braun." Available online. URL: http://baic.house.gov/member-profiles/profile.html?intID=59. Downloaded April 11, 2009.

D'Orio, Wayne. *Carol Moseley-Braun.* Philadelphia: Chelsea House Publishers, 2003.

Explorations in Black Leadership. "Carol Moseley Braun." Available online. URL: http://www.virginia.edu/publichistory/bl/index.php?uid=4. Downloaded April 11, 2009.

Foerstel, Karen. *Biographical Dictionary of Congressional Women.* New York: Greenwood Press, 1999.

Gill, LaVerne McCain. *African American Women in Congress: Forming and Transforming History.* New Brunswick, N.J.: Rutgers University Press, 1997.

Langston, Donna. *A to Z of American Women Leaders and Activists.* New York: Facts On File, 2002.

Motley, Constance
(Constance Baker Motley)
(1921–2005) *president of Manhattan borough, New York*

Constance Baker Motley was best known for her work in the judicial branch, both as a trial lawyer and as the first African-American woman to become a federal district judge. However, she also made her mark by being the first black woman to serve in the New York state senate and the first woman to serve as Manhattan borough president.

Motley was born Constance Baker on September 14, 1921, in New Haven, Connecticut. Her father, Willoughby, was a chef, and her mother, Rachel, was a homemaker. She had planned to become an interior designer after finishing high school, but the Great Depression was still going on when she graduated in 1939. Instead, she took a job with the National Youth Administration, which sought to provide young people with part-time jobs and financial assistance so they could continue their education. Part of her job involved giving public presentations in the New Haven area; one such presentation so impressed Clarence Blakeslee, a local businessman, that he offered to pay for her entire college education. She enrolled in Fisk University in 1941, transferred to New York University in 1942, received a B.A. in economics in 1943, and enrolled in Columbia University Law School in 1944. Two years later, she

Constance Motley represented Harlem in the New York State Senate. *(Library of Congress)*

received an LL.B. and married Joel Motley, with whom she had one child.

After graduating from law school, Motley went to work as a law clerk for Thurgood Marshall, at the time chief counsel for the National Association for the Advancement of Colored People's Legal Defense and Educational Fund. Marshall and the fund were attacking racial segregation in state and federal courts across the country, and over the next 20 years Motley became the fund's principal trial lawyer. In addition to arguing a number of cases concerning education, employment, housing, public accommodations, and transportation, she helped write the briefs for plaintiff Brown in *Brown v. Board of Education,* the landmark 1954 U.S. Supreme Court decision that marked the beginning of the end for segregated public schools.

Motley was also politically active as a member of the Democratic Party. Although her work for the fund frequently took her out of town, she campaigned whenever she could for the party's state and local candidates. By 1958, she was one of the most influential black women in New York. That same year, she became involved in the executive branch of government by taking on a part-time job as a member of the New York State Advisory Council on Employment and Unemployment Insurance. In 1963, she moved into the legislative branch when she was elected to complete the term of Harlem's representative in the New York state senate. She won a full term the following year and introduced several bills to eliminate segregation in education, employment, and housing. Before she could have much effect, however, she resigned in early 1965 after being elected to complete the term of the president of New York City's Manhattan borough. Reelected when her term expired later that year, she drew up a plan to revitalize several impoverished areas of Harlem and then won almost $1 million in federal funding to implement the plan.

In 1966, Motley resigned as borough president to accept an appointment as federal district judge for the Southern District of New York, thus ending her political career. She became the district's chief judge in 1982 and its senior judge in 1990. In 2001, she received the Presidential Citizens Medal, the second highest award for civilians in the United States, from President Bill Clinton. Motley died of heart failure in New York City on September 28, 2005.

Further Reading

Boyd, Herb. *Autobiography of a People: Three Centuries of African American History Told by Those Who Lived It.* New York: Doubleday, 2000.

Lamson, Peggy. *Few Are Chosen: American Women in Political Life.* Boston: Houghton Mifflin, 1968.

Martin, Douglas. "Constance Baker Motley, Civil Rights Trailblazer, Dies at 84." *New York Times,* September 29, 2005. Available online. URL: http://www.nytimes.com/2005/09/29/nyregion/29motley.html?_r=1. Downloaded April 11, 2009.

Motley, Constance B. *Equal Justice under Law: An Autobiography.* New York: Farrar, Straus and Giroux, 1999.

Wood, Jennifer. "Motley, Constance Baker." In *African American National Biography,* vol. 6, edited by Henry Louis Gates, Jr., and Evelyn Brooks Higginbotham. New York: Oxford University Press, 2008, pp. 65–67.

Murray, George

(George Washington Murray)
(1853–1926) *U.S. congressional representative from South Carolina*

George Murray was the last African American to represent South Carolina in the U.S. Congress in the 19th century. Murray was born on September 24, 1853, on a plantation near Rembert in Sumter County, South Carolina. His parents, whose names are unknown, were slaves. Nothing is known about his early life other than that he gained his freedom in 1865 as a result of the Civil War. In 1876, at age 21, he entered the University of South Carolina. Two years later, he returned to Sumter County where he operated a farm and taught school for 14 years. At some point, he married a woman named Cornelia, with whom he had two children.

Although few records exist to document his political career, it seems clear that Murray became extensively involved in local politics in the late 1870s or early 1880s as a member of the Republican Party. Otherwise, his appointment in 1890 as a federal customs inspector for Charleston makes little sense, as these positions were usually reserved for loyal, effective supporters of the political party in control of the White House. Shortly after his appointment, he ran for the U.S. House of Representatives but lost his party's nomination to Thomas Miller. Two years later, he took the nomination from Miller and defeated his Democratic opponent in the general election.

Murray was assigned to the committee on education and labor and the committee on expenditures in the Treasury Department. Unlike most freshmen congressmen, he addressed the full House early and often; his two most memorable speeches were in favor of free coinage of silver, a major political controversy during the election of 1896, and in favor of having the deceased body of Frederick Douglass, the famous black abolitionist, lie in state in the rotunda of the Capitol Building. He opposed in vain the efforts of southern Democrats to repeal the last of the Reconstruction Acts giving federal protection to African-American voters. A man of supreme confidence, he often engaged in heckling his colleagues while they spoke, peppering them with pointed questions they could rarely answer. He introduced bills to provide federal funding for teacher's colleges and industrial training schools, to exempt the Young Men's Christian Association from paying taxes, and to provide pensions for elderly and infirm freedmen; not surprisingly, given his penchant for heckling, none of them passed.

Murray was apparently denied reelection in 1894; however, he challenged the results and was eventually declared the winner by the House elections committee. Unfortunately for him, this decision did not come until June 1896, toward the end of the term. Undaunted, he took his seat anyway and called repeatedly for a federal investigation into political corruption in his home state. His reelection campaign in 1896 was unsuccessful.

In 1897, Murray returned to Sumter County, where he engineered a novel plan for evading South Carolina's disfranchisement of blacks. The state constitution of 1895 established a property requirement for voters, so he bought 10,000 acres, subdivided it into tracts of 25 acres, and sold them at reasonable terms to landless blacks. In 1905, he moved to Chicago, Illinois, and spent the rest of his life lecturing about race relations. He penned two books on the subject, *Race Ideals* (1914) and *Light in Dark Places* (1925). He died on April 21, 1926, in Chicago.

Further Reading

Biographical Directory of the United States Congress. "Murray, George Washington, 1853–1926." Available online. URL: http://bioguide.congress. gov/scripts/biodisplay.pl?index=M001106. Downloaded April 1, 2009.

Black Americans in Congress. "George Washington Murray." Available online. URL: http://baic. house.gov/member-profiles/profile.html?int ID=21. Downloaded April 1, 2009.

Gaboury, William J. "George Washington Murray and the Fight for Political Democracy in South Carolina." *Journal of Negro History* 62 (July 1977): 258–269.

Holt, Thomas C. *Black over White: Negro Political Leadership in South Carolina during Reconstruction.* Urbana: University of Illinois Press, 1977.

Marszalek, John F. *A Black Congressman in the Age of Jim Crow: South Carolina's George Washington Murray.* Gainesville: University of Florida Press, 2006.

N

Nagin, Ray
(C. Ray Nagin, Clarence Ray Nagin)
(1956–) *mayor of New Orleans, Louisiana*

Although his political career was filled with dramatic moments, Mayor Ray Nagin will always be remembered for his impassioned plea for help for New Orleans in the aftermath of the Hurricane Katrina disaster.

Clarence Ray Nagin was born in New Orleans on June 11, 1956. His family struggled financially, with both parents working sometimes two or three jobs to support the household. Nagin left Louisiana to attend Tuskegee University in Alabama on a baseball scholarship. In 1978, he graduated with a degree in accounting.

Nagin excelled in the corporate world. He worked first for General Motors in Detroit and then for Associates Corporation in Dallas. In 1982, Nagin married his wife Seletha, which whom he has three children.

Nagin returned to New Orleans in 1985 to work as controller for Cox Communications, the city's cable television franchise. Within four years, he had become vice president and general manager at Cox. During his tenure at the company, he increased customer service satisfaction, oversaw the creation of hundreds of jobs, and hosted a call-in television show for cable customers. Nagin also became known to the public as the spokesman for a group of investors behind the New Orleans Brass, a minor league hockey team. While at Cox, Nagin studied for his master's of business administration, which he received from New Orleans's Tulane University in 1994.

Although he had never held political office, Nagin announced his candidacy for mayor in December 2001. He said his teenage son inspired him to run. His son had complained that, with New Orleans's deteriorating economy, he could not envision a future in the city. Nagin promised that, as mayor, he would focus on cleaning up New Orleans's notoriously corrupt city government and on using his business acumen to improve the city's economy.

On election day, Nagin led the candidates with 29 percent of the vote, but it was not enough to avoid a runoff. The runoff pit him against the second-highest vote-getter, police chief Richard Pennington. Again, Nagin was victorious, winning the mayorship with 59 percent of the vote. His most enthusiastic support came from white voters. Nagin received 85 percent of the white vote, but only 40 percent of the black vote.

Early in his tenure as mayor, Nagin remained popular, as he worked to make good on his campaign promises. For his staff, he mostly chose business leaders to signal his commitment to improving New Orleans's struggling economy. He also pushed for the arrest of dozens of people on corruption charges, many of whom were taxi drivers who had bribed officials to obtain permits. The arrests were largely symbolic; most were thrown out of court for lack of evidence.

In September 2004, as Hurricane Ivan approached New Orleans, Nagin called for a voluntary evacuation of the city. His edict caused huge traffic jams. When the hurricane veered away from the city, leaving it unharmed, many citizens complained that Nagin had panicked in ordering the evacuation.

In August 2005, another hurricane, Katrina, had New Orleans in its sights. Nagin once again called for a voluntary evacuation. But when the situation looked more dire, he ordered the first mandatory evacuation in the city's history about 24 hours before Katrina hit ground. New Orleans residents unable to leave the city crowded into its Superdome arena. On the morning of August 29, the hurricane destroyed the city's levee system, and within hours most of New Orleans was flooded. For days, the federal government failed to send supplies or aid the relief effort for survivors in the city and in the Superdome. During a tearful radio interview, Nagin urged federal officials to "get off your asses and . . . do something . . . [to] fix the biggest goddamn crisis in the history of this country."

With much of New Orleans destroyed, Nagin came under criticism for delaying the call for a mandatory evacuation and for not doing enough to help the poor get out of the city. He further inflamed his critics with a series of impolitic remarks. In October 2005, he stated that he wanted to make sure that, in the rebuilding of New Orleans, the city was "not overrun by Mexican workers." In January 2006, Nagin declared that, despite the displacement of many African-American residents, New Orleans "should be a chocolate New Orleans. This city will be a majority-African-American city. It's the way God wants it to be." His comments alienated white and black residents alike. Some political experts predicted such rhetoric had destroyed Nagin's political career, but he managed to beat out lieutenant governor Mitch Landrieu to narrowly win reelection in the spring of 2006.

Nagin's second and last term, due to term limits, was also rife with controversy. Once a crusader against corruption, Nagin was questioned about a Hawaiian vacation his family took. It was allegedly funded by a business concern that had won contracts from the city. Many people complained that the mayor spent too much time outside of the New Orleans and was not doing enough to reduce crime and to oversee reconstruction efforts. In a February 2008 interview, Nagin further disturbed his critics by threatening to "cold cock" anyone who approached him, while he complained about the many threats received against himself and his family. In early 2009, a poll found that Nagin's overall approval rating was only 36 percent, with a meager 5 percent from the white residents who had once supported him so strongly. After leaving office in May 2010, Nagin embarked on a new career as a paid speaker about topics such as crisis management and economic development.

Further Reading

Henderson, Ashyia, Candace LaBalle, and Sara Pendergast. "Ray Nagin, 1956–   ." *Contemporary Black Biography* 57 (2007): 95–99.

Miester, Mark. "Ray Nagin." *Tulane University Magazine,* Spring 2003. Available online. URL: http://www2.tulane.edu/article_news_details.cfm?ArticleID=4713. Downloaded May 23, 2009.

Schwartz, John. "Term Limits Say New Orleans Mayor Can't Return; Residents Say They Don't Mind." *New York Times,* May 3, 2009. Available online. URL: http://www.nytimes.com/2009/05/04/us/04nagin.html?_r=1. Downloaded May 23, 2009.

Napier, James
(James Carroll Napier)
(1845–1940) *city councilman in Nashville, Tennessee*

James Napier was the most important black politician in 19th-century Tennessee. A gifted orator and a successful businessman with a good understanding of human nature, he achieved many gains for African Americans via conciliation and moderation. Although he did not hold elective office after 1899, he continued to be an important "behind-the-scenes" presence in state, local, and national politics well into the 20th century.

Napier was born on June 9, 1845, in Nashville, Tennessee. His parents, William and Jane, were slaves. At age three, he and his family were freed by their owner, Elias Napier, his paternal grandfather. His father immediately moved the family to Ohio, a free state, then in 1855 returned to Nashville to open a livery stable. He was educated in schools for free blacks in Nashville and Ohio, and at age 19 he enrolled in Wilberforce University. Two years later, he transferred to Oberlin College and graduated in 1868, whereupon he returned to Nashville.

Napier began his political career in 1868 when he joined the State Colored Men's Convention and the Republican Party. That same year, the Freedmen's Bureau appointed him to the commission of refugees and abandoned lands for Tennessee's Davidson County, which included Nashville. In 1870, he led a black delegation to the nation's capital to protest to the president and Congress white violence designed to contravene the Fifteenth Amendment, which guarantees freedmen the right to vote. While he was in Washington, JOHN LANGSTON, a friend of the family since its days in Ohio, convinced him to enroll in Howard University's law school. After graduating from Howard in 1872, he returned to Nashville and opened a law office.

Napier was one of the state's most prominent black Republicans by virtue of his education, and his legal and political careers flourished. In 1875, he was appointed to the first of several patronage positions with the Internal Revenue Service in Nashville. In 1878, the same year he married Langston's daughter, Nettie, he was elected to the Nashville city council. He served on the council through 1889 and for a brief period was its president. As a city councilman, he paid particular

attention to the educational needs of the city's African Americans, ensuring that black students went to school in first-class buildings staffed by competent black teachers. He was also responsible for getting the city to hire more black workers and succeeded in desegregating the fire department.

Napier was a member of the executive committee of the state Republican Party for almost 35 years, and he served as its secretary from 1882 until 1888. In 1882, he ran for circuit court clerk of Davidson County and for a seat in the state legislature but lost both contests. Undaunted, he continued to work behind the scenes for the political and economic advancement of black Tennesseans. In 1898, he ran for the U.S. House of Representatives, but he lost this race as well.

Despite these defeats, Napier remained one of the most prominent African-American politicians in the nation. He served as a member of the so-called black cabinet, which informally offered advice to Republican presidents on matters related to race. As a reward for his loyalty and support, in 1911 he was named register of the U.S. Treasury, and in this capacity he oversaw the day-to-day collection and dispersal of federal money. He resigned two years later to protest the segregationist hiring practices endorsed by Democratic president Woodrow Wilson.

Meanwhile, Napier continued to be one of Nashville's most prominent citizens. In 1903, he cofounded the Nashville One-Cent Savings Bank, today known as Citizens Savings Bank and Trust Company, which catered to the city's black clientele. In addition to his law practice, he became heavily involved in real estate and was responsible for the construction of Napier Court, a downtown office building that served as the business home for many black professionals. From 1915 to 1919, he was president of the National Negro Business League. He was a cofounder of Tennessee Agricultural and Industrial State Normal School (today known as Tennessee State University) and served as a trustee of Meharry Medical College, Fisk University, and Howard University. In 1938, at age 93, he was appointed to Nashville's housing authority. He died on April 21, 1940, in Nashville.

Further Reading

Clark, Herbert L. "James Carroll Napier: National Negro Leader." *Tennessee Historical Quarterly* 49 (1990): 243–252.

Foner, Eric. *Freedom Lawmakers: A Dictionary of Black Officeholders during Reconstruction.* New York: Oxford University Press, 1993.

Lamon, Lester C. *Blacks in Tennessee, 1791–1970.* Knoxville: University of Tennessee Press, 1981.

Scott, Mingo. *The Negro in Tennessee Politics and Governmental Affairs, 1865–1965: The Hundred Years Story.* Nashville: Rich Printing Co., 1965.

Nash, Charles

(Charles Edmund Nash)

(1844–1913) *U.S. congressional representative from Louisiana*

Charles Nash was the first African American from Louisiana to serve in the U.S. House of Representatives and the only black from his state to serve in Congress during Reconstruction. Surprisingly, his entire political career consisted of one term in the House, for he seems never to have been active in state or local politics before or after.

Nash was born on May 23, 1844, in Opelousas, Louisiana. His parents, Richard and Masie, were free blacks. Around 1860, he moved to New Orleans to work as a bricklayer. In 1863, he joined a unit of the Corps d'Afrique, an all-black unit in the Union army that was later renamed the Eighty-second U.S. Colored Infantry Regiment. For two years, he fought against Confederate forces in Louisiana, rising to the rank of sergeant major, and in 1865 he lost his right leg while storming Fort Blakely in Alabama. He was honorably discharged shortly thereafter and spent the next four years recuperating from his wounds. As a reward for his heroism, in 1869 he was hired as a night inspector at the New Orleans Custom House.

Located as it was in one of the nation's busiest ports, the New Orleans Customs House was a primary source of federal patronage, which also made it a hotbed of political activity. Nash seems not to have been involved in state or local politics prior to 1874; however, he clearly had made an impression on the political powers that be via his hobnobbing at the customs house. Consequently, when he ran for the U.S. House of Representatives in 1874, he easily won the Republican nomination and the general election. Shortly after the election, he married Martha Ann Wycoff. They had no children.

In Congress, Nash was assigned to the committee on education and labor. His lack of formal education and the pain he continued to feel from his war injury kept him from making an impact on his colleagues. He introduced only one bill, to conduct a survey of the bayous in his district, which failed to pass. He made only one speech, in which he decried the sorry state of race relations in Louisiana in particular and the nation at large while calling for renewed federal guarantees of African-American civil rights. He ran for reelection in 1876 but was defeated by his white Democratic opponent. He never held elective office again.

Nash returned to New Orleans after his congressional term expired in 1877 and resumed his career as a bricklayer. In 1882, he was appointed postmaster for Washington, Louisiana, but he resigned after less than three months on the job. He returned to Opelousas where his wife died in 1884. Later that year, he moved back to New Orleans; unable to work any longer as a bricklayer, he went to work as a cigar maker. In 1905, he married Julia Lucy Montplaisir. He died on June 21, 1913, in New Orleans.

Further Reading

Biographical Directory of the United States Congress. "Nash, Charles Edmund, 1844–1913." Available online. URL: http://bioguide.congress.gov/scripts/

biodisplay.pl?index=N000008. Downloaded April 10, 2009.

Black Americans in Congress. "Charles Edmund Nash." Available online. URL: http://baic.house.gov/member-profiles/profile.html?intID=9. Downloaded April 3, 2009.

Clay, William L. *Just Permanent Interests: Black Americans in Congress, 1870–1992.* New York: Amistad Press, 1993.

Miller, Chandra. "Charles Nash." In *African American National Biography,* vol. 6, edited by Henry Louis Gates, Jr., and Evelyn Brooks Higginbotham. New York: Oxford University Press, 2008, pp. 118–120.

Taylor, Joe G. *Louisiana Reconstructed, 1863–1877.* Baton Rouge: Louisiana State University Press, 1974.

Nix, Robert

(Robert Nelson Cornelius Nix)
(ca. 1898–1987) *U.S. congressional representative from Pennsylvania*

Robert Nix was the first African-American congressman from Pennsylvania. Although he was not a flamboyant personality, his quiet demeanor, ability to compromise, and deep devotion to the best interests of his constituents allowed him to serve in the House for more than 20 years.

Nix was born in Orangeburg, South Carolina, on August 9; the year of his birth has been given variously as 1898 (more likely) and 1905 (his claim). His father, Nelson, was a dean at the Colored Normal, Industrial, Agricultural and Mechanical College of South Carolina (modern South Carolina State University), and his mother, Sylvia, was a homemaker. His father did not believe that South Carolina provided a suitable public education for African-American children, so when Nix reached school age he was sent to live with relatives in Harlem in New York City. After completing high school, he enrolled in Lincoln University in Pennsylvania and received a B.A. in 1921. Three years later, he received a law degree from the University of Pennsylvania Law School. In 1925, he passed the state bar examination and opened a law office in Philadelphia. An able lawyer, from 1934 to 1938 he served as special deputy attorney general of the state's department of revenue. During this period he was also named special assistant deputy attorney general for the state, a position he held until his election to Congress.

Nix became involved in politics shortly after taking up the practice of law. He joined the Democratic Party and became one of its top recruiters. He was particularly successful at registering voters in the city's black-majority wards. In 1932, he was named to the 44th Ward's executive committee, and in 1950 he took over as its chairman. As a result of his active leadership, Philadelphia achieved the highest percentage of registered voters among its African-American population of all U.S. cities. He was further rewarded with important seats on the party's city campaign committee, and in 1956 he was named a delegate to the national convention. He was unable, however, to translate his success within the party to success at the polls in the several local elections in which he was a candidate.

In early 1958, Congressman Earl Chudoff resigned from the House to accept a Philadelphia judgeship. Nix won the special election to fill the few remaining months of his term. He used this victory as a springboard to reelection later that year, and was reelected to his seat nine more times. As a freshman congressman, he was assigned to the committees on the merchant marine and fisheries and veterans affairs. In 1961, he was put on the foreign affairs committee. In 1963, he was reassigned to the post office and civil service committee, and he served as its chairman during his last term (1977–79).

Nix was not a flamboyant congressman, nor was he particularly successful at getting his bills passed, most of which died in committee. He was highly effective, however, at using the powers of his office to benefit the citizens of Philadelphia, particularly the black and elderly. Every Sunday, he returned to

Robert Nix was the first African American to represent Pennsylvania in Congress. *(Library of Congress)*

Philadelphia to listen to the petitions of his constituents and then returned to Washington to use his influence to take care of them. He was especially interested in providing jobs for the unemployed and better jobs for the underemployed. He also worked to expand the civil rights of African Americans. In 1965, he joined other Democrats in attempting to deny seating to Mississippi's congressional delegation on the grounds that blacks could not vote in that state. That same year, he energetically supported the Voting Rights Act.

In 1971, Nix became a charter member of the Congressional Black Caucus. He proved to be considerably more moderate than the other members of the caucus, most of whom preferred a more confrontational stance vis-à-vis the rest of the federal government. The caucus was particularly incensed when Nix, as chairman of the civil service committee, did not oppose President Jimmy Carter's civil service reforms. Whereas the caucus

perceived that these reforms threatened to reduce the job security of African-American government employees, which they did, Nix perceived that the reforms promised to improve the job performances of all government employees, which they also did. In any event, Nix had gotten where he was by working as a moderate to achieve small gains, and he was not about to change that strategy toward the end of his career.

Despite his personal service to his constituents, by 1978 Nix had grown visibly old. His bid for reelection that year failed when he lost the party's nomination to BILL GRAY. He returned to Philadelphia when his term expired and continued his involvement in politics as a ward committeeman. He died on June 22, 1987, in Philadelphia.

Further Reading
Barker, Lucius J., and Mack H. Jones. *Black Americans and the Political System*. 3rd ed. Englewood Cliffs, N.J.: Prentice Hall, 1994.
Biographical Directory of the United States Congress. "Nix, Robert Nelson Cornelius, Sr., 1905–1987." Available online. URL: http://bioguide.congress. gov/scripts/biodisplay.pl?index=N000113. Downloaded April 2, 2009.
Black Americans in Congress. "Robert Nelson Cornelius Nix, Sr." Available online. URL: http://baic. house.gov/member-profiles/profile.html? intID=32. Downloaded April 2, 2009.
Clay, William L. *Just Permanent Interests: Black Americans in Congress, 1870–1992*. New York: Amistad Press, 1993.

Norton, Eleanor Holmes
(1937–   ) *delegate to the U.S. House from the District of Columbia*

Eleanor Norton was the second African American to serve as the District of Columbia's nonvoting delegate in the U.S. House of Representatives. She generated a bit of a controversy by calling repeatedly for D.C. statehood.

Norton was born Eleanor Holmes on June 13, 1937, in Washington, D.C. Her father, Coleman, was a civil servant with the D.C. government, and her mother, Vela, was a schoolteacher. After finishing high school in 1955, she enrolled in Antioch College and received a B.A. in 1960. She then attended Yale University where she received an M.A. in American studies in 1963 and an LL.B. in 1964. She spent the next year working as a law clerk for a federal judge in Philadelphia, Pennsylvania, then went to work for the American Civil Liberties Union as assistant legal director. Over the next five years, she defended the First Amendment rights of civil rights activists and white supremacists alike. In 1970, she was named chairwoman of New York City's Commission on Human Rights. In this position, she fought against discrimination against minorities, women, and the handicapped. She did such a good job that in 1977 Democratic president Jimmy Carter asked her to chair the U.S. Equal Employment Opportunity Commission. She resigned the position in 1981 following the election of Republican president Ronald Reagan. She worked for a year as a senior fellow at the Urban Institute, then in 1982 she became a professor of law at Georgetown University. In 1965, she married Edward Norton, with whom she had two children; they divorced in 1993.

Norton got involved in politics in 1988, when she represented JESSE JACKSON during the Democratic National Convention's platform debate. Two years later, WALTER FAUNTROY announced that he would not seek reelection as the District of Columbia's nonvoting delegate in the U.S. House of Representatives. After a narrow victory in the Democratic primary, during which it was disclosed that Norton and her husband owed thousands of dollars in back taxes to the district, she easily won in the general election. She took her seat in 1991 and was assigned to the committees on the District of Columbia and judiciary/education. She was reelected nine times.

During her first term, Norton focused on issues that related directly to D.C. Her first act was to win the right to vote on the House floor when it met as the Committee of the Whole; her predecessors could vote only in committee meetings away from the House floor. She also secured increased federal funding for the operation of the district's government, particularly for expanded police protection.

Throughout her career in Congress, Norton pushed hard for full voting rights for the District of Columbia's residents. They can vote for the president and local officials, but D.C.'s delegate to the House cannot vote on bills and residents are not represented in the Senate at all. To remedy this situation, Norton introduced a bill calling for D.C. statehood. The bill would give the new state, to be called New Columbia, two seats in the Senate and proportionate representation in the House. It would also give the district government control over all federal property within its limits except for a handful of federal buildings and monuments. The proposal was defended on the grounds that Washington, D.C., has a larger population than several states and therefore deserves fuller representation in Congress. The bill was defeated in the House of Representatives in November 1993.

Continuing the fight for D.C. voting rights, Norton introduced the District of Columbia House Voting Rights Act of 2009 in the House of Representatives on January 6, 2009. The act was introduced to the U.S. Senate on the same day. The bill called for a congressional seat with full voting rights in the House of Representatives to represent the citizens of the District of Columbia. The act was passed by the Senate in February 26, 2009.

Further Reading

Biographical Directory of the United States Congress. "Norton, Eleanor Holmes, 1937." Available online. URL: http://bioguide.congress.gov/scripts/biodisplay.pl?index=N000147. Downloaded October 19, 2010.

Congresswoman Eleanor Holmes Norton, Official Web Site. Available online. URL: http://www.norton.house.gov. Downloaded April 11, 2009.

Explorations in Black Leadership. "Eleanor Holmes Norton." Available online. URL: http://www.virginia.edu/publichistory/bl/index.php?uid=23. Downloaded April 12, 2009.

Gill, LaVerne McCain. *African American Women in Congress: Forming and Transforming History.* New Brunswick, N.J.: Rutgers University Press, 1997.

Lester, Joan Steinau. *Fire in My Soul: The Life of Eleanor Holmes Norton.* New York: Atria, 2004.

Smith, Jessie Carney. *Epic Lives: One Hundred Black Women Who Made a Difference.* Detroit: Visible Ink Press, 1993.

Nutter, Michael

(Michael A. Nutter)
(1957–   ) *mayor of Philadelphia, Pennsylvania*

In 2008, Michael Nutter became the third African American to serve as mayor of Philadelphia, Pennsylvania. Nutter was born in West Philadelphia on June 29, 1957. An excellent student, he received scholarships to the prestigious St. Joseph Preparatory School and to the University of Pennsylvania. Although he considered studying medicine, Nutter graduated with a bachelor's degree in business in 1979. In college, Nutter worked as a deejay at the Impulse Disco, a black-owned nightclub that frequently hosted fund-raisers for African-American politicians.

After graduation, Nutter became an investment manager with Pryor, Counts & Co. Interested in foreclosed properties as a potential investment, he began attending city council meetings. He ran several campaigns for council members, before running and winning his own seat in 1992. A year earlier, he married Lisa Johnson, a specialist in job training. Nutter has two children, one from his marriage and one from a previous relationship.

During his 15 years as a councilman, Nutter fought for stricter ethics laws, a smoking ban in public places, and a domestic partnership bill. He was known for his combative style, especially in his challenges to JOHN STREET, a fellow council member who was elected mayor in 1999.

Reelected in 2003, Street struggled in his second term. A corruption scandal in his administration preoccupied the mayor. Many critics complained that Street was not doing enough to solve Philadelphia's most pressing problems, particularly its extremely high rate of violent crime. Street was unable run for a third term because of term limits, and in 2007, five Democratic candidates—including Nutter—fought for their party's nomination. Nutter faced stiff competition: His rivals included two members of the U.S. Congress, a state legislator, and a billionaire entrepreneur. During the first few months of his campaign, polls consistently put him in last place in the Democratic field. To increase his name recognition, he took to handing out Nutter Butter cookies at campaign events.

Over time, Nutter won over a diverse group of voters, who responded to his promotion as a reform candidate. He also developed a reputation as a practical politician who was willing to work hard, presenting himself as a contrast to the supposedly uninvolved and unfocused Street. Nutter promised to address the crime issue by supporting a "stop, question, and frisk" policy for police to deal with anyone suspected of carrying a concealed weapon. When the policy was criticized for impinging on citizens' civil rights, Nutter, as quoted in the *New York Times*, said, "My view is that people also have a civil right not to get shot." To the surprise of many, Nutter overtook his competition to win the primary. He also won the general election by a landslide, taking 82 percent of the vote.

When Nutter took office, the expectations for the new mayor were high. But his first year in office proved difficult. His police department was severely criticized after a news helicopter took footage of policemen beating three African-American suspects in the murder of a police officer. Nutter was also faced with a city budget spiraling out of control. The problem was exasperated in late 2008, when a national financial downturn deepened Philadelphia's financial troubles. To decrease a projected budget gap of more than $1 billion over five years, Nutter pushed for several unpopular measures, including an increased sales tax and the closing of many public swimming pools and libraries. For the remainder of his term, Nutter worked to reconcile the reform ideology of his campaign with the budgetary restrictions placed on him once in office.

Further Reading

Fagone, Jason. "Michael Nutter's Dilemma." *Philadelphia Magazine,* January 2007. Available online. URL: http://www.phillymag.com/articles/michael_nutters_dilemma. Downloaded May 15, 2009.

Ifill, Gwen. *The Breakthrough: Politics and Race in the Age of Obama.* New York: Doubleday, 2009.

Volk, Steve. "Mike vs. Mike." *Philadelphia Magazine,* May 2009. Available online. URL: http://www.phillymag.com/articles/mike_vs_mike. Downloaded May 18, 2009.

O

Obama, Barack
(Barack Hussein Obama, Jr.)
(1961–   ) *president of the United States*

With his inspiring personal story, his keen intellect, his intense charisma, his stirring oratory, and his message of hope, Barack Obama convinced American voters to elect him to the highest office in the land. On January 20, 2009, he was inaugurated as the 44th president of the United States.

Obama's story began on August 4, 1961, in Honolulu, Hawaii. His father was Barack Obama, Sr., an economist from Kenya. His mother was Stanley Ann Dunham Obama, a white woman who grew up in a small town in Kansas. They met as students at the University of Hawaii.

When Barack Obama was two, his father left Hawaii to attend Harvard University in Cambridge, Massachusetts. His parents subsequently divorced, and Obama was left in the care of his mother and her parents. Obama's father wrote to him regularly, but they did not see each other again, except for a monthlong visit when Obama was 10 years old.

Ann Obama's second husband was an Indonesian businessman. From age six to 10, Obama lived in his stepfather's house in Jakarta. The boy then returned to Hawaii to live with his grandparents, who sent him to Punahou Academy, Hawaii's most prestigious private school. After graduating

in 1979, Obama attended Occidental College in Los Angeles, California, for two years. He then transferred to Columbia University in New York City, from which he received a bachelor of arts degree in political science in 1983.

In 1985, Obama moved to Chicago, Illinois, to work as a community organizer. Hired by the Calumet Community Religious Conference, he worked with poor residents to help them improve their neighborhoods. During this time, he also began attending the Trinity United Church of Christ.

Obama left Chicago in 1988 to attend Harvard Law School. There, he was elected president of the *Harvard Law Review,* the first African American ever chosen for that post. After graduating, he returned to Chicago and began practicing civil rights law. He also headed PROJECT VOTE, a voter registration drive. The program was credited with helping to elect CAROL MOSELEY BRAUN to the U.S. Senate.

In 1991, Obama married Michelle Robinson. Also an Ivy League–educated lawyer, Michelle Obama grew up in a working-class family on Chicago's South Side. The couple has two daughters— Malia and Natasha (nicknamed Sasha).

In 1995, Obama's memoir entitled *Dreams from My Father: A Story of Race and Inheritance* was published. In the book, Obama recounted his struggles to come to terms with his identity as a biracial man and with his feelings toward his largely absent father, who died in a car accident in 1982. The memoir also described Obama's brief teenage flirtation with marijuana and cocaine use. *Dreams from My Father* was a popular and critical success. The audio book version won Obama a Grammy Award in 2006 for Best Spoken Word Album.

For years, Obama taught constitutional law at the University of Chicago. But increasingly he became more interested in politics than in academia. In 1996, he was elected to the Illinois state senate from a district that includes the tony Hyde Park area and some of the poorest South Side neighborhoods. While a state senator, he pushed for increased access to early childhood education and for a state earned income tax credit to aid working families. He also led the senate in reforming death penalty prosecutions by requiring police to videotape all interrogations in capital cases.

After four years in state office, Obama ran for the U.S. House of Representatives. He challenged BOBBY RUSH, a four-term congressman who had once been a leader of the Black Panthers. Voters were fairly satisfied with Rush, so Obama had a difficult time convincing them to elect him instead. Rush beat Obama decisively in the Democratic primary.

In 2004, Obama decided to try again for national office, after Illinois senator Peter Fitzgerald announced that he was retiring. Obama joined six others competing in the Democratic primary. Several of his rivals bested him both in experience and in funding. For much of the primary season, Blair Hull, a financier who spent $29 million of his own money on his campaign, was in the lead. In contrast, Obama had to take out a second mortgage on his house to fund his Senate run.

Obama, however, did have one advantage over the other candidates. He proved extremely able at attracting dedicated volunteers to work for his campaign. Many were inspired to support Obama because of a speech he delivered at an antiwar rally in October 2002. He strongly criticized the administration of President George W. Bush,

In 2009, former Illinois senator Barack Obama took office as the 44th president of the United States. *(Office of the Clerk, U.S. House of Representatives)*

which was preparing for a military invasion of Iraq. Announcing his opposition to the upcoming Iraq War, Obama told the crowd, "I am not opposed to all wars. I'm opposed to dumb wars."

Hull remained in the lead until the last weeks of the campaign, when details of his contentious divorce became public. In March 2004, Obama won the primary election with 53 percent of the vote. In the general election, however, he faced stiff competition from Jack Ryan, a handsome, wealthy Republican who had spent the past three years working as a teacher in an inner-city Chicago school.

While still campaigning for the Senate, Obama got a chance to shine on the national political stage when he was invited to deliver the keynote address at the Democratic Party Convention in July 2004. His rousing speech was an enormous success. Immediately afterward, he was anointed a rising superstar of the Democratic Party.

Already leading in the polls, Obama's convention appearance further helped his campaign for Senate. But a confluence of events ended up making him a shoo-in to win. A court ordered the release of records of Jack Ryan's divorce from actress Geri Ryan, which revealed that he had asked his wife to accompany him to sex clubs. The resulting scandal forced Ryan out of the race. The Republican Party, scrambling for a replacement candidate, drafted ALAN KEYES, a controversial African-American political analyst, to run in Ryan's place. On election day, Obama, winning about 70 percent of the vote, beat Keyes in a landslide. Obama became the fifth African-American to serve in the U.S. Senate.

As the junior senator from Illinois, Obama was placed on several committees, including Environment and Public Works, Veterans' Affairs, and Foreign Relations. From 2007 to 2009, he was the chairman of the Foreign Relations Committee's Subcommittee on European Affairs. He focused on such issues as securing increased benefits for Iraq veterans, developing alternative energy sources, and decreasing the spread of nuclear weapons. While a sitting senator, Obama also published his second book, *The Audacity of Hope: Thoughts on Reclaiming the American Dream* (2006). The best seller outlined his beliefs about politics, faith, and family.

On February 10, 2007, Barack Obama announced that he would run for the Democratic nomination in the 2008 presidential election. It was a bold move, especially considering that, at that point, he had been in Washington, D.C., for only two years. Aside from the question of his political inexperience, Obama had to compete with two formidable opponents in the primary: New York senator Hillary Clinton and 2004 vice presidential nominee John Edwards. Both had more experience in national politics, and Clinton especially enjoyed strong support in the Washington establishment.

Obama, however, did have the advantage of having publicly opposed the Iraq War, a position that endeared him to many Democrats angered by the ongoing conflict. He also campaigned with an upbeat message of national unity that held special appeal to younger voters. In awe of Obama's oratory and excited by his optimistic vision of the future, many Obama supporters were so enthusiastic about their candidate that they were said to be caught up in Obamamania.

Many African Americans, however, remained skeptical of Obama's candidacy. They had trouble believing that a black man could win the primary, much less the presidency. His victory in the Iowa caucuses in January 2008 marked a turning point in the campaign. Having proven his appeal among the mostly white voters of Iowa, more African-American voters were willing to join Obama's camp.

Obama and his advisers tried to avoid discussing race in the campaign for fear of alienating white voters. But the issue reared its head after video footage surfaced showing Obama's pastor, Jeremiah Wright, making incendiary remarks about whites and about American foreign policy. Obama's rivals tried to tie Obama to Wright's angry, divisive comments in order to undermine the candidate's image as a calm, uniting figure. Obama countered by delivering a major speech on American racial relations—a speech that was considered one of the best of his career.

After a grueling five months of state primaries and caucuses, Obama finally won enough delegates to secure the Democrat nomination. At the Democratic convention, he accepted the nomination on August 28, 2008, the 45th anniversary of the famous "I Have a Dream" speech delivered by Martin Luther King, Jr., during the 1963 civil rights march in Washington, D.C. Fueled by an outpouring of contributions, mostly from small donors, Obama took on Senator John McCain in the general election. The race was close until late September, when a banking crisis threatened the nation's economic security. With voters more confident in the Democratic Party's ability to manage the economy, Obama moved into the lead. On November 4, 2008, he became the first African American elected to the presidency of the United States.

Obama's inauguration became an occasion for Americans to reflect on this enormous step toward breaching the nation's racial divide. But after the speeches and celebrations, the Obama administration was faced with the daunting task of dealing with the many serious problems facing the United States. First and foremost was the failing economy. Obama addressed the crisis by pushing for the American Recovery and Reinvestment Act of 2009. This unprecedented stimulus package, passed in Obama's second month in office, was an attempt to jump-start the economy by spending more than $700 billion dollars on education, health care, infrastructure, unemployment benefits, and other programs.

The next major legislative goal of the Obama administration was passage of a comprehensive health care reform bill. After almost a year of contentious debate in Congress, Obama signed into law the Affordable Health Care for America Act on March 23, 2010. The sweeping law guaranteed access to health insurance to an estimated 30 million Americans.

As Obama's presidency began its second year, he was still occupied with an array of pressing issues, including decreasing a high unemployment rate, managing wars in Iraq and Afghanistan, fighting international terrorism, combating a global climate change, reducing America's dependence on oil, and restoring damaged relations with foreign leaders. In addition, in spring 2010, his administration was forced to deal with an unexpected crisis when an oil rig exploded in the Gulf of Mexico, precipitating the greatest environmental disaster in American history. With so many difficulties to address on so many different fronts, Obama's presidency promised to be one of the most challenging of the modern era.

Further Reading

Change We Can Believe In: Barack Obama's Plan to Renew America's Promise. New York: Three Rivers Press, 2008.

Ifill, Gwen. *The Breakthrough: Politics and Race in the Age of Obama.* New York: Doubleday, 2009.

Obama, Barack. *The Audacity of Hope: Thoughts on Reclaiming the American Dream.* New York: Crown Publishers, 2006.

———. *Dreams from My Father: A Story of Race and Inheritance.* New York: Times Books, 1995.

Sabato, Larry J., ed. *The Year of Obama: How Barack Obama Won the White House.* Boston, Mass.: Longman, 2009.

Street, Paul. *Barack Obama and the Future of American Politics.* Boulder, Colo.: Paradigm Publishers, 2009.

O'Hara, James
(James Edward O'Hara)
(1844–1905) *U.S. congressional representative from North Carolina*

James O'Hara was the second African American to represent North Carolina in Congress. He was a talented speaker and able politician, and his persistence and assertiveness made him a role model for freedmen in his home state and a target for conservative whites seeking to keep African Americans "in their place."

O'Hara was born on February 26, 1844, in New York City. His father was an Irish merchant and his mother was a free black from the West Indies; their first names are unknown. At age six, he moved with his parents to the Danish West Indies (modern U.S. Virgin Islands) where he grew up. At age 18, he settled in eastern North Carolina, at the time occupied by the Union Army, and the following year he began teaching in freedmen's schools in New Bern and Goldsboro. In 1864, he married Ann Marie Harris; they had no children and were separated two years later. In 1869, the same year he married Elizabeth Harris, with whom he had one child, he moved to Washington, D.C., to work as a clerk in the U.S. Treasury Department while studying law at Howard University.

O'Hara began dabbling in politics in 1868, when he served as a clerk at the state constitutional convention. He also clerked during the first session of the state legislature the following year. Upon returning to North Carolina in 1872 and opening a law office in Enfield, Halifax County, he became actively involved in the Republican Party. That same year, he was appointed county attorney, and in 1874 he was elected chairman of the county board of commissioners. For the next four years, he worked to provide public education and poor relief to the county's indigent freedmen. His efforts drew fire from conservative whites, who succeeded in bringing him and an associate to trial on charges of corruption. Although the charges appeared to be politically motivated, he pleaded nolo contendere and agreed to reimburse the county for certain expenditures he had authorized. He left office in 1878 and spent the next five years concentrating on his law practice. During this period, he led a statewide fight against prohibition and vigorously opposed the patronage policies of state Republicans, who denied most party jobs and nominations to African Americans.

Meanwhile, O'Hara continued to pursue the political office he most wanted, a seat in the U.S. Congress representing the so-called Black Second District, in which African Americans constituted a majority. Denied the Republican nomination in 1874 and 1876, he secured it in 1878, only to have the party endorse a different candidate three weeks before the election. Undaunted, he ran as an independent; he would have won had not Democrat-controlled electoral boards in three counties thrown out a number of ballots naming him. In 1880, he failed again to gain the party's nomination. Finally, in 1882, on his fifth try for the office, he was elected to the House of Representatives. O'Hara served on the committee on mines and mining and the committee on expenditures on public buildings; however, most of his efforts were devoted to expanding and securing the civil rights of African Americans. When in 1883 the Supreme Court nullified the Civil Rights Act of 1875, which prohibited racial discrimination in places of public accommodation, he proposed a constitutional amendment to bar such discrimination. He also worked to ban racial discrimination in the District of Columbia and on railroad passenger cars operating within the purview of the Interstate Commerce Act of 1884. Other bills of his attempted to reimburse investors in the failed Freedmen's Savings and Trust Company, in which thousands of freedmen had deposited their meager savings in the belief that it was backed by the federal government, as well as to provide federal funding for public education. But, being a black Republican in a Congress controlled by white Democrats, he was rarely successful. He did manage, however, to gain passage for several bills providing economic relief for eastern North Carolina.

Reelected in 1884, O'Hara failed in his bid for a third term in 1886. He returned to Enfield where he published a newspaper and practiced law. Although he never held elective office again, he remained active in state politics and party affairs for the rest of his life. In 1890, he moved to New Bern where he practiced law until his death on September 15, 1905.

Further Reading

Anderson, Eric. *Race and Politics in North Carolina, 1872–1901: The Black Second.* Baton Rouge: Louisiana State University Press, 1981.

Biographical Directory of the United States Congress. "O'Hara, James Edward, 1844–1905." Available online. URL: http://bioguide.congress.gov/scripts/biodisplay.pl?index=0000054. Downloaded April 5, 2009.

Black Americans in Congress. "James Edward O'Hara." Available online. URL: http://baic.house.gov/member-profiles/profile.html?intID=10. Downloaded April 5, 2009.

Clay, William L. *Just Permanent Interests: Black Americans in Congress, 1870–1992.* New York: Amistad Press, 1993.

Rabinowitz, Howard N., ed. *Southern Black Leaders of the Reconstruction Era.* Urbana: University of Illinois Press, 1982.

O'Leary, Hazel
(Hazel Rollins O'Leary)
(1937–) *U.S. secretary of energy*

In 1993, Hazel O'Leary was one of four African Americans named to cabinet-level positions by President Bill Clinton. Her record as an administrator was marred by a scandal involving excessive travel expenses.

O'Leary was born Hazel Reid on May 17, 1937, in Newport News, Virginia. Her parents, Russell and Hazel, were physicians. They divorced when Reid was 18 months old, and she was raised by her father and her stepmother, Mattie, a schoolteacher. She attended a high school for the performing arts in Newark, New Jersey, where she boarded with an aunt. Upon graduating in 1955, she enrolled in Fisk University and received a B.A. in history four years later. In 1959, she married Carl Rollins, with whom she had one child. She returned with her husband to Newark, and in 1966 she received a J.D. from the Rutgers University School of Law. The following year, she passed the New Jersey bar examination and became an assistant prosecutor for Essex County. Over the next seven years, she became an assistant state attorney general, divorced her husband, and moved to Washington, D.C., to become a partner in Coopers and Lybrand, an accounting firm.

Reid first went to work for the federal government in 1974, when she was named director of the Federal Energy Administration's Office of Consumer Affairs. Two years later, she became the general counsel for the Community Services Administration. In 1977, she returned to the FEA as assistant administrator for conservation and environment. The following year, the FEA was incorporated into the new Department of Energy, and she was appointed director of the DOE's Economic Regulatory Administration, which oversaw the petroleum, natural gas, and electric industries.

In 1980, she married John O'Leary, a DOE deputy secretary. The following year, she and her husband formed their own energy consulting firm; she served as vice president and general counsel. In 1989, two years after her husband's death, she closed the firm and joined the Northern States Power Company as executive vice president for corporate affairs. In this position, she oversaw the company's activities regarding environmental policy, lobbying, public relations, and personnel.

When Bill Clinton was elected president in 1992, he was pressured by African Americans to appoint a number of blacks to important posts in his administration. To this end, he named four African Americans to his cabinet, one of them being O'Leary. Clinton admitted that she had been chosen partly because she was a black female. However, her knowledge of the energy industry and her background as a high-level administrator, both in and out of government, made her exceptionally qualified for the position.

O'Leary took over as DOE secretary in 1993. For the next four years, she worked to reform U.S. energy policy. She promoted the increased use of natural gas over other fossil fuels because it is cleaner, but at the same time she called for the increased use of nuclear power because it lessened U.S. reliance on foreign energy sources. She also stressed the need to conserve energy of all types, and to clean up nuclear waste in an environmentally safe manner. She drew praise for declassifying government policies and practices regarding the disposal of nuclear waste resulting from U.S. weapons programs. As secretary, she was successful at balancing the needs and demands of the various competing energy industries while promoting safety and conservation.

Despite her accomplishments, O'Leary was forced to resign in 1997. As secretary, she had made more than 100 overseas trips at government expense, usually with a large entourage of staffers and industry executives. Critics charged that she spent more time out of the country than in it, and her travel expenses greatly exceeded the DOE's budget for travel and entertainment. A Senate investigation cleared her of criminal wrongdoing, but the scandal crippled her effectiveness as the chief spokesperson for U.S. energy policy.

After leaving office, O'Leary opened another energy consulting firm. In 2000, she joined Blaylock & Partners, the nation's largest minority-owned investment bank, as its chief operating officer. O'Leary was named president of Fisk University in Nashville, Tennessee, in 2004.

Further Reading

Haywood, Richette L. "Secretary Hazel O'Leary: Bright, Charming, Tough." *Ebony* 50 (February 1995): 94–100.

Kearney, Janis F. "O'Leary, Hazel." In *African American National Biography*, vol. 6, edited by Henry Louis Gates, Jr., and Evelyn Brooks Higginbotham. New York: Oxford University Press, 2008, pp. 184–186.

Owens, Major
(Major Robert Odell Owens)
(1936–   )   *U.S. congressional representative from New York*

Major Owens was best known as Congress's "rap poet." The outspoken congressman wrote a number of rap poems expressing his disgust with various governmental and societal outrages, and more than a dozen were published in the *Congressional Record*. When not rhyming, he focused on improving education and preventing child abuse.

Owens was born on June 28, 1936, in Memphis, Tennessee, to Ezekial and Edna Owens. After graduating from high school, he enrolled in Morehouse College and received a B.A. in mathematics in 1956. The following year, he received an M.S. in library science from Atlanta University in 1957, and in 1958 he moved to New York City to work for the Brooklyn Public Library. Over the next eight years, he specialized in library education and information development. He also served for several years as the library's community coordinator. In 1966, he left the library to become executive director of the Brownsville Community Council.

Owens became involved in the Civil Rights movement shortly after moving to New York City. This involvement led him into local politics, and he became active in the affairs of the Democratic Party. In 1964, he was tapped to chair the Brooklyn Congress of Racial Equality and to serve as vice president of the Metropolitan Council on Housing. In 1968, he was appointed chairman of the city's community development agency, and in this capacity he administered the city's programs for fighting poverty.

In 1973, Owens was elected to the New York state senate. During his eight years in the senate, he championed civil rights and government reform. He also pushed for increased state funding of public and school libraries. He was particularly interested in getting librarians and educators to work together to develop state-of-the-art information delivery services. As a senator, he served on the governor's commission on libraries and information sciences.

In 1982, Owens declared his candidacy for the congressional seat being vacated by SHIRLEY CHISHOLM. The outspoken Owens had angered a number of state Democrats by denouncing them for foot-dragging on efforts to reform state government, and they denied him their support during his campaign. He managed to eke out a narrow victory in the election when it was disclosed that his opponent had connections to organized crime. He took his seat in 1983 and was appointed to the committees on education/labor and government operations.

As a congressman, Owens focused on issues pertaining to education. In his capacity as chairman of the subcommittee on select education and civil rights, he wrote the act that reorganized the Office of Educational Research and Improvement. He also advocated reducing the military budget, especially after the cold war ended, and spending the savings on education. Not surprisingly, many of his educational projects include increased federal funding for libraries, and he urged librarians across the country to form their own special interest group in order to gain more money for libraries via political action.

Owens's interest as a congressman was not confined to education. He fought for passage of the Child Abuse Prevention Challenge Grants Reauthorization Act, which protected federal funding for child abuse prevention programs. He played a major role in the enactment of the Americans with Disabilities Act, which mandates equal access in a number of areas for the physically disabled, and the Domestic Volunteer Service Act, which breathed new life into a number of national volunteer service programs. He also worked to increase the minimum wage, preserve the Occupational Safety and Health Administration, and defend the political rights of labor unions.

In 2004, Owens was reelected to a 12th term. Choosing not to seek another term in 2006, Owens retired from politics. Late that year, he accepted a post as a distinguished visiting scholar at the John W. Kluge Center at the Library of Congress. In 2009, Owens also joined the Dubois-Bunche Center for Public Policy at Medgar Evers College in New York City.

Further Reading
Biographical Directory of the United States Congress. "Owens, Major Robert Odell, 1936– ." Available online. URL: http://bioguide.congress.gov/scripts/biodisplay.pl?index=0000159. Downloaded April 11, 2009.

Black Americans in Congress. "Major Robert Odell Owens." Available online. URL: http://baic.house.gov/member-profiles/profile.html?intID=58. Downloaded April 10, 2009.

Clay, William L. *Just Permanent Interests: Black Americans in Congress, 1870–1992.* New York: Amistad Press, 1993.

P

Paige, Rod
(Roderick Raynor Paige)
(1933–   ) *U.S. secretary of education*

As the first African-American secretary of the Department of Education, Rod Paige helped oversee sweeping changes in education policy during the first term of the administration of President George W. Bush. Born on June 17, 1933, Paige grew up in Monticello, Mississippi. His father was a school principal and his mother was a librarian. Both stressed the importance of an education and instilled in him a passion to succeed.

Paige won an athletic scholarship to Jackson State University, a historically black institution in Jackson, Mississippi. After graduation, he became the university's football coach. While coaching, Paige began studying physical education at Indiana University, Bloomington. He earned a master's degree in 1964 and a doctoral degree in 1969.

After coaching at the University of Cincinnati, Paige was named the football coach and athletic director of Texas Southern University in Houston in 1984. He later became the dean of its college of education, serving in that post for 10 years. In 1989, Paige was elected to a seat on Houston's board of education. The city's school system was then the seventh largest in the United States. The

board appointed Paige the superintendent of schools in 1994.

Paige set about overhauling the entire school system. His education philosophy was described in a document titled "A Declaration of Beliefs and Visions." It called for decentralizing the school distinct, demanding more accountability from administrators and teachers, and developing a core curriculum. Paige also initiated the Peer Examination, Evaluation, and Redesign (PEER) program. Through PEER, Paige consulted with top businesses leaders for their ideas on how to improve Houston's schools. During his tenure as superintendent, Paige promoted incentive pay for teachers, hiring private companies to handle food preparation and other services, and the creation of special schools for violent students. A member of the Republican Party, Paige also endorsed the proposed Republican reform of providing tax-subsidized vouchers to help students in failing public schools enroll in private institutions.

Following the 2000 presidential election, president-elect George W. Bush, a longtime friend of Paige, asked him to head the Department of Education. In his formal nomination of Paige, Bush stated that he wanted the secretary to be "someone who is a reformer and someone who had a record of results." Houston's schools claimed that, under Paige's leadership, its students' test scores had risen by 20 percent and the system's dropout rate had been cut in half.

Once in Washington, D.C., Paige focused on implementing the educational policies set out in the No Child Left Behind Act (NCLB) of 2001. Echoing many of Paige's ideas, the federal law called for state and district funding to be tied to school performance as demonstrated by students' scores on standardized tests. The act proved controversial in education circles. Proponents claimed it applied research-based methods of identifying and improving failing schools. Detractors said it encouraged teachers to "teach to the test" and schools to fudge the numbers to ensure their funding was not reduced.

Paige also ran into controversy in early 2003 when the Texas Education Agency discovered that the dropout rate in Houston city schools was greatly underreported. Local and national media also found that at least one high school had knowing falsified the data it provided to district and state agencies. Paige claimed these charges did not diminish his record as school superintendent in Houston. He told the *New York Times*, "I wouldn't doubt that it a system as large as Houston, where you have 300 schools . . . that you're going to have some problems."

Paige was also criticized for a comment he made during a gathering of governors in February 2004. In a speech, he called the National Education Association, the United States' largest teacher's union, a "terrorist organization." Amid calls for his resignation, Paige acknowledged he had used a "poor choice of words" but did not apologize to the union.

In November 15, 2004, Paige announced his resignation and emphasized that it was his decision to leave the administration. He then served as a Public Policy Scholar at the Woodrow Wilson International Center for Scholars in Washington, D.C. In 2006, Paige became the cofounder and chairman of the Chartwell Education Group, a consulting firm focusing on education in the United States and abroad.

Further Reading

Bowers, Ryan Reid. "Rod Paige." In *African American National Biography*, vol. 4, edited by Henry Louis Gates, Jr., and Evelyn Brooks Higginbotham. New York: Oxford University Press, 2008, pp. 228–229.

Paige, Rod. *The War Against Hope: How Teachers' Unions Hurt Children, Hinder Teachers, and Endanger Public Education*. Nashville, Tenn.: Thomas Nelson, 2007.

Schemo, Diana Jean. "Secretary of Education Will Leave Bush Cabinet." *New York Times*, November 13, 2004. Available online. URL: http://www.nytimes.com/2004/11/13/politics/13paige.html?scp=12&sq=&st=nyt. Downloaded May 6, 2009.

Paterson, David

(David A. Paterson)
(1954–   ) *governor of New York*

In 2006, David Paterson became the first African-American governor of New York, when Governor Eliot Spitzer abruptly resigned amid a sex scandal.

Born on May 20, 1954, in New York City, David Paterson was the son of Basil Paterson, a labor lawyer prominent in New York politics. At various times, Basil Paterson served as a deputy mayor, state senator, and secretary of state of New York. When David Paterson was an infant, he fell ill with an infection that destroyed his sight in his left eye and left his vision seriously impaired in his right. Looking for a school that would not segregate Paterson from sighted students, his parents moved to Hempstead, New York. According to Paterson, the taunts of his classmates because of his disability instilled in him a deep desire to succeed.

After completing high school in three years, Paterson enrolled in Columbia University, where he received a degree in history in 1977. Paterson graduated from Hofstra Law School five years later. He worked in the district attorney's office of Queen's County before deciding to follow in his father's footsteps by delving into politics. In 1985, Paterson was elected to the New York State senate from New York City's 30th district, which includes Harlem. At 31, he became the youngest state senator in New York history.

During his 21-year tenure in the senate, Paterson became known as a reformer. A liberal Democrat, he pushed for legislation to expand voting rights, reduce domestic violence, increase education funding, and promote greater transparency in government. Paterson was also known for his intelligence and quick wit, which helped him get along with people across the political spectrum. In 2002, Paterson was unanimously elected senate minority leader, the first nonwhite so honored.

Four years later, Paterson surprised many political insiders by deciding to run for lieutenant governor on the ticket of New York attorney general Eliot Spitzer. Lieutenant governors traditionally held little power, but Paterson hoped to have more say in policy matters than most who had had the job. The hard-driving Spitzer valued Paterson's track record and affability and expected that Paterson could play a "good cop" role in dealing with the legislature.

Spitzer and Paterson won their election in November 2006. But Paterson would serve as lieutenant governor for just over a year. In March 2008, the *New York Times* and other news outlets reported that Spitzer had repeatedly visited prostitutes. When he was forced to resign, Paterson became the new governor of New York. He was not only the first African American in that position. He was also the second legally blind person to serve as a governor in the United States.

The day after his inauguration, Paterson appeared before the press and revealed that both he and his wife, Michelle Paige Paterson, had had extramarital affairs in the past. His forthright confession kept his adultery from becoming a career-destroying scandal.

During his first few months in office, Paterson remained a popular figure. However, he fell into trouble when he had to select someone to take over the U.S. Senate seat vacated by Hillary Clinton, who was named secretary of state by President-elect BARACK OBAMA. Paterson seemed to favor Caroline Kennedy, but the idea drew strong criticism. Many charged that she was being considered not because of her qualifications but because of her fame as the daughter of President John F. Kennedy. For weeks, Paterson vacillated, seemingly unable to make up his mind about the senate appointment. Only after Kennedy abruptly took her name out of the running did Paterson finally choose Representative Kirsten Gillibrand as Clinton's replacement. In the end, the affair was a substantial blow to Paterson's credibility by making him appear disorganized and unfocused.

A severe economic downturn in late 2008 also damaged the new governor's reputation. With decreasing tax revenues, he pushed for a punishing new budget that coupled tax increases and service cuts, especially in health care and education. Outrage over Paterson's plans eroded much of his support, particularly in the African-American community. By March 2009, his approval rating had fallen to 26 percent.

Despite his detractors, Paterson continued to promote significant changes in New York State policies. A strong supporter of gay rights, he pushed for legislation that would legalize same-sex marriage in the state. Paterson also proposed a cap on property taxes.

Fueled by anger over a major budget crisis and by Paterson's increasingly stormy relationship with the state legislature, the public continued to sour on Paterson—so much so that President Barack Obama asked him to give up his reelection bid. The governor, however, refused and declared his candidacy on February 20, 2010. In less than a week, he withdrew from the race. Allegations had surfaced that Paterson had pressured the girlfriend of one of his aides into keeping quiet about the aide's domestic abuse. In addition to dealing with massive budget problems as a lame duck governor, Paterson subsequently faced an investigation into his conduct by New York attorney General Andrew Cuomo, who had announced his own run for the governorship. In March 2010, the Commission on Public Integrity also charged that Paterson had testified falsely while under oath about a gift he had received of tickets to the 2009 World Series.

Further Reading

"David A. Paterson." *New York Times.* Available online. URL: http://topics.nytimes.com/top/reference/timestopics/people/p/david_a_paterson/index.html. Downloaded May 24, 2009.

"Governor David A. Paterson: Biography." New York State Web Site. Available online. URL: http://www.ny.gov/governor/bio/index.html. Downloaded May 24, 2009.

Smith, Chris. "Eliot's Problem Child." *New York*, March 1, 2009. Available online. URL: http://nymag.com/news/politics/citypolitic/55006. Downloaded May 23, 2009.

Patrick, Deval
(Deval L. Patrick)
(1956–   ) *governor of Massachusetts*

In 2006, the voters of Massachusetts chose Deval Patrick to be the governor their state. He was the second African American ever elected to a governorship. The first, DOUG WILDER of Virginia, was elected in 1989.

Patrick was born on July 31, 1956, in a poor area of Chicago, Illinois. His father abandoned his family when he was still a boy. Getting by on welfare, Patrick's family lived in an apartment in the Robert Taylor housing project, in which he, his mother, and his sister shared a bedroom. One of his earliest memories was of his mother taking him to hear Martin Luther King, Jr., give a speech at a Chicago park.

Despite his impoverished background, Patrick was an excellent student. A teacher recommended him to A Better Chance, a charitable organization that sends promising students to leading private schools. Patrick received a scholarship to Milton Academy, an elite preparatory boarding school near Boston, Massachusetts. While attending Milton, he made pocket money by delivering newspapers. Patrick later bought a house along his old paper route, where his mother and grandmother lived until their deaths.

Patrick attended Harvard University, becoming the first person in his family to go to college. Graduating in 1978, he spent a year in Africa, working for a youth training project sponsored by the United Nations. When Patrick returned to the United States, he enrolled in Harvard Law School, where he was president of the Legal Aid Bureau, a student-run organization that provided legal services.

After a year as a law clerk, Patrick took a job with the NAACP Legal Defense Fund in 1983. There, he worked on several voting rights cases, including a lawsuit brought against Arkansas for discriminatory election practices. While working on a settlement, Patrick got to know Bill Clinton, who was then Arkansas's governor. During his years at the NAACP, Patrick also met labor and employment lawyer Diane Bemus. Patrick and Bemus married and had two children.

In 1986, Patrick became a partner at Hill & Barlow, a Boston law firm. Six years later, President Bill Clinton asked Patrick to serve as the assistant U.S. attorney general for civil rights. In this post, he worked to prosecute cases involving employment discrimination and violence at abortion clinics. He also led an investigation into church burnings in the South during the mid-1990s.

Patrick returned to private practice in 1997. At the Boston firm of Berry & Howard, he served as the first chairperson of Texaco's Equality and Fairness Task Force, which was established as a result of a settlement in a race discrimination case. Texaco subsequently hired Patrick as a vice president in charge of global legal affairs. Starting in 2000, Patrick later spent six years as vice president and general counsel for Coca-Cola.

In 2005, Patrick announced that he was running for governor of Massachusetts. From the beginning, he was an underdog in the race. He had never held political office or even run for one. Many also wondered how his race would affect his candidacy. The population of Massachusetts was only 7 percent black, so Patrick could not expect a broad base of African-American support.

As a candidate outside the state's political establishment, Patrick opted to run a lengthy grassroots campaign, modeled on that of former Massachusetts governor Michael Dukakis. Patrick projected an infectious openness and optimism as he tried to appeal to a broad spectrum of voters with what he called the "politics of hope." If elected, he promised to establish all-day kindergartens and to fight crime by hiring more police officers. His message soon began to resonate with voters. He easily won the Democratic primary. Pitted against the popular Republican lieutenant governor Kerry Healey in the general election, Patrick won in a landslide with 56 percent of the vote to Healey's 37 percent.

Patrick was sworn in on January 4, 2007. Almost immediately, he made a series of missteps that would dog him his entire first term. Voters were angered by reports that he had spent $30,000 of taxpayer's money to decorate his office, with $12,000 going for drapes alone. He was also castigated for upgrading his official car to a Cadillac for an additional cost of $20,000. Patrick's ethics came under fire when it was reported that he had spoken with his friend Robert Rubin, the former treasury secretary who was then chairman of Citigroup, about making a deal with the controversial mortgage lender Ameriquest, on whose board Patrick had once served. Critics charged that it was inappropriate for a sitting governor to be so entangled in the business dealings of two large financial institutions.

An economic downturn also threatened Patrick's ambitious plans to hire more police and increase access to education and health care. As a solution, he launched a plan to allow three casinos to operate in Massachusetts. The legislature, however, overwhelmingly voted against this measure, which revealed a growing animosity between state lawmakers and the governor. In early 2009, they also butted heads over a proposed sales tax hike, which Patrick threatened to veto if passed.

During the 2008 presidential election, Patrick was an enthusiastic supporter of BARACK OBAMA. He also defended Obama from charges that the candidate had plagiarized a stump speech Patrick gave during his 2006 gubernatorial campaign. Given Patrick's decreasing approval numbers, many political insiders expected him to join Obama's administration after the election, perhaps in the attorney general post that eventually went to ERIC HOLDER. Instead, Patrick remained in Massachusetts. On November 2, 2010, he won his bid for reelection to a second term.

Further Reading

Cooper, Kenneth J. "Gov. Deval L. Patrick Takes Charge: Massachusetts' Chief Executive Makes History and Begins to Chart His Own Course." *Ebony* 62 (March 2007): 155–159.

Governor Deval Patrick, Official Web Site. Available online. URL: http://www.mass.gov/?pageID=gov3 utilities&sid=Agov3&U=Agov3_Deval_Patrick_ welcome_msg. Downloaded May 23, 2009.

Ifill, Gwen. *The Breakthrough: Politics and Race in the Age of Obama.* New York: Doubleday, 2009.

Payne, Donald

(Donald Milford Payne)
(1934–   ) *U.S. congressional representative from New Jersey*

Payne was the first African American to be elected to Congress from New Jersey. A former educator, he championed programs that promoted literacy and education reform.

Payne was born on July 16, 1934, in Newark, New Jersey. His father, William, was a dockworker, and his mother, Norma, was a homemaker. He finished high school in 1952 and received a B.A. in social studies from Seton Hall University in 1957. For the next seven years, he taught English and social studies in the Newark public school system. In 1958, he married Hazel Johnson, with whom he had three children. She died of cancer in 1963; in order to support himself and his children, the following year he gave up teaching to sell life insurance. He also did volunteer work with the Young Men's Christian Association, and in 1970 he was elected its national president. After serving in this position for three years, he was named chairman of its World Refugee and Rehabilitation Committee, and over the next eight years he traveled to more than 80 countries. In 1973, he became a vice president of Urban Data Systems in Newark, a position he held for 16 years.

Payne became involved in politics in 1954 while he was in college. His brother, William, was running for local office, and Payne served as manager of his successful campaign. He was too busy to pay much attention to politics again until the late 1960s, when he helped revitalize the Democratic Party's organization in Newark's South Ward. He served as chairman of the organization from 1970 until 1988 and played a key role getting SHARPE JAMES elected, then reelected, mayor of Newark. In 1972, Payne was elected to the Essex County Board of Chosen Freeholders, in effect the county board of supervisors. Six years later, the board named him its director, thus giving him primary responsibility for administering the county budget.

In 1982, Payne resigned as board director to run for the U.S. Congress. After being defeated in the primary by longtime incumbent Peter Rodino, he ran successfully for a seat on the Newark municipal council. He lost a second time to Rodino in 1986, but in 1988 Rodino announced his retirement effective at the end of his term, and

Donald Payne was the first African American to represent New Jersey in Congress. *(Donald M. Payne)*

this time Payne's campaign was successful. He took his seat in Congress in 1989 and was assigned to the committees on education/labor, foreign affairs, and government operations.

As a congressman, Payne focused on establishing programs to enhance public education. He played a key role in the passage of a number of education bills, including the Goals 2000 school-improvement initiative, the School-to-Work Opportunities Act, the National Service Act, and the Student Loan Act. He also helped establish the National Literacy Institute and worked to restore federal funding for Head Start, Summer Jobs for Youths, and Pell Grants, which provide college loans. He also sponsored the legislation that established National Literacy Day in 1990.

In terms of foreign affairs, Payne has worked to restore human rights in Africa and China. He coordinated the efforts of several pharmaceutical companies to donate millions of dollars of medical supplies to refugees in Somalia. He has headed presidential and congressional fact-finding commissions to refugee camps in the Balkans and Rwanda.

In 1995, Payne was elected to a one-year term as chair of the Congressional Black Caucus. Beginning in 2003, he served two consecutive terms as the Congressional delegate to the United Nations. Payne was reelected to his 12th congressional term in 2010.

Further Reading

Biographical Directory of the United States Congress. "Payne, Donald Milford, 1934– ." Available online. URL: http://bioguide.congress.gov/scripts/biodisplay.pl?index=P000149. Downloaded April 9, 2009.

Cheers, D. Michael. "Donald Payne: New Jersey's First Black Congressman." *Ebony* 44 (May 1989): 92.

Clay, William L. *Just Permanent Interests: Black Americans in Congress, 1870–1992.* New York: Amistad Press, 1993.

Congressman Donald M. Payne, Official Web Site. Available online. URL: http://www.house.gov/payne. Downloaded April 11, 2009.

Perry, Carrie
(Carrie Saxon, Carrie Saxon Perry)
(1931–   ) *mayor of Hartford, Connecticut*

Carrie Perry was the first African-American woman to serve as mayor of a New England city. She also served four terms in the lower house of the Connecticut state assembly.

Perry was born Carrie Saxon on August 10, 1931, in Hartford, Connecticut. She was raised by her mother, Mabel, and her maternal grandmother. After graduating from high school in 1949, she enrolled in Howard University and received a B.S. in political science four years later. She studied law at Howard Law School for two years, and then in 1955 she returned to Hartford. For the next 20 years, she did social work for the state of Connecticut. In this capacity, she held a number of positions, including assistant administrator for the Community Renewal Team of Greater Hartford and executive director of Amistad House. In 1955, she married James Perry, with whom she had one child; they later divorced.

As a social worker, Perry was faced with the constant reality that her clients had too many needs to fill with the resources she had at hand. She attempted to remedy this situation by lobbying state and local officials to increase funding for social outreach programs. Although her lobbying had some effect, she determined that the best way to get more funding was to get involved personally in the political process. In 1976, she declared her candidacy for a seat in the Connecticut state legislature. Despite her total lack of experience in politics and a lack of support from the Democratic Party, to which she belonged, she ran a tough race and narrowly lost. Undaunted, she tried again in 1980, and this time she won a narrow victory.

Perry's victory shocked the local political pundits. They were shocked a second time when, as a freshman legislator, she was appointed assistant majority leader of the lower house. Despite her lack of experience, she learned quickly how to play the political game. She got herself appointed chairwoman of the House subcommittee on bonding and then used her influence to obtain enough funding to rehabilitate several poor neighborhoods along Hartford's riverfront. She won set-asides for minority contractors in a number of state contracts. She also convinced the state to divest itself of its investments in South Africa so long as apartheid held sway in that country. She was reelected to three additional terms in the Connecticut House.

In 1987, Perry decided that she could best achieve her political goals by serving as mayor of Hartford. Her hometown had a large but silent minority population, as well as the usual urban problems of high crime and rundown neighborhoods, yet the local political establishment seemed unable and unwilling to tackle the problems. She declared her candidacy for the post that same year. This time she had the full support of the Democratic Party as well as the experience to run an aggressive campaign, and she easily defeated her Republican challenger in the general election. As mayor, she established after-school and day-care programs, improved public housing, and established a civilian review board to investigate charges of police brutality. She also established Operation Break, a job training program for residents of public housing.

Perry was less successful at reforming the school system, which was in woeful shape, and at recruiting new businesses into the city. This last failure contributed to her downfall. The country had entered into a major recession just as she took office, and the insurance companies that call Hartford home were hit particularly hard. She was unable to cope with the massive layoffs that followed or to reverse the economic decline, and this failure doomed her bid for reelection in 1991.

Perry returned to private life following the expiration of her term in 1992. She remained active in the affairs of the local Democratic Party. She also served on the board of directors of Efficacy, a nonprofit think tank and advocacy group that favors the legalization and regulation of drugs. She supports legalization on the grounds that, like Prohibition in the early 20th century, the "war against drugs" cannot be won, and that outlawing drugs serves only to promote violence and criminal behavior.

Further Reading

Hine, Darlene Clark, ed. *Black Women in America: An Historical Encyclopedia*, 2 vols. Brooklyn, N.Y.: Carlson Publishing Co., 1993.

Smith, Jessie Carney, ed. *Notable Black American Women*. Detroit: Gale Research, 1992.

Pinchback, P. B. S.
(Pinckney Benton Stewart Pinchback)
(1837–1921) *governor of Louisiana*

P. B. S. Pinchback was the first African American to serve as governor of any state. He was also the first person to be elected to both houses of the

U.S. Congress without being permitted to take his seat in either body.

Pinchback was born on May 10, 1837, in Macon, Georgia. His father, William Pinchback, owned plantations in Mississippi, Georgia, and Virginia. His mother, Eliza Stewart, was a former slave of William Pinchback's whom he had taken to Philadelphia, Pennsylvania, and set free shortly before Pinchback's birth. At age 10, he was sent to Cincinnati, Ohio, to get an education. His schooling was cut short the following year when his father died and he was refused any financial support from his father's relatives. To support himself and his mother and siblings, he went to work as a cabin boy on an Ohio canal boat. Several years later, he became a steward on a Mississippi riverboat. In 1860, he married Nina Hawthorne, with whom he had six children.

In 1862, Pinchback made his way to New Orleans, Louisiana, shortly after it had been captured by Union forces. He enlisted in the Union army as a private but was soon promoted to captain and assigned to recruit black soldiers for a unit of the Corps d'Afrique that was later renamed the 74th U.S. Colored Infantry Regiment. In 1863, he resigned his commission because the army discriminated against its African-American troops. He was persuaded to reenlist by General Nathaniel Banks, who wanted him to raise a black cavalry company, but he resigned again when Banks refused to restore him to his former rank.

Pinchback's political career began in 1863, shortly after he left the army. He began speaking at political rallies, declaring that African Americans should not be drafted unless they were also given the right to vote. When the Civil War ended, he went to Alabama to work for the establishment of public schools for blacks. Returning to New Orleans in 1867, he joined the Republican Party and became a member of its state executive committee. The following year, he served as a delegate to the state constitutional convention, where he was a vocal proponent of state-funded education, civil rights for freedmen, and voting

P. B. S. Pinchback *(shown in middle to the left of Frederick Douglass)* was the first African American to serve as a state governor. *(Library of Congress)*

rights for black men. The eloquent speeches he gave at this convention, as well as the provision he wrote into the constitution prohibiting racial discrimination in places of public accommodation, allowed him to emerge from the convention as one of Louisiana's leading black politicians.

In 1868, Pinchback was elected to the state senate. Over the next three years, he worked to improve the political and economic situation of freedmen while demonstrating a talent for compromise that impressed his white colleagues. As a result, in 1871 he was elected president pro tempore of the senate. He became lieutenant governor later that year when the incumbent died in office, and in 1872 he took over as acting governor when the new incumbent was impeached and removed from office.

Pinchback turned down the Republican nomination for governor in 1872 in the interest of party unity. As his reward, the party arranged for him to be elected to Louisiana's at-large seat in the U.S. House of Representatives. That election was contested by his white Democrat opponent, however, and while the outcome was pending he was elected by the state legislature to the U.S. Senate (prior to ratification of the Seventeenth Amendment in 1913, senators were elected by the state legislatures, not by the voters at large). This outcome was contested, too; ultimately, both the House and the Senate denied him a seat in Congress.

Pinchback continued to serve in the state senate until 1882. Although he was for the most part a devoted Republican, his true interest lay in obtaining better opportunities for freedmen. In 1877, when the newly elected Democratic governor promised to improve educational facilities for African Americans, Pinchback gave him his support, and in return was appointed to the state board of education. Two years later, as a delegate to the state's constitutional convention, he succeeded in including a provision for establishing Southern University as an all-black college.

Pinchback retired from politics in 1882, five years after the end of Reconstruction greatly diminished the prospects for African-American politicians. He concentrated on his business ventures, which included a Mississippi riverboat operation, a cotton mill, a brokerage and commission house, and a newspaper. From 1882 to 1886, he served as the U.S. Treasury Department's surveyor of customs for the port of New Orleans while earning a law degree from Straight University. In 1892, he moved to New York City where he worked as a U.S. marshal. In 1895, he moved to Washington, D.C., to practice law. He died there on December 21, 1921.

Further Reading

Haskins, James. *The First Black Governor, Pinckney Benton Stewart Pinchback.* Trenton, N.J.: Africa World Press, 1996.

Jackson, Eric R. "Pinchback, P. B. S." In *African American National Biography,* vol. 6, edited by Henry Louis Gates, Jr., and Evelyn Brooks Higginbotham. New York: Oxford University Press, 2008, pp. 354–356.

Vincent, Charles. *Black Legislators in Louisiana during Reconstruction.* Baton Rouge: Louisiana State University Press, 1976.

Powell, Adam Clayton, Jr.

(1908–1972) *U.S. congressional representative from New York*

Adam Clayton Powell, Jr., was the most powerful and influential African-American political leader of his day. As the first black city councilman for New York City and the first black congressman from New York State, he gained passage of dozens of bills that markedly improved life for African Americans across the country. At the same time, he was one of the most perplexing politicians of any race ever to hold elective office in the United States. While his successes thrilled his supporters and infuriated his enemies, his failures puzzled them all.

Powell was born on November 29, 1908, in New Haven, Connecticut. His father, Adam, Sr., was a minister, and his mother, Mattie, was a homemaker. As an infant, he moved with his family to New York City when his father took over as pastor of Abyssinian Baptist Church, one of the most prominent black churches in the nation. In 1923, his family and the church moved from lower Manhattan to Harlem. After graduating from Colgate University in 1930, he entered Union Theological Seminary and was appointed assistant pastor and business manager of his father's church. Not finding the seminary to his liking, he transferred to Columbia University and received an A.M. in religious education in 1932. The following year, he married Isabel Washington and adopted her child from a previous marriage.

Powell's congregation was sorely beset by the Great Depression of the 1930s, and he took it upon himself to provide economic relief for them as best he could. First, he organized a soup kitchen and "clothes closet" that fed and clothed thousands of African Americans who had lost their jobs. Next, he opened an unemployment service and formed adult education classes at the church's community center so that his flock could more easily find work. Then, when he discovered that racial discrimination kept his people, regardless of their qualifications, from being hired by white employers, he committed himself to securing equal employment for African Americans throughout the city. These efforts hit high gear after 1937, when he succeeded his father as pastor. In addition to speaking emphatically from the pulpit for the need for equal employment and economic justice, he started a "don't buy where you can't work" program and helped organize the Greater New York Coordinating Committee for Employment (GNYCCE), which brought together several different groups working toward the same goal. On numerous occasions, Powell himself led picketers as they demonstrated in front of stores and businesses that refused to hire blacks. The results were impressive; by 1942 Harlem Hospital had rehired five black physicians who had been dismissed to make room for whites, and significant numbers of

African-American men and women had been hired to work as clerks, secretaries, and salespeople for local merchants; as members of repair crews for the electric and telephone companies; as workers at the 1939 World's Fair; and as drivers and mechanics for the city transit system.

Powell's leadership of GNYCCE and his pastorship of Abyssinian Baptist made him the best-known African American in Harlem, perhaps in all of New York City. In 1941, he decided to capitalize on his fame by running for city council. Reorganizing the GNYCCE as the Harlem People's Committee and mobilizing it on behalf of his candidacy, he was easily elected. As a councilman, he redoubled his efforts to achieve economic justice for African Americans. To this end, he also cofounded and edited *People's Voice,* a Harlem newspaper that became his personal political organ, and cofounded with BEN DAVIS the Communist-backed National Negro Congress, which included as members several leaders of the National Association for the Advancement of Colored People.

In 1943, Powell declined to run for reelection, instead giving his support to Davis's candidacy. In fact, he had set his sights on being elected in 1944 to the U.S. House of Representatives from the Twenty-second District. This black-majority district centered on Harlem was created as a result of reapportionment necessitated by the census of 1940. A Democrat since 1932 when he had campaigned for Franklin D. Roosevelt, he easily gained his party's nomination, ran for Congress unopposed, and was sworn in in 1945. That same year, he divorced his first wife and married Hazel Scott, a jazz pianist and organist, with whom he had one child.

Powell was first assigned to the committees on Indian affairs and invalid pensions; in 1947, he was also named to the committee on education and labor. He spent most of his time, however, campaigning for expanded civil rights for African Americans. He demanded an end to the poll tax, which prevented many blacks from voting in state and federal elections, the permanent establishment of the wartime Fair Employment Practices Commission, and an end to segregated education, housing, transportation, and military facilities. He was responsible for desegregating the House press gallery and for gaining admission for black staff members to the congressional amenities to which white staffers routinely enjoyed access, and he began clamoring for what became known as the "Powell Amendment." This clause, which he strove to include in every piece of spending legislation, denied federal funds to any organization or project that in any way fostered or supported racial discrimination.

Powell's push for equality for blacks delighted his constituents, and they reelected him 11 times. At the same time, his flamboyant style and refusal to compromise on matters relating to racial discrimination earned him many enemies. In 1953, he alienated many Democrats when he began supporting the legislative agenda of Republican president Dwight D. Eisenhower in return for the administration's support for civil rights legislation. Shortly thereafter, Powell found himself being investigated for tax fraud. Undaunted, he ignored the warning, if indeed it was such, and in 1956 he supported Eisenhower's reelection campaign, thus further outraging his fellow Democrats. A grateful Eisenhower backed the Civil Rights Act of 1957, which, although watered down to a considerable degree, set the stage for the passage in the 1960s of civil rights bills with sharper teeth.

Meanwhile, the investigation continued, and in 1958 a federal grand jury indicted Powell on three counts of tax evasion. Shortly after the indictment, several New York Democrats initiated a drive to purge him from the party. His constituents backed him so loyally that he managed to avoid being expelled. In 1960, two counts of tax evasion were dropped for lack of evidence and the third count was dismissed when the jury could not reach a decision as to his guilt, but he did not escape scot-free; partly because of the trial, that same year his second wife filed for divorce.

Adam Clayton Powell, Jr., shown here with his wife Hazel, represented Harlem in the U.S. House of Representatives. *(Library of Congress)*

Powell rebounded from the divorce by marrying Yvette Flores Diago in 1960; they would have one child. In 1961, he rebounded from his near-divorce by the Democrats when, as senior member of the committee on education and labor, he assumed its chairmanship. During his seven-year tenure as chairman, he was a leading player in President John F. Kennedy's New Frontier and President Lyndon B. Johnson's Great Society, helping push through the committee and the House 48 pieces of social legislation with price tags of more than $14 billion. Among these bills were the Minimum Wage Act of 1961, the Manpower Development and Training Act of 1962, and in 1964 the Anti-Poverty Act, the Juvenile Delinquency Act, and the Vocational Education Act. Each of these acts contained something specific for African Americans, usually in the way of enhanced employment or educational opportunities. When the Civil Rights Act of 1964 became law, it was a particularly sweet victory for Powell because the act made the Powell Amendment part of all future federal legislation. As a result of his success at championing social justice for African Americans, he earned the sobriquet "Mr. Civil Rights."

Unfortunately, Powell's successes seemed to go to his head. He became increasingly boastful and began to abuse his privileges as a congressman, spending tax dollars on frivolous trips to the Caribbean and missing important roll call votes on the House floor. His undoing actually came about as the result of a needless insult to one of his constituents. In a 1960 television interview, he had called Esther James, a Harlem widow, a "bag woman," meaning that she collected and distributed bribes. Not surprisingly, she sued him for slander and won a judgment of $46,500. He refused to apologize or to pay or to appear in court to explain his refusal to pay. The court tolerated such behavior for six years, but in 1966 it ordered that he be arrested for contempt of court. He avoided jail only by fleeing to the island of Bimini in the Bahamas. Meanwhile, the James affair and Powell's flagrant mishandling of committee funds resulted in 1967 in his removal from the chairmanship and his expulsion from the House.

Powell refused to go away quietly. When a special election was held in 1967 to fill his vacant seat, he was reelected by a huge margin. When his seat came up for reelection in 1968, he was again reelected by a huge margin. The House refused to accept both results, so Powell took his case to the U.S. Supreme Court. In 1969, the Court ruled in *Powell v. McCormack* that his exclusion from Congress was unconstitutional. Prior to the ruling, however, he had paid James (via a community fund-raiser), thus removing the threat of jail time, and worked out a deal with the House whereby he gave up his seniority and chairmanship and paid a fine of $25,000 in return for being reseated.

In 1969, Powell was diagnosed with cancer, and he announced that he would retire in 1971 when his term expired. He later changed his mind and ran for reelection; however, by this time his constituents had grown tired of him and elected CHARLES RANGEL to take his place. In 1971, Powell left Congress, stepped down as Abyssinian Baptist's pastor, and retired to Bimini. He died on April 4, 1972, in Miami, Florida.

Further Reading

Biographical Directory of the United States Congress. "Powell., Adam Clayton, Jr., 1908–1972." Available online. URL: http://bioguide.congress.gov/scripts/biodisplay.pl?index=P000477. Downloaded April 1, 2009.

Black Americans in Congress. "Adam Clayton Powell, Jr." Available online. URL: http://baic.house.gov/member-profiles/profile.html?intID=33. Downloaded April 2, 2009.

Clay, William L. *Just Permanent Interests: Black Americans in Congress, 1870–1992.* New York: Amistad Press, 1993.

Hamilton, Charles V. *Adam Clayton Powell, Jr.: The Political Biography of an American Dilemma.* New York: Atheneum, 1991.

Powell, Adam C., Jr. *Adam by Adam: The Autobiography of Adam Clayton Powell, Jr.* New York: Dial Press, 1971.

Wallenstine, Peter. "Powell, Adam Clayton." In *African American National Biography,* vol. 6, edited by Henry Louis Gates, Jr., and Evelyn Brooks Higginbotham. New York: Oxford University Press, 2008, pp. 406–408.

Powell, Colin
(Colin Luther Powell)
(1937–   ) *U.S. secretary of state*

Colin Powell was the first African American to hold the post of chairman of the Joint Chiefs of Staff, and the first to hold the office of secretary of state.

Powell was born on April 5, 1937, in New York City. His father, Luther, was a shipping clerk, and his mother, Maud, was a seamstress. After graduating from high school in 1954, he enrolled in the City College of New York. While at CCNY, he joined the U.S. Army Reserve Officers' Training Corps, and upon graduating in 1958 he was commissioned a second lieutenant. Over the next 30 years, he rose up through the ranks until he was made a four-star general in 1989. During this period, he served overseas in West Germany, South Korea, and Vietnam. While in Vietnam, he received the Purple Heart and the Bronze Star; he also received the Soldier's Medal for rescuing several wounded soldiers from a helicopter that had crashed and was burning. He served at a number of army posts stateside, including the Command and General Staff College in Fort Leavenworth. In 1962, he married Alma Johnson, with whom he has three children.

Like most career army officers, Powell pulled several tours of duty in the nation's capital. During one tour, he received an M.B.A. from George Washington University in 1971. After serving in several advisory posts in the Pentagon and the Department of Energy, in 1983 he was appointed military assistant to Caspar Weinberger, the secretary of defense under Republican president Ronald Reagan. Four years later, he was named deputy director of the National Security Council, and shortly thereafter he was appointed national security adviser. In 1989, he was named chairman of the Joint Chiefs of Staff, an appointment that made him the nation's top military officer. He was the youngest person and the first African American to hold this position.

Powell first came to the nation's attention in 1989. That same year the U.S. military invaded Panama to oust its president, Manuel Noriega. Powell appeared on several nationally televised press conferences to address the nation about the purpose and the execution of the mission. His professional performance during these conferences contributed greatly to giving the public a favorable impression of the mission's necessity. In 1991, he turned in an even more impressive performance during Operation Desert Storm, the U.S./NATO invasion of Iraq following its invasion of Kuwait. Most military experts had expected the Iraqis to put up a determined struggle, and high casualties for U.S. troops had been predicted. Under Powell's overall direction, the invasion lasted six weeks and casualties were minimal. Once again, he appeared numerous times on tele-

vision and impressed the nation with his cool, calm, and collected demeanor as well as his sense of self-deprecating humor. After hostilities ended, he was awarded a gold medal by Congress.

Powell retired from the military in 1993. He was recruited by both major political parties to run for president in 1996. Powell certainly fit the mold of a successful presidential candidate; George Washington, Andrew Jackson, William Henry Harrison, Ulysses S. Grant, and Dwight D. Eisenhower had all made the transition from victorious general to president. But after several months of sober consideration, Powell declined to run, citing as one reason the intense scrutiny that would be brought to bear on his family. Instead, he opted to become chairman of America's Promise, the Alliance for Youth, in 1997. As chairman, he solicited millions of dollars from the nation's corporations, then oversaw the implementation of programs designed to "build and strengthen the character and compe-

Colin Powell was the first African American to serve as U.S. secretary of state. *(U.S. Department of State)*

tence of our youth." It was estimated that within two years America's Promise had made a positive impact on the lives of more than 10 million children in the United States.

Powell returned to public life in 2001 when he was appointed secretary of state by Republican president George W. Bush. The appointment made him the fifth most powerful person in the federal government and at the time marked the highest post ever held by an African American. Powell's appointment was welcomed by most Americans, who believed that he would bring to the post the same cool toughness he had demonstrated during Operation Desert Storm. Many observers were disappointed, however, by the lackluster performance he turned in during his first two years in office. Instead of serving as a major adviser and counselor to the president, he seemed rather to be little more than an errand boy who delivered the president's belligerent messages to an unreceptive world. In 2003, his credibility came under attack following the U.S.-led invasion of Iraq known as Operation Iraqi Freedom. Powell had gained congressional and public support for the invasion by claiming with the utmost confidence that Iraq possessed "weapons of massive destruction" in an address to the UN Security Council. These weapons were not found. In 2005, Powell admitted in a television interview with Barbara Walters that he considered his speech at the UN a "blot" on his public record. "It was painful. It's painful now," he stated.

Following Bush's reelection in 2004, Powell resigned as secretary of state. (He was replaced by CONDOLEEZZA RICE, the first African-American woman to hold that position.) Returning to private life, Powell joined the venture capital firm of Kleiner, Perkins, Caufield & Byers and began delivering motivational speeches.

Although his reputation was tarnished by his tenure in the Bush administration, Powell was frequently named as a possible Republican vice presidential nominee during the 2008 campaign. Shortly before the election, however, Powell endorsed the Democratic presidential nominee BARACK OBAMA.

Further Reading

DeYoung, Karen. *Soldier: The Life of Colin Powell.* New York: Vintage, 2007.

Gates, Henry Louis, and Cornel West. *The African-American Century: How Black Americans Have Shaped Our Country.* New York: Free Press, 2000.

Harari, Oren. *The Leadership Secrets of Colin Powell.* New York: McGraw-Hill, 2002.

O'Sullivan, Christopher D. *Colin Powell: American Power and Intervention from Vietnam to Iraq.* Lanham, Md.: Rowman and Littlefield, 2009.

Powell, Colin L., and Joseph E. Persico. *My American Journey.* New York: Random House, 1995.

Roth, David. *Sacred Honor: A Biography of Colin Powell.* Grand Rapids, Mich.: Zondervan Publishing, 1993.

Powell, Debra
(Debra Ann Powell)
(1964–   ) *mayor of East St. Louis, Illinois*

Debra Powell was the first female mayor of East St. Louis, Missouri. As with KWEISI MFUME and ALAN KEYES, a successful career in radio and television led her to run for political office.

Powell was born on April 30, 1964, in East St. Louis. Her father, James, was a construction worker, and her mother, Barbara, was a retail clerk. After graduating from high school in 1981, she received a basketball scholarship to the University of Nebraska in Lincoln. Four years later, she received a B.A. in speech communications. She then returned to East St. Louis where she was hired as a public relations assistant to the mayor, Carl Officer. Within a year, however, a controversy had arisen over Powell's employment. Officer had promised Powell while she was in high school that if she earned a bachelor's degree he would offer her a job with the city. When the city council objected to her employment, he paid her salary out of his own pocket. Needless to say, the whole episode was rather embarrassing for Powell. In 1986, after only a year on the job, she got married and moved to Pasadena, California, where she worked in public relations.

In 1990, Powell, by now the divorced mother of two children, returned to East St. Louis. She began reporting for the local newspaper and a radio station, and a year later she cocreated the East St. Louis Daily News Broadcast. Eventually, she was hired as a news anchor by a local cable television station. By 1998, she had become the station's news director. Throughout her career in television, she emphasized the news, good and bad, about her local community, thus helping local residents become more aware of themselves as East St. Louisans.

Powell began her political career in 1993 when she was elected to a seat on the East St. Louis city council. Over the next six years, she worked to boost the city's economy and to overcome the corruption and wastefulness she observed among city employees. In 1999, she decided to do more to improve life in the community of 40,000 by running for mayor. After a hard-fought battle against a better-funded competitor, she was able to win a narrow victory when it was disclosed that one of her opponent's major campaign contributors operated a string of topless night clubs.

As mayor, Powell focused on improving municipal services. She improved training for city employees and fired those employees who showed a lack of desire to serve the public. Before long, much-needed repairs to streets and school buildings began to take place. She secured millions of dollars in federal funding to refurbish the city's outdated sewer system. She improved public safety by overhauling the police officer training program, instituting a residency requirement for all fire and police personnel, and hiring more firefighters and police officers. In her fight against corruption within city government, she called to task three members of the fire and police commissioners'

Debra Powell was the mayor of East St. Louis, Illinois. *(Debra A. Powell)*

board for promoting people based on their politics and not their ability.

In terms of economic development, Powell helped put together a $500 million redevelopment plan. She championed the expansion of casino gambling along the city's Mississippi riverfront and lobbied for the construction of a new stadium for the National League's St. Louis Cardinals in East St. Louis. She oversaw the implementation of minority set-asides guaranteeing that 50 percent of all city construction contracts would go to minority contractors. She also secured enough funding to complete the refurbishment of 174 dilapidated homes in one of the city's oldest neighborhoods.

The highlight of Powell's efforts to improve the local economy was a visit by President Bill Clinton to East St. Louis. The occasion was the opening of a Walgreen's Drug Store in a newly constructed strip mall; it was the first retail establishment to open for business within the city limits in 40 years. At the ribbon-cutting ceremony, Clinton called on Congress to pass a bill to make available funding to high- unemployment, low-income cities like East St. Louis so that similar commercial projects could be completed. Powell was denied an opportunity to run for reelection in 2003 when she failed to file all necessary forms with the county clerk. After leaving office in 2003, she returned to private life.

Further Reading

Doig, Melissa W. "Debra A. Powell, 1964–   ." *Contemporary Black Biography* 23 (2000): 161–163.

R

Rainey, Joseph

(Joseph Hayne Rainey)
(1832–1887) *U.S. congressional representative from South Carolina*

Joseph Rainey was the first African American to serve in the U.S. House of Representatives. He also served longer in office—almost nine years—than any other black congressman during Reconstruction.

Rainey was born on June 21, 1832, in Georgetown, South Carolina. His parents, Edward and Gracia, were slaves. By 1850, Rainey's father had purchased the family's freedom and moved them to Charleston, where he opened a barber shop. Rainey assisted his father for several years, then moved to Philadelphia, Pennsylvania, where in 1859 he married a woman named Susan, with whom he had five children. The couple returned to South Carolina just in time for the outbreak of the Civil War.

Despite being free, Rainey was pressed into service as a military laborer by the Confederate government and helped construct fortifications around Charleston. He was later forced to serve as a cook and steward aboard a Confederate blockade runner. In 1862, he managed to stow away his wife aboard the ship, and when it landed in Bermuda the couple made good their escape. For the next three years, he worked as a barber in St.

George and Hamilton, then returned to Charleston after the war ended.

Almost immediately upon his return, Rainey became active in the Republican Party, the only major political party that welcomed participation by blacks. In 1865, he served as vice president of the Colored Peoples' Convention in Charleston, a meeting that endorsed legal rights for African Americans and political rights for black men and condemned the so-called Black Codes, legislation that tried to keep freedmen in a state of quasi slavery. Although the state legislature ignored the convention, in 1867 the establishment of Reconstruction in South Carolina essentially implemented everything it had called for, and Rainey's involvement in the convention made him a prominent figure among state Republicans.

In 1867, Rainey returned to Georgetown and became active in recruiting freedmen, who constituted a local majority, for the Republican Party. The following year he was named chairman of Georgetown County's Republican apparatus, appointed to the state Republican executive committee, served as a delegate to the state constitutional convention, and elected to represent his county in the state senate, where he was named chairman of the finance committee. In early 1870, he was elected to the U.S. House of Representatives as the replacement for Benjamin F. Whittemore, a carpetbagger from Massachusetts who had been forced by the House to forgo the remaining few months of his term for selling appointments to the military academies at West Point and Annapolis.

As a congressman, Rainey worked to expand the rights of African Americans while following a policy of cautious compromise. He was a vocal supporter of the Enforcement Act of 1872, which outlawed the intimidation and harassment of black voters by the Ku Klux Klan and related paramilitary groups. He called repeatedly for stricter federal enforcement of the Fourteenth and Fifteenth Amendments, which guaranteed the citizenship and voting rights of African Americans. He voted for general amnesty for former Confederates, a measure introduced by House Democrats, with the understanding that the Democrats would support passage of the Civil Rights Act of 1875, which outlawed discrimination against blacks on juries and in businesses that accommodated the general public.

Although he worked for legal and political equality for blacks, he opposed most measures that attempted to legislate social equality of the races, including legalization of interracial marriages. He supported the imposition of a poll tax that would disfranchise poor freedmen, although he did so with the understanding that the proceeds would go to fund integrated public education. Because of his nonradical stance, Rainey was respected by both sides of the House, and on one occasion in 1874, when the Speaker of the House was indisposed, he was chosen to preside in the speaker's place.

Rainey was reelected to the House for four full terms. By 1878, however, the Democrats has regained control of South Carolina politics, and that year he lost his bid for reelection. In 1879, he accepted a position as a special agent of the Treasury Department in South Carolina but resigned two years later. In 1881, he returned to Washington; failing in his bid to become clerk of the House, he instead opened a brokerage and banking firm. When the firm failed five years later, he became a partner in a Washington coal and wood yard. In 1887, his health having failed, he returned to Georgetown where he died on August 2.

Further Reading

Black Americans in Congress. "Joseph Hayne Rainey." Available online. URL: http://baic.house.gov/member-profiles/profile.html?intID=11. Downloaded April 2, 2009.

Clay, William L. *Just Permanent Interests: Black Americans in Congress, 1870–1992.* New York: Amistad Press, 1993.

Dray, Philip. *Capitol Men: The Epic Story of Reconstruction through the Lives of the First Black Congressmen.* Boston: Houghton Mifflin, 2008.

Holt, Thomas C. *Black over White: Negro Political Leadership in South Carolina during Reconstruction.* Urbana: University of Illinois Press, 1977.

Lamson, Peggy. *The Glorious Failure: Black Congressman Robert Brown Elliott and the Reconstruction of South Carolina.* New York: W. W. Norton, 1973.

Joseph Rainey was the first African American to serve in the U.S. House of Representatives. *(Library of Congress)*

Packwood, Cyril O. *Detour–Bermuda, Destination– U.S. House of Representatives: The Life of Joseph Hayne Rainey.* Hamilton, Bermuda: Baxter's, 1977.

Rangel, Charles
(Charles Bernard Rangel)
(1930–   ) *U.S. congressional representative from New York*

Charles Rangel has been a member of Congress for almost 40 years. Rangel was born on June 11, 1930, in Harlem, New York City. His father, Ralph, was a laborer, and his mother, Blanche, worked in a garment factory. At age 16, he dropped out of high school; several low-paying jobs later, in 1948 he joined the U.S. Army. He served in Korea during the Korean War and received the Bronze Star for leading 40 men to safety who had been trapped behind enemy lines for several days. Discharged with the rank of sergeant in 1952, he returned to Harlem to finish high school. A year later, he enrolled in New York University and received a B.S. in accounting in 1957. Three years later, he received an LL.B. from St. John's University Law School and opened a law office in Harlem. In 1961, he was appointed an assistant district attorney for the Southern District of New York. He resigned the following year, and for the next four years he served as legal counsel to various groups, including the New York City Housing and Redevelopment Board and the Neighborhood Conservation Bureau. In 1964, he married Alma Carter, with whom he has two children.

Rangel became involved in politics in 1960, when he joined the Carver Democratic Club. The Carver Club was a major vehicle for getting black politicians from Harlem elected to state and local offices, and for the next four years he paid his dues by loyally supporting the club's candidates. In 1964, he switched his allegiance to the John F. Kennedy Democratic Club, which he cofounded, in order to speed up his own political advancement. Two years later, with the Kennedy Club's

Charles Rangel took the congressional seat formerly held by the legendary Adam Clayton Powell, Jr. *(Charles B. Rangel)*

backing, he was elected to the state assembly from central Harlem. During his two terms, he championed legalized gambling in the form of a state lottery, since most of his constituents played the "numbers" game, from which many state lottery games are derived. He also vigorously opposed the rising use of narcotics, which he believed posed a greater threat to his constituents, some 30,000 of whom were addicted to heroin, than did the spread of Soviet communism, the preoccupation of most Americans during the cold war.

In 1969, Rangel ran for New York city council but came in last in a six-man race. Undaunted, the following year he decided to challenge ADAM CLAYTON POWELL, JR., for his seat in the U.S. House of Representatives. Powell had represented Harlem in Congress since 1945 and was immensely popular with his constituents. Over the last several years, however, he had gotten into trouble with federal authorities for various reasons; he had announced his retirement, but then decided to run for reelection. Rangel perceived that Powell had lost favor with Harlemites, and he ran a vigorous but gentlemanly campaign to replace him. His strategy succeeded; he beat Powell by 150 votes in the Democratic primary and then easily won the general election.

Rangel took his seat in Congress in 1971 and was assigned to the select committee on crime. He used this position to further his personal war on drugs. By the end of his first term, he had gained approval for an amendment that authorized the president to cut off all military and economic aid to any country that refused to cooperate with U.S. efforts to curtail the international drug trade. The amendment is credited with Turkey's decision to put an end to the production of opium poppies, from which heroin is produced, within its borders. In 1976, he was named to the select committee on narcotics abuse and control, and he served as its chairman from 1983 to 1993. His incessant and vociferous battle against drugs, which he claims affect every aspect of U.S. life in general and life in the African-American community in particular, eventually angered a number of government officials and curtailed his influence in this regard. In 1986, he was banned from a White House conference on drugs because he had lambasted President Ronald Reagan's antidrug record, and in 1993 the House voted to disband his committee. When Congress later established the Congressional Narcotics Abuse and Control Caucus, however, he was the clear choice to become its chairman.

Rangel also played an important role on the committee on ways and means, to which he was appointed in 1974. He authored legislation establishing low-income housing tax credits as a means of financing affordable housing for the poor, and he coauthored legislation creating federal "empowerment zones" as a means of revitalizing businesses in urban neighborhoods. He also worked to increase trade between the United States and the nations of Africa and the Caribbean; to this end he cosponsored the African

Growth and Opportunity Act and the Caribbean Basin Initiative.

In 1971, Rangel cofounded the Congressional Black Caucus, and he served as its chairman in 1974–75. In 1987, he helped change the internal revenue code so that U.S. businesses could not receive tax credits for taxes paid to the South African government. This measure is credited with inducing several large corporations to quit doing business in South Africa, thus helping to bring about an end to apartheid in that country. He sponsored legislation establishing a number of aids for African Americans, including the work opportunity tax credit and the office of minority affairs in the Department of Veterans Affairs. During the administration of George W. Bush, Rangel used his position as the ranking Democrat on the House Ways and Means Committee to oppose Bush's tax-cutting programs, particularly the reduction in the dividend tax. In the run-up to the Iraq War, he made the controversial proposal of reinstating the draft. Rangel argued that people from all backgrounds and income levels should serve in the military in time of war.

In 2008, Rangel became embroiled in several ethics investigations dealing with unpaid taxes and rental properties. Ethics questions have continued to dog Rangel. In February 2010, the House admonished him for accepting corporate-sponsored trips. In the wake of the scandal, Rangel resigned from his chairmanship of the House Ways and Means Committee. In July 2010, the House Ethics Committee charged Rangel with 13 violations of House rules. Nevertheless, in November of that year, he was reelected to a 21st term. After a formal investigation, Rangel was censured on 11 ethics violations on December 6, 2010.

Further Reading

Biographical Directory of the United States Congress. "Rangel, Charles Bernard, 1930." Available online. URL: http://bioguide.congress.gov/scripts/biodisplay.pl?index=R000053. Downloaded April 9, 2009.

Clay, William L. *Just Permanent Interests: Black Americans in Congress, 1870–1992.* New York: Amistad Press, 1993.

Jacobsen, Mark. "Chairman of the Money." In *American Gangster and Other Tales of New York.* New York: Grove Press, 2007, pp. 56–72.

Rangel, Charles B., and Leon Wynter. *And I Haven't Had a Bad Day Since: From the Streets of Harlem to the Halls of Congress.* New York: Thomas Dunne Books, 2007.

Thomas, Evan. *Charles B. Rangel, Democratic Representative from New York.* Washington: Grossman, 1972.

Ransier, Alonzo
(Alonzo Jacob Ransier)
(1834–1882) *U.S. congressional representative from South Carolina*

Alonzo Ransier's political career was meteoric. After rising to the highest state position ever held by an African American in South Carolina, he fell from the good graces of the electorate shortly thereafter and died in obscurity.

Ransier was born on January 3, 1834, in Charleston, South Carolina. Little is known about his parents except that they were freeborn Haitian immigrants. As a youth, he learned how to read and write, and at age 16 he went to work as a shipping clerk for a local mercantile firm. In 1856, he married Louisa Ann Carroll, with whom he had 11 children.

At the end of the Civil War, Ransier was appointed registrar of elections by the Union army of occupation. That same year, he attended the Colored Peoples' Convention in Charleston that called for equal political and economic rights for freedmen. In 1867, after the Reconstruction Acts were passed, he joined the Republican Party and was immediately elected vice president of the state executive committee. The following year, he was named president of the committee and served as a delegate to the state constitutional convention. He impressed the state's black voters by speaking out

forcefully against a clause to legalize debts owed for the purchase of slaves before the Civil War, as well as against a literacy requirement for voting. He also succeeded in having the word *white* struck from every state law. Shortly after the convention ended, he was elected to the state's lower house; later, in 1868 he was appointed auditor of Charleston County. In 1870, he became the highest-ranking black in South Carolina during Reconstruction when he was elected lieutenant governor. In this position, he successfully sponsored a bill that guaranteed blacks the same legal protections afforded to whites. He also supported voting rights for women, and as lieutenant governor he attended a woman suffrage convention in Columbia.

In early 1872, Ransier was elected to the U.S. House of Representatives to complete the term of ROBERT DELARGE, who had been expelled by the House for election fraud. Later that year, he was elected to a full term of his own. He served on the

Alonzo Ransier represented South Carolina in the U.S. Congress. *(Library of Congress)*

committee on manufactures and introduced several bills, none of which was enacted. He also worked hard to protect and expand the civil rights of African Americans. He gained a reputation as a vocal proponent of integrated public education, going so far as to abstain from voting on what became the Civil Rights Act of 1875 because it did not outlaw racial discrimination in schools.

In 1874, Ransier lost the Republican nomination to a white opponent, and so he was not returned to Congress. Instead, he accepted a position with the U.S. Treasury Department as collector of internal revenue for the Charleston district. But shortly after receiving the position, his life began to fall apart. In 1875 his wife died, in 1876 his term as collector expired, and that same year he lost his modest investments in real estate and railroad stocks. In 1879, he went to work as a night watchman at the Charleston custom house, but he lost this job for political reasons. He was working as a manual laborer for the Pacific Guano Company at the time of his death on August 17, 1882, in Charleston.

Further Reading

Biographical Directory of the United States Congress. "Ransier, Alonzo Jacob, 1834–1882." Available online. URL: http://bioguide.congress.gov/scripts/biodisplay.pl?index=R000060. Downloaded April 12, 2009.

Black Americans in Congress. "Alonzo Jacob Ransier." Available online. URL: http://baic.house.gov/member-profiles/profile.html?intID=12. Downloaded April 2, 2009.

Clay, William L. *Just Permanent Interests: Black Americans in Congress, 1870–1992.* New York: Amistad Press, 1993.

Hine, William C. "Ransier, Alonzo." In *African American National Biography,* vol. 6, edited by Henry Louis Gates, Jr., and Evelyn Brooks Higginbotham. New York: Oxford University Press, 2008, pp. 510–512.

Holt, Thomas C. *Black over White: Negro Political Leadership in South Carolina during Reconstruction.* Urbana: University of Illinois Press, 1977.

Rapier, James
(James Thomas Rapier)
(1837–1883) *U.S. congressional representative from Alabama*

James Rapier was one of the most able and moderate African-American politicians of the Reconstruction era. Despite his abilities, or perhaps because of them, he was harassed by white racists throughout his political career. He spent the last years of his life helping southern blacks escape racial prejudice by making better lives in the Midwest.

Rapier was born on November 13, 1837, in Florence, Alabama. His parents, John H. and Susan, were free blacks; his father made a living as a barber. At age five, he went to live with his grandmother and paternal uncle in Nashville, Tennessee, where he could be tutored privately. At age 19, he went to live with another paternal uncle in Buxton, Canada West (today Ontario), attending school there and in Toronto, where he also taught for several years.

In 1863, the same year the Union army secured Tennessee, Rapier returned to that state, leased 200 acres in Maury County, and began raising cotton. Two years later, shortly after the end of the Civil War, he got involved in politics by working to secure voting rights for freedmen. He quickly became a political leader of the state's African Americans, and in 1865 he delivered the keynote address at the Tennessee Negro Suffrage Convention in 1865. Because Tennessee had returned to the Union before Reconstruction began, black politicians never gained the opportunities there that they did in other southern states. In 1866, he returned to Florence, leased several hundred acres on Seven Mile Island in the Tennessee River, recruited almost two dozen tenant farmers, and began raising cotton. He soon became one of the most prosperous black planters in Alabama.

Rapier became involved in state politics in 1867, shortly after passage of the Reconstruction Acts. He joined the Republican Party, began recruiting freedmen to the party's ranks, and served as chairman of the platform committee at the party's state convention. Later that year, he attended the state's constitutional convention, where he impressed members of both parties with his moderate views. Although he insisted on equal political and economic rights and public education for African Americans, he opposed punishing former Confederates beyond what the U.S. Congress was willing to do. Despite his moderation, in 1868 Rapier drew the attention of the Ku Klux Klan. In their campaign to hound African Americans from Alabama politics, they attempted to lynch him along with several other blacks. He managed to escape but was forced to go into seclusion in Montgomery for a year.

Rapier emerged from hiding in 1869, and for the next three years he focused on alleviating the freedmen's economic problems. That same year, he attended the National Negro Labor Union (NNLU) convention in Washington, D.C. In 1870, he was elected the NNLU's vice president, and in this position he lobbied for a federal land bureau that would redistribute land to poor freedmen. He also organized a chapter of the NNLU in Alabama and served as its president and executive chairman. Meanwhile, he renewed his involvement in state politics by running as the Republican candidate for secretary of state in 1870. After his defeat, he received a federal appointment as assessor of internal revenue for the Montgomery district.

In 1872, Rapier ran a strong campaign for the U.S. House of Representatives. As a result of federal policing of the polls and prosecution of the Ku Klux Klan in federal courts, he was able to defeat a Confederate war hero by several thousand votes. As a member of the committee on education and labor, he introduced bills to provide federal funding for public education. He also played an important role in passing the Civil Rights Act of 1875, which made it a federal crime to discriminate against African Americans on juries and in places of public accommodation. He also intro-

duced a bill that resulted in making Montgomery a port of delivery; as a result, federal monies were made available for dredging the Alabama River all the way to Montgomery, thus greatly boosting the economy of northern and central Alabama.

Despite his accomplishments, Rapier was denied reelection in 1874. The Ku Klux Klan defied federal efforts to suppress it and waged a campaign of violence against Rapier on the grounds that no black man should represent the capital of the former Confederacy in Congress. After the election, he leased several cotton plantations in Lowndes County, which was in a different congressional district, and ran for the House again in 1876. He lost when he and JEREMIAH HARALSON split the black vote, thus giving the election to their white opponent. Although he never held elective office again, he remained active in the affairs of the Republican Party and served as a delegate to the 1880 convention. In 1877, he was appointed collector of internal revenue for the U.S. Treasury Department, a post he held for the next six years.

Meanwhile, Rapier had become increasingly disillusioned with the prospects for southern African Americans. While a congressman, he had represented Alabama at the Fifth International Exhibition in Vienna, Austria, and the United States at the World's Fair in Paris, France; the total lack of racial discrimination in Europe made him realize that dealing with racism did not have to be a part of the African-American life. He was further disgusted by the renewal of violence against blacks in the mid-1870s and the refusal—indeed, inability—of his white constituents to judge him by his accomplishments rather than his race. By 1879, when he chaired the emigration committee of the Southern States Negro Convention in Nashville, he had become a proponent of black exodus from the South. To this end, he purchased enough land in Wabaunsee County, Kansas, to establish a black community and gave a number of speeches urging blacks to emigrate to the Great Plains states. Before he could make his model community a reality, however, he contracted pulmonary tuberculosis. He died, having never married, on one of his plantations in Lowndes County on May 31, 1883.

Further Reading

Biographical Directory of the United States Congress. "Rapier, James Thomas, 1837–1883." Available online. URL: http://bioguide.congress.gov/scripts/biodisplay.pl?index=R000064. Downloaded March 30, 2009.

Black Americans in Congress. "James Thomas Rapier." Available online. URL: http://baic.house.gov/member-profiles/profile.html?intID=13. Downloaded March 30, 2009.

Clay, William L. *Just Permanent Interests: Black Americans in Congress, 1870–1992.* New York: Amistad Press, 1993.

Rabinowitz, Howard N., ed. *Southern Black Leaders of the Reconstruction Era.* Urbana: University of Illinois Press, 1982.

Schweninger, Loren. *James T. Rapier and Reconstruction.* Chicago: University of Chicago Press, 1978.

Revels, Hiram
(Hiram Rhoades Revels)
(1827–1901) *U.S. senator from Mississippi*

Hiram Revels was the first African American to serve in the U.S. Senate. Ironically, he was chosen by the Mississippi state legislature to complete the unexpired term of the seat once held by Jefferson Davis, former president of the Confederate States of America.

Revels was born on September 27, 1827 (although some sources claim 1822), in Fayetteville, North Carolina. His parents were free, not enslaved, and one may have been a full-blooded Indian; their names and occupations are unknown. He received his basic education at a private school for blacks in Fayetteville. In 1842, he moved with his family to Lincolnton, where he worked briefly as a barber. Two years later, he entered Beech

Grove Seminary in Liberty, Indiana; he continued his education at Darke County Seminary for Negroes in Ohio, and by 1847 he was an ordained minister of the African Methodist Episcopal (AME) Church.

For the next six years, Revels did missionary work in the Midwest and Upper South. Sometime during this period he married Phoeba A. Bass, with whom he had six children. In 1853, he was made head of an AME congregation in St. Louis, Missouri, but he left a year later to become pastor of the Madison Street Presbyterian Church in Baltimore, Maryland. Except for a year spent at the Knox Academy in Galesburg, Illinois, he held that position for the next nine years while also serving as principal of an all-black high school.

In 1863, Revels became involved in the Civil War by recruiting blacks to serve in work battalions in the Union army. That same year, he returned to St. Louis where he opened a school for freedmen and helped raise Missouri's first black regiment. He served briefly as the regiment's chaplain and then spent the remainder of the war in Mississippi establishing churches and Freedmen's Bureau schools and working for the provost marshal's office in Vicksburg and Jackson. After the war, he served as pastor of AME churches in Leavenworth, Kansas, Louisville, Kentucky, and New Orleans, Louisiana. In 1868, he returned to Mississippi to become the presiding elder of an AME church in Natchez.

Revels became involved in politics in 1868 when Adelbert Ames, the military governor of Mississippi, appointed him to the Natchez board of aldermen. (After the Civil War, Mississippi was ruled by a military governor until it was readmitted to the Union.) The following year, he was elected as a Republican to represent Natchez and Adams County, which was 75 percent African American, in the Mississippi state senate. Meanwhile, Mississippi was in the process of being readmitted to the Union, and one of the legislature's top orders of business was to fill the state's two

Hiram Revels *(right)* was the first African American to serve in the U.S. Senate. (Frederick Douglass is featured in the center, and on the left is U.S. senator Blanche Bruce.) *(Library of Congress)*

seats in the U.S. Senate that had been vacant since 1861 (prior to ratification of the Seventeenth Amendment in 1913, senators were elected by the state legislatures, not the voters at large). The legislature's black members insisted that one of the seats go to an African American. Revels had impressed the entire body with the invocation he had given to open the session, and on the seventh ballot he was chosen to represent Mississippi in Washington.

Revels's election created a stir in the nation's capital. Several senators opposed seating him because of his race, and for three days the U.S. Senate debated whether or not to accept his credentials. Finally, by a vote of 48-8, he was sworn in and seated on February 25, 1870.

Revels served in the Senate for a little over a year. He was appointed to two relatively unimportant committees, District of Columbia and Education and Labor. He proposed five bills, mostly to fund transportation projects in Mississippi and Louisiana, but only the one petitioning for the removal of civil and political penalties for an ex-Confederate passed. He nominated the first African American to the U.S. Military Academy, but the candidate, Michael Howard, failed to pass the entrance examination and was denied admission. Toward the end of his term, he became an advocate of general amnesty for all Confederates, a stance that disappointed many of his fellow African Americans.

Revels returned to Mississippi when his term expired on March 3, 1871. Shortly thereafter,

James L. Alcorn, governor of Mississippi, appointed him president of a college for black males, later named Alcorn State University. He served in this position until 1874, when he was forced to resign for political reasons. He spent the next two years at churches in Holly Springs, Mississippi, and New Orleans, while editing a religious newspaper, the *Southwestern Christian Advocate*. He returned as Alcorn's president in 1876 and served in that capacity for another six years. In 1882, he was forced out a second time because of the college's dismal financial situation. He spent his remaining years teaching theology at Rust College in Holly Springs and serving as assistant pastor of his church. He died on January 16, 1901, in Aberdeen, Mississippi, while attending an AME conference.

Further Reading

Biographical Directory of the United States Congress. "Revels, Hiram Rhodes, 1827–1901." Available online. URL: http://bioguide.congress.gov/scripts/biodisplay.pl?index=R000166. Downloaded October 20, 2010.

Black Americans in Congress. "Hiram Rhodes Revels." Available online. URL: http://baic.house.gov/member-profiles/profile.html?intID=14. Downloaded April 2, 2009.

Clay, William L. *Just Permanent Interests: Black Americans in Congress, 1870–1992.* New York: Amistad Press, 1993.

Dray, Philip. *Capitol Men: The Epic Story of Reconstruction through the Lives of the First Black Congressmen.* Boston: Houghton Mifflin, 2008.

Thompson, Julius E. *Hiram R. Revels, 1827–1901: A Biography.* New York: Arno Press, 1982.

Rice, Condoleezza
(Condi Rice)
(1954–   ) *U.S. secretary of state*

From January 2005 to January 2009, Condoleezza Rice served as the secretary of state. She was the first African-American woman to hold this position.

Rice was born on November 14, 1954, in Birmingham, Alabama. Both of her parents were educators. Her mother, a music teacher, gave her her unusual name. It was derived from the Italian musical direction *con dolcezza,* meaning "with sweetness." Rice's mother taught her to play the piano when she was still a little girl. As a young child, she also developed a fascination with politics. She especially enjoyed discussing political issues with her father, a staunch Republican.

In 1968, the Rice family moved to Denver, Colorado, so her father could take an administrative post at the University of Denver. Having skipped two grades, Rice enrolled at the university at the age of 15. Initially, she studied piano performance, but later changed her major to political science after she became interested in the politics of the Soviet Union. After receiving her bachelor's degree in 1974, she continued her education at Notre Dame University in Notre Dame, Indiana, where she earned a master's in international studies. She then returned to the University of Denver for her Ph.D. Rice's doctoral dissertation, *Uncertain Allegiance: The Soviet Union and Czechoslovak Army,* was published in 1984.

In 1981, Rice began her academic career as an assistant professor at Stanford University in Palo Alto, California. There, she became acquainted with Brent Scowcroft, an expert in military affairs who had served as the National Security Advisor under President Gerald Ford. In 1989, he joined the administration of President George H. W. Bush in the same capacity. On Scowcroft's recommendation, Rice, now a tenured professor, was named director of Soviet and East European Affairs on the National Security Council. As the Soviet Union was collapsing, her expertise in Soviet politics, language, and history proved an invaluable resource to the White House.

After the election of President Bill Clinton in 1992, Rice returned to academia. From 1993 to 1999, she served as the provost of Stanford. Rice

Condoleezza Rice was the second African American and the second woman to head the U.S. Department of State. *(U.S. Department of State)*

was both the first woman and the first African American to hold this prestigious post. With Philip D. Zelikow, she also wrote *Germany Unified and Europe Transformed: A Study in Statecraft* (1999).

Through her connections with the former president Bush, Rice was hired by the 2000 presidential campaign of his son, Texas governor George W. Bush. As the younger Bush's national security expert, she tutored the candidate on a wide range of foreign policy issues. Rice and Bush developed a tight personal bond during this time. When Bush won the presidency, he asked Rice to return to Washington and become the first woman to serve as National Security Advisor.

Rice proved to be extremely loyal to President Bush. She supported his preemptive war on Iraq, citing the belief that Saddam Hussein possessed nuclear weapons as its justification. Famously, during an interview on CNN, she stated, "We don't want the smoking gun to be a mushroom cloud." After the military invasion, Bush placed Rice in charge of the Iraq Stabilization Group, in October 2003. In April 2004, she testified before the 9/11 Commission, which conducted an investigation into the events surrounding the terrorist acts in the United States on September 11, 2001.

After Bush's reelection in November 2004, he named Rice to replace the exiting COLIN POWELL as secretary of state. The continuing war in Iraq dominated her tenure. She supported an increase in troop levels in 2007 and tried to encourage the emerging democratic government in Iraq. Rice traveled the globe in an effort to rebuild diplomatic relations with world leaders troubled by the U.S. Iraq policies. Rice also worked to bring an end to the Israeli-Palestinian conflict and to stall nuclear weapons development in Iran and North Korea. In 2008, *Forbes* magazine named Rice the seventh most powerful woman in the world.

During the run-up to the 2008 presidential election, Rice was often mentioned as a possible vice presidential candidate on the Republican ticket. She, however, said that she had no interest in running for any office. Following the election of BARACK OBAMA, she left Washington, D.C., and returned to Stanford to teach political science. She was also named a senior fellow on public policy at the Hoover Institution, a conservative think tank located on Stanford's campus. In February 2009, Crown Publishers announced that they had Rice under contract to write two memoirs, one about her experiences in the Bush administration and one about her youth in Birmingham during the Civil Rights era. Her book *Extraordinary, Ordinary People: A Memoir of Family* was published in October 2010.

Further Reading

Bumiller, Elizabeth. *Condoleezza Rice: An American Life*. New York: Random House, 2007.

Felix, Antonia. *Condi: The Condoleezza Rice Story.* Updated ed. New York: Newmarket Press, 2005.

Kessler, Glenn. *The Confidante: Condoleezza Rice and the Creation of the Bush Legacy.* New York: St. Martin's Press, 2007.

Mabry, Marcus. *Twice as Good: Condoleezza Rice and Her Path to Power.* New York: Modern Times, 2007.

Mann, James. *Rise of the Vulcans: The History of Bush's War Cabinet.* New York: Viking Books, 2004.

Rice, Condoleezza. *Extraordinary, Ordinary People: A Memoir of Family.* New York: Crown Publishers, 2010.

Rice, Norm
(Norman Blann Rice)
(1943–) *mayor of Seattle, Washington*

Norm Rice was the first African-American mayor of Seattle, Washington. He served two terms as mayor before retiring to private life.

Rice was born on May 4, 1943, in Denver, Colorado. His father, Otha, was a railroad porter, and his mother, Irene, was a maid. After finishing high school, he attended the University of Colorado at Boulder for two years before dropping out in 1963. For the next six years, he worked as a hospital orderly and meter reader. Part of his income went to help support his mother, who had divorced his father while he was a teenager. In 1969, he visited Seattle and fell in love with the city. He moved there that same year, enrolled in the University of Washington under the Economic Opportunity Program, and received a B.A. in communications in 1972 and an M.A. in public administration two years later. As an undergraduate, he worked as a television reporter, and as a graduate student he worked as the assistant director and public relations coordinator for the Seattle Urban League. In 1974, he was named executive assistant director of government services for the Puget Sound Council of Governments. Two years later, he became the manager of corporate communications for Rainier National Bank. In 1973, he married Constance Williams, with whom he has one child.

Rice, a Democrat, began his political career in 1978 when he was appointed to fill a vacancy on the Seattle city council. He won a full term of his own the following year. During his 11 years on the council, he earned a reputation for being a fence-sitter; rather than speak his mind forcefully on a given subject, he would work to build consensus. To an extent, the style served him well. In 1983, after only five years on the council, he was elected council president, a position he held for seven years. At the same time, it served him poorly. Twice he was defeated in his bid for higher office, once in 1985 when he ran for mayor and again in 1987 when he ran for the U.S. Congress. After both defeats, he considered getting out of politics and going back to work in the private sector, but both times his supporters convinced him to stay and run again.

In 1989, Rice again declared his candidacy for mayor. This time, he had an issue he felt passionately about, Initiative 34. This initiative proposed to end school busing for desegregation purposes in Seattle, and its champion was Doug Jewett, the Republican candidate for mayor. An impassioned Rice condemned the initiative as morally wrong and vowed as mayor to do everything in his power to undo the damage he was sure the initiative would do. Although Initiative 34 was passed by Seattle's voters (it was later turned down by the local school board), those same voters were impressed by the new Rice despite his opposition to the initiative, and they voted him into office by a 57-43 margin. Perhaps surprisingly, given that desegregation was a key issue and that Seattle's population is less than 10 percent African American, Rice's race was never an issue during the campaign.

After taking office in early 1990, Rice reached out to city council in a way that few Seattle mayors had ever done. In the process, he was able to bring about consensus on a surprisingly large number of issues. At the same time, he demonstrated the ability to speak his own mind confidently and convincingly, and in turn city council began taking its lead from him on more and more issues. One idea that came about from this jointly cooperative effort was the Families in Education Levy, a fundraising process that raised more than $25 million to pay the salaries of school nurses, family counselors, and after-school activities supervisors.

Rice's economic development policies focused on making Seattle an international city. To this end, he invited entrepreneurs from all over the world, but especially from the Pacific Rim nations, to set up shop in Seattle. One result was that the city was able to weather the national economic downturn of the early 1990s better than most communities of similar size.

Rice was reelected in 1993. In 1996, he ran for governor of Washington but was defeated in the Democratic primary. After the reelection of President Bill Clinton that same year, it was rumored that Rice would be appointed secretary of the U.S. Department of Housing and Urban Development. By that time, he had decided to leave public service, however, and he did not pursue the appointment. He declined to run for reelection in 1997. After leaving office, he was the president and chief executive officer of the Federal Home Loan Bank of Seattle from 1998 to 2004. He later served as a distinguished practitioner-in-residence at the University of Washington's Evans School of Public Affairs. In 2010, Rice was named president and CEO of the Seattle Foundation, which awards grants to nonprofit organizations.

Further Reading
Sobol, Richard. *Mayor: In the Company of Norman Rice, Mayor of Seattle.* San Francisco: Cobblehill Books, 1996.

Rice, Susan E.
(1964–) *U.S. ambassador to the United Nations*

In January 2009, Susan E. Rice became the first African-American woman to serve as the U.S. ambassador to the United Nations. Rice was born in Washington, D.C., on November 17, 1964. Her father was an economics professor and a governor of the Federal Reserve Board. Her mother was an expert in education policy.

Rice attended National Cathedral School, an elite preparatory academy. During her high school years, she was a star basketball player, student body president, and class valedictorian. Rice continued her education at Stanford University in Palo Alto, California, where she earned a bachelor's degree in history in 1986. At Stanford, she met her future husband, television news producer Ian Cameron. The couple has two children.

After graduation, Rice attended New College at Oxford University in England as a Rhodes Scholar. There, she received master's and doctoral degrees in international relations. Back in the United States, Rice briefly served as a management consultant for McKinsey and Company.

In 1993, she began her career in public service by joining the administration of President Bill Clinton. A member of the National Security Council, she was named first director for international organizations and peacekeeping and later senior director for African affairs. She was awarded the council's Samuel Nelson Drew Memorial Ward in 2000 for her contributions to forming peaceful relationships among nations.

In 1997, at the age of 32, she became the assistant secretary of state for African affairs. Rice served under her mentor and family friend Madeleine K. Albright. While at the Department of State, Rice traveled to 48 African countries. She also acquired experience in dealing with the al-Qaeda terrorist group after the 1998 bombings of U.S. embassies in Tanzania and Kenya. During her service in the Clinton administration, Rice earned a reputation for her no-nonsense approach. As she said in an interview in the Stanford alumni magazine, "I guess you could say I'm plainspoken. I can be diplomatic when I have to be. But I don't have a lot of patience for BS."

In late 2002, Rice joined the Brookings Institution as a senior fellow. She kept her hand in politics, however. Rice was a senior adviser on national security affairs during the 2004 presidential campaign of John Kerry. In 2008, Rice, an early supporter of presidential contender BARACK OBAMA, served as Obama's foreign policy adviser. After he won the election, she was named as co-leader of the national security group of his transition team.

In December 2008, president-elect Obama nominated Rice to be the U.S. ambassador to the United Nations. She was confirmed on January 22, 2009. During the confirmation hearings in the U.S. Senate, she stated that her priorities at the UN would be to improve the organization's peacekeeping operations, lead on the world's response to climate change, help prevent the spread of nuclear weapons, and work to alleviate poverty throughout the world.

Further Reading

Blunt, Martha. "Into Africa." *Stanford Magazine*, January/February 2000. Available online. URL: http://www.stanfordalumni.org/news/magazine/2000/janfeb/articles/rice.html. Downloaded May 20, 2009.

Savage, Charles. "Susan E. Rice." *New York Times*, November 6, 2008. Available online. URL: http://www.nytimes.com/2008/11/07/us/politics/06rice.html?_r=1. Downloaded May 20, 2009.

Rogers, Joe
(Joseph B. Rogers)
(1964–   ) *lieutenant governor of Colorado*

At the time of his election, Joe Rogers was the youngest lieutenant governor in the United States. His political inexperience got him into trouble with the governor and the state legislature, and his political career came to a temporary end at the end of his first term.

Rogers was born on July 8, 1964, in Omaha, Nebraska. When he was two years old, he moved with his mother to Denver, Colorado; shortly thereafter she divorced his father, who was in the military. After finishing high school, he enrolled in Colorado State University where he received a B.S. in business in 1986. Three years later, he received a J.D. from the Arizona State University Law School and joined a Denver law firm. After practicing law for four years, in 1993 he moved to Washington, D.C., to work as a legal counsel to Hank Brown, a former U.S. senator from Colorado.

In 1995, Rogers returned to Denver to run for political office. The popular Democratic congresswoman Pat Schroeder had decided to retire from public office, and Rogers ran as a Republican for her seat. Despite his inexperience, he ran a tough race before losing 58-42 in the 1996 general election, a good showing for a political neophyte.

Rogers ran well enough in 1996 to earn a shot at the Republican nomination for lieutenant governor in 1998. His chief opponent was state senator Jim Congrove, a conservative who took a strong stance against abortion and gun control. Meanwhile, Rogers ran a clean, middle-of-the-road campaign and defeated Congrove handily. Then, in the general election, he bested his Democratic opponent, thus becoming at age 34 the youngest lieutenant governor in the country.

Almost immediately, Rogers ran afoul of the newly elected governor, Republican Bill Owens. Rather than keep his opinions to himself when they differed from those of the chief executive, Rogers criticized Owens whenever he disagreed with the governor. Owens responded by exercising his authority over Rogers in ways that only a governor can, such as holding up the paychecks for Rogers's staff. By 1999, Rogers's office manager had sued the governor for her pay, and Owens had released a list of spending by Rogers's office, which included a number of questionable expenditures. In late 1999, Rogers and Owens met and reportedly ironed out their differences, and from then on they seemed to work better together.

However, Rogers's actions had cost him much in terms of his relationship with the state legislature, which believed he had embarrassed the state by his actions.

In 2000, the Colorado legislature passed a bill that changed the way the state's lieutenant governor is selected. Rather than being chosen independently of the governor in the primaries and general election, and thus opening the possibility of having a governor and lieutenant governor of opposite parties, the bill gave the gubernatorial nominees the right to name their own running mates. In effect, the position of lieutenant governor was changed from an elective to an appointive position. Then, to further drive home the point that Rogers's actions had been unacceptable, the state legislature cut the budget of the lieutenant governor's office by 25 percent. In 2002, Owens ran for reelection as governor, but he dumped Rogers as his running mate.

The census of 2000 led to the creation of a seventh congressional district in Colorado. In 2002, Rogers declared his candidacy for the newly created seat. He lost the primary to Bob Beauprez, the eventual winner in the general election, after which Rogers returned to private life. He and his wife, Juanita, have three children.

Further Reading

Watkins, Michael J. "Joe Rogers, 1964– ." *Contemporary Black Biography* 27 (2001): 157–159.

Whitaker, Charles. "America's Youngest Lieutenant Governor." *Ebony* 55 (March 2000): 140–146.

Ross, Don
(Don R. Ross)
(1941–) *Oklahoma state representative*

Don Ross served in the Oklahoma state legislature for more than 20 years. He is best known for his efforts to keep alive the memory of the Tulsa Race Riot and to award reparations to its survivors.

Ross was born on March 11, 1941, in Tulsa, Oklahoma, to Israel and Pearline Ross. In 1959, he graduated from high school and enlisted in the U.S. Air Force. Honorably discharged four years later, he returned to Tulsa and found a job as a baker. Shortly thereafter, he began studying journalism at Central State University; by the time he received his B.S. in 1986, the school was known as the University of Central Oklahoma. In 1963, he began writing a weekly column about social and urban issues for the *Oklahoma Eagle,* a newspaper for and about African Americans; he continued to write the column into the 21st century. In 1967, he became the labor affairs director of the Tulsa Urban League. In 1972, he moved to Gary, Indiana, to become the assistant managing editor of the Gary *Post-Tribune,* thus becoming one of the first black newspaper editors in the country. Five years later, he returned to Tulsa to become vice president and general manager of the *Eagle.* He left in 1978 to form Don Ross & Associates, a public relations firm that he renamed Ebony Partners in 1995. He found time along the way to get married and help raise six children.

Ross became involved in politics in 1982 when he was elected as a Democrat to a seat in the Oklahoma lower house. He would go on to hold that seat for more than 20 years. As a state legislator, he authored the state's first affirmative action law; it gave preference to minority vendors wishing to do business with the state. He later wrote the law that set affirmative action goals for the state's institutions of higher learning. He played a major role in making Dr. Martin Luther King's birthday a state holiday, and he cosponsored a bill requiring that public schools teach the history of the state's minorities. He also led the fight to remove the Confederate flag from atop the state capitol. As a result, in 1989 Oklahoma became the first state in the nation to stop flying the Confederate flag over governmental buildings. In other areas, he focused on improving state funding for health and social services for African Americans, and he helped overhaul the state's laws regarding child labor.

Ross chaired the health and social services committee's subcommittee on appropriations and budget, which oversees the spending of more than $1 billion annually. He chaired the House of Representatives Democratic Caucus and the Oklahoma Legislative Black Caucus, vice-chaired the Tulsa County Democratic Party, and cochaired the Oklahoma Task Force on African-American Males.

Ross is best known for his efforts to publicize the facts surrounding the Tulsa Race Riot of 1921. The riot began after a black man was arrested for assaulting a white woman in an elevator. Although the sources are vague as to what actually happened, they suggest that the "assault" involved nothing more than the man accidentally stepping on the woman's foot. By the time the riot was over, marauding gangs of rifle-toting whites had shot and killed dozens of blacks and set fire to Greenwood, the African-American neighborhood on the north side of Tulsa. The fire destroyed 200 black-owned businesses and countless numbers of black residences.

Ross first wrote about the Tulsa Race Riot in 1968. Almost immediately, he was criticized vehemently by both blacks and whites for dredging up a sordid incident from the past that was best forgotten. Undaunted, he continued to investigate and publicize his findings about the riot, and in 1997 he wrote the bill that created the state-sponsored Tulsa Race Riot Commission. Ross has insisted that part of the commission's work should be to award reparations to the riot's survivors, many of whom were still living, and indeed, in 2001, the commission recommended that the state pay reparations to 130 survivors. Instead the legislature opted to build a race riot memorial, but without appropriating any funds for that purpose.

Further Reading

Golus, Carrie. "Don Ross, 1941– ." *Contemporary Black Biography* 27 (2001): 171–173.

Rush, Bobby

(Bobby L. Rush)
(1946–) *U.S. congressional representative from Illinois*

In 1993, Bobby Rush took office as the Illinois First District's representative in Congress. In so doing, he became the eighth straight African American to hold the seat since OSCAR DEPRIEST was elected to it in 1929.

Rush was born on November 23, 1946, in Albany, Georgia. His father, Jimmy, worked odd jobs, and his mother, Cora, was a beautician. At age seven, his parents separated, and he moved with his mother and siblings to Chicago, Illinois, where he grew up. In 1963, at age 17, he dropped out of high school and joined the U.S. Army. During part of his enlistment, he was stationed in Alabama, where he became involved in the Civil Rights movement. In 1966, he joined the Student Nonviolent Coordinating Committee and participated in a number of demonstrations in the Deep South. He eventually went AWOL to work for the movement full-time; rather than prosecute him as a deserter, and in the process risk blackening its own eye, the army gave him an honorable discharge.

In 1967, Rush founded the Chicago chapter of the Black Panther Party. This group of African-American militants was originally founded in 1966 in Oakland, California, as a means of protecting that city's black residents from police brutality. As they spread to other cities, the Black Panthers began espousing Marxist revolutionary theory and advocating that black people arm themselves for the coming struggle with racist whites. As the Black Panthers' defense minister, Rush devoted himself full-time to the group's activities. He narrowly missed being assassinated during a police raid of a party "safe house" in 1969, during which two Black Panthers were shot and killed.

Following the raid, Rush directed the party into more peaceful projects such as the Free Breakfast for Children and the Free Medical Clinic. The clinic tested African Americans for sickle-cell anemia; it also drew the health care community's attention to the problem, which led to a national research program into sickle-cell anemia's causes, effects, and solutions. Meanwhile, he enrolled in Chicago's Roosevelt University. His classwork was interrupted briefly in 1972 when he was jailed for six months on a weapons charge, but the following year he received a B.A. in general studies. He took a job selling life insurance and gradually distanced himself from the Black Panthers, quitting the group for good in 1974.

Despite leaving the Black Panthers, Rush still wanted to effect positive change for Chicago's blacks. In 1974, he ran for a seat on the city board of aldermen but was defeated. He remained interested in politics nevertheless and gradually drifted into the camp of HAROLD WASHINGTON. At the time, Washington was an Illinois state senator, and he had also worked to end police brutality in Chicago. Rush helped get out the vote for Washington

Former black militant Bobby Rush represents Chicago in the U.S. House of Representatives. *(Bobby Rush)*

when he ran successfully for Congress in 1980. Rush also helped Washington get elected mayor of Chicago in 1983, at the same time getting himself elected alderman from the Second Ward. He served in this position for nine years while also serving as a ward committeeman for the Democratic Party. These two positions allowed him to build up a large and loyal following, thus making him an influential figure in local politics.

In 1992, Rush challenged CHARLES HAYES for his seat in Congress. Hayes was vulnerable because of his involvement in the House banking scandal, during which hundreds of congresspeople had overdrawn their House checking accounts, in effect taking out interest-free loans at taxpayer expense. Rush narrowly defeated Hayes in the Democratic primary and then breezed to victory in the general election. He took his seat in 1993 and was assigned to the committees on banking/finance/urban affairs and government operations.

As a congressman, Rush continued to work primarily for the interests of the African-American community. He got the Justice Department to investigate charges that the Chicago police department routinely violated the civil rights of the city's black residents. His idea to establish federally funded community banks to foster economic development in inner-city neighborhoods was eventually incorporated into the Community Development and Regulatory Act. He introduced a bill to establish a coordinated attack against cockroaches, a major cause of asthma in inner-city children. He supported the implementation of the earned income tax credit for low-income families. Reassigned to the committee on energy and commerce, he introduced the Program for Investment in Microentrepreneurs (PRIME) Act that provided funding for training and technical assistance for small business owners.

While serving in Congress, Rush continued to grow and evolve. He received an M.A. in political science from the University of Illinois in Chicago in 1994, an M.A. in theological studies from McCormick Seminary in 1998, and was ordained a Baptist minister in 1999. That same year, he ran for mayor of Chicago but was soundly beaten by the incumbent, Richard M. Daley. In 1999, Rush's son was shot to death by robbers outside his Chicago home; afterward, Rush became a proponent of gun control, a complete but understandable turnabout from the way he had thought as a Black Panther. In addition to working to reduce violent crime, Rush has also become an important critic of human rights abuses in Sudan and an advocate for increasing access to technology. In 2010 he was reelected to a 10th term in Congress. He and his wife Carolyn have five children.

Further Reading

Biographical Directory of the United States Congress. "Rush, Bobby L., 1946–   ." Available online. URL: http://bioguide.congress.gov/scripts/biodis-play. pl?index=R000515. Downloaded April 15, 2009.

Congressman Bobby L. Rush, Official Web Site. Available online. URL: http://www.house.gov/rush. Downloaded April 23, 2009.

Idani, Michaeljulius. "Rush, Bobby." In *African American National Biography*, vol. 7, edited by Henry Louis Gates, Jr., and Evelyn Brooks Higginbotham. New York: Oxford University Press, 2008, pp. 35–36.

Krauss, Clifford. "The Hard Journey of Bobby Rush." *Gentlemen's Quarterly* 63 (August 1993): 162–170.

McCormick, John, and Peter Annin. "A Father's Anguished Journey." *Newsweek* 134, no. 22 (November 29, 1999): 52–53.

S

Savage, Gus
(Gustavus Savage)
(1925–) *U.S. congressional representative from Illinois*

First elected to Congress in 1980, Gus Savage was a throwback to the early days of the Civil Rights movement. He was known as "The Warrior" for his combative style and militant rhetoric, but by the end of his career these characteristics, which had made him successful, led to his downfall.

Savage was born on October 30, 1925, in Detroit, Michigan. At age five, he moved with his parents, Thomas and Molly, to Chicago, Illinois, where he grew up. After finishing high school in 1943, he joined the U.S. Army and served through the end of World War II. In 1946, he returned to Chicago and married Eunice King, with whom he had three children. That same year, he enrolled in Roosevelt University, graduating with a B.A. in philosophy in 1951. He spent a year doing graduate work at Roosevelt and a year studying law at Chicago-Kent College of Law, the law school of the Illinois Institute of Technology, before becoming a journalist in 1953. In 1965, he founded Citizen Newspapers and began editing and publishing weekly journals for a number of black communities in the Chicago area. Over the next 12 years, these papers emerged as powerful voices for equal opportunity and social justice.

Savage became involved in politics in 1948, when he worked as an organizer for Henry Wallace, the Progressive Party candidate for president. He remained involved during the 1950s by working for civil rights, particularly by picketing city hall for equal housing for minorities. In the 1960s, he served as chairman of the South End Voters Conference and Protest at the Polls, and as campaign manager of the Midwest League of Negro Voters, all of which sought to achieve a greater voice for African Americans in the political process in the North Central states. In 1976, he chaired the Committee for a Black Mayor of Chicago, and in this capacity he served as campaign manager for HAROLD WASHINGTON in his unsuccessful first attempt to become Chicago's mayor.

Savage first ran for office in 1968, when he challenged Democratic incumbent William T. Murphy for his seat in the U.S. House of Representatives. Murphy was backed by Mayor Richard J. Daley's political machine, and he easily defeated Savage in the primary. Undaunted, Savage ran against Murphy again two years later, with the same result. When Murphy announced that he would not seek reelection in 1980, Savage ran against three other candidates for the seat. Despite not being endorsed by the Daley machine, he won the primary and the general election. He took his seat in 1981 and was assigned to the committee on public works and transportation.

As a congressman, Savage continued to work for equal opportunity. His most impressive contribution in this regard came in 1987, when he successfully amended that year's defense appropriations bill to include a 5 percent set-aside for minority-owned businesses. This amendment alone put more than $100 million into the pockets of minority contractors.

In foreign affairs, Savage was a bit of a maverick. He opposed the U.S. invasions of Grenada, Panama, Kuwait, and Iraq, and he was one of the few advocates in Congress for the creation of a Palestinian state. He was also one of Congress's most vocal opponents of U.S. support for Israel, and he complained bitterly about the $3 billion annual subsidy provided to it by the United States. His opposition to Israel led him to make a number of intemperate remarks that were offensive to Jews, and he gained a reputation for being anti-Semitic.

This reputation came back to haunt Savage during his 1992 reelection campaign. Illinois's congressional districts had just been redrawn in accordance with the census of 1990, and his former black-majority district now included a number of Jewish-majority communities. In addition, the American Israel Public Affairs Committee targeted Savage for defeat and contributed generously to his opponent's campaign. Meanwhile, Savage's militant rhetoric had come to irritate African-American voters, many of whom now believed that greater political gains for blacks could be achieved by cooperating with whites than by confronting them. Other voters were put off by Savage when he was investigated by the Ethics Committee on charges of sexual harassment. His reelection bid was doomed, however, several days before the primary, when the car of his opponent, Mel Reynolds, was fired upon by drive-by shooters. Although no one blamed Savage directly for the incident, many voters blamed his militant rhetoric for creating an atmosphere that encouraged violence. Defeated in the primary, he retired after his term expired in 1993.

Further Reading

Biographical Directory of the United States Congress. "Savage, Gus, 1925– ." Available online. URL: http://bioguide.congress.gov/scripts/biodisplay.pl?index=S000081. Downloaded April 11, 2009.

Black Americans in Congress. "Gus Savage." Available online. URL: http://baic.house.gov/member-profiles/profile.html?intID=56. Downloaded April 2, 2009.

Clay, William L. *Just Permanent Interests: Black Americans in Congress, 1870–1992.* New York: Amistad Press, 1993.

Schmoke, Kurt
(Kurt Lidell Schmoke)
(1949–) *mayor of Baltimore, Maryland*

Kurt Schmoke was the first African-American mayor of Baltimore, Maryland. After leaving office, he became dean of his alma mater, the Howard University Law School.

Schmoke was born on December 1, 1949, in Baltimore. His father, Murray, was a chemist, and his mother, Irene, was a clerk-typist. After graduating from high school, he enrolled in Yale University and received a B.A. in 1971. He spent the next two years at Oxford University as a Rhodes Scholar and then entered Harvard University Law School, receiving a J.D. in 1976. He then returned to Baltimore where he joined a prestigious law firm. A year later, he was recruited to join President Jimmy Carter's domestic policy staff. In 1979, he returned to Baltimore, this time to work as a prosecutor in the U.S. district attorney's office. While in law school, he married Patricia Locks, with whom he has two children.

In a sense, Schmoke's political career began in high school, when he was elected student body president of his mostly white school. Indeed, at age 14 he had declared his ambition to one day become mayor of Baltimore. This ambition led him to forgo a brilliant legal career as well as one in the federal government so that he could enter local politics and make a run at the coveted office.

In 1982, Schmoke made his first major step toward the mayor's office by getting elected state's attorney for the city of Baltimore. Over the next four years, he oversaw the activities of more than 100 prosecutors. As state's attorney, he worked hard to combat the city's growing traffic in illegal drugs, seeking the death penalty for drug dealers who murdered undercover investigators.

In 1987, Baltimore's popular mayor, William Donald Schaefer, left office to become the governor of Maryland. He was succeeded as mayor by Clarence Burns, the city council president. Later that year, Schmoke declared his candidacy for the Democratic nomination for mayor, despite the common assumption that Burns, as Schaefer's right-hand man, would be easily elected. As mayor, Schaefer had done much to revitalize downtown Baltimore, but he had done little for the people living in the city's poor neighborhoods. Schmoke appealed directly to these people during the campaign by declaring that Schaefer had made Baltimore "prettier but poorer." He also attacked Schaefer's record on social problems, especially the growing rates of teen pregnancies and high school dropouts. Schmoke beat Burns in a close race by garnering most of the black votes in this black-majority city and a considerable number of the white votes as well. He easily won the general election and took office that same year.

As mayor, Schmoke focused on solving the social problems that Schaefer had largely ignored. He established reading centers to combat adult illiteracy, and he founded the Baltimore Commonwealth, a partnership between the city school board and various private businesses and organizations that established an endowment fund for assisting college students with their tuition. He created the Community Development Financing Corporation as a means of providing low-interest loans for low-income renters who wanted to purchase and renovate abandoned houses.

Like most mayors, Schmoke generated considerable controversy during his tenure. Shortly after taking office, he went on record as favoring the legalization of some forms of drug use. He made the remarks on the grounds that drug abuse should be considered a public health issue and not just a criminal justice concern. As a prosecutor, he had come to realize that drug dealing was too lucrative to ever be stamped out; consequently, it made sense to legalize certain aspects of it so that drug usage could be regulated from the standpoint of public health. In this regard, he proposed the establishment of a needle exchange program as a way of combating the spread of HIV/AIDS and of administering low dosages of narcotics to addicts at government-run centers, so as to hold down the cost of emergency medical care for addicts. Not surprisingly, such proposals outraged a number of Baltimoreans. Among the most livid were African Americans who considered the dealing of illegal drugs to be a form of genocide directed against blacks.

The drug-legalization flap eventually died down, but a more persistent criticism of Schmoke throughout his tenure as mayor was his style of governing. Schaefer, his predecessor, had been a gregarious leader who was seen and heard all over Baltimore. As befits a former Rhodes Scholar, Schmoke was more thoughtful and measured in his consideration of the various options and in his dealings with the body politic. His scholarly approach to government and to people was often mistaken for aloofness. Another perceived problem, at least in the African-American community, was his failure to do more about "black" issues; indeed, many of his programs were designed to help lower-income Baltimoreans regardless of race. His refusal to pander to one race or the other, however, earned him the respect of most city residents, who reelected him to two more terms.

Throughout his administration, Schmoke struggled to combat Baltimore's rising homicide rate. Despite early achievements, he also seemed unable to develop a satisfactory plan for reversing decades of urban decay. He lost his bid for a fourth term when he was defeated in the 1999 Democratic primary. After leaving office, that same year, he returned to the private practice of law. In 2002, he was named dean of the Howard University Law School in Washington, D.C.

Further Reading

Cheers, D. Michael. "Baltimore Breakthrough." *Ebony* 43 (February 1988): 180.

Harris, Jessica Christina. "Schmoke, Kurt." In *African American National Biography,* vol. 7, edited by Henry Louis Gates, Jr., and Evelyn Brooks Higginbotham. New York: Oxford University Press, 2008, pp. 96–97.

"Schmoke, Kurt L." *Current Biography* 56 (February 1995): 38–41.

Scott, Bobby

(Robert Cortez Scott)
(1947–   ) *U.S. congressional representative from Virginia*

In 1993, Bobby Scott was elected to the U.S. House of Representatives from Virginia. It was the first time since JOHN LANGSTON had left office in 1891 that an African American had represented the state in Congress.

Scott was born on April 30, 1947, in Washington, D.C. His father, Charles, was a physician, and his mother, Mae, was a teacher. As a young boy, he moved with his family to Newport News, Virginia, where he grew up. He attended Groton School, a prestigious private school in Massachusetts, received a B.A. from Harvard University in 1969, and a J.D. from Boston College Law School in 1973. He then returned to Newport News where he opened a law practice. He specialized in civil rights cases, and in 1974 he was elected president of the Newport News branch of the National Association for the Advancement of Colored People.

In 1978, Scott was elected as a Democrat to the Virginia General Assembly's lower house. He served there until 1983, when he was elected to the state senate. As a state legislator, he played a major role in enacting bills to raise the state's minimum wage, increase Medicaid health care benefits for women and children, increase unemployment benefits, and provide liability insurance for small businesses. He introduced the Neighborhood Assistance Act, which provides tax breaks to companies that donate to certain social service and crime prevention programs. During his 10 years as a state senator, he earned a reputation for being an able legislator and a moderate.

Scott first ran for Congress in 1984, when he narrowly lost to a popular incumbent, Herbert Bateman. In 1992, he ran again, with a different result. The census of 1990 had mandated that Virginia redraw its congressional districts, and in the process the state legislature created a black-majority district that included Scott's neighborhood. He countered his lack of support by the state Democratic organization with his popularity in the African-American neighborhoods in Richmond and the Tidewater area and an endorsement from JESSE JACKSON. He defeated two other black contenders in the Democratic primary and easily won the general election. He took his seat in 1993 and was assigned to the committees on the judiciary, science/space/technology, and education/labor.

As a congressman, Scott sided with the moderate Democrats. He worked to prevent police brutality by sponsoring the Death in Custody Act, which requires law enforcement officials to investigate the deaths of anyone under arrest or in jail. He has consistently supported crime prevention programs, but not those that call for an increased reliance on the death penalty. He sponsored the Individuals with Disability Education Act, which guarantees the rights of disabled children to receive an appropriate education at public expense. Although he opposed the Iraq War, he has been a good friend to defense contractors, largely because the nation's largest naval shipyard and several defense installations are located in his district.

In 1997, the U.S. Supreme Court invalidated the boundaries of Scott's district on the grounds that it had been gerrymandered in terms of race. By 1998, the district had been realigned, but in such a way that it still encompassed a black majority. Scott was easily reelected that year. In 2010, he was returned to Congress for a 10th term.

Further Reading

Biographical Directory of the United States Congress. "Scott, Robert Cortez, 1947– ." Available online. URL: http://bioguide.congress.gov/scripts/biodisplay.pl?index=S000185. Downloaded April 11, 2009.

Clay, William L. *Just Permanent Interests: Black Americans in Congress, 1870–1992.* New York: Amistad Press, 1993.

Congressman Bobby Scott, Official Web Site. Available online. URL: http://www.bobbyscott.house.gov. Downloaded April 11, 2009.

"Robert C. Scott." *Congressional Quarterly Weekly Report* 51 (January 16, 1993, supplement): 141.

Sharpton, Al
(Alfred Charles Sharpton, Jr.)
(1954–) *presidential candidate*

Best known for his activism and for his flamboyant personality, Al Sharpton has occasionally entered the political arena, most notably in 2004, when he ran for president of the United States.

Born in Brooklyn on October 3, 1954, Sharpton became a public figure at an early age. At four, he was regularly preaching at his parents' church. When he was 10, his pastor ordained him as a minister. Known as the Wonderboy, Sharpton made appearances throughout the New York area and went on tour with gospel singer Mahalia Jackson.

When he was 12, Sharpton went to see Reverend ADAM CLAYTON POWELL, JR., preach. The first African-American congressman from New York, Powell greatly impressed the young Sharpton. The boy negotiated his way into a face-to-face meeting with Powell, whose style and swagger greatly influenced Sharpton.

While still in high school, Sharpton became involved in community protests and became acquainted with famed activist JESSE JACKSON. In 1971, he founded the National Youth Movement, an organization charged with combating police brutality. The next year, he graduated from Tipton High School and then attended Brooklyn College for two years. In 1978, Sharpton planned a run for a seat on the state legislature, but his bid was aborted when a judge found he did not meet the necessary residency requirements.

Sharpton was a dynamic speaker, with a reputation for drawing large crowds. But he did not become a national figure until he became involved in the Bernard Goetz case in 1985. Goetz, a white man, shot several young African-American men on the New York subway. Sharpton organized a series of demonstrations seeking justice for the black victims. Throughout the 1980s and 1990s, Sharpton drew attention to a variety of other cases in which African Americans were physically harmed or killed by white assailants. For instance, he organized rallies in the name of Michael Griffith, who was killed by whites in Howard Beach, Brooklyn, in 1986; Abner Louima, who was brutalized in police custody in 1997; and Amadou Diallo, who was shot with 19 bullets by police officers in 1999.

Most notoriously, however, Sharpton in 1987 became a champion of Tawana Brawley, a black teenager who claimed she had been abducted, tortured, and raped by a gang of white men. Sharpton inflamed public opinion over Brawley's shocking charges. He and her other supporters went so far as to assert that the Dutchess County assistant district attorney Steven Pagones was one of Brawley's rapists. A grand jury report found that Brawley's charges had no merit and deemed the entire episode a hoax. Pagones sued Sharpton for defamation of character, and after a lengthy court battle Sharpton was ordered to pay Pagones

$65,000. He refused to admit wrongdoing and had wealthy supporters pay the judgment.

Tarnished in the press by the Brawley affair, Sharpton nevertheless remained in the public eye. In 1990s, Sharpton ran for the U.S. Senate from New York several times without success. In 1997, he entered the Democratic primary for mayor of New York City. He lost the contest, although he did win 32 percent of the vote.

As the 2004 presidential election approached, Sharpton announced that he would compete for the Democratic nomination. Although he was judged to have no chance of winning, he was able to appear in televised debates, during which he often delivered entertaining and unexpected answers in the otherwise staid forums. Supporters praised Sharpton for entering the race because he forced the leading candidates to confront issues they might otherwise have ignored, such as the high rate of incarceration for African-American men. Detractors condemned Sharpton as irrelevant, claiming that the African-American community had long ago abandoned his brand of divisive politics.

In March 2004, Sharpton conceded the race to the Democratic nominee, Senator John Kerry. He has since been involved in the high profile cases of Sean Bell, a young black man killed by undercover officers in New York City in 2006, and the Jena Six, a group of African-American youths in Jena, Louisiana, accused of attempted murder. Sharpton is also a regular guest on televised public affairs programs and the host of his own daily radio show, "Keepin' It Real with Al Sharpton."

Since the mid-1980s, Sharpton has been married to singer Kathy Jordan. They have two children.

Further Reading

Sharpton, Al, and Anthony Walton. *Go and Tell Pharoah: The Autobiography of the Reverend Al Sharpton.* New York: Doubleday, 1996.
———, with Karen Hunter. *Al on America.* New York: Dafina Books, 2002.

Slater, Rodney
(Rodney Earl Slater)
(1955–) *U.S. secretary of transportation*

In 1997, Rodney Slater and ALEXIS HERMAN were appointed by Democratic president Bill Clinton to posts in the U.S. cabinet. Slater achieved his position largely as a result of having worked for a number of years as a Clinton aide in Arkansas and Washington.

Slater was born on February 23, 1955, in Tutwyler, Mississippi. Shortly after his birth, his mother, Velma, married Earl Brewer, a mechanic and maintenance man, and the family moved to Marianna, Arkansas, where he grew up. As a boy, he helped his mother pick cotton and peaches to make ends meet. A star athlete in high school, he won a football scholarship to Eastern Michigan University and received a B.S. in 1977. He then enrolled in the University of Arkansas School of Law and received a J.D. three years later. While in law school, he married Cassandra Wilkins, with whom he has one child.

Slater's father-in-law was Henry Wilkins, an Arkansas state legislator, and in 1979 Wilkins introduced Slater to Bill Clinton, at the time the newly elected governor of Arkansas. Upon graduating from law school, Slater was helped by Clinton to obtain a position as an assistant attorney general. Slater resigned in 1982 to work on Clinton's reelection campaign; after Clinton's victory, Slater stayed on as the governor's special assistant for community and minority affairs. In 1987, he was appointed to the state highway commission, and in 1992 he was named to chair the commission. Later that year, he joined Clinton's presidential campaign team as deputy campaign manager and senior traveling adviser.

Following Clinton's inauguration, Slater was appointed to head the Federal Highway Administration. In this position, he helped develop an innovative financing program that allowed many highway construction projects to be completed on time and under budget, and he trimmed the agency's staff so that more funds could be diverted to highway construction and repair. He made a name for himself in 1994 when he quickly developed a plan for rebuilding freeways damaged in an earthquake in southern California. His critics deplored his efforts to double the maximum allowable weight for trucks on interstate highways and to abolish the 55-mile-per-hour national speed limit that had been imposed following the oil shortages of the 1970s.

In 1997, Clinton appointed Slater as secretary of the Department of Transportation. In this capacity, he oversaw the nation's highways, its commercial aviation and mass transportation systems, and the U.S. Coast Guard, and managed more than 100,000 employees and a budget of approximately $40 billion. Upon taking office, he determined that transportation in general was not keeping up with state-of-the-art developments in communications and computer technology. To remedy this situation, he founded the Morgan Technology and Transportation Futures Program. Named in honor of African-American inventor Garrett Morgan, who invented the first traffic light, this education program provided additional training in mathematics and science for students interested in a career in transportation. In terms of safety, he urged the states to pass tougher laws against drunk driving, and he made the public aware of the dangers of air bags to small children. He was a major player in Clinton's Africa Initiative, by which the United States sought to strengthen its economic ties with the developing nations of sub-Saharan Africa. Slater, in particular, sought to help improve the safety of their commercial airlines while also expanding regular air and water transportation between Africa and North America.

Slater resigned as secretary of transportation in 2001, following the election of Republican president George W. Bush. He became a partner in the law firm of Patton Boggs and headed its transportation practice group in Washington.

Further Reading
Patton Boggs LLP. "Rodney E. Slater." Available online. URL: http://www.pattonboggs.com/rslater. Downloaded April 25, 2009.
Thompson, Cliff, ed. "Slater, Rodney." *Current Biography Yearbook 1999.* New York: H. W. Wilson, 1999.

Smalls, Robert
(1839–1915) *U.S. congressional representative from South Carolina*

Robert Smalls was the last of six African-American congressmen from South Carolina to serve during Reconstruction. In terms of his ability to "deliver the goods," he was probably the most successful.

Smalls was born on April 5, 1839, in Beaufort, South Carolina. His mother, Lydia, was a slave, and his father was probably Lydia's master, John McKee. At age 12, he was sent to live with McKee's relatives in Charleston. He was allowed to hire out his services to whomever he desired and to retain part of the money he earned to spend as he pleased. He taught himself how to read and write and briefly attended a school for free blacks. In 1856, he married Hannah Jones, with whom he had three children.

By 1861, Smalls had become a skilled seaman and pilot. When the Civil War broke out, he was put to work by the Confederate government on the *Planter,* a dispatch boat; within a year he had become the vessel's pilot. In May 1862, he and the ship's black crewmen snuck their families on board in the middle of the night and sailed the *Planter* out to where the Union navy was blockading Charleston Harbor. As a result of his exploits, he became a hero throughout the North. In addition to being rewarded financially by the U.S. government for delivering the *Planter,* he was kept on as its pilot after it was commissioned into the Union navy and put into use as a transport ship. He claimed that he had also served as the ship's captain after it was retrofitted into a gunboat in

Robert Smalls represented South Carolina in the U.S. House of Representatives. *(Library of Congress)*

1863, but he could never produce satisfactory evidence to substantiate the claim.

The *Planter* operated out of Beaufort, which had been captured by Union forces in 1862, and before the war ended Smalls had opened a store there that catered to freedmen. After the war ended, he was able to buy McKee's house from the government at a fraction of its value. By 1870, he owned a considerable amount of property and exercised a considerable amount of influence among both black and white residents in the Beaufort area.

Smalls began his political career in 1868 when he served as a delegate to the state constitutional convention. At the convention, he drafted the resolution that led to the creation of state-funded public education in South Carolina. That same year, he joined the Republican Party and was elected to the state's lower house. Two years later, he was elected to the state senate, where he served

for the next four years. For most of his tenure in the senate, he chaired the printing committee, which oversaw the bidding out of the state's printing requirements.

In 1874, Smalls was elected to the U.S. House of Representatives, where he served off and on until 1887. In 1877, following his reelection to Congress, he was convicted of accepting a $5,000 bribe from a South Carolina printer while chairing the printing committee. He was sentenced to three years' hard labor but served only three days, having been pardoned by the governor. His criminal record and the renewed activities of the Red Shirts, South Carolina's version of the Ku Klux Klan, kept him from being reelected in 1878. In 1880, he was defeated again, but this time he contested the results and won, taking his seat toward the end of the term. He declined to run in 1884, but when the winner died shortly after the election Smalls was chosen to finish out the remainder of the term.

Although Smalls served on the agricultural committee and the War Claims Commission, he spent most of his time on affairs that affected South Carolina. He successfully introduced bills to improve naval facilities at Port Royal and to return The Citadel, South Carolina's military college, to state control. He was also a vocal and successful proponent of keeping federal troops in South Carolina, where they were needed to protect freedmen from the depredations of the Red Shirts and related groups. He also managed to get a bill passed that provided for the construction of several government buildings in Beaufort. In matters such as these, he demonstrated more political ability than did most of his fellow African-American congressmen, but in matters regarding civil rights, he was less successful. He introduced bills prohibiting racial discrimination in the U.S. armed forces and outlawing racial discrimination in public establishments in the District of Columbia, both of which failed to pass.

Smalls was denied reelection in 1886, and he never held elected office again. Nevertheless, he remained politically active for a number of years.

He helped THOMAS MILLER get elected to Congress in 1890, and he served as one of five black delegates to the state constitutional convention in 1895, where he fought a losing battle against the disfranchisement of African-American voters. Meanwhile, he served as collector of customs for the port of Beaufort under every Republican president from 1889 to 1913. In 1890, he married Annie Wigg, with whom he had one child (his first wife had died seven years earlier).

Smalls remained a determined supporter of civil rights for African Americans until his last days. In 1913, at age 74, he managed to prevent the lynching of two black prisoners in Beaufort jail. A former brigadier general in the state militia who had been invited to serve as colonel of an African-American regiment in the Spanish-American War, he threatened to raise and lead a black lynch mob on a rampage through the white part of town if the prisoners were harmed in any way. He died on February 23, 1915, in Beaufort.

Further Reading

Billingsley, Andrew. *Yearning to Breathe Free: Robert Smalls of South Carolina and his Families.* Columbia: University of South Carolina Press, 2007.

Biographical Directory of the United States Congress. "Smalls, Robert, 1839–1915." Available online. URL: http://bioguide.congress.gov/scripts/bio display. pl?index=S000502. Downloaded April 1, 2009.

Black Americans in Congress. "Robert Smalls." Available online. URL: http://baic.house.gov/member-profiles/profile.html?intID=15. Downloaded April 2, 2009.

Miller, Edward A. *Gullah Statesman: Robert Smalls from Slavery to Congress, 1839–1915.* Columbia: University of South Carolina Press, 1995.

Robert Smalls Official Web Site and Information Center. Available online. URL: http://www.robert smalls.org. Downloaded March 29, 2009.

Uya, Okun E. *From Slavery to Political Service: Robert Smalls, 1839–1915.* New York: Oxford University Press, 1971.

Steele, Michael

(1958–) *Republican National Committee chairman*

Colorful and controversial, Michael Steele in January 2009 was elected chairman of the Republican National Committee (RNC), becoming the first African American to head that organization in its 155-year history.

On October 19, 1958, Steele was born at Andrews Air Force Base in Prince George's County, Maryland. As a baby, he was adopted by William and Maebell Steele. After William Steele's death, Maebell Steele eked out a living as a laundress. But, as Michael Steele later recalled, she refused to go on welfare. According to Steele, she said she wanted her child to be raised by his mother, not by the government.

One of the first people in his family to go to college, Steele attended Johns Hopkins University in Baltimore, Maryland, where he was voted student body president. He received a bachelor's degree in international relations in 1981. Steele studied for the priesthood for several years before deciding instead to pursue a career in public service. In 1985, he married Andrea Derritt, a bank executive. The couple has two sons.

Steele enrolled in Georgetown University in Washington, D.C., and earned his law degree in 1991. The same year, he joined the Washington law firm of Cleary, Gottlieb, Steen, and Hamilton. In 1997, he went to work at Mills Corporation, a real estate development company, and in 1998, he founded the Steele Group, a consulting firm.

Beginning in the Reagan administration, Steele developed an interest in politics. Between 1994 and 2000, he served as the chair of the Republican committee of Prince George's County. After a failed campaign for comptroller, Steele became the chair of Maryland's Republican Party in 2000.

In July 2002, Steele decided to run for lieutenant governor of Maryland, joining the ticket of Republican gubernatorial candidate Rob Ehrich.

At a campaign debate, staffers of their Democratic opponents were accused of passing out Oreo cookies as a means of insinuating Steele lacked empathy with and involvement in the black community. Eyewitness reports varied greatly about the Oreo cookie incident. Some have held that Oreos were thrown at Steele. Others have denied the entire Oreo story. Despite the controversy, Ehrich and Steele won the election. Steele became the first African American elected to statewide office in Maryland.

When Maryland senator Paul Sarbanes chose not to run for reelection in 2006, Steele made a bid for his seat. He won the Republican primary but was defeated in the general election by the Democratic candidate, former representative Benjamin L. Cardin. Steele then reportedly sought the chairmanship of the RNC, the organization that coordinates the Republican Party's platform and fund-raising. He lost that post to Senator Mel Martinez of Florida, although he was named chairman of the Republican political action committee GOPAC in 2007.

In January 2009, Steele again campaigned to be named chairman of the RNC. In a spirited contest between six contenders, he won the position on the sixth ballot. Following the Republican electoral defeats of November 2008, Steele promised to reinvigorate the party. But in his first few months as RNC chairman, he instead courted controversy with a series of embarrassing gaffes. For instance, in an interview with GQ magazine, he suggested that he fell on the pro-choice side of the abortion debate, while the RNC was officially against abortion. Steele was also compelled to apologize after he called the popular radio show of right-wing personality Rush Limbaugh "incendiary" and "ugly." While some Republicans called for Steele's resignation, the conservative magazine National Review came to his defense: "Some Republicans are urging Steele to avoid the spotlight and instead work on fund-raising and organization. It's bad advice. Steele won the RNC chairmanship largely on the strength of his com-

munication skills. He ought to be able to master both the low-profile and high-profile aspects of his job."

Even as the Republican Party became accustomed to Steele's gaffes, he came under fire in March 2010 with the news that the RNC paid a $2,000 bill at a strip club. In July 2010, Steele was once again in the hot seat for stating that the U.S. war in Afghanistan was "a war of [President Barack] Obama's choosing," although the conflict was initiated during the administration of OBAMA's Republican predecessor. Despite calls for his dismissal, Steele managed to hold on to his chairmanship.

Further Reading
Burton, Danielle. "10 Things You Didn't Know About Michael Steele." *U.S. News & World Report*, April 7, 2008. Available online. URL: http://www.usnews.com/articles/news/politics/2008/04/07/10-things-you-didnt-know-about-michael-steele.html. Downloaded May 26, 2009.
Nagourney, Adam. "New Face of G.O.P. Brings a Brash Style." *New York Times*, February 4, 2009. Available online. URL: http://www.nytimes.com/2009/02/04/us/politics/03web-nagourney.html. Downloaded May 26, 2009.

Stokes, Carl
(Carl Burton Stokes)
(1927–1996) *mayor of Cleveland, Ohio*

Carl Stokes was the first African American to be elected mayor of a major U.S. city. Although his tenure as mayor was short-lived, his victory demonstrated that African Americans could be elected to major offices despite their race.

Stokes was born on June 21, 1927, in Cleveland, Ohio. His father, Charles, worked in a laundry, and his mother, Louise, was a homemaker. When Carl was two, his father died, and his mother supported the family as a domestic worker. At age 17, he dropped out of high school, and he spent the next year hustling pool, training as a boxer, and inspecting valves for a local manufacturer. In 1945, he was drafted into the U.S. Army and served in Germany during World War II. Discharged as a corporal in 1946, he returned to Cleveland, completed high school, and used the G.I. Bill to pay his way through college. After one year at West Virginia State College and two years at Case Western Reserve University, in 1950 he went to work as an enforcement officer for the Ohio Department of Liquor Control and began raiding unlicensed "gin joints" run by African Americans. The following year, he married Edith Smith. They had no children.

In 1953, Stokes almost got shot by a bootlegger during a raid. Two things happened as a result: His wife left him, and he returned to school, this time the University of Minnesota. After receiving a B.S. in law in 1954, he enrolled in Cleveland-Marshall College of Law at Cleveland State University and received an LL.B. in 1956. The following year, he passed the bar examination and formed a legal practice in Cleveland with his brother, LOUIS STOKES. In 1958, he married Shirley Edwards, with whom he had three children.

Stokes became interested in politics while a student at Case Western. John Holly, a black politician who was recruiting black voters for the 1949 Democratic gubernatorial candidate, hired Stokes to drive him around northern Ohio. The spectacle of Holly in action so fascinated Stokes that he dropped out of school so he could travel the entire state with Holly. He put what he learned to use while a student at Minnesota, where he managed the unsuccessful campaign of a black policeman running for the Minneapolis city council. Shortly after taking up the practice of law, he joined the Young Democrats and managed Lowell Henry's successful bid for a seat on Cleveland's city council.

In 1958, Holly managed to get Stokes appointed assistant city police prosecutor. This position freed him from his law practice and gave him the time to concentrate on his own political career. That same year, he ran for the state senate, and in 1960 he campaigned for a seat in the lower house, but

both times he lost in the Democratic primary. By 1962, he had made himself known to the voters, and that year he was elected state representative. Reelected twice, he established a reputation as a moderate while working successfully for gun control, improved mental health services, cleaner air, and equal rights for African Americans.

In 1965, Stokes made his first run for mayor of Cleveland. Ralph Locher, the Democratic incumbent, had fallen into disfavor with the city's black populace for a number of reasons. The unemployment rate in their neighborhoods was rising with no end in sight, the city's urban renewal program was displacing large numbers of them from their neighborhoods without finding them new homes, and they perceived that the police were hassling them for no good reason. Denied the support of the Democratic Party, Stokes obtained the backing of the United Freedom Movement, a local civil rights coalition, and ran as an independent. In the three-way general election, he came in second to Locher by less than 3,000 votes. Encouraged by his near-defeat, he immediately began campaigning for the 1967 race. His chances were buoyed tremendously in 1966, when Locher performed poorly during a three-day race riot. Stokes easily bested Locher in the primary, then eked out a narrow victory over his Republican challenger.

As mayor, Stokes worked hard to revitalize Cleveland. He used his friendship with Vice President Hubert H. Humphrey to secure a $10 million federal urban renewal grant. He got the business community to create Cleveland Now!, which raised $4 million to fund various community improvement projects. He equalized city services in all the neighborhoods, black and white, inaugurated a major hiring program to put a proportionate number of African Americans on the city payroll, and eased tensions between the police department and the black community by hiring more black police officers. Then, in 1968, disaster struck. Another race riot broke out when the police and a black nationalist group got into a shootout. Before the riot ended, nine people were killed, more than during the riot of two years earlier. To make matters worse, it was disclosed that the black nationalists had purchased their weapons with money raised by Cleveland Now!, thus killing that program as well.

Although Stokes was reelected in 1969 by a wider margin than before, the riot hung over his second term like a black cloud. It soured his relations with the chief of police, the city council president, the business community, and white residents. Meanwhile, the city's economy worsened, and when the voters rejected a tax increase, thousands of city workers were laid off indefinitely, thus souring his relationship with the black community. By 1971, he realized he could not win a third term, so he announced his retirement from politics.

When his term expired in 1972, Stokes left Cleveland to take a job as a television news correspondent and anchorman in New York City. The following year he divorced his wife. In 1981, he married Raija Kostadinov and returned to Cleveland to renew his legal career. In 1983, he was elected to the bench of the Cleveland Municipal Court, and he became its chief judge three years later. In 1994, he was appointed ambassador to the Republic of the Seychelles, an island nation in the West Indian Ocean. He died on April 3, 1996, in Cleveland.

Further Reading

"Carl & Louis Stokes." The Western Reserve Historical Society. Available online. URL: http://www.stokescleveland.org/index.htm. Downloaded March 29, 2009.

Colburn, David R., and Jeffrey S. Adler. *African-American Mayors: Race, Politics, and the American City.* Urbana: University of Illinois Press, 2001.

Haskins, James. *A Piece of the Power: Four Black Mayors.* New York: Dial Press, 1972.

Moore, Leonard N. *Carl B. Stokes and the Rise of Black National Power.* Urbana: University of Illinois Press, 2002.

Stokes, Carl. *Promises of Power: A Political Autobiography.* New York: Simon & Schuster, 1973.

Weinberg, Kenneth G. *Black Victory: Carl Stokes and the Winning of Cleveland.* Chicago: Quadrangle Books, 1968.

Zannes, Estelle, and Mary Jean Thomas. *Checkmate in Cleveland: The Rhetoric of Confrontation during the Stokes Years.* Cleveland: Press of Case Western Reserve University, 1972.

Stokes, Louis

(1925–) *U.S. congressional representative from Ohio*

Louis Stokes was the first African-American congressman from Ohio. During his 30 years in Congress, he was a strong supporter of civil rights and equal opportunity. He also chaired several highly visible investigative committees.

Stokes was born on February 23, 1925, in Cleveland, Ohio. His father, Charles, worked in a laundry, and his mother, Louise, was a homemaker. When Louis was four, his father died, and his mother supported the family as a domestic worker. After graduating from high school in 1943, he joined the U.S. Army. Discharged in 1946, he returned to Cleveland and enrolled in Case Western Reserve University. He received a B.A. in 1948, then studied at the Cleveland-Marshall College of Law at Cleveland State University. He received an LL.B. in 1953, and the following year he passed the bar examination and became a partner in a Cleveland law firm. The firm handled all types of cases, but his specialty was civil rights. In 1960, he married Jeannette Jay, with whom he had four children.

Stokes got involved in politics in 1962 when his brother, CARL STOKES, was elected to the Ohio state legislature. He served as Carl's chief adviser and campaign worker in this election and again in 1967, when Carl was elected mayor of Cleveland. Carl's success got him interested in running for office himself. Meanwhile, the Ohio legislature had redistricted the state, and his home congressional district, the 21st, had been transformed from a black-minority to a black-majority district. Despite having never held elected office before, in 1968 he decided to run as a Democrat for Congress. His record as a civil rights attorney, coupled with Carl's popularity as mayor, resulted in a resounding victory. He took his seat in Congress in 1969 and was assigned to the committees on internal security and on education and labor. Later in his career, he was reassigned to the powerful committees on intelligence and appropriations.

As a congressman, Stokes continued to be involved in civil rights. He joined with other African-American members of Congress to oppose President Richard M. Nixon's attempts to undo the gains blacks had made during the Kennedy and Johnson administrations. One of the things Nixon wanted to do was weaken the Voting Rights Act of 1965, which outlawed a number of voting abuses that technically were constitutional. Stokes opposed Nixon on this issue by observing firsthand the harassment of black voters during the 1969 state and local elections in Mississippi and reporting back to the full House. In 1971, he became a founding member of the Congressional Black Caucus.

For Stokes, civil rights also meant decent employment. His district had the lowest median income in the Midwest, so he worked hard to ensure that African Americans in all parts of the country had equal opportunity to get hired for jobs for which they were qualified, and to get trained for those they were not. He fought for more public housing and to end discrimination in the sale and rental of housing. He was a prime mover in the enactment of the Disadvantaged Minority Health Improvement Act of 1989. He sponsored legislation that created training programs for African Americans wanting to do biomedical research and that set aside a certain percentage of government-funded scientific and technological research projects for minority businesses and black colleges. His commitment to equal opportunity led to his chairing the Congressional Black Caucus for a number of years.

Louis Stokes was the first African American to represent Ohio in Congress. *(Library of Congress)*

Stokes also played a prominent role in several high-profile congressional investigations. In 1977, he was named chairman of the select committee on assassinations, which looked into the deaths of President John F. Kennedy and Martin Luther King, Jr. Stokes criticized the Warren Commission for not releasing most of the relevant documents concerning Kennedy's assassination into the public domain. He also belittled its assertion that Lee Harvey Oswald had acted alone in killing Kennedy, as he was convinced that organized crime had something to do with the president's death. As chairman of the committee on intelligence, he served on the 1987–88 Iran-Contra Investigating Committee. This investigation sought to determine who in the executive branch, including President Ronald Reagan, was involved in selling arms to Iran and then using the proceeds to fund Nicaraguan freedom fighters, thus contravening an act of Congress. In 1991, he was named chairman of the House Ethics Committee, which faced a full agenda of cases involving questionable behavior, both financial and sexual, on the parts of congresspeople.

Stokes was reelected 14 times. In 1998, he declined to run for reelection on account of his age. When his term expired in 1999, he returned to the private practice of law with Squire, Sanders, and Dempsey, a prestigious firm in Washington, D.C. In 2007, the Louis Stokes Museum, featuring memorabilia and displays devoted to Stokes's career, opened in the Outhwaite housing project in Cleveland, Ohio.

Further Reading

Biographical Directory of the United States Congress. "Stokes, Louis, 1925–   ." Available online. URL: http://bioguide.congress.gov/scripts/biodisplay. pl?index=S000948. Downloaded April 15, 2009.
Black Americans in Congress. "Louis Stokes." Available online. URL: http://baic.house.gov/member-profiles/profile.html?intID=34. Downloaded April 13, 2009.
"Carl & Louis Stokes." The Western Reserve Historical Society. Available online. URL: http://www. stokescleveland.org/index.htm. Downloaded March 29, 2009.
Clay, William L. Just Permanent Interests: Black Americans in Congress, 1870–1992. New York: Amistad Press, 1993.
Fenno, Richard F. Going Home: Black Representatives and Their Constituents. 2nd ed. Chicago: University of Chicago Press, 2003.

Street, John

(John F. Street)
(1943–   ) mayor of Philadelphia, Pennsylvania

John Street was the second African American to serve as mayor of Philadelphia. He is probably the only big-city mayor who ever earned a living as a sidewalk vendor and cabdriver.

Street was born in 1943 in Norristown, Pennsylvania. His father, James, was a factory worker, and his mother, Elizabeth, was a homemaker. Not long after his birth his parents leased a farm with another family outside Conshohocken, Pennsylvania, where he grew up. After finishing high school in 1961, he attended Oakland College in Huntsville, Alabama, receiving a B.A. in English three years later. He remained in Huntsville for two years after graduation, supporting himself by doing manual labor. In 1966, he returned to Philadelphia, and over the next nine years he earned a living by driving a taxicab, teaching school as a substitute, and selling hot dogs on the street corner with his brother, Milton Street. Meanwhile, he applied annually to the Temple University Law School. In 1972, his application was finally accepted, and he received a J.D. three years later. In 1975, he passed the Pennsylvania bar examination and opened his own law office.

Street became involved in politics through his brother Milton. In the late 1970s, the city had toughened its laws regulating street vendors, and Milton had organized several demonstrations to protest those laws. Street joined his brother during some of the demonstrations, and he accompanied Milton to several city council meetings to further protest the new laws. Eventually, the Streets broadened their attacks on city council to include charges of misuse of federal funds earmarked for urban redevelopment. In 1978, Milton won a seat in the state legislature, and Street helped with the campaign.

Buoyed by Milton's victory, the following year Street defeated three other contenders to win a seat on city council, a seat he would hold for almost 20 years. His career as an elected official began inauspiciously; shortly after his victory, he was arrested and jailed for dozens of unpaid parking tickets. It was soon revealed that he also owed considerable sums of money to the Internal Revenue Service, the city utilities department, and Temple University. He was able to dispel the negative publicity resulting from these revelations, however, by focusing on representing his constituents in a rather dramatic fashion. One thing that happened in his favor was the so-called Abscam scandal. Agents of the Federal Bureau of Investigation (FBI) posing as oil-rich Arabs attempted to obtain political favors by bribing elected officials. Among those "stung" in the operation were several members of the Philadelphia city council. Street made much political hay by repeatedly haranguing those members who had been caught by the FBI. In 1981, he made the national news by getting into a fistfight with two other council members when the council president refused to let council vote on Street's measure to rescue the city's financially strapped public schools.

John Street was the second African-American mayor of Philadelphia, Pennsylvania. *(John F. Street)*

Following this sordid incident, Street vowed to change his combative ways. Instead of complaining vociferously about things he did not like, he worked to change them by becoming an expert on the city charter, municipal ordinances, and state law regarding cities. He then coupled this knowledge with his newly developed conciliatory skills to effect real change for the neighborhood in North Philadelphia where he lived and which he represented. He was able to gain funding for a number of community development projects, each of which provided a considerable amount for minority contractor set-asides. His greatest accomplishment was convincing the council to pass legislation allowing squatters to take legal possession of abandoned houses if the squatters agreed to rehabilitate the houses. This measure alone vastly improved the housing situation for thousands of low-income Philadelphians. He also sponsored a bill that created a liquor-by-the-drink tax and earmarked the $23 million per year the tax raised for the school budget.

In 1992, Street was chosen unanimously by his fellow council members to serve as council president. In this capacity, he worked closely with Mayor Edward G. Rendell to address the host of financial problems facing the city. Their alliance resulted in new measures, such as cutting the business and wage tax, that brought new business to the city. They also reduced expenses by tightening the budget via such measures as negotiating a new contract with the municipal workers' union. By decade's end, a $250 million deficit had been turned into the largest surplus in the city's history, and a number of new jobs had been created.

In late 1998, Street resigned from city council to campaign for mayor. He beat four other contenders in the 1999 Democratic primary and then narrowly edged his Republican challenger in the general election. After taking office in early 2000, Street worked to improve Philadelphia public schools, revitalize city neighborhoods, increase funding for after-school programs, construct a city-wide wi-fi network, and establish the Office of

Health and Fitness within the city government. He also attempted to reduce Philadelphia's high murder rate.

Street was reelected in 2003, although corruption scandals involving close associates surfaced during his reelection campaign. Although Street was not formally charged with any crime, the scandals marred his second term and led *Time* magazine to name Street one of the three worst mayors in the United States in 2005.

Barred by term limits, Street did not seek a third term as mayor. After leaving office in 2008, he joined the faculty of the department of political science at Temple University. Divorced twice, he is married to the former Naomi Post and has four children.

Further Reading

Brennan, Carol. "John F. Street, 1943– ." *Contemporary Black Biography* 24 (2000): 163–166.

Gurwitt, Rob. "Betting on the Bulldozer." *Governing* 15 (July 2002): 28–34.

Issenberg, Sasha. "The Great Days of John Street." *Philadelphia,* May 2005. Available online. URL: http://www.phillymag.com/articles/feature_the_great_days_of_john_street. Downloaded April 23, 2009.

Sullivan, Louis

(Louis Wade Sullivan)

(1933–) *U.S. secretary of health and human services*

Louis Sullivan was the only African American to serve in President George H. W. Bush's cabinet. As secretary of the Department of Health and Human Services, he became involved in several controversies. However, he did not let any of them distract him from his mission to improve health care for minorities and the needy.

Sullivan was born on November 3, 1933, in Atlanta, Georgia. His father, Walter, was an insurance salesman, and his mother, Lubirda, was a homemaker. As a young boy, he moved with his family to Blakely, a small town in southwest Georgia. Because of the racist attitude of Blakely's white residents, he attended school in Atlanta while boarding with family friends. After finishing high school in 1950, he enrolled in Morehouse College and received a B.S. in 1954. He then entered Boston University Medical School and received an M.D. in 1958. Over the next eight years, he completed his internship and residency at New York Hospital-Cornell Medical Center in New York City, studied pathology at Massachusetts General Hospital in Boston, studied hematology at Harvard Medical School, and taught medicine at Harvard and Seton Hall (later New Jersey) College of Medicine. In 1966, he joined the staff at the Boston University Medical Center, and over the next nine years he taught medicine while specializing in sickle-cell anemia and blood disorders related to vitamin deficiencies. In 1955, he married Eve Williamson, with whom he has three children.

In 1975, Sullivan was recruited by Morehouse College officials and alumni to develop a medical education program for blacks in Atlanta. By 1978, he had obtained enough funding from the Carter Administration (many of whose members were from Georgia), the Georgia state legislature, the Atlanta city council, the Fulton County board of commissioners, and local businesses and individuals to establish a two-year program at Atlanta University Center College. By 1981, this program had grown into the Morehouse School of Medicine, with Sullivan as its dean. As one of three predominantly black medical schools in the United States (the others are Howard University College of Medicine in Washington, D.C., and Meharry Medical College in Nashville, Tennessee), Morehouse specialized in conditions related to African Americans, such as sickle-cell anemia.

In the course of his fund-raising activities, Sullivan met Vice President George H. W. Bush and his wife, Barbara. Sullivan and Mrs. Bush became friends, and he invited her to serve as a Morehouse trustee, thus boosting the vice president's image in the African-American community. In return, Bush invited Sullivan to serve on an official delegation to seven African nations in 1982, and to introduce Mrs. Bush to the Republican National Convention in 1988. That same year, Bush was elected president, and he floated Sullivan's name as a candidate for secretary of the Department of Health and Human Services (HHS). While no one questioned Sullivan's qualifications to oversee the department's multibillion-dollar budget, many conservatives objected to him on the grounds of his pro-abortion stance. After making several confusing and contradictory remarks about his personal views on abortion, he was confirmed by the U.S. Senate and took office in 1989.

Sullivan became embroiled in other controversies while secretary of HHS. One week after taking office, he endorsed a needle-exchange program whereby intravenous drug users could turn in their old hypodermic needles for ones that were not contaminated with AIDS. The program was attacked by conservatives who saw it as encouraging drug use rather than addressing the growing AIDS epidemic. Later, he came out in favor of fetal tissue research programs, which conservatives strongly opposed. In both cases, he smoothed things over by making remarks that could be interpreted to suit the listener. He also became a champion of antismoking activists. Again, he was opposed by conservatives, but this time he did not backpedal. He battled ardently and successfully to restore funding for antismoking campaigns, and he attacked tobacco companies whose advertising targeted teenage smokers.

Sullivan made preventive medicine and minority health care HHS's top priorities. He was able to restore much of the funding for medical scholarships and research, as well as for occupational health programs that benefited minorities, that had been cut during the Reagan Administration. He endorsed plans to eradicate tuberculosis, a disease that disproportionately affects the inner-city poor and the institutionalized, by 2010. He also fought the repeal of the Medicare Catastrophic Coverage Act, which provided expanded health care to the elderly. In 1993, following the election of Democrat Bill Clinton to the presidency, he resigned his secretaryship and returned to the Morehouse School of Medicine as its president. In 2002, he became the school's president emeritus. Sullivan has served as the chairman of the board of the National Health Museum in Washington, D.C., and the cochair of the President's Commission on HIV and AIDS.

Further Reading

Creelan, Marilee. "Louis Sullivan (b. 1933)." New Georgia Encyclopedia. Available online. URL: http://www.georgiaencyclopedia.org/nge/Article.jsp?id=h-1229. Downloaded March 28, 2009.
Kosterlitz, Julie. "A Doctor in the Pulpit." *National Journal* 22, no. 41 (October 13, 1990).

T

Thompson, Bennie
(Bennie G. Thompson)
(1948–) *U.S. congressional representative from Mississippi*

Like many African-American political leaders, Bennie Thompson became involved in politics via the Civil Rights movement. First elected to office in 1969, Thompson spent the next 40 years working to make life better for black Mississippians.

Thompson was born on January 28, 1948, in Bolton, Mississippi. His father, Will, was an auto mechanic, and his mother, Annie, was a teacher. After finishing high school he enrolled in Tougaloo College, receiving a B.A. in political science in 1968. He taught school in Madison, Mississippi, for a year, and then enrolled in Jackson State University where he received an M.S. in educational administration and supervision in 1972.

While in college, Thompson joined the Student Nonviolent Coordinating Committee and participated in a number of civil rights protest marches and voter registration drives. He also worked on Fannie Lou Hamer's 1968 campaign for Congress. Although Hamer failed to get elected, her example inspired Thompson to pursue a career in politics. In 1969, he and two other African Americans were elected to Bolton's board of aldermen. The town's white mayor and aldermen, however, refused to seat Thompson and his black colleagues. The

three black aldermen had to sue the town in court before they could take office. Meanwhile, Thompson was fired from his teaching position and drafted by the local Selective Service board. Again, he sued in court on the grounds that both moves were racially motivated. He stayed out of the military, but he never taught again.

By 1973, the Civil Rights movement's voter registration drives were beginning to have a noticeable impact on local politics in Mississippi. That same year, Thompson was elected mayor of Bolton while all of the successful candidates for the board of aldermen were black. Again, the winners had to sue in court to ensure their victory, but eventually they were able to take control of the town. During Thompson's tenure as mayor, the town paved its streets, built a new city hall, and renovated dilapidated property. It also bought its first fire engine and provided professional training for its volunteer fire department. Thompson also ordered a reappraisal of all real estate in Bolton. During the reappraisal, it was discovered that property owned by whites had been undervalued for years in order to hold down their property taxes. Thompson saw to it that this situation was quickly rectified. In 1979, he was elected to the Hinds County Board of Supervisors, a position he held for the next 13 years. As supervisor, he played a prominent role in winning a federal grant with which to provide the county with public transportation.

In 1993, MIKE ESPY resigned his seat in Congress to become the secretary of agriculture. A special election was held that same year to replace him, and Thompson declared his candidacy. He defeated six other Democratic contenders in the primary, including UNITA BLACKWELL and Espy's brother Henry, and then narrowly beat his Republican challenger in the election. Unlike Mike Espy, a moderate who forged alliances with white political leaders to get elected, Thompson relied solely on his popularity and reputation within the black community to win. He took his seat that same year and was assigned to the committees on the budget and agriculture.

As a congressman, Thompson continued to work to improve the quality of life for rural African Americans. He used his position on the House Agriculture Committee to get the Department of Agriculture to increase funding for rural housing programs, and to get the Mississippi Department of Wildlife, Fisheries, and Parks to improve its dismal employment record concerning blacks. As a member of the National Council on Health Planning and Development, he worked for

Bennie Thompson represents Mississippi in the U.S. House of Representatives. *(Bennie G. Thompson)*

affordable, quality health care programs of benefit to the rural poor. He opposed vigorously all attempts to cut spending for federal poverty programs, particularly when such cuts were to be used to fund a tax cut for the wealthy. He opposed federal efforts to curtail drastically the consumption of tobacco in the United States on the grounds that many African-American small farmers and family farmers rely on tobacco to keep their operations profitable. Thompson also introduced a bill that called for the implementation of the remaining recommendations of the 9/11 Commission. It was signed into law in August 2007.

In 2010, Thompson was reelected to a 10th term. He is married to the former London Johnson, with whom he has one child.

Further Reading

Biographical Directory of the United States Congress. "Thompson, Bennie, 1948– ." Available online. URL: http://bioguide.congress.gov/scripts/bio display.pl?index=T000193. Downloaded April 11, 2009.

Clay, William L. *Just Permanent Interests: Black Americans in Congress, 1870–1992.* New York: Amistad Press, 1993.

Congressman Bennie Thompson, Official Web Site. Available online. URL: http://benniethompson. house.gov. Downloaded April 11, 2009.

Klein, Joe. "The Emancipation of Bolton, Mississippi." *Esquire* 104 (December 1985): 258–262.

"New Member Profile: Bennie Thompson, D-Miss. (2)." *Congressional Quarterly Weekly Report* 51 (April 17, 1993): 971.

Towns, Edolphus
(1934–) *U.S. congressional representative from New York*

In 1982, Edolphus Towns became one of two African Americans to be elected to Congress from Brooklyn, New York. He has since been reelected 13 times.

Towns was born on July 21, 1934, in Chadbourn, North Carolina. His parents, Dolphus and Vergie, were farmers. He finished high school in 1952, then enrolled in North Carolina Agricultural and Technical State University. In 1956 he received a B.S. and joined the U.S. Army as an officer. Upon being discharged two years later, he took a job as a teacher in the New York City public school system and taught in Brooklyn for the next seven years. In 1965, he left teaching to become a deputy hospital administrator at Beth Israel Medical Center, a position he held for six years. In 1971, he enrolled in Adelphi University; two years later he received a master's degree in social work and took a position with the city as a facilitator in the development of new neighborhood housing projects. In 1960, he married Gwendolyn Forbes, with whom he has two children.

Ever since settling in Brooklyn, Towns has been active in the affairs of the local Democratic Party, rising up through the party's ranks to become a state committeeman. After almost 18 years of working to elect other people, in 1976 he got himself elected deputy borough president of Brooklyn. For the next six years, he functioned much like a deputy mayor would, assisting the borough president in matters related to transportation, housing, and other social services.

In 1982, the representative from Towns's congressional district, Frederick W. Richmond, announced his retirement after being charged with tax evasion. Running in a district with a Hispanic majority, Towns defeated two Hispanic candidates in the Democratic primary, then easily defeated his Republican opponent in the general election. He took his seat in 1983 and was assigned to the committees on public works and government operations.

One of the first issues Towns addressed as a congressman was the plight of the family farm. Many small farmers were African Americans, like his parents, and the rise of agribusiness threatened the continued existence of small farmers. To remedy this situation, he fought to increase, rather than reduce, federal subsidies for family farms.

Towns's other major interests have been education and health care. In terms of education, he is best remembered for writing the Student Right to Know Act, which forces colleges and universities to make public the percentage of their student athletes who graduate on time. He also sponsored legislation to provide increased federal funding for bilingual education, teacher training, and special education. His health initiatives include enhancing the Medicare reimbursement rates for such mid-level services as midwives and home care and maintaining federal funding for mammography testing and rural health clinics.

In 1991, Towns was chosen to chair the Congressional Black Caucus. The following year, he was named to the committee on energy and commerce. As a member of this committee, he cosponsored legislation to create the Telecommunications Development Fund, which provides low-interest loans to small and minority-owned companies in the telecommunications industry. He also served as a conferee on the bill creating a national energy strategy. In 2010 he was reelected to a 15th term.

Further Reading

Biographical Directory of the United States Congress. "Towns, Edolphus, 1934– ." Available online. URL: http://bioguide.congress.gov/scripts/bio display.pl?index=T000326. Downloaded April 11, 2009.

Clay, William L. *Just Permanent Interests: Black Americans in Congress, 1870–1992.* New York: Amistad Press, 1993.

Congressman Edolphus Towns, Official Web Site. Available online. URL: http://www.house.gov/towns. Downloaded April 11, 2009.

Tubbs Jones, Stephanie

(1949–2008) *U.S. congressional representative from Ohio*

In 1998, Stephanie Tubbs Jones became the second African American to represent Ohio in the

U.S. Congress. She did so by replacing the first, LOUIS STOKES, upon his retirement.

Tubbs Jones was born Stephanie Tubbs on September 10, 1949, in Cleveland, Ohio. Her father, Andrew, was a skycap for United Airlines, and her mother, Mary, was a homemaker. After finishing high school, she accepted a full scholarship to Case Western Reserve University and received a B.A. in sociology in 1971. Three years later she received a J.D. from Case Western's law school. As a law student, she had worked as a legal clerk for the Northeast Ohio Regional Sewer District, and after graduation she was hired full-time as the district's assistant general counsel and equal opportunity administrator. In 1976, she became an assistant prosecutor in the Cuyahoga County prosecutor's office. Three years later, she went to work for the Equal Employment Opportunity Commission's Cleveland office as a trial attorney. In 1976, she married Mervyn Jones, with whom she had one child.

Tubbs Jones got involved in politics in 1979 when she helped a friend get elected to a minor public office. The experience convinced her to run for office, too, and two years later she defeated four other candidates for a judgeship on the Cleveland municipal court. In 1984, she was elected to the Cuyahoga County court of common pleas and then reelected four years later. By this time she had drawn the attention of the state Democratic Party, to which she belonged, and its leaders drafted her to run for the Ohio Supreme Court in 1990. Her narrow defeat gained her more name recognition, and the following year she was easily elected to the highly visible office of Cuyahoga County chief prosecutor. The office employed 150 attorneys and argued cases before 34 different judges. As chief prosecutor, she oversaw the computerization of the office and implemented a supplemental education program for county attorneys and law enforcement officials in her jurisdictions. She also focused the office's attention on child welfare by prosecuting negligent parents and fathers who refused to pay child support.

In 1998, Louis Stokes decided to retire from Congress after almost 30 years in office. Tubbs Jones was one of five Democrats to declare their candidacies for his seat. She easily defeated the other four in the primary, and then swept to victory in the general election. She took her seat in 1999 and was assigned to the committees on banking/financial services, small business, and ethics.

As a congresswoman, Tubbs Jones focused on the safety and welfare of children. She authored the Child Abuse Prevention and Enforcement (CAPE) Act, which reforms the enforcement of federal statutes regarding the protection of children. The act's most innovative feature funds training for child advocacy centers and child care providers by using forfeited assets and bail bonds as well as fines paid for violating child protection laws, thus costing the taxpayer next to nothing. In related areas, she introduced legislation to regulate research efforts concerning uterine fibroids and to outfit college dormitories and student residences with adequate fire protection. She served on task forces related to violent crime and drug abuse, worked to close loopholes in existing gun control laws, and took steps to stimulate the local economy in Cleveland, especially as it pertains to minority- and female-owned businesses. In 2008, she was reelected to a fifth term. On August 20, 2008, Tubbs Jones died suddenly of a ruptured brain aneurysm. She was 58 years old.

Further Reading

Biographical Directory of the United States Congress. "Jones, Stephanie Tubbs, 1949– ." Available online. URL: http://bioguide.congress.gov/scripts/biodisplay.pl?index=J000284. Downloaded April 11, 2009.

Black Americans in Congress. "Stephanie Tubbs Jones." Available online. URL: http://baic.house.gov/member-profiles/profile.html?intID=100. Downloaded April 12, 2009.

Fenno, Richard F. *Going Home: Black Representatives and Their Constituents.* Chicago: University of Chicago Press, 2003.

Foerstel, Karen. *Biographical Dictionary of Congressional Women.* New York: Greenwood Press, 1999.

Hevesi, Dennis. "Stephanie Tubbs Jones, Lawmaker, Dies at 58." *New York Times,* August 20, 2008. Available online. URL: http://www.nytimes.com/2008/08/21/washington/21jones.html?scp=2&sq=stephanie%20tubbs%20jones&st=cse. Downloaded April 11, 2009.

"Stephanie Tubbs Jones, D-Ohio (11). New Member Profile." *CQ Weekly* 56 (November 7, 1998): 3,021.

Turner, Benjamin
(Benjamin Sterling Turner)
(1825–1894) *U.S. congressional representative from Alabama*

Benjamin Turner was the first African American to represent Alabama in Congress. *(Library of Congress)*

Benjamin Turner was the first African American to represent Alabama in the U.S. Congress. While in Congress, he proved to be a moderate with a vision; unfortunately, none of his bills was enacted into law.

Turner was born on March 17, 1825, near Weldon, North Carolina. His parents, whose names are unknown, were slaves owned by Elizabeth Turner. At age five, he relocated with Elizabeth Turner to a plantation near Selma, Alabama. Fifteen years later, she sold him to her stepdaughter's husband, W. H. Gee. Gee put him to work in his Selma hotel, and Gee's children taught him to read and write. When Gee died, Turner became the property of his brother, James T. Gee, who made him the manager of another Selma hotel. At some point, probably during the late 1850s, he married a slave woman named Independence, with whom he may have had one child; the relationship ended when a white man bought the woman for his sexual gratification.

When the Civil War broke out, Selma became a manufacturing center and supply base for the Confederacy. As a result, Turner's businesses thrived to the point that he was able to invest in Confederate bonds, but when the Union army captured Selma, it burned down most of the town. Turner lost his businesses, which were worth about $8,000. This unfortunate event did not ruin him financially, however, for shortly after the war ended he opened a school for the children of freedmen with his own money. He also opened his own mercantile business.

With the abolition of slavery, much confusion existed as to the proper working relationship between black laborers and white employers. Turner assisted both parties by helping African Americans in and around Selma enter into equitable work contracts with their bosses. His good business sense, as demonstrated in this and other matters, endeared him to both races, and in 1867 he was appointed tax collector for Dallas County, which includes Selma. The following year, he was elected to city council as an independent. By 1868, he had become alarmed at the racist inclinations of the Democratic Party, so he became a

Republican and recruited many freedmen into that organization. Meanwhile, his business affairs had recovered from the war; according to the census of 1870 he was worth $10,000, a considerable amount for that day.

In 1870, Turner was elected to the U.S. House of Representatives. He served on the Committee on Invalid Pensions, an important committee in the years following the Civil War. He gained a reputation as a moderate by supporting bills in favor of the expansion of civil rights for African Americans as well as universal amnesty for former Confederates. Being an astute businessman, however, Turner devoted most of his time in Congress to bettering economic conditions in Alabama in general and Selma in particular. He introduced bills to provide federal funding for rebuilding structures destroyed by the Union army as well as for constructing new government buildings. He worked for the reimbursement of a federal tax on cotton, in essence a war reparations measure, which extracted $250 million from the South between 1866 and 1888. He argued that the tax was impeding the South's recovery and damaging the efforts of freedmen to get ahead economically. He introduced a bill, which unfortunately never made it out of committee, to authorize the redistribution of land to landless southerners of both races in small tracts for 10 percent down and 10 percent per year. Had such a measure been enacted, it would have mitigated the negative effects of decades of tenant farming and sharecropping on the South.

Turner lost his bid for reelection in 1872. Although he never held public office again, he remained active in local politics through 1880. During that period, he served on the state Republican executive committee and was a delegate to the national convention and a presidential elector. Meanwhile, the financial panic of 1873 forced his mercantile business into bankruptcy, and for the next 20 years he farmed on 300 acres in Dallas County. He died on March 21, 1894, in Selma.

Further Reading

Bailey, Richard. *Neither Carpetbaggers nor Scalawags: Black Officeholders during the Reconstruction of Alabama, 1867–1878.* 5th ed. Montgomery, Ala.: NewSouth Books, 2007.

Biographical Directory of the United States Congress. "Turner, Benjamin Sterling, 1825–1894." Available online. URL: http://bioguide.congress.gov/scripts/biodisplay.pl?index=T000414. Downloaded April 23, 2009.

Black Americans in Congress. "Benjamin Sterling Turner." Available online. URL: http://baic.house.gov/member-profiles/profile.html?intID=16. Downloaded April 7, 2009.

Clay, William L. *Just Permanent Interests: Black Americans in Congress, 1870–1992.* New York: Amistad Press, 1993.

Dray, Philip. *Capitol Men: The Epic Story of Reconstruction through the Lives of the First Black Congressmen.* Boston: Houghton Mifflin, 2008.

U

Usry, James
(James Leroy Usry)
(1922–2002) *mayor of Atlantic City, New Jersey*

James Usry was mayor of one of the United States's most famous vacation destinations for six years. During that time, he did much to make the city a better place to live and a better place to visit. Unfortunately, he was politically naive, having had little involvement in elected politics before becoming mayor, and his inexperience led to his political downfall.

Usry was born on February 2, 1922, in Athens, Georgia. As an infant, he moved with his parents to Atlantic City, New Jersey, a thriving oceanside resort that would later fall on hard times. In 1939, he graduated from high school and enrolled in Lincoln University in Pennsylvania, but he left school after three years to enlist in the U.S. Army. After serving in North Africa and Italy during World War II, he returned to Lincoln and received a B.A. in 1946. For the next five years, he played professional basketball for the New York Renaissance, an all-black team that played most of its games on the road. In 1952, he returned to Atlantic City to teach school. He later received an M.A. from New Jersey's Glassboro State College (now Rowan University) and was named a school principal, and by 1982 he had become assistant super-

intendent of Atlantic City's public schools. In 1984, he married Laverne Young.

Usry got involved in politics in 1982, when the black community persuaded him to run for mayor of Atlantic City. Four years earlier, the state had legalized casino gambling in the hope that it would reinvigorate Atlantic City's flagging economy. Developers quickly built casinos there. Although the casinos did indeed provide more jobs and tax revenue, they did little to improve life for the city's African Americans, who constituted 55 percent of the city's population. Moreover, the "easy money" from the casinos contributed further to Atlantic City's unsavory reputation for being corrupt and incompetent. Municipal employees were perceived as being overpaid and underworked, and two of Atlantic City's previous four mayors had been convicted of official misconduct on charges related to bribery and corruption.

Running as a Republican, Usry promised that, if elected, he would spend a sizable proportion of the city's take from the casinos to renovate the city's most run-down neighborhoods. He also vowed to clean up city hall. After losing to his white opponent, Michael J. Matthews, by fewer than 400 votes, he tried to have the results overturned in court by charging Matthews with vote fraud. The suit was dismissed for lack of evidence; however, shortly thereafter, Matthews was indicted by the federal government for accepting a bribe (he eventually served time in prison on this charge). In 1983, Usry began a petition campaign to have Matthews removed from office, and the following year Matthews was recalled and Usry was elected to take his place. He was reelected to a full four-year term in 1986.

As mayor, Usry succeeded in renovating much of Atlantic City's run-down infrastructure, mostly by getting the state Casino Reinvestment Development Authority to earmark more funds for Atlantic City. Although much of this money went to protect the beach and repair the oceanfront boardwalk, a significant amount was spent fixing up the city's worst examples of urban blight. He managed to block the expansion of the casinos into the North East Inlet area and then oversaw the development of plans to erect much-needed housing in their place. In 1989, he was elected to a one-year term as president of the National Conference of Black Mayors, and he brought its annual convention to Atlantic City, much to the delight of the mayors and city residents alike. His political inexperience, however, prevented him from doing much about reforming the city's government. He developed a plan to change the way the city hired new employees, only to see it bog down in city council before a watered-down version was passed almost two years later. Other attempts to reduce the influence of the city's political machine similarly came to naught. Toward the end of his second term, a casino-funded audit showed that few of the city's governmental problems had changed during his tenure.

In 1988, Usry committed political suicide by endorsing JESSE JACKSON, a Democratic candidate for president. Prior to the endorsement, Usry had been the darling of New Jersey Republicans because they believed he could deliver African-American votes to party candidates for state and national offices. After the endorsement, he lost the party's support entirely. Coincidentally, the following year he was caught up in a statewide investigation of corrupt practices in local governments called ComServe. He and four other Atlantic City officials were arrested and charged with 13 counts of bribery and corruption, the very things he had promised to eliminate from municipal affairs. In 1991, he pled guilty to one count of accepting an unreported campaign contribution; the other charges were dropped. The negative publicity surrounding his involvement in ComServe ruined his chances of serving a third term as mayor, and he lost his 1990 reelection bid. After completing his term, he retired to his home in Atlantic City, where he remained a respected and involved member of the black community. He died in a nursing home in Galloway Township, New Jersey, on January 25, 2002.

Further Reading
"James L. Usry, the First Black Mayor of Atlantic City, Succumbs at 79." *Jet* 101, no. 10 (February 25, 2002): 54.
Johnson, Kirk. "James L. Usry, Atlantic City Mayor in 1980's, Dies at 79." *New York Times* (January 28, 2002): B7.

W

Walls, Josiah
(Josiah Thomas Walls)
(1842–1905) *U.S. congressional representative from Florida*

Josiah Walls was the only black from Florida to serve in Congress during Reconstruction. Unlike other states such as South Carolina and Mississippi, Florida did not have a majority of black voters. Nevertheless, Walls was able to win election to state and federal office because his pragmatic politics appealed to the economic interests of both races.

Walls was born on December 30, 1842, near Winchester, Virginia. The names and occupations of his parents are unknown. In all likelihood, his mother was a slave whose master was Dr. John Walls, a Winchester physician. It has been suggested that Dr. Walls was his father as well as his master, but later photographs of Congressman Walls show him with skin too dark to have resulted from a biracial union.

In 1861, Walls was kidnapped by Confederate soldiers who made him work as a servant to an artillery battery. In May 1862, he escaped when Union troops overran the battery at Yorktown, Virginia, during the Peninsular Campaign. He was sent by his liberators to Harrisburg, Pennsylvania, where he attended school for a year. In July 1863 he joined the Third Infantry Regiment,

U.S. Colored Troops (USCT) and participated in the bloody but successful siege of Charleston, South Carolina. At war's end, he was a first sergeant and artillery instructor with the Thirty-fifth Regiment, USCT, in Picolata, Florida, where in 1864 he had married Helen Ferguson. They had one child. Discharged from the army in October 1865, he settled in Florida's Alachua County. Over the next three years, he worked as a lumberer and as a teacher in a Freedman's Bureau school.

During the early years of Reconstruction in Florida, the voting rights of whites were curtailed while those of blacks were expanded, thus making it possible for freedmen, even ones of modest means, to get involved in politics. In 1867, Walls attended the state Republican convention as a delegate. In 1868, the same year he bought an 80-acre farm in Newnansville, he served as a delegate to the state constitutional convention and was elected to Florida's lower house. The following year, he was one of five blacks who were elected to the 24-seat senate.

By 1870, most white voters in Florida had been reenfranchised, and white supremacist groups such as the Ku Klux Klan were using violence against blacks to keep them from voting. Nevertheless, that same year Walls was elected to serve as the state's only representative in the U.S. House. His white opponent successfully contested the results, but not until Walls had almost completed a full two-year term. In 1872, Walls was returned to Washington; during the summer recess of 1873 he was also elected mayor of Gainesville. He was reelected to Congress in 1874 but was again forced from office toward the end of the term when his opponent's challenge was upheld.

Walls was not a flamboyant legislator. Having acquired only one year of formal education, he did not speak confidently before his colleagues in the House and usually read his remarks from a prepared text. Nevertheless, he was an energetic sponsor of measures that benefited the economic conditions of all Floridians. He introduced bills to provide federal funding for a railroad along Florida's Atlantic coast and to improve the navigability of the state's harbors and rivers. He also promoted the construction of customhouses, courthouses, and post offices throughout his adopted state,

worked to acquire tariff protection for the state's nascent citrus fruit industry, and helped establish a land grant agricultural college. He was also a strong supporter of public education. He argued for a national education fund, financed by the sale of federal land, that would help the states establish elementary schools for all children, like the schools that had been operated by the Freedmen's Bureau.

By 1876, white Floridians had regained control of the state's Republican Party, and they denied Walls that year's nomination for Congress. Undaunted, that same year he ran for and won a seat in the state senate, where he served until retiring from state politics in 1879. For the next five years, he concentrated on his business interests, which now included 1,500 acres of tomato and orange groves, a sawmill, a newspaper, and a law practice, while serving on the Alachua County Commission and School Board. He ran as an independent for Congress in 1884 and for the state senate in 1890, but was soundly defeated both times.

In 1885, Walls's first wife died, and that same year he married her cousin, Ella Angeline Gass. In 1895, his crops were killed by an early frost, and as a result he lost his business enterprises. That same year, he moved to Tallahassee where he took a job as director of the farm at the Florida Normal College. He died on May 15, 1905, in Tallahassee.

Further Reading

Biographical Directory of the United States Congress. "Walls, Josiah Thomas, 1842–1905." Available online. URL: http://bioguide.congress.gov/scripts/biodisplay.pl?index=W000093. Downloaded April 5, 2009.

Black Americans in Congress. "Josiah Thomas Walls." Available online. URL: http://baic.house.gov/member-profiles/profile.html?intID=17. Downloaded April 6, 2009.

Clay, William L. *Just Permanent Interests: Black Americans in Congress, 1870–1992.* New York: Amistad Press, 1993.

Josiah Walls was the first African American to represent Florida in Congress. *(Library of Congress)*

Dray, Philip. *Capitol Men: The Epic Story of Reconstruction through the Lives of the First Black Congressmen.* Boston: Houghton Mifflin, 2008.

Klingman, Peter D. *Josiah Walls: Florida's Black Congressman.* Gainesville: University Presses of Florida, 1976.

Richardson, Joe M. *The Negro in the Reconstruction of Florida, 1865–1877.* Tampa, Fla.: Trend House, 1973.

Washington, Harold

(1922–1987) *mayor of Chicago, Illinois*

Harold Washington was the first African-American mayor of Chicago. His victory and subsequent administration were hailed as victories for black politicians in general and signaled the dawning of a new era for African Americans. Unfortunately, his untimely death precluded him from achieving even greater victories.

Washington was born on April 15, 1922, in Chicago, Illinois. His father, Roy, was a meatpacker who later became a lawyer and clergyman, and his mother, Bertha, was a homemaker. He dropped out of high school in 1939 and joined the Civilian Conservation Corps; he later worked briefly as a meatpacker and as a clerk for the U.S. Treasury Department in Chicago. In 1942, he married Nancy Finch; they divorced in 1950. In 1943, he was drafted into the U.S. Army and served with the Army Air Corps in the Pacific theater. He returned to Chicago after the war and enrolled in Roosevelt University, having earned his high school equivalency degree while in the military. He received a B.A. in political science and economics in 1949, then enrolled in the Northwestern University School of Law. He received a J.D. in 1952, passed the bar examination in 1953, and went to work as an assistant city prosecutor in Chicago in 1954. In 1958, he was named an arbitrator for the Illinois State Industrial Commission, a position he held for six years.

Washington got involved in politics through his father, who had been a Democratic precinct captain since the 1920s. When his father died in 1954, Washington took over his position in the party and became an important cog in Chicago's Democratic machine. After working tirelessly for other candidates for 10 years, in 1964 he made his first run for office and was elected to the state house of representatives. He served six terms in the lower house before being elected to the state senate in 1976. During his 15 years in the state legislature, he focused on gaining more and better public housing and on putting an end to police brutality in Chicago. He also played a prominent role in founding the state legislature's first black caucus, establishing the Illinois Fair Employment Practices Commission, and getting the birthday of Martin Luther King, Jr., declared a state holiday. Meanwhile, he had declared his independence from the Chicago machine, thus earning its enmity in upcoming elections.

In 1980, Washington ran for the U.S. House of Representatives against Bennett Stewart, who had taken RALPH METCALFE's seat after the latter died two years earlier. Although Stewart had the support of the Democratic machine, Washington had earned the respect of the voters while in the state legislature, and he easily won the primary and the general election. He took his seat in 1981 and was assigned to the committees on education and labor, government operations, and the judiciary.

As a congressman, Washington opposed the rising tide of conservatism that followed in the wake of Ronald Reagan's election as president in 1980. Along with his fellow members in the Congressional Black Caucus, he worked to preserve funding for social services, voted against increases in military spending, and campaigned successfully for an extension of the Voting Rights Act of 1965. He was reelected in 1982.

In 1983, Washington decided to campaign for mayor of Chicago. He had run for this post once before, in 1976, but he had received only 11 percent of the vote in the Democratic primary. Since then, however, the number of registered African-American voters had risen considerably, and his chances of victory seemed good. He frightened many Democrats by vowing to put an end to machine politics, and he terrified many whites because of his race. However, he polled virtually all of the black and Hispanic votes, and these votes gave him a slight edge in both the primary and the general election.

Upon taking office in 1983, Washington set out to make good on his campaign promises. He hired a number of blacks to important city positions, including chief of police. He reduced the city's budget deficit by laying off 700 workers and cutting his own salary by 20 percent. He enacted the so-called Shakman decree, which replaced political patronage with a merit system of hiring and firing. He oversaw major improvements to the city's neighborhoods, but especially where blacks and Hispanics lived. By the end of his first term, the city had changed for the better in a number of ways, and Washington had gained the grudging respect, if not support, of most of the city's political leaders.

Washington was reelected in 1987. He died of a heart attack in his office at city hall on November 25, 1987.

Further Reading

Biographical Directory of the United States Congress. "Washington, Harold, 1922–1987." Available online. URL: http://bioguide.congress.gov/scripts/biodisplay.pl?index=W000180. Downloaded April 10, 2009.

Black Americans in Congress. "Harold Washington." Available online. URL: http://baic.house.gov/member-profiles/profile.html?intID=51. Downloaded April 9, 2009.

Clavel, Pierre, and Wim Wiewel. *Harold Washington and the Neighborhoods: Progressive City Government in Chicago, 1983–1987.* New Brunswick, N.J.: Rutgers University Press, 1991.

Clay, William L. *Just Permanent Interests: Black Americans in Congress, 1870–1992.* New York: Amistad Press, 1993.

Kleppner, Paul. *Chicago Divided: The Making of a Black Mayor.* DeKalb: Northern Illinois University Press, 1985.

Miller, Alton. *Harold Washington: The Mayor, the Man.* Chicago: Bonus Books, 1989.

Muwakkil, Salim. *Harold!: Photographs from the Harold Washington Years.* Evanston, Ill.: Northwestern University Press, 2007.

Rivlin, Gary. *Fire on the Prairie: Chicago's Harold Washington and the Politics of Race.* New York: Henry Holt, 1992.

Washington, Walter
(Walter Edward Washington)
(1915–2003) *mayor of Washington, D.C.*

Walter Washington was the first elected mayor of the nation's capital since Congress took over the city's administration in 1874. Under his guidance, the District of Columbia worked hard to end its status as "America's last colony."

Washington was born on April 15, 1915, in Dawson, Georgia. His father, William, was a factory worker, and his mother, Willie Mae, was a teacher. It was the custom of the day for an African-American mother living in the North to have her baby in the southern community where she had been raised; shortly after his birth, his mother took him home to Jamestown, New York, where he grew up. After graduating from high school, he enrolled in Howard University and received a B.A. in 1938. He then entered American University's graduate program in public administration, but he dropped out after several years to study law. In 1941, he married Bennetta Bullock, with whom he had one child.

That same year, Washington went to work for the District of Columbia's Alley Housing Authority as a junior housing assistant. At the time,

D.C.'s black servants did not live in their white employers' homes but rather in dilapidated shacks in the alleys behind. His job was to help these alley-dwellers find other housing so that the shacks could be demolished. After receiving his LL.B. from Howard Law School in 1948, he was made housing unit manager of a turnkey project for senior citizens that the agency, now known as the National Capital Housing Authority, had arranged to buy from a private developer. Over the next 13 years, he worked his way up through the ranks, and in 1961 President John F. Kennedy appointed him executive director.

One of the problems the District of Columbia faced was that, unlike other major cities, it was not self-governing. Rather, it was funded by federal appropriations from congressional committees and administered by a three-member commission of presidential appointees. In essence, its mayor was the president and its city council was Congress, and its residents exercised less control over their lives than did residents of Puerto Rico or the Virgin Islands. Consequently, the workings of government in D.C. were even more confused than in a city of similar size. In 1966, President Lyndon B. Johnson sought to rectify this situation by giving the city limited home rule, and he offered Walter Washington the post as president of the board of commissioners, thus making him the city's mayor. Washington turned him down because, under Johnson's plan, the chief commissioner would not have control over the city's police or fire departments. Instead, he accepted an offer to become chairman of the New York City Housing Authority.

Shortly thereafter, Johnson decided to expand the chief commissioner's powers as Washington had suggested, and in 1967 Washington accepted the position. Over the next seven years, he struggled to reorganize the city's government from top to bottom by eliminating duplicate agencies, streamlining others, and getting all agencies to work together under his direction. In addition to this daunting task, he also was faced with two huge challenges. Because it is the nation's capital, D.C. faces crowd control problems unlike those of any other city. This problem was exacerbated during the 1960s by numerous protests concerning the Vietnam War and the Civil Rights movement. In 1968, following the assassination of Martin Luther King, Jr., D.C., like more than 100 other cities, erupted in an orgy of rioting and looting that destroyed many parts of its residential and shopping districts. Rebuilding the city and dealing with hordes of often-unruly visitors while trying to reinvent city government strained the coping ability of Washington, the city and the man, almost to the breaking point.

By 1973, however, both Washingtons had made impressive headway. That same year, Congress enacted legislation to give D.C.'s residents greater control over city government, including the right to elect their own mayor. In 1974, Washington won the first mayoral election under the new law, and the following year he officially became Mayor Washington of Washington, D.C. Reelected in 1976, he continued to reorganize the government while addressing the city's housing, unemployment, and poverty problems.

Washington declined to run for reelection in 1978. When his term expired the following year, he joined a New York law firm and opened a branch office of the firm in D.C. Washington died on October 27, 2003, at the age of 88. Three years later, the Walter E. Washington Convention Center in Washington, D.C., was named in his honor.

Further Reading

District of Columbia Bar. "Legends in the Law: A Conversation with Walter Washington." Available online. URL: http://www.dcbar.org/for_lawyers/resources/legends_in_the_law/washington.cfm. Downloaded April 12, 2009.

Joint Center for Political Studies. *Profiles of Black Mayors in America*. Chicago: Johnson Publishing, 1977.

Martin, Douglas. "Walter Washington, 88, Former Mayor of Washington, Dies." *New York Times*,

October 28, 2003. Available online. URL: http://
www.nytimes.com/2003/10/28/national/28WASH.
html?scp=2&sq=walter%20washington&st=cse.
Downloaded April 13, 2009.

Picott, J. Rupert, et al. *Walter Washington, the District of
Columbia's First Elected Mayor since Reconstruction.*
Washington: Associated Publishers, 1976.

Waters, Maxine
(Maxine Moore)
(1938–) *U.S. congressional representative
from California*

During her 14 years in the California state assembly, Maxine Waters was one of the most powerful women in California. She later became one of the most powerful women in the U.S. Congress.

Waters was born Maxine Moore on August 31, 1938, in St. Louis, Missouri. Her father, Remus, was a laborer, and her mother, Velma, was a homemaker. When Moore was two, her parents divorced; shortly thereafter, her mother remarried and Moore was raised by her mother and stepfather. In 1956, she graduated from high school; married Edward Waters, with whom she had two children; and went to work in a factory. After five years, she and her husband decided to seek their fortunes in Los Angeles, California. Little changed, however; for the next four years Waters worked in a factory and as a telephone operator.

In 1965, the Head Start program came to Los Angeles. The program helped prepare youngsters for school, and Waters landed a job as an assistant Head Start teacher. The position opened her eyes to the necessity of furthering her own education. In 1968, she enrolled in California State University and received a B.A. in sociology four years later. In 1972, she and her husband divorced; five years later she married Sidney Williams.

Waters had become politically involved as a Head Start teacher. Despite the program's good intentions, it was underfunded, and it did not always suit the needs of the community. To rem-

edy this situation, she urged parents to lobby their elected officials in order to improve the program. Her activities in this regard brought her to the attention of the local Democratic Party, and in 1972 she was chosen to serve as a delegate to the Democratic National Convention. The following year, she went to work for Los Angeles city councilman David Cunningham as his chief deputy. For the next three years, she managed Cunningham's reelection campaigns while immersing herself in the legislative doings of city council. She also made valuable contacts while working for the campaigns of Senator Alan Cranston and Mayor TOM BRADLEY.

In 1976, Waters decided to run for a seat in the California state legislature. With the active support of Cranston and Bradley, she easily won. As a representative, Waters championed the interests of the downtrodden. She won passage of legislation establishing the nation's first child abuse prevention training program and prohibiting strip searches of those arrested on misdemeanor charges. She won set-asides for minority- and female-owned businesses in state contracts and got the state to divest itself of its investments in South Africa so long as apartheid held sway in that nation. She cofounded the Black Women's Forum as a vehicle for making the voices of California's African-American women heard. On the local level, she won funding for Project Build, which provided educational and job training services to public housing residents in Los Angeles. Reelected to six additional terms, she served on several important committees while winning a term as chair of the Democratic caucus.

Waters became actively involved in national politics as well. In 1980, she won a seat on the Democratic National Committee and seconded the nomination of Senator Edward Kennedy for president. In 1984, she cofounded the National Political Congress of Black Women to do nationally what the Black Women's Forum did in California. She cochaired the presidential campaigns of JESSE JACKSON in 1984 and 1988.

In 1990, AUGUSTUS HAWKINS announced that he would not seek reelection to Congress. Waters declared her candidacy for his seat, despite not having the support of the local Democratic organization. Because of her 14-year performance in the state assembly, she easily won the Democratic primary and the general election. She took her seat in 1991 and was assigned to the committees on veteran affairs and banking/finance/urban development. She has been reelected six times.

As a congresswoman, Waters continued to push for legislation that benefited minorities. She won passage of the Emergency Development Loan Guarantee Program in 1992, which made it easier for urban small businesses to get funding as well as for urban residents to purchase their own homes. The following year, her Youth Fair Chance Program was enacted; this $50-million program provides job and life skill training to unskilled and unemployed people between the ages of 17 and 30. In 1994, she became a vocal opponent of sexually explicit lyrics in so-called gangsta rap. In 1996, she was elected to a one-year term as chair of the Congressional Black Caucus. Like a growing number of African-American political leaders, she supports shifting funding from the "war on drugs" into prevention and treatment programs. Waters also voted against the Iraq War Resolution in 2002 and has since been a vocal critic of the war. In 2010, she was reelected to an 11th term by 79 percent of the vote.

Further Reading

Biographical Directory of the United States Congress. "Waters, Maxine, 1938– ." Available online. URL: http://bioguide.congress.gov/scripts/bio display.pl?index=W000187. Downloaded April 2, 2009.

Clarke, Caroline V. *Take a Lesson: Today's Black Achievers on How They Made It and What They Learned Along the Way.* New York: John Wiley, 2001.

Clay, William L. *Just Permanent Interests: Black Americans in Congress, 1870–1992.* New York: Amistad Press, 1993.

Congresswoman Maxine Waters, Official Web Site. Available online. URL: http://www.house.gov/ waters. Downloaded April 12, 2009.

Gill, LaVerne McCain. *African American Women in Congress: Forming and Transforming History.* New Brunswick, N.J.: Rutgers University Press, 1997.

Smith, Jessie Carney. *Black Heroes of the 20th Century.* Detroit: Visible Ink Press, 1998.

Watson, Diane
(Diane Edith Watson)
(1933–   ) *U.S. congressional representative from California*

Like her fellow Californian JUANITA MILLENDER-MCDONALD, Diane Watson arrived in the halls of Congress after a long teaching career. Watson's experiences prior to serving in Congress also included a stint as a U.S. ambassador.

Watson was born on November 12, 1933, in Los Angeles, California. Her father, William, was a police officer, and her mother, Dorothy, was a postal worker. After finishing high school, she attended Los Angeles City College before transferring to UCLA, where she received a B.A. in education in 1956. She then went to work for the Los Angeles Unified School District as an elementary school teacher. Between 1969 and 1971, she directed UCLA's secondary school allied health professions project, and from 1971 to 1973 she worked for the state department of education as a health occupation specialist. In 1987, she received an M.A. in school psychology from California State University and a Ph.D. in educational administration from Claremont Graduate University, after which she worked as a school psychologist and assistant superintendent of child welfare. At various times during her teaching career, she taught gifted children in France and Japan, authored a book about careers in health care, and wrote several chapters in a textbook about health occupations.

Watson became involved in politics in 1975 when she was elected to a three-year term on the

Los Angeles Unified School District board of education. During her tenure, she focused on upgrading the district's academic expectations of all its students. In 1978, she was elected as a Democrat to the state senate, where she served for 20 years. From 1981 to 1998, she chaired the senate health and human services committee. In this capacity, she played a major role in enacting a number of her own legislative initiatives. These included acts to fund research concerning birth defects and breast cancer, establish and enforce standards for nursing homes and assisted-living residences, and toughen food safety requirements for restaurants. She pushed through legislation that reformed the state's welfare programs by providing training, jobs, and child care to recipients as a means of helping them become self-sufficient, and she worked to obtain funding for a similar program aimed at single mothers.

In 1999, Democratic president Bill Clinton appointed Watson ambassador to the Federated States of Micronesia, an island nation in the western Pacific Ocean. She resigned two years later after the inauguration of Republican president George W. Bush. In 2001, JULIAN DIXON, who represented Watson's district in the U.S. Congress, died in office. Watson ran in the special election to fill the unexpired portion of his term and won. She took her seat that same year and was assigned to the committees on international relations and government reform.

As a congresswoman, Watson focused on improving health care benefits for senior citizens by working to include comprehensive prescription drug coverage through Medicare. She worked to preserve the Temporary Assistance for Needy Families program by restoring benefits for legal immigrants and by using a flexible, commonsense approach to reforming the work requirements for welfare recipients. She spoke out against the Bush administration's handling of the war on terrorism, claiming that President George W. Bush's homeland security program was seriously flawed, and that the president was using the war on terrorism and against Iraq as excuses to raid Medicare and

Diane Watson served as a teacher and U.S. ambassador before being elected to Congress. *(Diane E. Watson)*

Social Security funds. Watson is also concerned with relieving traffic congestion and treating obesity and other health problems. In 2008, she was reelected to her fourth full term. Watson later announced her plans to retire following the 11th congressional session.

Further Reading

Biographical Directory of the United States Congress. "Watson, Diane Edith, 1933– ." Available online. URL: http://bioguide.congress.gov/scripts/biodisplay.pl?index=W000794. Downloaded April 12, 2009.

Congresswoman Diane E. Watson, Official Web Site. Available online. URL: http://www.house.gov/watson/index.shtml. Downloaded April 12, 2009.

"Diane Watson Wins House Seat of Late Julian Dixon; Becomes 15th Black Woman Serving in U.S. Congress." *Jet* 100 (June 25, 2001): 30.

Explorations in Black Leadership. "Diane Watson." Available online. URL: http://www.virginia.edu/publichistory/bl/index.php?uid=32. Downloaded April 12, 2009.

"Longtime Political Activist, Experienced State Legislator Is Elected to Succeed Rep. Dixon." *CQ Weekly* 59 (June 9, 2001): 1,389.

Watt, Mel
(Melvin Luther Watt)
(1945–   ) *U.S. congressional representative from North Carolina*

In 1993, Mel Watt and EVA CLAYTON were elected to the U.S. House of Representatives from North Carolina. It was the first time since GEORGE WHITE had left office in 1901 that an African American had represented the state in Congress.

Watt was born on August 26, 1945, in Steele Creek, North Carolina. When he was three, his parents separated; he eventually moved with his mother and two brothers to Charlotte, where he grew up. After graduating from high school, he enrolled in the University of North Carolina at Chapel Hill and received a B.S. in business administration in 1967. Three years later, he received a J.D. from Yale University Law School. After spending a year in Washington, D.C., where he passed the bar examination, in 1971 he returned to Charlotte and joined a law firm. In 1968, he married Eulada Paysour, with whom he has two children.

As a lawyer, Watt became involved in the affairs of the local Democratic Party. He became the right-hand assistant to HARVEY GANTT, a maverick politician who generated much support from the state's lower classes. Watt served as Gantt's campaign manager during the 1980s, when Gantt won a seat on the Charlotte city council and then was elected mayor. In 1990, Watt managed Gantt's senatorial campaign, which shocked the nation's political pundits by

Mel Watt represented a white-majority district in Congress. *(Melvin L. Watt)*

almost unseating the longtime incumbent, conservative Republican Jesse Helms. Meanwhile, Watt had served a term as state senator. In 1985, the Democratic candidate from Watt's district, who was also the front-runner, died just before the election. Watt was prevailed upon to take the deceased candidate's place, and he won. He refused to stand for reelection, however, as he insisted on spending time with his children while they were still in high school.

By 1992, Watt's children were in college, and he was ready to run for office again. By coincidence, the state legislature had just redrawn North Carolina's congressional districts, in the process creating a black-majority district that encompassed that part of Charlotte in which Watt lived. He declared his candidacy for Congress, handily defeated three other candidates in the Democratic primary, and then breezed to victory in the general election. He took his seat in 1993 and was assigned to the committees on the judiciary and banking/financial services.

As a congressman, Watt became known for his outspoken, liberal views. He supported gun control, abortion rights, and socialized medicine. He upheld the legal rights of juvenile offenders and convicted sex offenders and opposed the death penalty. He fought against measures to reduce illegal immigration from Mexico. As a member of the banking/financial services committee, he consistently took the side of consumers whenever their interests clashed with those of the big banks and financial services corporations. Perhaps most surprising of all was his stance against the tobacco interests that wielded considerable influence in his home state.

Throughout his tenure in Congress, Watt has had to battle with the courts concerning the boundaries of his district. Long and narrow, it originally snaked its way from the South Carolina border south of Charlotte to Durham in the north central portion of the state. One wag commented that a person could get within earshot of everyone in the district simply by driving up and down I-85, the interstate highway that cuts the state roughly in half. In 1996, the U.S. Supreme Court ruled that the district's boundaries were unconstitutional because the district had been gerrymandered for racial purposes. It was redrawn in time for the election of 1998 so that it had a white majority. Watt confounded the experts by winning reelection anyway. After the election, a federal district judge ruled that the district's new boundaries were also unconstitutional and ordered them to be redrawn yet again, but the Supreme Court overturned this decision. Regardless of the racial makeup of his district, Watt continued to be returned to office. In 2010, he was reelected to a 10th term.

Further Reading

Biographical Directory of the United States Congress. "Watt, Melvin L., 1945– ." Available online. URL: http://bioguide.congress.gov/scripts/bio display.pl?index=W000207. Downloaded April 12, 2009.

Clay, William L. *Just Permanent Interests: Black Americans in Congress, 1870–1992.* New York: Amistad Press, 1993.

Congressman Mel Watt, Official Web Site. Available online. URL: http://www.watt.house.gov. Downloaded April 12, 2009.

Lacayo, Richard. "The Outsiders." *Time* 140 (November 2, 1992): 44–46.

"Melvin Watt." *CQ Weekly* 57, no. 42 (October 30, 1999, supplement): 48–49.

Watts, J. C.
(Julius Caesar Watts, Jr.)
(1957–) *U.S. congressional representative from Oklahoma*

In 1995, J. C. Watts joined GARY FRANKS as the only African-American Republicans in the U.S. House. His election offered further evidence of a growing conservatism among black political leaders and a potential shift of many African Americans back to the "party of Lincoln."

Watts was born on November 18, 1957, in Eufaula, Oklahoma. His father, Julius Caesar, Sr., was a policeman, and his mother, Helen, was a homemaker. After graduating from high school in 1976, he went to the University of Oklahoma on a football scholarship. In 1981 he received a B.A. in journalism, and he spent the next five years playing professional football in Canada. During the off-season, he resided in Norman, Oklahoma, and he returned there once his playing days ended in 1985. Over the next two years, he lost most of his earnings from football in a string of oil and real estate deals. In 1987, he became a youth minister at Sunnylane Baptist Church in Del City, Oklahoma. Seven years later, he was named the church's associate pastor. In 1977, he married Frankie Jones, with whom he has five children. He also fathered a child by an unknown woman while he was in high school; the child was adopted and raised by his uncle.

Watts developed an interest in politics as a boy, when his father served on the Eufaula city council. Like most African Americans, he was originally a Democrat. However, his conservative views on issues such as abortion, gun control, and gay rights led him into the Republican Party. In 1990, he successfully ran for one of three seats on the State Corporation Commission, which, among other duties, regulates the state's utilities and its powerful oil and gas industries. In 1993,

J. C. Watts was one of a few African-American Republicans to serve in Congress in the 20th century. *(J. C. Watts, Jr.)*

he was named the commission's chairman. During his five-year tenure on the commission, he was criticized for developing too-close ties with the leaders of several businesses he was supposed to be regulating. He admitted to accepting $100,000 from them, which is not illegal under state law, and he was later investigated without being charged for bribery.

In 1994, Watts declared his candidacy for a House seat from a district that was 90 percent white. He was still remembered by many as a football hero, but his conservative stand on the issues got him elected. He took his seat in 1995 and was assigned to the committee on transportation and the services committee.

The election of 1994 gave Republicans control of the House, and Watts became one of the party's most visible congressmen. Like most Republicans, he embraced the Contract with America, which called for tax breaks for the wealthy, spending cuts for social programs, a balanced budget, a strong military, and welfare reform. Watts was put in charge of a special congressional task force on minority relations, and he used this position to urge blacks to rely less on the federal government and more on themselves. Fewer than 10 percent of African Americans considered themselves to be Republicans, and Watts was pegged as the party's "Great Black Hope." He toured the country speaking to groups of African Americans, promoting conservative values and the Republican agenda of less government and more privatization. To further boost his visibility, in 1997 he was chosen to give the party's rebuttal to President Bill Clinton's state of the union address. In 1998, he was elected to chair the House Republican Conference, thus giving him a major role in overseeing the party's communications and image building efforts in Congress. In 2000 he was named honorary cochairman of the Republican National Convention.

Not surprisingly, Watts was attacked repeatedly by the Democrats, usually on the old charges of corruption. He was accused of improperly using his position as a congressman to obtain a government-backed loan for an apartment complex he wanted to purchase. He was also criticized for not reporting his wife's income on his tax returns one year, but the charges never stuck, as Watts was reelected three times.

In 2002, Watts announced that he would not seek reelection to a fifth term. He was begged by a number of high-ranking party officials to reconsider, as they believed he attracted a number of black voters to the party. After leaving office in 2003, he formed the J. C. Watts Companies; based in Arlington, Virginia, the companies conduct public opinion research and offer a variety of consulting services. Watts remained in the public eye as a popular speaker, a syndicated newspaper columnist, and a political analyst on radio and television programs. In July 2008, he announced his plans to launch the Black Television News Channel, the first cable news channel geared specifically to an African-American audience. Watts briefly considered running in the 2010 Oklahoma gubernatorial race, but gave up the idea of returning to politics, citing his various business obligations as the reason.

Further Reading

Biographical Directory of the United States Congress. "Watts, Julius Caesar, Jr. (J. C.), 1957– ." Available online. URL: http://bioguide.congress. gov/scripts/biodisplay.pl?index=W000210. Downloaded April 3, 2009.

Black Americans in Congress. "Julius Caesar (J. C.) Watts, Jr." Available online. URL: http://baic.house.gov/member-profiles/profile.html?intID=50. Downloaded April 13, 2009.

"J. C. Watts, Nation's Only Black Republican in Congress, Says He Won't Seek Fifth Term." *Jet* 102 (July 22, 2002), pp. 34–36.

Watts, J. C., with Chriss Winston. *What Color Is Conservative?: My Life in Politics.* New York: HarperCollins, 2002.

Weaver, Robert
(Robert Clifton Weaver)
(1907–1997) *U.S. secretary of housing and urban development*

Robert Weaver was the first African American to serve as a U.S. cabinet officer. Although he never ran for public office, he was active politically as an opinion leader and behind-the-scenes party worker.

Weaver was born on December 29, 1907, in Washington, D.C. His father, Mortimer, was a postal clerk, and his mother, Florence, was a homemaker. As a boy, he was fascinated with electricity, and by his senior year in high school he was working as a self-employed electrician. Upon graduating in 1925, he tried to get a union card but was turned down because he was black. Undaunted, he enrolled in Harvard University to study economics and received a B.A. in 1929 and an M.A. in 1931. After teaching at North Carolina Agricultural and Technical College (now State University) for a year, he returned to Harvard and received a Ph.D. in 1934. In 1935, he married Edith Haith, with whom he had one child.

In 1934, Weaver returned to Washington to work in the Department of Interior's Public Works Administration as an adviser on minority problems for the Tennessee Valley Authority, the Advisory Committee on Education, and the National Youth Administration. His task was to make sure that African-American employees and clients were treated fairly, particularly in terms of receiving their share of public housing. He also served informally as the leader of President Franklin D. Roosevelt's "black cabinet," a group of prominent African Americans who advised the president on minority affairs. In large part because of the black cabinet's recommendations, and because of its members' influence with black voters, Roosevelt offered more help to African Americans through the New Deal, hired more blacks for federal government clerkships and entry-level positions, and appointed the nation's first African-American general, Benjamin O. Davis, Sr.

In 1938, Weaver was appointed special assistant to the head of the National Housing Authority. This agency sought to provide housing for millions of America's poor, and again he worked to make sure that blacks got their fair share. In 1940, with World War II on the horizon, he became assistant to the head of the National Defense Advisory Committee. During the war he served on the War Production Board and the Negro Manpower Commission. His job with all three was to drum up African-American support for the war and get blacks more involved in the war effort. Weaver performed well in these assignments, but by war's end he had become disillusioned with the federal government's commitment to racial equality. Although Roosevelt had done more to improve the quality of life for African Americans than any previous president, he refused to press for an integrated society.

In 1944, Weaver moved to Chicago, Illinois, to work for integration as executive director of the Mayor's Commission on Race Relations. A year later, he became director of community services for the American Council of Race Relations. Having decided that segregation might best be attacked where people live, thus eliminating it in all aspects of life, he also became a board member of the city's Metropolitan Housing Council and executive committeeman of the National Committee on Housing.

In 1948, Weaver published *The Negro Ghetto*, a book that spoke out against the condition of segregated slums in the northern cities. That same year, he moved to New York City to teach at New York University and to direct the John Hay Whitney Foundation's Opportunity Fellowships Program. He continued his struggle against segregated housing by becoming involved in the affairs of the Democratic Party in city and state.

In 1955, the newly elected Democratic governor of New York asked Weaver to become state rent commissioner, thus giving him the power to do something about segregated housing. To this end, he tried to keep middle-class whites from moving out of the cities by controlling rents in integrated neighborhoods and by encouraging middle-class blacks to move to the suburbs. In 1959, he was named vice chairman of the New York City Housing and Development Board, thus giving him some authority over the city's slums, but before he could make much progress, he accepted newly elected Democratic president John F. Kennedy's offer to serve as head of the Federal Housing and Home Finance Agency, taking office in 1961. Since this agency was responsible for federal programs related to urban renewal and public housing, he was now in an ideal position to begin rectifying on a nationwide basis the conditions he had attacked in his book.

Weaver demonstrated his seriousness of purpose by moving into a modest apartment in Capitol Park, an urban redevelopment project in Washington. One of his first actions was to write the Housing Act of 1961, which gave him greater control over the activities of the agency's divisions while providing for billions of dollars for public housing and urban renewal projects. Knowing that Congress was not ready to ban segregated public housing, he sought an executive order to that effect. He preferred to renovate slums rather than clear them, because this only moved the residents to other slums since they generally could not afford the higher rents that new housing commanded. He developed a plan to integrate the suburbs by using Federal Housing Administration mortgage insurance. He campaigned for his enlightened but controversial approach to the nation's urban housing problem by writing *The Urban Complex: Human Values in Urban Life* (1964) and *Dilemmas of Urban America* (1965). When President Lyndon B. Johnson combined several agencies into the Department of Housing and Urban Development (HUD) in 1966, Weaver was named its secretary and, as such became a member of Johnson's cabinet, with all the power and prestige such a position embodies. His work was further facilitated by passage of Johnson's Model Cities program, which provided federal subsidies for urban redevelopment projects.

Weaver resigned from HUD in 1969 when Republican president Richard M. Nixon took office. He returned to New York City to become president of Baruch College of the City University of New York, then in 1970 began teaching in Hunter College's Urban Affairs Research Center. In 1978, he retired to his home in Manhattan, but in 1982 he became part of a board to oversee New York City's rent-stabilized apartments. He died on July 17, 1997, in New York City.

Further Reading

Bowser, Benjamin P., and Louis Kushnick, eds. *Against the Odds: Scholars Who Challenged Racism in the Twentieth Century.* Amherst: University of Massachusetts Press, 2002.

Pritchett, Wendell E. "Weaver, Robert." In *African American National Biography*, vol. 8, edited by Henry Louis Gates, Jr., and Evelyn Brooks Higginbotham. New York: Oxford University Press, 2008, pp. 179–181.

Smith, Jessie Carney. *Black Heroes of the 20th Century.* Detroit: Visible Ink, 1998.

Webb, Wellington
(Wellington E. Webb)
(1941–) *mayor of Denver, Colorado*

In 1991, Wellington Webb became the first African-American mayor of Denver, Colorado. Reelected to two terms, he played a major role in rebuilding the city's economy and improving its basic services.

Webb was born on February 17, 1941, in Chicago, Illinois. His father, Wellington, was a railroad porter, and his mother, Mardina, was a homemaker. He suffered from asthma as a youngster, and at age seven he was sent to live with his grandmother in Denver in the hope that the mountain air would improve his health. It did,

and he remained in Colorado for the rest of his life. After finishing high school, he attended Colorado State College, receiving a B.A. in sociology in 1964. Over the next seven years, he taught emotionally disturbed children and counseled welfare recipients while doing graduate work in sociology at the University of Northern Colorado. He received an M.A. in 1971 and briefly returned to teaching in Denver.

Webb got involved in politics through his grandmother, who was active in the local Democratic Party. With her assistance, in 1972 he ran a successful campaign for the Colorado state legislature. As a member of the lower house from 1973 to 1977, he pushed for legislation related to welfare and health care, and he coauthored the state's first civil rights bill for the handicapped.

In 1976, Webb chaired Jimmy Carter's presidential campaign in Colorado. Upon being inaugurated the following year, Carter appointed Webb principal regional director of the Department of Health, Education and Welfare's Region 8, which included Colorado, Wyoming, Montana, Utah, and the Dakotas. In this capacity, he managed a $3 billion budget and administered thousands of social services programs. Among them were many of the programs for Native Americans living on 23 reservations. For four years he worked hard to address the many problems they faced, including alcoholism, unemployment, illiteracy, teen pregnancy, and suicide. When Carter left office in 1981, Webb resigned and accepted an appointment as executive director of the Colorado Department of Regulatory Agencies, a position he held for six years.

In 1983, Webb returned to the political arena by running for mayor of Denver. He lost to Federico Peña, who served two terms before being named U.S. secretary of transportation in 1993. In the mid-1980s, Denver's office of city auditor had come under investigation because of various charges of corruption. In 1987, Webb ran successfully for city auditor, and over the next four years he made a name for himself by overhauling the department and making it operate in accordance with standard accounting and auditing practices.

In 1991, Peña decided not to seek reelection as mayor, and Webb joined a host of other candidates vying for his post. Toward the end of the campaign, he was trailing most of the other hopefuls and lacked the campaign funds with which to buy splashy media advertisements. Undaunted, he took to the streets to meet personally as many prospective voters as he could. For 39 days, he walked the city without returning to his home, spending the night in homeless shelters and in the homes of whoever would take him in. Not surprisingly, the unorthodox campaign generated a great deal of media attention (all of it free). However, it demonstrated to the people of Denver, only 12 percent of whom were African Americans, that Webb was sincere in his desire to serve them. It also brought him into closer contact with the people who most needed to be served, and gave him a better appreciation of the city's needs. He pulled off an upset victory, which he called "a victory of shoe leather over airwaves."

When Webb took office in 1991, Denver was just emerging from a rather long economic downturn. The city was $3 billion in debt, and the central business district was decaying. Webb responded to these problems by concentrating on the "nuts and bolts" of local government. He oversaw improvements in such mundane services as garbage collection and snow removal, which he paid for via an innovative mix of public and private financing. These improvements helped revitalize downtown Denver, and businesses that had once abandoned the city for the suburbs began to return. As they returned, the local tax base increased, thus providing the city with enough money to reduce its debt without raising taxes.

Webb's administration was not without its difficulties. His efforts to boost Denver's economy were hampered in 1993 when the voters of Colorado amended the state constitution so as to negate city ordinances prohibiting discrimination against homosexuals. As a result, many national groups that had planned to hold conventions in Denver began canceling them. Although Webb worked hard to assure the nation that Denver residents did not support the amendment, he was unable to avoid the loss of approximately $30 million in convention revenue. One group that did not cancel was the Roman Catholic Church, which held its annual World Youth Day in Denver that same year; the event drew more than 500,000 visitors, including Pope John Paul II and President Bill Clinton. Despite the cancellations, Denver's economic star continued to rise, and by mid-decade several of the nation's business magazines had given the city and its mayor high marks for being business-friendly.

Webb was reelected in 1995 and 1999. In 2000, he was elected to a two-year term as president of the National Conference of Black Mayors. During his later terms as mayor, Webb gained recognition for his successful summer and after-school programs for young people and for his aggressive position on gang violence. He also oversaw improvements to the Denver Medical Health Center that helped make the institution financially stable.

Webb left the mayor's office in 2003. He has since established Webb Group International, a consulting firm that concentrates on the economic development of urban centers. In 2007, his autobiography—*Wellington Webb: The Man, the Mayor and the Making of Modern Denver*—was published. He is married to the former Wilma Gerdine; he has two children by a previous marriage.

Further Reading

Balliette, James Fargo. "Webb, Wellington." In *African American National Biography*, vol. 8, edited by Henry Louis Gates, Jr., and Evelyn Brooks Higginbotham. New York: Oxford University Press, 2008, pp. 158–159.

Norment, Lynn. "Denver's Walking Mayor." *Ebony* 49 (December 1993): 29–32.

"Webb, Wellington E." *Current Biography* 60 (August 1999): 49–51.

Webb, Wellington, with Cindy Brovsky. *Wellington Webb: The Man, the Mayor and the Making of Modern Denver.* Golden, Colo.: Fulcrum Publishing, 2007.

Wheat, Alan

(Alan Dupree Wheat)

(1951–) *U.S. congressional representative from Missouri*

Alan Wheat was one of the first African-American politicians whose voter base was not predominantly black. For 12 years, he represented a congressional district that was 75 percent white; this is one of the highest nonminority percentages in any district represented by an African American. His success demonstrated the willingness of white voters to ignore race when their legislator represents their interests.

Wheat was born on October 16, 1951, in San Antonio, Texas. His father, James, was an Air Force colonel, and his mother, Emogene, was a homemaker. As a "military brat," he received his elementary and secondary education at various schools in the United States and Europe. After graduating from high school in Bossier City, Louisiana, in 1968, he enrolled in Grinnell College in Iowa and received a B.A. in economics four years later. In 1972, he moved to Kansas City, Missouri; over the next three years he worked as an economist for the U.S. Department of Housing and Urban Development and the Mid-America Regional Council. In 1975, he became the legislative aide to the county executive of Jackson County, which includes portions of Kansas City.

In 1977, Wheat was elected as a Democrat to the Missouri house of representatives. He was reelected twice, and during his third term he chaired the urban affairs committee and the Legislative Black Caucus. In 1982, the representative from Wheat's congressional district, Richard Bolling, announced his retirement. Of the seven Democrats vying for their party's nomination for Bolling's seat, Wheat was the youngest and the only African American. Nevertheless, he outpolled the others and then defeated his Republican opponent in the general election. He took his seat in Congress in 1983 and was assigned to the committee on rules.

During his 12 years in Congress, Wheat was one of its most liberal members. He supported federal aid for the homeless, federal initiatives to curtail hunger, strict controls on the purchase of handguns, unpaid family and medical leave, and cutting back on defense spending so that social programs could receive increased funding. He opposed U.S. investments in South Africa while apartheid was in force, the space station program, and the Persian Gulf War. He is best remembered for his role in passing the Civil Rights Act of 1990; as manager of the rule controlling debate on the floor, he was able to hold off conservative efforts to weaken the bill. Unlike many liberals, he supported the Violent Crime Control and Law Enforcement Act of 1994, because it promised to reduce crime and violence in black neighborhoods.

In 1992, Wheat's reputation was tarnished a bit when he became involved in the House banking scandal. Like many other representatives, Wheat had overdrawn his congressional banking account on numerous occasions. However, the scandal did not prevent him from being reelected later that year for the fourth time. In fact, he remained popular with his constituents because over the years he had paid careful attention to the needs of his district. His most important successes in this area were to obtain millions of dollars of federal money for flood control and transportation projects for Kansas City.

In 1994, John Danforth, U.S. senator from Missouri, announced his retirement. Wheat declined to run for reelection in order to campaign for Danforth's seat. He emerged victorious from the seven-way Democratic primary, but lost the general election to John Ashcroft, former governor and future U.S. attorney general.

Wheat retired from elected politics when his House term expired in 1995. That same year, he became vice president of public policy and government relations for the CARE Foundation, an international relief and development organization. The following year, he took a position as vice president for federal relations for Smith-Kline Beecham, a national pharmaceutical corporation. In 1996, he served as deputy campaign manager for the development of minority support for President Bill Clinton's reelection campaign. In 1997, he founded Wheat Government Relations, a lobbying firm based in Arlington, Virginia.

Further Reading

Biographical Directory of the United States Congress. "Wheat, Alan Dupree, 1951– ." Available online. URL: http://bioguide.congress.gov/scripts/biodisplay.pl?index=W000326. Downloaded April 12, 2009.

Black Americans in Congress. "Alan Dupree Wheat." Available online. URL: http://baic.house.gov/member-profiles/profile.html?intID=49. Downloaded April 11, 2009.

Clay, William L. *Just Permanent Interests: Black Americans in Congress, 1870–1992.* New York: Amistad Press, 1993.

Ruffin, David C. "Whole Wheat." *Black Enterprise* 17 (August 1986): 48.

White, George

(George Henry White)
(1852–1918) *U.S. congressional representative from North Carolina*

George White was the last African-American congressman of the 19th century. Despite his best efforts, he could not forestall the disfranchisement of black voters across the South, not even in his home state. After he left office in 1901, it was 28 years before another black politician, OSCAR DEPRIEST, was elected to Congress.

White was born on December 18, 1852, in Rosindale in Bladen County, North Carolina. His parents, Wiley and Mary, were slaves. By age 13, he had gained his freedom as a result of the Civil War, and he spent the next eight years working on the family farm and making barrels while sporadically attending public school. By 1873, he had saved enough money to enroll in Howard University. He graduated four years later and moved to New Bern, where he became principal of the state's only teachers' college for African Americans. He also took up the study of law, and by 1880 he had passed the bar examination and opened a law office in New Bern. At some point, he married Fannie Randolph, with whom he had one child; after she died he married Cora Cherry (the sister-in-law of HENRY CHEATHAM), with whom he had three children.

Upon settling in New Bern, White joined the Republican Party and became involved in local politics. In 1880, he was elected to the state legislature's lower house; while in office he gained state funding for four new black teachers' colleges. He was not reelected in 1882, but two years later the voters sent him to the state senate where he served on the committees pertaining to insurance, the judiciary, and the state insane asylum. In 1885, he was also elected solicitor and prosecutor for the judicial district encompassing the six counties in the state's northeastern corner, and for the next nine years he discharged his duties with considerable ability.

In 1894, White moved to Tarboro, where he had opened a second law office. That same year, he unsuccessfully challenged Cheatham for the Republican nomination to his brother-in-law's former seat in the U.S. House of Representatives. Two years later, however, he gained the nomination and won the election, thus becoming the third African American to represent eastern North Carolina in Congress since the end of Reconstruction. He was reelected in 1898.

As the only African American in Congress, White was the highest elected black official in the United States, and he saw himself as the representative of African Americans all across the country. He missed no opportunity to debate his racist colleagues on the House floor as they attempted to constrict the civil rights of black people. He introduced the first federal anti-lynching bill, a measure that would have reduced the congressional representation of states that disfranchised African Americans, and a bill to expand opportunities for blacks in the U.S. Army, none of which passed. He was more successful in gaining federal jobs for his constituents, and he managed to secure almost two dozen postmasterships in North Carolina for African Americans.

White was denied reelection in 1900, and he never held elective office again. When the North Carolina legislature disfranchised most African Americans that same year, he moved his law office and his residence to Washington, D.C., in 1901 and from there to Philadelphia, Pennsylvania, four years later. The latter move brought him closer to Whitesboro, an all-black community he had helped to establish. In 1899, he and two partners had purchased 1,700 acres in Cape May County, New Jersey, where the community was located. By 1906, the town's population included 300 families living in homes that had been financed via low-interest loans through the People's Savings Bank, which White had cofounded in 1905 in Philadelphia. He died on December 28, 1918, in Philadelphia.

Further Reading

Anderson, Eric. *Race and Politics in North Carolina, 1872–1901: The Black Second.* Baton Rouge: Louisiana State University Press, 1981.
Biographical Directory of the United States Congress. "White, George Henry, 1852–1918." Available online. URL: http://bioguide.congress.gov/scripts/biodisplay.pl?index=W000372. Downloaded April 20, 2009.
Black Americans in Congress. "George Henry White." Available online. URL: http://baic.house.gov/member-profiles/profile.html?intID=22. Downloaded April 3, 2009.
Clay, William L. *Just Permanent Interests: Black Americans in Congress, 1870–1992.* New York: Amistad Press, 1993.
Justesen, Benjamin R. *George Henry White: An Even Chance in the Race of Life.* Baton Rouge: Louisiana State University Press, 2001.

White, Jesse
(Jesse Clark White, Jr.)
(1934–) *secretary of state of Illinois*

Jesse White is the first African American to be elected to a statewide position in Illinois. Before being elected Illinois secretary of state, he served for more than 20 years as an elected official in state and county government.

White was born on June 23, 1934, in Alton, Illinois. His father, Jesse, was a laborer, and his mother, Julia, was a homemaker. At age four, he moved with his family to Chicago. After graduating from high school in 1952, he attended Alabama State College on an athletic scholarship and received a B.S. in 1956. He then signed a contract to play professional baseball with the Chicago Cubs, but he was drafted into the U.S. Army and never got a chance to play in the major leagues. Discharged in 1959, he returned to Chicago and went to work as a physical education teacher in one of the city's elementary schools. That same year, he founded the Jesse White Tumblers, a performing gymnastics team composed mostly of youngsters from Chicago's housing projects. Eventually, the Tumblers became world-renowned, and for the next 40-plus years they toured the nation and the world. Meanwhile, he continued to work in the school system as a teacher and administrator until 1992. He and his wife Sylvia had two children before they were divorced.

White got involved in politics in 1974 when he was elected as a Democrat to the state legislature. He was voted out of office in 1976 but returned two years later and was reelected through 1993. As a legislator, he sponsored a number of pro-education and anti-crime bills. Toward the end of his tenure, he was named chairman of the human services committee, which oversees the state's social services programs. In 1992, he was elected recorder of deeds for Cook County, which includes Chicago. He pushed for and then oversaw the computerization of the recorder's office, which saved the taxpayers time and money.

In 1998, White resigned as recorder to run for Illinois secretary of state. One of the duties of that office is to issue drivers' licenses, and at the time the office was being investigated by the U.S. Justice Department for allegedly accepting bribes from long-haul truckers who could not otherwise obtain commercial driver's licenses. White's reputation for honesty and competence carried him through the Democratic primary and the general election with ease; he was endorsed by virtually everyone, including the Republican candidate for governor.

Once elected, White focused on improving the state's motor vehicle safety record. He helped the legislature remove loopholes from the motor vehicle code, thus preventing incompetent drivers from obtaining commercial driver's licenses. He also lobbied successfully for programs to improve traffic safety and state roads.

In Illinois, secretary of state is a high-visibility position, and its holder often gets elected governor. White has eschewed any desire to do so, however, saying that when he leaves the office he will leave elected politics. In 2002 and 2006, he was overwhelmingly reelected.

Following BARACK OBAMA's election to the presidency in November 2008, White found himself at the center of a national controversy. Illinois governor Rod Blagojevich, after being arrested for corruption, appointed former state attorney general ROLAND BURRIS to the U.S. Senate seat previously held by Obama. White opposed Blagojevich's action and, as secretary of state, refused to sign the certificate of appointment. However, in the case of *Burris v. White*, the Illinois Supreme Court found that the certificate of appointment was valid without White's signature. Burris was sworn into the U.S. Senate on January 12, 2009.

Further Reading

Davis, Rick. *They Call Heroes Mister: The Jesse White Story*. Richton Park, Ill.: Lumen-us Publications, 2006.

Hawkins, Walter J. *African-American Biographies*. Chicago: McFarland & Co., 1992., pp. 442–43.

Hulse, Carl, and David Stout. "Burris, Blocked From Taking Seat, Gains New Support." *New York Times*, January 6, 2009. Available online. URL: http://www.nytimes.com/2009/01/07/us/politics/07burris.html?hp. Downloaded April 19, 2009.

Joens, David A. "White, Jesse Clark, Jr." In *African American National Biography*, vol. 8, edited by Henry Louis Gates, Jr., and Evelyn Brooks Higginbotham. New York: Oxford University Press, 2008, pp. 250–251.

White, Michael

(Michael Reed White)
(1951–   ) *mayor of Cleveland, Ohio*

Michael White was elected mayor of Cleveland in 1989. He won office after a hard-fought battle with his political mentor, George L. Forbes, then was reelected to two terms.

White was born on August 13, 1951, in Cleveland, Ohio, to Robert and Audrey White. After graduating from high school in 1969, he attended Ohio State University, receiving a B.A. in education in 1973 and an M.P.A. (master's degree of public administration) in 1974. He returned to Cleveland and worked for two years as a special assistant to the mayor. In 1976, he accepted a position as administrative assistant to the Cleveland city council.

White's political career began in college, when he was elected president of the student government. While working for the city council, he impressed councilman George L. Forbes, who took White under his wing and encouraged him to run as a Democrat for office himself. With Forbes's help, White won a seat on city council in 1977. Over the next six years, he served on the council's finance committee and chaired the community development committee. Like his mentor Forbes, he also gained a reputation for being verbally intemperate and racially combative; he once called one of his council colleagues a "white-folks nigger."

In 1984, White was appointed to a vacant seat in the Ohio state senate. As a state legislator, he authored several antidrug bills, sponsored measures to help the elderly pay for prescription medications, and worked to toughen the laws against rape. He toned down his racial rhetoric in order to appeal to his white constituents, and in 1986 he was elected to a full term of his own.

In 1989, White declared his candidacy for mayor of Cleveland. His principal opponent was his old mentor, George Forbes. During the campaign, White did a better job than Forbes of assuring the city's white voters that he would do more to protect their interests. After a bitter mudslinging campaign that did credit to neither side, White was elected by a wide margin.

As mayor, White made it a priority to revitalize Cleveland's downtown. He oversaw efforts to build a new stadium for major league baseball's Cleveland Indians, thus preventing them from moving to Tampa, Florida. The new stadium, Jacobs Field, was part of the Gateway Sports Complex, which included a new arena for the National Basketball Association's Cleveland Cavaliers, thus inducing them to return to the city from the suburbs where they had played for years. When the National Football League's (NFL) Cleveland Browns left town for Baltimore, Maryland, in 1996, he helped retain the team's name and colors and elicited a promise from the NFL to put an expansion team in Cleveland in 1999. He played an instrumental role in attracting the Rock and Roll Hall of Fame to Cleveland; a number of people around the country were amused, or stunned, to think of Cleveland as a major music center. Nevertheless, the Hall of Fame began attracting large numbers of visitors to the city almost as soon as it was completed, and it did much to enhance Cleveland's image. He also brought together various private investment groups representing more than $1 billion and streamlined the workings of city government so that they could develop rundown parts of the central business district.

White also paid attention to the deteriorating conditions in the city's residential neighborhoods, particularly the ones where minorities lived. He encouraged private investors to develop new housing projects, and he worked hard to improve municipal services such as garbage pickup and police protection. He improved conditions in the city's East Side by working with CSX Corporation, one of the nation's major railroads, to reduce noise and improve safety by cutting down on the number of long trains it ran through the neighborhood each day.

White was presented with a more difficult challenge by the city's public school system. Many schools had been allowed to deteriorate over the years, and White struggled to find the money to renovate them. After years of struggling with a recalcitrant school board, in 1997 he convinced the Ohio state legislature to give the mayor's office almost total control over the school system. This development allowed him to experiment with several innovative ways of financing educational improvements.

In 1997, White was reelected to a third term. He declined to run for reelection in 2001, citing a need to spend more time with his family, and he returned to private life after leaving office in early 2002. He and his wife, Tamera Kay, have four children.

Further Reading

The Encyclopedia of Cleveland History. "The Mayoral Administration of Michael R. White." Available online. URL: http://ech.cwru.edu/ech-cgi/article.pl?id=MAOMRW. Downloaded April 25, 2009.
"White, Michael R." *Current Biography* 60 (March 1999): 53–56.

Wilder, Doug

(Lawrence Douglas Wilder)
(1931–) *governor of Virginia, mayor of Richmond, Virginia*

Lawrence Douglas "Doug" Wilder was the first popularly elected black governor in the history of the United States. During his four years as governor, he was the highest-ranking elected African American in the nation. An able governor, he was unable to translate his success into a national office.

Wilder was born on January 17, 1931, in Richmond, Virginia. His father, Robert, was an insurance salesman, and his mother, Beulah, was a homemaker. In 1947, at age 16, he enrolled in Virginia Union University, receiving a B.S. in chemistry in 1951. That same year, he joined the U.S. Army and was sent to Korea, where he earned a Bronze Star for heroism during the Korean War. Discharged in 1953, he returned to Richmond to work as a toxicologist in the state medical examiner's office. Three years later, he enrolled in Howard University Law School; in 1959 he received an LL.B. and opened a law office in Richmond. In 1958, he married Eunice Montgomery, with whom he had three children; they were divorced in 1978.

Wilder had entertained political ambitions since college, but Virginia's traditional attitudes regarding race prevented him from pursuing them. The passage of the Voting Rights Act of 1965 began to change that situation, however, and in 1969 he saw his opportunity to get involved in politics. The state senator for his district, in which blacks barely outnumbered whites, resigned to campaign for a higher office. Before the special election to fill his

unexpired term could be announced, Wilder declared his candidacy for the vacant office. He had the good fortune to be opposed by two white candidates, who split the white vote between them while Wilder garnered virtually all of the black votes. When he took office later that year, he became the first African American to serve in the Virginia senate since Reconstruction.

Wilder, a Democrat, immediately gained a reputation as an "angry young black." Sporting a bushy Afro hairdo during his maiden speech in the senate, he attacked the state song, "Carry Me Back to Old Virginia," for its racist lyrics and demanded that it be changed. Reelected to a term of his own in 1970, he pressed the senate to enact fair housing laws, to repeal the death penalty because blacks were far more likely to be executed than whites, and to repeal the sales tax on food and nonprescription drugs because they fell unfairly on minorities and the elderly. He demanded that Lee-Jackson Day, one of the state's most hallowed holidays because it honored Confederate generals Robert E. Lee and Thomas "Stonewall" Jackson, be amended to honor Martin Luther King, Jr., as well, a proposal so audacious that it outraged virtually every white person in the state. Yet Wilder had a more politic side as well, which he displayed in closed committee meetings. During his 16 years in the senate, he gradually played down his blackness while learning to compromise without abandoning his principles, and by 1985 he was considered one of the senate's most influential figures.

In 1981, Wilder had campaigned vigorously among African Americans for Chuck Robb, the Democratic candidate for governor. Wilder's influence proved to be the difference in Robb's victory, the first for a Democrat in a statewide contest in 16 years. Four years later, Wilder decided to run for lieutenant governor. Democrats were lukewarm about his candidacy because they did not think an African American could win a statewide popular election; indeed, no black had ever won such a contest anywhere in the South. They supported him anyway because he had demonstrated an ability to mobilize African-American voters, and they did not want to lose his support in future elections. During the campaign, Wilder developed an image as a populist by canvassing the entire state by car, meeting and shaking hands with voters (most of whom were white) in virtually every little hamlet he visited. In a state that was 19 percent black, he won with 52 percent of the vote.

Wilder devoted his four-year term to preparing for a run at the state house. Although he remained a loyal Democrat, he feuded just enough with Democratic governor Gerald Baliles to establish himself in the eyes of the voters as his own man. In 1989 he easily won the party's nomination for governor, and in the ensuing campaign he successfully depicted his Republican opponent, Marshall Coleman, as a right-wing radical. To their credit, neither candidate called attention to their own or the other's race. The election was so close that a recount was called, which Wilder won by fewer than 7,000 votes. He took office in 1990.

As governor, Wilder surprised his supporters and critics alike. He fired many of Robb's and Baliles's appointees from state boards, then replaced them not with African Americans but with whites who had supported his campaign. Rather than embark on a grandiose agenda of social spending, as many critics feared he would, he transformed the state's deficit into a surplus by trimming the budget and raising taxes modestly. When the census of 1990 mandated that Virginia redraw its congressional districts, he opposed the creation of a black-majority district on the grounds that it was unnecessary, as his own elections had proven. When the economy began to cool off, thus resulting in lowered state revenues, he refused to raise taxes to make up the difference, choosing instead to cut appropriations to state agencies and lay off workers. In all, his four-year tenure was an exercise in fiscal and social conservatism. His most liberal venture was to order state agencies and universities to divest themselves of investments in corporations doing business in South Africa until apartheid was abolished.

In 1991, his second year as governor, Wilder declared his candidacy for president. He cam-

paigned as part of what he called the "New Mainstream," urging the nation's Democrats to divest themselves of their image as free-spenders and become more fiscally responsible if they intended to win elections. To position himself as the first choice of African Americans, he began criticizing JESSE JACKSON, who had twice run for president, for being too liberal and therefore unelectable. This ploy, however, angered more blacks than it attracted, and it diminished Wilder's stature in the national black community. To make himself known outside Virginia, in 1992 he campaigned for and won a one-year term as chairman of the Southern Governors' Association. He also began making public appearances across the United States, traveling so extensively that he was out of the state for days at a time. His frequent absences angered those Virginians who thought that being governor should be a full-time job, and his popularity rating at home suffered as a result. By 1992, it was clear that Wilder's campaign was headed nowhere, so he withdrew from the race to focus on his duties as governor.

After leaving office in 1994 (by law, Virginia governors are limited to one term), Wilder became the host of a radio talk show that lasted only a few months before it was canceled. That same year he decided to run for the U.S. Senate against Robb, the incumbent. When he was denied the Democratic nomination, Wilder stayed in the race as an independent, thus angering most of his long-time supporters who were also staunch Democrats. He dropped out of the race before the general election and announced his retirement from politics. From 1998 to 2003, he was president of his alma mater, Virginia Union.

Wilder was hired as professor of public policy at Virginia Commonwealth University. In 2004, the university named its School of Government and Public Affairs in his honor. Wilder was also instrumental in establishing the National Slavery Museum and raising funds for a permanent facility in Fredericksburg, Virginia.

Wilder returned to politics in May 2004, by announcing his candidacy for mayor of Richmond in the city's first direct election for the post.

Wilder won the election by approximately 79 percent of the vote. His term was marked by a series of battles with the city council and school board. In May 2008, Wilder declared that he would not seek another term as mayor, marking the end of his long political career.

Further Reading

Baker, Donald P. *Wilder: Hold Fast to Dreams: A Biography of L. Douglas Wilder.* Cabin John, Md.: Seven Locks Press, 1989.

Edds, Margaret. *Claiming the Dream: The Victorious Campaign of Douglas Wilder of Virginia.* Chapel Hill, N.C.: Algonquin Books, 1990.

Explorations in Black Leadership. "L. Douglas Wilder." Available online. URL: http://www.virginia.edu/publichistory/bl/index.php?uid=42. Downloaded April 20, 2009.

Jeffries, J. L. *Virginia's Native Son: The Election and Administration of Governor L. Douglas Wilder.* West Lafayette, Ind.: Purdue University Press, 2000.

Lazarus, Jeremy M. "Richmond Mayor Doug Wilder Ends 40-Year Public Service Career with Mixed Legacy." *Richmond Free Press,* May 17, 2008. Available online. URL: http://www.louisianaweekly.com/news.php?viewStory=76. Downloaded April 20, 2009.

Yancey, Dwayne. *When Hell Froze Over: The Untold Story of Doug Wilder: A Black Politician's Rise to Power in the South.* Dallas, Tex.: Taylor Publishing Co., 1988.

Williams, Anthony

(Anthony Stephen Eggleton,
Anthony Allan Williams)
(1951–   ) *mayor of Washington, D.C.*

Like SHARON PRATT DIXON KELLY, Anthony Williams was elected to replace MARION BARRY as mayor of Washington, D.C. Unlike Kelly, Williams possessed considerable skill as an administrator, which allowed him to overcome his political inexperience and win reelection to a second term.

Williams was born Anthony Stephen Eggleton on July 28, 1951, in Los Angeles, California. Placed in a foster home as an infant, at age three he was adopted by Lewis and Virginia Williams, postal workers, and renamed. After graduating from high school in 1969, he attended Santa Clara University for two years before dropping out to join the U.S. Air Force. He received an honorable discharge in 1974, and a year later, he enrolled in Yale University. While attending school he held several jobs and received a B.A. in economics in 1982. He then enrolled in Harvard University, and by 1987 he had received two graduate degrees in public finance.

In 1988, Williams was hired by Chris Grace, a former classmate at Harvard and head of the Boston (Mass.) Redevelopment Authority, to head the authority's neighborhood housing and development program. Two years later, Grace, now the director of development in St. Louis, Missouri, enticed Williams to join him as head of the city's community development agency. About a year into the job, Williams refused to pay two contractors on the grounds that they had done shoddy work. They assaulted him, broke his nose, and went to jail, and Williams returned to New England. In 1991, he was hired as deputy comptroller for the state of Connecticut. He received such favorable reviews in this position that he came to the attention of the Clinton Administration. In 1993, he was hired as chief financial officer of the U.S Department of Agriculture and served briefly under MIKE ESPY. As CFO, he oversaw a budget of more than $60 billion and helped keep tabs on more than two dozen agencies.

In 1995, Williams applied for an even more challenging position, that of chief financial officer of the District of Columbia. As Washington's primary landlord, the federal government had run all aspects of D.C.'s government until 1974, when home rule gave control of local government to local residents. Even so, the city had to apply annually to Congress for operating funds, since it could not collect real estate taxes on federal property. Congress generally hemmed and hawed before allocating such funds and did not always provide enough funds. Meanwhile, the city government had become bloated with mid-level managers, many of whom showed little interest in getting the job done. By 1995, the city was $1 billion in debt, a figure that was expected to increase by about $100 million each year. To solve the problem, Congress created an oversight committee that took control of the district's financial affairs. Daily oversight was to be delegated to a chief financial officer who would be hired by the mayor but could be fired only by the committee. Williams contacted then-mayor Marion Barry to apply for the position and went to work in 1995.

As CFO, Williams exercised more control over the workings of D.C.'s government than did Mayor Barry. Williams oversaw a successful program to collect delinquent income and property taxes, and he implemented the highest standard of accounting and audit practices. He also fired 300 mid-level managers who he deemed were performing unsatisfactorily. By 1997, these practices and others had halted the city's financial hemorrhaging and created an annual budget surplus of $186 million. Williams performed so well that in 1998 a citizens group convinced him to run for mayor.

Williams's candidacy was criticized by many on the ground that he had lived in the district for only five years and that he lacked political experience. In fact, he had held public office before, having won a term in 1981 on the New Haven (Conn.) board of aldermen while attending Yale. Despite the criticism, he easily defeated three other contenders in the Democratic primary, swept to victory in the general election, and took office in 1999.

Williams's first act as mayor was to have each department head establish goals for improving the department's service to the public. He then published the goals and worked relentlessly to make sure that they were met. Next, he won important concessions from Congress regarding the return of full-fledged home rule to the district. Greatly impressed by Williams's performance to date,

Congress agreed to return control of the city's financial affairs to the mayor after he had balanced four consecutive budgets. Two years later, Congress returned control of the district's finances to the Williams administration.

Williams's expertise as a financial manager helped him solve a great many of the district's problems. However, his political inexperience got him into trouble several times. Shortly after Williams took office, a white homosexual aide publicly used the word *niggardly,* which outraged many of the city's African-American residents. Williams immediately accepted the aide's resignation, which outraged the city's gay community. Williams then rehired the aide, only to be charged with indecisiveness. Later errors were less comedic. In 1999, he was charged with failing to declare $40,000 in income he had received as a consultant on the financial disclosure form he had filed for the 1998 election. He was fined a nominal sum by the local office of campaign finance, but the incident cast a shadow on his reputation for being financially irreproachable. In 2002, it was discovered that the petition Williams had filed to run for reelection in the Democratic primary contained a number of forged signatures, so many that he was denied a spot on the ballot.

Despite these problems, Williams remained very popular with district voters. He ran as a write-in candidate in the 2002 Democratic primary and easily won. In that year's general election, he was reelected by a wide margin. During his second term, Williams helped arrange for the Montreal Expos, a major league baseball team, to move to Washington, D.C., despite initial opposition from the city council. In 2005, the Washington Nationals played their first game in the U.S. capital.

The same year, Williams announced that he would not seek reelection. After leaving office, he founded Premium Public Realty Trust, a real estate investment firm. In 2009, Premium was dissolved, and Williams joined the law firm Arent Fox in Washington, D.C. He is married to the former Diane Simmons, with whom he has one child.

Further Reading

Explorations in Black Leadership. "Anthony Williams Interview." Available online. URL: http://www.virginia.edu/publichistory/bl/index.php?uid=29. Downloaded April 9, 2009.

Rosenberg, Debra. "D.C.'s Mr. Clean Takes a Mud Bath." *Newsweek* 140 (August 2002): 37.

Walters, Jonathan. "Capital Gains." *Governing* 15 (August 2002): 28–31.

"Williams, Anthony A." *Current Biography* 60 (October 1999): 52–55.

Williams, Avon
(Avon Nyanza Williams, Jr.)
(1921–1994) *Tennessee state senator*

Avon Williams was a leading figure in Tennessee politics during the civil rights era. While serving in the state senate for more than 20 years, he introduced a number of bills that improved life for the state's minorities.

Williams was born on December 22, 1921, in Knoxville, Tennessee, to Avon and Carrie Williams. After finishing high school, he enrolled in North Carolina's Johnson C. Smith University and received an A.B. in 1940. He briefly attended Boston University School of Law but left before graduating to serve in the U.S. Army during World War II. He returned to school after the war and received an LL.B. in 1948. That same year, he moved to Nashville, Tennessee, to work as an intern for ALEXANDER LOOBY, and in 1949 he returned to Knoxville to open a law office of his own. Four years later, he rejoined Looby in Nashville, and the two men remained associates until 1969, when Williams established a separate practice. As an attorney, he specialized in civil rights cases, and was involved with Looby in much of the litigation involving the desegregation of Tennessee's public schools. Possessed of a caustic and fiery personality, he was jailed several times for contempt of court because he refused to kowtow to racist judges. In 1956, he married Joan Marie Bontemps, with whom he had two children.

Williams became involved in politics in 1962 when he cofounded the Davidson County Independent Political Council. After serving as its president for four years, in 1966 he cofounded the Tennessee Voters Council, and served as its general chairman for almost 20 years. The two organizations were established to provide a home for African-American voters, who were not recruited by either of the two major political parties in the mid-1960s. He first ran for office in 1968 and was elected to the state senate.

Williams served in the senate from 1969 to 1991. As a senator, he continued to champion equal opportunity for minorities. He introduced the bill that created the state's housing development agency, and he had African-American studies introduced into the public schools. He was the moving force behind the state's allocation of millions of dollars to Meharry Medical College, a black institution. He also wrote legislation that forced the state's utility districts to lay water lines to black communities. Perhaps most importantly, he was the author of Tennessee's first civil rights act. Passed in 1978, it prohibited discrimination on the basis of race, religion, gender, or national origin.

In 1985, Williams developed a motor neuron disease known as pseudobular palsy, which affected his ability to speak and walk. Undaunted, he bought a wheelchair and hired a translator, who accompanied him to committee hearings and onto the senate floor. His feistiness impressed his constituents, who reelected him the following year. By 1990, however, his health had declined to the point that he could no longer serve, and he declined to run for reelection that year. After leaving office in 1991, he retired to his home in Nashville, where he died on August 29, 1994.

Further Reading

Doyle, Don H. *Nashville since the 1920s.* Knoxville: University of Tennessee Press, 1985.

Lovett, Bobby L., and Linda T. Wynn. *Profiles of African Americans in Tennessee.* Nashville, Tenn.: Local Conference on Afro-American Culture and History, 1996.

The Tennessee Encyclopedia of History and Culture. "Avon N. Williams, Jr., 1921–1994." Available online. URL: http://tennesseeencyclopedia.net/imagegallery.php?EntryID=W065. Downloaded April 20, 2009.

Tennessee State University Digital Library. "Avon Nyanza Williams, Jr. (1921–1994)." Available online. URL: http://www.tnstate.edu/library/digital/williama.htm. Downloaded March 29, 2009.

Williams, George
(George Washington Williams)
(1849–1891) *Ohio state legislator*

George Williams was the first African American to serve in the Ohio state legislature. He is also remembered as being the "father of black history" and for exposing the abuses of European colonialism in Africa.

Williams was born on October 16, 1849, in Bedford Springs, Pennsylvania. His parents, Thomas and Ellen, were free blacks. His father supported the family variously as a boatman, barber, and minister, and as a result the family moved to Johnstown, Newcastle, and other western Pennsylvania towns. Consequently, young George rarely attended school, instead picking up the rudiments of the barbering trade. In 1863, at age 14, he lied about his age, temporarily assumed his uncle's name, and joined the Union army. Serving under General Ulysses S. Grant, he took part in the sieges of Richmond and Petersburg and was wounded in action at Fort Harrison, Virginia. When the Civil War ended, he went to Texas and ended up helping the Mexicans overthrow Maximilian, their French-backed emperor. In 1867, he reenlisted in the U.S. Army and saw service in Indian Territory as a member of the fabled 10th Cavalry, an all-black unit known to the Indians they chased as "buffalo soldiers." He received a medical discharge the following year after being shot in the leg under mysterious circumstances.

Williams drifted through Missouri and Illinois before enrolling in Howard University in 1869.

Shortly thereafter, he felt the calling to become a minister, and after briefly attending Wayland Seminary in Washington, D.C., he transferred to Newton Theological Institution in Massachusetts. In 1874, he graduated from Newton, married Sarah Sterret (with whom he had one child), and became pastor of Boston's Twelfth Baptist Church. He resigned a year later and returned to Washington to edit a black newspaper, *The Commoner*. The paper folded within six months, and in 1876 he went to Cincinnati, Ohio, to become pastor of the Union Baptist Church. In addition to pastoring, he studied law at the Cincinnati Law School and wrote articles for the *Cincinnati Commercial Tribune*.

Williams's political career began shortly after he arrived in Cincinnati. He became involved with the local Republican Party, and in 1877 he ran for the state legislature. After losing the election, he resigned his pastorate and supported himself as a store clerk and auditor's assistant while planning a second campaign. In 1879, with the full support of the local Republican leadership, he ran again and narrowly won a seat in the lower house, thus becoming the first African American to serve in the Ohio state legislature.

Williams's sole term was a colorful one. He outraged whites by insisting on eating at a restaurant in Columbus, the state capital, that catered to legislators. He also outraged blacks by voting to condemn an African-American cemetery as a health hazard in order to remove it to make room for a white-sponsored development project. He introduced bills to legalize interracial marriage, to regulate the police in the state's larger cities, and to restrict liquor sales, none of which passed. He declined to run for reelection in 1881 and never held public office again.

Williams passed the Ohio bar examination in 1881 and opened a law office in Cincinnati. He also took up the writing of black history. In 1882, G. P. Putnam's Sons published his two-volume work, the meticulously researched *History of the Negro Race in America from 1619 to 1880: Negroes as Slaves, as Soldiers, and as Citizens*. The work was unique in that it was the first scholarly history of African Americans, as well as one of the first to make extensive use of newspapers as primary sources. It was so highly praised by both black and white reviewers that he wrote *A History of the Negro Troops in the War of the Rebellion, 1861–1865*. Published in 1887, it also received praise for its scholarly approach.

In 1883, Williams had relocated his law practice to Boston. He also became involved in a scheme to recruit African Americans to work in Africa's Congo Free State, at the time the personal possession of King Leopold II of Belgium. Upon inspecting the country, however, Williams found Leopold's administration over native Africans to be rife with cruelty and exploitation. Instead of serving as a recruiter, in 1890 he published *An Open Letter to His Serene Majesty, Leopold II, King of the Belgians*, in which he told the world how the Belgians were repressing Africans. He contracted tuberculosis during the trip and died while returning to the United States on August 2, 1891, in Blackpool, England.

Further Reading

Franklin, John Hope. *George Washington Williams: A Biography*. Durham, N.C.: Duke University Press, 1998.

George Washington Williams: An Ohio Legislator. Available online. URL: http://www.georgewashing tonwilliams.org/index.cfm. Downloaded March 29, 2009.

Infoplease. "George Washington Williams." Available online. URL: http://www.infoplease.com/ipa/ A0878504.html. Downloaded May 20, 2002.

Williams, Hosea
(Hosea Lorenzo Williams)
(1926–2000) *Georgia state senator*

Hosea Williams was one of the Civil Rights movement's most fearless leaders. However, the militancy that served him so well in the movement did not serve him well as a politician. Although he held various elected offices for 20 years, his political effectiveness was hampered by his inability to put the movement behind him.

Williams was born on January 5, 1926, in Attapulgus, Georgia. His father was blind and his mother died a few years after Williams was born, so he was raised by his grandfather, Turner Williams, a farmer. By age 14, he had had enough of farming, so he ran away. After three years of earning a living by working odd jobs across the Florida panhandle, he joined the U.S. Army. During World War II, he served in Germany, where he was seriously wounded. After the war, he returned to Attapulgus and reenrolled in high school, receiving his diploma in 1947. Four years later, he received a B.A. in chemistry from Morris Brown College in Atlanta, then took a job teaching high school chemistry in Douglasville. In 1952, he moved to Savannah to work for the U.S. Department of Agriculture as a research chemist, a position he held for 11 years. That same year, he married Juanita Terry, with whom he had five children and adopted four more.

In 1952, Williams joined the National Association for the Advancement of Colored People, thus involving himself in the Civil Rights movement. He also joined the Southern Christian Leadership Conference (SCLC), and in 1960 he led an SCLC-sponsored boycott of Savannah stores with lunch counters that would not serve blacks. In 1961, he began publishing the *Chatham County Crusader*, a pro-civil rights newspaper in Savannah. Two years later, he moved to Atlanta to become the SCLC's special projects director, a position he held for seven years. As director, he served as a valued assistant to Martin Luther King, Jr., and he became known as King's "field general." His "special projects" included organizing the 1965 march from Selma to Montgomery, Alabama, that ended in "Bloody Sunday" when state troopers attacked and injured 80 demonstrators on the outskirts of Selma. By 1971, when he resigned as SCLC's executive director, he had led dozens of protest marches, been arrested dozens of times, and spent weeks in jail.

Williams made his first foray into politics in 1968, when he ran for the Georgia legislature as a Democrat. Undaunted by his defeat, two years later he ran again, this time as a Republican for Georgia secretary of state. Losing again, in 1972 he returned to the Democratic Party to seek its nomination for U.S. senator. This bid failed, as did the one the following year for the party's nomination for mayor of Atlanta. Finally, in 1974, he was elected to represent southeast Atlanta in the state senate.

As a senator, Williams continued to focus on expanding the civil rights of African Americans. He limited his effectiveness, however, by being a political gadfly. In 1980, he shocked Georgia's Democrats by endorsing Ronald Reagan, the Republican candidate for president, instead of President Jimmy Carter, his fellow Democrat and Georgian, on the grounds that Carter had done little to further civil rights. When Reagan proved to be downright antagonistic toward civil rights, in 1984 Williams backed the presidential candidacy of JESSE JACKSON. That same year, he ran for the U.S. House of Representatives; the party had neither forgotten nor forgiven his apostasy of four years earlier, however, and its lack of support cost him the election.

In 1985, Williams relinquished his seat in the senate, having won a seat on the Atlanta city council. Again, the focus of his tenure, this time for five years, was on civil rights. In 1987, he led two controversial and confrontational marches in Forsyth County, to the northeast of Atlanta, that generated much media attention but little racial harmony. In 1989, he again ran for mayor of Atlanta but lost the Democratic nomination to former mayor MAYNARD JACKSON. Incensed by the party's lack of support, Williams turned once again to the Republicans for help, asking them to open their minds and hearts to black voters who were "sick and tired of being hostages to the Democratic Party." The bid failed, and he lost the election. The following year, however, he was elected to Georgia's DeKalb County commission by a

landslide. His effectiveness in this position was marred by repeated arrests for various traffic and handgun violations, and by charges that he had voted for a small-business grant to a chemical manufacturing and distribution firm founded by him and codirected by one of his daughters. In 1994, in the middle of his reelection campaign, he retired from politics.

Williams spent his retirement leading protest marches. In 1995, he helped organize the Million Man March in Washington, D.C. Later that year, he tried to organize a similar march in Atlanta, but only 400 marchers showed up. Undaunted, in 1996 he led a march on the state capital to protest the state flag's incorporation of the Confederate battle flag. He died on November 16, 2000, in Atlanta.

Further Reading

Kirkland, W. Michael. "Hosea Williams (1926–2000)." New Georgia Encyclopedia. Available online. URL: http://www.georgiaencyclopedia.org/nge/Article.jsp?id−h-2721. Downloaded March 29, 2009.

Williams, Juan. *Eyes on the Prize: America's Civil Rights Years, 1954–1965.* New York: Viking, 1987.

Wynn, Albert
(Albert Russell Wynn)
(1951–) *U.S. congressional representative from Maryland*

Albert Wynn was one of a growing breed of moderate Democrats. He was also the first African American to represent a black-majority district that was predominantly suburban and middle class.

Wynn was born on September 10, 1951, in Philadelphia, Pennsylvania. As a boy he moved with his family to North Carolina and from there to Glenarden in Prince George's County, Maryland, a suburb of Washington, D.C. He graduated from high school in 1969, then attended the Uni-

Albert Wynn represented the Maryland suburbs of Washington, D.C., in Congress. *(Albert R. Wynn)*

George's County, which borders Washington to the east. The county experienced many growing pains as the percentage of its African-American residents slowly rose until 1980, when a majority of the county's residents were black. A majority of these blacks were middle class, and in 1982 they gave Wynn his first political victory when they elected him to one of the county's seats in the Maryland House of Delegates. In 1986, he was elected to the state senate, and four years later he was reelected. In the senate, he served on the ways and means committee and the budget and taxation committee.

As a state legislator, Wynn worked for the interests of the black middle class. These African Americans appreciated the help that had been given them by the federal government, and they welcomed the continuation of certain government initiatives. Specifically, they wanted the government to ensure equal opportunity at the polls, ban discrimination in the workplace, and stimulate the development of minority-owned small businesses. Many of them, however, were less enamored with other government welfare programs, which they perceived as undermining the ability of black people to help themselves. Wynn's middle-class African-American constituents wanted to do as much for themselves as they could, and to this end he pressed the state government to help blacks without taking away their pride or their incentive to better themselves.

Following the census of 1990, the Maryland legislature redrew the state's congressional districts. In the process, it created a black-majority district centered around Prince George's County. In 1992, Wynn declared his candidacy for this seat. He survived a 12-candidate race to win the Democratic primary and then easily defeated his Republican opponent in the general election. He took his seat in 1993 and was assigned to the committees on foreign affairs, banking/finance/urban affairs, and post office/civil service.

As a congressman, Wynn continued to fight for the black middle class. He battled the National

versity of Pittsburgh on a debating scholarship. Four years later, he received a B.S. in political science. After a year of studying public administration at Howard University, in 1974 he enrolled in Georgetown University Law School, receiving a J.D. three years later. In 1977, he was named executive director of Prince George's County consumer protection commission, a position he held until 1981, when he opened a law firm in the county.

Most government workers in the District of Columbia are African Americans, and many of them serve as clerks and mid-level managers. The middle-class wages that these positions began paying after World War II made it possible for many black government workers to buy homes in Prince

Institutes of Health, the Library of Congress, and the Voice of America over their poor record of promoting African Americans to management positions. He successfully initiated a simplified process for filing and reconciling complaints with the Equal Employment Opportunity Commission. He worked to reduce the amount of paperwork the government required small businesses to complete and file, and he sought to establish a system for tracking the number of loans banks and mortgage lenders offered to consumers living in minority neighborhoods. He pushed to increase the percentage of government contract set-asides for minority-owned businesses from 20 percent to 23 percent, which more closely approximates the percentage of African-American citizens in the United States.

In 2002, Wynn was reelected to a sixth term. In 2003, he helped secure a federal grant to improve security at the Port of Baltimore in Maryland, and he helped to expand the child care tax credit to low-income Americans.

Wynn was again reelected in 2004, but before the 2006 election, his district was redrawn to include several conservative-leaning suburbs. He narrowly defeated DONNA EDWARDS in the Democratic primary, and won the general election with 80 percent of the vote. However, Wynn lost the next primary to Edwards in February 2008 and resigned from office four months later to accept a partnership with the Washington law firm Dickstein Shapiro. He has been married and divorced and is the father of one child.

Further Reading

"Albert R. Wynn." *Congressional Quarterly Weekly Report* 51 (January 16, 1993 supplement): 91.

Biographical Directory of the United States Congress. "Wynn, Albert Russell, 1951– ." Available online. URL: http://bioguide.congress.gov/scripts/biodisplay.pl?index=W000784. Downloaded April 14, 2009.

Black Americans in Congress. "Albert R. Wynn." Available online. URL: http://baic.house.gov/member-profiles/profile.html?intID=119. Downloaded April 13, 2009.

Clay, William L. *Just Permanent Interests: Black Americans in Congress, 1870–1992.* New York: Amistad Press, 1993.

Helderman, Rosalind S., and Jeffrey H. Birnbaum. "Wynn Decides to Leave Congress Months Before His Term Expires." *Washington Post,* March 28, 2008. Available online. URL: http://www.washingtonpost.com/wp-dyn/content/article/2008/03/27/AR2008032702136.html. Downloaded April 14, 2009.

Y

Young, Andy
(Andrew Jackson Young, Jr.)
(1932–   ) *U.S. ambassador to the United Nations, mayor, congressional representative*

Andy Young is the only American to have served as mayor, congressman, and U.N. ambassador. He also headed a successful campaign to bring the Olympic Games to Atlanta, Georgia, where he now teaches public policy.

Young was born on March 12, 1932, in New Orleans, Louisiana. His father, Andrew, was a dentist, and his mother, Daisy, was a teacher. He finished high school in 1947, then enrolled in Dillard University in New Orleans. A year later, he transferred to Howard University to study premedicine. After receiving a B.S. in 1951, he enrolled in Connecticut's Hartford Theological Seminary and received a B.D. four years later. In 1955, he was ordained a minister in the United Church of Christ. After serving for two years as pastor of congregations in Thomasville and Beachton, Georgia, in 1957 he became associate director of the National Council of Churches Department of Youth Work in New York City. In 1961, the NCC started a project to register and educate African-American voters in the South, and Young moved to Atlanta, Georgia, to oversee the campaign. During the campaign, he met Martin Luther King, Jr., leader of the Southern Chris-

tian Leadership Conference, and in 1962 Young left the NCC to work for civil rights as King's administrative assistant. In 1964, he was named the SCLC's executive director, and in 1967 he became its executive vice president. In 1954, he married Jean Childs, with whom he had four children. She died in 1994, and in 1996 he married Carolyn Watson.

King's assassination in 1968 led Young to conclude that the next step in the struggle to gain civil rights was political action. In 1970, he resigned from the SCLC to campaign for the U.S. Congress. Although he won the Democratic primary, he lost badly in the general election, mostly because he was relatively unknown in Atlanta. Following the election, he became chairman of the Atlanta Community Relations Commission, and in this capacity he was able to increase his recognition among the voters. In 1972, he ran again, and this time he was elected, thus becoming the first African American to represent Georgia in Congress since Reconstruction. He was assigned to the committee on banking and currency.

As a congressman, Young gained a reputation as a skillful compromiser. His ability to see both sides of an issue and to proceed in a manner that was fair to all parties earned him a reassignment to the powerful Rules Committee. It also helped him achieve the gains he wanted most, such as the strengthening of the Voting Rights Act of 1965 to provide for increased federal enforcement. He voted consistently against increasing the military budget and to restrict U.S. investments in South Africa so long as apartheid remained in force. He also opposed the Nixon administration's efforts to cut spending on programs aimed at helping the poor. He was reelected easily to two additional terms.

In 1976, Young became the first nationally known politician to endorse the presidential candidacy of Georgia's Jimmy Carter. He did so because he believed that Carter, of all the Democratic hopefuls, would do the most to advance civil rights. At the time, Carter was a political unknown, but with Young leading his campaign in the African-American community he was able to win the nomination and the election. In 1977, President Carter rewarded Young for his support by naming him U.S. ambassador to the United Nations.

In addition to attending to his official duties as ambassador, Young lobbied to change U.S. policy toward the continent of Africa and developing countries globally. He was most interested in getting the United States to improve its commercial relations with underdeveloped nations while using its influence to effect a peaceful transition from white to black rule. His opponents criticized him for exceeding the bounds within which his predecessors had stayed, but he enjoyed the full support of Carter, who himself had a strong interest in the human rights of the world's disadvantaged. Young's undoing came in 1979, when he met with representatives of the Palestine Liberation Organization as a means to bring about peace in the Middle East. Such a meeting had been expressly forbidden by act of Congress, and Young was forced to resign later that year.

Young returned to Atlanta where he founded a consulting firm, Young Ideas. In 1981, he was induced to run for mayor of Atlanta to succeed MAYNARD JACKSON, who was prohibited by law from seeking a third consecutive term. After a

Andy Young served as a UN ambassador, a U.S. congressman, and the mayor of Atlanta. *(Library of Congress)*

tough campaign in both primary and general election, Young was elected and took office in 1982. As mayor of a predominantly black city that whites controlled economically, he walked a political tightrope as he tried to get both sides to work together for the betterment of both. Using all of his skills as a diplomat, he achieved success in this endeavor while also managing to lower the crime rate and attract new businesses to town. He was reelected handily to a second term. After stepping down as mayor in 1990, Young campaigned for governor of Georgia. He polled well in Atlanta and other cities, but he fared poorly in the rural areas and lost.

Although Young retired from politics after his defeat, he remained involved in public policy and international affairs. He served as chairman of the Atlanta Organizing Committee, which attracted the 1996 Centennial Olympic Games to Atlanta largely because Young drew heavily on his personal acquaintanceship with many prominent individuals on the International Olympic Committee. In 1994, he was named chairman of the

Southern Africa Enterprise Development Fund, which lends equity capital to African nations. He founded and served as chairman of GoodWorks International, a consulting firm that provides strategic services to corporations and governments operating in the global economy. Young's company drew fire for defending the labor practices of Nike, one of its largest clients, after Nike was accused of running sweatshops in Asia. Young was also criticized for controversial remarks he made while serving on the national steering committee for Working Families for Wal-Mart.

Young is a Distinguished Senior Fellow at Georgia State University's Andrew Young School of Policy Studies. The Andrew Young Center for International Affairs at Morehouse College is also named in his honor.

Further Reading

Black Americans in Congress. "Andrew Jackson Young, Jr." Available online. URL: http://baic.house.gov/member-profiles/profile.html?intID=48. Downloaded April 11, 2009.

Colburn, David R., and Jeffrey S. Adler. *African-American Mayors: Race, Politics, and the American City.* Urbana: University of Illinois Press, 2001.

DeRoche, Andrew J. *Andrew Young: Civil Rights Ambassador.* Wilmington, Del.: SR Books, 2003.

Gardner, Carl. *Andrew Young: A Biography.* New York: Drake, 1978.

Hornsby, Alton, Jr. "Young, Andrew." In *African American National Biography,* vol. 8, edited by Henry Louis Gates, Jr., and Evelyn Brooks Higginbotham. New York: Oxford University Press, 2008, pp. 477–479.

Jones, Bartlett C. *Flawed Triumphs: Andy Young at the United Nations.* Lanham, Md.: University Press of America, 1996.

Young, Andrew. *A Way Out of No Way: The Spiritual Memoirs of Andrew Young.* Nashville, Tenn.: Thomas Nelson Publishers, 1994.

———. *An Easy Burden: The Civil Rights Movement and the Transformation of America.* 2nd ed. Waco, Tex.: Baylor University Press, 2008.

Young, Coleman

(Coleman Alexander Young)
(1918–1997) *mayor of Detroit, Michigan*

Coleman Young was the first black mayor of Detroit. He took over at a time when the city's economic and social situation could hardly have been bleaker. Nevertheless, he convinced most of the city's residents to put their differences behind them and to work together for the common good. In the process, Detroit was transformed from a decaying city into a vibrant one.

Young was born on May 24, 1918, in Tuscaloosa, Alabama. His father, Coleman, was a tailor, and his mother, Ida, was a homemaker. As a young boy he moved with his family to Huntsville. His family got so tired of being harassed by the Ku Klux Klan that in 1926 they moved to Detroit, where his father opened a dry cleaning business. After graduating from high school in 1936, Young was offered a partial scholarship to attend the University of Michigan; unable to pay the difference or to find anyone who would lend it to him, he enrolled in the Ford Motor Company's electricians' apprentice school instead. Upon completing the program, he discovered that Ford had only one opening for an electrician. Having finished at the head of the class, he believed the job would be his; instead, it went to a white apprentice while Young was put to work on the assembly line. Angered by this blatant display of racism, he became a union and civil rights activist. This involvement, however, led to on-the-job harassment and dismissal. In 1940, he went to work for the U.S. Postal Service but was fired two years later for calling his white supervisor "Hitler." Drafted shortly thereafter into the U.S. Army Air Corps, he became a second lieutenant with the all-black Tuskegee Airmen and flew missions over Europe as a bombardier-navigator.

After World War II, Young returned to the Postal Service while becoming more heavily involved in union activities. In 1947, he married Marion McClellan (they had no children), and he was named organizational secretary for the local chapter of the Congress of Industrial Organizations (now the AFL-CIO). He lost this position the following year, however, when he ran afoul of Walter Reuther, head of the United Automobile Workers, for demanding equal employment opportunities for African Americans in Detroit's auto factories. In 1948, he campaigned for Henry Wallace, the Progressive candidate for president who was rumored to be "soft" on communism. In 1950, he left the Postal Service to open a dry cleaning store like his father's.

In 1951, Young founded the National Negro Labor Council to lobby large employers across the country to hire more African Americans, and he enjoyed some conspicuous successes in Chicago and San Francisco. Unfortunately, these successes occurred during the McCarthy era, when virtually all black self-help groups were thought to be communist fronts. In 1952, he was called before the House Un-American Activities Committee and ordered to hand over the group's membership list. He refused repeatedly to comply, even after the council was placed on the subversive list, and in 1956 he closed it down. Meanwhile, his dry cleaning business had failed and his marriage had ended in divorce.

In 1957, Young went to work as an insurance salesman and joined the Democratic Party. Selling insurance brought him into contact with the voters of his district; he gained a better understanding of their problems while they gained a better appreciation for his vision and abilities. In 1960 he was named a delegate to the state constitutional convention, and in 1964 he was elected to the state senate. Reelected three times, he became a powerful voice in the senate for more public housing and less discrimination at school and work. In 1968, he became the first African American elected to the Democratic National Committee.

In 1973, Young declared his candidacy for mayor of Detroit. His opponent was John F. Nichols, the white commissioner of police who was running on a "law and order" platform. Young stole his thunder by promising to get rid of all kinds of crime, including police brutality. The polls indicated that more than 90 percent of the whites favored Nichols while more than 90 percent of the blacks favored Young. Since African Americans barely outnumbered whites in Detroit, Young won by a few thousand votes.

As mayor, Young hired more black police officers, firefighters, and municipal clerks, and he required all city employees to live in the city. He also opened police substations in high crime districts in an effort to rid Detroit of the nickname "Murder City." He brought business and labor leaders together in an effort to attract new industries while retaining the existing ones. During his 20 years as mayor, Detroit renovated much of its downtown and riverfront; new projects included the Joe Louis Arena, the Renaissance Center hotel-office complex, the Millender Center residential- retail complex, and the People Mover monorail system. The city also refurbished Belle Isle Park in the Detroit River, rebuilt several decaying neighborhoods, and convinced General Motors and Chrysler to build new plants in Detroit. These efforts were aided tremendously by the influx of federal funding between 1977 and 1981; during this period, Democratic president Jimmy Carter was in office and Young served as vice-chairman of the Democratic National Committee. He also brought blacks and whites together in an effort to create racial harmony where little had existed before. As a reward for his leadership, Young was reelected four times, each time by a landslide.

Despite his accomplishments, Young also experienced some "hard stuff" as mayor. In 1989, a former city worker won a large money settlement against him for fathering her child out of wedlock. Two years later, he was faced with a major scandal in the police department when its chief was indicted for embezzling $2 million. In 1992, his intemperate remarks on television heightened racial tensions following the beating death of Malice Green, a young black man, by two white police officers. His management style came under attack during his fifth term for not being open enough and for being too confrontational, particularly in matters concerning the mostly black city's mostly white suburbs. Perhaps worst of all, he was criticized for his failure to combat Detroit's economic downturn that began in the late 1980s. As a result, the city's tax revenues dwindled, which led in part to a decline in city services and a rise in crime.

Young declined to run for reelection in 1993 because of poor health. After his term expired, he taught at Wayne State University and joined an investment group that wanted to build a casino on the waterfront. He died on November 30, 1997, in Detroit.

Further Reading

Colburn, David R., and Jeffrey S. Adler, eds. *African-American Mayors: Race, Politics, and the American City.* Urbana: University of Illinois Press, 2001.

Harp, Andrea S. "Coleman A. Young: Social and Political Powerbroker." Available online. URL: http://www.is.wayne.edu/mnissani/elephant/young.htm. Downloaded March 29, 2009.

Preston, Michael B., et al., eds. *The New Black Politics: The Search for Political Power,* 2nd ed. New York: Longman, 1987.

Young, Coleman A. *The Quotations of Mayor Coleman A. Young.* Detroit: Wayne State University Press, 2008.

Young, Coleman A., with Lonnie Wheeler. *Hard Stuff: The Autobiography of Coleman Young.* New York: Viking, 1994.

BIBLIOGRAPHY AND RECOMMENDED SOURCES

BOOKS

Bailey, Harry A., ed. *Negro Politics in America.* Columbus, Ohio: C. E. Merrill Books, 1967.

Bailey, Richard. *Neither Carpetbaggers nor Scalawags: Black Officeholders during the Reconstruction of Alabama, 1867–1878.* 5th ed. Montgomery, Ala.: NewSouth Books, 2007.

Barker, Lucius J., and Jesse J. McCorry, Jr. *Black Americans and the Political System.* 2nd ed. Boston: Little, Brown, 1982.

Bositis, David A. *Changing of the Guard: Generational Differences among Black Elected Officials.* Washington: Joint Center for Political and Economic Studies, 2001.

Burns, Peter F. *Electoral Politics Is Not Enough: Racial and Ethnic Minorities and Urban Politics.* Albany: State University of New York Press, 2006.

Christopher, Maurine. *Black Americans in Congress,* rev. and expanded ed. New York: T. Y. Crowell, 1976.

Clay, William L. *Just Permanent Interests: Black Americans in Congress, 1870–1992.* New York: Amistad Press, 1993.

Clayton, Edward T. *The Negro Politician—His Success and Failure.* Chicago: Johnson Publishing Co., 1964.

Colburn, David R., and Jeffrey S. Adler. *African-American Mayors: Race, Politics, and the American City.* Urbana: University of Illinois Press, 2001.

Concise Dictionary of American Biography. New York: Scribner; Simon & Schuster and Prentice Hall International, 1997.

Contemporary Black Biography, Profiles from the International Black Community. Detroit: Gale Research, 1992– .

Current Biography. New York: H. W. Wilson, 1940– .

Davis, John, ed. *Perspectives in Black Politics and Black Leadership.* Lanham, Md.: University Press of America, 2007.

Dawson, M. C. *Behind the Mule: Race and Class in African-American Politics.* Princeton, N.J.: Princeton University Press, 1994.

Dictionary of American Biography. New York: Charles Scribner's Sons, 1996.

Drago, Edmund L. *Black Politicians and Reconstruction in Georgia: A Splendid Failure.* Athens: University of Georgia Press, 1992.

Dray, Philip. *Capitol Men: The Epic Story of Reconstruction through the Lives of the First Black Congressmen.* Boston: Houghton Mifflin, 2008.

Dymally, Mervyn M., ed. *The Black Politician: His Struggle for Power.* Belmont, Calif.: Duxbury Press, 1971.

Elliot, Jeffrey M. *Black Voices in American Politics.* New York: Harcourt Brace Jovanovich, 1986.

Fenno, Richard F. *Going Home: Black Representatives and Their Constituents.* 2nd ed. Chicago: University of Chicago Press, 2003.

Foerstel, Karen. *Biographical Dictionary of Congressional Women.* New York: Greenwood Press, 1999.

Foner, Eric. *Freedom Lawmakers: A Dictionary of Black Officeholders During Reconstruction.* New York: Oxford University Press, 1993.

Foster, William Z. *History of the Communist Party of the United States.* New York: Greenwood Press, 1968.

Garraty, John A., and Mark C. Carnes, eds. *American National Biography.* New York: Oxford University Press, 1999.

Gates, Henry Louis, Jr., and Evelyn Brooks Higginbotham, eds. 8 vols. *African American National Biography.* New York: Oxford University Press, 2008.

Gill, LaVerne McCain. *African American Women in Congress: Forming and Transforming History.* New Brunswick, N.J.: Rutgers University Press, 1997.

Gosnell, Harold F. *Negro Politicians: The Rise of Negro Politics in Chicago.* Chicago: University of Chicago Press, 1967.

Haskins, James. *Distinguished African-American Political and Governmental Leaders.* Phoenix, Ariz.: Oryx Press, 1999.

———. *A Piece of the Power: Four Black Mayors.* New York: Dial Press, 1972.

Hawkins, Walter J. *African-American Biographies.* Chicago: McFarland & Co., 1992.

Haynie, Kerry L. *African American Legislators in the American States.* New York: Columbia University Press, 2001.

Hine, Darlene C., ed. *Facts On File Encyclopedia of Black Women in America.* New York: Facts On File, 1997.

Holt, Thomas C. *Black over White: Negro Political Leadership in South Carolina during Recon-* struction. Urbana: University of Illinois Press, 1977.

Ifill, Gwen. *The Breakthrough: Politics and Race in the Age of Obama.* New York: Doubleday, 2009.

Jennings, James. *The Politics of Black Empowerment: The Transformation of Black Activism in Urban America.* Detroit: Wayne State University Press, 2001.

Johnson, Cedric. *Revolutionaries to Race Leaders: Black Power and the Making of African American Politics.* Minneapolis: University of Minnesota Press, 2007.

Joint Center for Political Studies. *Profiles of Black Mayors in America.* Chicago: Johnson Publishing Co., 1977.

Kaptur, Marcy. *Women in Congress, 1917–2006.* Washington, D.C.: Government Printing Office, 2006.

Langston, Donna. *A to Z of American Women Leaders and Activists.* New York: Facts On File, 2002.

Litwack, Leon F., and August Meier. *Black Leaders of the Nineteenth Century.* Urbana: University of Illinois Press, 1991.

Logan, Rayford W., and Michael R. Winston, eds. *Dictionary of American Negro Biography.* New York: W. W. Norton, 1982.

Marable, Manning. *Beyond Black and White: Transforming African-American Politics.* New York: Verso, 2009.

Menifield, Charles E., and Stephen D. Shaffer. *Politics in the New South: Representation of African Americans in South State Legislatures.* Albany: State University of New York Press, 2005.

Middleton, Stephen, ed. *Black Congressmen During Reconstruction: A Documentary Sourcebook.* Westport, Conn.: Greenwood Press, 2002.

Perry, Huey. *Race, Politics, and Governance in the United States.* Gainesville: University of Florida Press, 1996.

Persons, Georgia, ed. *Beyond the Boundaries: A New Structure of Ambition in African Ameri-*

can Politics. Piscataway, N.J.: Transaction Publishers, 2009.

Preston, Michael B. et al., eds. *The New Black Politics: The Search for Political Power,* 2nd ed. New York: Longman, 1987.

Rabinowitz, Howard N., ed. *Southern Black Leaders of the Reconstruction Era.* Urbana: University of Illinois Press, 1982.

Rueter, Ted. *The Politics of Race: African Americans and the Political System.* Armonk, N.Y.: M. E. Sharpe, 1995.

Schultz, Jeffrey D., Kerry L. Haynie, Anne M. McCulloch, and Andrew L. Aoki, eds. *Encyclopedia of Minorities in American Politics: African Americans and Asian Americans,* vol. 1. Phoenix, Ariz.: Oryx Press, 2000.

Scott, Mingo. *The Negro in Tennessee Politics and Governmental Affairs, 1865–1965: The Hundred Years Story.* Nashville: Rich Printing Co., 1965.

Singh, Robert. *The Congressional Black Caucus: Racial Politics in the U.S. Congress.* Thousand Oaks, Calif.: Sage Publications, 1997.

Smith, Jessie Carney. *Notable Black American Women.* Detroit: Gale Research, 1992.

———. *Black Heroes of the 20th Century.* Detroit: Visible Ink Press, 1998.

Smith, Robert C. *Encyclopedia of African-American Politics.* New York: Facts On File, 2003.

Swain, Carol M. *Black Faces, Black Interests: The Representation of African Americans in Congress,* enlarged ed. Washington, D.C.: University Press of America, 2006.

Tate, Katherine. *Black Faces in the Mirror: African Americans and Their Representatives in the U.S. Congress.* Princeton, N.J.: Princeton University Press, 2004.

Thompson, J. Phillip. *Double Trouble: Black Mayors, Black Communities, and the Call for a Deep Democracy.* New York: Oxford University Press, 2005.

Udogu, E. Ike. *African American Politics in Rural America: Theory, Practice, and Case Studies from Florence County, South Carolina.* Lanham, Md.: University Press of America, 2006.

Walton, Hanes. *Black Republicans: The Politics of the Black and Tans.* Metuchen, N.J.: Scarecrow Press, 1975.

WEB SITES

"African Americans and American Politics." Schomburg Center for Research in Black Culture, New York Public Library. URL: http://exhibitions.nypl.org/african-americans-in-politics.

Avoice: African American Voices in Congress. URL: http://www.avoiceonline.org.

"Black Americans in Congress." Office of the Clerk of the U.S. Capitol." URL: http://baic.house.gov.

"Breaking New Ground: African American Senators." United States Senate. URL: http://www.senate.gov/pagelayout/history/h_multi_sections_and_teasers/Photo_Exhibit_African_American_Senators.htm.

Center for the Study of African-American Politics, University of Rochester. URL: http://www.rochester.edu/college/PSC/CSAAP/index.html.

Congressional Black Caucus Foundation, Inc. URL: http://www.cbcfinc.org.

National Black Caucus of State Legislators. URL: http://www.nbcsl.org.

National Conference of Black Mayors. URL: http://ncbm.org.

National Conference of Black Political Scientists. URL: http://www.ncobps.org.

National Organization of Black County Officials. URL: http://www.nobcoinc.org.

Entries by Office Held

U.S. President
Obama, Barack

U.S. Secretary/Attorney General
Brown, Ron
Espy, Mike
Harris, Patricia Roberts
Herman, Alexis
Holder, Eric
Jackson, Alphonso
Jackson, Lisa P.
O'Leary, Hazel
Paige, Rod
Powell, Colin
Rice, Condoleezza
Slater, Rodney
Sullivan, Louis
Weaver, Robert

U.S. Senator
Brooke, Edward
Bruce, Blanche
Burris, Roland
Moseley Braun, Carol
Obama, Barack
Revels, Hiram

Governor/Lieutenant Governor
Evans, Melvin

Hastie, William H.
Paterson, David
Patrick, Deval
Pinchback, P. B. S.
Rogers, Joe
Steele, Michael
Wilder, Doug

State Secretary/Attorney General
Allen, Ethel
Baker, Thurbert E.
Blackwell, Ken
Burris, Roland
Cardozo, Francis
McCall, Carl
White, Jesse

U.S. Representative
Ballance, Frank
Bishop, Sanford
Blackwell, Lucien
Brown, Corrine
Burke, Yvonne
Cain, Richard
Carson, André
Carson, Julia
Cheatham, Henry
Chisholm, Shirley
Christian-Christensen, Donna

Clarke, Yvette D.
Clay, William
Clay, William, Jr.
Clayton, Eva
Cleaver, Emanuel
Clyburn, James
Collins, Barbara-Rose
Collins, Cardiss
Conyers, John
Crockett, George W.
Cummings, Elijah
Davis, Artur
Davis, Danny K.
Dawson, William
DeLarge, Robert
Dellums, Ron
DePriest, Oscar
Diggs, Charles
Dixon, Julian
Dymally Mervyn
Elliott, Robert
Ellison, Keith
Espy, Mike
Fattah, Chaka
Fauntroy, Walter
Fields, Cleo
Flake, Floyd
Ford, Harold
Ford, Harold, Jr.
Franks, Gary
Fudge, Marcia L.

Gray, Bill
Hall, Katie
Haralson, Jeremiah
Hastings, Alcee
Hawkins, Augustus
Hayes, Charles
Hilliard, Earl
Hyman, John
Jackson, Jesse, Jr.
Jefferson, William
Johnson, Eddie Bernice
Jordan, Barbara
Kilpatrick, Carolyn
Langston, John
Lee, Barbara
Leland, Mickey
Lewis, John
Long, Jefferson
Lynch, John
Majette, Denise
McKinney, Cynthia
Meek, Carrie
Meek, Kendrick
Meeks, Gregory
Metcalfe, Ralph
Mfume, Kweisi
Millender-McDonald,
   Juanita
Miller, Thomas
Mitchell, Arthur
Mitchell, Parren
Moore, Gwen
Murray, George
Nash, Charles
Nix, Robert
Norton, Eleanor Holmes
O'Hara, James
Owens, Major
Payne, Donald
Powell, Adam Clayton, Jr.
Rainey, Joseph
Rangel, Charles
Ransier, Alonzo
Rapier, James

Rush, Bobby
Smalls, Robert
Stokes, Louis
Thompson, Bennie
Towns, Edolphus
Tubbs Jones, Stephanie
Turner, Benjamin
Walls, Josiah
Washington, Harold
Waters, Maxine
Watson, Diane
Watt, Mel
Watts, J. C.
Wheat, Alan
White, George
Wynn, Albert
Young, Andy

STATE/LOCAL LEGISLATOR
Anderson, Charles W., Jr.
Arnett, Benjamin
Bond, Julian
Brown, Willie
Davis, Ben
Henry, Aaron
Jack, Hulan
Looby, Alexander
Mitchell, Charles
Motley, Constance
Napier, James
Ross, Don
Williams, Avon
Williams, George
Williams, Hosea

MAYOR
Archer, Dennis
Arrington, Richard
Barry, Marion
Belton, Sharon
Berry, Ted
Blackwell, Unita
Booker, Cory
Bosley, Freeman

Bradley, Tom
Brown, Lee
Brown, Willie
Campbell, Bill
Cleaver, Emanuel
Dellums, Ron
Dinkins, David
Dixon, Sheila
Evers, Charles
Fenty, Adrian M.
Franklin, Shirley
Fudge, Marcia L.
Gantt, Harvey
Gibson, Kenneth
Goode, W. W.
Harmon, Clarence
Hatcher, Richard
Hayes, James
Herenton, Willie
Jackson, Maynard
James, Sharpe
Johnson, Harvey
Kelly, Sharon Pratt Dixon
Kilpatrick, Kwame
Kirk, Ron
Marsh, Henry
Morial, Dutch
Nagin, Ray
Nutter, Michael
Perry, Carrie
Powell, Debra
Rice, Norm
Schmoke, Kurt
Stokes, Carl
Street, John
Ursy, James
Washington, Harold
Washington, Walter
Webb, Wellington
White, Michael
Wilder, Doug
Williams, Anthony
Young, Andy
Young, Coleman

PRESIDENTIAL/VICE PRESIDENTIAL CANDIDATE
Chisholm, Shirley
Ford, James
Foster, Ezola
Fulani, Lenora
Gregory, Dick
Jackson, Jesse

Keyes, Alan
McKinney, Cynthia
Moseley Braun, Carol
Sharpton, Al

POLITICAL PARTY OFFICIAL
Anderson, Charles W.
Baker, Ella

Church, Robert
Davis, Benjamin J.
Howard, Perry
Martin, Louis
Steele, Michael

Entries by Year of Birth

1820–1829
Cain, Richard
Langston, John
Mitchell, Charles
Revels, Hiram
Turner, Benjamin

1830–1839
Arnett, Benjamin
Cardozo, Francis
Long, Jefferson
Pinchback, P. B. S.
Rainey, Joseph
Ransier, Alonzo
Rapier, James
Smalls, Robert

1840–1849
Bruce, Blanche
DeLarge, Robert
Elliott, Robert
Haralson, Jeremiah
Hyman, John
Lynch, John
Miller, Thomas
Napier, James
Nash, Charles
O'Hara, James
Walls, Josiah
Williams, George

1850–1899
Anderson, Charles W.
Cheatham, Henry
Church, Robert
Davis, Benjamin J.
Dawson, William
DePriest, Oscar
Ford, James
Howard, Perry
Looby, Alexander
Mitchell, Arthur
Murray, George
Nix, Robert
White, George

1900–1909
Anderson, Charles W., Jr.
Baker, Ella
Berry, Ted
Crockett, George W.
Davis, Ben
Hastie, William H.
Hawkins, Augustus
Jack, Hulan
Powell, Adam Clayton, Jr.
Weaver, Robert

1910–1919
Bradley, Tom
Brooke, Edward

Evans, Melvin
Hayes, Charles
Martin, Louis
Metcalfe, Ralph
Washington, Walter
Young, Coleman

1920–1924
Chisholm, Shirley
Diggs, Charles
Evers, Charles
Harris, Patricia Roberts
Henry, Aaron
Mitchell, Parren
Motley, Constance
Usry, James
Washington, Harold
Williams, Avon

1925–1929
Allen, Ethel
Conyers, John
Dinkins, David
Dymally, Mervyn
Meek, Carrie
Morial, Dutch
Savage, Gus
Stokes, Carl
Stokes, Louis
Williams, Hosea

1930–1932
Blackwell, Lucien
Burke, Yvonne
Clay, William
Collins, Cardiss
Gibson, Kenneth
Gregory, Dick
Perry, Carrie
Rangel, Charles
Wilder, Doug
Young, Andy

1933–1934
Arrington, Richard
Blackwell, Unita
Brown, Willie
Clayton, Eva
Dixon, Julian
Fauntroy, Walter
Hatcher, Richard
Marsh, Henry
Paige, Rod
Payne, Donald
Sullivan, Louis
Towns, Edolphus
Watson, Diane
White, Jesse

1935–1937
Barry, Marion
Brown, Lee
Burris, Roland
Dellums, Ron
Hastings, Alcee
James, Sharpe
Johnson, Eddie Bernice
Jordan, Barbara
Norton, Eleanor Holmes
O'Leary, Hazel
Owens, Major
Powell, Colin

1938–1939
Carson, Julia

Collins, Barbara-Rose
Foster, Ezola
Goode, W. W.
Hall, Katie
Jackson, Maynard
McCall, Carl
Millender-McDonald, Juanita
Waters, Maxine

1940–1941
Bond, Julian
Brown, Ron
Clyburn, James
Davis, Danny K.
Gray, Bill
Harmon, Clarence
Herenton, Willie
Jackson, Jesse
Lewis, John
Ross, Don
Webb, Wellington

1942–1944
Archer, Dennis
Ballance, Frank
Cleaver, Emanuel
Gantt, Harvey
Hilliard, Earl
Kelly, Sharon Pratt Dixon
Leland, Mickey
Rice, Norm
Street, John

1945–1946
Brown, Corrine
Christian-Christensen, Donna
Flake, Floyd
Ford, Harold
Franklin, Shirley
Hayes, James
Jackson, Alphonso
Kilpatrick, Carolyn
Lee, Barbara

Rush, Bobby
Watt, Mel

1947–1949
Bishop, Sanford
Blackwell, Ken
Butterfield, G. K.
Herman, Alexis
Jefferson, William
Johnson, Harvey
Mfume, Kweisi
Moseley Braun, Carol
Schmoke, Kurt
Scott, Bobby
Thompson, Bennie
Tubbs Jones, Stephanie

1950–1951
Belton, Sharon
Cummings, Elijah
Fulani, Lenora
Holder, Eric
Jackson Lee, Sheila
Keyes, Alan
Moore, Gwen
Wheat, Alan
White, Michael
Williams, Anthony
Wynn, Albert

1952–1953
Baker, Thurbert E.
Campbell, Bill
Dixon, Sheila
Espy, Mike
Franks, Gary
Fudge, Marcia L.
Meeks, Gregory

1954–1955
Bosley, Freeman
Coleman, Michael
Kirk, Ron
Majette, Denise

McKinney, Cynthia
Paterson, David
Rice, Condoleezza
Sharpton, Al
Slater, Rodney

1956–1959
Clay, William, Jr.
Fattah, Chaka
Nagin, Ray
Nutter, Michael
Patrick, Deval

Steele, Michael
Watts, J. C.

1960–1964
Clarke, Yvette D.
Ellison, Keith
Fields, Cleo
Jackson, Lisa P.
Obama, Barack
Powell, Debra
Rice, Susan E.
Rogers, Joe

1965–1975
Booker, Cory
Carson, André
Davis, Artur
Fenty, Adrian M.
Ford, Harold, Jr.
Jackson, Jesse, Jr.
Kilpatrick, Kwame
Meek, Kendrick

INDEX

Page numbers in *italic* indicate photos or illustrations. Entries and page numbers in **boldface** indicate major treatment of a topic.

A

Abacha, Sani 217
Abdullah, Patrice 48
abolition 6, 213, 221. *See also* antislavery movement
abortion rights 67, 99, 109, 177, 284, 291, 309, 310
Abscam scandal 289
Abyssinian Baptist Church (New York City) 250, 252
ACLU. *See* American Civil Liberties Union (ACLU)
ACTION volunteer organization 188
Addabbo, Joseph 110
Addonizio, Hugh 125
advertising 67, 72, 77, 98–99, 179, 291. *See also* campaign advertising
Advisory Committee on Education 311
affirmative action xii
  Anderson, Charles W., Jr. 4
  Campbell, Bill 45
  Clay, William 57
  Cleaver, Emanuel 61
  Clyburn, James 63
  Davis, Danny K. 79
  Fields, Cleo 109
  Foster, Ezola 116
  Gibson, Kenneth 125
  Jackson, Maynard 164
  Lewis, John 188

  Meek, Kendrick 203
  Ross, Don 271
Affordable Health Care for America Act of 2010 235
Afghanistan, U.S. war in xv, 284
AFL-CIO 333
Africa. *See also* South Africa; *specific country*
  Campbell, Bill 45
  Diggs, Charles 88
  Dymally, Mervyn 93, 94
  Fattah, Chaka 104
  Gray, Bill 128
  Jackson, Jesse 160
  Jackson, Jesse, Jr. 162
  Jefferson, William 169
  Leland, Mickey 186, 187
  McKinney, Cynthia 200
  Mitchell, Parren 215
  Moseley Braun, Carol 217
  Patrick, Deval 243
  Payne, Donald 246
  Rangel, Charles 260
  Rice, Susan E. 269
  Slater, Rodney 281
  Sullivan, Louis 291
  Williams, George 326
  Young, Andy (Andrew) 331, 332
Africa Growth and Opportunity Act 169

Africa Initiative 281
African American People's Convention (Memphis) 147–148
African Development Bank 215
African Development Foundation 128, 166
African Growth and Opportunity Act 260
African Methodist Episcopal (AME) Church 6, 43, 110, 111, 264
Agnew, Spiro T. 57, 84, 173
Agriculture, U.S. Department of (USDA)
  Clayton, Eva 60
  Espy, Mike 98, 99
  Hyman, John 155
  Thompson, Bennie 293
  Williams, Anthony 322
  Williams, Hosea 326
Agriculture Research Act 60
aides, congressional 64, 181, 184–185, 280
AIDS
  Brown, Willie 36
  Cummings, Elijah 72
  Jackson, Jesse, Jr. 162
  Jackson, Maynard 164
  Johnson, Eddie Bernice 170, 171

  Lee, Barbara 186
  McKinney, Cynthia 200
  Schmoke, Kurt 277
  Sullivan, Louis 291
AIP. *See* American Independent Party (AIP)
Air America (radio) 37
Air Force, U.S. 271, 322. *See also* Army Air Corps, U.S.
Airport and Airway Safety, Capacity and Expansion Act of 1987 67
Alabama 73–74, 132–134, 150–151, 262–264, 296–297
Alameda Corridor 209
Alan Keyes is Making Sense (TV) 177
"Alan Keyes Show" (radio) 177
Alaska 144–145
Alaska Pipeline Bill 40
Albright, Madeleine K. 269
Alcorn, James L. 266
Alexander, Fred 123
Allen, Ethel **1–2**
Alliance for Youth 253–254
al-Qaeda. *See under* Q
Amalgamated Press (Fleetway Press) 197
ambassadors. *See* diplomacy

AME Church. *See* African Methodist Episcopal (AME) Church
American Cancer Society 9
American Civil Liberties Union (ACLU) 229
American Communist Party. *See* Communist Party
American Council for Human Rights 135
American Council on Race Relations 312
American Independent Party (AIP) 178
American Israel Public Affairs Committee 276
American Legion Boys Nation 177
American Militarism (Conyers) 69
American Negro Labor Congress 115
American Recovery and Reinvestment Act of 2009 235
Americans with Disabilities Act 208, 239
America's Promise 253–254
AmeriCorps 113
Ameriquest 244
Ames, Adelbert 193, 264
Amtrak 49
Anatomy of an Undeclared War (Conyers) 69
Anderson, Charles W. ix, **2–3**
Anderson, Charles W., Jr. **3–4**
Andrews, Carl 56
Angola 88
Anti-Apartheid Acts of 1985 and 1986 128
antilynching law 4, 86, 212, 317
Anti-Poverty Act 251
Anti-Saloon League 7
antislavery movement vii–viii, 183
antismoking activism 291
antiterrorism. *See* homeland security

apartheid. *See also* divestiture; economic sanctions
Brown, Willie 36
Crockett, George W. 70–71
Dellums, Ron 84
Diggs, Charles 88
Fauntroy, Walter 107
Gray, Bill 128
Keyes, Alan 177
Leland, Mickey 187
Mfume, Kweisi 208
Moseley Braun, Carol 217
Perry, Carrie 246
Rangel, Charles 260
Waters, Maxine 305
Wheat, Alan 315
Wilder, Doug 321
Young, Andy (Andrew) 331
Appalachia 187
Arabia Mountain (Georgia) 195
Arafat, Yasser 160
Archer, Dennis **4–6**, 180
Aristide, Jean-Bertrand 128
Arkansas 280
armed forces, U.S. 137, 282. *See also specific branch*
Arms Transfers Code of Conduct of 1997 200
Armstrong Agricultural College 211
Army, U.S. *See also* Confederate military; Union army
Blackwell, Lucien 20
Brooke, Edward 28
Brown, Ron 34
Bruce, Blanche 38
Clay, William 57
Dawson, William 79
Diggs, Charles 87
Dinkins, David 89
Dixon, Julian 91
Espy, Mike 98
Evers, Charles 101
Fattah, Chaka 103
Ford, James 114
Gibson, Kenneth 125
Goode, W. W. 126

Gregory, Dick 129
Harmon, Clarence 134
Henry, Aaron 145
Jackson Lee, Sheila 166
James, Sharpe 167
Lynch, John 194
Metcalfe, Ralph 206
Mitchell, Arthur 211–212
Mitchell, Parren 214
Morial, Dutch 216
Powell, Colin 252–253
Rangel, Charles 259
Rush, Bobby 272
Savage, Gus 275
Stokes, Carl 285
Stokes, Louis 286
Towns, Edolphus 294
Usry, James 298
Washington, Harold 302
White, George 317
White, Jesse 317
Wilder, Doug 320
Williams, Avon 324
Williams, George 325
Williams, Hosea 326
Army Air Corps, U.S. 16, 87, 137, 302, 332
Army National Guard, U.S. 68
Arnett, Benjamin ix, **6–7**
Arrington, Richard **7–8**
Ashcroft, John 316
Atlanta (Georgia)
Baker, Ella 10
Bond, Julian 22
Brown, Lee 32
Campbell, Bill 44, 45–46
Davis, Ben 74–75
Davis, Benjamin J. 77
Franklin, Shirley 117–118
Jackson, Maynard 163–165
Lewis, John 188–189
McKinney, Cynthia 200–201
Williams, Hosea 326–327
Young, Andy (Andrew) 330–332

Atlanta Committee on Appeal for Human Rights 22
Atlanta Inquirer 22
Atlanta Organizing Committee 331
Atlantic City (New Jersey) 298–299
Atomic Energy Commission 1
Attorney General, U.S. 151–153. *See also* Justice, U.S. Department of
attorneys. *See also* district attorneys
Anderson, Charles W., Jr. 3–4
Archer, Dennis 5
Baker, Thurbert E. 10–11
Ballance, Frank 11–12
Berry, Ted 15–17
Bishop, Sanford 17
Booker, Cory 24
Bosley, Freeman 25, 26
Bradley, Tom 27
Brooke, Edward 28, 29, 30
Brown, Ron 34
Brown, Willie 35
Burke, Yvonne 39
Burris, Roland 41
Campbell, Bill 44, 46
Coleman, Michael 64
Conyers, John 68
Crockett, George W. 70
Cummings, Elijah 71
Davis, Artur 73
Davis, Ben 74
Dawson, William 79
Dinkins, David 89
Dixon, Julian 91
Elliot, Robert 95
Ellison, Keith 97
Espy, Mike 98, 99
Fenty, Adrian M. 107
Fields, Cleo 108
Ford, Harold, Jr. 113
Fudge, Marcia L. 120
Harris, Patricia Roberts 135, 136
Hastie, William H. 136
Hastings, Alcee 138

Hatcher, Richard 140
Hayes, Charles 143
Hilliard, Earl 150
Holder, Eric 151–153
Howard, Perry 153
Jackson, Maynard 164
Jackson Lee, Sheila 165
Jefferson, William 168
Jordan, Barbara 173
Kelly, Sharon Pratt Dixon 175
Kirk, Ron 181
Langston, John 183
Looby, Alexander 191–192
Lynch, John 193–194
Majette, Denise 195
Marsh, Henry 196
Meeks, Gregory 204–205
Miller, Thomas 210
Mitchell, Arthur 212
Morial, Dutch 216–217
Moseley Braun, Carol 217
Motley, Constance 219, 220
Napier, James 225
Nix, Robert 227
Norton, Eleanor Holmes 229
Obama, Barack 232
O'Hara, James 236
Patrick, Deval 243
Pinchback, P. B. S. 249
Rangel, Charles 259
Rogers, Joe 270
Schmoke, Kurt 276
Scott, Bobby 278
Slater, Rodney 281
Steele, Michael 283
Stokes, Carl 285
Stokes, Louis 286, 288
Street, John 288
Tubbs Jones, Stephanie 295
Washington, Harold 302
Washington, Walter 304
Watt, Mel 308
White, George 316
Wilder, Doug 320

Williams, Avon 324
Williams, George 325–326
Wynn, Albert 328, 329
attorneys general
Baker, Thurbert E. 10–11
Brooke, Edward 28
Burris, Roland 40, 41
Elliot, Robert 96
Holder, Eric 151–153
Howard, Perry 153
O'Leary, Hazel 237
Patrick, Deval 243
Audacity of Hope: Thoughts on Reclaiming the American Dream, The (Obama) 234
automobile industry 5, 332–333

B
Baker, Ella **9–10,** 13, 101, 147
Baker, Harry 212
Baker, Thurbert E. **10–11**
Baker v. Carr x, x–xi
Baldwin, Chuck 178
Baliles, Gerald 321
Balkans 35, 246
Ballance, Frank **11–12**
Baltimore (Maryland) 71–72, 92–93, 207–208, 214–215, 275, 276–278
Bank Enterprise Act of 1994 110
banking industry 54, 110, 178, 208, 225, 236, 317, 329. *See also* House banking scandal
Banks, Nathaniel 247
Barefootin': Life Lessons from the Road to Freedom (Blackwell) 22
Barry, Marion **12–14,** 92, 136, 175–176, 188, 322, 323
baseball 33, 76, 157, 255, 317, 319, 323
basketball 124, 298, 319
Bateman, Herbert 278
Baton Rouge (Louisiana) 109
B-1 bomber 84
Beatty, Christine 180

Beauprez, Bob 271
Beck, Glenn 97
Bedford-Stuyvesant Political League 51
Belgium 326
Bell, Sean 280
Belton, Sharon **14–15**
Benham, Robert 195
Benjamin, Adam, Jr. 131
Bentsen, Lloyd 34, 160, 181
Berkeley (California) 83
Berry, Ted **15–17**
Biden, Joe 152
Bill of Rights 162
Birmingham (Alabama) 7–8, 150–151
Bishop, Sanford **17–18,** 18
Black Americans for Family Values 116
Black Belt 73, 190
black cabinet ix, xiv, 225, 311
Black Codes 6, 46, 81–82, 257
"Black Laws" (Ohio) 6
black middle class xii–xiii
Black Muslims 13
black nationalism 82, 88, 286
Black Panther Party 27, 83, 130, 207, 233, 272, 273
Black Power movement 83, 103
"Black Second" district (North Carolina) ix, 49, 50, 236
Black Television News Channel 311
Blackwell, Ken **19**
Blackwell, Lucien **20–21,** 104
Blackwell, Unita **21–22,** 101, 147, 292
Black Women Mayors' Conference (BWMC) 21
Black Women's Forum 305
Blagojevich, Rod 41, 79, 162, 318
"Bloody Sunday" 326
Bloomberg, Michael 122

Blue Dog Coalition xiii, 18, 114
Blueprint: Obama's Plan to Subvert the Constitution and Build and Imperial Presidency, The (Ken Blackwell and Klukowski) 19
Boggs, Lindy 168
Bolling, Richard 315
Bolton (Mississippi) 292
Bond, Julian **22–23,** 188
Bonus March 115
Booker, Cory xiv, **23–25**
borough presidents (NYC)
Dinkins, David 90
Jack, Hulan 156–157
Motley, Constance 220
Towns, Edolphus 294
Bosley, Freeman **25–26,** 134
Bosley, Freeman, Sr. 25
Boston Finance Committee 29
Boston (Massachusetts) 213, 325
Bowen, Christopher C. 82, 83
Bowers, Michael 11
boycotts 9, 10, 13, 29, 101, 146, 250, 326
Boy Scouts of America 41
Bradley, Tom **26–28,** 305
Brawley, Tawana 279–280
Bread 'n Butter Party 159
breast cancer 67, 307
Brick Towers (Newark) 24
Britain 95, 137. *See also* Rhodes scholars
British Petroleum 152
Bronx Empowerment Zone 56
Brooke, Edward x, **28–30,** 29, 80, 106
Brookings Institution 269
Brooklyn (New York) 51–52, 294
Browder, Earl 115
Browhhelm Township (Ohio) vii
Brown, Corrine **31–32,** 202
Brown, John 183–184
Brown, Lee **32–33,** 134

Brown, Ron xiii, **33–35,** 149
Brown, Shantrel 31
Brown, Willie **35–37,** 36
Brown v. Board of Education 21, 88, 220
Bruce, Blanche viii, **37–39,** 38
Buchanan, Pat 116–117, 121–122
"buffalo soldiers" 325
Burke, Yvonne 39, **39–40,** 91
Burns, Clarence 277
Burris, Roland xi, **40–42,** 162, 318
Burris v. White 318
Burrows, Daniel 89
Bush, Barbara 290–291
Bush, George H. W. xii, 19, 70, 113, 266, 290–291
Bush, George W. xiv
  Brooke, Edward 30
  Conyers, John 69
  Fattah, Chaka 104
  Herman, Alexis 150
  Jackson, Alphonso 157, 158
  Jackson, Lisa P. 163
  Lee, Barbara 186
  Majette, Denise 195
  McKinney, Cynthia 200–201
  Moseley Braun, Carol 219
  Obama, Barack 233
  Paige, Rod 240–241
  Powell, Colin 254
  Rangel, Charles 260
  Rice, Condoleezza 267
  Slater, Rodney 281
  Watson, Diane 307
Bush, Jeb 203
business and industry 101, 223, 225, 249, 296, 297, 301. *See also* free markets; minority-owned businesses; privatization; small business; *specific company or industry*
busing 9, 192, 268
BWMC. *See* Black Women Mayors' Conference (BWMC)

C
cabinet secretaries xi, xiii, xiv
  Brown, Ron 34–35
  Espy, Mike 98, 99
  Harris, Patricia Roberts 135–136
  Herman, Alexis 149–150
  Jackson, Alphonso 157–158
  Jackson, Lisa P. 162–163
  O'Leary, Hazel 237–238
  Paige, Rod 240–241
  Powell, Colin 252–254
  Rice, Condoleezza 266–268
  Slater, Rodney 280–281
  Sullivan, Louis 290–291
  Weaver, Robert 311–313
Cain, Richard **43–44,** 95
Califano, Joseph A. 136
California
  Brown, Willie 35–37
  Burke, Yvonne 39–40
  Dellums, Ron 83–85
  Dixon, Julian 91–92
  Dymally, Mervyn 93–94
  Foster, Ezola 116
  Hawkins, Augustus 141–143
  Lee, Barbara 184–186
  Millender-McDonald, Juanita 208–209
  Waters, Maxine 305–306
  Watson, Diane 306–308
Cameron, Ian 269
campaign advertising xv, 114, 314
Campbell, Bill **44–46,** 117
Canada 309
Cao, Anh 169
CAPE. *See* Child Abuse Prevention and Enforcement Act (CAPE)

Capitol, U.S. 201
Cardin, Benjamin L. 284
Cardozo, Francis viii, **46–47,** 82
CARE Foundation 316
Caribbean 94, 104, 260. *See also* Virgin Islands, U.S.
Caribbean Advisory Committee 137
Caribbean-Americans 56
Caribbean Basin Initiative 260
Carson, André **47–48,** 97
Carson, Julia 47, **48–49**
Carter, Jimmy
  Bond, Julian 23
  Harris, Patricia Roberts 136
  Hastings, Alcee 138
  Herman, Alexis 149
  Johnson, Eddie Bernice 170
  Lewis, John 188
  Marsh, Henry 197
  Martin, Louis 198
  Nix, Robert 228
  Norton, Eleanor Holmes 229
  Schmoke, Kurt 276
  Sullivan, Louis 290
  Webb, Wellington 313
  Williams, Hosea 327
  Young, Andy (Andrew) 331
  Young, Coleman 333
Carver Democratic Club 89, 259
casino development 5, 255, 298, 299, 334
Casino Reinvestment Development Authority (CRDA) 299
Castro, Fidel 94, 186, 187
CBTU. *See* Coalition of Black Trade Unionists (CBTU)
CCC. *See* Civilian Conservation Corps, U.S. (CCC)
Census Bureau, U.S. 203
Center for Voting and Democracy (Cincinnati) 17
Central Intelligence Agency (CIA) 209

Cesar Chavez Workplace Fairness Act 139
Challenge of Change: Crisis in Our Two-Party System, The (Brooke) 29
Charleston (South Carolina) 261–262
Charlotte Hornets 124
Charlotte (North Carolina) 123–124, 308–309
Chatham County Crusader 326
Cheatham, Henry viii–ix, **49–50,** 316
Cherokee Indians 154
Chicago (Illinois) x
  Burris, Roland 41
  Church, Robert 55
  Collins, Cardiss 66–67
  Davis, Danny K. 78
  Dawson, William 79–81
  DePriest, Oscar 85–86
  Evers, Charles 101
  Ford, James 114–115
  Gregory, Dick 129–130
  Harris, Patricia Roberts 135
  Hayes, Charles 143–144
  Jackson, Jesse 159
  Jackson, Jesse, Jr. 161–162
  Metcalfe, Ralph 205–207
  Mitchell, Arthur 212
  Moseley Braun, Carol 217–219
  Obama, Barack 232–235
  Rush, Bobby 272–274
  Savage, Gus 275–276
  Washington, Harold 302–303
  Weaver, Robert 312
  White, Jesse 317–318
Chicago Cubs 317
Chicago Defender 197, 198
Chicago Urban League 41
child abuse prevention 238, 239, 295, 305
Child Abuse Prevention and Enforcement Act (CAPE) 295

Child Abuse Prevention Challenge Grants Reauthorization Act 239
children 66, 67, 124, 125, 166, 238, 239, 253–254, 295, 305. *See also* education
Child Safety Protection Act of 1993 67
China 21–22, 35, 99, 245
Chisholm, Shirley **51–53,** 52, 56, 117, 219, 238
Christian-Christensen, Donna **53–54**
Christian right 177. *See also* conservatism
Chrysler 5, 333
Chudoff, Earl 227
church. *See* ministry; *specific church*
Church, Robert **54–56**
CIA. *See* Central Intelligence Agency (CIA)
Cincinnati Commercial Tribune 325
Cincinnati (Ohio) 15–17, 19, 325–326
CIO. *See* Congress of Industrial Organizations (CIO)
Cisneros, Henry G. 99
Citicorp 244
Citizen Newspapers 275
Citizen's Against Government Waste 177
city council
  Allen, Ethel 1–2
  Arrington, Richard 7
  Barry, Marion 13
  Belton, Sharon 15
  Berry, Ted 15–17
  Blackwell, Ken 19
  Blackwell, Lucien 20
  Bradley, Tom 27
  Campbell, Bill 45
  Carson, André 48
  Clarke, Yvette D. 56
  Clay, William 57
  Cleaver, Emanuel 61
  Coleman, Michael 64
  Collins, Barbara-Rose 65, 66
  Davis, Ben 74–76

Davis, Danny K. 78
Dawson, William 80
Dellums, Ron 83
DePriest, Oscar 87
Dinkins, David 90
Dixon, Sheila 92
Fauntroy, Walter 105
Fenty, Adrian M. 107–108
Franks, Gary 119
Gantt, Harvey 123
Hatcher, Richard 140
Hayes, James 145
Jackson Lee, Sheila 165–166
James, Sharpe 167
Kilpatrick, Carolyn 178
Lewis, John 188
Looby, Alexander 191–192
Marsh, Henry 196
Metcalfe, Ralph 206
Mfume, Kweisi 207–208
Millender-McDonald, Juanita 209
Morial, Dutch 217
Napier, James 225
Nutter, Michael 230
Powell, Adam Clayton, Jr. 249, 250
Powell, Debra 255
Rangel, Charles 259
Rice, Norm 268–269
Rush, Bobby 273
Stokes, Carl 285
Street, John 288
Thompson, Bennie 292
Turner, Benjamin 296–297
White, Michael 318–319
Williams, Hosea 327
city government. *See also* city council; mayors; *specific city*
  Archer, Dennis 4–6
  Booker, Cory 23–25
  Bosley, Freeman 25–26
  Burke, Yvonne 39
  Cheatham, Henry 50
  Chisholm, Shirley 51
  Church, Robert 54

Collins, Barbara-Rose 65
Collins, Cardiss 66–67
Crockett, George W. 70
Davis, Danny K. 78
DePriest, Oscar 86
Evers, Charles 102
Fattah, Chaka 103
Fields, Cleo 108–109
Franklin, Shirley 117
Fudge, Marcia L. 120
Goode, W. W. 126–127
Hall, Katie 131
Harmon, Clarence 134
Jack, Hulan 156–157
Jackson, Jesse 159
Kelly, Sharon Pratt Dixon 175–176
Kilpatrick, Kwame 180
Kirk, Ron 181
Langston, John 183
McCall, Carl 199
Meeks, Gregory 204–205
Mitchell, Parren 214
Moore, Gwen 216
Motley, Constance 220
Nix, Robert 227
Owens, Major 238
Payne, Donald 245
Schmoke, Kurt 277
Towns, Edolphus 294
Usry, James 298
Walls, Josiah 301
Washington, Harold 302
Washington, Walter 304
Waters, Maxine 305
Weaver, Robert 312
Webb, Wellington 313–314
Young, Andy (Andrew) 330–331
city government reform 164, 176, 236, 255, 298, 299, 304, 313–314, 322–323
Civilian Conservation Corps, U.S. (CCC) 86, 302

civil liberties 69, 201, 229
civil rights vii–viii, xii. *See also* Civil Rights movement
  Bishop, Sanford 17
  Bond, Julian 22
  Brown, Willie 36
  Cain, Richard 43, 44
  Cardozo, Francis 46
  Cheatham, Henry 50
  Church, Robert 55
  Clay, William 57
  Clayton, Eva 60
  Collins, Cardiss 66
  Conyers, John 68–69
  Davis, Ben 74–76
  DeLarge, Robert 82–83
  Dellums, Ron 84–85
  DePriest, Oscar 85
  Diggs, Charles 87, 88
  Elliot, Robert 96
  Hastie, William H. 136, 137, 138
  Hawkins, Augustus 142
  Hyman, John 154
  Jordan, Barbara 173
  Langston, John 183
  Lynch, John 193
  Marsh, Henry 196
  Metcalfe, Ralph 206
  Nash, Charles 226
  Nix, Robert 228
  Norton, Eleanor Holmes 229
  Nutter, Michael 230
  Obama, Barack 232
  O'Hara, James 236
  Pinchback, P. B. S. 247–249
  Powell, Adam Clayton, Jr. 250–251
  Rainey, Joseph 257, 258
  Ransier, Alonzo 261, 262
  Scott, Bobby 278
  Smalls, Robert 282
  Turner, Benjamin 297
  White, George 317
  Williams, Avon 324
Civil Rights Act of 1875 96, 132, 133, 184, 193, 236, 258, 262, 264

Civil Rights Act of 1957
251
Civil Rights Act of 1964
142, 198, 251
Civil Rights Act of 1965
136. *See also* Voting
Rights Act of 1965
Civil Rights Act of 1968
30
Civil Rights Act of 1990
119, 315
Civil Rights Act of 1991
69, 208
Civil Rights Driving Tour
(Jackson, Mississippi)
172
Civil Rights movement x–
xi, xv. *See also* boycotts;
demonstrations and
protests; riots; sit-ins
Anderson, Charles W.,
Jr. 4
Arrington, Richard 7
Baker, Ella 9–10
Ballance, Frank 11
Barry, Marion 13
Berry, Ted 16
Blackwell, Unita 21
Bond, Julian 22
Brooke, Edward 28
Brown, Ron 34
Cleaver, Emanuel 61
Crockett, George W.
70
Dawson, William
80–81
Evers, Charles 101,
102
Fauntroy, Walter 105
Ford, Harold, Jr.
113–114
Gregory, Dick 129
Hatcher, Richard 140
Henry, Aaron 145–146
Hilliard, Earl 150, 151
Jackson, Jesse 159
Johnson, Harvey 172
Kilpatrick, Carolyn
179
Leland, Mickey 186
Lewis, John 187–188
Looby, Alexander 192
Majette, Denise 195
Owens, Major 238
Rush, Bobby 272

Savage, Gus 275
Stokes, Carl 285
Thompson, Bennie
292
Washington, Walter
304
Williams, Hosea 326
Young, Andy (Andrew)
330
Civil Service, U.S. 212
civil service reform 212,
228
Civil War, U.S. vii–viii.
See also Confederate
military;
Reconstruction; Union
army
Bruce, Blanche 37
Cheatham, Henry 50
DeLarge, Robert 81
Hyman, John 154
Langston, John
183–184
Long, Jefferson
190–191
Lynch, John 193
Miller, Thomas 210
Mitchell, Charles 213
Murray, George 221
Pinchback, P. B. S.
247
Rainey, Joseph 257
Ransier, Alonzo 261
Rapier, James 263
Revels, Hiram 264
Smalls, Robert
281–282
Turner, Benjamin 296
Walls, Josiah 300
White, George 316
Williams, George 325
Clarke, Hansen 179
Clarke, Una S. T. 56
Clarke, Yvette D. 56
Clarksdale (Mississippi)
146
Clay, William **57–58**
Clay, William, Jr. **58–59,**
59
Clayton, Eva 12, **59–61,**
308
Cleaver, Emanuel **61–62**
Cleveland (Ohio) x, 119–
120, 284–286, 295,
318–320

Cleveland, Grover 38
Cleveland Browns 319
Cleveland Cavaliers 319
Cleveland Indians 319
climate change 163, 271
Clinton, Bill xiii
Archer, Dennis 6
Brown, Lee 32
Brown, Ron 34–35
Chisholm, Shirley 52
Cleaver, Emanuel 62
Davis, Danny K. 78
Espy, Mike 99
Ford, Harold 112
Ford, Harold, Jr. 113
Gray, Bill 128
Herman, Alexis 149
Holder, Eric 152
Jackson, Jesse 160
Jackson Lee, Sheila
166
Jefferson, William 168
Mfume, Kweisi 208
Motley, Constance
220
O'Leary, Hazel 237
Patrick, Deval 243
Powell, Debra 255–256
Rice, Condoleezza 266
Rice, Norm 269
Rice, Susan E. 269
Slater, Rodney 280
Sullivan, Louis 291
Watson, Diane 307
Watts, J. C. 310
Webb, Wellington 314
Wheat, Alan 316
Williams, Anthony
322
Clinton, Hilary 74, 91,
188, 234, 242
Clyburn, James **62–64**
CNN 97
Coalition of Black Trade
Unionists (CBTU) 143
Coast Guard, U.S. 139
Cockrel, Kenneth, Jr. 180
COFO. *See* Council of
Federated Organizations
(COFO)
Cohen, Steve 148
Coleman, Marshall 321
Coleman, Michael 64,
64–65
College Fund/UNCF 128

Collins, Barbara-Rose
65–66, 178
Collins, Cardiss **66–68,**
78
Collins, George 66–67
Colorado 270–271,
313–315
Colored Citizens
Association of Memphis
54
Colored Normal,
Industrial, Agricultural
and Mechanical College
of South Carolina 210,
227
Colored People's
Convention (South
Carolina, 1865) 43, 46,
81–82, 257, 261
Colquitt, Alfred H. 191
Columbus (Ohio) 64–65
comedians 129
Commerce, U.S.
Department of 33, 35,
113
Commission on the Status
of Puerto Rico 136
Committee for a Unified
Independent Party 122
Commoner, The 325
communications 57, 67,
171–172, 199, 281. *See
also* film and television;
radio
communism 66, 70,
74–75, 76, 114–115, 115,
333
Communist International's
Negro Commission 115
Communist Party x,
74–75, 76, 114–115, 250
Community Action
Committee (Cincinnati)
16
Community Development
and Regulatory Act 273
Community for New
Politics 83
Community Renewal Act
110–111
comptrollers, state xi, 40,
198–200, 322
computers 166, 169, 281,
318
Compuware 5

ComServe 299
Confederate flag 172, 218, 271, 327
Confederate military 257, 300
confirmation hearings 149–150, 163, 218, 219, 270, 291
Congo Free State 326
Congress. *See* House of Representatives, U.S.; Senate, U.S.
Congressional Black Caucus xi, xiii
  Brooke, Edward 30
  Brown, Corrine 32
  Burke, Yvonne 40
  Chisholm, Shirley 52
  Clay, William 57
  Clyburn, James 63
  Collins, Cardiss 67
  Conyers, John 68
  Dawson, William 81
  Dellums, Ron 85
  Diggs, Charles 87, 88–89
  Dixon, Julian 91
  Dymally, Mervyn 94
  Fauntroy, Walter 106
  Flake, Floyd 111
  Ford, Harold, Jr. 113
  Franks, Gary 119
  Hall, Katie 131
  Hawkins, Augustus 142
  Herman, Alexis 149
  Johnson, Eddie Bernice 169, 171
  Kilpatrick, Carolyn 179
  Lee, Barbara 186
  Leland, Mickey 187
  Metcalfe, Ralph 206
  Mfume, Kweisi 208
  Mitchell, Parren 215
  Nix, Robert 228
  Payne, Donald 246
  Rangel, Charles 260
  Stokes, Louis 287
  Towns, Edolphus 294
  Washington, Harold 302
  Waters, Maxine 306
congressional candidates. *See* House candidates; Senate candidates

Congressional Children's Caucus 166
Congressional Classroom 109
congressional committees. *See specific House or Senate committee*
Congressional Narcotics Abuse and Control Caucus 260
Congressional Urban Caucus 189
Congress of Industrial Organizations (CIO) 333
Congress of Racial Equality (CORE) 51, 146, 159, 238
Congrove, Jim 270
Connecticut 118–119, 246–247, 322
conservatism. *See also* fiscal conservatism
  Brooke, Edward 29
  Dellums, Ron 85
  Evers, Charles 102
  Flake, Floyd 111
  Foster, Ezola 116
  Keyes, Alan 177
  Mitchell, Arthur 212
  Sullivan, Louis 291
  Washington, Harold 302
  Watts, J. C. 309, 310
Con Son prison (Vietnam) 142
Constitution in Crisis, The (Conyers) 69
Constitution Party 117, 178
consul generals 184
consumer advocacy 10, 29, 67, 309, 328
Contract with America 110, 188, 310
Conyers, John **68–70,** 161
cooperatives, food 9
CORE. *See* Congress of Racial Equality (CORE)
Corker, Bob 114
Cornyn, John 182
Corps d'Afrique 226, 247
Corps of Engineers, U.S. 68

corruption viii. *See also* scandals
  Arrington, Richard 8
  Ballance, Frank 11, 12
  Barry, Marion 13–14
  Brooke, Edward 29
  Burris, Roland 41
  Campbell, Bill 45–46
  Cardozo, Francis 47
  Carson, Julia 49
  Church, Robert 55
  DeLarge, Robert 82
  DePriest, Oscar 86
  Diggs, Charles 87, 89
  Dixon, Sheila 93
  Espy, Mike 99
  Fields, Cleo 109
  Ford, Harold 112
  Gibson, Kenneth 125, 126
  Hall, Katie 132
  Harmon, Clarence 134
  Hastings, Alcee 138–139
  Hatcher, Richard 140
  Hayes, James 145
  Hilliard, Earl 151
  Howard, Perry 153
  Hyman, John 154, 155
  Jack, Hulan 156, 157
  Jackson, Alphonso 158
  Jackson, Jesse 159
  Jackson, Jesse, Jr. 161
  James, Sharpe 167
  Jefferson, William 169
  Jordan, Barbara 173
  Kilpatrick, Carolyn 178, 179
  Kilpatrick, Kwame 180
  Moseley Braun, Carol 217
  Murray, George 221
  Nagin, Ray 223–224
  Nutter, Michael 230
  O'Hara, James 236
  Powell, Adam Clayton, Jr. 251
  Powell, Debra 255
  Rangel, Charles 260
  Smalls, Robert 282
  Street, John 290
  Usry, James 298–299
  Watts, J. C. 311

  Webb, Wellington 313–314
  White, Jesse 318
  Williams, Hosea 327
Corzine, Jon 163
cotton industry 262, 263, 264, 297
Council of Federated Organizations (COFO) 146–147
Countrywide Financial 158
county government
  Burke, Yvonne 39, 40
  Cheatham, Henry 50
  Clayton, Eva 60
  Davis, Danny K. 78
  DePriest, Oscar 85–86
  Elliot, Robert 95
  Gibson, Kenneth 126
  Hatcher, Richard 140
  Jordan, Barbara 173
  Looby, Alexander 192
  O'Hara, James 236
  Payne, Donald 245
  Rainey, Joseph 257
  Ransier, Alonzo 261
  Thompson, Bennie 292
  Tubbs Jones, Stephanie 295
  Walls, Josiah 301
  White, Jesse 318
  Williams, Hosea 327
  Wynn, Albert 328
courts. *See* judges; *specific case or court*
Cranston, Alan 305
CRDA. *See* Casino Reinvestment Development Authority (CRDA)
crime and violence. *See also* police brutality
  Baker, Thurbert E. 11
  Belton, Sharon 15
  Booker, Cory 24
  Bradley, Tom 27–28
  Brooke, Edward 30
  Dellums, Ron 85
  Evans, Melvin 100
  Kilpatrick, Kwame 180
  Mfume, Kweisi 207
  Moore, Gwen 216
  Owens, Major 239
  Rush, Bobby 274

crime prevention. *See also* child abuse prevention; domestic violence prevention
  Baker, Ethel 1
  Blackwell, Lucien 20
  Booker, Cory 24–25
  Bosley, Freeman 26
  Clay, William, Jr. 59
  Dellums, Ron 85
  Gibson, Kenneth 125
  Harmon, Clarence 134
  Herenton, Willie 148
  Jackson, Maynard 164
  James, Sharpe 167
  Kirk, Ron 181
  Lee, Barbara 185
  Nutter, Michael 230
  Schmoke, Kurt 277
  Scott, Bobby 278
  Stokes, Carl 285–286
  Watt, Mel 309
  Wheat, Alan 315
  White, Jesse 318
  Young, Coleman 333–334
Crisis Intervention Network 20
Crockett, George W. 5, 66, **70–71**
Cropp, Linda 108
Crump, Edward H. 54, 55
CSX Corporation 319
Cuba 94, 186, 187
Cummings, Elijah 71, **71–72**
Cunningham. David 305
Cuomo, Andrew 243

D

Dahmer, Jeffrey 216
Daily Worker 75
Daley, Richard J. 81, 130, 159, 206–207, 275
Daley, Richard M. 41, 78, 162, 274
Dallas Mavericks 181
Dallas (Texas) 157–158, 181–182
Danforth, John 315–316
Darfur 166
Date Rape Prevention Drug Act 166

Davis, Artur xiv, **73–74,** 151
Davis, Ben **74–76,** 75, 77, 115, 250
Davis, Benjamin J. 55, 74, **76–78**
Davis, Benjamin O., Sr. 312
Davis, Danny K. **78–79**
Davis, Jefferson 133, 264
Dawson, William **79–81,** 80, 205
DEA. *See* Drug Enforcement Agency, U.S. (DEA)
Death in Custody Act 278
death penalty reform 161–162, 217, 233, 320
Defense, U.S. Department of (DoD) 67, 80, 83, 84, 179, 253. *See also* armed forces, U.S.; military aid; military desegregation; military-industrial complex; military spending
Defense Sense: The Search for a Rational Military Policy (Dellums) 84
DeLarge, Robert 47, **81–83,** 82, 96, 261
Dellums, Ron **83–85,** 84, 184–185
Delta Sigma Theta sorority 135, 136
Democrat-Farm-Labor Party (DFL) 15, 97
Democratic Leadership Council xiii, 114
Democratic National Committee (DNC) x
  Brown, Ron 34
  Christian-Christensen, Donna 53
  Cleaver, Emanuel 62
  Dawson, William 81
  Herman, Alexis 149
  Jackson, Maynard 165
  Kelly, Sharon Pratt Dixon 175
  Martin, Louis 197–198
  Waters, Maxine 305
  Young, Coleman 333
Democratic National Convention (1936) 212

Democratic National Convention (1948) 1, 81
Democratic National Convention (1956) 227
Democratic National Convention (1964) 21, 136, 147
Democratic National Convention (1968) 23, 147
Democratic National Convention (1972) 40, 52, 147, 305
Democratic National Convention (1976) 173
Democratic National Convention (1980) 305
Democratic National Convention (1984) 92, 159, 209
Democratic National Convention (1988) xii, 34, 158, 160, 161, 229
Democratic National Convention (1992) 34, 149, 174
Democratic National Convention (1996) 6
Democratic National Convention (2000) 113
Democratic National Convention (2004) 233–234
Democratic National Convention (2008) 234
Democratic Party viii, ix–x, xii
  Allen, Ethel 1
  Archer, Dennis 6
  Arrington, Richard 7
  Baker, Ella 10
  Baker, Thurbert E. 10–11
  Ballance, Frank 12
  Barry, Marion 13, 14
  Bishop, Sanford 17
  Blackwell, Lucien 20
  Blackwell, Unita 21
  Bond, Julian 23
  Bosley, Freeman 25
  Bradley, Tom 27
  Brooke, Edward 29
  Brown, Corrine 31
  Brown, Lee 33

  Brown, Ron 34
  Brown, Willie 35, 36
  Burke, Yvonne 39–40
  Burris, Roland 41
  Campbell, Bill 45
  Carson, Julia 49
  Chisholm, Shirley 51
  Christian-Christensen, Donna 53
  Clarke, Yvette D. 56
  Clay, William 57
  Clay, William, Jr. 58
  Clayton, Eva 60
  Cleaver, Emanuel 61–62
  Clyburn, James 63
  Coleman, Michael 64
  Collins, Barbara-Rose 65
  Collins, Cardiss 67
  Conyers, John 68
  Crockett, George W. 70
  Cummings, Elijah 71
  Davis, Artur 73
  Davis, Danny K. 78, 79
  Dawson, William 80
  Dellums, Ron 83
  Diggs, Charles 87–88
  Dinkins, David 89
  Dixon, Julian 91
  Dymally, Mervyn 93
  Espy, Mike 98
  Evers, Charles 101
  Fattah, Chaka 104
  Fauntroy, Walter 105
  Fenty, Adrian M. 107
  Fields, Cleo 108
  Flake, Floyd 110
  Ford, Harold 111
  Ford, Harold, Jr. 113–114
  Foster, Ezola 116
  Franklin, Shirley 117
  Fudge, Marcia L. 120
  Fulani, Lenora 121
  Gantt, Harvey 124
  Goode, W. W. 126
  Gray, Bill 128
  Hall, Katie 131
  Haralson, Jeremiah 132
  Harmon, Clarence 134
  Harris, Patricia Roberts 135–136

Hastings, Alcee 138
Hatcher, Richard 140
Hawkins, Augustus 141
Hayes, Charles 143
Hayes, James 145
Henry, Aaron 147
Herenton, Willie 148
Herman, Alexis 149
Hilliard, Earl 150
Jack, Hulan 156
Jackson, Jesse 158, 160
Jackson, Jesse, Jr. 161–162
Jackson, Maynard 164
James, Sharpe 167
Jefferson, William 168
Johnson, Eddie Bernice 170
Johnson, Harvey 171
Jordan, Barbara 173
Kelly, Sharon Pratt Dixon 175
Kilpatrick, Kwame 180
Kirk, Ron 181
Lee, Barbara 185
Lewis, John 188
Majette, Denise 195, 196
Marsh, Henry 196
Martin, Louis 197–198
McCall, Carl 199
McKinney, Cynthia 201
Meeks, Gregory 205
Metcalfe, Ralph 206
Mfume, Kweisi 208
Millender-McDonald, Juanita 209
Mitchell, Arthur 211, 212
Mitchell, Parren 214
Moore, Gwen 216
Morial, Dutch 217
Moseley Braun, Carol 217
Motley, Constance 220
Nix, Robert 227
Norton, Eleanor Holmes 229
Nutter, Michael 230
Obama, Barack 233–234
Owens, Major 238
Paterson, David 242

Patrick, Deval 244
Payne, Donald 245
Perry, Carrie 246, 247
Powell, Adam Clayton, Jr. 250
Rangel, Charles 259, 260
Rice, Norm 268, 269
Ross, Don 271
Rush, Bobby 273
Savage, Gus 275
Schmoke, Kurt 277
Scott, Bobby 278
Sharpton, Al 280
Stokes, Carl 285
Stokes, Louis 287
Thompson, Bennie 292
Towns, Edolphus 294
Tubbs Jones, Stephanie 295
Turner, Benjamin 296–297
Washington, Harold 302
Waters, Maxine 305
Watson, Diane 307
Watt, Mel 308
Watts, J. C. 310
Weaver, Robert 312
Webb, Wellington 313
Wheat, Alan 315
White, Jesse 318
White, Michael 319
Wilder, Doug 320
Williams, Anthony 323
Williams, Hosea 327
Wynn, Albert 328
Young, Andy (Andrew) 330
Young, Coleman 333
Democratic Select Committee 81. See also Congressional Black Caucus
demonstrations and protests. See also boycotts; riots; sit-ins; sleep-ins
Ballance, Frank 11
Blackwell, Lucien 20
Clay, William 57
Crockett, George W. 70

Davis, Ben 74
Dinkins, David 90
Fauntroy, Walter 105
Ford, James 115
Jackson, Jesse 159
Jackson Lee, Sheila 166
Street, John 288
Williams, Avon 324
Williams, Hosea 327
Denver (Colorado) 313–315
departments, U.S. See under name of department, e.g., Agriculture, U.S. Department of (USDA)
DePriest, Oscar x, 80, 85–87, 86, 205, 212, 272, 316
desegregation. See military desegregation; school desegregation; segregation and desegregation
Detroit (Michigan)
  Archer, Dennis 4–6
  Collins, Barbara-Rose 65, 66
  Conyers, John 68, 69
  Crockett, George W. 70
  Diggs, Charles 87–88
  Kilpatrick, Carolyn 178
  Kilpatrick, Kwame 179–181
  Young, Coleman 332–334
Detroit Lions 5
Detroit Tigers 5
Deukmejian, George 27
DFL. See Democrat-Farm-Labor Party (DFL)
Diallo, Amadou 279
Diggs, Charles 57, 70, 87–89, 88, 94
Diggs, Charles, Sr. 87
digital divide 169
Dingall, John, Jr. 68
Dinkins, David 32, 34, 89–91
diplomacy
  Blackwell, Ken 19
  Chisholm, Shirley 52
  Evans, Melvin 99, 100

Harris, Patricia Roberts 135
Jackson, Jesse 160
Keyes, Alan 176–177
Langston, John 184
McCall, Carl 199
Moseley Braun, Carol 219
Payne, Donald 246
Rice, Susan E. 269–270
Stokes, Carl 286
Watson, Diane 306
Young, Andy (Andrew) 330, 331
disability rights 63, 142, 229, 278, 313
Disadvantaged Minority Health Improvement Act of 1989 287
discrimination vii–viii, ix, x
  Brown, Willie 36
  Burke, Yvonne 40
  Clay, William 57
  Clyburn, James 63
  Collins, Barbara-Rose 66
  DePriest, Oscar 86–87
  Elliot, Robert 96
  Haralson, Jeremiah 132
  Harmon, Clarence 134
  Hastie, William H. 137, 138
  Hastings, Alcee 139
  Hawkins, Augustus 142
  Johnson, Eddie Bernice 170
  Jordan, Barbara 173
  Lynch, John 193
  Millender-McDonald, Juanita 209
  Mitchell, Arthur 212
  Mitchell, Parren 214
  Moseley Braun, Carol 217
  Norton, Eleanor Holmes 229
  O'Hara, James 236
  Patrick, Deval 243–244
  Pinchback, P. B. S. 247, 249

Powell, Adam Clayton, Jr. 250
Rainey, Joseph 258
Ransier, Alonzo 262
Rapier, James 264
Smalls, Robert 282
Stokes, Louis 287
Webb, Wellington 314
Williams, Avon 324
Young, Coleman 332, 333
disenfranchisement
Elliot, Robert 96
Howard, Perry 153
Langston, John 184
Miller, Thomas 210
Moore, Gwen 216
Murray, George 221
Rainey, Joseph 258
Smalls, Robert 283
White, George 316
Displaced Homemakers Act of 1977 40
district attorneys
Meeks, Gregory 204
Morial, Dutch 216–217
Paterson, David 242
Rangel, Charles 259
Schmoke, Kurt 276
District of Columbia x, xi. *See also* home rule (for District of Columbia)
Baker, Ella 10
Barry, Marion 12–14
Bruce, Blanche 38
Cardozo, Francis 47
Cheatham, Henry 50
Dellums, Ron 84, 85
Diggs, Charles 88
Dixon, Julian 92
Fattah, Chaka 104
Fauntroy, Walter 105–107
Fenty, Adrian M. 107–108
Harris, Patricia Roberts 135–136
Howard, Perry 153
Hyman, John 154
Jackson, Jesse 159, 160
Kelly, Sharon Pratt Dixon 175–176
Langston, John 184

Norton, Eleanor Holmes 228–229
O'Hara, James 236
O'Leary, Hazel 237
Powell, Colin 253
Washington, Walter 303–305
Williams, Anthony 322–324
District of Columbia Delegation Act of 1970 105
District of Columbia House Voting Rights Act of 2009 229
Ditto, Diane 171
diversity 172, 181. *See also* affirmative action
divestiture
Brown, Willie 36
Dellums, Ron 84
Gray, Bill 128
Mfume, Kweisi 208
Moseley Braun, Carol 217
Perry, Carrie 246
Rangel, Charles 260
Waters, Maxine 305
Wheat, Alan 315
Wilder, Doug 321
Dixon, Alan J. 217
Dixon, Julian **91–92**, 117, 307
Dixon, Sharon Pratt. *See* Kelly, Sharon Pratt Dixon
Dixon, Sheila **92–93**
DNC. *See* Democratic National Committee (DNC)
DoD. *See* Defense, U.S. Department of (DoD)
Dodd, Christopher 119
DOE. *See* Energy, U.S. Department of (DOE)
domestic violence prevention 11, 15, 72, 195, 242
Domestic Volunteer Service Act 239
DoT. *See* Transportation, U.S. Department of (DoT)
Douglass, Frederick 221
Downtown Now! (St. Louis) 135

Dreams of My Father: A Story of Race and Inheritance (Obama) 232–233
driver's licenses 318
drug abuse prevention 72, 104, 109, 139, 259, 260, 277, 306. *See also* needle-exchange programs
Drug Enforcement Agency, U.S. (DEA) 14
drug law reform 70, 145, 247, 277
drug trade 209, 260
Dukakis, Michael xii, 34, 160, 217, 244
Dymally, Mervyn 91, **93–94**

E

East Africa 186, 187. *See also specific country*
Economic Bill of Rights 143–144
economic development
Archer, Dennis 5
Arrington, Richard 8
Barry, Marion 13
Belton, Sharon 15
Bosley, Freeman 26
Campbell, Bill 45
Clayton, Eva 60
Cleaver, Emanuel 62
Clyburn, James 63
Coleman, Michael 65
Espy, Mike 98
Gantt, Harvey 124
Harmon, Clarence 134–135
Hatcher, Richard 140–141
Herenton, Willie 148
Jackson, Maynard 164
James, Sharpe 167
Johnson, Harvey 171–172
Kirk, Ron 181
Marsh, Henry 197
Meeks, Gregory 205
Morial, Dutch 217
Nagin, Ray 224
Obama, Barack 235
Perry, Carrie 246
Powell, Debra 255

Rangel, Charles 260
Rice, Norm 269
Rush, Bobby 273
Stokes, Carl 285
Usry, James 298, 299
Webb, Wellington 314
White, Michael 319
Young, Coleman 333, 334
Economic Development Administration (Commerce, U.S. Department of) 113
Economic Growth and Tax Relief Reconciliation Act of 2001 113
economic opportunity 202, 287
economic sanctions 91, 177. *See also* divestiture
education. *See also* Head Start; public education
Anderson, Charles W., Jr. 4
Arrington, Richard 7
Brown, Lee 32
Cheatham, Henry 50
Chisholm, Shirley 51, 52
Clyburn, James 62
Collins, Barbara-Rose 65, 66
Davis, Artur 73
Davis, Danny K. 78
Dixon, Sheila 92
Dymally, Mervyn 93
Evers, Charles 101
Fattah, Chaka 103, 104
Fenty, Adrian M. 108
Fields, Cleo 109
Foster, Ezola 116
Hall, Katie 131
Hawkins, Augustus 142
Hayes, Charles 144
Hayes, James 144
Herenton, Willie 147
Hilliard, Earl 150, 151
Howard, Perry 153
Jackson Lee, Sheila 166
James, Sharpe 167
Johnson, Harvey 171
Kilpatrick, Carolyn 178

Langston, John vii, 184
Leland, Mickey 186
McKinney, Cynthia 200
Meek, Carrie 202
Metcalfe, Ralph 206
Millender-McDonald, Juanita 208, 209
Miller, Thomas 210
Mitchell, Arthur 211
Mitchell, Parren 214, 215
Moseley Braun, Carol 219
Murray, George 221
Napier, James 225
Norton, Eleanor Holmes 229
Obama, Barack 233
O'Hara, James 236
Owens, Major 238, 239
Paige, Rod 240–241
Perry, Carrie 247
Pinchback, P. B. S. 249
Powell, Adam Clayton, Jr. 251
Ransier, Alonzo 262
Rapier, James 263
Revels, Hiram 264
Rice, Condoleezza 266–267, 267
Rice, Norm 269
Ross, Don 271
Schmoke, Kurt 277
Stokes, Louis 287
Sullivan, Louis 290
Thompson, Bennie 292
Towns, Edolphus 294
Usry, James 298
Walls, Josiah 301
Watson, Diane 306–307
Webb, Wellington 313
White, George 316
White, Jesse 317–318
White, Michael 319
Wilder, Doug 321
Williams, Avon 324
Williams, Hosea 326
Education, U.S.
  Department of 127, 136, 219, 240–241. See also Health, Education, and Welfare, U.S. Department of (HEW)

Edwards, Donna 329
Edwards, John 234
EEOC. See Equal Employment Opportunity Commission (EEOC)
Ehrich, Rob 283–284
Eighty-second U.S. Colored Infantry Regiment 226
Eisenhower, Dwight D. 1, 4, 251
Elders, Jocelyn 149
election of 1868 190
election of 1870 96, 132, 191, 257–258, 297, 300–301
election of 1872 154, 193, 249, 261, 264, 297, 301
election of 1874 133, 154, 226, 263, 282, 301
election of 1876 264
election of 1878 133
election of 1882 193, 236
election of 1884 236, 282, 301
election of 1888 184, 210
election of 1890 210
election of 1892 221
election of 1896 221
election of 1928 80, 211
election of 1932 55, 115, 141
election of 1934 87, 211
election of 1936 115
election of 1938 115
election of 1940 115
election of 1942 80
election of 1944 250
election of 1948 81, 275, 333
election of 1950 87–88
election of 1952 1, 35
election of 1954 88
election of 1956 251
election of 1960 81, 93, 173, 198
election of 1962 93
election of 1964 29, 68, 147, 198
election of 1966 125, 140
election of 1968
  Clay, William 57
  Clayton, Eva 60
  Evers, Charles 101

Gregory, Dick 130
Jackson, Maynard 164
Martin, Louis 198
Mitchell, Parren 214
Powell, Adam Clayton, Jr. 252
Savage, Gus 275
Stokes, Louis 287
election of 1970 84, 105, 125, 206, 214, 259–260, 330
election of 1972 52, 67, 106, 173, 330
election of 1974 93, 100, 111–112, 125, 173
election of 1976 60, 125, 128, 188, 207, 313, 331
election of 1978 91, 100, 103, 125, 128, 186, 207
election of 1980 34, 70, 94, 100, 157, 275, 302, 327
election of 1982
  Archer, Dennis 5
  Clayton, Eva 60
  Fattah, Chaka 103–104
  Gibson, Kenneth 125
  Hall, Katie 131
  Henry, Aaron 147
  Owens, Major 238
  Payne, Donald 245
  Towns, Edolphus 294
  Washington, Harold 302
  Wheat, Alan 315
election of 1984
  Chisholm, Shirley 52
  Davis, Danny K. 78
  Fauntroy, Walter 105, 106–107
  Hall, Katie 132
  Jackson, Jesse 159–160
  Scott, Bobby 278
  Waters, Maxine 305
  Williams, Hosea 327
election of 1986 78, 98, 108, 110, 125, 188, 208
election of 1988
  Brown, Ron 34
  Chisholm, Shirley 52
  Collins, Barbara-Rose 66
  Fattah, Chaka 104
  Fulani, Lenora 120–121

Jackson, Jesse 160
Jackson, Jesse, Jr. 161
Keyes, Alan 177
Morial, Dutch 217
Moseley Braun, Carol 218
Norton, Eleanor Holmes 229
Payne, Donald 245
Usry, James 299
Waters, Maxine 305
election of 1990
  Collins, Barbara-Rose 66
  Fields, Cleo 109
  Franks, Gary 119
  Gantt, Harvey 124
  Hastings, Alcee 138
  Jackson, Jesse 160
  Jefferson, William 168
  Johnson, Eddie Bernice 170–171
  Waters, Maxine 306
  Watt, Mel 308
election of 1992 xiii
  Brown, Corrine 32
  Brown, Ron 34–35
  Clayton, Eva 60
  Cleaver, Emanuel 62
  Clyburn, James 63
  Davis, Danny K. 78
  Fields, Cleo 109
  Fulani, Lenora 121
  Hastings, Alcee 138–139
  Hayes, Charles 144
  Hayes, James 145
  Herman, Alexis 149
  Hilliard, Earl 151
  Jackson, Jesse 160
  Jefferson, William 168
  Johnson, Eddie Bernice 171
  Keyes, Alan 177
  McKinney, Cynthia 200
  Meek, Carrie 202
  Moseley Braun, Carol 217
  Rush, Bobby 273
  Savage, Gus 276
  Scott, Bobby 278
  Slater, Rodney 280
  Watt, Mel 308–309
  Wheat, Alan 315
  Wynn, Albert 328

election of 1994 104, 121,
166, 201, 310, 315–316
election of 1996
Carson, Julia 49
Christian-Christensen,
Donna 53
Cummings, Elijah 72
Davis, Danny K. 78–79
Fields, Cleo 109
Ford, Harold, Jr. 113
Foster, Ezola 116–117
Franks, Gary 119
Fulani, Lenora 121
Harmon, Clarence 134
Herman, Alexis 149
Keyes, Alan 177
Kilpatrick, Carolyn
178
Millender-McDonald,
Juanita 209
Powell, Colin 253
Rogers, Joe 270
Wheat, Alan 316
election of 1998 119, 121,
145, 185, 205, 217, 295
election of 2000
Blackwell, Ken 19
Brown, Corrine 31
Clay, William, Jr. 59
Clayton, Eva 60–61
Conyers, John 69
Foster, Ezola 116
Fulani, Lenora
121–122
McKinney, Cynthia
201
Moseley Braun, Carol
219
Obama, Barack 233
election of 2002 xiv
Conyers, John 69
Davis, Artur 73
Dymally, Mervyn 94
Hilliard, Earl 151
Jefferson, William 169
Kirk, Ron 182
Majette, Denise 195
Meek, Carrie 203
Watson, Diane 307
Wynn, Albert 329
election of 2004
Cleaver, Emanuel 62
Conyers, John 69
Ford, Harold, Jr. 113
Jefferson, William 169

Keyes, Alan 177
Majette, Denise 196
McKinney, Cynthia
201
Moore, Gwen 216
Obama, Barack 233
Rice, Susan E. 270
Sharpton, Al 279
Wynn, Albert 329
election of 2006 xv
Clyburn, James 63
Ellison, Keith 97
Ford, Harold, Jr. 114
Jefferson, William 169
Kilpatrick, Carolyn
179
Kilpatrick, Kwame 180
McKinney, Cynthia
201
Millender-McDonald,
Juanita 209
Patrick, Deval 244
election of 2008 xv–xvi
Burris, Roland 41
Davis, Artur 73, 74
Davis, Danny K. 79
Dinkins, David 91
Dymally, Mervyn 94
Ellison, Keith 97
Fattah, Chaka 104,
105
Fudge, Marcia L. 120
Holder, Eric 152
Jackson, Jesse, Jr. 162
Keyes, Alan 178
Kilpatrick, Carolyn
179
Kilpatrick, Kwame 179
McKinney, Cynthia
201
Moore, Gwen 216
Obama, Barack 232,
234–235
Patrick, Deval 244
Powell, Colin 254
Rice, Susan E. 270
Scott, Bobby 279
Tubbs Jones, Stephanie
295
Watson, Diane 307
White, Jesse 318
Wynn, Albert 329
election of 2010
Baker, Robert 11
Bishop, Sanford 18

Booker, Cory 25
Brown, Corrine 32
Carson, André 48
Clarke, Yvette D. 56
Clay, William, Jr. 59
Cleaver, Emanuel 62
Clyburn, James 63
Conyers, John 69
Davis, Ben 74
Davis, Danny K. 79
Dellums, Ron 85
Ellison, Keith 97
Fattah, Chaka 105
Ford, Harold, Jr. 114
Fudge, Marcia L. 120
Hastings, Alcee 139
Jackson, Jesse, Jr. 162
Jackson Lee, Sheila 166
Johnson, Eddie Bernice
171
Kilpatrick, Carolyn
179
Lee, Barbara 186
Lewis, John 189
Meek, Kendrick 204
Meeks, Gregory 205
Moseley Braun, Carol
219
Paterson, David 242
Patrick, Deval 244
Payne, Donald 246
Rangel, Charles 260
Rush, Bobby 274
Thompson, Bennie
293
Towns, Edolphus 294
Waters, Maxine 306
Watt, Mel 309
Watts, J. C. 311
election reform 69
Elementary and Secondary
Education Act of 1970
142, 215
Elementary and Secondary
School Improvement
Amendment of 1988
142
Elliot, Robert 43, **95–96**
Ellison, Keith 48, **97–98**
El Salvador 71
Emergency Development
Loan Guarantee
Program of 1992 306
emergency management
224

emigration 264–265
employment. *See* job
programs and training
empowerment zones 5, 45,
260
Energy, U.S. Department
of (DOE) 237–238, 253
energy policy 27, 163, 234,
237–238, 253, 294
Enforcement Act of 1872
96, 258
engineers 125
enterprise zones 62, 63,
151
environmentalism 29, 52,
109, 140–141, 162–163,
169, 173, 237–238
Environmental Protection
Agency, U.S. (EPA) 10,
31, 162–163
envoys (Jesse Jackson) 160
EPA. *See* Environmental
Protection Agency, U.S.
(EPA)
Equal Employment
Opportunity
Commission (EEOC)
142, 229, 295, 329
equal opportunity
Allen, Ethel 1–2
Clay, William 57
Collins, Cardiss 67
Crockett, George W.
70
Dixon, Julian 91
Dymally, Mervyn 93,
94
Hawkins, Augustus
142
Hilliard, Earl 150
Jordan, Barbara 173
Langston, John 183
Leland, Mickey 186
McKinney, Cynthia
200
Powell, Adam Clayton,
Jr. 250
Rainey, Joseph 258
Rapier, James 264
Savage, Gus 275, 276
Stokes, Louis 287
Thompson, Bennie
293
Tubbs Jones, Stephanie
295

Williams, Avon 324
Wynn, Albert 328, 329
Young, Coleman 333
Equity in Athletics
Disclosure Act of 1993
67
Espy, Ben 64
Espy, Henry 293
Espy, Mike xiii, 64,
98–99, 293, 322
Ethiopia 166, 187
Europe 54, 264. *See also
specific country*
European Union 54
Evans, Melvin xi, **99–101**
Evers, Charles **101–102,**
147, 172
Evers, Medgar 101, 146,
172
Exodusters 38
*Extraordinary, Ordinary
People: A Memoir of
Family* (Rice) 267

F

FAA. *See* Federal Aviation
Administration (FAA)
Fairbanks (Alaska)
144–145
Fair Employment Practices
Commission 251, 302
Fair Employment Practices
Committee 55, 70
Fair Housing Amendments
Act of 1988 142
Families in Education Levy
269
Family and Medical Leave
Act of 1991 31, 67
Family Development
Accounts 59
Farmer, James 51–52
farm subsidies 18, 50, 60,
294
Fattah, Chaka 20, **103–
105,** *104*
Fauntroy, Walter **105–
107,** *106,* 229
Fayette (Mississippi)
101–102
FBI. *See* Federal Bureau of
Investigation (FBI)
FCC. *See* Federal
Communications
Commission (FCC)

FEA. *See* Federal Energy
Administration (FEA)
Federal Aviation
Administration (FAA)
209
Federal Bureau of
Investigation (FBI) 12,
41, 45–46, 140, 158, 289
Federal Communications
Commission (FCC) 57
Federal Energy
Administration (FEA)
237
Federal Highway
Administration (FHA)
280–281
Federal Housing
Administration 312
Federal Housing and
Home Finance Agency
312
Federal Reserve Board
142
Federal Trade
Commission, U.S.
(FTC) 67
Federated States of
Micronesia 307
Federation of Independent
Voters 121
Fenty, Adrian M. xiv,
107–108
Ferrer, Fernando 91
fetal tissue research 291
FHA. *See* Federal Highway
Administration (FHA)
Field Foundation 188
Fields, Cleo **108–110**
Fifteenth Amendment
viii, 225, 258
55th Massachusetts
Infantry 213
film and television
Booker, Cory 24
Coleman, Michael 65
Collins, Cardiss 67
Ellison, Keith 97
Ford, Harold, Jr. 114
Fulani, Lenora 122
Gregory, Dick 129
Keyes, Alan 177
Leland, Mickey 187
McCall, Carl 199
Powell, Debra 254
Rice, Norm 268

Sharpton, Al 280
Stokes, Carl 286
Watts, J. C. 311
Financial Institutions
Reform and Recovery
Act 208
First Amendment 229
fiscal conservatism 17, 18,
19, 114, 119, 145, 321
Fitzgerald, Peter 233
flags 172, 218, 271, 327
Flake, Floyd **110–111,** 205
Fleetway Press 197
flooding 25
Florida 31–32, 138–139,
202–204, 300–302
football 26, 309, 319
Forbes, George L. 318, 319
Forbes, Steve 19
Ford, Emmitt 112, 113
Ford, Gerald R. 2, 173
Ford, Harold **111–112,**
113, 147, 148
Ford, Harold, Jr. xv, 58,
112–114, 147
Ford, James 112, 113,
114–116
Ford, Joe 148
Ford, John 112, 113
Ford, Michael 112, 113
Ford Motor Company 332
foreign aid 66, 88, 94, 204,
260
foreign policy. *See also*
diplomacy
Crockett, George W.
70–71
Davis, Artur 73
Davis, Ben 76
Dellums, Ron 83, 84
Diggs, Charles 88
Dymally, Mervyn 94
Fauntroy, Walter 107
Langston, John 184
Lee, Barbara 185–186
Majette, Denise 195
McKinney, Cynthia
200–201
Obama, Barack 234,
235
Payne, Donald
245–246
Rangel, Charles 260
Rice, Condoleezza
266–268

Savage, Gus 276
Wheat, Alan 315
Young, Andy (Andrew)
331
Foster, Ezola xiii, **116–117**
Foster, Mike 109, 169
Foster, William Z. 115
Fourteenth Amendment
viii, ix, 82, 258
Fourth Circuit Court of
Appeals 217
Fowler, Wynche 188
FOX news (TV) 114
France 306
Franklin, Shirley **117–118**
Franks, Gary **118–119,** 309
Fraser, Don 15
Frazer, Victor O. 53
"Freaknik" 45
Frederick D. Patterson
Research Institute 128
free blacks 46, 81, 183,
210, 225, 226, 262, 281,
325
"Free D.C." movement 13
freedmen vii, viii
Cain, Richard 43, 44
Cardozo, Francis 46,
47
Hyman, John 154
Long, Jefferson
190–191
Lynch, John 193
Miller, Thomas
210–211
O'Hara, James 235,
236
Pinchback, P. B. S.
247–249
Rainey, Joseph 257
Rapier, James 263–264
Smalls, Robert 282
Turner, Benjamin 297
Walls, Josiah 300
Freedmen's Bureau 81,
184, 225, 264, 300, 301
Freedmen's Convention of
North Carolina (1866)
154
Freedmen's Savings and
Trust Company 38, 236
Freedom and Peace Party
130
Freedom Riders 146,
187–188

"Freedom Summer" 147
"Freedom to Farm" 60
"Freedom Vote" 146–147
free markets 17, 111, 204.
    See also fiscal
    conservatism
free-markets 110, 111
Free-Soil Party 183
Friedel, Samuel N. 214
Friedler, Carl 214
FTC. *See* Federal Trade
    Commission, U.S.
    (FTC)
Fudge, Marcia L. **119–120**
Fulani, Lenora xiii,
    120–122

G
G. P. Putnam's Sons
    325–326
Gainesville (Florida) 301
gambling 259. *See also*
    casino development
Gantt, Harvey **123–124,**
    308
Garrison, William Lloyd
    213
Gary (Indiana) x, 131–
    132, 139–141
gay rights 33, 37, 59, 121,
    242, 310, 314. *See also*
    same-sex marriage
GEAR UP 104
Gees Bend (Alabama)
    151
General Motors 5, 333
genocide 166
George, Walter 77
Georgia viii
    Baker, Thurbert E.
        10–11
    Bishop, Sanford 17–18
    Bond, Julian 22–23
    Davis, Benjamin J.
        76–78
    Lewis, John 187–189
    Long, Jefferson
        189–191
    Majette, Denise
        195–196
    McKinney, Cynthia
        200–202
    Sullivan, Louis 290
    Williams, Hosea
        326–327

Georgia Equal Rights and
    Education Association
    190
Germany 285, 326
*Germany Unified and
    Europe Transformed: A
    Study in Statecraft* (Rice
    & Zelikow) 267
gerrymandering 18, 31,
    109, 171, 279, 309
Gibson, Kenneth **124–
    126,** 167
Gillibrand, Kirsten 242
Gingrich, Newt 162
Giulinani. Rudolph 90,
    199
global warming 163, 270
GNYCCE. *See* Greater
    New York Coordinating
    Committee for
    Employment
    (GNYCCE)
Goals 2000 school-
    improvement initiative
    245
Goetz, Bernard 279
Goldwater, Barry 29
Goode, W. W. **126–127**
Good Fight, The
    (Chisholm) 52
GoodWorks International
    332
Gove, Samuel F. 190
Government Accounting
    Office 67
government reform 238.
    See also city government
    reform
governors xiv, xv. *See also*
    gubernatorial
    candidates; lieutenant
    governors
    Evans, Melvin 99–101
    Hastie, William H.
        136–138
    Paterson, David
        241–243
    Patrick, Deval 244
    Pinchback, P. B. S.
        247–249
    Wilder, Doug 320–322
Grace, Chris 322
Gramm, Phil 182
Grand Army of the
    Republic 213

Grant, Ulysses S. 325
Gray, Bill 20, 103, 104,
    127–129, 228
Gray, Frizzell. *See* Mfume,
    Kweisi
Gray, Vincent C. 108
Great Depression ix, 55, 86,
    135, 141, 212, 219, 250
Greater New York
    Coordinating
    Committee for
    Employment
    (GNYCCE) 250
Great Exodus 85
Great Migration ix, x
Great Society 30, 69, 83,
    214, 251
Green, Katie Beatrice. *See*
    Hall, Katie
Green, Malice 333–334
Green, Mark 90–91
Green Party 201
Gregory, Dick xi, *129,*
    129–130
Grenada 71, 186, 276
Griffith, Michael 279
gubernatorial candidates
    Baker, Thurbert E. 11
    Blackwell, Ken 19
    Bradley, Tom 27
    Burris, Roland 41
    Coleman, Michael 65
    Davis, Artur 74
    Evers, Charles 102
    Fields, Cleo 108, 109
    Fulani, Lenora 121
    Gibson, Kenneth 125
    Jefferson, William 169
    McCall, Carl 199
    Paterson, David 242
    Rice, Norm 269
    Young, Andy (Andrew)
        331
Gulf of Mexico oil spill
    (2010) 152, 163, 235
Gulf War (1991) 254, 276,
    278, 315
gun control 27, 49, 93, 99,
    274, 295, 309, 310

H
Hackett, Richard 148
Hagelin, John 122
Haiti 107, 115, 128, 184,
    203, 204

Hall, Katie **131–132**
Hamer, Fannie Lou 292
handicapped rights. *See*
    disability rights
Hanrahan, Edward 207
Haralson, Jeremiah **132–
    134,** *133,* 264
Harding, Warren G. 3,
    153
Harlem Liberator 75
Harlem (New York City)
    75–76, 89, 115, 116, 156,
    199, 220, 242, 250,
    259–260
Harlem People's
    Committee 250
Harmon, Clarence 25, 26,
    134–135
Harper's Ferry raid
    183–184
Harris, Patricia Roberts
    xi, **135–136,** 175
Harrison, Benjamin 38, 50
Hartford (Connecticut)
    246–247
Harvard Law Review 232
Hastie, William H. **136–
    138,** *137*
Hastings, Alcee 31, **138–
    139,** *139,* 202
Hatch Act of 1939 58
Hatcher, Charles 17
Hatcher, Richard x, 131,
    139–141
hate crime legislation 59,
    68–69
Hate Crimes Statistics Act
    of 1971 68–69
Hawkins, Augustus **141–
    143,** 306
Hayes, Charles **143–144,**
    273
Hayes, James **144–145**
Head Start 16, 31, 110,
    195, 245, 305
Healey, Kerry 244
Health, Education, and
    Welfare, U.S.
    Department of (HEW)
    136, 170, 313. *See also*
    Education, U.S.
    Department of; Health
    and Human Services,
    U.S. Department of
    (HHS)

Health and Human
    Services, U.S.
    Department of (HHS)
    136, 290–291. *See also*
    Health, Education, and
    Welfare, U.S.
    Department of (HEW)
health and medicine. *See
    also* Medicare;
    prescription drug
    coverage
    Allen, Ethel 1–2
    Baker, Thurbert E. 11
    Brown, Corrine 31
    Christian-Christensen,
        Donna 53, 54
    Clarke, Yvette D. 56
    Conyers, John 69
    Cummings, Elijah 72
    Davis, Artur 73
    Evans, Melvin 100
    Fields, Cleo 109
    Ford, Harold 112
    Fulani, Lenora 121
    Gibson, Kenneth 124,
        125
    Henry, Aaron 145
    Hilliard, Earl 151
    Jackson, Jesse, Jr. 162
    Jackson Lee, Sheila
        166
    Johnson, Eddie Bernice
        170, 171
    Lee, Barbara 186
    Leland, Mickey 186
    Metcalfe, Ralph 206
    Obama, Barack 235
    Rush, Bobby 273
    Schmoke, Kurt 277
    Stokes, Louis 287
    Sullivan, Louis
        290–291
    Thompson, Bennie
        293
    Watt, Mel 309
Heflin, Howell 73
Heflin, James 86–87
Helms, Jesse 124, 217, 308
Henry, Aaron 88, 101,
    145–147, *146*
Henry, Lowell 285
Herenton, Willie **147–
149,** *148*
Herman, Alexis xiii, **149–
150,** 280

Herndon, Angelo 74–75
HEW. *See* Health,
    Education, and Welfare,
    U.S. Department of
    (HEW)
HHS. *See* Health and
    Human Services, U.S.
    Department of (HHS)
Higher Education Grant
    104
highways 280–281
Hill, Anita 217
Hill, Oliver W. 196
Hill, Tony 203
Hilliard, Earl xiv, 73,
    150–151
Hispanic voters 139, 141,
    173, 181, 182, 294, 303
historians 325–326
*History of the Negro Race in
    America from 1619 to
    1880: Negroes as Slaves,
    as Soldiers, and as
    Citizens* (George
    Williams) 325–326
*History of the Negro Troops
    in the War of the
    Rebellion, 1861–1865*
    (George Williams) 326
HIV Prevention Outreach
    Act of 1997 72
Hofeld, Al 217
Holden, William H. 154
Holder, Eric **151–153,**
    244
Holder, Wesley M. 51
Holly, John 285
Holmes, David 178
Holt, Curtis 196
homeland security 33, 48,
    56, 176, 179, 307
Homeland Security
    Committee 56
homelessness 20, 61, 187,
    315
home ownership 182, 186,
    206, 277, 306
Home Ownership Plan
    Encouragement Act 110
home rule (for District of
    Columbia) 87, 106, 229,
    304, 323
Hoover, Herbert ix, 55, 77,
    153, 212
Hoover Institution 267

HOPE college tuition tax
    credit 11
HOPE for Africa Act of
    1999 162
House Agriculture
    Committee 52, 60, 293
House AIDS Working
    Group 72
House Appropriations
    Committee 63, 162,
    178–179, 202–203
House Banking
    Committee 107, 205,
    309
House banking scandal 17,
    144, 273, 315
House candidates
    Blackwell, Unita 22
    Bond, Julian 23
    Gantt, Harvey 124
    Herenton, Willie 148
    Napier, James 225
    Obama, Barack 233
    Rogers, Joe 270
    Williams, Hosea 327
House Committee on
    Armed Services 84
House Committee on
    Elections 82–83
House Committee on
    Foreign Affairs 70
House Committee on
    Foreign Relations 88
House Committee on
    Government Operations
    80
House Committee on
    Government Reform 79
House Committee on
    Intelligence 84, 287
House Committee on
    Invalid Pensions 297
House Committee on
    Oversight and
    Government Reform
    152
House Committee on
    Small Business 79
House Committee on the
    District of Columbia
    84, 85, 88, 92, 105–106
House Committee on the
    Militia 96
House Democratic Caucus
    63

House Education and
    Labor Committee 56,
    96, 251, 263
House Energy and
    Commerce Committee
    67
House Ethics Committee
    31, 66, 92, 151, 162, 260,
    276, 288
House Financial Services
    Committee 59, 62
House Foreign Relations
    Committee 234
House Government
    Operations Committee
    67
House Government
    Reform Committee 59
House Judiciary Committee
    69, 70, 166, 173
House Labor Committee
    56
House of Representatives,
    U.S. viii–ix, xi, xii, xiii
    Allen, Ethel 2
    Ballance, Frank 12
    Bishop, Sanford 17–18
    Blackwell, Lucien 20
    Brown, Corrine 31–32
    Burke, Yvonne 39–40
    Cain, Richard 43–44
    Carson, André 47–48
    Carson, Julia 48–49
    Cheatham, Henry
        49–50
    Chisholm, Shirley
        51–52
    Christian-Christensen,
        Donna 53
    Clarke, Yvette D. 56
    Clay, William 57–58
    Clay, William, Jr.
        58–59
    Clayton, Eva 59–61
    Cleaver, Emanuel
        61–62
    Clyburn, James 62–64
    Collins, Barbara-Rose
        66
    Collins, Cardiss 67
    Conyers, John 68–70
    Crockett, George W.
        70–71
    Cummings, Elijah
        71–72

Davis, Artur 73–74
Davis, Danny K. 78–79
Dawson, William
  79–81
DeLarge, Robert 81,
  82–83
Dellums, Ron 83–85
DePriest, Oscar 86–87
Diggs, Charles 87–89
Dixon, Julian 91–92
Dymally, Mervyn
  93–94
Elliot, Robert 95–96
Ellison, Keith 97
Espy, Mike 98–99
Evans, Melvin 100
Fattah, Chaka
  103–105
Fauntroy, Walter
  105–106
Fields, Cleo 108–110
Flake, Floyd 110–111
Ford, Harold 111–112
Ford, Harold, Jr.
  112–114
Franks, Gary 118–119
Fudge, Marcia L.
  119–120
Gray, Bill 128
Hall, Katie 131–132
Haralson, Jeremiah
  132–134
Hastings, Alcee
  138–139
Hawkins, Augustus
  141–143
Hayes, Charles
  143–144
Henry, Aaron 147
Hilliard, Earl 150–151
Hyman, John 154–155
Jackson, Jesse, Jr.
  161–162
Jackson Lee, Sheila
  165–166
Jefferson, William
  168–169
Johnson, Eddie Bernice
  169–171
Jordan, Barbara
  172–174
Kilpatrick, Carolyn
  178–179
Langston, John
  183–184

Lee, Barbara 184–186
Leland, Mickey
  186–187
Lewis, John 187–189
Long, Jefferson
  189–191
Lynch, John 192–194
Majette, Denise
  195–196
McKinney, Cynthia
  200–202
Meek, Carrie 202–203
Meek, Kendrick 204
Meeks, Gregory
  204–205
Metcalfe, Ralph
  206–207
Mfume, Kweisi 208
Millender-McDonald,
  Juanita 208–209
Miller, Thomas
  210–211
Mitchell, Arthur 212
Mitchell, Parren
  214–215
Moore, Gwen 216
Murray, George 221
Nash, Charles 226
Nix, Robert 227–228
Norton, Eleanor
  Holmes 228–229
O'Hara, James 236
Owens, Major
  238–239
Payne, Donald
  244–246
Pinchback, P. B. S. 249
Powell, Adam Clayton,
  Jr. 249–252
Rainey, Joseph
  257–258
Rangel, Charles
  259–260
Ransier, Alonzo
  261–262
Rapier, James 263–264
Rush, Bobby 272–274
Savage, Gus 275–276
Scott, Bobby 278–279
Smalls, Robert
  281–283
Stokes, Louis 286–288
Thompson, Bennie
  292–293
Towns, Edolphus 293

Tubbs Jones, Stephanie
  294–295
Turner, Benjamin
  296–297
Walls, Josiah 300–302
Washington, Harold
  302
Waters, Maxine
  305–306
Watson, Diane
  306–308
Watt, Mel 308–309
Watts, J. C. 309–311
Wheat, Alan 315–316
White, George
  316–317
Wynn, Albert 327–329
Young, Andy (Andrew)
  330–332
House of Umoja
  (Philadelphia) 103
House Post Office and
  Civil Service
  Committee 57, 66
House Public Works and
  Transportation
  Committee 66
House Republican
  Conference 310
House Resolution 64 186
House Rules Committee
  330–331
House Select Committee
  on Assassinations 165,
  287
House Select Committee
  on Hunger 187
House Speaker's Select
  Committee on Energy
  Independence and
  Global Warming 62
House Subcommittee on
  Military Installations
  and Facilities 84
House Un-American
  Activities Committee
  (HUAC) 333
House Ways and Means
  Committee 52, 73, 112,
  168–169, 188, 204, 260
housing. See also home
  ownership; public
  housing
  Blackwell, Unita 21
  Brown, Willie 35

Clayton, Eva 60
Flake, Floyd 110
Gibson, Kenneth 125
Harris, Patricia Roberts
  135, 136
Hawkins, Augustus
  142
Jackson, Alphonso
  157–158
Johnson, Eddie Bernice
  170
Rangel, Charles 260
Stokes, Louis 287
Street, John 289
Thompson, Bennie
  293
Washington, Harold
  302
Washington, Walter
  303–305
Weaver, Robert
  311–313
White, Michael 319
Wilder, Doug 320
Williams, Anthony
  322
Young, Coleman 333
Housing Act of 1961 312
Housing and Community
  Development Act of
  1990 98
Housing and Urban
  Development, U.S.
  Department of (HUD)
  Blackwell, Ken 19
  Blackwell, Unita 21
  Campbell, Bill 45
  Clayton, Eva 60
  Cleaver, Emanuel 62
  Harris, Patricia Roberts
  135, 136
  Jackson, Alphonso
  157–158
  Kilpatrick, Carolyn
  178
  Weaver, Robert
  311–313
  Wheat, Alan 315
Housing Programs
  Reauthorization Act
  110
Houston Astros 33
Houston (Texas) 32–33,
  116, 165–166, 173,
  240–241

Howard, Michael 265
Howard, Perry 55,
  153–154
Howard University
  Brown, Lee 32
  DePriest, Oscar 86
  Harris, Patricia Roberts
    135, 136
  Hastie, William H.
    137
  Langston, John 184
  Martin, Louis 198
  Napier, James 225
  Schmoke, Kurt 278
  Sullivan, Louis 290
HUAC. *See* House
  Un-American Activities
  Committee (HUAC)
HUD. *See* Housing and
  Urban Development,
  U.S. Department of
  (HUD)
Hull, Blair 233
human rights
  Baker, Ella 10
  Blackwell, Ken 19
  Fauntroy, Walter 107
  Jackson, Jesse 160
  Jackson Lee, Sheila
    166
  Leland, Mickey 186,
    187
  McKinney, Cynthia
    200
  Moseley Braun, Carol
    217
  Payne, Donald
    245–246
  Rush, Bobby 274
  Young, Andy (Andrew)
    332
Humphrey, Hubert H. xi,
  140, 285
Humphrey-Hawkins Full-
  Employment and
  Balanced Growth Act of
  1978 142
hunger 187
Hunt, Jim 60
hurricanes 158, 201, 203,
  223, 224
Hussein, Saddam 267
Hyde Amendment 67
Hyman, John 12,
  154–155

I

Illinois xi
  Burris, Roland 40–42
  Collins, Cardiss 66–68
  Davis, Danny K. 78–79
  Dawson, William
    79–81
  DePriest, Oscar 85–87
  Hayes, Charles
    143–144
  Jackson, Jesse, Jr.
    161–162
  Keyes, Alan 177
  Metcalfe, Ralph
    205–207
  Mitchell, Arthur
    211–212
  Moseley Braun, Carol
    217–219
  Obama, Barack
    232–235
  Rush, Bobby 272–274
  Savage, Gus 275–276
  White, Jesse 317–318
ILU. *See* International
  Labor Union (ILU)
immigration 27, 139, 166,
  203, 309
Immigration and
  Naturalization Service,
  U.S. (INS) 139
impeachment 138, 152,
  166
Impulse Disco 230
Independence Party 122
Independent 77
independent candidates
  Berry, Ted 16
  Haralson, Jeremiah
    132, 133
  Hatcher, Richard 140
  Henry, Aaron 147
  O'Hara, James 236
  Turner, Benjamin 296
  Wilder, Doug 321
Independents for
  Buchanan 117
Indiana 47–48, 48–49,
  131–132
Indianapolis (Indiana)
  48–49
Indian Territory 325
Individuals with Disability
  Education Act 278

industry. *See* business and
  industry
infant mortality 124, 125
inflation 142
In Friendship 9
Initiative 34 (Seattle,
  Washington) 268
INS. *See* Immigration and
  Naturalization Service,
  U.S. (INS)
integration 4, 7–8, 11,
  192, 258. *See also*
  military desegregation;
  school desegregation;
  segregation and
  desegregation
Interior, U.S. Department
  of 133, 137, 193, 311
Intermediate Nuclear
  Forces Treaty of 1987
  84
Internal Revenue Service,
  U.S. (IRS) 2, 77, 225,
  260, 288
International Labor Union
  (ILU) 115
International
  Longshoremen's
  Association 20
International United Auto
  Workers 70
Internet access 72
interracial marriage 258,
  325
Interstate Commerce Act
  of 1884 236
Iran 267
Iran-contra investigation
  287–288
Iraq, U.S. invasion of
  (1991) 253, 276, 278,
  315
Iraq Stabilization Group
  267
Iraq War (2003–) xv
  Carson, André 48
  Carson, Julia 49
  Clay, William, Jr. 59
  Conyers, John 69
  Fattah, Chaka 104
  Jackson, Jesse, Jr. 162
  Lee, Barbara 185, 186
  McKinney, Cynthia
    201

Obama, Barack 233,
  234
Powell, Colin 254
Rangel, Charles 260
Rice, Condoleezza 267
Waters, Maxine 306
Watson, Diane 307
Iraq War Resolution 306
IRS. *See* Internal Revenue
  Service, U.S. (IRS)
Isakson, Johnny 196
Islam 97
Israel 73, 76, 201, 267, 276
Italy 298
Ivan (hurricane) 224

J

Jack, Hulan **156–157**
Jackson, Alphonso xiv,
  157–158
Jackson, Jesse xii, 24,
  158–160. *See also*
  Operation PUSH
  Brown, Ron 34
  Burris, Roland 41
  Chisholm, Shirley 52
  Dixon, Julian 92
  Fauntroy, Walter 105,
    106–107
  Fulani, Lenora 121
  Jackson, Jesse, Jr. 161
  Norton, Eleanor
    Holmes 229
  Scott, Bobby 278
  Sharpton, Al 279
  Usry, James 299
  Waters, Maxine 305
  Wilder, Doug 321
  Williams, Hosea 327
Jackson, Jesse, Jr. *161*,
  161–162
Jackson, Lisa P. **162–163**
Jackson, Mahalia 279
Jackson, Maynard 32, 45,
  77, 117, **163–165**, 327,
  331
Jackson, Thomas
  "Stonewall" 320
Jackson Lee, Sheila *165*,
  165–166
Jackson (Mississippi) 146,
  171–172
Jackson State College
  shootings 30
Jacobs, Andy 48–49

Jakarta 232
Jamaica 52, 56
James, Esther 252
James, Sharpe 24, 125,
    166–167, 245
Japan 306
Jarvis, Charlene Drew 107
Jefferson, William *168,*
    168–169
Jena (Alabama) Six 280
Jesse White Tumblers 317
Jewett, Doug 268
Job Corps 16, 147
job programs and training
    Archer, Dennis 5
    Belton, Sharon 15
    Clay, William, Jr.
        58–59
    Herenton, Willie 148
    Herman, Alexis 149
    Kirk, Ron 181
    Meek, Carrie 202
    Mitchell, Parren 215
    Morial, Dutch 217
    Nix, Robert 228
    Perry, Carrie 247
    Powell, Adam Clayton,
        Jr. 251
    Waters, Maxine 305,
        306
John A. Hyman Memorial
    Youth Foundation 12
John Birch Society 116
John F. Kennedy
    Democratic Club 259
John Paul II (pope) 314
Johnson, Eddie Bernice
    169–171, *170*
Johnson, Hank 201
Johnson, Harvey **171–172**
Johnson, J. Bennett 168
Johnson, Lyndon B. x
    Berry, Ted 16
    Brooke, Edward 30
    Clay, William 57
    Conyers, John 68, 69
    Dawson, William 80
    Dellums, Ron 83
    Fauntroy, Walter 105
    Harris, Patricia Roberts
        136
    Martin, Louis 198
    Mitchell, Parren 214
    Powell, Adam Clayton,
        Jr. 251

Washington, Walter
    304
Weaver, Robert
    312–313
Joint Center for Political
    and Economic Studies
    198
Joint Center for Political
    Studies 175
Joint Chiefs of Staff 252,
    253
Jones, J. Raymond 89
Jones, Walter B. 60
Jordan, Barbara 114, **172–**
    174, *173,* 186
journalism
    Cain, Richard 43
    Davis, Ben 74, 75
    Davis, Benjamin J.
        76–77
    Elliot, Robert 95
    Martin, Louis 197–198
    Powell, Debra 255
    Rice, Norm 268
    Ross, Don 271
    Savage, Gus 275
    Williams, George 325
judges
    Archer, Dennis 5
    Crockett, George W.
        70
    Hastie, William H.
        136, 138
    Hastings, Alcee
        138–139
    Majette, Denise 195
    Martin, Louis 198
    Morial, Dutch 217
    Motley, Constance 220
    Tubbs Jones, Stephanie
        295
Justice, U.S. Department
    of
    Brown, Ron 35
    Campbell, Bill 44
    Collins, Barbara-Rose
        66
    Collins, Cardiss 67
    Conyers, John 68–69
    Crockett, George W.
        70
    Harris, Patricia Roberts
        135
    Hatcher, Richard 140
    Holder, Eric 151–153

Jackson, Alphonso 158
Rush, Bobby 273
White, Jesse 318
Just Permanent Interests:
    Black Americans in Con-
    gress (William Clay) 58
Juvenile Delinquency Act
    251

K

Kansas 263–264
Kansas City (Missouri)
    61–62
Katrina (hurricane) 158,
    201, 223, 224
Katz, Martin 140
"Keepin' It Real with Al
    Sharpton" (radio) 280
Kelly, Edward J. 80
Kelly, Sharon Pratt Dixon
    14, 107, **175–176,** 322
Kennedy, Caroline 242
Kennedy, Edward (Ted)
    29, 34, 305
Kennedy, John F. x
    Clay, William 57
    Conyers, John 68
    Dawson, William 81
    Dymally, Mervyn 93
    Harris, Patricia Roberts
        136
    Jordan, Barbara 173
    Martin, Louis 198
    Paterson, David 242
    Powell, Adam Clayton,
        Jr. 251
    Stokes, Louis 287
    Washington, Walter
        304
    Weaver, Robert 312
Kennedy, Peggy Wallace
    74
Kentucky 3–4
Kentucky Commission on
    Human Rights 4
Kenya 232, 269
Kerry, John 270, 280
Keyes, Alan **176–178,** 234
Khalid Sheik Mohammed
    152
Kilpatrick, Carolyn 66,
    178–179, *179,* 180
Kilpatrick, Kwame
    179–181
King, Coretta Scott 198

King, Martin Luther, Jr.
    Baker, Ella 9–10
    Bond, Julian 23
    Brooke, Edward 30
    Cleaver, Emanuel 61
    Conyers, John 68
    Dawson, William
        80–81
    Fauntroy, Walter 105
    Jackson, Jesse 159
    Jackson, Maynard 164
    Martin, Louis 198
    Obama, Barack 234
    Patrick, Deval 243
    Stokes, Louis 287
    Washington, Walter
        304
    Wilder, Doug 320
    Williams, Hosea 326
    Young, Andy (Andrew)
        330
King, Martin Luther, III
    73
King, Rodney 27–28, 90,
    116
King Birthday Holiday
    legislation 68, 106, 131–
    132, 271, 302
Kirk, Ron xiv, **181–182**
Koch, Edward I. 90, 110
Korean War 20, 68, 101,
    259, 320
Ku Klux Klan 77, 95, 96,
    154, 190–191, 264, 300,
    332
Kuwait 253, 276
Kuykendall, Daniel 112

L

Labor, U.S. Department of
    70, 149–150
Labor Statistics, U.S.
    Bureau of 66
labor unions 5, 20, 57, 68,
    70, 115, 143, 239,
    332–333
land redistribution viii,
    43–44, 46, 47, 82, 297
Landrieu, Mitch 224
Lane, Mark 130
Langston, John vii, **183–**
    184, 225, 278
LAPD. *See* Los Angeles
    Police Department
    (LAPD)

LaRouche, Lyndon H. 157
Latin America 186
law enforcement 27–28,
    32–33, 134, 285, 295.
    See also crime
    prevention; police
lawyers. *See* attorneys
Lebanon 160
Lee, Barbara 48, **184–
    186,** *185*
Lee, Robert E. 320
Lee-Jackson Day 320
Leland, Mickey **186–187**
Leopold II (king of the
    Belgians) 326
Lewinsky, Monica 152
Lewis, John xvi, 23, **187–
    189,** *188*
liberal Democrats 151,
    242, 309, 315
liberalism 34, 63, 78, 79,
    109, 189
Liberator, The 213
Liberia 44, 200
libraries 238, 239
Library of Congress 329
lieutenant governors
    Dymally, Mervyn 93,
        94
    Fulani, Lenora 121
    Moseley Braun, Carol
        218
    Paterson, David 242
    Pinchback, P. B. S. 249
    Ransier, Alonzo 261
    Rogers, Joe 270–271
    Steele, Michael
        283–284
    Wilder, Doug 320
Light in Dark Places
    (Murray) 221
Limbaugh, Rush 284
Lincoln, Abraham vii–viii
Lincoln League 54–55
Lincolnville 44
literacy 245, 277
literacy tests 82, 95, 261
Livable Wage Act of 1995
    63
lobbying 20, 34, 85, 107,
    112, 182, 237, 246, 316
local government xii, xiv,
    140, 299. *See also* city
    government; county
    government

Locher, Ralph 285
Long, Jefferson **189–191,**
    190
Looby, Alexander **191–
    192,** 324
Los Angeles (California)
    Bradley, Tom 26,
        27–28
    Burke, Yvonne 39–40
    Dixon, Julian 91, 92
    Dymally, Mervyn 93,
        94
    Foster, Ezola 116
    Gregory, Dick 129
    Hawkins, Augustus
        141–143
    Millender-McDonald,
        Juanita 208–209
    Waters, Maxine
        305–306
    Watson, Diane
        306–307
Los Angeles Police
    Department (LAPD)
    27–28, 116
Los Angeles Rams 26
Los Angeles riots 27, 39,
    129
lotteries 259
Louima, Abner 279
Louisiana viii, 108–110,
    168–169, 226, 247–249
Lower Mississippi Delta
    Congressional Caucus
    98
Lower Mississippi River
    Valley Delta
    Development Act of
    1988 98
Loyalist Democrats 102,
    147
Loyless, Tom 76
Luxembourg 136
Lynch, John viii, **192–194**
lynching 263, 283. *See also*
    antilynching law
Lyons, Henry 31

M
machine politics 2–3, 8,
    81, 112, 113, 205, 206,
    275, 299, 302
MacLaine, Shirley 21
Madden, Martin B. 80,
    85–86

Majette, Denise **195–196,**
    201
Malcolm X 97
Mandela Freedom
    Resolution 70–71
Manhattan (New York)
    90, 156–157, 220
Manpower Development
    and Training Act of
    1962 (and 1964) 251
marches. *See*
    demonstrations and
    protests; specific *march*
March on Washington
    (1963) 105, 188
Marine Corps, U.S. 83,
    89
marriage 242, 258, 325
Marsh, Henry **196–197**
Marshall, Thurgood 198,
    220
Martin, Louis x, **197–198**
Martinez, Mel 158, 204,
    284
Marxism 115. *See also*
    Communist Party
Maryland 71–72, 177,
    207–208, 214–215, 283–
    284, 327–329
Maryland Legislative Black
    Caucus 71
Masell, Sam 164
Massachusetts vii, x, xv,
    28–30, 213, 243–244
Matthews, Michael J.
    298–299
Maximilian 325
Mayersville (Mississippi)
    21
mayoral candidates
    Burris, Roland 41
    Davis, Danny K. 78
    Fattah, Chaka 104
    Fauntroy, Walter 107
    Fulani, Lenora 121
    Gregory, Dick 129–130
    Harris, Patricia Roberts
        136
    Hatcher, Richard 141
    Jackson, Jesse 159
    Jackson, Maynard 164
    Jefferson, William 168
    Johnson, Harvey 171
    Moseley Braun, Carol
        219

Rush, Bobby 274
Sharpton, Al 280
Williams, Hosea 327
mayors x, xi, xiv. *See also*
    mayoral candidates
    Archer, Dennis 4–6
    Arrington, Richard
        7–8
    Barry, Marion 12–14
    Belton, Sharon 14–15
    Berry, Ted 15–17
    Blackwell, Ken 19
    Blackwell, Unita 21
    Booker, Cory 23–25
    Bosley, Freeman 25–26
    Bradley, Tom 26–28
    Brown, Lee 32–33
    Brown, Willie 35
    Campbell, Bill 44,
        45–46
    Cleaver, Emanuel
        61–62
    Coleman, Michael
        64–65
    Dellums, Ron 83, 85
    Dinkins, David 89,
        90–91
    Dixon, Sheila 92–93
    Evers, Charles 101–102
    Fenty, Adrian M.
        107–108
    Franklin, Shirley
        117–118
    Fudge, Marcia L. 120
    Gantt, Harvey
        123–124
    Gibson, Kenneth
        124–126
    Goode, W. W. 126–127
    Harmon, Clarence
        134–135
    Hatcher, Richard
        139–141
    Hayes, James 144–145
    Herenton, Willie
        147–149
    Jackson, Maynard
        163–165
    James, Sharpe 166–167
    Johnson, Harvey
        171–172
    Kelly, Sharon Pratt
        Dixon 175–176
    Kilpatrick, Kwame
        179–181

Kirk, Ron 181–182
Marsh, Henry 196–197
Morial, Dutch 216–217
Nagin, Ray 223–224
Nutter, Michael
230–231
Perry, Carrie 246–247
Powell, Debra 254–256
Rice, Norm 268
Schmoke, Kurt
276–278
Stokes, Carl 284–286
Street, John 288–290
Thompson, Bennie
292
Usry, James 298–299
Walls, Josiah 301
Washington, Harold
302–303
Washington, Walter
303–305
Webb, Wellington
313–315
White, Michael
318–320
Wilder, Doug 320–322
Williams, Anthony
322–324
Young, Andy (Andrew)
330–332
Young, Coleman
332–334
McCain, John 178,
234–235
McCall, Carl xiv,
198–200
McCarran Internal
Security Act 76
McCarthyism 333
McGovern, George 52
McKinley, William 6, 7,
38
McKinley Tariff 50
McKinney, Billy 200
McKinney, Cynthia 195,
200–202, *201*
McKissick, Floyd 60, 123.
See also Soul City
Foundation
McMillan, John L. 106
*McSwain v. Board of
Anderson County,
Tennessee* 192
Medicare 67, 113, 291,
294, 307

Medicare Catastrophic
Coverage Act 291
medicine. *See* health and
medicine
Meek, Carrie 31, **202–
203**
Meek, Kendrick **203–204**
Meeks, Gregory *204,*
204–205
Melton, Frank 172
Memphis (Tennessee)
54–55, 111, 112–114,
147–149, 159
Merrill Lynch 114
Metcalfe, Ralph 81, **205–
207,** *206,* 302
Mexico 325
MFDP. *See* Mississippi
Freedom Democratic
Party (MFDP)
Mfume, Kweisi 71, 72, 92,
207–208
Miami (Florida) 202
Michigan 65–66, 68–71,
87–89, 178–179, 180
Michigan Chronicle 197,
198
Michigan Legislative Black
Caucus 65
Micronesia 307
Mid-America Regional
Council 315
middle class xii–xiii
Middle East 160
Mikulski, Barbara 177
military aid 88
military desegregation 38,
57, 137, 282
military-industrial complex
84
military spending
Dellums, Ron 83, 84
Espy, Mike 99
Fields, Cleo 109
Fulani, Lenora 121
Gray, Bill 128
Lee, Barbara 186
Owens, Major 239
Savage, Gus 276
Washington, Harold
302
Young, Andy (Andrew)
331
Millender-McDonald,
Juanita 208–210, 306

Miller, Thomas **210–211,**
221, 283
Miller, Zell 11, 196
Million Man March (1995)
327
Minimum Wage Act of
1961 251
minimum wage law 4, 63,
79, 215, 239, 251, 278
ministry
Arnett, Benjamin 6, 7
Cain, Richard 43, 44
Cardozo, Francis 46
Cleaver, Emanuel 61
Fauntroy, Walter 105,
107
Flake, Floyd 110, 111
Goode, W. W. 127
Gray, Bill 128
Hayes, James 144
Jackson, Jesse 159
McCall, Carl 199
Powell, Adam Clayton,
Jr. 250
Revels, Hiram 264
Rush, Bobby 273–274
Sharpton, Al 279
Watts, J. C. 309–310
Williams, George 325
Young, Andy (Andrew)
330
Minneapolis (Minnesota)
14–15, 97
Minnesota 15, 97
Minority Business
Development Act 208
Minority Business
Enterprise Legal
Defense and Education
Fund 215
minority-owned businesses
Collins, Cardiss 67
Dymally, Mervyn 94
Gray, Bill 128
Herenton, Willie 148
Jackson, Maynard 164
Johnson, Harvey
171–172
Kilpatrick, Carolyn
179
Leland, Mickey 187
Meek, Carrie 202
Meeks, Gregory 205
Metcalfe, Ralph 206
Mfume, Kweisi 208

Mitchell, Parren 214,
215
Morial, Dutch 217
Perry, Carrie 246
Powell, Debra 255
Ross, Don 271
Savage, Gus 276
Stokes, Louis 287
Street, John 289
Towns, Edolphus 294
Tubbs Jones, Stephanie
295
Waters, Maxine 305
Wynn, Albert 328, 329
minority set-asides. *See*
set-asides
miscegenation xv. *See also*
interracial marriage
missiles 84
Mississippi viii
Baker, Ella 9–10
Blackwell, Unita 21–
22
Bruce, Blanche 37–39
Diggs, Charles 88
Espy, Mike 98–99
Evers, Charles 101–102
Gregory, Dick 129
Henry, Aaron 145–147
Howard, Perry 153
Johnson, Harvey
171–172
Lynch, John 192–194
Revels, Hiram
264–266
Thompson, Bennie
292–293
Mississippi Action
Community Education
21
Mississippi Delta 98, 101
Mississippi Freedom
Democratic Party
(MFDP) x, 9, 10, 21,
68, 101, 102, 147
Mississippi Project of the
National Lawyers Guild
70
Missouri 25–26, 57–58,
58–59, 61–62, 315–316
Mitchell, Arthur 71, 80,
87, 205, **211–213**
Mitchell, Charles vii, **213**
Mitchell, Parren 207, 208,
214, **214–215**

Mitchell v. United States et al. (1941) 212
Model Cities program 202, 313
moderate Democrats 168, 204, 205, 228, 278, 296, 321, 327
Moffett, Toby 119
Montgomery (Alabama) 9, 159, 188, 326
Montreal Expos 323
Moore, Gwen **215–216**
Morales, Victor 182
Morehouse College 290–291, 332
More Perfect Union: Advancing New American Rights, A (Jesse Jackson, Jr.) 162
Morgan, Garrett 281
Morgan Technology and Transportation Futures Program 281
Morial, Dutch 168, **216–217**
Morial, Marc 168, 216
mortgage crisis 158. *See also* home ownership
Mosbacher, Robert, Jr. 33
Moseley Braun, Carol 40, **217–219,** 232
Motley, Constance **219–221,** 220
motor vehicle safety 318
MOVE (Philadelphia) 127
Mozambique 88
MSNBC (TV) 114, 177
Muigwithania 140
municipal services 126, 171–172, 255, 285, 314, 319
Murphy, William T. 275
Murray, George 62, 211, **221–222**
music 238, 306, 319
Muslims xiv, 48, 97

N

NAACP. *See* National Association for the Advancement of Colored People (NAACP)
NAFTA. *See* North American Free Trade Agreement (NAFTA)

Nagin, Ray **223–224**
NAP. *See* New Alliance Party (NAP)
Napier, James ix, **224–226**
NASA. *See* National Aeronautics and Space Administration (NASA)
Nash, Charles **226–227**
Nashville (Tennessee) 13, 191–192, 224–226, 324
National Aeronautics and Space Administration (NASA) 179
National Association for the Advancement of Colored People (NAACP)
  Anderson, Charles W., Jr. 4
  Baker, Ella 9
  Barry, Marion 13
  Berry, Ted 16, 17
  Bond, Julian 23
  Bosley, Freeman 26
  Brown, Willie 35
  Burris, Roland 41
  Davis, Ben 75
  DePriest, Oscar 86
  Evers, Charles 101
  Harmon, Clarence 134
  Henry, Aaron 145–146
  Mfume, Kweisi 72, 208
  Motley, Constance 220
  Patrick, Deval 243
  Powell, Adam Clayton, Jr. 250
  Scott, Bobby 278
  Williams, Hosea 326
National Basketball Association (NBA) 124, 181
National Breast Cancer Awareness Month 67
National Campaign to Prevent Teenage Pregnancy 60
National Capital Housing Authority 304
National Catfish Day 98
National Coalition Against Sexual Assault 15

National Commission on the International Year of the Child 22
National Conference of Black Mayors (NCBM) xi, 13, 21, 62, 102, 141, 299, 314
National Council of Churches (NCC) 330
National Council of Negro Women 21
National Council on Health Planning and Development 293
National Defense Advisory Committee 312
National Defense Rail Act 49
National Democratic Club 140
National Endowment for the Humanities (NEH) 67
National Equal Rights League (NERL) 6, 184
National Football League (NFL) 319
National Housing Authority 312
National Housing Trust Fund 59
National Institutes of Health 328–329
National Labor Relations Board (NLRB) 164
National Lawyers Guild 70
National League of Cities 167
National Literacy Institute 245
National Medical Association 208
National Negro Business League 225
National Negro Congress (NNC) 75, 250
National Negro Labor Council 333
National Negro Labor Union (NNLU) 264
National Newspaper Publishers Association 197
National Political Congress of Black Women 52, 305

National Rifle Association (NRA) 18, 99
National Science Foundation 166
National Security Advisor 267
National Security Council 253, 266, 269
National Service Act 245
National Slavery Museum 321
National Urban League 35
National Voter Registration Act of 1993 69
National Women's Committee for Civil Rights 136
National Youth Administration 311
National Youth Movement 279
Native Americans 129, 130, 154, 187, 313
Natural Law Party 122
Navy, U.S. 193
NBA. *See* National Basketball Association (NBA)
NCBM. *See* National Conference of Black Mayors (NCBM)
NCC. *See* National Council of Churches (NCC)
needle-exchange programs 72, 277, 291
Neely, Matthew M. 70
Negro Ghetto, The (Weaver) 312
Negro Liberator 75
Negro Manpower Commission 312
NEH. *See* National Endowment for the Humanities (NEH)
neighborhood associations 24, 32–33, 64, 107, 205
Neighborhood Oriented Policing (NOP) 32–33
Neilsen Media Research 67
Nelson, Wayne 145
NERL. *See* National Equal Rights League (NERL)

New Alliance Party
(NAP) xiii, 121. *See
also* Reform Party
Newark (New Jersey)
23–25, 124–126, 166–
167, 245
Newark Now 24
New Deal ix–x, 80, 87,
197–198, 212, 311–312
New Democratic Coalition
114
New Frontier 251
New Jersey 162–163, 237,
244–246
New Jersey Conference of
Mayors 167
New Markets Initiative 169
New Orleans (Louisiana)
158, 168, 169, 216–217,
223–224, 226, 247. *See
also* Katrina (hurricane)
"New South" 124, 171
New Towns program 60
New York City x. *See also*
September 11, 2001
Anderson, Charles W.
2–3
Brown, Lee 32
Brown, Ron 34
Chisholm, Shirley 51
Davis, Ben 74–76
Dinkins, David 89–91
Flake, Floyd 110
Ford, James 115
Fulani, Lenora 121–122
Jack, Hulan 156–157
McCall, Carl 199
Meeks, Gregory
204–205
Motley, Constance
219–220
Owens, Major
238–239
Paterson, David 242
Powell, Adam Clayton,
Jr. 249–252
Rangel, Charles
259–260
Sharpton, Al 279–280
Towns, Edolphus 294
Usry, James 298
Washington, Walter
304
Weaver, Robert 312,
313

New York City Colored
Republican Club 3
New York City Housing
and Development Board
312
New York City Housing
Authority 304
New York Civil Rights Law
of 1895 3
New York Giants 157
New York Renaissance
(basketball team) 298
New York State
Anderson, Charles W.
2–3
Chisholm, Shirley
51–52
Clarke, Yvette D. 56
Flake, Floyd 110–111
Fulani, Lenora
120–122
Jack, Hulan 156
McCall, Carl 198–200
Meeks, Gregory
204–205
Motley, Constance 220
Owens, Major
238–239
Paterson, David
241–243
Powell, Adam Clayton,
Jr. 249–252
Rangel, Charles 259
Sharpton, Al 280
Towns, Edolphus 293
New Zealand 219
NFL. *See* National Football
League (NFL)
Nicaragua 287–288
Nichols, John F. 333
Nigeria 217
Nike 332
9/11 Commission 267, 293.
See also September 11,
2001
Nix, Robert 128, **227–
228**, *228*
Nixon, Richard M. xi, xii
Brooke, Edward 30
Clay, William 57
Conyers, John 68
Dellums, Ron 84, 85
Diggs, Charles 88
Evans, Melvin 100
Ford, Harold 112

Hawkins, Augustus 142
Jordan, Barbara 173
Lewis, John 188
Martin, Louis 198
Stokes, Louis 287
Weaver, Robert 313
Young, Andy (Andrew)
331
NLRB (National Labor
Relations Board) 164
NNC. *See* National Negro
Congress (NNC)
NNLU. *See* National
Negro Labor Union
(NNLU)
No Child Left Behind Act
of 2001 113, 240–241
NOP. *See* Neighborhood
Oriented Policing (NOP)
Noriega, Manuel 253
North Africa 298
North American Free
Trade Agreement
(NAFTA) 60, 181
North Carolina viii–ix,
11–12, 49–50, 59–61,
154–155, 235–236, 308–
309, 316–317
North Carolina Hunger
Forum 61
North Carolina
Intercollegiate Council
on Human Rights 159
North Carolina
Orphanage for Negros
50
North Korea 267
Norton, Eleanor Holmes
228–230
NRA. *See* National Rifle
Association (NRA)
nuclear power 126
nuclear waste 237
nuclear weapons 83, 84,
234, 267
Nutter, Michael xiv,
230–231

O

Oakland (California) 83,
85, 184–186
Obama, Barack xv–xvi,
232–235, *233*
Brooke, Edward 30
Burris, Roland 41

Conyers, John 69
Davis, Artur 73, 74
Davis, Danny K. 79
Fattah, Chaka 104
Holder, Eric 152
Jackson, Jesse, Jr. 162
Jackson, Lisa P. 163
Keyes, Alan 177
Kirk, Ron 182
Lewis, John 188
Paterson, David 242
Patrick, Deval 244
Powell, Colin 254
Rice, Condoleezza 267
Rice, Susan E. 270
Steele, Michael 284
White, Jesse 318
Oberlin College vii, ix, 37,
183
Occupational Safety and
Health Administration
(OSHA) 239
Odd Fellows Block
(Atlanta) 77
Office of Economic
Opportunity (OEO) 16
Officer, Carl 254
O'Hara, James viii–ix, 50,
235–237
Ohio vii, ix, 6–7, 19, 69,
119–120, 183, 286–288,
294–295, 325–326
Ohio State Anti-Slavery
Society 183
oil spills 152, 163, 235
Oklahoma 271–272,
309–311
Oklahoma Eagle 271
O'Leary, Hazel xiii,
237–238
O'Leary, John 237
Olympic Games 27, 45,
205–206, 330, 331
O'Malley, Martin 92
"One Florida" program
203
*Open Letter to His Serene
Majesty, Leopold II, King
of the Belgians, An*
(George Williams) 326
Operation Breadbasket
159
Operation Break
(Hartford, Connecticut)
247

Operation Desert Storm 253, 254

Operation Iraqi Freedom 254

Operation PUSH (People United to Save Humanity) 41, 159, 161

Oregon 32, 33

organized labor. *See* labor unions

OSHA. *See* Occupational Safety and Health Administration (OSHA)

Oswald, Lee Harvey 287

Owens, Bill 270–271

Owens, Chris 56

Owens, Major 56, **238–239**

P

Pagones, Steven 279–280

Paige, Rod xiv, **240–241**

Palestine 160, 201, 267, 276

Palestine Liberation Organization (PLO) 71, 331

Panama 71, 206, 253, 276

Panama Canal 206

Parental and Medical Leave Act of 1993 58

Parks, Rosa 6, 179

Paterson, Basil 241

Paterson, David **241–243**

Patrick, Deval xiv, xv, **243–244**

Patriot Party. *See* Reform Party

patronage ix
  Anderson, Charles W. 2–3
  Arrington, Richard 8
  Brooke, Edward 29
  Church, Robert 54, 55
  Davis, Benjamin J. 76, 77
  Davis, Danny K. 78
  Dawson, William 81
  DePriest, Oscar 86
  Haralson, Jeremiah 133
  Howard, Perry 153
  Metcalfe, Ralph 206
  Murray, George 221
  Napier, James 225

Nash, Charles 226

O'Hara, James 236

Washington, Harold 302

Patton, Boggs and Blow 34

Payne, Donald **244–246,** *245*

Peace Dividend Housing Act of 1990 110

Pell grants 245

Peña, Federico 313, 314

Pennington, Richard 223

Pennsylvania 1, 20, 227–228

pensions 58, 86, 133, 142, 221, 297. *See also* Social Security

People's Voice 250

Perot, H. Ross 117, 121

Perry, Carrie **246–247**

Philadelphia (Mississippi) 101

Philadelphia (Pennsylvania) 1–2, 20, 55, 103–105, 126–127, 127–129, 227–228, 230–231, 288–290

Pinchback, P. B. S. viii, 109, **247–249,** *248*

Pitts, Rob 118

Platt, Thomas C. 3

Plessy v. Ferguson (1896) 212

PLO. *See* Palestine Liberation Organization (PLO)

police
  Barry, Marion 13
  Bosley, Freeman 26
  Bradley, Tom 26–27
  Brown, Lee 32–33
  Dellums, Ron 85
  Foster, Ezola 116
  Gregory, Dick 130
  Harmon, Clarence 134
  Jackson, Maynard 164
  Kilpatrick, Kwame 180
  Meek, Kendrick 203
  Moore, Gwen 216
  Nutter, Michael 230
  Perry, Carrie 247
  Stokes, Carl 285

police brutality
  Arrington, Richard 7
  Bradley, Tom 27–28

  Brown, Lee 32–33
  Clay, William 57
  Coleman, Michael 65
  Conyers, John 68–69
  Davis, Ben 76
  Metcalfe, Ralph 206–207
  Rush, Bobby 273
  Scott, Bobby 278
  Sharpton, Al 279, 280
  Washington, Harold 302
  Young, Coleman 333–334

political establishment, changes in xv

political machines. *See* machine politics

poll taxes 80, 95, 250–251, 258

Poor People's Campaign 159

"poor power" 83

Portugal 88

postal system 57, 66, 115, 332, 333

postracism xv

Post-Tribune (Gary, Indiana) 271

poverty 16, 24, 63, 83–84, 202, 216, 236, 251

Powell, Adam Clayton, Jr. 75–76, **249–252,** *251,* 259–260, 279

Powell, Colin xiv, 74, **252–254,** *253,* 267

Powell, Debra **254–256,** *255*

"Powell Amendment" 251

Powell v. McCormack 252

Prager, Dennis 97

Pratt, Sharon. *See* Kelly, Sharon Pratt Dixon

prescription drug coverage 59, 113, 307, 320

presidential candidates xi, xii, xiii, xv–xvi. *See also* vice presidential candidates
  Chisholm, Shirley 51, 52
  Fulani, Lenora 120–122
  Gregory, Dick 129–130
  Jackson, Jesse 158–160

  Keyes, Alan 176, 177–178
  McKinney, Cynthia 201
  Moseley Braun, Carol 219
  Sharpton, Al 279–280

Presidential Medal of Freedom 30, 160

presidents, U.S. (Barack Obama) 232–235

President's Commission on HIV and AIDS 291

PRIME. *See* Program for Investment in Microentrepreneurs (PRIME)

Prince George's County (Maryland) 328

privatization 45, 310

Program for Investment in Microentrepreneurs (PRIME) 273

Progressive Party 275, 333

Project Build (Los Angeles) 305

PROJECT VOTE 232

Proposition 187 (California) 116

public education viii
  Cain, Richard 44
  Cardozo, Francis 46–47
  Clay, William, Jr. 59
  Cummings, Elijah 72
  DeLarge, Robert 82
  Flake, Floyd 111
  Ford, Harold, Jr. 113
  Foster, Ezola 117
  Jackson, Alphonso 157–158
  Jackson, Jesse, Jr. 162
  Kilpatrick, Kwame 179
  Lee, Barbara 186
  Meek, Kendrick 203–204
  Owens, Major 238
  Payne, Donald 245
  Rapier, James 264

public housing 24, 73, 79, 110, 136, 140, 157, 167

public transportation 31, 49, 79, 157, 167

Pucciarelli, Nicholas 103–104

Puerto Rico 54, 136, 137
PUSH. *See* Operation
   PUSH
PUSH-Excel 159

Q
al-Qaeda 269
Queens (New York City)
   110–111, 204–205
Qur'an 97

R
Race Ideals (Murray) 221
race relations 137, 171,
   221, 226, 234, 312
race riots. *See* riots
racial profiling 15, 69, 72.
   See also Traffic Stops
   Statistics Study Act of
   1999
racism ix, x. *See also*
   apartheid;
   discrimination; white
   supremacy
   Arrington, Richard
      7–8
   Bradley, Tom 27–28
   Cleaver, Emanuel 61
   Davis, Ben 75, 76
   Davis, Benjamin J. 77
   Dawson, William 80
   Dellums, Ron 84
   Gregory, Dick 130
   Harris, Patricia Roberts
      135
   Jackson, Alphonso
      158
   Jackson, Maynard 164
   Mitchell, Arthur 212
   Young, Coleman
      333–334
Radical Republicans viii,
   96
radio 37, 46, 67, 97, 114–
   115, 122, 254, 311, 329.
   See also talk radio
railroad industry 49, 209,
   212, 236, 301, 319
Rainbow Coalition 159,
   160, 161
Rainey, Joseph 96, **257–
   259,** 258
Ralston-Purina 26, 134
Rangel, Charles 113, 252,
   259, **259–261**

Ransier, Alonzo *261,*
   261–262
Rapier, James 133,
   262–264
rap music 238, 306
Read to Lead 104
Reagan, Ronald xii, 52
   Chisholm, Shirley 52
   Conyers, John 69
   Crockett, George W.
      70, 71
   Dellums, Ron 85
   Evans, Melvin 100
   Fauntroy, Walter 106
   Ford, Harold, Jr. 113
   Gray, Bill 128
   Hall, Katie 132
   Harris, Patricia Roberts
      136
   Hawkins, Augustus
      142
   Herman, Alexis 149
   Holder, Eric 152
   Johnson, Eddie Bernice
      170
   Keyes, Alan 177
   Lewis, John 188
   Marsh, Henry 197
   Norton, Eleanor
      Holmes 229
   Powell, Colin 253
   Rangel, Charles 260
   Steele, Michael 283
   Stokes, Louis 287–288
   Sullivan, Louis 291
   Washington, Harold
      302
   Williams, Hosea 327
"Reagan Revolution" 142
reapportionment
   (redistricting). *See also*
   gerrymandering
   Ballance, Frank 12
   Bishop, Sanford 17–18
   Bond, Julian 22
   Brown, Corrine 31
   Burke, Yvonne 40
   Cheatham, Henry 50
   Chisholm, Shirley 51
   Clay, William 57
   Clyburn, James 63
   Davis, Artur 73
   Davis, Ben 75
   Fields, Cleo 109
   Henry, Aaron 147

Hilliard, Earl 151
Johnson, Eddie Bernice
   170–171
Jordan, Barbara 173
Lewis, John 189
Lynch, John 193
Marsh, Henry 196
McKinney, Cynthia
   200, 201
Mitchell, Parren 215
Moseley Braun, Carol
   217
Powell, Adam Clayton,
   Jr. 250
Rogers, Joe 271
Savage, Gus 276
Scott, Bobby 278, 279
Stokes, Louis 286–287
Watt, Mel 308–309
Wilder, Doug 321
Wynn, Albert 328, 329
Reconstruction vii–viii
   Bruce, Blanche 37, 38
   Cain, Richard 43
   Cardozo, Francis 46,
      47
   Church, Robert 55
   DeLarge, Robert 81, 82
   Elliot, Robert 95, 96
   Haralson, Jeremiah
      132
   Lynch, John 193, 194
   Miller, Thomas 210
   Murray, George 221
   Nash, Charles 226
   Pinchback, P. B. S. 249
   Rainey, Joseph 257
   Ransier, Alonzo 261
   Rapier, James 263–264
   Smalls, Robert 281
   Walls, Josiah 300
Reconstruction Acts 221,
   261
"redlining" 206
Red Shirts 282
Reform Party xiii, 116–
   117, 121–122
Regan, Edward 199
Reid, Hazel. *See* O'Leary,
   Hazel
religion. *See* ministry;
   specific church
Rendell, Edward G. 289
Reno, Janet 152
reparations 151, 272, 297

representatives, U.S. *See*
   House of
   Representatives, U.S.
Republican American
   Committee 55, 191
Republican National
   Committee (RNC) 19,
   283–284
Republican National
   Convention (1870) 96
Republican National
   Convention (1872) 191
Republican National
   Convention (1880) 263,
   296
Republican National
   Convention (1884) 193
Republican National
   Convention (1892) 50
Republican National
   Convention (1896) 7
Republican National
   Convention (1908) 77
Republican National
   Convention (1912) 153
Republican National
   Convention (1916) 77
Republican National
   Convention (1920) 86
Republican National
   Convention (1936) 87
Republican National
   Convention (1964) 29
Republican National
   Convention (1976) 2
Republican National
   Convention (1988) 291
Republican National
   Convention (2000) 310
Republican Party vii–viii,
   ix, x, xiv, xv
   Allen, Ethel 1–2
   Anderson, Charles W.
      2–3
   Anderson, Charles W.,
      Jr. 4
   Arnett, Benjamin 6
   Baker, Ella 10
   Ballance, Frank 12
   Blackwell, Ken 19
   Brooke, Edward 28, 29
   Bruce, Blanche 38
   Cain, Richard 43
   Cardozo, Francis 46
   Cheatham, Henry 50

Church, Robert 54–55
Clayton, Eva 60
Davis, Ben 74
Davis, Benjamin J. 76, 77
Dawson, William 80
DeLarge, Robert 81, 82
DePriest, Oscar 85–86
Elliot, Robert 95, 96
Evans, Melvin 100
Evers, Charles 102
Foster, Ezola 116
Franks, Gary 118
Haralson, Jeremiah 132
Howard, Perry 153–154
Hyman, John 154
Jackson, Alphonso 157
Keyes, Alan 176
Langston, John 184
Long, Jefferson 190
Looby, Alexander 192
Lynch, John 193
Miller, Thomas 210
Mitchell, Arthur 212
Mitchell, Charles 213
Murray, George 221
Napier, James 225
O'Hara, James 236
Paige, Rod 240
Pinchback, P. B. S. 247
Powell, Adam Clayton, Jr. 251
Rainey, Joseph 257
Ransier, Alonzo 261
Rapier, James 263
Revels, Hiram 264
Rogers, Joe 270
Smalls, Robert 282
Turner, Benjamin 297
Usry, James 298
Walls, Josiah 301
Watts, J. C. 310
White, George 316
Williams, George 325
Williams, Hosea 327
Reserve Officers Training Corps (ROTC) 28, 34, 252
Responsible Fatherhood Act 49
Resurrection City 159
Reuther, Walter 333

Revels, Hiram viii, **264–266,** 265
Reynolds, Mel 161, 276
Reynolds v. Sims x–xi
Rhodesia (Zimbabwe) 88
Rhodes scholars 24, 269, 276, 277
Rice, Condoleezza xiv, 74, 97, 254, **266–268,** 267
Rice, Norm **268–269**
Rice, Ronald 24
Rice, Susan E. **269–270**
Rice University 32
Rich, Marc 152
Richmond, Frederick W. 294
Richmond (Virginia) 196–197, 321–322
riots
   Barry, Marion 13
   Bradley, Tom 27–28
   Brooke, Edward 30
   Burke, Yvonne 39
   Gibson, Kenneth 125
   Gregory, Dick 129
   Hilliard, Earl 151
   Ross, Don 271, 272
   Stokes, Carl 285–286
   Washington, Walter 304
RNC. *See* Republican National Committee (RNC)
Robb, Chuck 320, 321
Rock and Roll Hall of Fame 319
Rodino, Peter 245
Rogers, Joe **270–271**
Roman Catholic Church 314
Roosevelt, Eleanor 55
Roosevelt, Franklin D. ix, 55, 115, 137, 141, 143–144, 212, 250, 311–312
Roosevelt, Theodore 3
Ross, Don **271–272**
Rostenkowski, Dan 152
ROTC. *See* Reserve Officers Training Corps (ROTC)
Rubin, Robert 244
rum industry 54
Rush, Bobby 144, 233, **272–274,** 273
Rwanda 246

Ryan, Geri 234
Ryan, Jack 177, 233, 234

S
Sabo, Martin 97
Sahel 88
Saltonstall, Leverett 29
same-sex marriage 242
Sanchez, Tony 182
sanctions 91, 177, 187. *See also* divestiture
San Francisco (California) 35, 36–37, 83
Sarbanes, Paul 177, 284
Savage, Gus **275–276**
Savannah (Georgia) 326
SBA. *See* Small Business Administration (SBA)
scandals. *See also* corruption
   Ballance, Frank 11, 12
   Barry, Marion 13, 14
   Bishop, Sanford 17–18
   Blackwell, Ken 19
   Brown, Corrine 31
   Brown, Ron 35
   Collins, Barbara-Rose 66
   Conyers, John 69
   DePriest, Oscar 86–87
   Hayes, Charles 144
   Jack, Hulan 156, 157
   McKinney, Cynthia 200–201, 201
   Murray, George 221
   Obama, Barack 234
   O'Leary, Hazel 237, 238
   Paige, Rod 241
   Paterson, David 241, 242–243
   Patrick, Deval 244
   Powell, Adam Clayton, Jr. 252
   Steele, Michael 284
   Street, John 288–289
   Williams, Anthony 323
   Williams, Hosea 327
   Young, Coleman 333–334
Schaefer, William Donald 277
Schafer, Donald 207–208
Schmoke, Kurt **276–278**

Schoemehl, Vincent 25
school desegregation xiii
   Blackwell, Unita 21
   Bosley, Freeman 26
   Clay, William, Jr. 58
   Cleaver, Emanuel 61
   DeLarge, Robert 82
   Diggs, Charles 88
   Herman, Alexis 149
   Looby, Alexander 192
   Marsh, Henry 196
   Motley, Constance 220
   Ransier, Alonzo 262
   Rice, Norm 268
   Williams, Avon 324
School Improvement Act of 1987 144
school prayer 117
School-to-Work Opportunities Act 245
school vouchers 72, 111, 240
Schroeder, Pat 270
SCLC. *See* Southern Christian Leadership Conference (SCLC)
Scott, Bobby **278–279**
Scowcroft, Brent 266
Search for Education, Elevation, and Knowledge (SEEK) 51, 52
Seattle (Washington) 268
Seattle Foundation 269
Seattle Urban League 268
secretaries. *See* cabinet secretaries; state, secretaries of
Secret Service 200
SEEK. *See* Search for Education, Elevation, and Knowledge (SEEK)
segregation and desegregation. *See also* military desegregation; school desegregation
   Anderson, Charles W., Jr. 4
   Arnett, Benjamin 6
   Baker, Ella 9, 10
   Blackwell, Unita 21
   Bosley, Freeman 26
   Brooke, Edward 29
   Brown, Willie 35
   Bruce, Blanche 38

Burris, Roland 41
Clay, William 57
Cleaver, Emanuel 61
Davis, Ben 76
Dawson, William 80
DeLarge, Robert 82
Diggs, Charles 88
Evers, Charles 101
Gantt, Harvey 123
Hastie, William H. 137
Henry, Aaron 146
Herman, Alexis 149
Lewis, John 187–188
Looby, Alexander 192
Marsh, Henry 196
Morial, Dutch 216–217
Motley, Constance 220
Napier, James 225
Powell, Adam Clayton,
   Jr. 251
Rice, Norm 268
Weaver, Robert 312
Williams, Avon 324
Williams, George 325
Selma (Alabama) 151,
   159, 188, 296–297, 326
Senate, U.S. viii, x, xiv, xv
Brooke, Edward 28–30
Bruce, Blanche 37–39
Burris, Roland 41
Davis, Benjamin J. 77
DePriest, Oscar 86–87
Fauntroy, Walter 106
Henry, Aaron 147
Moseley Braun, Carol
   218–219
Obama, Barack 233
Pinchback, P. B. S. 249
Revels, Hiram
   264–266
Senate candidates
Burris, Roland 41
Ford, Harold, Jr. 114
Ford, James 115
Franks, Gary 119
Gantt, Harvey 123,
   124
Keyes, Alan 177
Kirk, Ron 182
Majette, Denise 196
Meek, Kendrick 204
Mfume, Kweisi 208
Sharpton, Al 280
Wilder, Doug 321
Williams, Hosea 327

Senate Ethics Committee
   41
Senate Judiciary
   Committee 34
"separate but equal" 212
September 11, 2001 152,
   186, 195, 201, 267, 293
Serbia 185
set-asides
Burke, Yvonne 40
Collins, Cardiss 67
Dymally, Mervyn 94
Gray, Bill 128
Herenton, Willie 148
Jackson, Maynard 164
Lewis, John 188
Meek, Carrie 202
Mfume, Kweisi 208
Millender-McDonald,
   Juanita 209
Mitchell, Parren 214,
   215
Powell, Debra 255
Savage, Gus 276
Street, John 289
Waters, Maxine 305
Wynn, Albert 329
Seventeenth Amendment
   249
74th U.S. Colored Infantry
   Regiment 247
sexual harassment 166,
   217, 276
Seychelles 286
Shakman decree 303
sharecropping 21, 145, 202
Sharpton, Al 24, 73,
   279–280
Shriver, R. Sargent, Jr. 16
sickle-cell anemia 173,
   273, 290
Sickle Cell Disease
   Control Month 173
Sinclair, Upton 141
Sissoko, Foutanga 31
sit-ins 10, 13, 22, 35, 192,
   203
Slater, Rodney xiii,
   280–281
slavery. *See also* abolition;
   antislavery movement
Bruce, Blanche 37
Cain, Richard 44
Cheatham, Henry 50
Conyers, John 69

DePriest, Oscar 86
Haralson, Jeremiah
   132
Hilliard, Earl 151
Hyman, John 154
Langston, John 183
Long, Jefferson 190
Lynch, John 192–193
Pinchback, P. B. S.
   247
Rainey, Joseph 257
Smalls, Robert 281
Turner, Benjamin 296
Walls, Josiah 300
White, George 316
Slay, Francis 26, 135
sleep-ins 61
Slim-Safe Bahamian Diet
   130
Small Business
   Administration (SBA)
   171, 215
small businesses 171, 181,
   215, 216, 273, 278, 306,
   329. *See also* minority-
   owned businesses
Smalls, Robert 210, **281–
   283,** *282*
Smith Act 76
Smith-Kline Beecham 316
SNCC. *See* Student
   Nonviolent
   Coordinating
   Committee (SNCC)
Snow, Butler 172
socialism 121
socialized medicine. *See*
   health and medicine
Social Security 203, 307.
   See also pensions
sociology 32, 214
Somalia 245
Soul City Foundation 60,
   123
South Africa 36. *See also*
   apartheid; divestiture
Crockett, George W.
   70–71
Dellums, Ron 84
Diggs, Charles 88
Dixon, Julian 91
Fauntroy, Walter 107
Gray, Bill 128
Keyes, Alan 177
Leland, Mickey 187

Mfume, Kweisi 208
Moseley Braun, Carol
   217
Perry, Carrie 246
Rangel, Charles 260
Waters, Maxine 305
Wheat, Alan 315
Wilder, Doug 321
Young, Andy (Andrew)
   331
South Carolina viii, ix
Cain, Richard 43–44
Cardozo, Francis
   46–47
Clyburn, James 62–64
DeLarge, Robert
   81–83
Elliot, Robert 95–96
Miller, Thomas
   210–211
Murray, George 221
Rainey, Joseph
   257–258
Ransier, Alonzo
   261–262
Smalls, Robert
   281–283
South Carolina Leader 43,
   95
South Carolina State
   University 210, 227
Southern Africa Enterprise
   Development Fund 332
Southern Christian
   Leadership Conference
   (SCLC) 9–10, 61, 105,
   146, 159, 326, 330
Southern Conference of
   Black Mayors xi. *See*
   also National
   Conference of Black
   Mayors (NCBM)
Southern Governors'
   Association 100, 321
Southern Pacific Railroad
   209
Southern Poverty Law
   Center 73
Southern Regional
   Council 149, 188, 212
South Korea 253
South Side (Chicago) 80,
   81, 143, 233
*Southwestern Christian
   Advocate* 264

Soviet Union 76, 84, 115, 266
Spanish-American War 194, 213, 283
Spanish language 187
Sparks, Ron 74
Spitzer, Eliot 241, 242
Spock, Benjamin 130
sports. *See* Olympic Games; *specific sport or team*
sports stadiums
    Archer, Dennis 5
    Booker, Cory 24
    Brown, Lee 33
    Jack, Hulan 157
    Kirk, Ron 181
    Powell, Debra 255
    White, Michael 319
St. Louis Cardinals 26, 255
St. Louis (Missouri) 25–26, 57, 58–59, 134–135, 254–256
Starr, Kenneth 152
state, secretaries of
    Illinois (Jesse White) 317–318
    Ohio (Ken Blackwell) 19
    Pennsylvania (Ethel Allen) 1–2
    South Carolina (Francis Cardozo) 47
    Texas (Ron Kirk) 181
State, U.S. Department of 176–177, 252–254, 266–268, 269
state government vii, viii, ix, xi, xii, xiv. *See also* governors; *specific state*
    Anderson, Charles W. 2–3
    Anderson, Charles W., Jr. 3–4
    Arnett, Benjamin 6–7
    Baker, Thurbert E. 10–11
    Bishop, Sanford 17–18
    Blackwell, Lucien 20
    Bond, Julian 22–23
    Brooke, Edward 29–30
    Brown, Corrine 31
    Brown, Willie 35–36
    Brown, Yvonne 39–40

Bruce, Blanche 37–38
Carson, André 47–48
Chisholm, Shirley 51–52
Clay, William, Jr. 58
Clyburn, James 63
Coleman, Michael 64
Collins, Barbara-Rose 65
Collins, Cardiss 66
Conyers, John 68
Cummings, Elijah 71–72
DeLarge, Robert 82
Dellums, Ron 83
DePriest, Oscar 86
Diggs, Charles 87–88
Dinkins, David 89
Dixon, Julian 91
Dixon, Sheila 92
Dymally, Mervyn 93
Elliot, Robert 95–96
Espy, Mike 98
Evans, Melvin 100
Fattah, Chaka 103–104
Fields, Cleo 108, 109
Ford, Harold 111–112
Fudge, Marcia L. 120
Fulani, Lenora 121
Gibson, Kenneth 125
Goode, W. W. 126
Hall, Katie 131
Haralson, Jeremiah 132–133
Hastings, Alcee 138
Hawkins, Augustus 141–142
Hayes, James 144
Henry, Aaron 145–147
Herman, Alexis 149
Hilliard, Earl 150–151
Hyman, John 154
Jack, Hulan 156
Jackson, Lisa P. 162–163
James, Sharpe 167
Jefferson, William 168
Johnson, Eddie Bernice 170
Johnson, Harvey 171
Jordan, Barbara 173, 174
Keyes, Alan 177
Kilpatrick, Carolyn 178

Kilpatrick, Kwame 180
Kirk, Ron 181
Langston, John 184
Lee, Barbara 185
Leland, Mickey 186
Lynch, John 193
Majette, Denise 195
Marsh, Henry 197
McCall, Carl 198–200
McKinney, Cynthia 200
Meek, Carrie 202
Meek, Kendrick 203–204
Metcalfe, Ralph 206
Millender-McDonald, Juanita 209
Miller, Thomas 210
Mitchell, Charles 213
Mitchell, Parren 214
Moore, Gwen 216
Morial, Dutch 217
Moseley Braun, Carol 217
Motley, Constance 219, 220
Napier, James 225
Nix, Robert 227
Obama, Barack 233
O'Hara, James 236
O'Leary, Hazel 237
Owens, Major 238
Paterson, David 241–243
Perry, Carrie 246
Pinchback, P. B. S. 247–249
Powell, Adam Clayton, Jr. 249
Rangel, Charles 259
Ransier, Alonzo 261
Rapier, James 263–264
Revels, Hiram 264–265
Rogers, Joe 270–271
Ross, Don 271–272
Scott, Bobby 278
Slater, Rodney 280
Smalls, Robert 282
Steele, Michael 283–284
Stokes, Carl 285
Stokes, Louis 286
Street, John 288

Tubbs Jones, Stephanie 295
Walls, Josiah 301
Washington, Harold 302
Waters, Maxine 305
Watson, Diane 307
Watt, Mel 308–309
Watts, J. C. 310
Webb, Wellington 313
Wheat, Alan 315
White, George 316
White, Jesse 317–318
White, Michael 319
Wilder, Doug 320
Williams, Avon 324
Williams, George 325–326
Williams, Hosea 326–327
Wynn, Albert 328
Young, Coleman 333
Steele, Michael 19, **283–284**
Stephens, Alexander 96
Stevens, Ted 152
Stevenson, Adlai 35
Stewart, Bennett 302
Stewart B. McKinney Homeless Assistance Act 187
Stimson, Henry L. 137
Stokes, Carl x, **284–286**
Stokes, Louis 120, 285, **286–288,** 287, 295
Stoneham, Horace 157
Strategic Defense Initiative 69
Street, John 230, **288–290,** 289
Street, Milton 288
Street Fight (documentary) 24
strikes 150
Student Loan Act 245
Student Nonviolent Coordinating Committee (SNCC) 10, 13, 21, 22, 146, 187–188, 272, 292
Student Right to Know Act 294
Student Voice 22
Sudan 166, 274
suffrage. *See* voting rights; women's suffrage

Sullivan, Louis **290–291**
Summer Jobs for Youths 245
Sumner, Charles 184
Sun-Diamond Growers 99
Superfund 162
Supreme Court, U.S. x–xi. *See also specific case*
  Berry, Ted 16
  Bishop, Sanford 18
  Bond, Julian 23
  Brooke, Edward 30
  Brown, Corrine 31
  Diggs, Charles 89
  Hastings, Alcee 138, 139
  Looby, Alexander 192
  McKinney, Cynthia 201
  Mitchell, Arthur 212
  Moseley Braun, Carol 217
  Motley, Constance 220
  O'Hara, James 236
  Powell, Adam Clayton, Jr. 252
  Scott, Bobby 279
  Watt, Mel 309
Surface Transportation Assistance Act 215
sweatshops 332
Syracuse Convention of 1864 43, 46
Syria 160

T
talk radio 177, 207, 280, 284, 321
Tallon, Robin 63
Talmadge, Herman 164
TANF. *See* Temporary Assistance for Needy Families (TANF)
Tanzania 269
tariffs 54, 301
Task Force on Television Measurement 67
tax credits 11, 31, 150, 233, 260, 273, 329
tax evasion 46, 89, 125, 126, 152, 180, 251, 294
teachers. *See* education
technology 72, 274, 281. *See also* computers

Telecommunications Development Fund 294
telecommunications industry 171–172, 179, 187, 294
television. *See* film and television
temperance 7
Temple University 290
Temporary Assistance for Needy Families (TANF) 307
Tennessee 54–55, 111–114, 147–149, 224–225, 262, 324
Tennessee Agricultural and Industrial State Normal School (Tennessee State University) 225
Tennessee Negro Suffrage Convention (1865) 262
Tennessee State University 225
Tennessee Valley Authority (TVA) 311
Tennessee Voters Council 324
10th Cavalry 325
terrorism 269, 307. *See also* September 11, 2001
Texaco 243–244
Texas 165–166, 169–174, 186–187, 240–241
There's Hope for the World (Arrington) 8
Third Circuit Court of Appeals 138
Third World debt 107
Thirteenth Amendment viii
Thomas, Clarence 217
Thompson, Bennie 22, **292–293**, 293
Thompson, William "Big Bill" 86
Thornburgh, Richard 2
366th Combat Infantry Regiment 28
Three Mile Island nuclear power plant 126
Thurgood Marshall Regular Democratic Club 205
Title IX program 67

tobacco industry 11, 50, 60, 63, 291, 293, 309
Tobago 100
Towns, Edolphus **293–294**
trade, global 33, 35, 60, 99, 169, 181, 182, 186, 260
Trade Representative, U.S. 182
Trade Union Educational League 115
Trade Union Unity League 115
Traffic Stops Statistics Study Act of 1999 69, 72
transportation 209, 215, 280–281. *See also* public transportation
Transportation, U.S. Department of (DoT) 280–281
treasurers, state 19, 46, 47
Treasury Department, U.S.
  Bruce, Blanche 38
  Burris, Roland 41
  Cardozo, Francis 47
  Elliot, Robert 96
  Gregory, Dick 130
  Haralson, Jeremiah 133
  Hyman, John 154
  Mitchell, Charles 213
  Murray, George 221
  Napier, James 225
  O'Hara, James 236
  Pinchback, P. B. S. 249
  Rainey, Joseph 258
  Ransier, Alonzo 262
  Rapier, James 264
  Washington, Harold 302
Trinidad 100
Truman, Harry S. 81, 137
"truth commission" 69
Tsongas, Paul 30
Tubbs Jones, Stephanie 119, 120, **294–296**
tuberculosis 291, 326
Tucker, Samuel 196
Tucker, Sterling 13
Tucker, Walter 209
Tulsa Race Riot 271, 272
Tulsa Urban League 271
Turkey 260

Turner, Benjamin 132, *296*, **296–297**
Turnley, Richard 108
Tuskegee Airman 16, 332
Tuskegee Institute 211
TVA. *See* Tennessee Valley Authority (TVA)
Twelfth Baptist Church (Boston) 325
two-strikes bill 11
Tyson Foods 99

U
UAW. *See* United Auto Workers (UAW)
UDC. *See* United Daughters of the Confederacy (UDC)
UFCWU. *See* United Food and Commercial Workers Union (UFCWU)
Unbought and Unbossed (Chisholm) 52
Uncertain Alliance: The Soviet Union and Czechoslovak Army, The (Rice) 266
UNCF. *See* College Fund/ UNCF
UNIA. *See* Universal Negro Improvement Association (UNIA)
Union army 183–184, 193, 213, 226, 247, 261, 264, 300, 325
Union Baptist Church (Cincinnati) 325
Union Brotherhood Lodge 191
unions. *See* labor unions
United Auto Workers (UAW) 333
United Daughters of the Confederacy (UDC) 217
United Food and Commercial Workers Union (UFCWU) 143
United Freeman Movement 285
United Nations
  Anderson, Charles W., Jr. 4
  Blackwell, Ken 19

Clayton, Eva 61
Harris, Patricia Roberts
    136
Keyes, Alan 177
McCall, Carl 199
Patrick, Deval 243
Payne, Donald 246
Powell, Colin 254
Rice, Susan E.
    269–270
Young, Andy (Andrew)
    330, 331
United Negro College
    Fund (UNCF). See
    College Fund/UNCF
United Packinghouse
    Workers of America
    (UPWA) 143
United Parcel Service
    (UPS) 150
Unity Democratic Club 51
universal health care. See
    health and medicine
Universal Negro
    Improvement
    Association (UNIA)
    156
Unremunerated Work Act
    66
UPS. See United Parcel
    Service (UPS)
UPWA. See United
    Packinghouse Workers
    of America (UPWA)
Urban Complex: Human
    Values in Urban Life,
    The (Weaver) 312
Urban Homesteading Plan
    136
Urban Institute 229
urban redevelopment and
    renewal
    Booker, Cory 24
    Bosley, Freeman 25
    Coleman, Michael 65
    Harris, Patricia Roberts
        136
    James, Sharpe 167
    Johnson, Harvey
        171–172
    Meek, Carrie 202
    Motley, Constance 220
    Perry, Carrie 246
    Powell, Debra 255
    Stokes, Carl 285

Weaver, Robert
    312–313
White, Michael 319
Young, Coleman 333,
    334
U.S.-China People's
    Friendship Association
    21–22
U.S. Colored Troops
    (USCT) 300
U.S. Conference of Mayors
    124
USDA. See Agriculture,
    U.S. Department of
    (USDA)
Usry, James **298–299**
U.S. Steel 141

V

veterans 115, 213, 234,
    260
Veterans Affairs, U.S.
    Department of 260
vice presidential
    candidates
    Ford, James 114, 116
    Foster, Ezola 116–117
Vietnam War
    Bond, Julian 23
    Brooke, Edward 30
    Chisholm, Shirley 52
    Clay, William 57
    Conyers, John 69
    Dawson, William 80
    Dellums, Ron 84
    Gregory, Dick 129, 130
    Hawkins, Augustus
        142
    Keyes, Alan 177
    Powell, Colin 253
    Washington, Walter
        304
violence. See crime and
    violence
Violence Against Women
    Act of 1999 72
Violence Against Women
    Committee of the
    National Association of
    Attorneys General 11
Violent Crime Control and
    Law Enforcement Act of
    1994 315
Virginia 183–184, 278–
    279, 320–322

Virgin Islands, U.S. xi,
    53–54, 99–101, 136–138
Virgin Islands Organic Act
    of 1936 137
VISTA 215–216
Vocational Education Act
    251
Voice of America (radio)
    329
Volpe, John A. 29
volunteerism 239
voter education 146, 188,
    330
voter registration xi
    Baker, Ella 10
    Ballance, Frank 12
    Blackwell, Unita 21
    Church, Robert 55
    Conyers, John 69
    Evers, Charles 101
    Fattah, Chaka 103
    Gregory, Dick 129
    Hatcher, Richard 140
    Henry, Aaron 146
    Hilliard, Earl 150
    Hyman, John 154
    Jackson, Jesse 159
    Lewis, John 188
    Nix, Robert 227
    Obama, Barack 232
    Thompson, Bennie
        292
    Young, Andy (Andrew)
        330
voting rights ix, xi. See
    also women's suffrage
    Church, Robert 54
    Conyers, John 69
    Dawson, William 80, 81
    DeLarge, Robert 82
    Elliot, Robert 95
    Fauntroy, Walter 105,
        106
    Jordan, Barbara 173
    Langston, John 184
    Miller, Thomas 210,
        211
    Morial, Dutch 217
    Napier, James 225
    Norton, Eleanor
        Holmes 229
    Patrick, Deval 243
    Pinchback, P. B. S. 247
    Powell, Adam Clayton,
        Jr. 250–251

Rainey, Joseph 258
Ransier, Alonzo 261
Rapier, James 262, 263
Savage, Gus 275
Stokes, Louis 287
Walls, Josiah 300
Voting Rights Act of 1965
    xi
    Conyers, John 68
    Evers, Charles 101
    Jordan, Barbara 173
    Martin, Louis 198
    McKinney, Cynthia 201
    Nix, Robert 228
    Stokes, Louis 287
    Washington, Harold
        302
    Wilder, Doug 320
    Young, Andy (Andrew)
        331
vouchers. See school
    vouchers

W

Waldon, Alton R. 110
Walker, Dan 41
Walker, Edward G. vii,
    213
Wallace, George 74
Wallace, Henry 275, 333
Walls, Josiah 31, **300–
    302,** *301*
Walters, Barbara 30, 254
war. See specific war
War Claims Commission
    282
War Crimes and the
    American Conscience
    (Conyers) 69
War on Poverty 16, 52, 84
War Production Board 312
Warren Commission 287
Warrensville Heights
    (Ohio) 120
Washington, Booker T.
    Ford, James 115
    Franks, Gary 119
    Mitchell, Arthur 211,
        212
Washington, Craig 166
Washington, D.C. See
    District of Columbia
Washington, Harold 78,
    143, 159, 217, 273, 275,
    302–303

Washington, Roy 302
Washington, Walter x, xi, 13, 106, **303–305**
Washington Nationals 323
Waterbury (Connecticut) 118, 119
Watergate affair 30, 112, 173
Waters, Maxine 116, 161, **305–306**
Watson, Diane **306–308,** 307
Watt, Mel 59–60, *308,* **308–309**
Watts, J. C. **309–311,** *310*
Watts riots (1969) 27, 39, 129
"weapons of mass destruction" 254, 267
Weaver, Robert 137, 198, **311–313**
Webb, Wellington **313–315**
Weinberger, Caspar 253
welfare reform 11, 17, 49, 79, 112, 119, 307
Wellington Webb: The Man, the Mayor and the Making of Modern Denver (Webb) 314
West, John 63
West, Roy A. 197
West Germany 253
West Point Military Academy 38
Westside Association for Community Action (Chicago) 78
What Went Wrong in Ohio (House Judiciary Committee) 69
Wheat, Alan **315–316**
White, George viii–ix, 60, 308, **316–317**

White, Jesse **317–318**
White, Michael **318–320**
"white flight" 65, 125, 172, 196, 312
White House Office of National Drug Control Policy 32
White House security personal 200
white middle class xiii
Whitesboro (New Jersey) 317
white supremacy viii, 96, 229, 300
white voters ix, xii, xv
  Arrington, Richard 7
  Berry, Ted 16
  Bradley, Tom 26
  Church, Robert 55
  DeLarge, Robert 82
  DePriest, Oscar 87
  Gantt, Harvey 123–124
  Goode, W. W. 126
  Harmon, Clarence 134, 135
  Hatcher, Richard 140
  Jackson, Maynard 164
  Long, Jefferson 191
  Mitchell, Arthur 212
  Mitchell, Parren 214
  Nagin, Ray 223
  Obama, Barack 234
  Schmoke, Kurt 277
  Walls, Josiah 300
  Wheat, Alan 315
  White, Michael 319
  Wilder, Doug 320
Whittemore, Benjamin F. 257–258
Wilberforce University ix, 6, 111
Wilder, Doug 34, 196, 243, **320–322**

Wilkins, Henry 280
Williams, Anthony 192, **322–324**
Williams, Avon **324–325**
Williams, George ix, **325–326**
Williams, Hardy 103
Williams, Hosea **326–327**
Williams, Robert L. 101
Wilson, Woodrow 3, 225
Wisconsin 215–216
WNET-TV 199
Women's Bureau (Labor, U.S. Department of) 149
Women's Caucus Task Force on Children, Youth and Families 200
women's rights 1–2, 39, 40, 57, 66, 67, 136
women's suffrage 44, 261
Woods, Crip 79
Working Families for Wal-Mart 332
Workplace Investment Act of 1998 150
World War I 79, 114, 115, 211–212
World War II
  Brooke, Edward 28
  Davis, Ben 76
  Diggs, Charles 87
  Evers, Charles 101
  Harmon, Clarence 134
  Henry, Aaron 145
  Metcalfe, Ralph 206
  Mitchell, Parren 214
  Savage, Gus 275
  Stokes, Carl 285
  Usry, James 298

Washington, Harold 302
Weaver, Robert 312
Williams, Avon 324
Williams, Hosea 326
Young, Coleman 332
World Youth Day 314
Wright, Jeremiah 234
Wright, Jim 92
Wynn, Albert **327–329,** *328*

Y

Yassky, David 56
YMCA 61, 221, 245
Yorty, Sam 27
Young, Andy (Andrew) xi, 117, 164, 188, *188,* **330–332,** *331*
Young, Coleman 5, 69, 70, 178, **332–334**
Young Democrats 35, 68, 285
Young Men's Christian Association. *See* YMCA
Young Men's Colored Republican Club of New York County 2
Young Men's Republican Club of Georgia 77
Young Negroes' Cooperative League 9
Youth Fair Chance Program 306
Youth Movement to Clean Up Politics 35
Youth Pride, Inc. 13, 14

Z

Zaire 107
Zelikow, Philip D. 267
Zimbabwe (formerly Rhodesia) 88